Environmental Law in Property Transactions

Fourth edition

Waite and Jewell

Environmental Law in Property Transactions

Fourth edition

Andrew Waite
Solicitor, Consultant, Head of Environment Group, Ashurst LLP

Gregory Jones QC
Barrister of Lincoln's Inn, King's Inns, Dublin
and the Inn of Court Northern Ireland
Fellow of the Centre of European law, King's College, London
Practising at FTB
Francis Taylor Building, Temple

and

Valerie Fogleman
Consultant, Stevens & Bolton LLP
Professor of Law, School of Law and Politics, Cardiff University

Foreword by The Right Hon Lord Carnwath of Notting Hill, CVO Justice of the Supreme Court

Bloomsbury Professional

Published by
**Bloomsbury Professional Ltd, Maxwelton House, 41–43 Boltro Road,
Haywards Heath, West Sussex, RH16 1BJ**

© Bloomsbury Professional Ltd 2016

Bloomsbury Professional is an imprint of Bloomsbury Publishing Plc

British Library Cataloguing-in-Publication Data.
A CIP Catalogue record for this book is available from the British Library.

ISBN 978 1 78043 329 5

Typeset by Phoenix Photosetting, Chatham, Kent
Printed and bound in Great Britain by CPI Group (UK) Ltd, Croydon, CR0 4YY

CONTENTS

Foreword by Lord Carnwath JSC	xi
Preface	xiii
Authors and Contributors	xv
Table of Statutes	xix
Table of Statutory Instruments	xxxiii
Table of Cases	xliii

PART I APPROACHING THE TRANSACTION

Chapter 1 Introduction (Alexa Seagroatt) — 3
The conveyancing context of environmental law — 3
The meaning and significance of environmental law — 3
The parties affected by environmental concerns — 4
Money laundering offences — 10
Framework of environmental law — 13
European Community environmental law — 15
UK environmental policy and the emergence of principle — 19
Statutory regulators — 34

Chapter 2 Dealing with information – the caveat emptor rule and environmental issues (Andrew Waite) — 37
Protecting the parties — 37
The *caveat emptor* (buyer beware) rule — 38
Misdescription — 39
Misrepresentation — 40
Fraudulent concealment — 42
Duty of disclosure — 42
Negligent workmanship by the seller — 49
Liability for defective building operations — 49
Leaving waste on the premises — 50
The effect of the transfer of property on environmental liabilities – the limits of *caveat emptor* — 51
Standard contractual terms relating to the *caveat emptor* rule — 52
Environmental information – the position of the seller — 54

Chapter 3 Preliminary enquiries (Andrew Waite) — 57
Information from the seller — 57
Additional environmental enquiries: industrial properties and/or heavily contaminated land — 64

**Chapter 4 Freedom of access to environmental information
(Gregory Jones QC and Juan Lopez)**   67
  Introduction   67
  Environmental Information Regulations 2004   69
  Environmental information   74
  Exceptions   76
  Time limits   94
  Criminal offences   97
  Remedies   97
  Duty to organise and disseminate environmental information   99

Chapter 5 Local land charges search (Alison Murrin)   **101**
  Introduction   101
  The local land charges register   102

**Chapter 6 Local authority and water company enquiries
(Andrew Waite and Mark Westmoreland Smith)**   **113**
  Introduction   113
  Rights of way   114
  Drainage matters   115
  Outstanding notices   115
  Tree preservation order   116
  Conservation area   116
  Contaminated land   117
  Radon gas precautions   117
  Parks and countryside   118
  Noise abatement   119
  Hazardous substance consents   120
  Environmental and pollution notices   121
  Hedgerow notices   121
  Flood defence and land drainage consents   122
  Standard drainage and water enquiries   122
  Foul and surface drainage   122
  Adoption agreement   123
  Sewers within the property   124
  Nearby sewers   124

Chapter 7 Other sources of information (Andrew Waite)   **127**
  Introduction   127
  Public registers   127
  Pollution inventory   129
  Enquiries of other authorities   129

Chapter 8 Environmental survey (Andrew Waite)   **143**
  Importance of an environmental survey   143
  Types of environmental survey   143
  Who should commission the survey?   146

Disadvantages of a survey 147
Selecting the right consultant 148
The buyer and existing reports 152

**Chapter 9 Assessing and managing environmental risk: contractual
protection and environmental insurance (Andrew Waite and
Valerie Fogleman)** **153**
Analysing the information – assessing the risk 153
Effect of environmental liabilities on the transaction 153
Dealing with liabilities in the contract 154
Warranties 158
Indemnities 158
Environmental insurance 182

**Chapter 10 Particular transactions – leases, lending and securitisation
(Andrew Waite)** **189**
Leases 189
Lender liability issues 213

Chapter 11 Agreements for remedial works (Andrew Waite) **223**
Remedial works 223
Remediation method statement 225

Chapter 12 Transferring permits (Andrew Waite) **231**
Environmental permits 231
Petrol storage certificates and licenses 232
Hazardous substances consent 233
The delayed transfer problem 234

PART II THE BROADER CONTEXT

Chapter 13 Civil liability (Valerie Fogleman) 247
Introduction 247
Nuisance 248
Trespass to land 268
Negligence 269
Limitation of action and remedies 270
Liability for the torts of independent contractors 274
Causation and contribution 274

**Chapter 14 Statutory nuisance (Gregory Jones QC, Melissa Murphy
and Caroline Daly)** 277
Introduction 277
The definition of statutory nuisances 279
The power to seek injunctions 288
Summary proceedings by a 'person aggrieved' 305
Construction site noise 309

Contents

Chapter 15 Contaminated land (Valerie Fogleman)   **311**
Introduction   311
The general policy position   312
Guiding principles   313
Contaminated land and planning powers   314
Amenity notices   320
Contaminated land and waste management   322
Contaminated land and statutory nuisance   323
Remediation of contaminated land – Part 2A of the Environmental
      Protection Act 1990   324
Environmental Liability Directive   364

Chapter 16 Waste (Gregory Jones QC and Sarah Sackman)   **367**
Introduction   367
European Waste Framework Directive   369
What is waste?   371
Waste disposal and planning   380
Waste duty of care   381
The Environmental permitting system   384
Waste offences   385
Hazardous waste   388
Landfill   389
Landfill tax   390

**Chapter 17 Water (Gregory Jones QC, Cain Ormondroyd and
Annabel Graham Paul)**   **393**
Water supply   393
Water abstraction and abstraction licensing   401
Water discharge activities   409
Protection of controlled waters   425
Discharge of trade effluent into public sewers   432
Trade effluent containing special category effluent   436
EC directive on urban waste water treatment   442
Sensitive areas and high natural dispersion areas   443
Sewers   444
Sewers for new developments   445

**Chapter 18 Built environment (Gregory Jones QC, John Joliffe and
Rebecca Clutten)**   **459**
Introduction   459
Planning authorities   460
General policy position   463
Development plans   464
Development control   467

**Chapter 19 Nature conservation (Gregory Jones QC, Jeremy Pike and
Ned Westaway)**   **483**
Introduction   483

FOREWORD

The need for a new edition of this book is demonstrated by the continuing development of environmental law in the seven years since the last edition appeared. The environmental permitting regime has encompassed ever more regulatory schemes within its scope. The Supreme Court decisions in *Coventry v Lawrence* (in which I participated) have altered lawyers' understanding of the common law of nuisance and there has been increasing regulation of energy use in the name of climate change mitigation. There are many more examples.

Contrary to common perceptions, environmental law is not only a product of the last 40 years or so. Of course, that period has witnessed one of the periods of greatest growth in this area of the law and has seen it develop as a discrete area of study and practice. However, its origins stretch back beyond the great nineteenth century legislation on public health and pollution control to the common law of nuisance which aims to protect the integrity and amenity of property. The two way operation of nuisance law benefiting both landowners and their neighbours was the foundation stone on which much of our subsequent environmental law has been built. First statutory nuisance, then sectoral controls and finally more holistic regulation have both restricted the rights of landowners to impose 'externalities' on their neighbours and protected them from the excesses of others. From the narrow base of the protection of property rights the law has extended its protective umbrella to all persons affected by the environmental depredations of others, from the local to the global community and beyond that and to the wider environment which merits protection for its own sake. In recent years this trend has been enhanced by the rights to information, participation in decision making and access to justice under the Aarhus Convention.

The interaction between property and environmental law is an important area for lawyers and their clients. It is perhaps surprising that this book provides the only up to date, comprehensive exploration of this field. For that reason alone I would commend it. In addition, the authors are not afraid to analyse aspects which have not been dealt with adequately elsewhere in the cases or the books and to suggest their own conclusions. Good examples of this are to be found in the sections on leaving waste (and contamination) on the property in Chapter 2, the discussion on contractual protection in Chapter 9 and the analysis of the effect of common leasehold covenants on environmental liabilities and the impact of statutory appeal provisions on the landlord's ability to claim under leasehold covenants in Chapter 10. Chapter 12 contains a useful summary table of the requirements for transferring permits as well as a solution to the common problem of regulators' failure to transfer permits by the date of completion.

The book is in three parts: Approaching the transaction (which explains how environmental issues are dealt with in the context of property and conveyancing law and practice), the Broader Context (which explains the aspects of environmental law which are most relevant in property transactions) and finally a useful selection of precedents.

This volume will be a valuable addition to the libraries of property and environmental lawyers.

Robert Carnwath
Supreme Court, United Kingdom
Whitsun 2016

PREFACE TO THE FOURTH EDITION

It is now seven years since the last edition of this book appeared. Much has happened since then. It is with sadness that we record the death of Lord (Christopher) Kingsland QC who wrote the foreword to the 3rd edition and died a few months after its publication. Christopher was a great environmental lawyer, politician and economist. Always, kind, patient and courteous, he had a facility for unravelling the knottiest legal problems. He is greatly missed. Lord Carnwath JSC has kindly prepared the foreword to this edition and our thanks are due to him.

There has been a welter of new legislation and case law which in some areas has transformed the legal landscape, notably the Environmental Permitting (England and Wales) Regulations and numerous amending regulations which have expanded the areas covered by this regime and improved the enforcement tools available to the regulators. On the common law side, the Supreme Court decisions in *Coventry v Lawrence* in 2014 have significantly altered our understanding of the law of nuisance which has potential consequences for property transactions. That scourge of legal writers, the propensity of the law for constant change (particularly in the final stages of a book) has afflicted us as it does many others. However, we have attempted to state the law as at 31 March 2016 although some later changes have also been included.

This is the first edition in which Tim Jewell has not been actively involved, but his work lives on in the text and justifies his inclusion in the title.

In preparing this edition our thanks are due to the many people who have made it possible, particularly our fellow contributors who are listed on another page, the staff at Bloomsbury: Leanne Barrett, Jane Bradford, Juliet Smith and Claire Banyard for their unfailing help and patience throughout this long process, and also Jim Mitchell whose photographic and other talents will never be eclipsed.

Andrew would like to thank his colleagues at Ashurst for their support and for discussing many of the ideas which have found their way into this edition. Particular thanks are due to Lisa Smith for typing and organising successive chapter versions with amendments and re-amendments cheerfully and without complaint, Alison Murrin for editing Chapter 5 and for her thoughts and comments on many points, Chris Vigrass for reviewing the section on money laundering and the library staff, David, Julia and Anita for their assistance in updating footnotes and retrieving materials. Finally, Andrew would like to thank his family for their continued love and support: his wife Cheryl, their children and partners Darren, Keiko, Tracey, Rachel, Olly and Ben, and their grandchildren: Huw, Sam, Mischa, Mirai and Rafaela (who was born just before this edition was completed) and his parents who he hopes would have been proud of this edition.

Valerie would like to thank her colleagues at Stevens & Bolton and the University of Cardiff School of Law and Politics for their encouragement. A special note of thanks goes to Andrew Waite and the staff at Bloomsbury for their patience. Finally, Valerie would like to thank her family for their love and forbearing; her children: Nicole, David and Tanya and her grandchildren: Emily, Katherine, Lauren, Joshua and Austin, as well as her late parents for starting and encouraging her on the path to environmental law.

Gregory would like to thank his colleagues at Francis Taylor Building who have assisted in the production of this edition of the book and to his family Rosali, Phoebe and Felicity. Gregory also expresses his grateful thanks to his fellow authors and staff at Bloomsbury for the great patience they have shown when the demands of practice have delayed delivery of text. Finally, Gregory would also like to dedicate his own contribution to the memory of his father Colin Frederick Jones who passed away since the production of the third edition of this book.

Andrew Waite
London

Valerie Fogleman
Guildford

Gregory Jones
London

Whitsun 2016

AUTHORS AND CONTRIBUTORS

AUTHORS

Andrew Waite, MA (Oxon) is a practising solicitor and consultant at Ashurst where he heads the firm's environment group in London. He has a wide practice in environmental law both contentious and non-contentious, specialising in the overlapping area of environmental and property law. He is a former Lecturer in Law at Southampton University, was Visiting Professor of Law at the University of Georgia, and has lectured at a number of universities around the world. He was also a partner and head of the environment group at Berwin Leighton Paisner LLP. He is co-founder and former Secretary of the UK Environmental Law Association and former President of the European Environmental Law Association and was Vice Chair for Western Europe of the Commission on Environmental Law of the International Union for the Conservation of Nature. He is the editor of the *Environmental Law Handbook* (4th edn, Bloomsbury Professional 2013) and has published many articles on environmental and property law.

Valerie Fogleman, BLA, MSc, JD, LLM, LLD was Natural Resources Law Fellow at Lewis & Clark Law School in Portland, Oregon, a Fellow at the University of Illinois College of Law and in private practice in Corpus Christi, Texas, prior to returning to England in 1992. She was subsequently partner and Head of the Environment Group at Barlow Lyde & Gilbert (now Clyde & Co) and a Consultant at Lovells (now Hogan Lovells). She is currently a Consultant at Stevens & Bolton LLP and a Professor of Law at Cardiff University School of Law and Politics. Valerie advises clients on environmental, climate change, insurance, and health and safety law. Her work includes various projects (some with BIO by Deloitte) for the European Commission, including five projects on the Environmental Liability Directive. She is an Honorary Member of the Royal Institution for Chartered Surveyors, member and former Vice Chair of the City of London Law Society Planning and Environment Committee, member and former Council member of the United Kingdom Environmental Law Association and member of the Texas State Bar, the American Bar Association and the Association of Insurance and Risk Managers. She is listed as a leading environmental lawyer in the directories. Valerie has written three books and over 200 articles on environmental and insurance law.

Gregory Jones QC, MA (Oxon), LLM (Lond.) is a member of the Bars of England & Wales, Ireland and Northern Ireland. Practicing in planning, environmental, local government, public and property law from Francis Taylor Building, Temple, London, Gregory is identified as a leading silk in *Planning Magazine* and various directories. He has acted in many of the leading environmental cases, including *Tarmac*, *Wakil* and *Cogent* in England and *Seaport* and *The Alternative A5 Alliance* in Northern Ireland. Gregory is a Fellow of the Royal Geographical Society, the *Centre* of *European* Law, King's College, London, the Institute of Quarrying, and the Linnean Society. He is a Legal Associate of the Royal Town Planning Institute. His published work includes G. Jones (ed.) *The Habitats Directive: a developer's obstacle course?* (Hart, 2012), Gregory Jones and David Graham, 'Maritime Spatial Planning' in Soyer & Tettenborn (eds.), *Offshore Contracts and Liabilities* (Taylor & Francis, 2014), and Robert McCracken, Gregory Jones and James Pereira, *Statutory Nuisance* (3rd edn, Bloomsbury Professional 2012). In July 2015 Gregory was appointed by the Irish government to chair the independent review of *An Bord Pleanála* which reported in February 2016.

CONTRIBUTORS

Rebecca Clutten is a barrister at Francis Taylor Building, Temple, London. She was called to the Bar in 2008 and is currently ranked 2nd in the top planning juniors under 35 (The Law Survey 2014–2015, *Planning Magazine* 2015), having held a top 5 position for the last three years and a top 10 position for the last five. Rebecca is also listed in Chambers and Partners Guide to the UK Bar (2016).

Caroline Daly is a barrister at Francis Taylor Building, Temple, London. She has a broad planning and environmental practice ranging from judicial reviews in the High Court to criminal cases in the Magistrates' Court.

Annabel Graham Paul is a barrister at Francis Taylor Building, Temple, London. Her practice encompasses infrastructure, planning, compulsory purchase, compensation and land valuation, judicial review, environmental law (including environmental impact assessment, waste, water and nuisance), property (including rating, highways, commons and greens), licensing, advertising, trees, ecclesiastical and education law. She is recommended by *Chambers & Partners* 2015 and *Legal 500* (2013 and 2014). Annabel has been consistently ranked as a leading planning junior barrister in England and Wales under the age of 35 by *Planning Magazine*.

John Jolliffe is a barrister at Francis Taylor Building, Temple, London. He has a wide ranging environmental law practice. He is part of the counsel team promoting the HS2 railway before Parliament, and he has advised on environmental issues including habitats, ecology and EIA. He is a member of the council of the United Kingdom Environmental Law Association, and has been appointed to the Attorney General's panel of counsel.

Juan Lopez is a barrister at Francis Taylor Building, Temple, London. His practice encompasses environmental law (including *Aarhus*, EIA and SEA, contaminated land, nuisance and water), property, compulsory purchase, compensation and valuation, and infrastructure, in addition to general planning. Juan has been regularly recommended in *Chambers and Partners* and *Legal*

500 directories, and regularly acts on behalf of clients including water services providers, electricity distribution operators, and national infrastructure bodies.

Alison Murrin is Expertise Counsel at Ashurst LLP in the real estate department. Alison was a transactional lawyer at Ashurst for over ten years and advised on development projects, investment transactions, and landlord and tenant matters. As Expertise Counsel she oversees lawyer training, drafts precedents and delivers client seminars on a wide range of real estate topics.

Cain Ormondroyd is a barrister at Francis Taylor Building, Temple, London He is listed by *Planning Magazine* as a leading barrister under the age of 35 and is a member of the Attorney General's Panel of Counsel. Cain also works with Friends of the Earth, the Environmental Law Foundation and other public interest groups.

Melissa Murphy is a barrister at Francis Taylor Building, Temple, London She specialises in planning, administrative law, compulsory purchase and compensation. She is rated as a leading junior for planning, in both *Chambers and Partners* and the *Legal 500*. She was named 'top planning barrister under the age of 35' for two years running in the annual *Planning Magazine survey* (2011 and 2012) and is now among the 'top rated juniors' in the most recent edition.

Jeremy Pike is a barrister at Francis Taylor Building, Temple, London. His practice covers planning and environmental law (including Development Consent Orders under the Planning Act 2008, compulsory purchase and compensation, transport and works orders, and private bills) judicial review and statutory challenge, public law and local government law (including non-domestic rating and the council tax, and licensing) commons and village greens. He has particular expertise in renewable energy, infrastructure and environmental impact assessment. Jeremy has been regularly recommended in *Chambers and Partners* and *Legal 500* directories.

Sarah Sackman is a barrister at Francis Taylor Building, Temple, London, specialising in public, planning and environmental law. She has been a member of the Attorney General's panel of counsel since 2013 and acts for government, private clients and NGOs. Sarah has held fellowships at Cambridge and Harvard universities and currently lectures on the LSE Cities Programme.

Alexa Seagroatt is a lawyer in the Cabinet Office and Central Commercial Team of the Commercial Law Group in the Government Legal Department. She was previously an associate at Ashurst LLP and Watson, Farley & Williams. Her main expertise is in the area of land acquisitions, receivership sales and administrations, development agreements, lease negotiations and real estate aspects of energy, transport and infrastructure projects. She also has an interest in environmental law, land rights and international human rights.

Ned Westaway is a barrister specialising in environmental and planning law at Francis Taylor Building, Temple, London. He regularly talks and writes on environmental law. He is a visiting researcher at the UCL Centre for Law and the Environment. Ned is a Trustee of the United Kingdom Environmental Law Association and acts as counsel for the Campaign for National Parks.

Mark Westmoreland Smith is a barrister specialising in environmental and planning law at Francis Taylor Building, Temple, London. He was recognised as one of the top five planning junior barristers in the *Planning Magazine Survey* (2016). His practice focuses on all aspects of planning, infrastructure, land valuation and compensation. He acts for developers, the Government and interested parties on a wide range of schemes in planning inquiries, development consent examinations and in the courts.

TABLE OF STATUTES

Agriculture Act 1947
  s 109.. 14.04
Agriculture Act 1970
  s 29.. 19.41
Agriculture Act 1986
  s 18.. 5.28
    (1), (3)–(8)........................ 19.60
Ancient Monuments and Archae-
  ological Areas Act 1979 .... 5.33
  s 1(2), (9).............................. 5.31
    2(3) 5.31
    7....................................... 5.31
    8(2)(b)............................... 5.31
    (2A), (6) 5.31
    12(1), (1A), (2), (7).............. 5.31
    16(4), (8)............................ 5.31
    17(5) 19.18
    33..................................... 5.31
  Sch 1
    para 1(2)............................. 5.31
Anti-social Behaviour, Crime and
  Policing Act 2014................. 14.02

Building Act 1984 .... 3.10; 5.07
  s 21.. 17.145
    (3)..................................... 17.144
    (4), (5).......... 6.50; 17.144, 17.147
    (6) 17.144, 17.147
    22...................... 5.11; 17.145
    (1)–(6) 17.145
    25(1), (4)–(6)....................... 17.15
    59.. 17.146P
    (1) 17.147
      (a)–(d)................... 5.11; 10.24
    (2) 5.11
    (3) 17.147
    60....................................... 17.151
    64–66................................. 5.12
    84....................................... 10.24
    99....................................... 17.152
    (1) 17.147
    (2) 17.149
    102...................... 10.24; 17.145,
                            17.148, 17.152
    103..................................... 17.152
    (2) 17.145, 17.148

Building Act 1984 – *contd*
  s 103(3) 17.148
    107..................................... 5.08
    126..................................... 17.151

Civil Aviation Act 1982
  s 76...................................... 3.19
Civil Evidence Act 1995
  s 12...................................... 14.44
Civil Liability (Contribution) Act
    1978 .... 2.36; 8.16; 13.60
  s 1.. 13.60
Clean Air Act 1956 .... 20.32
Clean Air Act 1968 .... 20.32
Clean Air Act 1993 ... 3.20; 14.04; 20.03,
                        20.32, 20.33, 20.34
  s 1.. 20.33
    (1), (2)................................ 20.32
    2................................ 20.32, 20.33
    4....................................... 20.32
    (4) 20.33
    5, 6............................ 20.32, 20.33
    14................................ 5.29; 20.34
    15....................................... 5.29
    18............................... 5.29; 20.34
    20, 21................................. 20.34
    24............................... 5.17; 10.24
    41A.................................... 20.32
Clean Neighbourhoods and Envi-
  ronment Act 2005........ 15.30, 15.34
  Pt 5 (ss 35–54)........................ 16.19
  s 35...................................... 16.19
    86....................................... 14.14
    102..................................... 14.04
    104..................................... 15.71
Climate Change Act 2008 .... 1.16
Coast Protection Act 1949 .... 5.06
  s 8(8) 5.06, 5.07, 5.15, 5.22
    10....................................... 5.15
    12....................................... 5.15
    13....................................... 5.15
    (6) 5.06, 5.07, 5.15, 5.22
Companies Act 2006
  s 1159................................... 15.85
Compensation Act 2006
  s 3 .... 13.61

Competition and Service (Utilities) Act 1992
s 35(11) 17.154
43(1) 17.05
Conservation of Seals Act 1970... 19.16
Constitutional Reform Act 2005
s 15(1) 5.03
Sch 4
Pt 1
para 82, 83 .... 5.03
Consumer Insurance (Disclosure and Representations) Act 2012 .... 9.43
Contracts (Rights of Third Parties) Act 1999 ..... 9.07; 10.10, 10.19; 11.02, 11.12
s 1 .... 8.16
(2) 8.16
Control of Pollution Act 1974 ..... 6.33; 14.04, 14.20, 14.73; 15.30; 16.04
s 1(3) 16.19
3(1)(a) 17.48
5 .... 16.119
16 .... 15.30
Pt III (ss 60–74) 3.19; 14.02, 14.74
s 60 .... 6.34; 14.04, 14.38, 14.50, 14.73, 14.75
(3) 14.73
(5 .... 14.75
(7) 14.74
(8) 14.76
61 .... 14.04, 14.38, 14.73, 14.76
(8) 14.76
63 .... 6.27, 6.29; 14.56
64 .... 6.28, 6.29; 7.02; 14.56
65 .... 6.29; 14.38, 14.56
66 .... 6.29, 6.30, 6.34; 7.02; 14.38, 14.56
67 .... 6.29, 6.30; 14.38, 14.56
72 .... 14.74
Control of Pollution (Amendment) Act 1989
s 1(1), (5) 16.19
Corporation Tax Act 2009
s 1144, 1177 .... 9.02, 9.04
Countryside Act 1968 .... 19.06, 19.40
s 15 .... 19.39
(2)–(4) 19.40

Countryside and Rights of Way Act 2000 .... 19.13, 19.23, 19.27, 19.28, 19.38
s 73(1) 19.06
75(3) 19.40
Pt IV (ss 82–93) 6.24
s 82 .... 6.22
85 .... 6.24
103(2) 19.27
Courts Act 1971
s 52 .... 14.49
Courts and Legal Services Act 1990
s 58 .... 14.72
Criminal Justice Act 1982
s 37 .... 14.76; 15.25, 15.60; 16.19
Data Protection Act 1984 .... 4.25
s 1(1) 4.25
7 .... 4.27
Deer Act 1991 .... 19.16
Defective Premises Act 1972
s 1, 2 .... 2.28
6(3) 2.28
Deregulation Act 2015
s 59, 63–65 .... 6.29
Sch 13
Pt 5 (paras 9–15) 6.29
Energy Act 2011 .... 1.16; 3.06
Enterprise Act 2002 .... 10.55
Environment Act 1995 .. 1.16, 1.30, 1.42; 14.02; 15.04; 17.01, 17.81; 18.03
Pt I (ss 1–56) 1.42; 18.03
s 2 .... 1.42; 7.04
(1)(a) 18.03
(3) 17.01
4 .... 1.31
(1), (3) 1.30
7(1) 19.09
31(2) 1.30
37 .... 7.13
39 .... 15.69
(1) 1.31
41 .... 17.40, 17.78
42 .... 17.40
57 .... 2.25, 2.40, 2.41; 7.04; 9.13; 10.05, 10.43, 10.49, 10.52, 10.56; 14.02; 15.04, 15.08, 15.34, 15.35

Environment Act 1995 – *contd*
s 58.. 15.80
    63.. 18.03
    80.. 20.04
    81.............................. 20.04, 20.05
    (1) 20.05
    82.. 20.05
    83.. 20.05
    (1) 20.05
    84.. 20.05
    93.. 16.07
    108.............................. 15.53; 16.19
    (4)(k)................................... 8.11
    109.. 16.19
    112.. 17.27
    114.. 17.75
    120............................ 14.36; 15.103;
                                        17.37, 17.86
    (3) 15.14; 17.27
Sch 9
    para 5 .... 17.27
Sch 13.. 18.32
Sch 14.. 18.32
Sch 17
    para 5 .... 14.03
Sch 22.. 10.04
    para 89 .... 14.04; 15.32
    103 .... 17.134
    121 .... 17.126
    128 .... 17.37
    162 .... 10.43; 14.36;
                                        17.47, 17.86
    170 .... 15.103
    173 .... 17.81
Sch 24................. 10.13; 15.14; 17.27
Environment (Wales) Act 2016.... 18.03
Environmental   Protection   Act
    1990 .... 1.16; 6.16, 6.33;
                                10.50, 10.53; 13.13;
                                14.03, 14.13, 14.50,
                                14.60, 14.61, 14.66;
                                16.11, 16.30; 17.81;
                                19.07; 20.01, 20.32
Pt I (ss 1–28)........ 3.20; 14.04; 17.116;
                                20.01, 20.02, 20.07,
                                20.09, 20.10
s 2.. 20.10
    3................................. 18.20; 20.04
    4.. 20.02
    7(2) 18.20
    9.. 12.14
Pt II (ss 29–78) 15.31; 20.06

Environmental   Protection   Act
    1990 – *contd*
s 33...................... 16.11, 16.17, 16.23,
                                16.24, 16.26
    (1) 16.26; 17.47
    (a) 16.24
    (c) 16.23
    (6) 7.14
    (7) 16.25
    (8) 16.26
    33B, 33C, 33ZA.................... 16.26
    34.............................. 3.20; 16.17
    (2A)................................... 16.18
    (10) 16.17
    34A.............................. 6.33; 16.17
    40.. 12.14
    47ZA 6.33
    59.......................... 3.11; 6.33, 6.34;
                                7.14; 10.52; 15.02,
                                15.30, 15.65, 16.26
    (3) 15.31
    59A.. 7.14
    59ZA 2.25; 15.30
    (5).................................... 15.31
    62A(1)................................... 16.27
    71.. 8.11; 16.19
    73(6) 16.26
    75(5) 16.18
Pt IIA (ss 78A–78YC) 1.13; 2.11,
                                2.36, 2.40, 2.45;
                                3.01, 3.11; 5.20;
                                6.16, 6.18, 6.33;
                                7.02, 7.04; 9.03,
                                9.09, 9.13, 9.39,
                                9.42; 10.10, 10.25,
                                10.27, 10.43, 10.46;
                                11.07; 15.04, 15.05,
                                15.06, 15.08, 15.13,
                                15.15, 15.16, 15.18,
                                15.29, 15.30, 15.31,
                                15.32, 15.33, 15.34,
                                15.35, 15.37, 15.38,
                                15.39, 15.42, 15.53,
                                15.68, 15.74, 15.76,
                                15.77, 15.80, 15.81,
                                15.91, 15.100, 15.102,
                                15.104, 15.106; 17.47,
                                17.87; 20.23
s 78A...................................... 15.37
    (2)........................ 15.38, 15.40,
                                15.47, 15.48
    (b) 15.40

Environmental Protection Act
 1990 – *contd*
s 78A(4).......................... 15.40, 15.47
  (5)........................... 15.39, 15.40,
                              15.47, 15.49
  (7)........................... 15.04, 15.40
  (9)............................. 9.12; 10.36,
                              10.49; 15.15,
                              15.49, 15.51,
                              15.53, 15.75,
                              15.78, 15.88
78B 2.25; 15.37
  (1).................................. 15.53
  (2).................................. 15.38
  (3), (4)............................. 15.53
78C.............................. 2.25; 7.15;
                              15.37, 15.51
  (1)–(4) 15.54
  (10)................................. 15.51
78D.............................. 7.15; 15.37,
                                    15.51
  (3), (4) 15.54
78E 2.25; 7.15; 10.08;
                              15.37, 15.65
  (1)........................... 15.60, 15.74
  (2).................................. 15.62
  (4).............. 15.60, 15.68, 15.98
  (5).................................. 15.38
78F.............................. 9.03; 10.52;
                              15.37, 15.91
  (1) 15.74, 15.93
  (2) 9.21; 15.5,
                              15.77, 15.93
  (3) 15.75, 15.93;
                                    17.47
  (4) 10.05; 15.09,
                              15.78, 15.93
  (5) 15.78, 15.93
  (6) 8.10; 9.03, 9.04;
                        10.05, 10.36; 15.09,
                        15.38, 15.63, 15.84
  (7) 15.38, 15.93
  (9) 9.09
78G.................................. 15.60
  (3) 6.16
78H.................................. 15.37
  (1) 15.39, 15.64
  (3)................................. 15.64
  (4) 15.64, 15.73
  (5) 15.65, 15.72,
                                    15.97
     (a)............................... 15.65

Environmental Protection Act
 1990 – *contd*
s 78H(5)(b)..................... 15.15, 15.39,
                              15.64, 15.65
     (c) 15.65
     (d)..................... 15.65, 15.66
  (6)–(8), (10)..................... 15.67
  (7) 2.25
  (10) 15.65
78J 15.37
  (2)–(6)............................. 15.80
78K.................................. 15.37
  (1)........................ 15.75, 15.82,
                                    15.91
  (3)–(5) 15.82, 15.91
78L 15.34, 15.37,
                                    15.71
  (4), (5)............................ 15.71
78M.................................. 15.37
  (1), (3)–(5) 15.60
78N........................ 15.37, 15.65,
                              15.72, 15.97
  (3) 15.83
     (a), (c) 15.97
     (b).............................. 15.97
     (c) 2.24
     (e) 15.66
78O.................................. 15.37
78P...................... 2.25; 5.20; 10.56;
                              15.37, 15.66,
                              15.74, 15.98
  (2) 15.38, 15.66, 15.69,
                        15.96, 15.97, 15.98
  (3) 2.24; 15.101
  (4)................................. 2.24
  (5)–(11), (14)................... 15.101
78Q.................................. 15.37
  (4) 15.51
  (6) 15.38
78QA 15.37
78R...................... 2.25; 6.15, 6.17;
                        7.02, 7.15; 15.102
  (j), (j), (l) 15.102
78S........................ 15.37, 15.102
  (1), (2) 15.103
78T 15.37, 15.102,
                                    15.103
78TA.............................. 15.102
78U........................ 15.37, 15.104
  (2), 93) 15.104
78V..............................7.15; 15.37
  (1), (2) 15.38

Environmental Protection Act
1990 – *contd*

s 78W 15.37
   (2) 15.38
78X 15.37
   (3) 10.55; 15.81
   (4) 15.81
78YA 15.37
78YB 15.65
   (2) 15.29
   (3) 15.30, 15.65
78YC 15.37
Pt III (ss 79–85) 3.10, 3.16,
                3.17, 3.19; 5.19;
                6.33; 10.06; 14.02,
                14.04, 14.07, 14.34,
                14.62, 14.65; 18.23
s 79(1) 13.04; 14.04,
                14.14; 15.13
   (a) 14.03, 14.38
   (b) 14.03, 14.19
   (c) 14.03
   (d), (e) 14.03, 14.19,
                14.38
   (f) 14.03
   (fa) 14.03, 14.38
   (fb) 14.03, 14.19
   (g) 14.03, 14.19,
                14.38
   (h) 14.03
   (1A) 14.02, 14.04;
                15.32
   (1B) 15.33
   (2) 14.04
   (2A)(b) 14.14
   (2C)(a), (b) 14.17
   (2D) 14.16
   (2E) 14.17
   (3) 14.04
     (i)–(iv) 14.04
   (4) 14.04
   (5A), (5B) 14.04
   (6A) 14.04
   (7) 10.06, 10.48;
                13.13; 14.04,
                14.06, 14.30,
                14.57
   (7C) 14.04
     (e) 14.04
   (7D) 14.04
   (9) 14.55
     (a), (b) 14.55

Environmental Protection Act
1990 – *contd*

s 79(10) 14.04, 14.19
80 .... 2.25, 2.40, 2.41;
                6.10; 9.31;
                10.08, 10.52;
                14.14, 14.38,
                14.63
   (1) 13.04; 14.12,
                14.23, 14.25,
                14.26, 14.64
    (a) 14.18
   (2) 13.13; 14.30,
                14.34, 14.58
    (b), (c) 10.06; 14.30
   (2A)(b) 10.27
   (3) 10.24, 10.26;
                14.38
   (4) 14.50, 14.54,
                14.57
   (5) 14.57; 15.60
   (6) 14.57
   (7) 14.04, 14.39,
                14.54
   (8) 14.04
    (a), (aza), (b) 14.04
    (c) 14.54
   (8B), (8C) 14.04
   (9) 14.56
80A 14.04
81(1) 14.30, 14.37
   (3) 5.19; 10.06;
                14.58
   (4) 2.24, 2.25; 5.19;
                10.06; 14.37,
                14.58, 14.60,
                14.61
   (5) 14.20, 14.22,
                14.23, 14.24
81A 2.25; 5.19; 10.56;
                14.03, 14.34, 14.61
   (1), (3)–(8) 14.61
   (9) 10.49; 14.62
   (10) 14.03
81B 14.61, 14.62
82 .... 9.31; 13.04;
                14.01, 14.19,
                14.63, 14.64,
                14.67, 14.68,
                14.69
   (2) 14.63, 14.64,
                14.67

Environmental Protection Act
1990 – *contd*
s 82(4)(a) 14.53
(6) 14.64, 14.67
(7) 14.64
(9) 14.64
(10) 14.64
(aza) 14.04
(10A) 14.04
(12) 14.70, 14.72
75 .... 7.02
95 .... 7.02
122 .... 7.02
Pt VII (ss 128–139) 19.06
s 130 .... 19.08
131(6) 19.06
132 .... 19.06, 19.07
(1) 19.07
143 .... 10.13; 15.14
160 .... 14.68, 14.69
(3), (5) 14.68
Sch 6 .... 19.06
Sch 9 .... 19.06
para 4(1) 19.40
European Communities Act
1972 .... 20.07
s 2(2) 4.02
Explosives Act 1875 .... 3.24

Factory and Workshop Act 1891. 10.23,
10.25
s 7(2) 10.23, 10.24
Finance Act 1996 .... 16.01, 16.29
s 40 .... 16.29
43A, 43B 15.09
64 .... 16.30
Fire and Rescue Services Act 2004
s 43 .... 17.20
(1), (4) 17.16
Flood and Water Management Act
2010
s 30 .... 2.25
Sch 1 .... 6.10
para 5 .... 5.32
Sch 3
para 7, 9, 10 .... 6.08
11 .... 6.08
(3) 6.08
12, 16, 17 .... 6.08
Food and Environment Protection
Act 1985 .... 16.22

Freedom of Information Act
2000 .... 4.01, 4.11, 4.19,
4.20, 4.28, 4.29,
4.30, 4.31, 4.37,
4.39, 4.40; 6.01
s 1(1) 4.02
2 .... 4.02
(2), (3) 4.02
3(1) 4.06
(2) 4.08
5 .... 4.06
6 .... 4.06, 4.10
14 .... 4.15
Pt II (ss 22–44) 4.02
s 26(1) 4.28
27 .... 4.19
(1) 4.29
29(1) 4.29
33(1) 4.28
36(2) 4.28
38(1) 4.28
39 .... 4.02
41 .... 4.25
43(1), (2) 4.28
44 .... 4.25
50(1) 4.35
57, 58 .... 4.39
63 .... 4.10
74 .... 4.02
Sch 1 .... 4.06
Sch 3 .... 4.37
Gas Act 1948 .... 15.76
Gas Act 1972 .... 15.76
Gas Act 1986 .... 15.76
Greater London Authority Act
1999 .... 18.04
Health and Safety at Work etc Act
1974
s 2–4 .... 3.16, 3.17
Highways Act 1980 .... 5.07
s 38 .... 3.09
Housing Act 1957 .... 14.13
Housing Act 1985
s 609 .... 19.18
Housing and Planning Act 2016.. 18.03,
18.04
Housing Grants, Construction
and Regeneration Act 1996
Pt II (ss 104–113) 8.16; 11.14
s 104(2)(b) 8.16

Housing Grants, Construction
and Regeneration Act 1996 – *contd*
s 105...................................... 8.16
(2).................................. 8.16
108–113............................ 8.16
Human Rights Act 1998......... 1.36, 1.37,
1.38
s 2–4...................................... 1.37
6.................................... 4.06
(3)................................ 1.37
Sch 1...................................... 1.37

Infrastructure Act 2015............... 5.03
s 34–36................................... 5.03
Sch 5...................................... 5.03
Insolvency Act 1986
s 44(1)(a).............................. 10.55
Sch B1
para 69 .... 10.55
Insurance Act 2015 .... 9.43
Interpretation Act 1978
s 6.. 10.06
17(2)................................... 5.07

Land Charges Act 1972
s 2.. 19.18
Land Compensation Act 1961
s 5.. 17.92
Land Drainage Act 1991 .... 7.04
s 4.. 7.13
14(5), (6)............................ 13.19
14A(11)............................... 13.19
18(1) 5.34
23...................... 7.13; 12.09, 12.14
(1A)............................... 12.14
52...................................... 7.02
66...................................... 7.13
Landlord and Tenant Act 1927
s 18.. 10.13
19(1)................................... 10.15
(1A)............................... 10.17
Landlord and Tenant (Covenants)
Act 1995............................. 10.17
s 22.. 10.17
Land Registration Act 1925
s 70(1)(a).............................. 17.10
Land Registration Act 2002
s 23.. 10.50
55...................................... 5.22
58, 59................................. 7.11
Sch 1..................................... 19.18
Sch 3..................................... 19.18

Latent Damage Act 1986............ 13.50
Law of Property Act 1925........... 2.21
s 79.. 19.18
84...................................... 18.24
85.................................. 5.22; 10.50
86, 87................................ 10.50
109(2)................................ 10.55
198.................................... 2.21
Law of Property Act 1969
s 24.. 2.21
Law of Property (Miscellaneous
Provisions) Act 1989............ 18.25
s 2.. 18.25
Law Reform (Contributory Negli-
gence) Act 1945
s 1.. 13.59
Legal Aid, Sentencing and Punish-
ment of Offenders Act 2012
s 85................................ 14.57, 14.64;
15.60; 17.81
Limitation Act 1980.................... 9.17
s 2.. 13.50
14A, 14B............................. 13.50
Local Democracy, Economic Development and Construction
Act 2009...................... 8.16; 11.14
Local Government (Access to Information) Act 1985 .... 4.23
Local Government Act 1972
Pt VII (ss 111–146A) 4.23
s 222...................................... 13.35
(1) 14.22
Local Government Act 2003
s 93.. 18.15
Local Government (Miscellaneous
Provisions) Act 1982............ 5.11
s 27.. 17.150
Local Government (Wales) Act
1994 .... 18.03
Localism Act 2011 .... 18.03
s 33A..................................... 16.16
109...................................... 18.03
Local Land Charges Act 1975 ..... 2.21,
2.25; 5.01, 5.07,
5.25; 7.02
s 1.. 5.01
(1)(a)............................... 5.07
(2)................................... 5.09
2.. 5.01
(e)................................. 5.24, 5.25
3, 5..................................... 5.02
7.. 5.22

Local Land Charges Act 1975 – *contd*
s 10.. 5.04
 13A(7), (9) 5.03
London Building Acts (Amend-
 ment) Act 1905 .... 10.23
s 33, 35, 107............................ 10.23

Marine and Coastal Access Act
 2009 .... 19.07, 19.14,
 19.23, 19.42
s 71(5) 12.14
 72(7), (8) 12.11, 12.14
Misrepresentation Act 1967
s 1.. 2.11
 (b) 2.15
 2(1) 2.15

National Parks and Access to the
 Countryside Act 1949 .... 6.05, 6.24;
 19.06, 19.58
s 1.. 19.08
 (4).. 19.08
 2(1), (2).............................. 19.07
 5.. 19.09
 7............................... 6.23; 19.58
 15.. 19.58
 (1)(b) 19.22
 16...............................19.18, 19.29,
 19.58
 (3).. 19.40
 17.. 19.58
 19................................ 19.21, 19.58
 20.. 19.58
 (2).. 19.58
 21...................... 5.28; 19.21, 19.22,
 19.58, 19.59
Pt IV (ss 27–58)...................... 6.04
s 31(a) 19.07
 34(2)(a), (c) 19.07
 35(1) 19.07
 (2) 19.58
 64–66.................................. 5.28
 87, 88.................................. 6.24
 114(1) 19.34
Sch 4....................................... 19.07
 para 1(c) 19.07
National Trust Act 1937
s 8.. 19.18
Natural Environment and Rural
 Communities Act 2006 .... 19.07
s 2................................ 1.29; 19.07
 7.. 19.39

Natural Environment and Rural
 Communities Act 2006 – *contd*
s 11.. 18.35
 16.. 19.39
 18, 33.................................. 1.29
 40(1) 19.09
 88.. 1.29
Natural Heritage (Scotland) Act
 1991 .... 19.06, 19.07
s 12.. 19.28
Nature Conservation (Scotland)
 Act 2004 .... 19.23
Noise Act 1996 .... 3.19; 14.02,
 14.04
Noise and Statutory Nuisance Act
 1993 .... 14.02
s 10(2) 10.49, 10.56;
 14.03
Sch 2
 para 1 .... 14.38
Nuclear Installations Act 1965.... 15.34,
 15.66
s 7–9............................. 13.01, 13.54
 10.. 13.54
Nuisances Removal Act for Eng-
 land 1855............................. 14.10

Occupiers' Liability Act 1957...... 3.11,
 3.16; 9.09; 10.53
Occupiers' Liability Act 1984...... 3.11,
 3.16; 9.09

Planning Act 2008.............. 18.03, 18.04;
 19.57
Pt 3 (ss 14–30A) 18.04
Planning and Compensation Act
 1991
s 12.. 18.24
 22.. 18.31
Sch 2....................................... 18.31
Planning and Compulsory Pur-
 chase Act 2004............. 18.03, 18.08
s 17(7)(za) 18.09
 33A.. 18.08
 36(3) 18.08
 38.. 18.03
 (6) 18.03, 18.07
 38A.. 18.03
Planning (Hazardous Substances)
 Act 1990 ....3.10, 3.11, 3.20
s 6................................ 12.06, 12.14
 10, 11.................................. 5.24

Planning (Hazardous Substances)
  Act 1990 – *contd*
s 17.. 12.14
  24.. 5.24
  28.................................... 6.31; 7.02
Planning (Listed Buildings and
  Conservation Areas) Act 1990
s 2.................................... 5.23, 5.33
  3... 5.24
  7... 5.33
  17, 38...................................... 5.24
  69.................................. 5.24; 18.12
  70–72...................................... 18.12
Pollution Prevention and Control
  Act 1999.................... 17.81; 20.01,
                                20.06, 20.07
s 1.. 20.10
  3.. 20.08
  5(3)... 20.08
  6.................................... 14.04; 17.81,
                                        17.126
  (2)......................... 17.116; 20.01
Sch 1.. 20.08
Sch 2
  para 6........................ 14.04, 14.19
     8.................................... 17.81
Sch 3.. 17.82
Sch 4.. 18.32
Powers of Criminal Courts (Sen-
  tencing) Act 2000
s 130.............................. 13.04; 14.63,
                                        14.70
Prevention of Damage by Pests Act
  1949
s 7.. 5.16
Proceeds of Crime Act 2002........ 1.14
s 327... 1.14
  328... 1.14
     (2)(a).............................. 1.14
  329... 1.14
  330... 1.14
     (6)(b).............................. 1.14
  331, 332............................... 1.14
  333(1)................................... 1.14
  335... 1.14
     (5), (6)............................ 1.14
  340(2), (3), (11)..................... 1.14
  342(2)..................................... 1.14
Protection of Badgers Act 1992.... 19.16
Public Health Act 1875...... 10.08; 14.07,
                                14.10; 19.22
s 94, 95.................................. 14.36

Public Health Act 1936......... 5.07, 5.21;
                                10.24, 10.50;
                                14.10, 14.13
s 18.. 6.46
  36... 5.11
  38, 39..................................... 5.11
  44... 5.12
  45.................................. 5.12; 10.24
  46, 47..................................... 5.12
  50.................................. 5.11; 6.10;
                                        10.24
  (1)–(3)............................. 17.153
  56... 5.11
  83.................................. 5.16; 6.10
  95, 96..................................... 5.19
  141.. 14.04
  259... 5.21
  (1)..................................... 14.04
  264.................................. 5.13; 10.24
  265... 5.21
  275... 5.21
  290.. 10.24
  (3), (6), (7)..................... 17.153
  291... 5.08
  300.. 17.153
  343.. 14.34
Public Health Act 1961......... 5.07; 10.24
s 17.................................. 5.11; 10.24;
                                        17.146
  35... 5.16
  73.................................. 5.18; 10.24
Public Health (Drainage of Trade
  Premises) Act 1937............... 5.07
Public Health (Scotland) Act
  1897.......................... 14.02, 14.38
s 111, 112............................... 14.04

Radioactive Substances Act
  1993...................................... 13.55
s 7, 13, 14, 16, 16A................ 12.14
Regulatory Enforcement and
  Sanctions Act 2008............. 17.28
Pt 1 (ss 1–21)......................... 1.35
Pt 2 (ss 22–35)....................... 1.35
Pt 3 (ss 36–71)....................... 1.35
s 50, 63–65............................. 19.12
Pt 4 (ss 72, 73)....................... 1.35
Reservoirs Act 1975
s 2(2)(b)................................. 7.02
Rivers (Prevention of Pollution)
  Act 1951............................... 17.50
s 85... 17.52

Scotland Act 1998
  s 53.................................... 20.08
Senior Courts Act 1981
  s 31(3) 1.40
Statute of Marlborough 1267...... 10.30
  s 2............................. 10.28, 10.30

Town and Country Planning Act
  1947 .... 16.04
Town and Country Planning Act
  1990 .... 15.104
  s 1..................................... 18.03
  4, 5.................................... 18.03
  54A.................................... 18.07
  55(1)........................ 16.16; 17.14
    (2)(c) 17.14
    (3)(b)............................... 16.16
  61G.................................... 18.03
  70............................. 5.24; 18.16
    (2) 18.07
  72...................................... 18.16
  106................... 3.09; 4.20; 5.24;
                    15.21; 18.24; 19.18
    (1)(d)............................... 18.27
    (3), (11)........................... 18.24
  106A(10)............................. 18.24
  179..................................... 19.34
  198..................................... 6.12
    (1), (3), (6).................... 5.24
  215............................. 5.24; 15.23
    (1) 15.24
  216(2)–(5)........................... 15.25
  217(1), (2).......................... 15.25
    (3)–(5)............................. 15.26
  218..................................... 15.26
  219(1), (2).......................... 15.27
Town   and   Country   Planning
  (Scotland) Act 1972
  s 18A.................................. 18.07
Transport Act 1968
  s 108.................................. 14.04
Transport Act 2000
  s 108.................................. 18.11

Water Act 1989........................ 5.07
  s 4..................................... 5.07
Water Act 2003.................. 17.03, 17.05,
                        17.25, 17.26,
                        17.27, 17.30,
                        17.31, 17.39,
                        17.41, 17.81,
                            17.138

Water Act 2003 – *contd*
  s 36.................................... 7.22
  39...................................... 1.29
  86....................... 15.40, 15.49;
                            17.87
  88..................................... 17.108
  101(1)................................ 17.81
Water Act 2014 .... 17.01, 17.03, 17.06,
                        17.07, 17.17
  s 17.................................... 17.03
  18................................ 17.03, 17.17
    (4) 17.07
  19, 20, 38......................... 17.03
Water Consolidation (Consequen-
  tial Provisions) Act 1991...... 5.11;
                            17.116
  s 3..................................... 5.07
  Sch 2
    para 1 .... 17.124
       (1), (2)...................... 5.11
  Sch 3................................. 5.07
Water Industry Act 1991 .... 1.38; 2.22;
                    5.07; 15.15; 17.01,
                    17.103, 17.104,
                    17.126, 17.158,
                    17.159; 20.06
  s 2(3) 17.157
  2(2A), (3) 17.124
  37(1) 17.02
  41..................................... 17.133
    (1) 17.02
      (b), (c)......................... 17.03
    (2) 17.02
    (4) 17.04
  42............................. 17.03, 17.133
  43............................. 17.03, 17.133
  44..................................... 17.133
    (1), (2)............................ 17.04
    (3)(b).............................. 17.04
    (4) 17.05
  45(1), (1A) 17.05
    (2) 17.17
    (3)(a), (b)........................ 17.05
    (6) 17.17
  46(1)–(4)............................ 17.07
    (5), (6)............................ 17.08
  47(1)–(3)............................ 17.06
  51(1)(a), (b)....................... 17.09
    (2) 17.09
    (3), (4)............................ 17.10
    (5) 17.09
  51D(1) 17.05

Water Industry Act 1991 – *contd*
s 52(1)–(4) 17.18
    (4A) 17.18
        (c) 17.18
    (5), (6) 17.18
54 .... 17.18
55 .... 17.159
    (1)–(3) 17.19
56(1) 17.19
58(1), (4) 17.20
60 .... 17.21
61 .... 17.21
    (1A) 17.21
62 .... 17.21
63A 17.21
64(1), (2) 17.13
    (3) 17.13
        (a), (b) 17.13
    (4) 17.13
65 .... 17.159
66 .... 5.14; 17.159
68(1) 17.22
70 .... 17.22
82 .... 5.14
94 .... 17.128
    (1) 17.132, 17.133
        (a) 13.18
97(1) 17.132, 17.154
    (2) 17.132
98, 99 .... 17.133
100 .... 17.133
    (4) 17.133
101 .... 17.133
    (1) 17.133
101A 17.134
102(1)–(5), (7) 17.137
103 .... 17.137
104 .... 3.09; 6.45, 6.46
    (1)–(4) 17.137
    (5) 17.136
    (6) 17.137
    (7) 17.136
105(2)–(7) 17.137
105A 17.107
    B(2) 17.107
    B(4) 17.107
106 .... 6.08; 17.103,
                                  17.140
    (1), (2) 17.138
    (3)–(6), (8) 17.139
107 .... 5.11
    (1)–(4), (4A) 17.140

Water Industry Act 1991 – *contd*
s 108(1), (2) 17.141
109(2) 17.141
112(1), (2), (5), (6) 17.142
113(1), (3)–(5) 17.154
114 .... 17.154
115(1)(a) 17.155
117(1) 17.133
118 .... 3.10, 3.20; 7.22,
                               7.23; 12.14;
                         17.122, 17.127
    (1) 17.108
    (3), (4) 17.103
119 .... 17.108, 17.122,
                                  17.127
120 .... 17.127
    (1)–(3), (9) 17.117
121 .... 7.22; 17.127
    (1), (2) 17.109
122 .... 7.22; 17.109,
                          17.111, 17.118,
                                  17.127
123 .... 17.118, 17.127
124 .... 7.23; 17.127
    (1)–(3) 7.22; 17.112
    (4) 7.22
    (5)–(7) 17.112
125 .... 17.127
    (1)–(3) 17.112
126 .... 7.22; 17.127
    (1)–(6) 17.113
127 .... 17.127
    (1)–(3) 17.118, 17.119
128 .... 17.127
129 .... 7.22; 12.07, 12.14;
                          17.117, 17.127
130 .... 7.22; 17.127
    (1)–(3), (7) 17.117
131 .... 7.22; 17.127
    (1)–(4) 17.119
132 .... 17.127
    (2)–(5) 17.119
133 .... 17.127
134 .... 17.121, 17.127
135–137 .... 17.127
138 .... 7.22; 17.116,
                                  17.127
    (2) 17.116
139, 140 .... 17.127
141(1), (2) 17.108
142(1), (2) 17.156
    (4) 17.157

Water Industry Act 1991 – *contd*
s 143.................................... 7.24
　(1) 17.123
　　(b)............................. 17.123
　(3) 17.123
　(5) 17.123
　　(b)............................. 17.124
144(1)–(4) 17.157
146(3) 17.137
158.................................. 17.142
159(1), (2)....................... 17.07
161(1) 17.142
196.............................. 7.02, 7.22,
　　　　　　　　7.23; 17.125
199.............................. 6.48, 6.51;
　　　　　　　　　　17.143
206.............................. 7.23; 17.81
　(1)–(3), (7)...................... 17.126
209.................................. 17.159
　(1) 17.159
218.................................. 17.02
219(1) 17.02, 17.04,
　　　　　　　　17.05, 17.131
Sch 4A 17.21
Sch 8 .... 7.24
Water Industry Act 1999 .... 17.21
s 3(1)–(2), (4)........................ 17.123
s 4................................... 7.24
s 5................................... 17.157
Water Industry Act 2011
s 105B(3)............................. 17.107
Water Resources Act 1991 ... 9.39; 10.08,
　　　　　　　　10.43; 12.14;
　　　　　　　　17.01, 17.43,
　　　　　　　　17.44, 17.46,
　　　　　　　　17.57, 17.87,
　　　　　　　　17.95, 17.125;
　　　　　　　　　　20.06
Pt II (ss 19–81) 3.10; 7.04,
　　　　　　　　7.11; 17.25
s 21................................. 17.34
24.................................. 3.21
　(1)–(3)............................ 17.26
　(4) 17.26
　　(a), (b)......................... 17.27
　(5) 17.26
24A 17.31
25.................................. 3.21
　(1) 17.39
　(2)(b)............................. 17.39
　(3) 17.39
　(8) 17.39

Water Resources Act 1991 – *contd*
s 26, 27............................. 3.21
27A................................ 17.26
28.................................. 3.21
29.............................. 3.21; 17.26
　(2A)............................. 17.26
30–33.............................. 3.21
34.............................. 3.21; 17.32
　(3) 17.33
35.................................. 3.21
　(2)–(4)............................ 17.29
36.................................. 3.21
37.............................. 3.21; 17.32
38.................................. 3.21
　(1) 17.33
　(2) 17.35
　　(b)............................. 7.11
　(3) 17.34
39.............................. 3.21; 7.11
　(1), (2)............................ 17.34
39A................................ 17.34
40.............................. 3.21; 7.11; 17.34
　(2) 17.34
41.............................. 3.21; 17.36
42–44.......................... 3.21; 17.36
45.................................. 3.21
46.................................. 3.21
　(2)–(5)............................ 17.35
47.................................. 3.21
　(1) 17.35
48.............................. 3.21, 17.29
49, 50............................ 3.21; 12.14
51–56.......................... 3.21; 7.11; 17.37
57.............................. 3.21; 17.37
58.................................. 3.21
59.............................. 3.21; 7.11
59A.......................... 7.11; 12.08, 12.14
　(5)............................... 17.41
59B 7.11; 17.41
59C........................... 7.11; 12.08,
　　　　　　　　12.14; 17.41
59D................................ 7.11
60.................................. 3.21
61.............................. 3.21; 17.37
62–68.............................. 3.21
69.............................. 3.21; 17.38
70.............................. 3.21; 17.29
71, 72.............................. 3.21
Pt III (ss 82–104) 7.04
s 84................................. 17.72
85.................................. 7.31
91A, 91B........................... 15.80

Water Resources Act 1991 – *contd*

s 92...................................... 17.82
93.. 17.94
97.. 3.11
104.............................. 7.12; 9.11;
15.33; 17.43
Pt IV (ss 105–113).................. 7.04
s 107.................................... 7.13
109........................... 7.13; 12.09,
12.14; 20.18
(1), (2).......................... 7.13
110.......................... 12.09, 12.14
(2)(c)........................... 12.14
Pt V (ss 114–116)................... 7.04
s 118(5)............................... 17.118
121(5)............................... 17.118
129.................................... 17.119
158(3), (4)........................... 7.11
161...................... 2.25; 3.11, 3.20;
9.03, 9.22, 9.23,
9.24; 10.04,
10.43, 10.56;
15.110; 17.47,
17.83, 17.84,
17.86, 17.88
(1A)............................... 17.47
(2), (3).......................... 17.83
(4)–(6)........................... 17.84
161A..................... 2.25; 3.11, 3.20;
9.03, 9.22; 10.04,
10.08, 10.25, 10.43;
14.36; 17.86,
17.88, 17.91
(1)....................... 17.47, 17.88
(2)(a), (b)...................... 17.88
161AA(1), (2), (4)............... 17.89
161B 2.25; 3.11, 3.20;
9.03, 9.22; 10.04,
10.25, 10.43; 14.37;
17.86, 17.89, 17.92
(1)–(5).......................... 17.91
161C..................... 2.25; 3.11, 3.20;
9.03, 9.22; 10.04,
10.25, 10.43; 17.86
161D..................... 2.25; 3.11, 3.20;
9.03, 9.22; 10.04,
10.25, 10.43,
10.56; 17.86
(1), (2)................. 10.04; 17.93
(3), (4)......................... 17.93
161ZA 17.85, 17.88
(4)............................... 17.88

Water Resources Act 1991 – *contd*

s 161ZC(1)............................. 17.83
(2).............................. 17.84
189................................ 7.02, 7.11
(1)............................... 17.42
190................................ 2.25; 7.12
191A(2)............................... 15.103
193................................ 7.02; 7.13
193A–193E.......................... 7.02
196(1)............................... 17.115
201.................................... 17.27
204.................................... 17.81
(2)(a)........................... 17.81
206......................... 17.27, 17.81
(4), (5)......................... 17.27
208.................................... 17.159
210................................ 7.13, 7.19
216(2)................................ 17.28
217.................................... 17.28
221.................................... 7.20
(1)....................... 17.26, 17.39
Sch 10
para 11 .... 12.14; 17.122
Sch 11.................................. 17.94
Sch 25
para 5 .... 7.13
6 .... 7.19
Wildlife and Countryside Act
1981 .... 4.25; 19.06, 19.10,
19.14, 19.15, 19.23,
19.28, 19.31, 19.32,
19.33, 19.42, 19.49,
19.52, 19.55
Pt I (ss 1–27ZA) 19.13, 19.16
s 1..................................... 19.14
(1)–(3)........................... 19.14
2..................................... 19.14
3................................ 19.14, 19.16
4................................ 19.14, 19.16
(2)(c)........................... 19.14
5..................................... 19.14
(4), (4A) 19.14
6–8................................ 19.14
9................................ 19.15, 19.16
(1), (3), (4), (10) 19.16
10(3)(c) 19.16
(5)............................... 19.15
11(1), (2)....................... 19.15
13(1), (3)....................... 19.15
14................................ 7.16; 19.16
(2)............................... 9.09
(4A)....................... 2.25; 7.16

Wildlife and Countryside Act
1981 – *contd*

s 16(1)	19.14
(3)	19.16
19ZA, 19ZB	19.32
21	19.14
(1)	19.14
27(1)	19.14, 19.15
28	2.25; 7.26; 10.52; 19.21, 19.23, 19.25, 19.26, 19.34, 19.35, 19.36, 19.37
(1)	1.24
(b)	10.51
(3)	19.25
(4)	19.24
(5)	19.25
(9)	5.28
(11)	19.36
28A	2.25
28B, 28C	2.25; 19.23
28D	2.25; 19.28
28E	2.25; 10.51; 19.29
(1), (7), (8)	19.29
28F	2.25; 19.29
28G	2.25; 19.33, 19.38
28H	2.25; 19.29, 19.33
28I	2.25; 19.33
28J, 28K	2.25; 7.28; 19.29, 19.30
28L	2.25; 19.30
(2)	19.31
(4)	19.30
(7)	19.31
28M	2.25; 19.29

Wildlife and Countryside Act
1981 – *contd*

s 28N	2.25; 19.32
(2)–(4)	19.32
28O	2.25
28P	2.25; 10.51; 19.29
(2)	19.29, 19.38
(3)	19.29
(4)	19.29, 19.62
(6), (6A)	19.29
28Q	2.25
(1)–(4)	7.28
28R	2.25
31(1)	19.29
34	2.25
35	19.21
(1), (5)	19.59
37A	19.28
39	5.28; 19.39
(2)	19.40
(3)	19.18, 19.40
40	19.61
50(2), (3)	19.41
51(1)	19.32
52(4)	19.34
Pt III (ss 53–66)	6.05
s 53	6.05
56	6.04
57	6.05
59	6.06
Sch 5	14.04; 19.15
Sch 8	19.15
Sch 9	19.16
Pt II	9.09
Sch 9A	2.25; 7.16

TABLE OF STATUTORY INSTRUMENTS

Air Quality (England) Regulations 2000, SI 2000/928 .... 20.05
Air Quality (Scotland) Regulations 2000, SI 2000/97 .... 20.05
Air Quality (Wales) Regulations 2000, SI 2000/1940 .... 20.05
Anti-Pollution Works Regulations 1999, SI 1999/1006 .... 9.22; 17.89
  reg 2 .... 17.89
    (e) 17.90
    3 .... 10.25; 17.90
      (4) 10.25
    4–6 .... 17.90
    7 .... 17.92
  Schedule 17.92
    para 2, 4 .... 17.92
      5(2) 17.92
      6 .... 17.92

Building (Amendment) Regulations 2001, SI 2001/3335 ..... 17.144
  Sch 1
    para H4 .... 5.30; 6.51
Building Regulations 2000, SI 2000/2531 .... 17.143
  Sch 1
    paras H1, H3 .... 17.144
Building Regulations 2010, SI 2010/2214 .... 15.18
  reg 15(3) 6.51
    (b) 6.48
  Sch 1 .... 6.20, 6.51
Business Protection from Misleading Marketing Regulations 2008, SI 2008/1276
  reg 3 .... 2.16

CRC Energy Efficiency Scheme Order 2013, SI 2013/1119 ... 3.07; 10.31
  art 3, 5, 36 .... 10.31
  Sch 1
    para 14(3) 10.31
      16(1), (2) 10.31
      (3)(b) 10.31

Civil Procedure Rules 1998, SI 1998/3132 .... 1.40
Clean Neighbourhoods and Environment Act 2005 (Commencement No 2) (England) order 2006, SI 2006/1361 .... 15.34
Community Infrastructure Levy Regulations 2010, SI 2010/948
  reg 122 .... 18.25
    123 .... 18.26
Conservation (Natural Habitats etc) Regulations 1994, SI 1994/2716 .... 2.25; 19.57
  reg 14 .... 5.28
Conservation of Habitats and Species (Amendment) Regulations 2012, SI 2012/1927
  reg 12 .... 19.52
Conservation of Habitats and Species Regulations 2010, SI 2010/490 .... 2.25; 19.22, 19.42, 19.49, 19.50, 19.52, 19.53
  reg 9 .... 19.49
    13 .... 19.50, 19.51
    14, 16 .... 19.51
    20, 21 .... 19.52
    25–29 .... 7.26
    61 .... 19.55
    63 .... 7.12; 19.56
    73–76, 81–101 .... 19.57
Construction Contracts (England and Wales) Exclusion Order 1998, SI 1998/648 .... 8.16
Consumer Trading from Unfair Trading Regulations 2008, SI 2008/1277
  reg 4, 11, 16 .... 2.16
Contaminated Land (England) (Amendment) Regulations 2001, SI 2001/663 .... 15.34
Contaminated Land (England) Regulations 2000, SI 2000/227 .... 15.34

Contaminated Land (England) Regulations 2006, SI 2006/1380 .... 15.34
reg 2 .... 15.52
    (1)(k), (l) 15.52
3 .... 15.52
4 .... 15.61, 15.74
    (1)(g)................................. 15.61
    (h) 15.62
    (i), (j) 15.61
6 .... 15.60
7 .... 10.25; 15.71
    (1)(h), (i) 15.72
8(2)(a)................................... 15.73
9 .... 15.73
10(2)..................................... 15.73
12(1)..................................... 15.73
13 .... 7.02; 15.102
Sch 1...................................... 15.52
Sch 2...................................... 15.60
Sch 3............................. 7.02; 15.102
    para 12–14........................ 15.102
    15 .... 2.25; 15.102
    16 .... 15.102
Contaminated Land (Scotland) Regulations 2000, SI 2000/178 .... 15.04
Controlled Waste (England and Wales) Regulations 2012, SI 2012/811
reg 3 .... 16.11
Sch 1...................................... 16.17
Control of Asbestos Regulations 2012, SI 2012/632 .... 3.06; 9.09
reg 4 .... 3.06
Control of Major Accident Hazards Regulations 2015, SI 2015/483 .... 3.20
Control of Noise (Appeals) Regulations 1975, SI 1975/2116 .. 14.74
Control of Noise (Codes of Practice for Construction and Open Sites) Order 1984, SI 1984/1992 .... 14.56
Control of Noise (Code of Practice for Construction and Open Sites) Order 1987, SI 1987/1730 .... 14.56; 14.74
Control of Noise (Measurement and Registers) Regulations 1976, SI 1976/37 .... 7.02

Control of Pollution (Oil Storage) (England) Regulations 2001, SI 2001/2954 .... 3.11; 17.82
reg 2(2).................................... 3.11
9 .... 3.11
Control of Trade in Endangered Species (Enforcement) Regulations 1997, SI 1997/1372 .. 19.16
Countryside Stewardship Regulations 1998, SI 1998/1327 ..... 19.61
reg 3(1)................................... 19.61
4, 9 .... 19.61

Dangerous Substances (Notification and Marketing of Sites) Regulations 1990, SI 1990/304 .... 3.20
Development Commission (Transfer of Functions and Miscellaneous Provisions) Order 1999, SI 1999/416 .... 19.08

End-of-Life Vehicles Regulations 2003, SI 2003/2635 .... 7.02
Energy Performance of Buildings (England and Wales) Regulations 2012, SI 2012/3118 ..... 2.06
reg 6 .... 10.32
9(1), (2) 10.32
18 .... 3.10
27 .... 10.32
Environment Act 1995 (Commencement No 5) Order 1996, SI 1996/186 .... 7.04
Environment Act 1995 (Commencement No 15) Order 1999, SI 1999/1301 .... 17.86
Environment Act 1995 (Commencement No 16 and Saving Provision) (England) Order 2000, SI 2000/340 .... 15.04, 15.35
Environment Act 1995 (Commencement No 17 and Savings Provision) (Scotland) Order 2000, SI 2000/180 ..... 15.35
Environment Act 1995 (Commencement No 20 and Saving Provision) (Wales) Order 2001, SI 2001/3211 .... 15.04, 15.35

Environmental Assessment of Plans and Programmes Regulations 2004, SI 2004/1633 .. 18.37, 18.38
reg 4 .... 18.39
  5(1)–(3)............................... 18.37
  8 .... 18.39
  9, 10 .... 18.38
Pt 3 (regs 12–15) 18.39
reg 12(2)..................................... 18.39
  13 .... 18.39
Sch 1.. 18.38
Sch 2.............................. 18.39, 18.40
Environmental Civil Sanctions (England) Order 2010, SI 2010/1157 .... 17.28; 19.12
Sch 4.. 19.12
para 7(3)...................................... 19.12
Environmental Civil Sanctions (Miscellaneous Amendments) (England) Regulations 2010, SI 2010/1159 .... 19.12
Environmental Damage (Prevention and Remediation) Regulations 2009, SI 2009/153 .... 1.25
Environmental Damage (Prevention and Remediation) (England) Regulations 2015, SI 2015/810 .... 15.106, 15.106, 15.107, 15.110
reg 2(6)...................................... 15.106
  3(1)... 15.106
  4(1)(a).................................... 15.108
  (c).. 15.107
  (2)–(4).................................. 15.108
  (5).. 15.107
  5(1), (2) 15.106, 15.108
  8(1)... 15.105
  13, 14, 16, 18...................... 15.106
Sch 1
para 1 .... 15.108
Sch 3
para 4(2), (3) 15.109
  5... 15.109
Sch 4........................... 15.107, 15.108
Environmental Damage (Prevention and Remediation) (Wales) Regulations 2009, SI 2009/995 .... 15.105
Environmental Information Regulations 1992, SI 1992/3240 .. 4.29; 6.01; 17.79, 17.81

Environmental Information Regulations 2004, SI 2004/3391 .. 1.40; 4.01, 4.02, 4.03, 4.04, 4.05, 4.06, 4.07, 4.09, 4.10, 4.11, 4.15, 4.19, 4.20, 4.25, 4.26, 4.30, 4.32, 4.35, 4.37, 4.39, 4.40; 6.01; 7.23; 15.104; 17.126; 20.27
reg 2 .... 4.09
  (1).................... 4.06, 4.20, 4.30
  (a), (c)......................... 4.20
  (2)............................... 4.06; 7.23
  (a)............................. 4.09, 4.20
  (c)............................. 4.06, 4.20
  (d) 4.06
  (3)............................... 4.08
  3(3)............................... 4.07
  4 .... 4.40; 20.27
  (1)............................... 4.08
  5(1)............................... 4.08
  (2)............................... 4.31
  (3)............................... 4.27
  (4)............................... 4.29
  (6).......................... 4.20, 4.23, 4.25
  6 .... 4.34
  (1)(b) 4.34
  7................................. 4.31
  8................................. 4.35
  (3)............................... 4.35
  (5)–(7)........................ 4.35
  9 .... 4.12, 4.16
  11 .... 4.38
  (1), (2), (4) 4.32
  12 .... 4.11, 4.25
  (1)............................... 4.11
  (4)............................... 4.11
  (a)............................. 4.14
  (b) 4.15
  (d) 4.17
  (e)............................. 4.18
  (5).................... 4.11, 4.12, 4.28
  (a).................... 4.19, 4.23
  (b) 4.05, 4.09, 4.20, 4.25
  (c)............................. 4.21
  (d) 4.20, 4.22, 4.23
  (e)......................... 4.22, 4.24

Environmental Information Regulations 2004 – *contd*
reg 12(5)(f) 4.22, 4.25
    (g)................................. 4.22
    (6)................................. 4.32
    (8)................................. 4.18
    (9)................................. 4.23
    (10)............................... 4.06
    (11)............................... 4.13
  13 .... 4.25, 4.27
  14 .... 4.38
    (1), (2), (5) 4.32
  15 .... 4.19
  16 .... 4.03
  17 .... 4.10
  18 .... 4.39
    (1)................................. 4.32
    (3)................................. 4.32
    (4)................................. 4.32
      (a)............................. 4.35
    (6)........................... 4.32, 4.35
  19 .... 4.36
  20 .... 4.02
  26 .... 4.09
  Sch 5
  para 5–11........................... 1.40
Environmental Liability (Prevention and Remediation) Regulations (Northern Ireland) 2009, SI 2009/252 .... 15.105
Environmental Liability (Scotland) Regulations 2009, SSI 2009/266 .... 15.105
Environmental Licences (Suspension and Revocation) Regulations 1996, SI 1996/508 .... 17.37
Environmentally Sensitive Areas (England) Designation Orders (Amendment) Regulations 1996, SI 1996/3104 ..... 19.60
Environmental Permitting (England and Wales) (Amendment) (No 2) Regulations 2016, SI 2016/475 ...... 16.20; 20.10, 20.17, 20.18
Environmental Permitting (England and Wales) Regulations 2007, SI 2007/3538 .... 15.29; 17.49; 20.01, 20.10
  reg 21 .... 12.14
  Sch 1
  Pt I.................................... 7.15

Environmental Permitting (England and Wales) Regulations 2010, SI 2010/675 .... 3.10, 3.20, 3.23; 6.34; 7.03, 7.04, 7.13; 10.21, 10.34, 10.44; 12.04, 12.13; 15.29; 16.01, 16.08, 16.20, 16.23, 16.28; 17.43, 17.44, 17.45, 17.46, 17.57, 17.68, 17.71, 17.79, 17.100; 20.01, 20.10, 20.11, 20.17, 20.18, 20.22, 20.25, 20.26, 20.28, 20.32
  reg 2 .... 17.100; 20.18
    (1)........................... 15.01; 20.12
  3 .... 15.106
  4 .... 16.22
  5 .... 17.44; 20.18
  7 .... 20.19
  8 .... 12.04; 17.45; 20.12, 20.13, 20.18
    (2)................................. 20.18
  Pt 2 (regs 11–31) 17.69
  reg 12 .... 7.13, 7.14; 10.21; 20.13
    (1)................................. 7.17
      (a)............................. 17.45
      (b) 9.03; 17.44
  13 .... 20.19, 20.20
    (1)................................. 20.13
  15 .... 17.71
  19 .... 17.76
  20 .... 3.20; 7.17; 17.74; 20.15
    (1)–(5), (7) 20.24
  21 .... 12.04, 12.14; 17.77, 17.122; 20.15, 20.22
    (1)(a)–(c)........................ 12.04
    (4)................................. 12.04
      (a)–(c)........................ 12.04
  22 .... 2.22; 7.17; 17.74; 20.15, 20.28
  24 .... 20.23
  25 .... 3.20; 20.23

Environmental Permitting (England and Wales) Regulations 2010 – *contd*

reg 26	20.25
(4)	20.25
27(3)	20.25
28–30	20.25
31	12.04; 17.74; 20.31
(9)	20.31
32	20.12
34	17.74; 20.15
(2)	20.28
35	17.76
(2)(d)	16.28
Pt 4 (regs 36–44A)	20.16
reg 36	2.22; 7.12, 7.18; 20.28
37	2.22; 7.18
(2)	20.28
38	7.14, 7.18; 16.23, 16.26; 20.28
(1)	3.20; 7.12, 7.17; 12.04; 17.45, 17.68
(a)	10.03, 10.46
(b)	17.57
(2)	7.12; 10.03
(3)	17.45; 20.28
(4)	17.45
(a)	17.45
(5)	17.45
39	16.23, 16.26
(1), (3), (4)	17.46
40	16.25; 17.59
(1)	16.67
(2), (3)	7.31
42	16.26; 20.28
44	16.26; 20.28
44A	20.28
Pt 5 (regs 45–56)	20.16
reg 46	17.79; 20.27
(2), (8), (9)	20.27
47	17.79
(3)	17.79
48	17.79; 20.27
(1)	17.80
51	17.80; 20.27
(2)(b)	17.80
53	20.31
(1)	20.31
55	17.80
56	17.80
Pt 6 (regs 57–66B)	20.16

Environmental Permitting (England and Wales) Regulations 2010 – *contd*

reg 57	16.26; 20.30
(4)–(6)	20.30
57A	20.30
59	20.26
61	17.73
62	17.73
(3)	17.73
67A	12.04; 17.76
68	16.23
Sch 1	20.18
Pt 2	7.17; 20.12
Sch 2	17.44
para 3	3.20; 16.22
(1)(b)(ii)	12.04, 12.14
4(b)	12.04, 12.14
5	12.04, 12.14
7	7.02, 7.14
15	20.28
Sch 3	7.14; 12.04, 12.14; 16.22; 20.18
Pt 2	17.44
Pt 4	20.18
Sch 5	17.69; 20.11, 20.19
Pt 1	
para 1	20.26
3	20.20
4	20.19
5	20.24
(1)–(4)	20.26
6	20.26
9	20.21
11	20.26
12(2)	20.21
13	20.20, 20.22
(3)	20.20
14	20.23
15	20.19, 20.22
17	20.19
20	20.21, 20.30
Pt 2	17.71; 20.21
para 3, 4	17.69
5, 6	1.40; 17.69
12	17.70
(2)	17.71
13, 15	12.04
Sch 6	17.75; 20.11
para 3	20.31
(1)	17.75
5(1)	17.75

Environmental Permitting (England and Wales) Regulations 2010 – *contd*
Sch 7A.......................... 10.21; 20.11
Sch 8.............................. 10.21; 20.11
Sch 8A...................................... 20.11
Sch 9................................. 3.20; 10.21; 16.08; 20.11
    para 2 .... 16.16
Sch 9A.. 3.20
Sch 10............................... 3.20; 7.14; 16.28; 20.11
    para 1 .... 16.28
Sch 11.. 20.11
Sch 12.. 20.11
Sch 13A...................................... 20.11
Sch 14.. 20.11
Sch 15A...................................... 20.11
Sch 16.. 20.11
Sch 17A...................................... 20.11
Sch 18.. 20.11
Sch 19.. 20.11
Sch 21............................... 3.20; 7.22; 17.44; 20.11
    para 6 .... 17.68
      (2)–(6)........................ 17.68
Sch 22............................... 3.20; 20.11
    para 3 .... 17.101
      4, 5 .... 17.100
      6, 8 .... 17.102
Sch 23... 7.17
Sch 23ZA 7.13; 20.18, 20.28
Sch 24................................ 7.02, 7.17, 7.18; 17.79
    para 1 .... 20.27
Sch 25.. 16.23
Environmental Protection (Disposal of Polychlorinated Biphenyls and other Dangerous Substances) (England and Wales) Regulations 2000, SI 2000/1043 .... 3.22
Environmental Protection (Duty of Care) Regulations 1991, SI 1991/2839 .... 16.17
Environmental Protection (Prescribed Processes and Substances) Regulations 1991, SI 1991/472 .... 3.20
Explosives Regulations 2014, SI 2014/1638 .... 3.24

Greenhouse Gas Emissions Trading Scheme Regulations 2012, SI 2012/3038 .... 12.14
    reg 9 .... 12.10
    reg 12 .... 12.10
    reg 16 .... 12.10
    reg 41 .... 12.10
Groundwater Regulations 1998, SI 1998/2746 .... 12.14; 17.100
    reg 18 .... 12.14
Hazardous Waste (England and Wales) (Amendment) Regulations 2016, SI 2016/336 .... 13.12
    reg 2(3)................................. 12.12
Hazardous Waste (England and Wales) Regulations 2005, SI 2005/894 .... 16.27
    reg 4 .... 16.27
      6 .... 16.27
      21 .... 12.14; 16.27
      (1)–(3)............................. 12.12
      22–23, 35–38, 47–51, 65, 65A, 66, 69, 70 .... 16.27
Hazardous Waste (Miscellaneous Amendments) Regulations 2015, SI 2015/1360 .... 16.27
Health and Safety (Enforcing Authority) Regulations 1998, SI 1998/494 .... 14.66
Hedgerows Regulations 1997, SI 1997/1160
    reg 5(1)–(9)............................. 6.37
      10 .... 6.35, 6.36
Human Rights Act 1998 (Commencement No 2) Order 2000, SI 2000/1851 .... 1.36

Landfill Tax (Contaminated Land) Order 1996, SI 1996/1529 ... 16.29
Landfill Tax (Material from Contaminated Land) (Phasing out of Exemption) Order 2008, SI 2008/2669 .... 15.09
Landfill Tax (Qualifying Material) Order 2011, SI 2011/1017 ... 16.29, 16.31
Landfill Tax Regulations 1996, SI 1996/1527 .... 16.01, 16.29
Landfill Tax (Site Restoration and Quarries) Order 1999, SI 1999/2075 .... 16.31

Land Registration Rules 1925, SI 1925/1093

r 258.. 17.10

Local Authorities (Executive Arrangements) (Meetings and Access to Information) (England) Regulations 2012, SI 2012/2089 .... 4.23

Local Land Charges Rules 1977, SI 1977/985 .... 5.02

r 2(2) 5.06, 5.07, 5.15, 5.23

3.............................. 5.05, 5.23, 5.26

Magistrates' Court (Hearsay Evidence in Civil Proceedings) Rules 1999, SI 1999/681 .... 14.44

National Assembly for Wales (Transfer of Functions) Order 1999, SI 1999/672 .... 18.04

Natural Resources Body for Wales (Establishment) Order 2013, SI 2013/1903 .... 18.03

Natural Resources Body for Wales (Functions) Order 2013, SI 2013/755 .... 18.03

art 4(2) 1.42; 7.04, 7.29

Sch 4

para 246 .... 1.42; 7.04

247(a) 1.42; 7.04

Sch 5

para 80(1)............................ 7.29

Nitrate Pollution Prevention (Amendment) and Water Resources (Control of Pollution) (Silage, Slurry and Agricultural Fuel Oil) (England) (Amendment) Regulations 2013, SI 2013/1001 .... 17.82

Nitrate Pollution Prevention Regulations 2008, SI 2008/2349 .... 17.95

Pts 3–8.................................... 17.97

reg 11B.................................. 17.96

48 .... 17.97

Noise Act 1996 (Commencement No 1) Order 1996, SI 1996/2219 .... 14.02

Notification of Cooling Towers and Evaporative Condensers Regulations 1992, SI 1992/2225 .... 3.16

Notification of Installations Handling Hazardous Substances Regulations 1982, SI 1982/1357 .... 9.12

Nuclear Installations (Liability for Damage) Order 2016, SI 2016/562 .... 13.54

Petroleum (Consolidation) Regulations 2014, SI 2014/1637 .. 3.11

reg 9, 10 .... 12.05, 12.14

14(8)........................ 12.05, 12.14

Planning (Hazardous Substances) Regulations 1992, SI 1992/656 .... 9.12

Planning (Hazardous Substances) Regulations 2015, SI 2015/627 .... 3.10, 3.11, 3.20; 7.02

reg 3, 20 .... 6.32

Sch 1.................................... 6.32

Pollution Prevention and Control (England and Wales) Regulations 2000, SI 2000/1973 ..... 3.20; 18.32; 20.01, 20.10, 20.13

reg 18 .... 12.14

64 .... 20.12

Sch 5.................................... 20.12

Sch 10

para 7 .... 14.19

Pollution Prevention and Control (Public Participation) (England and Wales) Regulations 2005, SI 2005/1448 .... 1.40

Pollution Prevention and Control (Scotland) Regulations 2012, SI 2012/360 .... 20.08

Private Water Supplies Regulations 2009, SI 2009/3101 ..... 17.22

Producer Responsibility Obligations (Packaging Waste) Regulations 2007, SI 2007/871 .. 1.33; 16.07

Radioactive Contaminated Land (Enabling Powers) (England) Regulations 2005, SI 2005/3467 .... 15.34

Radioactive Contaminated Land
(Modification of Enactments)
(England) Regulations 2006,
SI 2006/1379 .... 15.34, 15.45
reg 5 .... 15.45
　(1), (4), (6), (8) 15.40
　6 .... 15.41, 15.45
　7 .... 15.45, 15.57
　8 .... 15.45, 15.60,
　　　　　　　　　　　　　　 15.68
　9 .... 15.45, 15.75
　10 .... 15.45, 15.60
　11, 12 .... 15.45
　13 .... 15.45, 15.75
　14 .... 15.45, 15.65
　15–17 .... 15.45
Radioactive Contaminated Land
Regulations (Northern Ire-
land) 2006/345 .... 15.35
Registers of Drainage Boards
Regulations 1968, SI 1968/
1672 .... 7.02

Scheme for Construction Con-
tracts (England and Wales)
Regulations 1998, SI 1998/
649 .... 8.16
Smoke Control Areas (Author-
ised Fuels) (England) (No 2)
Regulations 2014, SI 2014/
2366 .... 20.34
Smoke Control Areas (Exempted
Fireplaces) (England) Order
2015, SI 2015/307 .... 20.34
Statutory Nuisance (Appeals)
(Amendment) (England) Regulations 2006, SI 2006/771 .. 14.38
Statutory Nuisance (Appeals)
Regulations 1995, SI 1995/
2644 .... 10.06; 14.38
reg 2 .... 10.24
　(2)(c)...................... 10.26; 14.29
　　(i) 10.24
　　(j) 10.07, 10.24
　　　(ii)............................ 14.35
　(3), (5) 14.47
　(6)........................... 10.24, 10.25
　(7)........................... 10.24, 10.25
　　(a)...................... 14.47, 14.60
3(1).. 15.73
　(b)(i), (ii)...................... 14.40
　(2).. 15.73

Statutory Nuisance (Appeals)
Regulations 1995 – *contd*
reg 3(2 (a)................................ 14.41
　　(i), (ii)...................... 14.41
　　(b) 14.41
　(3).. 15.73
Statutory Nuisance (Appeals)
(Scotland) Regulations 1996,
SI 1996/1076 .... 14.38
Statutory Nuisance (Miscella-
neous Provisions) (Wales)
Regulations 2007, SI 2007/
117 .... 14.38
Statutory Nuisances (Insects)
Regulations 2006, SI 2006/
770 .... 14.04
Surface Waters (Abstraction for
Drinking Water) (Classifi-
cation) Regulations 1996,
SI 1996/3001 .... 17.22

Town and Country Planning (As-
sessment of Environmental
Effects) Regulations 1988,
SI 1988/1199 .... 18.28
Town and Country Planning
(Development Management
Procedure) (Wales) Order
2012, SI 2012/801
art 14(1) 7.29
Table Sch 4(q)........................ 7.29
Town and Country Planning
(Development Management
Procedure) (England) Order
2015, SI 2015/595
art 18(1) 7.29
Sch 4
　Table (w)............................ 7.29
Town and Country Planning
(Environmental Impact As-
sessment) (England and
Wales) Regulations 1999,
SI 1999/293 .... 18.28
Town and Country Planning
(Environmental Impact
Assessment) Regulations
2011, SI 2011/1824 .....18.28, 18.29,
　　　　　　　　　　　　 18.34, 18.35,
　　　　　　　　　　　　 18.36, 18.37
reg 2(1)........................... 18.33, 18.36
Pt 2 (regs 4–6) 18.34
reg 4(5).................................... 18.36

Town and Country Planning (Environmental Impact Assessment) Regulations 2011 – *contd*
Pt 4 (regs 13–15) 18.34
reg 13(4), (6) 18.34
Pt 5 (regs 16–22) 18.29
reg 37, 39, 40 .... 18.29
Sch 1...................................... 18.33
Sch 2............................ 18.33, 18.34, 18.36
Sch 3...................................... 18.36
Sch 4...................................... 18.36
Town and Country Planning (General Permitted Development) Order 1995, SI 1995/418 ..... 17.14; 19.57
art 4....................................... 5.24
Sch 2...................................... 17.14
Town and Country Planning (General Permitted Development) Order 2015, SI 2015/596 ..... 19.56, 19.57
Town and Country Planning (Local Planning) (England) Regulations 2012, SI 2012/767 .... 18.08
reg 4, 5, 9 .... 18.09
10....................................... 18.11
Town and Country Planning (London Spatial Development Strategy) Regulations 2000, SI 2000/1491 .... 18.04
Town and Country Planning (Mayor of London) Order 2008, SI 2008/580 .... 18.04
Town and Country Planning (Prescription of County Matters) (England) Regulations 2003, SI 2003/1003 .... 16.16
Trade Effluents (Prescribed Processes and Substances) (Amendment) Regulations 1990, SI 1990/1629 ..... 7.22; 17.116
Trade Effluents (Prescribed Processes and Substances) Regulations 1989, SI 1989/1156 .. 3.20; 7.22
reg 3, 4 .... 17.116
5.. 17.120
Sch 1...................................... 17.116
Sch 2...................................... 17.116

Trade Effluents (Prescribed Processes and Substances) Regulations 1992, SI 1992/339 .... 17.116
Unauthorised Deposit of Waste (Fixed Penalties) Regulations 2016, SI 2016/334 .... 16.26
Urban Waste Water Treatment (England and Wales) Regulations 1994, SI 1994/2841 ..... 17.127
reg 2(1)........................ 17.127, 17.128
3 .... 17.129
4 .... 17.128
5 .... 17.129
(2)....................................... 17.129
(5)(b) 17.129
6 .... 17.128
7 .... 17.127
(4)....................................... 17.130
11 .... 17.130
Sch 1
Pt 1 .... 17.129
Sch 2..................................... 17.128
Sch 3
Table 1.................................. 17.128
Urban Waste Water Treatment (Scotland) Regulations 1994, SI 1994/2842 .... 17.127

Waste and Contaminated Land (Northern Ireland) Order 1997, SI 1997/2778
Pt III (arts 49–71) 15.35
Waste (England and Wales) Regulations 2011, SI 2011/988 .... 16.05, 16.08, 16.19; 18.11
reg 2 .... 16.13
12 .... 16.05, 16.17
13, 14 .... 16.06
15 .... 16.05
18 .... 16.16
25 .... 16.17
26 .... 16.19
28 .... 16.17
29 .... 16.19
(5)..................................... 16.19
35 .... 16.05
75(2)................................... 15.30
Water Act 1989 (Commencement No 1) Order 19889, SI 1989/1146
art 4....................................... 17.17

Water Act 2003 (Commencement No 11) Order 2012, SI 2012/264 .... 15.40

Water Authorities (Transfer of Functions) (Appointed Day) Order 1989, SI 1989/1530 ... 5.07

Water Industry Act 1999 (Commencement No 2) Order 1999, SI 1999/3440 .... 17.123

Water Industry (Charges) (Vulnerable Groups) Regulations 1999, SI 1999/3441 ..... 17.123

Water Industry (Schemes for Adoption of Private Sewers) Regulations 2011, SI 2011/1566 .... 17.104

Water Protection Zone (River Dee Catchment) Designation Order 1999, SI 1999/915 ..... 17.94

Water Resources (Abstraction and Impounding) Regulations 2006, SI 2006/641 .... 3.21; 17.33
Pt 2 (regs 3–13) 17.33
reg 3, 6 .... 17.32
reg 10 .... 17.36

Water Resources (Abstraction and Impounding) Regulations 2006 – *contd*
12 .... 17.36
17(1)–(5)............................. 17.42
34 .... 7.02

Water Resources (Succession to Licences) Regulations 1969, SI 1969/976
reg 4–7 .... 12.14

Water Resources (Control of Pollution) (Silage, Slurry and Agricultural Fuel Oil) (England) Regulations 2010, SI 2010/639 .... 3.11; 7.12; 17.82
reg 6–8 .... 7.12
Sch 1....................................... 7.12
Sch 2....................................... 7.12
Sch 3....................................... 7.12

Water Supply (Water Quality) Regulations 2000, SI 2000/3184 .... 17.22

Wildlife and Countryside Act 1981 (Variation of Schedule 9) Order 1997, SI 1997/226 . 19.16

TABLE OF CASES

A

AMEC Building Ltd & Squibb & Davies Ltd v Camden London Borough Council (1996) 55 Con LR 82, [1997] JPL B82, [1997] Env LR 330 .... 14.52, 14.75

ARCO Chemie Nederland Ltd v Minister van Volkshuisvesting, Ruimtelijke Ordening en Milieubeheer (C-418/97); *sub nom* Epon, Re (C-419/97); Vereniging Dorpsbelang Hees v Directeur van de dienst Milieu en Water van de provincie Gelderland (C-419/97) [2002] QB 646, [2002] 2 WLR 1240, [2003] All ER (EC) 237, [2000] ECR I-4475, [2003] Env LR 2, [2001] Env LR D6 .... 16.11

Aannemersbedrijf PK Kraaijeveld BV v Gedeputeerde Staten van Zuid-Holland: C-72/95 [1997] All ER (EC) 134, [1996] ECR I-5403, [1997] Env LR 265 .... 18.31

Alcock v Wraith [1991] NPC 135, 59 BLR 16, [1991] EGCS 137, [1992] BLM (April) 9-11.. 13.57

Aldin v Latimer Clark, Muirhead & Co [1894] 2 Ch 437, 63 LJ Ch 601, 8 R 352, 42 WR 553, 38 SJ 458, 71 LT 119, 10 TLR 452 .... 10.34

Allen v Gulf Oil Refining Ltd [1981] AC 1001, [1981] 1 All ER 353, [1981] 2 WLR 188, 125 SJ 101, [1981] RVR 70 .... 13.41, 13.42

Alphacell Ltd v Woodward [1972] AC 824, [1972] 2 All ER 475, [1972] 2 WLR 1320, 136 JP 505, 70 LGR 455, 116 SJ 431, 223 Estates Gazette 1271 .... 10.04, 10.46, 10.47; 15.78; 17.48, 17.50, 17.52, 17.53, 17.54, 17.58, 17.59, 17.60, 17.61, 17.62

American Cyanamid Co v Ethicon Ltd [1975] AC 396, [1975] 1 All ER 504, [1975] 2 WLR 316, [1975] FSR 101, [1975] RPC 513, 119 SJ 136............ 13.52

American Express International Banking Corpn v Hurley [1985] 3 All ER 564, [1985] FLR 350, [1986] BCLC 52, 2 BCC 98, 993, [1985] NLJ Rep 1034 .... 10.55

Amway Corp v Eurway International Ltd [1973] FSR 213, [1974] RPC 82 ...... 4.24

Andreae v Selfridge & Co Ltd [1938] Ch 1, [1937] 3 All ER 255, 107 LJ Ch 126, 81 SJ 525, 157 LT 317 .... 13.06

Anglian Water Services Ltd v Crawshaw Robbins & Co Ltd [2001] BLR 173, [2001] NPC 32 .... 17.159

Anstruther Gough Calthorpe v McOscar [1924] 1 KB 716 .... 10.13

Arscott v Coal Authority 2004] EWCA Civ 892, [2005] Env LR 6, (2004) 148 SJLB 880, [2004] NPC 114.. 13.10

Ashburn Anstalt v Arnold [1989] Ch 1, [1988] 2 All ER 147, [1988] 2 WLR 706, 55 P & CR 137, [1987] 2 EGLR 71, 284 Estates Gazette 1375, 132 SJ 416, [1988] 16 LS Gaz R 43 .... 17.10

Ashby v White (1703) 1 Bro Parl Cas 62, 2 Ld Raym 938, 955, 6 Mod Rep 45, 54, 1 Salk 19, 3 Salk 17, Holt KB 524, 1 Smith LC 266, 14 State Tr 695; on appeal (1704) 3 Ld Raym 320 .... 13.47

Ashcroft v Cambro Waste Products [1981] 1 WLR 1349, [1981] 3 All ER 699, 79 LGR 612, [1982] JPL 176, (1981) 125 SJ 288 .... 16.23

Ashcroft v Michael McErlain Ltd (unreported, 30 Januay 1985)...................... 16.13

Askey v Golden Wine Co Ltd [1948] 2 All ER 35, 64 TLR 379, (1948) 92
SJ 411, KBD 9.10
Associated Provincial Picture Houses Ltd v Wednesbury Corpn [1948] 1 KB
223, [1947] 2 All ER 680, 112 JP 55, 45 LGR 635, [1948] LJR 190, 92
SJ 26, 177 LT 641, 63 TLR 623 .... 18.16
Attersoll v Stevens (1808) 1 Taunt 183, [1803–13] All ER Rep 603 .... 13.47
A-G (on the relation of Glamorgan County Council & Pontardawe RDC) v
PYA Quarries Ltd [1957] 2 QB 169, [1957] 1 All ER 894, [1957] 2 WLR
770, 121 JP 323, 55 LGR 208, 101 SJ 338 .... 13.04, 13.34, 13.35
A-G's Reference (No 1 of 1994) [1995] 2 All ER 1007, [1995] 1 WLR 599, 159
JP 584 .... 10.03; 17.58, 17.59, 17.62,
17.63
Austria v European Parliament (C161/04) [2006] ECR IA-7183 .... 1.24
Avestapolarit Chrome Oy v Lapin Ymparistokeskus (Case C-114/01) [2003]
ECR I-8725, [2004] Env LR 44 .... 16.11

B
BHP Petroleum Ltd v British Steel Plc [2000] 2 All ER (Comm) 133, [2000]
2 Lloyd's Rep 277, [2000] CLC 1162, 74 Con LR 63 (Civ Div); *affirming*
[1999] 2 All ER (Comm) 544, [1999] 2 Lloyd's Rep 583 .... 9.10
BP Oil New Zealand Ltd v Ports of Auckland Ltd [2004] NZLR 208 ..... 10.11, 10.28,
10.30
Bal 1996 Ltd v British Alcan Aluminium Plc [2006] Env LR 26 .... 9.10, 9.14
Ballard v Tomlinson (1885) 29 Ch D 115, [1881–5] All ER Rep 688, 54 LJ Ch
454, 49 JP 692, 33 WR 533, 52 LT 942, 1 TLR 270 .... 13.26
Bamford v Turnley (1860) 3 B & S 62; on appeal (1862) 3 B & S 66, [1861–73]
All ER Rep 706, 31 LJQB 286, 9 Jur NS 377, 10 WR 803, 6 LT 721,
Ex Ch 14.08
Barker v Corus UK Ltd [2006] UKHL 20, [2006] 2 AC 572, [2006] 2 WLR
1027 .... 13.61
Barnes v Irwell Valley Water Board [1939] 1 KB 21, [1938] 2 All ER 650,
107 LJKB 629, 102 JP 373, 36 LGR 493, 82 SJ 394, 159 LT 125, 54
TLR 815 .... 13.48
Barns (NE) Ltd v Newcastle upon Tyne City Council; *sub nom* Newcastle upon
Tyne City Council v Barns (NE) Ltd [2005] EWCA Civ 1274, [2006] Env
LR 25, (2005) 102(44) LSG 31 .... 14.12, 14.23,
14.24
Barr v Biffa Waste Services Ltd [2012] EWCA Civ 312, [2013] QB 455, [2012]
3 WLR 795 .... 13.46
Barraclough v Brown [1897] AC 615, [1895–9] All ER Rep 239, 66 LJQB 672,
62 JP 275, 8 Asp MLC 290, 2 Com Cas 249, 76 LT 797, 13 TLR 527 .... 10.23
Bartoline Ltd v Royal & Sun Alliance Insurance Plc; *sub nom* Bartoline Ltd v
Royal Sun Alliance Plc [2006] EWHC 3598 (QB), [2007] 1 All ER (Comm)
1043, [2008] Env LR 1, [2007] Lloyd's Rep IR 423 .... 9.34
Baxter v Camden London Borough Council (1997) 30 HLR 501, [1998] 2
EGLR 29, [1998] 22 EG 150, [1997] EGCS 102, [1998] Env LR 270 .... 10.33
Baxter v Camden London Borough Council *see* Southwark LBC v Mills
Baylis v Jiggens [1898] 2 QB 315, 67 LJQB 793, 79 LT 78, 14 TLR 493 .... 10.08
Belcham & Gawley's Contract, Re [1930] 1 Ch 56, 99 LJ Ch 37, 142 LT 182 .. 2.18
Bellefield Computer Services Ltd v E Turner & Sons Ltd [2000] BLR 97, [2000]
NPC 9 .... 2.30

Belvedere Fish Guano Co Ltd v Rainham Chemical Works Ltd, Feldman &
  Partridge [1920] 2 KB 487, 89 LJKB 631, 84 JP 185, 18 LGR 517, 123 LT
  211, 36 TLR 362; *aff'd sub nom* Rainham Chemical Works Ltd v Belvedere
  Fish Guano Co [1921] 2 AC 465, [1921] All ER Rep 48, 90 LJKB 1252, 19
  LGR 657, 66 SJ 7, 126 LT 70, 37 TLR 973 .... 13.27, 13.32
Benjamin v Storr (1874) LR 9 CP 400, [1874-80] All ER Rep Ext 2000, 43
  LJCP 162, 22 WR 631, 30 LT 362 .... 13.35
Berkeley v Secretary of State for the Environment, Transport & the Regions
  (No 1) [2001] 2 AC 603, [2000] 3 WLR 420, [2000] 3 All ER 897, [2001]
  2 CMLR 38, [2001] Env LR 16, (2001) 81 P & CR 35, [2000] 3 PLR 111,
  [2001] JPL 58, [2000] EG 86 (CS), [2000] NPC 77 .... 18.30, 18.32
Beyfus v Lodge [1925] Ch 350, [1925] All ER Rep 552, 95 LJ Ch 27, 69 SJ 507,
  133 LT 265, 41 TLR 429 .... 2.23
Biggin & Co Ltd v Permanite Ltd [1951] 2 KB 314, [1951] 2 All ER 191, [1951]
  2 TLR 159 .... 9.10
Bird v Elwes (1868) LR 3 Exch 225, 37 LJ Ex 91, 32 JP 694, 16 WR 1120, 18
  LT 727 .... 10.08, 10.11
Birmingham City Council v Oakley *see* Oakley v Birmingham City Council
Birmingham Development Co Ltd v Tyler [2008] EWCA Civ 859, [2008] BLR
  445, 122 Con LR 207 .... 13.05
Birmingham District Council v Kelly (1985) 17 HLR 572, [1986] 2 EGLR 239 ..... 10.06
Birmingham District Council v Kelly [1986] 2 EGLR 239 .... 14.31
Birmingham, Dudley & District Banking Co v Ross (1888) 38 Ch D 295, 57 LJ
  Ch 601, 36 WR 914, 59 LT 609, 4 TLR 437 .... 10.34
Bishop Auckland Local Board v Bishop Auckland Iron & Steel Co Ltd (1882-
  83) LR 10 QBD 138 .... 14.10
Blackburn v ARC Ltd [1998] Env LR 469 .... 13.45; 14.11
Blackland Park Exploration v Environment Agency [2003] EWCA Civ 1795,
  [2004] Env LR 33, [2004] JPL 1131 .... 16.28
Blair & Sumner v Deakin (1887) 52 JP 327, 57 LT 522, 3 TLR 757 .... 13.58
Bliss v Hall (1838) 4 Bing NC 183, 7 LJCP 122, 1 Arn 19, 5 Scott 500, *sub nom*
  Bliss v Hay 6 Dowl 442, 2 Jur 110 .... 13.37
Blue Circle Industries plc v Ministry of Defence; *sub nom* Ministry of Defence v
  Blue Circle Industries Plc [1999] Ch 289, [1999] 2 WLR 295, [1998] 3 All
  ER 385, [1999] Env LR 22, [1998] EG 93 (CS), [1998] NPC 100, *affirming*
  [1997] Env LR 341, (1998) 76 P & CR 251, [1996] EG 190 (CS), (1997)
  94(2) LSG 25, (1997) 141 SJLB 11, [1996] NPC 170 .... 9.10, 9.17; 13.50,
  13.54, 13.55
Boddington v British Transport Police [1999] 2 AC 143, [1998] 2 All ER 203,
  [1998] 2 WLR 639, 162 JP 455, [1998] NLJR 515 .... 14.52; 15.26; 17.66
Bolton v Stone *see* Stone v Bolton
Bone v Seale [1975] 1 All ER 787, [1975] 1 WLR 797, 119 SJ 137 .... 13.53
Botross v London Borough of Hammersmith & Fulham (1994) 93 LGR 269,
  27 HLR 179, 16 Cr App Rep (S) 622, [1994] NPC 134, [1995] COD 169,
  [1995] Env LR 217 .... 14.63
Bower v Peate (1876) 1 QBD 321, [1874–80] All ER Rep 905, 45 LJQB 446, 40
  JP 789, 35 LT 321 .... 13.13
Bowles v Round (1800) 5 Ves 508 .... 2.18
Bowyer Philpott & Payne Ltd v Mather [1919] 1 KB 419, KBD 14.21
Brasserie du Pêcheur SA v Germany: C-46/93 [1996] QB 404, [1996] All ER
  (EC) 301, [1996] 2 WLR 506, [1996] ECR I-1029, [1996] 1 CMLR 889,
  [1996] IRLR 267 .... 1.26

Brett v Rogers [1897] 1 QB 525, 66 LJQB 287, 45 WR 334, 41 SJ 258, 76 LT
26, 13 TLR 175 .... 10.09
Brew Bros Ltd v Snax (Ross) Ltd [1970] 1 QB 612, [1970] 1 All ER 587, [1969]
3 WLR 657, 20 P & CR 829, 113 SJ 795............................. 10.01; 13.20, 13.37
Brewer & Hankins's Contract, Re (1899) 80 LT 127 .... 2.18
Bridlington Relay Ltd v Yorkshire Electricity Board [1965] Ch 436, [1965] 1 All
ER 264, [1965] 2 WLR 349, 109 SJ 12... 13.06
Bristol Corpn v Sinnott [1918] 1 Ch 62, [1916–17] All ER Rep Ext 1179, 82 JP
9, 15 LGR 871, 62 SJ 53, 117 LT 644... 14.25
British Celanese Ltd v A H Hunt (Capacitors) Ltd [1969] 2 All ER 1252, [1969]
1 WLR 959, 113 SJ 368 .... 13.05, 13.29
British Sugar Plc v NEI Power Projects Ltd, 87 BLR 42, [1997-98] Info TLR
353, [1998] ITCLR 125, (1998) 14 Const LJ 365 .... 9.10
British Waterways Board v National Rivers Authority [1993] Env LR 239 .... 17.26
Bromley v IC & The Environment Agency (Unreported, 31 August 2007) 4.39
Brown v Secretary of State for Transport, Local Government & the Regions
2 [2003] EWCA Civ 1170, [2004] Env LR 26, [2004] 2 P & CR 7, [2003]
3 PLR 100... 19.45
Browne v Flower [1911] 1 Ch 219, [1908–10] All ER Rep 545, 80 LJ Ch 181,
55 SJ 108, 103 LT 557.. 10.34
Bruton & the National Rivers Authority v Clarke (1995) 7 Environmental Law
& Management 93.. 17.84
Bryan v United Kingdom (A/335-A) (1995) 21 EHRR 342, [1996] 1 PLR 47,
[1996] 2 EGLR 123, [1996] 28 EG 137, [1996] JPL 386, ECHR.............. 1.38
Budd v Colchester Borough Council (1999) 97 LGR 601, [1999] NPC 30,
[1999] JPL 717, 143 SJLB 96, [1999] BLGR 601, [1999] EHLR 347,
[1999] Env LR 739 .... 14.04, 14.26, 14.27
Budd v Marshall (1880) 5 CPD 481, 50 LJQB 24, 44 JP 584, 29 WR 148, 42 LT
793 .... 10.09
Burgess v IC & Stafford Borough Council (Unreported, 7 June 2007).......... 4.20, 4.23
Burmah Oil Co Ltd v Bank of England [1980] AC 1090, [1979] 3 WLR 722,
[1979] 3 All ER 700, (1979) 123 SJ 786 .... 4.25
Burnie Port Authority v General Jones Property Ltd (1994) 120 ALR 42 (Aus-
tralian HC) 13.24
Butcher Robinson & Staples Ltd v London Regional Transport (1999) 79 P &
CR 523, [1999] 3 EGLR 63, [1999] 36 EG 165, [1999] EGCS 71 .... 13.12
Butuyuyu v Hammersmith & Fulham London Borough Council (1996) 29
HLR 584, [1997] Env LR D13.. 14.50, 14.51

C
CPC (UK) Ltd v National Rivers Authority [1995] Env LR 131, [1995] Journal
of Environmental Law 69 .... 17.55, 17.58,
17.61
Caballero v Henty (1873-74) LR 9 Ch App 447... 2.21
Caledonia North Sea Ltd v London Bridge Engineering Ltd; *sub nom* Caledonia
North Sea Ltd v BT Plc; Caledonia North Sea Ltd v British Telecommunications Plc; Caledonia North Sea Ltd v Norton (No 2) Ltd (In Liquidation); EE Caledonia Ltd v London Bridge Engineering Ltd [2002] UKHL
4, [2002] 1 All ER (Comm) 321, [2002] 1 Lloyd's Rep 553, 2002 SC (HL)
117, 2002 SLT 278, 2002 SCLR 346, [2002] CLC 741, [2002] BLR 139,
[2002] Lloyd's Rep IR 261, 2002 GWD 6-178... 9.10

Cambridge Water Co v Eastern Counties Leather plc [1994] 2 AC 264, [1994] 1
    All ER 53, [1994] 2 WLR 53, [1994] 1 Lloyd's Rep 261, [1994] 11 LS Gaz
    R 36, [1994] NLJR 15, 138 SJLB 24...... 13.02, 13.05, 13.08, 13.09, 13.24, 13.25,
                                            13.29, 13.30, 13.32, 13.49, 13.50; 14.08
Camden London Borough Council v Gunby [1999] 4 All ER 602, [2000]
    1 WLR 465, 32 HLR 572, [1999] 3 EGLR 13, [1999] 44 EG 147, [1999]
    29 LS Gaz R 30, [1999] NLJR 1146, [2000] Env LR D10 .... 10.49; 14.34, 14.35;
                                                              15.78; 19.34
Camden London Borough Council v London Underground Ltd [2000] Env LR
    369, [2000] 01 LS Gaz R 25, ENDS Report 300, p 47...................... 14.11, 14.71
Camden London Borough Council v Shortlife Community Housing Ltd (1992)
    90 LGR 358, 25 HLR 330 .... 17.10
Canada Steamship Lines Ltd v R [1952] AC 192, [1952] 1 All ER 305, [1952]
    1 Lloyd's Rep 1 .... 9.10
Canterbury City Council v Ferris [1997] Env LR D14 .... 15.60
Cargill v Gotts [1981] 1 All ER 682, [1981] 1 WLR 441, 41 P & CR 300, 125
    SJ 99 ....13.38; 17.23, 17.29
Carlish v Salt [1906] 1 Ch 335, 75 LJ Ch 175, 94 LT 58.............................. 2.23
Castle Cement Ltd v Environment Agency [2001] EWHC Admin 224, [2001]
    2 CMLR 19, [2001] Env LR 46 .... 16.11
Celsteel Ltd v Alton House Holdings Ltd [1985] 2 All ER 562, [1985] 1 WLR
    204, 49 P & CR 165, 129 SJ 115, [1985] LS Gaz R 1168; on appeal [1986]
    1 All ER 608, [1986] 1 WLR 512, 130 SJ 204, [1986] LS Gaz R 700 .... 17.10
Century National Merchant Bank & Trust Co Ltd v Davies [1998] AC 628,
    [1998] 2 WLR 779, 142 SJLB 110, PC.. 10.23
Chandler Lines v Wilson & Horton Ltd [1981] 2 NZLR 600 .... 4.23
Chartered Trust plc v Davies (1997) 76 P & CR 396, [1997] 2 EGLR 83, [1997]
    49 EG 135, [1997] NPC 125, 75 P & CR D6 .... 10.34
Cheshire County Council v Secretary of State for the Environment & Rathbone
    [1996] JPL 410, [1995] Env LR 316 .... 15.11
Chetwynd v Tunmore [2016] EWHC 156 (QB) 13.61
Chorley Borough Council v Ribble Motor Services Ltd (1996) 74 P &
    CR 182 .... 10.20
Circular Facilities (London) Ltd v Sevenoaks DC [2005] EWHC 865 (Admin),
    [2005] Env LR 35, [2005] JPL 1624 .... 10.47; 15.71, 15.75,
                                                                      15.77, 15.91
City of London Corpn v Bovis Construction Ltd [1992] 3 All ER 697, 86 LGR
    660, 49 BLR 1, [1989] JPL 263, 4 Const LJ 203 .... 14.50, 14.76
Citytowns Ltd v Bohemian Properties Ltd [1986] 2 EGLR 258...................... 2.23
Clark v Newsam (1847) 16 LJ Ex 296, 11 JP 840, 5 Ry & Can Cas 69, 1 Exch
    131, 9 LTOS 199... 13.58
Clayton v Sale UDC [1926] 1 KB 415, [1925] All ER Rep 279, 95 LJKB 178, 90
    JP 5, 24 LGR 34, 134 LT 147, 42 TLR 72 ....14.31, 14.33
Cocking v Eacott [2016] EWCA Civ 140, [2016] HLR 15 .... 10.02; 13.23
Codemasters Software Co Ltd v Automobile Club de L'Ouest [2009] EWHC
    2361 (Ch), [2009] Info TLR 203, [2010] FSR 12 .... 9.08, 9.10
Coedbach Action Team Ltd v Secretary of State for Energy & Climate Change
    [2010] EWHC 2312 (Admin), [2011] 1 Costs LR 70, [2011] Env LR 11 ... 1.40
Cointat v Myham & Son [1913] 2 KB 220, KBD.. 9.10
Commission of the European Communities v Council of the European Union
    (C-176/03) [2006] All ER (EC) 1, [2005] ECR I-7879, [2005] 3 CMLR 20,
    [2006] Env LR 18 .... 1.24

Commission of the European Communities v France Case (C-166/97) [1999] Env LR 781 .... 19.45

Commission of the European Communities v France Case (C-96/98) [2000] 2 CMLR 681 .... 19.45

Commission of the European Communities v Germany (C-57/89) [1991] ECR I-883 .... 19.43, 19.48

Commission of the European Communities v Netherlands (C-3/96) [1998] ECR I-3031, [1999] Env LR 147 .... 19.45, 19.46

Commission of the European Communities v Spain (C-355/90) [1993] ECR I-4221 .... 19.43, 19.45

Commission of the European Communities v United Kingdom (C-305/03) [2007] STC 1211, [2006] STI 383 .... 18.32

Cook v Taylor [1942] Ch 349, [1942] 2 All ER 85, 111 LJ Ch 214, 86 SJ 217, 167 LT 87, 58 TLR 278 .... 2.33

Corby Group Litigation Claimants v Corby BC[2008] EWCA Civ 463, [2008] CP Rep 32, [2008] BLR 411, [2008] PIQR P16, [2008] CILL 2597, [2008] 19 EG 204 (CS), (2008) 152(21) SJLB 32, [2008] NPC 58 .... 13.36, 13.48

Council of Civil Service Unions v Minister for the Civil Service [1985] AC 374, [1984] 3 WLR 1174, [1984] 3 All ER 935, [1985] ICR 14, [1985] IRLR 28, (1985) 82 LSG 437, (1984) 128 SJ 837 .... 1.40

Council of the European Union v Hautala (C-353/99 P) [2002] 1 WLR 1930, [2001] ECR I-9565, [2002] 1 CMLR 15, [2002] CEC 127 .... 4.11

County Properties Ltd v Scottish Ministers 2000 SLT 965, Ct of Sess 1.38

Coventry (t/a RDC Promotions) v Lawrence; Lawrence v Fen Tigers Ltd [2014] UKSC 13, [2014] AC 822, [2014] 2 WLR 433 .... 9.31; 13.06, 13.40, 13.45, 13.51; 14.11, 14.20; 18.23

Coventry v Lawrence (No 2) [2014] UKSC 46, [2015] AC 106, [2014] 3 WLR 555 .... 10.02, 10.16, 10.33, 10.34, 10.36; 13.23

Coventry City Council v Cartwright [1975] 1 WLR 845, [1975] 2 All ER 99, 73 LGR 218, (1975) 119 SJ 235 .... 14.04, 14.07

Crabb v Arun District Council [1976] Ch 179, [1975] 3 All ER 865, [1975] 3 WLR 847, 119 SJ 711 .... 17.10

Crédit Suisse v Beegas Nominees Ltd [1994] 4 All ER 803, 69 P & CR 177, [1994] 1 EGLR 76, [1994] 11 EG 151, 12 EG 189 .... 10.13

Creery v Summersell & Flowerdew & Co Ltd [1949] Ch 751, [1949] LJR 1166, 93 SJ 357 .... 10.16

Criminal Proceedings against Tombesi (C304/94); Criminal Proceedings against Santella (C330/94); Criminal Proceedings against Muzi (C342/94); Criminal Proceedings against Savini (C224/95) [1997] All ER (EC) 639, [1997] ECR I-3561, [1997] 3 CMLR 673, [1998] Env LR 59 .... 16.11

Criminal Proceedings against Van de Walle (C1/03); *sub nom* Ministere Public v Van de Walle (C1/03); Van De Walle v Texaco Belgium SA (C1/03); Criminal Proceedings against Texaco Belgium SA (C1/03) [2005] All ER (EC) 1139, [2004] ECR I-7613, [2005] 1 CMLR 8, [2005] Env LR 24, [2004] NPC 137 .... 2.32; 16.11

Criminal Proceedings against Vessoso (C206/88); Criminal Proceedings against Zanetti (C207/88) [1990] ECR I-1461 .... 16.11

Crossley & Sons Ltd v Lightowler (1867) 2 Ch App 478, 36 LJ Ch 584, 15 WR 801, 16 LT 438 .... 13.39

Crown River Cruises Ltd v Kimbolton Fireworks Ltd & London Fire & Civil Defence Authority [1996] 2 Lloyd's Rep 533 .... 10.20; 13.05, 13.06

Cumberland Consolidated Holdings Ltd v Ireland [1946] KB 264, [1946] 1 All
ER 284, 115 LJKB 301, 174 LT 257, 62 TLR 215 .... 2.33, 2.38
Cunningham v Birmingham City Council (1997) 96 LGR 231, 30 HLR 158,
[1998] Env LR 1 .... 14.07

D

D & F Estates Ltd v Church Comrs for England [1989] AC 177, [1988] 2 All ER
992, [1988] 3 WLR 368, [1988] 2 EGLR 262, [1988] NLJR 210, 15 Con
LR 35, 41 BLR 1, 132 SJ 1092 .... 2.30
DCLG v IC & Robinson [2012] UKUT 103 (AAC), [2012] 2 Info LR 43 .... 4.20
Dainton v IC & Lincolnshire County Council (Unreported, 10 September
2007) 4.25
Day v Harland & Wolff Ltd [1953] 2 All ER 387, [1953] 1 WLR 906, [1953]
2 Lloyd's Rep 58, 97 SJ 473 .... 10.12
Dayani v Bromley LBC (No 1) [1999] 3 EGLR 144, [1999] EG 135 (CS), (1999)
96(45) LSG 35 .... 10.29
Dear v Thames Water (1992) 33 Con LR 43 .... 13.17
Deepak Fertilisers & Petrochemicals Corp Ltd v Davy McKee (London) Ltd;
sub nom Deepak Fertilisers & Petrochemicals Corp Ltd v ICI Chemicals &
Polymers Ltd; Deepak Fertilisers & Petrochemical Corp Ltd v Davy McKee
(UK) London Ltd [1999] 1 All ER (Comm) 69, [1999] 1 Lloyd's Rep 387,
[1999] BLR 41, (1999) 1 TCLR 200, 62 Con LR 86 .... 9.10
Delaware Mansions Ltd & Flecksun Ltd v City of Westminster [2000] BLR 1,
[1999] 3 EGLR 68, [1999] 46 EG 194, [1999] EGCS 110 .... 13.50
Dennis v Ministry of Defence [2003] EWHC 793 (QB), [2003] Env LR 34,
[2003] EHLR 17, [2003] 2 EGLR 121, [2006] RVR 45, [2003] JPL 1577,
[2003] 19 EG 118 (CS), (2003) 153 NLJ 634, [2003] NPC 55 .... 13.51
Department of the Environment & Heritage Service v Felix O'Hare & Co Ltd
& James Phillips [2007] NICA 45 .... 16.13
Department of Transport v North West Water Authority [1984] AC 336, [1983]
1 All ER 892, [1983] 3 WLR 105, 81 LGR 599, 127 SJ 426; revsd [1984]
AC 336, [1983] 3 All ER 273, [1983] 3 WLR 707, 82 LGR 207, 127 SJ
713 .... 13.41, 13.42
Derwentside District Council v Wheeler [1994] PAD 403 .... 18.18
Dilieto v Ealing London Borough Council [2000] QB 381, [1998] 2 All ER 885,
[1998] 3 WLR 1403, [1998] PLCR 212 .... 14.52
Dobson v Thames Water Utilities Ltd [2007] EWHC 2021 (TCC), [2008] 2 All
ER 362, [2007] BLR 465, [2007] TCLR 7, 116 Con LR 135, [2008] Env
LR 21, [2007] HRLR 45, [2007] CILL 2518, [2007] NPC 102 .... 1.38; 13.53
Dodd v Crown Estate Comrs [1995] NPC 29, [1995] EGCS 35 .... 2.13, 2.15; 3.02
Draper v Sperring (1861) 25 JP 566 .... 14.04
Drinking Water Inspectorate & Secretary of State v Severn Trent Water (1995)
243 ENDS Report 45 .... 17.22
Duke of Bedford v University College Medical School [1974] CLY 2063 .... 10.23
Duke of Devonshire v Brookside [1899] 81 LT 83 .... 10.21
Dunlop Slazenger International Ltd v Joe Bloggs Sports Ltd [2003] EWCA Civ
901 .... 4.23
Durham County Council v Peter Connors Industrial Services Ltd [1993] Env
LR 197, [1992] Crim LR 743, [1992] COD 487 .... 16.25

E

ER Ives Investment Ltd v High [1967] 2 QB 379, [1967] 2 WLR 789, [1967] 1
All ER 504 .... 17.10

Earl of Pembroke v Warren [1896] 1 IR 76 .... 10.21

East Dorset DC v Eaglebeam Ltd [2006] EWHC 2378 (QB), [2007] Env LR
D9 .... 14.23, 14.24

East Riding of Yorkshire Council v Yorkshire Water Services Ltd [2001] Env LR
7, [2000] COD 446 .... 14.04

East Staffordshire Borough Council v Fairless (1998) 31 HLR 677, [1998] 41
LS Gaz R 46, [1999] EHLR 128, [1999] Env LR 525, [1998] EGCS 140 ... 14.67

Eastern Counties Leather Plc v Eastern Counties Leather Group Ltd [2002]
EWCA Civ 1636, [2003] Env LR 13 (Civ Div); *affirming* [2002] EWHC
494 (Ch), [2002] Env LR 34 .... 9.14, 9.17, 9.22, 9.28;

EC Commission v Germany: C-57/89 [1991] ECR I-883 .... 19.43

EC Commission v Germany: C-217/97 [1999] 3 CMLR 277 .... 4.35

Edinburgh City Council v Secretary of State for Scotland [1997] 1 WLR 1447,
[1998] 1 All ER 174, 1998 SC (HL) 33 .... 18.07

Edler v Auerbach [1950] 1 KB 359, [1949] 2 All ER 692, 93 SJ 727, 65 TLR
645 .... 2.06

Edwards v National Coal Board [1949] 1 KB 704, [1949] 1 All ER 743, 65 TLR
430, (1949) 93 SJ 337 .... 20.32

Elvanite Full Circle Ltd v AMEC Earth & Environmental (UK) Ltd [2013]
EWHC 1191 (TCC), 148 Con LR 127 .... 9.10

Empress Car Co (Abertillery) Ltd v National Rivers Authority *see* Environment
Agency (formerly National Rivers Authority) v Empress Car Co (Abertillery) Ltd

Englefield Holdings & Sinclair's Contract, Re; *sub nom* Rosslyn & Lorimer
Estates v Englefield Holdings [1962] 1 WLR 1119, [1962] 3 All ER 503,
(1962) 106 SJ 72 .... 2.23

Envirocor Waste Holdings Ltd v Secretary of State for the Environment [1996]
JPL 489 .... 18.22

Environment Agency v Brock plc [1998] 4 PLR 37, [1998] JPL 968, [1998] Env
LR 607 .... 17.56

Environment Agency v ICI Chemicals & Polymers Ltd (unreported 1998) 1.33

Environment Agency v Inglenorth Ltd [2009] EWHC 670 (Admin), [2009] Env
LR 33, [2009] LLR 389 .... 16.11, 16.13

Environment Agency v Short [1999] Env LR 300, [1999] EHLR 3, [1999] JPL
263 .... 16.25

Environment Agency v Thorn International UK Ltd [2008] EWHC 2595 (Ad-
min), [2009] PTSR 906, [2009] Env LR 10 .... 16.11, 16.13

Environment Agency (formerly National Rivers Authority) v Empress Car Co
(Abertillery) Ltd; *sub nom* Empress Car Co (Abertillery) Ltd v National
Rivers Authority [1999] 2 AC 22, [1998] 2 WLR 350, [1998] 1 All ER 481,
[1998] Env LR 396, [1988] EHLR 3, [1998] EG 16 (CS), (1998) 95(8) LSG
32, (1998) 148 NLJ 206, (1998) 142 SJLB 69, [1998] NPC 16 .... 10.03, 10.46;
17.52, 17.53, 17.54, 17.55, 17.56,
17.58, 17.60, 17.61, 17.63

Esso Petroleum Co Ltd v Southport Corpn [1956] AC 218, [1955] 3 All ER 864,
[1956] 2 WLR 81, 120 JP 54, 54 LGR 91, [1955] 2 Lloyd's Rep 655, 100
SJ 32 .... 13.47

Express Ltd (t/a Express Dairies Distribution) v Environment Agency [2003]
EWHC 448 (Admin), [2004] 1 WLR 579, [2003] 2 All ER 778, [2003] Env
LR 29, [2003] EHLR 11, [2003] ACD 58 .... 17.60

Express Ltd (t/a Express Dairies Distribution) v Environment Agency [2004]
EWHC 1710 (Admin), [2005] 1 WLR 223, [2005] Env LR 7, [2005] JPL
242, [2005] ACD 26 .... 17.44

F

Fairchild v Glenhaven Funeral Services Ltd (t/a GH Dovener & Son) [2002]
UKHL 22, [2003] 1 AC 32, [2002] 3 WLR 89 .... 13.61
Farley v Skinner [2000] PNLR 441, [2000] 15 LS Gaz R 41, [2000] EGCS 52... 13.48
Farlow v Stevenson [1900] 1 Ch 128, 69 LJ Ch 106, 48 WR 213, 44 SJ 73, 81
LT 589, 16 TLR 57 .... 10.09
Federated Homes Ltd v Mill Lodge Properties Ltd [1980] 1 All ER 371, [1980]
1 WLR 594, 124 SJ 412 .... 19.19
Fisher v English Nature *see* R (on the application of Fisher) v English Nature
Fish Legal v Information Comr (Case C-279/12) [2014] QB 521, [2014] 2 WLR
568, [2014] 2 CMLR 36 .... 4.06
Flachglas Torgau GmbH v Federal Republic of Germany (Case C-204/09)
[2013] QB 212, [2013] 2 WLR 105, [2012] 2 CMLR 17 .... 4.06
Flight v Booth (1834) 1 Bing NC 370, [1824-34] All ER Rep 43, 4 LJCP 66,
1 Scott 190 .... 2.07
Forsey & Hollebone's Contract, Re [1927] 2 Ch 379 .... 2.21
Foster v British Gas Plc (C-188/89) [1991] 1 QB 405, [1991] 2 WLR 258,
[1990] 3 All ER 897, [1990] ECR I-3313, [1990] 2 CMLR 833, [1991]
ICR 84, [1990] IRLR 353 .... 4.06
Foulger v Arding [1902] 1 KB 700, 71 LJKB 499, 50 WR 417, 46 SJ 356, 86 LT
488, 18 TLR 422 .... 10.08; 14.59
Francovich & Bonifaci v Italy: C-6, 9/90 [1991] ECR I-5357, [1993] 2 CMLR
66, [1995] ICR 722, [1992] IRLR 84 .... 1.26
Friends of the Earth v IC & Exports Credits Guarantee Department (unreport-
ed, 20 August 2007) 4.18
Frost v King Edward VII Welsh National Memorial Association for Prevention
Treatment & Abolition of Tuberculosis [1918] 2 Ch 180 .... 10.21

G

Gadd's Land Transfer, Re, Cornmill Developments Ltd v Bridle Lane (Estates)
Ltd [1966] Ch 56, [1965] 2 All ER 800, [1965] 3 WLR 325, 109 SJ 555... 19.18
Galer v Morrissey *see* Morrissey v Galer
Gateshead MBC v Secretary of State for the Environment; Gateshead MBC v
Northumbrian Water Group Plc 1995] Env LR 37, (1996) 71 P & CR 350,
[1994] 1 PLR 85, [1995] JPL 432, [1994] EG 92 (CS) 15.15; 18.17, 18.19,
18.20, 18.22
Gateway Professional Services (Management) Ltd v Kingston upon Hull City
Council [2004] EWHC 597 (Admin), [2004] Env LR 42, [2004] LLR 448.. 16.17
Gee v National Trust for Places of Historic Interest & Natural Beauty [1966]
1 All ER 954, [1966] 1 WLR 170, 17 P & CR 6, 109 SJ 935 .... 19.18
Gemeinde Altrip v Land Rheinland-Pfalz (Vertreter des Bundesinteresses beim
Bundesverwaltungsgericht intervening) Case C-72/12 [2014] PTSR 311.... 18.32
Gersten v Municipality of Metropolitan Toronto (1973) 41 DLR (3d) 646,
2 OR (2d) 1 .... 13.29
Gibbons v South West Water Services Ltd [1993] QB 507, *sub nom* AB v South
West Water Services Ltd [1993] 1 All ER 609, [1993] 2 WLR 507, [1993]
PIQR P 167, [1993] NLJR 235 .... 13.35, 13.49, 13.53
Gillingham Borough Council v Medway (Chatham) Dock Co Ltd [1993] QB
343, [1992] 3 All ER 923, [1992] 3 WLR 449, 91 LGR 160, 63 P & CR
205, [1992] 1 PLR 113, [1992] JPL 458 .... 13.06, 13.35, 13.43,
13.44, 13.45; 14.11

Goldman v Hargrave [1967] 1 AC 645, [1966] 2 All ER 989, [1966] 3 WLR
513, [1966] 2 Lloyd's Rep 65, 110 SJ 527, [1967] ALR 113, PC...... 13.14, 13.19;
17.158
Goodhart v Hyett (1883) 25 Ch D 182, 53 LJ Ch 219, 48 JP 293, 32 WR 165,
50 LT 95 .... 17.11
Gordon v Selico Co Ltd (1986) 18 HLR 219, [1986] 1 EGLR 71, 278 Estates
Gazette 53.. 2.17
Gosling v Anderson (1971) 220 Estates Gazette 1117; revsd (1972) 223 Estates
Gazette 1743, 122 NLJ 152 .... 2.22
Graham v Rechem International [1996] Env LR 158, ENDS June 1995, p 18... 13.05
Granby (Marquis) v Bakewell UDC (1923) 87 JP 105, 21 LGR 329 .... 13.53
Green v Matthews & Co (1930) 46 TLR 206 .... 13.38
Greetings Oxford Koala Hotel Pty Ltd v Oxford Square Investments Pty Ltd
(1989) 18 NSWLR 33... 10.12
Griffin v South West Water Services Ltd [1995] IRLR 15 .... 4.06
Griffiths v Pembrokeshire CC [2000] Env LR 622, [2000] EHLR 359, (2000)
97(18) LSG 36, (2000) 150 NLJ 512, [2000] NPC 38 .... 14.04
Grosvenor Hotel Co v Hamilton [1894] 2 QB 836, [1891–4] All ER Rep 1188,
63 LJQB 661, 9 R 819, 42 WR 626, 71 LT 362, 10 TLR 506 .... 10.34

H

H v Schering Chemicals Ltd [1983] 1 All ER 849, [1983] 1 WLR 143, 127
SJ 88 .... 8.11
Hackney LBC v Issa; *sub nom* Issa v Hackney LBC [1997] 1 WLR 956, [1997]
1 All ER 999, [1997] Env LR 157, (1997) 29 HLR 640, [1996] EG 184
(CS), (1997) 94(1) LSG 24, (1996) 140 SJLB 262, [1996] NPC 167 .... 14.04,
14.65
Hadley v Baxendale, 156 ER 145, (1854) 9 Ex 341, Ex Ct............................ 9.10
Hall v Kingston upon Hull City Council *see* R v Birmingham City Council, ex
p Ireland
Hampstead & Suburban Properties Ltd v Diomedous [1969] 1 Ch 248, [1968]
3 All ER 545, [1968] 3 WLR 990, 19 P & CR 880, 112 SJ 656 .... 10.19
Haringey London Borough Council v Jowett [1999] EHLR 410, (2000) 32
HLR 308, [1999] BLGR 667, [1999] EG 64 (CS), [1999] NPC 52, (1999)
78 P & CR D24, [2000] Env LR D6 .... 14.04, 14.32
Harmer v Jumbil (Nigeria) Tin Areas Ltd [1921] 1 Ch 200, [1920] All ER Rep
113, 90 LJ Ch 140, 65 SJ 93, 124 LT 418, 37 TLR 91 .... 10.34
Harper v GN Haden & Sons [1933] Ch 298, [1932] All ER Rep 59, 102 LJ Ch
6, 96 JP 525, 31 LGR 18, 76 SJ 849, 148 LT 303 .... 13.53
Harris v Hickman [1904] 1 KB 13, 73 LJKB 31, 68 JP 65, 2 LGR 1, 48 SJ 69,
89 LT 722, 20 TLR 18 .... 10.27; 14.48,
14.59
Harris v James (1876) 45 LJQB 545, [1874-80] All ER Rep 1142, 40 JP 663, 35
LT 240 .... 13.21
Hart v Swaine (1877) 7 Ch D 42, 47 LJ Ch 5, 26 WR 30, 37 LT 376 .... 2.20
Hatton v United Kingdom (36022/97) (2003) 37 EHRR 28, 15 BHRC 259,
ECHR.. 1.38
Hautala v Council of the European Union *see* Council of the European Union
v Hautala
Haywood v Brunswick Permanent Benefit Building Society (1881) 8 QBD 403,
51 LJQB 73, 46 JP 356, 30 WR 299, 45 LT 699 .... 19.18

Hazlett v Sefton Metropolitan Borough Council [2000] 4 All ER 887, [1999] NLJR 1869 .... 14.72

Heap v Ind Coope & Allsopp Ltd [1940] 2 KB 476, [1940] 3 All ER 634, 109 LJKB 724, 84 SJ 536, 163 LT 169, 56 TLR 948 .... 10.36

Heath v Brighton Corpn (1908) 72 JP 225, 98 LT 718, 24 TLR 414 .... 13.06

Heath v Keys [1984] CLY 3568, 134 NLJ 888 .... 13.53

Hedley Byrne & Co Ltd v Heller & Partners Ltd [1964] AC 465, [1963] 3 WLR 101, [1963] 2 All ER 575, [1963] 1 Lloyd's Rep 485, (1963) 107 SJ 454 ... 8.17; 11.10

Henderson v Merrett Syndicates Ltd [1995] 2 AC 145, [1994] 3 All ER 506, [1994] 3 WLR 761, [1994] NLJR 1204 .... 10.30

Heronslea (Mill Hill) Ltd v Kwik Fit Properties Ltd [2009] EWHC 295 (QB), [2009] Env LR 28, [2009] NPC 30 .... 10.22

Hewlings v Mclean Homes East Anglia Ltd [2001] 2 All ER 281, [2001] Env LR 17, [2001] EHLR 2, (2001) 33 HLR 50, [2001] JPL 226 (Note), [2001] JPL 425, [2000] EG 100 (CS), (2000) 97(39) LSG 41 .... 14.69

Hill v Harris [1965] 2 QB 601, [1965] 2 All ER 358, [1965] 2 WLR 1331, 109 SJ 333 .... 2.06

Hilton v James Smith & Sons (Norwood) Ltd [1979] 2 EGLR 44, (1979) 257 EG 1063 .... 10.33

Holbeck Hall Hotel Ltd v Scarborough Borough Council [1997] 2 EGLR 213; revsd [2000] QB 836, [2000] 2 All ER 705, [2000] 2 WLR 1396, [2000] NLJR 307, [2000] BLR 109, [2000] EGCS 29, 144 SJLB 109 ... 13.10, 13.16, 13.19

Holding & Management Ltd v Property Holding & Investment Trust plc [1990] 1 All ER 938, [1989] 1 WLR 1313, 21 HLR 596, [1990] 1 EGLR 65, [1990] 05 EG 75, 134 SJ 262 .... 10.12

Holywell Union & Halkyn Parish v Halkyn Drainage Co [1895] AC 117, [1891–94] All ER Rep 158, 64 LJMC 113, 59 JP 566, 11 R 98, 71 LT 818, 11 TLR 132 .... 17.12

Hone v Benson (1978) 248 Estates Gazette 1013 .... 2.27

Hopkins Developments Ltd v First Secretary of State; *sub nom* Hopkins Development Ltd v First Secretary of State [2006] EWHC 2823 (Admin), [2007] Env LR 14, [2007] 1 P & CR 25, [2007] JPL 1056, [2006] NPC 125 .... 18.19

Horlick v Scully [1927] 2 Ch 150 .... 10.13

Horner v Franklin [1904] 2 KB 877; *aff'd* [1905] 1 KB 479, 74 LJKB 291, 69 JP 117, 3 LGR 423, 92 LT 178, 21 TLR 225 .... 10.08, 10.23, 10.24, 10.25, 10.26; 14.60

Hotel Services Ltd v Hilton International Hotels (UK) Ltd 2000] 1 All ER (Comm) 750, [2000] BLR 235 .... 9.10

Hounslow LBC v Thames Water Utilities Ltd [2003] EWHC 1197 (Admin), [2004] QB 212, [2003] 3 WLR 1243, [2004] Env LR 4, [2003] EHLR 18, [2004] JPL 301, [2003] 24 EG 162 (CS), (2003) 100(27) LSG 37 .... 14.04

Howe v Botwood [1913] 2 KB 387, 82 LJKB 569, 108 LT 767, 29 TLR 437.... 10.08; 14.59

Hudson v Cripps [1896] 1 Ch 265, [1895-9] All ER Rep 917, 65 LJ Ch 328, 60 JP 393, 44 WR 200, 40 SJ 131, 73 LT 741, 12 TLR 102 .... 10.33

Hudson v Nicholson (1839) 5 M&W 437 .... 2.32

Hughes v Kingston upon Hull City Council [1999] QB 1193, [1999] 2 All ER 49, [1999] 2 WLR 1229, 31 HLR 779, [1999] Env LR 579, [1998] 44 LS Gaz R 36, 143 SJLB 54 .... 14.72

Hulley v Silversprings Bleaching & Dyeing Co Ltd [1922] 2 Ch 268, [1922] All ER Rep 683, 91 LJ Ch 207, 86 JP 30, 66 SJ 195, 126 LT 499 .... 13.39

Hunter v Canary Wharf Ltd; *sub nom* Hunter v London Docklands Develop-
    ment Corp, [1997] AC 655, [1997] 2 WLR 684, [1997] 2 All ER 426,
    [1997] CLC 1045, 84 BLR 1, 54 Con LR 12, [1997] Env LR 488, [1997] 2
    FLR 342, (1998) 30 HLR 409, [1997] Fam Law 601, [1997] EG 59 (CS),
    (1997) 94(19) LSG 25, (1997) 147 NLJ 634, (1997) 141 SJLB 108, [1997]
    NPC 64; *affirming* [1996] 2 WLR 348, [1996] 1 All ER 482, [1996] CLC
    197, 75 BLR 27, 47 Con LR 136, [1996] Env LR 138, (1996) 28 HLR 383,
    [1995] EG 153 (CS), (1995) 92(39) LSG 28, (1995) 145 NLJ 1645, (1995)
    139 SJLB 214, [1995] NPC 155 .... 13.05, 13.11, 13.12, 13.43, 13.56;
    14.10, 14.11, 14.73
Hussain v Lancaster City Council [2000] QB 1, [1999] 4 All ER 125, [1999]
    2 WLR 1142, 96 LGR 663, 77 P & CR 89, 31 HLR 164, [1998] 23 LS Gaz
    R 27, 142 SJLB 173, [1998] EGCS 86, 76 P & CR D31 .... 13.22
Hynes v Vaughan (1985) 50 P & CR 444 .... 2.33, 2.38

I

Impress (Worcester) Ltd v Rees [1971] 2 All ER 357, 69 LGR 305, 219 Estates
    Gazette 455, 115 SJ 245 .... 17.60
Inter-Environnement Wallonie ASBL v Région Wallonie: C-129/96 [1998] All
    ER (EC) 155, [1997] ECR I-7411, [1998] 1 CMLR 1057, [1998] Env LR
    623 .... 16.11
International Drilling Fluids Ltd v Louisville Investments (Uxbridge) Ltd [1986]
    Ch 513, [1986] 1 All ER 321, [1986] 2 WLR 581, 51 P & CR 187, [1986]
    1 EGLR 39, 277 Estates Gazette 62, 129 SJ 854 .... 10.16
International Energy Group Ltd v Zurich Insurance plc UK [2015] UKSC 33,
    [2015] 2 WLR 1471, [2015] 4 All ER 813 .... 13.61
Issa v Hackney LBC *see* Hackney LBC v Issa; *sub nom* Issa v Hackney LBC

J

Jelson Ltd v Derby City Council [1999] 4 PLR 11, [1999] 3 EGLR 91, [1999]
    39 EG 149, [2000] JPL 203, [1999] EG 88 (CS), (1999) 96(26) LSG 30,
    [1999] NPC 68 .... 18.25
Jenkins v Jackson (1888) 40 Ch D 71, 58 LJ Ch 124, 37 WR 253, 60 LT 105, 4
    TLR 747 .... 10.33
Jervis v Harris [1996] Ch 195, [1996] 2 WLR 220, [1996] 1 All ER 303, [1996]
    1 EGLR 78, [1996] 10 EG 159, [1995] EG 177 (CS), (1996) 93(3) LSG 30,
    (1996) 140 SJLB 13, [1995] NPC 171... 10.13
Johnsons News of London v Ealing London Borough Council (1989) 154 JP 33,
    [1990] COD 135... 14.39, 14.42, 14.57
Jones v Hill (1817) 7 Taunt 392, 1 Moore CP 100... 10.30
Jones v IC & Environment Agency [2012] 2 Info LR 129 .... 4.24
Jones v Llanrwst UDC [1911] 1 Ch 393, [1908–10] All ER Rep 922, 80 LJ Ch
    145, 75 JP 68, 9 LGR 222, 55 SJ 125, 103 LT 751, 27 TLR 133................ 13.47

I

Inter-Environnement Bruxelles ASBL v Region de Bruxelles-Capitale (Case
    C-567/10) [2012] 2 CMLR 30, [2012] Env LR 30.................................... 18.

K

Kavanagh v Chief Constable of Devon & Cornwall; *sub nom* Bankrupt,
    ex p v Chief Constable of Devon & Cornwall; Kavanagh, Re [1974] QB
    624, [1974] 2 WLR 762, [1974] 2 All ER 697, (1974) 118 SJ 347............. 14.45

Khorasandjian v Bush [1993] QB 727, [1993] 3 All ER 669, [1993] 3 WLR 476,
  [1993] 2 FCR 257, [1993] 2 FLR 66, [1993] Fam Law 679, 25 HLR 392,
  [1993] 15 LS Gaz R 40, [1993] NLJR 329, 137 SJLB 88 .... 13.11
King v David Allen & Sons (Billposting) Ltd [1916] 2 AC 54, [1916–17] All ER
  Rep 268, 85 LJPC 229, 114 LT 762 .... 17.10
Kirkaldie v Information Commissioner (Unreported, 4 July 2006) 4.20, 4.23
Kirklees MBC v Field (1998) 162 JP 88, [1998] Env LR 337, (1998) 30 HLR
  869, (1998) 10 Admin LR 49, (1998) 162 JPN 48, [1997] EG 151 (CS),
  (1997) 94(45) LSG 28, (1997) 141 SJLB 246, [1997] NPC 152 .... 14.27, 14.29
Kauffmann v Credit Lyonnais Bank (1995) CLC 300, (1995) 7 Admin LR
  669 .... 4.25
Konskier v B Goodman Ltd [1928] 1 KB 421 .... 2.32

L

L (A Minor) (Police Investigation: Privilege), Re; *sub nom* L (Minors) (Disclosure of Medical Reports), Re; L (Minors) (Police Investigation: Privilege),
  Re [1997] AC 16, [1996] 2 WLR 395, [1996] 2 All ER 78, [1996] 1 FLR
  731, [1996] 2 FCR 145, (1996) 32 BMLR 160, [1996] Fam Law 400,
  (1996) 160 LG Rev 417, (1996) 93(15) LSG 30, (1996) 146 NLJ 441,
  (1996) 140 SJLB 116 .... 4.20
Lambert v Barratt Homes Ltd [2010] EWCA Civ 681, [2010] BLR 527, 131
  Con LR 29 .... 13.19
Lambert (A) Flat Management Ltd v Lomas [1981] 2 All ER 280, [1981] 1
  WLR 898, 125 SJ 218f 14.50, 14.51
Lambson Fine Chemicals Ltd v Merlion Capital Housing Ltd [2008] EWHC
  168 (TCC), [2008] Env LR 37 .... 2.14, 2.15, 2.42; 13.48
Lambton v Mellish [1894] 3 Ch 163 .... 13.37
Landelijke Vereniging tot Behoud van de Waddenzee v Staatssecretaris van
  Landbouw, Natuurbeheer en Visserij (C127/02) [2005] All ER (EC) 353,
  [2004] ECR I-7405, [2005] 2 CMLR 31, [2005] Env LR 14, [2004] NPC
  136 .... 19.48, 19.53
Lawrence v Fen Tigers Ltd *see* Coventry (t/a RDC Promotions) v Lawrence
Leakey v National Trust for Places of Historic Interest or Natural Beauty [1980]
  QB 485, [1980] 1 All ER 17, [1980] 2 WLR 65, 78 LGR 100, 123 SJ 606... 13.10,
                                                                        13.19; 17.156
Leeds v Islington London Borough Council (1998) 31 HLR 545, [1998] Env LR
  657, [1998] COD 293, [1998] 07 LS Gaz R 33 .... 14.68
Legge (George) & Son Ltd v Wenlock Corpn [1938] AC 204, [1938] 1 All ER
  37, 107 LJ Ch 72, 102 JP 93, 36 LGR 117, 82 SJ 133, 158 LT 265, 54 TLR
  315 .... 13.38
Leigh Land Reclamation Ltd v Walsall MBC (1991) 155 JP 547, [1993] Env LR
  16, [1991] JPL 867, [1991] Crim LR 298, [1991] COD 152, (1991) 155
  JPN 332, (1991) 155 LG Rev 507 .... 16.24
Levy v Environment Agency [2002] EWHC 1663 (Admin), [2003] Env
  LR 11 .... 20.20
Lewisham London Borough v Fenner [1995] 248 ENDS Report 44, (1996)
  8 Environmental Law & Management 11 .... 14.07, 14.63
Lictor Anstalt v MIR Steel UK Ltd [2012] EWCA Civ 1397, [2013] 2 All ER
  (Comm) 54, [2013] CP Rep 7 .... 9.10
Lippiatt v South Gloucestershire Council [2000] QB 51, [1999] 4 All ER 149,
  [1999] 3 WLR 137, 31 HLR 1114, [1999] 15 LS Gaz R 31 .... 13.22

Liverpool Corpn v H Coghill & Son Ltd [1918] 1 Ch 307, 87 LJ Ch 186, 82 JP
129, 16 LGR 91, 118 LT 336, 34 TLR 159 .... 13.39
London & North Eastern Railway Co (LNER) v Berriman; *sub nom* Berriman
v London & North Eastern Railway Co (LNER) [1946] AC 278 .... 10.12
Lord Baker v Information Commissioner & the Department for Communities
& Local Government (Unreported, 1 June 2007) 4.18

M

MWH Associates Ltd v Wrexham CBC [2012] EWCA Civ 1884, [2013] Env LR
27, [2013] RVR 112 .... 19.04
McCarthy & Stone (Developments) Ltd v Richmond upon Thames LBC; *sub
nom* R v Richmond upon Thames LBC, ex p McCarthy & Stone (Developments) Ltd [1992] 2 AC 48, [1991] 3 WLR 941, [1991] 4 All ER 897, 90
LGR 1, (1992) 4 Admin LR 223, (1992) 63 P & CR 234; [1992] 1 PLR
131; [1992] JPL 467, [1991] EG 118 (CS), (1992) 89(3) LSG 33, (1991)
141 NLJ 1589, (1991) 135 SJLB 206; [1991] NPC 118; reversing [1990]
2 WLR 1294, [1990] 2 All ER 852, (1990) 60 P & CR 174, [1990] 1 PLR
109, [1990] COD 449, (1990) 154 LG Rev 796, [1990] EG 30 (CS), (1990)
140 NLJ 362; *affirming* (1989) 1 Admin LR 3, (1989) 58 P & CR 434,
[1989] 2 PLR 22, [1990] JPL 41, [1989] EG 14 (CS) 15.17; 18.15
McCartney v Londonderry & Lough Swilly Railway Co Ltd [1904] AC 301
(UK-Irl) 17.23
McCullough v IC & NI Water (EA/2012/0082) 4.20
McKinnon Industries Ltd v Walker [1951] WN 401, 95 SJ 559, 3 DLR 577,
PC 13.08
McLeod (or Houston) v Buchanan [1940] 2 All ER 179, 1940 SC (HL) 17, 1940
SLT 232, 1940 SN 20, 84 SJ 452 .... 17.48
Maguire v Leigh-on-Sea UDC (1906) 70 JP 479, 34 LGR 979, 95 LT 319 .... 10.50
Malone v Laskey [1907] 2 KB 141, [1904–7] All ER Rep 304, 76 LJKB 1134,
51 SJ 356, 97 LT 324, 23 TLR 399 .... 13.11
Malton Board of Health v Malton Manure Co (1879) 4 Ex D 302 .... 14.06
Mancetter Developments Ltd v Garmanson Ltd [1986] QB 1212, [1986] 1 All
ER 449, [1986] 2 WLR 871, [1986] BCLC 196, 2 BCC 98, 924, [1986]
1 EGLR 240, 130 SJ 129, [1986] LS Gaz R 612 .... 10.30
Manchester Bonded Warehouse Co Ltd v Carr (1879-80) LR 5 CPD 507,
CPD 10.28
Manchester Corpn v Markland [1936] AC 360 .... 17.159
Manley v New Forest DC [2000] EHLR 113, [1999] 4 PLR 36, (1999) 96(31)
LSG 44, [2000] Env LR D11 .... 14.04, 14.26, 14.55
Manley v New Forest DC [2007] EWHC 3188 (Admin), [2008] Env LR 26 ..... 14.04
Marcic v Thames Water Utilities Ltd; *sub nom* Thames Water Utilities Ltd v
Marcic [2003] UKHL 66, [2004] 2 AC 42, [2003] 3 WLR 1603, [2004]
1 All ER 135, [2004] BLR 1, 91 Con LR 1, [2004] Env LR 25, [2004]
HRLR 10, [2004] UKHRR 253, [2003] 50 EG 95 (CS), (2004) 101(4) LSG
32, (2003) 153 NLJ 1869, (2003) 147 SJLB 1429, [2003] NPC 150: 1.38;
13.18; 17.158
Margereson & Hancock v J W Roberts Ltd [1996] PIQR P 358, [1996] Env LR
304, [1996] 22 LS Gaz R 27 .... 3.06; 13.48, 13.49
Marker v Kenrick (1853) 13 CB 188, 22 LJCP 129, 17 Jur 44, 20 LTOS 223 ... 10.30
Markinson v the Information Commissioner (Unreported, 28 March 2006) 4.35
Marlborough Properties Ltd v Marlborough Fibreglass Ltd [1981] 1 NZLR
464 .... 10.30

Marleasing SA v La Comercial Internacional de Alimentación SA: C-106/89 [1990] ECR I-4135, [1992] 1 CMLR 305, [1993] BCC 421, 135 SJ 15 .... 1.26

Marsden v Edward Heyes Ltd [1927] 2 KB 1, [1926] All ER Rep 329, 97 LJKB 410, 136 LT 593 .... 10.28

Matania v National Provincial Bank Ltd & Elevenist Syndicate Ltd [1936] 2 All ER 633, 106 LJKB 113, 80 SJ 532, 155 LT 74 .... 13.13

Matos e Silva Lda v Portugal (1996) 24 EHRR 573, ECHR............................. 1.38

Mecklenburg (Wilhelm) v Kreis Pinneberg–Der Landsrat: C-321/96 [1999] All ER (EC) 166, [1998] ECR I-3809, [1999] 2 CMLR 418, [1998] 34 LS Gaz R 33 .... 4.09

Merlin v British Nuclear Fuels plc [1990] 2 QB 557, [1990] 3 All ER 711, [1990] 3 WLR 383, [1990] 31 LS Gaz R 33... 13.54

Merthyr Tydfil Car Auction Ltd v Thomas [2013] EWCA Civ 815, 149 Con LR 105, [2014] Env LR 4 .... 13.45

Metropolitian Asylum District Managers v Hill (1881) 6 App Cas 193........... 14.04

Metropolitan Rly Co v Fowler [1893] AC 416, 62 LJQB 533, 57 JP 756, 1 R 264, 42 WR 270, 68 LT 390, 9 TLR 610 .... 17.12

Midland Bank Ltd v Conway Borough Council (or Corpn) [1965] 2 All ER 972, [1965] 1 WLR 1165, 129 JP 466, 63 LGR 346, 109 SJ 494 .... 10.50

Midland Bank Ltd v Farmpride Hatcheries Ltd [1981] 2 EGLR 147, 260 EG 493 .... 2.33

Miller v Jackson [1977] QB 966, [1977] 3 All ER 338, [1977] 3 WLR 20, 121 SJ 287.. 13.37, 13.52

Milton Keynes DC v Fuller [2011] EWHC 1967 (Admin), [2011] Env LR 31, [2012] LLR 172.. 16.24

Miner (or Minor) v Gilmour (1859) 12 Moo PCC 131, 7 WR 328, 33 LTOS 98, PC:.. 17.23

Ministerial Planning Appeal Decision Ref T/APP/K1745/A/94/233729/P7 [1994] JPL 864 .... 14.04

Ministerio dell'Ambiente e della Tutela del Territorio e del Mare v Fipa Group Srl (Case C-534/13) [2015] Env LR 32, [2015] PTSR D43........................ 15.105

Mint v Good [1951] 1 KB 517, [1950] 2 All ER 1159, 49 LGR 495, 94 SJ 822, 66 (pt 2) TLR 1110.. 10.36

Mitchell v Beacon Estates (Finsbury Park) Ltd (1949) 1 P & CR 32 .... 2.22

Monk v Arnold [1902] 1 KB 761, 71 LJKB 441, 50 WR 667, 46 SJ 340, 86 LT 580 .... 10.23; 14.60

Monro v Lord Burghclere [1918] 1 KB 291, 87 LJKB 366, 82 JP 86, 16 LGR 210, 62 SJ 231, 118 LT 343, 34 TLR 131 .... 10.23; 14.60

Montford v IC & BBC (EA/2009/0114)... 4.06

Morgan v Hinton Organics (Wessex) Ltd [2009] EWCA Civ 107, [2009] CP Rep 26, [2010] 1 Costs LR 1... 1.40

Morrissey v Galer; *sub nom* Galer v Morrissey [1955] 1 WLR 110, [1955] 1 All ER 380, (1955) 119 JP 165, 53 LGR 303, (1955) 99 SJ 113 .... 14.04

Mountpace Ltd v Haringay LBC [2012] EWHC 698 (Admin), [2013] PTSR 664, [2012] Env LR 32 .... 16.17

Murdoch v Glacier Metal Co Ltd [1998] Env LR 732, [1998] EHLR 198, [1998] EG 6 (CS), (1998) 95(7) LSG 31... 14.06

Murphy v Brentwood District Council [1991] 1 AC 398, [1990] 2 All ER 908, [1990] 3 WLR 414, 89 LGR 24, [1990] 2 Lloyd's Rep 467, 22 HLR 502, 21 Con LR 1, 50 BLR 1, 134 SJ 1076, [1990] NLJR 1111........ 2.30; 13.49, 13.53

Myatt v Teignbridge District Council [1994] Env LR 78 .... 14.26

N

Nathan v Rouse [1905] 1 KB 527, 74 LJKB 285, 69 JP 135, 3 LGR 354, 92 LT
321, 21 TLR 222 .... 14.58
National Coal Board v Neath BC [1976] 2 All ER 478 .... 14.09
National Coal Board v Thorne 1976] 1 WLR 543, 74 LGR 429, (1976) 239 EG
121, (1976) 120 SJ 234 .... 14.10
National Rivers Authority v Biffa Waste Services Ltd (1995) 160 JP 497, [1996]
Env LR 227 .... 17.44
National Rivers Authority v Welsh Development Agency (1992) 158 JP 506,
[1993] Env LR 407 .... 17.62, 17.63, 17.64
National Rivers Authority v Wright Engineering Co Ltd [1994] 4 All ER 281,
[1994] Crim LR 453, [1994] Env LR 186 .... 17.60
National Rivers Authority v Yorkshire Water Services Ltd [1995] 1 AC 444, [1995]
1 All ER 225, [1994] 3 WLR 1202, 159 JP 573, [1995] NLJR 17 .... 10.03, 10.46
Natural England v Day [2014] EWCA Crim 2683, [2015] 1 Cr App R (S) 53,
[2015] Env LR 15 .... 19.29
Neath RDC v Williams [1951] 1 KB 115, [1950] 2 All ER 625, 49 LGR 177,
114 JP 464, 94 SJ 568, 66 (pt 2) TLR 539 .... 10.48
Network Housing Association Ltd v Westminster City Council [1995] Env LR
176, (1995) 27 HLR 189, 93 LGR 280, [1994] EG 173 (CS) 14.04, 14.26,
14.28, 14.31
Network Rail Ltd v IC & Network Rail Infrastructure Ltd (unreported, 17 July
2007) 4.06
Newbury District Council v Secretary of State for the Environment [1981] AC
578, [1980] 1 All ER 731, [1980] 2 WLR 379, 144 JP 249, 78 LGR 306,
40 P & CR 148, 124 SJ 186, [1980] JPL 325 .... 18.16
Newcastle-under-Lyme Corpn v Wolstanton Ltd [1947] Ch 427, [1947] 1 All
ER 218, 111 JP 102, 45 LGR 221, [1947] LJR 1311, 91 SJ 84, 176 LT 242,
63 TLR 162; reversing [1947] Ch 92, [1946] 2 All ER 447 .... 13.11
Newman v Real Estate Debenture Corpn Ltd & Flower Decorations Ltd [1940]
1 All ER 131, 162 LT 183 .... 10.34
Newport BC v Secretary of State for Wales [1998] Env LR 174, [1998] 1 PLR
47, [1998] JPL 377 .... 18.21, 18.22
North Uist Fisheries Ltd v Secretary of State for Scotland, 1992 SC 33, 1992
SLT 333, IH 19.24
Northumbrian Water Ltd v Sir Robert McAlpine Ltd [2014] EWCA Civ 685,
[2014] BLR 605, 154 Con LR 26 .... 13.05
Nottingham City DC v Newton; *sub nom* Nottingham Friendship Housing
Association vNewton; Nottingham Corp v Newton [1974] 1 WLR 923,
[1974] 2 All ER 760, 72 LGR 535, (1974) 118 SJ 462 .... 14.13
Nottingham Patent Brick & Tile Co v Butler (1885) 15 QBD 261; *aff'd* (1886)
16 QBD 778, [1886–90] All ER Rep 1075, 55 LJQB 280, 34 WR 405, 54
LT 444, 2 TLR 391 .... 2.12, 2.19
Nuttall v Bracewell (1866) LR 2 Exch 1, [1861–73] All ER Rep Ext 2013, 36 LJ
Ex 1, 31 JP 8, 4 H & C 714, 12 Jur NS 989, 15 LT 313 .... 17.11

O

OSS Group Ltd v Environment Agency; *sub nom* R (on the application of OSS
Group Ltd) v Environment Agency; Solvent Resource Management Ltd v
Environment Agency [2007] EWCA Civ 611, [2007] Bus LR 1732, [2007]
3 CMLR 30, [2008] Env LR 8, [2007] JPL 1597, (2007) 104(28) LSG 26,
(2007) 151 SJLB 892, [2007] NPC 80 .... 16.11

Oakley v Birmingham City Council; *sub nom* Birmingham City Council v Oakley [2001] 1 AC 617, [2000] 3 WLR 1936, [2001] 1 All ER 385, [2001] Env LR 37, [2001] EHLR 8, (2001) 33 HLR 30, [2001] BLGR 110, [2000] EG 144 (CS), (2000) 97(48) LSG 38, (2000) 150 NLJ 1824, (2000) 144 SJLB 290, [2000] NPC 136 .... 14.04

Ofcom v IC [2011] 2 Info LR 1...4.12

Office of Communications v Information Commissioner & T Mobile (Unreported, 4 September 2007).. 4.34

Oliver v Mills, 144 Mo 852 (1926) 13.58

Osman v Moss (J Ralph) [1970] 1 Lloyd's Rep 313 .... 9.10

O'Toole v Knowsley MBC [1999] EHLR 420, (2000) 32 HLR 420, (1999) 96(22) LSG 36, [1999] Env LR D29 .... 14.07, 14.46

Overseas Tankship (UK) Ltd v Miller Steamship Co Pty, The Wagon Mound (No 2) [1967] 1 AC 617, [1966] 2 All ER 709, [1966] 3 WLR 498, [1966] 1 Lloyd's Rep 657, 110 SJ 447, [1967] ALR 97, [1966] 1 NSWR 411, PC..... 13.09, 13.27

P

Packaging Centre Ltd v Poland Street Estate Ltd (1961) 178 Estates Gazette 189 .... 10.16

Page v Smith [1996] AC 155, [1995] 2 WLR 644, [1995] 2 All ER 736, [1995] 2 Lloyd's Rep 95, [1995] RTR 210, [1995] PIQR P329, (1995) 92(23) LSG 33, (1995) 145 NLJ 723, (1995) 139 SJLB 173..................................... 13.49

Palin Granit Oy v Lounais-Suomen Ymparistokeskus (C-9/00); *sub nom* Palin Granit Oy'sApplication, Re (C-9/00); Palin Granit Oy v Vehmassalon Kansanterveystyon Kuntayhtyman Hallitus (C-9/00) [2002] 1 WLR 2644, [2003] All ER (EC) 366, [2002] ECR I-3533, [2002] 2 CMLR 24, [2002] Env LR 35 .... 16.11

Parker v Inge (1886) 17 QBD 584, 55 LJMC 149, 51 JP 20, 55 LT 300........... 14.36

Parkwood Landfill Ltd v Customs & Excise Commissioners; *sub nom* Customs & Excise Commissioners v Parkwood Landfill Ltd [2002] EWCA Civ 1707, [2003] 1 WLR 697, [2003] 1 All ER 579, [2002] STC 1536, [2003] Env LR 19, [2002] BTC 8045, [2003] JPL 861, [2002] STI 1653, (2003) 100(6) LSG 26, (2002) 146 SJLB 278, [2002] NPC 155 .... 16.31

Patel v Mehtab (1981-82) 5 HLR 78... 14.07

Payne v Rogers (1794) 2 Hy Bl 350 .... 10.36; 13.20

Pearshouse v Birmingham City Council (1998) 96 LGR 169, 31 HLR 756, [1999] COD 132, [1999] JPL 725, [1999] EHLR 140, [1999] BLGR 169, [1999] Env LR 536 .... 14.67, 14.70

Pegler Ltd v Wang (UK) Ltd (No 1) [2000] BLR 218, 70 Con LR 68, [2000] ITCLR 617, [2000] Masons CLR 19.. 9.10

Pemberton v Southwark London Borough Council [2000] 3 All ER 924, [2000] 1 WLR 1672, [2000] 2 EGLR 33, [2000] 21 EG 135, [2000] EGCS 56 ..... 13.12

Perrins v Information Commissioner (Unreported, 9 January 2007)................. 4.20

Persimmon Homes v Ove Arup & Partners Ltd [2015] EWHC 3573 (TCC), [2016] BLR 112, 163 Con LR 191... 9.10

Petra Investments Ltd v Jeffrey Rogers plc [2000] EGCS 66, [2000] NPC 61.... 10.34

Polychronakis v Richards & Jerrom Ltd [1998] Env LR 346, [1998] JPL 588 ... 14.50

Port of London Authority v Information Commissioner & John Hibbert (unreported, 31 May 2007).. 4.06

Post Office v Aquarius Properties Ltd [1987] 1 All ER 1055, 54 P & CR 61, [1987] 1 EGLR 40, 281 Estates Gazette 798, [1987] LS Gaz R 820........... 10.12

Premier Confectionery (London) Co Ltd v London Commercial Sale Rooms Ltd
    [1933] Ch 904, [1933] All ER Rep 579, 102 LJ Ch 353, 77 SJ 523, 149 LT
    479 .... 10.16
Price v Cromack [1975] 2 All ER 113, [1975] 1 WLR 988, 139 JP 423, 119 SJ
    458 .... 10.47; 17.54
Pride of Derby & Derbyshire Angling Association Ltd v British Celanese Ltd
    [1952] 1 All ER 1326, 50 LGR 448, [1952] WN 227, 96 SJ 263, [1952]
    1 TLR 1013; *aff'd* [1953] Ch 149, [1953] 1 All ER 179, [1953] 2 WLR 58,
    117 JP 52, 51 LGR 121, 97 SJ 28 .... 13.29, 13.37, 13.52, 13.58
Property Alliance Group Ltd v Royal Bank of Scotland plc [2015] EWHC 3187
    (Ch), [2016] 1 WLR 992... 8.11
Proudfoot v Hart (1890) 25 QBD 42, [1886–90] All ER Rep 782, 59 LJQB 389,
    55 JP 20, 38 WR 730, 63 LT 171, 6 TLR 305 .... 10.12, 10.13
Prudential Assurance Co Ltd v London Residuary Body [1992] 2 AC 386,
    [1992] 3 All ER 504, [1992] 3 WLR 279, 64 P & CR 193, [1992] 2 EGLR
    56, [1992] 36 EG 129, [1992] 33 LS Gaz R 36, [1992] NLJR 1087, 136
    SJLB 229... 17.10
Puckett & Smith's Contract, Re [1902] 2 Ch 258, [1900–3] All ER Rep 114, 71
    LJ Ch 666, 50 WR 532, 87 LT 189 .... 2.08
Pyx Granite Co Ltd v Ministry of Housing & Local Government [1960] AC
    260, [1959] 3 WLR 346, [1959] 3 All ER 1, (1959) 123 JP 429, 58 LGR
    1, (1959) 10 P & CR 319, (1959) 103 SJ 633; reversing [1958] 1 QB 554,
    [1958] 2 WLR 371, [1958] 1 All ER 625, (1958) 122 JP 182, 56 LGR 171,
    (1958) 9 P & CR 204, (1958) 102 SJ 175 .... 10.23; 18.16

Q

Quick v Taff Ely Borough Council [1986] QB 809, [1985] 3 All ER 321, [1985]
    3 WLR 981, 84 LGR 498, 18 HLR 66, [1985] 2 EGLR 50, 276 Estates
    Gazette 452, [1985] NLJ Rep 848, 129 SJ 685 .... 10.12; 13.20
Quigley v Liverpool Housing Trust [2000] EHLR 130, [1999] EG 94 (CS),
    [2000] Env LR D9 .... 14.53

R

R v Birmingham City Council, ex p Ireland; *sub nom* Hall v Kingston upon Hull
    City Council; Ireland v Birmingham City Council; Baker v Birmingham
    City Council; R v Kingston City Council, ex p Hall; R v Kingston City
    Council, ex p Baker [1999] 2 All ER 609, (2000) 164 JP 9, [1999] EHLR
    243, (1999) 31 HLR 1078, [1999] BLGR 184, (1999) 163 JPN 894, [1999]
    EG 4 (CS), (1999) 149 NLJ 122, [1999] NPC 5, [1999] Env LR D19 .... 14.01,
                                                                                                          14.68
R v Bolton Metropolitan Council, ex p Kirkman (1997) 76 P & CR 548, [1997]
    NPC 188; on appeal [1998] Env LR 719, [1998] JPL 787, [1998] NPC
    80 .... 16.08; 18.19
R v Bristol City Council, ex p Everett [1999] 2 All ER 193, [1999] 1 WLR 1170,
    31 HLR 1102, [1999] 3 PLR 14, [1999] NPC 28, [1999] 13 LS Gaz R 31,
    [1999] NLJR 370, [1999] EGCS 33, 143 SJLB 104, [1999] BLGR 513,
    [1999] Env LR 587, [1999] EHLR 265.. 14.07, 14.28
R v British Coal Corpn, ex p Ibstock Brick Building Products Ltd [1994] NPC
    133, [1995] JPL 836, [1995] Env LR 277 .... 4.09
R v Broadland District Council & St Matthew Society Ltd & Peddars Way
    Housing Association, ex p Dove [1998] PLCR 119..................................... 18.21

R v Bromley London Borough Council, ex p Barker [2000] EGCS 51, [2000]
PLCR 399 .... 18.32

R v Cardiff City Council, ex p Cross (1981) 45 P & CR 156, 1 HLR 54, [1981]
RVR 155, [1981] JPL 748; *aff'd* (1982) 81 LGR 105, 6 HLR 1, [1982] RVR
270, [1983] JPL 245 .... 14.66

R v Carrick District Council, ex p Shelley (1996) 95 LGR 620, [1996] JPL 857,
[1996] Env LR 273 .... 14.04, 14.12, 14.13

R v Birmingham Justices, ex p Guppy (1988) 152 JP 159, 86 LGR 264, (1988)
152 LG Rev 713 .... 14.25

R v Crown Court at Oxford, ex p Smith (1989) 154 JP 422, 154 LGR 458,
[1990] COD 211, [1990] 2 Admin LR 389 .... 15.26

R v Cumberland Justices, ex p Trimble (1877) 41 JP 454, 36 LT 508:..... 14.36, 14.37

R v Daly (James Joseph) 1974] 1 WLR 133, [1974] 1 All ER 290, (1974) 58 Cr
App R 333, [1974] Crim LR 263, (1973) 118 SJ 66.............................. 14.70

R v Daventry DC; *sub nom* Thornby Farms Ltd *see* R (on the application of
Thornby Farms Ltd) v Daventry DC

R v Derby Magistrates Court, ex p B [1996] AC 487, [1995] 3 WLR 681, [1995]
4 All ER 526, [1996] 1 Cr App R 385, (1995) 159 JP 785, [1996] 1 FLR
513, [1996] Fam Law 210, (1995) 159 JPN 778, (1995) 145 NLJ 1575,
[1995] 139 SJLB 219 .... 4.20

R v Director-General of Water Services, ex p Lancashire County Council (1998)
96 LGR 396, 31 HLR 224, [1999] Env LR 114 .... 17.21

R v Dudley Magistrates' Court, ex p Hollis [1998] 1 All ER 759, [1999] 1 WLR
642, 30 HLR 902, [1998] 2 EGLR 19, [1998] 18 EG 133, [1998] JPL
652 .... 14.25, 14.70

R v Durham County Council, ex p Huddleston [2000] 1 WLR 1484, [2000]
2 CMLR 313, [2000] 13 LS Gaz R 43, [2000] EGCS 39, 144 SJLB 149 .... 18.31

R v Ettrick Trout Co Ltd & Baxter [1994] Env LR 165 .... 17.66

R v Falmouth & Truro Port Health Authority, ex p South West Water Services
(1999) 163 JP 589, [1999] EGCS 62, [1999] Env LR 833; *aff'd* [2000]
3 All ER 306, [2000] 3 WLR 1464, [2000] EGCS 50 .... 14.27, 14.28, 14.29

R v Fenny Stratford Justices, ex p Watney Mann (Midlands) Ltd [1976] 2 All
ER 888, [1976] 1 WLR 1101, 140 JP 474, 75 LGR 72, 238 Estates Gazette
417, 120 SJ 201 .... 14.28

R v Hertfordshire County Council, ex p Green Environmental Industries Ltd
[2000] 2 AC 412, [2000] 1 All ER 773, [2000] 2 WLR 373, [2000] 09 LS
Gaz R 42, [2000] NLJR 277, [2000] EGCS 27, [2000] Env LR 426 ..... 1.38; 8.11

R v Highbury Corner Magistrates' Court, ex p Edwards (1994) 26 HLR 682,
[1994] Env LR 215, [1995] Crim LR 65 .... 10.06; 14.31

R v Inland Revenue Commissioners, ex p National Federation of Self Employed
& Small Businesses Ltd; *sub nom* Inland Revenue Commissioners v National Federation of Self Employed & Small Businesses Ltd [1982] AC 617,
[1981] 2 WLR 722, [1981] 2 All ER 93, [1981] STC 260, 55 TC 133,
(1981) 125 SJ 325.. 1.40

R v Inspectorate of Pollution, ex p Greenpeace Ltd (No 2); R v Ministry of Agriculture, Fisheries & Food, ex p Greenpeace Ltd [1994] 4 All ER 329, [1994]
2 CMLR 548, [1994] Env LR 76, [1994] COD 116, [1993] NPC 126......... 1.40

R v Jagger [2015] Enc LR 25 .... 16.11

R v Jones [1978] 2 All ER 718, [1978] 1 WLR 195, 142 JP 453, 66 Cr App Rep
246, 122 SJ 94 .... 8.11

R v Kennet District Council, ex p Somerfield Property Co Ltd [1999] JPL 361,
[1999] Env LR D13 .... 18.20

R v Kingston upon Hull City Council, ex p Hall *see* Hall v Kingston upon Hull
    City Council
R v Leicestershire CC, ex p Blackfordby & Boothorpe Action Group Ltd; *sub
    nom* R v Leicester City Council, ex p Blackfordby & Boothcorpe Action
    Group Ltd; R v Leicestershire CC, ex p Blackfordby & Boothcorpe Action
    Group Ltdm [2001] Env LR 2, [2000] EHLR 215, [2000] JPL 1266 .... 18.19
R v Leighton & Town & Country Refuse Collections Ltd [1997] Env LR 411.. 16.23;
                                                                            17.48
R v Leominster DC, ex p Pothecary (1998) 10 Admin LR 484, (1998) 76 P &
    CR 346, [1997] 3 PLR 91, [1998] JPL 335, (1997) 94(45) LSG 28, [1997]
    NPC 151; reversing [1997] JPL 835, [1997] EG 2 (CS)............................. 18.07
R v Madden [1975] 3 All ER 155, [1975] 1 WLR 1379, 139 JP 685, 61 Cr App
    Rep 254, 119 SJ 657 .... 13.04, 13.34
R v Metropolitan Stipendiary Magistrate, ex p London Waste Regulation Author-
    ity; Berkshire CC v Scott [1993] 3 All ER 113, [1993] Env LR 417...... 14.04; 16.24
R v Miller (Raymond Karl); R v Glennie (Alastair Kincaid) [1983] 1 WLR 1056,
    [1983] 3 All ER 186, (1984) 78 Cr App R 71, [1983] Crim LR 615, (1983)
    133 NLJ 745, (1983) 127 SJ 580 .... 14.72
R v Nature Conservancy Council, ex p Bolton Metropolitan Borough Council
    [1996] JPL 203 .... 19.10, 19.25
R v Nature Conservancy Council, ex p London Brick Property Ltd [1996] JPL
    227 .... 19.25
R v Newham East Magistrates, ex p London Borough of Newham [1995] Env
    LR 113.. 14.32
R v Newham Justices, ex p Hunt [1976] 1 All ER 839, [1976] 1 WLR 420, 74
    LGR 305, 120 SJ 131.. 14.65
R v North Yorkshire County Council, ex p Brown [2000] 1 AC 397, [1999] 1 All
    ER 969, [1999] 2 WLR 452, [1999] 22 LS Gaz R 34, 143 SJLB 150.... 18.31, 18.32
R v Parlby (1889) LR 22 QBD 520 .... 14.04, 14.07
R v Plymouth City Council, ex p Plymouth & South Devon Co-operative
    Society Ltd (1993) 67 P & CR 78, [1993] 2 EGLR 206, [1993] 36 EG 135,
    [1993] JPL 1099 .... 18.25
R v Poole Borough Council, ex p Beebee [1991] 2 PLR 27, [1991] COD 264,
    [1991] JPL 643 .... 18.33
R v Rimmington (Anthony); R v Goldstein (Harry Chaim) [2005] UKHL 63,
    [2006] 1 AC 459, [2005] 3 WLR 982, [2006] 2 All ER 257, [2006] 1 Cr
    App R 17, [2006] HRLR 3, [2006] UKHRR 1, [2006] Crim LR 153, (2005)
    102(43) LSG 28, (2005) 155 NLJ 1685, [2006] Env LR D3 .... 14.10
R v Rochdale Metropolitan Borough Council, ex p Tew [1999] 3 PLR 74 .... 18.32
R v St Edmundsbury Borough Council, ex p Walton [1999] 3 PLR 51, [1999]
    JPL 805, 11 Admin LR 648, [1999] Env LR 879, [1999] NPC 44, 143 SJLB
    175, [1999] EGCS 53.. 18.33
R v Secretary of State for the Environment, ex p Friends of the Earth Ltd 1996]
    1 CMLR 117, [1996] Env LR 198, (1995) 7 Admin LR 793, [1996] COD
    35 (Civ Div); *affirming* [1994] 2 CMLR 760, [1995] Env LR 11, (1995)
    7 Admin LR 26 .... 1.40
R v Secretary of State for the Environment, ex p Hillingdon LBC [1986] 1 WLR
    807, [1986] 2 All ER 273, (1988) 55 P & CR 241, [1987] RVR 6, [1987]
    JPL 717, (1986) 83 LSG 2331, (1986) 130 SJ 481 (Civ Div); *affirming*
    [1986] 1 WLR 192, [1986] 1 All ER 810, (1986) 52 P & CR 409, [1987]
    RVR 6, [1986] JPL 363, (1986) 83 LSG 525, (1986) 136 NLJ 16, (1986)
    130 SJ 89 .... 14.21

R v Secretary of State for the Environment, ex p Kingston-upon-Hull City
Council [2000] Env LR 248 .... 17.128
R v Secretary of State for the Environment, ex p Rose Theatre Trust Co (No 2)
[1990] 1 QB 504, [1990] 2 WLR 186, [1990] 1 All ER 754, (1990) 59 P &
CR 257, [1990] 1 PLR 39, [1990] JPL 360, [1990] COD 186, [1989] EG
107 (CS), (1990) 87(6) LSG 41, (1990) 134 SJ 425 .... 1.40
R v Secretary of State for the Environment, ex p Royal Society for the Protection
of Birds: C-44/95 [1997] QB 206, [1997] 2 WLR 123, [1997] ECR I-3805,
[1996] 3 CMLR 411 .... 1.26; 19.43, 19.45
R v Secretary of State for the Environment, ex p Standley (National Farmers'
Union intervening): C-293/97 [1999] QB 1279, [1999] All ER (EC) 412,
[1999] 3 WLR 744, [1999] ECR I-2603, [1999] 2 CMLR 902 .... 17.98
R v Secretary of State for the Environment, Transport & the Regions, ex p First Corporate Shipping Ltd (C371/98); *sub nom* R (on the application of First Corporate Shipping Ltd) v Secretary of State for the Environment, Transport & the Re-
gions (C371/98) [2001] All ER (EC) 177, [2000] ECR I-9235, [2001] 1 CMLR
19, [2001] Env LR 34, [2001] 4 PLR 1, [2000] NPC 131 .... 1.24; 19.45, 19.47
R v Secretary of State for the Environment, Transport & the Regions, ex p
Marson [1999] 1 CMLR 268, [1998] Env LR 761, (1999) 77 P & CR 202,
[1998] 3 PLR 90, [1998] JPL 869, [1998] NPC 81 .... 18.34
R v Secretary of State for the Environment, Transport & the Regions, ex p
Alliance Against the Birmingham Northern Relief Road (No 1); *sub nom*
Alliance against the Birmingham Northern Relief Road v Secretary of State
for the Environment, Transport & the Regions (No 1) [1999] Env LR 447,
[1999] JPL 231, [1999] COD 45, [1998] NPC 129 .... 4.09
R v Secretary of State for Trade & Industry, ex p Duddridge [1995] 3 CMLR
231, [1995] Env LR 151; *aff'd* [1996] 2 CMLR 361 .... 1.30
R v Secretary of State for Trade & Industry, ex p Greenpeace Ltd (No 2) [2000]
2 CMLR 94, [2000] Eu LR 196, [2000] Env LR 221, [2000] COD 141 .... 19.47
R v Sellafield Ltd [2014] EWCA Crim 49, [2014] Env LR 19, [2014] LLR 572... 19.29
R v Shorrock [1994] QB 279, [1993] 3 All ER 917, [1993] 3 WLR 698, 98 Cr
App Rep 67, [1993] NLJR 511n 13.34
R v Staines Local Board (1888) 53 JP 358, 60 LT 261, 5 TLR 25 .... 10.48
R v Swale Borough Council & Medway Ports, ex p Royal Society for the Protec-
tion of Birds [1991] 1 PLR 6, [1990] COD 263, [1991] JPL 39 .... 18.33
R v Tandridge DC. ex p Al-Fayed [2000] EHLR 257, (2000) 80 P & CR 90,
[2000] 1 PLR 58, [2000] JPL 604, [2000] EG 1 (CS), [1999] NPC 161,
[2000] Env LR D23 .... 1.30; 18.22
R v Tirado (1974) 59 Cr App Rep 80 .... 8.11
R v Tunbridge Wells Justices, ex p Tunbridge Wells Borough Council (1995) 160
JP 574, 8 Admin LR 453, [1996] Env LR 88 .... 14.25
R v W [2010] EWCA Crim 927, [2011] 3 All ER 691, [2012] PTSR 617 .... 16.13
R v Wicks [1998] AC 92, [1997] 2 All ER 801, [1997] 2 WLR 876, 161 JP 433,
[1997] JPL 1049, [1997] 35 LS Gaz R 34, [1997] NLJR 883, 141 SJLB
127 .... 14.52; 15.26
R v Wigg (1705) 2 Salk 460 .... 14.04
R (on the application of Aggregate Industries UK Ltd) v English Nature; *sub
nom* Aggregate Industries UK Ltd v English Nature [2002] EWHC 908
(Admin), [2003] Env LR 3, [2002] ACD 67, [2002] NPC 58 .... 19.25
R (on the application of Alconbury Developments Ltd) v Secretary of State for
the Environment, Transport & the Regions) [2001] UKHL 23, [2003] 2 AC
295, [2001] 2 WLR 1389 .... 1.38

R (on the application of Ardagh Glass Ltd) v Cheshire West & Cheshire Council
[2010] EWCA Civ 172, [2011] 1 All ER 476, [2011] PTSR 1498 .... 18.32
R (on the application of Barker) v Bromley LBC; *sub nom* R v Bromley LBC, ex
p Baker; R v Bromley LBC, ex p Barker [2006] UKHL 52, [2007] 1 AC 470,
[2006] 3 WLR 1209, [2007] 1 All ER 1183, [2007] Env LR 20, [2007] JPL
744, [2006] 50 EG 85 (CS), (2007) 151 SJLB 28, [2006] NPC 129 .... 18.32
R (on the application of Blewett) v Derbyshire CC; *sub nom* Blewitt v Derbyshire Waste Ltd; Derbyshire Waste Ltd v Blewett [2004] EWCA Civ
1508, [2005] Env LR 15, [2005] 1 PLR 54, [2005] JPL 620, (2004) 148
SJLB 1369, [2004] NPC 171, CA; *affirming* [2003] EWHC 2775 (Admin),
[2004] Env LR 29, [2004] JPL 751 .... 16.08; 18.32
R (on the application of Boggis) v Natural England [2009] EWCA Civ 1061,
[2010] 1 All ER 159, [2010] PTSR 725 .... 19.25
R (on the application of Buckinghamshire CC) v Secretary of State for Transport [2014] UKSC 3, [2014] 1 WLR 324, [2014] 2 All ER 109 .... 18.40
R (on the application of Cala Homes (South) Ltd) v Secretary of State for Communities & Local Government [2011] EWCA Civ 639, [2011] 2 EGLR 75,
[2011] 34 EG 68 .... 18.03
R (on the application of Corner House Research) v Secretary of State for Trade
& Industry [2005] EWCA Civ 192, [2005] 1 WLR 2600, [2005] 4 All ER
1, [2005] CP Rep 28, [2005] 3 Costs LR 455, [2005] ACD 100, (2005)
102(17) LSG 31, (2005) 149 SJLB 297 .... 1.40
R (on the application of Davies) v Stafford Borough Council [2012] EWHC 971
(Admin) 18.14
R (on the application of Delena Wells) v Secretary of State for Transport, Local
Government & the Regions [2004] 1 CMLR 31 .... 18.31
R (on the application of Edwards) v Environment Agency (No 2); *sub nom*
Edwards v Environment Agency [2008] UKHL 22, [2008] 1 WLR 1587,
[2008] Env LR 34, [2008] 16 EG 153 (CS), (2008) 152(16) SJLB 29, [2008]
NPC 44 .... 18.32
R (on the application of England) v Tower Hamlets LBC (Permission to Appeal)
[2006] EWCA Civ 1742 .... 1.40
R (on the application of Fisher) v English Nature; *sub nom* Fisher v English
Nature, [2004] EWCA Civ 663, [2005] 1 WLR 147, [2004] 4 All ER 861,
[2005] Env LR 10, [2004] 2 P & CR 32, [2004] 3 PLR 98, [2005] JPL 83,
[2004] 23 EG 121 (CS), [2004] NPC 84 (Civ Div); *affirming* [2003] EWHC
1599 (Admin), [2004] 1 WLR 503, [2003] 4 All ER 366, [2004] Env LR 7,
[2003] 4 PLR 41, [2004] JPL 217, [2003] NPC 84 .... 19.25
R (on the application of Garner) v Elbridge Borough Council [2010] EWCA Civ
1006, [2011] 3 All ER 418, [2012] PTSR 250 .... 1.40
R (on the application of Hereford Waste Watchers Ltd) v Herefordshire CC; *sub
nom* Hereford Waste Watchers Ltd v Hereford Council [2005] EWHC 191
(Admin), [2005] Env LR 29, [2005] JPL 1469, [2005] 9 EG 188 (CS) 18.34
R (on the application of Jones) v Mansfield DC [2003] EWCA Civ 1408,
[2004] Env LR 21, [2004] 2 P & CR 14, (2003) 147 SJLB 1209, [2003]
NPC 119 .... 18.34
R (on the application of Lichfield Securities Ltd) v Lichfield DC; *sub nom* R v
Lichfield DC, ex p Lichfield Securities Ltd [2001] EWCA Civ 304, (2001)
3 LGLR 35, [2001] 3 PLR 33, [2001] PLCR 32, [2001] JPL 1434 (Note),
[2001] 11 EG 171 (CS), (2001) 98(17) LSG 37, (2001) 145 SJLB 78 .... 4.17
R (on the application of McMorn) v Natural England [2015] EWHC 3297
(Admin), [2016] Env LR 14 .... 19.03, 19.10

R (on the application of May) v Rother DC [2014] EWHC 456 (Admin), [2014] LLR 535, [2015] ECA 610 .... 18.21

R (on the application of Mayer Parry Recycling Ltd) v Environment Agency (C444/00); *sub nom* R v Environment Agency, ex p Mayer Parry Recycling Ltd (C444/00) [2004] 1 WLR 538, [2005] All ER (EC) 647, [2003] ECR I-6163, [2003] 3 CMLR 8, [2004] Env LR 6 .... 16.11

R (on the application of Medway Council) v Secretary of State for Transport, Local Government & the Regions; R (on the application of Essex CC) v Secretary of State for Transport, Local Government & the Regions; R (on the application of Mead) v Secretary of State for Transport, Local Government & the Regions [2002] EWHC 2516 (Admin), [2003] JPL 583, [2002] 49 EG 123 (CS), [2002] NPC 152 .... 19.48

R (on the application of Morge) v Hampshire CC [2011] UKSC 2, [2011] 1 WLR 268, [2011] 1 All ER 744 .... 19.11

R (on the application of National Grid Gas Plc (formerly Transco Plc)) v Environment Agency [2007] UKHL 30, [2007] 1 WLR 1780, [2007] Bus LR 1708, [2007] 3 All ER 877, [2008] Env LR 4, [2007] 3 EGLR 5, [2007] 41 EG 202, [2007] JPL 1737, [2007] 27 EG 302 (CS), (2007) 157 NLJ 974, (2007) 151 SJLB 893, [2007] NPC 77 .... 15.01, 15.76

R (on the application of Office of Communications v Information Comr) v Information Commission [2008] EWHC 1445 (Admin), [2009] Env LR 1, [2008] ACD 65 .... 4.21, 4.28

R (on the application of Rackham Ltd) v Swaffham Magistrates Court [2004] EWHC 1417 (Admin), [2005] JPL 224 .... 16.11

R (on the application of Redland Minerals) v Secretary of State for Environment, Food & Rural Affairs [2010] EWHC 913 (Admin), [2011] Env LR 2 .... 15.76, 15.88

R (on the application of Seiont, Swyfrai & Llyfni Anglers' Society) v Natural Resources Wales v Dwr Cymru Cyfyngedig t/a Dwr Cymru Welsh Water, First Hydro Co Ltd [2015] EWHC 3578 (Admin), [2016] 2 All ER 396, [2016] ACD 31 .... 15.105

R (on the application of An Taisce (National Trust for Ireland)) v Secretary of State for Energy & Climate Change [2013] EWHC 4161 (Admin) 18.19, 18.36

R (on the application of Tarmac Aggregates Ltd) v The Secretary of State for Environment, Food and Rural Affairs & Anor [2015] EWCA Civ 1149; [2016] Env LR 15 .... 20.18

R (on the application of Technoprint plc) v Leeds City Council [2010] EWHC 581 (Admin), [2010] JPL 1244, [2011] Env LR D5 .... 15.18

R (on the application of Thames Water Utilities Ltd) v Bromley Magistrates' Court Environment Agency (interested party) [2007] 1 WLR 1945, [2007] ECR I-3883, [2007] 3 CMLR 2 .... 17.127

R (on the application of Thames Water Utilities Ltd) v Bromley Magistrates' Court (C-252/05) *sub nom* Thames Water Utilities Ltd v Bromley Magistrates Court (C-252/05) [2007] 1 WLR 1945, [2007] 3 CMLR 2, [2008] Env LR 3, [2007] 20 EG 295 (CS) 16.24

R (on the application of Thornby Farms Ltd) v Daventry DC; *sub nom* Thornby Farms Ltd v Daventry DC; R v Daventry DC, ex p Thornby Farms; R (on the application of Murray) v Derbyshire DC; R (on the application of Murray) v Derbyshire CC [2002] EWCA Civ 31, [2003] QB 503, [2002] 3 WLR 875, [2002] Env LR 28, [2003] EHLR 4, [2002] 2 PLR 21, [2002] JPL 937, [2002] ACD 53, [2002] 5 EG 131 (CS), [2002] 5 EG 132 (CS), (2002) 99(11) LSG 35, (2002) 146 SJLB 52, [2002] NPC 13 .... 16.08

R (on the application of Trailer & Marina (Leven) Ltd) v Secretary of State for the Environment, Food & Rural Affairs; *sub nom* Trailer & Marina (Leven) Ltd v Secretary of State for the Environment, Food & Rural Affairs [2004] EWCA Civ 1580, [2005] 1 WLR 1267, [2005] Env LR 27, [2005] 1 P & CR 28, [2005] JPL 1086, (2005) 102(5) LSG 26, (2005) 149 SJLB 60 .... 19.25

R (on the application of Vella) v Lambeth LBC; *sub nom* Vella v Lambeth LBC [2005] EWHC 2473 (Admin), [2006] Env LR 33, [2006] HLR 12, [2006] JPL 1373, [2005] 47 EG 144 (CS).. 14.04

R (Champion) v North Norfolk DC [2015] 1 WLR 3710 .... 18.32

R (Forge Field) v Sevenoaks District Council [2014] EWHC 1895 (Admin ......) 18.12

R (HS2 Action Alliance Ltd) v Secretary of State for Transport [2014] UKSC 3 .... 18.40

R Leslie Ltd v Reliable Advertising & Addressing Agency Ltd [1915] 1 KB 652, KBD... 9.10

Raffinerie Mediterramee (ERG) SpA v Minsterio dello Sviluppo economico [2010] ECR I-1919 .... 15.105

Rahman v Arearose Ltd [2001] QB 351, [2000] 3 WLR 1184, (2001) 62 BMLR 84 .... 13.58

Rainham Chemical Works Ltd v Belvedere Fish Guano Co *see* Belvedere Fish Guano Co Ltd v Rainham Chemical Works Ltd, Feldman & Partridge

Rance v Elvin (1983) 49 P & CR 65, 127 SJ 732; revsd (1985) 50 P & CR 9 ... 17.12

Rawlins v Briggs (1878) 3 CPD 368, 47 LJQB 487, 42 JP 791, 27 WR 138 ...... 10.08

Raymond v Young [2015] EWCA Civ 456, [2015] HLR 41 .... 13.53

Read v J Lyons & Co Ltd [1947] AC 156, [1946] 2 All ER 471, [1947] LJR 39, 91 SJ 54, 175 LT 413, 62 TLR 646 .... 13.27, 13.29

Redland Bricks Ltd v Morris [1970] AC 652, [1969] 2 All ER 576, [1969] 2 WLR 1437, 211 Estates Gazette 153, 113 SJ 405.................................... 13.52

Rhone v Stephens [1994] 2 AC 310, [1994] 2 All ER 65, [1994] 2 WLR 429, [1994] 2 EGLR 181, [1994] 37 EG 151, [1994] NLJR 460, 138 SJLB 77.. 19.18

Rickards v Lothian [1913] AC 263, [1911–13] All ER Rep 71, 82 LJPC 42, 57 SJ 281, 108 LT 225, 29 TLR 281 .... 13.28

Riddell v Spear (1879) 43 JP 317, 40 LT 130 .... 14.33

Ridge v Crawley (1959) 173 EG 959 .... 2.17

Rignall Developments Ltd v Halil [1988] Ch 190, [1987] 3 All ER 170, [1987] 3 WLR 394, 54 P & CR 245, 20 HLR 7, [1987] 1 EGLR 193, 282 Estates Gazette 1414, 131 SJ 1039, [1987] LS Gaz R 2273 .... 2.12, 2.18, 2.19, 2.21

Rivers v Cutting [1982] 3 All ER 69, [1982] 1 WLR 1146, [1983] RTR 105, [1982] Crim LR 525, 126 SJ 362, [1982] LS Gaz R 954 .... 13.13

Roake v Chadha [1983] 3 All ER 503, [1984] 1 WLR 40, 47 P & CR 27, 128 SJ 32 .... 19.19

Robb v Dundee City Council, 2002 SC 301, 2002 SLT 853, [2002] Env LR 33, [2003] EHLR 9, 2002 Hous LR 26, 2002 GWD 7-244, IH..... 14.07, 14.09, 14.10

Robert Lindley Ltd v East Riding of Yorkshire Council [2016] UKUT 6 (LC), 2016 WL 2355... 13.19

Robinson v Kilvert (1889) 41 Ch D 88, 58 LJ Ch 392, 37 WR 545, 61 LT 60 .. 10.34; 13.06

Rookes v Barnard [1964] AC 1129, [1964] 1 All ER 367, [1964] 2 WLR 269, [1964] 1 Lloyd's Rep 28, 108 SJ 93... 13.53

Roper v Tussauds Theme Parks Ltd [2007] EWHC 624 (Admin), [2007] Env LR 31 .... 14.11, 14.65

Rosewell v Prior (1701) 1 Ld Raym 713, 6 Mod Rep 116, 2 Salk 460, *sub nom*
Roswell v Prior 12 Mod Rep 635, Holt KB 500................................. 2.34; 13.13
Roux Restaurants Ltd v Jaison Property Development Co Ltd; *sub nom* Jaison
Property Development Co Ltd v Roux Restaurants Ltd (1997) 74 P & CR
357, [1996] EG 118 (CS), [1996] NPC 111 .... 10.16
Royal Greek Government v Minister of Transport (1949) 83 Ll L Rep 228, 66
(pt 1) TLR 504.. 17.55
Royal Society for the Protection of Birds v Secretary of State for Scotland (2000)
GWD 26-961; Times 12 September... 19.14
Royal Society for the Protection of Birds v Secretary of State for Scotland;
sub nom: RSPB, Petitioners, 2000 SLT 1272, 2000 SCLR 1045, [2000]
3 CMLR 1157, [2001] Env LR 19, [2000] 4 PLR 120, 2000 GWD 26-961,
IH 19.48
Royal Society for the Protection of Birds v Secretary of State for the Environ-
ment, Food & Rural Affairs [2014] EWHC 1645 (Admin), [2014] Env LR
29 .... 19.23
Royscot Trust Ltd v Rogerson [1991] 2 QB 297, [1991] 3 All ER 294, [1991]
3 WLR 57, 135 SJ 444, [1991] NLJR 493.. 2.15
Rugby Joint Water Board v Walters [1967] Ch 397, [1966] 3 All ER 497, [1966]
3 WLR 934, 110 SJ 635 .... 17.23
Rust Consulting Ltd (in liquidation) v PB Ltd [2012] EWCA Civ 1070, [2012]
BLR 427, 144 Con LR 63 .... 9.10
Rylands v Fletcher; *sub nom* Fletcher v Rylands (1868) LR 3 HL 330; *affirming*
(1865-66) LR 1 Ex 265, [1865-66] All ER Rep 1, (1866) 4 Hurl & C 263,
ex Chamber 9.03, 9.22; 13.01, 13.05, 13.09,
13.23, 13.24, 13.25, 13.26, 13.27,
13.30, 13.31, 13.32, 13.33, 13.37,
13.49, 13.53; 17.158

S

SFI Group plc (formerly Surrey Free Inns) v Gosport Borough Council [1999]
Env LR 750, [1999] BLGR 610, [1999] EGCS 51 .... 14.26, 14.27, 14.29, 14.39,
14.42, 14.57
St Anne's Well Brewery Co v Roberts (1928) 92 JP 180, [1928] All ER Rep 28,
26 LGR 638, 140 LT 1, 44 TLR 703.. 13.20
St Helen's Smelting Co v Tipping (1865) 35 LJQB 66, [1861–73] All ER Rep
Ext 1389, 29 JP 579, 11 HL Cas 642, 11 Jur NS 785, 13 WR 1083, 11 ER
1483, 12 LT 776 .... 13.06
Saddleworth UDC v Aggregate & Sand Ltd (1970) 69 LGR 103, 114 SJ 931 ... 14.50
Safeway Stores Ltd v Twigger [2010] EWCA Civ 1472, [2011] 2 All ER 841,
[2011] Bus LR 1629.. 9.10
Sakkas v Donford Ltd (1982) 46 P & CR 290 .... 2.09, 2.22
Salford City Council v McNally [1976] AC 379, [1975] 2 All ER 860, [1975]
3 WLR 87, 139 JP 694, 73 LGR 408, 236 Estates Gazette 555, 119 SJ
475 .... 14.06, 14.07, 14.10,
14.65
Sampson v Hodson-Pressinger [1981] 3 All ER 710, 12 HLR 40, 261 Estates
Gazette 891, 125 SJ 623 .... 10.33; 13.07, 13.20
Savage v Fairclough [2000] Env LR 183 .... 13.08
Seaport Investments Ltd's Application for Judicial Review, Re [2007] NIQB 62,
[2008] Env LR 23 (NI).. 18.40

Sedleigh-Denfield v O'Callagan (Trustees for St Joseph's Society for Foreign Missions) [1940] AC 880, [1940] 3 All ER 349 .... 2.36; 7.31; 9.03, 9.09; 10.19; 13.13, 13.14, 13.19; 14.31; 17.158

Scarborough Corpn v Scarborough Rural Sanitary Authority (1876) 1 Ex D 344, 40 JP 726, 34 LT 768 .... 14.36

Schwann v Cotton [1916] 2 Ch 459, [1916–17] All ER Rep 368, 85 LJ Ch 689, 60 SJ 654, 115 LT 168 .... 17.11

Scottish Power Generation Ltd v Scottish Environment Protection Agency (No 1) 2005 SLT 98, [2005] Eu LR 449, [2005] Env LR 38, 2005 GWD 1-1 .... 16.11

Scott-Whitehead v National Coal Board (1985) 53 P & CR 263, [1987] 2 EGLR 227... 13.39, 13.48

Sevenoaks District Council v Brands Hatch Leisure Group Ltd [2001] Env LR 5, [2001] EHLR 7 .... 14.28

Shanks & McEwan (Midlands) Ltd v Wrexham Maelor BC (1996) 160 JP Rep 969, [1996] NPC 53, [1996] Env LR D26.. 16.23

Shanks & McEwan (Teesside) Ltd v Environment Agency [1999] QB 333, [1998] 2 WLR 452, [1997] 2 All ER 332, [1997] Env LR 305, [1997] JPL 824, [1997] Crim LR 684 .... 16.23

Shelfer v City of London Electric Lighting Co [1895] 1 Ch 287, [1891–4] All ER Rep 838, 64 LJ Ch 216, 12 R 112, 43 WR 238, 39 SJ 132, 72 LT 34, 11 TLR 137 .... 13.51; 14.20

Shillito v Thompson (1875) 1 QBD 12, 45 LJMC 18, 40 JP 535, 24 WR 57, 33 LT 506 .... 13.04

Shoreham-By-Sea UDC v Dolphin Canadian Proteins Ltd (1972) 71 LGR 261: 13.52

Sienkiewicz v Greif (UK) Ltd [2011] UKSC 10, [2011] 2 AC 229, [2011] 2 WLR 523 .... 13.61

Sindall (William) plc v Cambridgeshire County Council [1994] 3 All ER 932, [1994] 1 WLR 1016, 92 LGR 121, [1993] NPC 82 .... 2.12, 2.18

Skandia Property (UK) v Thames Water Utilities Ltd [1999] All ER (D) 881, [1999] BLR 338.. 17.159

Smeaton v Ilford Corpn [1954] Ch 450, [1954] 1 All ER 923, [1954] 2 WLR 668, 118 JP 290, 52 LGR 253, 98 SJ 251... 13.29

Smedley v Chumley & Hawke Ltd (1981) 44 P & CR 50, [1982] 1 EGLR 47, 261 Estates Gazette 775, 126 SJ 33... 10.13

Smith v South Wales Switchgear Co Ltd; Smith v UMB Chrysler (Scotland) Ltd [1978] 1 WLR 165, [1978] 1 All ER 18, 1978 SC (HL) 1 .... 9.10

Smith & Snipes Hall Farm Ltd v River Douglas Catchment Board [1949] 2 KB 500, [1949] 2 All ER 179, 113 JP 388, 47 LGR 627, 93 SJ 525, 65 TLR 628 .... 19.19

Smith New Court Securities Ltd v Citibank NA; *sub nom* Smith New Court Securities Ltd v Scrimgeour Vickers (Asset Management) Ltd 1997] AC 254, [1996] 3 WLR 1051, [1996] 4 All ER 769, [1997] 1 BCLC 350, [1996] CLC 1958, (1996) 93(46) LSG 28, (1996) 146 NLJ 1722, (1997) 141 SJLB 5... 2.15

Solvay v Region Wallone (Case C-182/10) [2012] 2 CMLR 19, [2012] Env LR 27... 4.01

Southern Water Authority v Nature Conservancy Council [1992] 3 All ER 481, [1992] 1 WLR 775, 65 P & CR 55, [1992] 32 LS Gaz R 36, 136 SJLB 230 .... 10.53; 15.78; 19.04, 19.11, 19.35, 19.38

Southwark LBC v Mills; *sub nom* Southwark LBC v Tanner; Baxter v Camden
    LBC (No 2) [2001] 1 AC 1, [1999] 3 WLR 939, [1999] 4 All ER 449, [2000]
    Env LR 112, (2000) 32 HLR 148, [2000] BLGR 138, [2000] L & TR 159,
    [1999] 3 EGLR 35, [1999] 45 EG 179, [1999] EG 122 (CS), (1999) 96(42)
    LSG 41, (1999) 96(42) LSG 45, (1999) 149 NLJ 1618, (1999) 143 SJLB
    249, [1999] NPC 123, (2000) 79 P & CR D13 .... 10.33, 10.34; 13.05, 13.07;
                                                                      14.03, 14.08, 14.31
Southwark LBC v Simpson (1998) 31 HLR 725, [1999] Env LR 553 .... 14.07,
                                                                      14.46
Sovereign Rubber Ltd v Stockport Metropolitan Borough Council [2000] Env
    LR 194, [2000] EHLR 154, [1999] NPC 84 .... 14.43, 14.47
Spicer v Smee [1946] 1 All ER 489, 175 LT 163.. 13.20
Standard Chartered Bank Ltd v Walker [1982] 3 All ER 938, [1982] 1 WLR
    1410, [1982] Com LR 233, 126 SJ 479, [1982] LS Gaz R 1137, 264 Estates
    Gazette 345.. 10.55
Stanley v London Borough of Ealing [2000] EHLR 172................................ 14.26
Stannard (t/a Wyvern Tyres) v Gore [2012] EWCA Civ 1248, [2014] QB 1,
    [2013] 3 WLR 623... 13.31, 13.33
Stapley v Gypsum Mines Ltd [1953] AC 663, [1953] 2 All ER 478, [1953]
    3 WLR 279, 97 SJ 486 .... 13.59
Steers v Manton (1893) 57 JP 584 .... 14.04
Stent v Monmouth District Council (1987) 54 P & CR 193, 19 HLR 269,
    [1987] 1 EGLR 59, 282 Estates Gazette 705.. 10.12
Sterling Homes (Midlands) Ltd v Birmingham City Council [1996] Env LR
    121 .... 14.28, 14.52
Stichting Greenpeace Council (Greenpeace International) v EC Commission:
    C-321/95P [1998] All ER (EC) 620, [1998] ECR I-1651, [1998] 3 CMLR
    1, [1999] Env LR 181 .... 1.26
Stockdale v Ascherberg [1904] 1 KB 447, [1904–7] All ER Rep 153, 73 LJKB
    206, 68 JP 241, 2 LGR 529, 52 WR 289, 48 SJ 244, 90 LT 111, 20 TLR
    235 .... 10.08; 14.59
Stone v Bolton [1950] 1 KB 201, [1949] 2 All ER 851, 48 LGR 107, 93 SJ 710,
    65 TLR 683; on appeal *sub nom* Bolton v Stone [1951] AC 850, [1951] 1
    All ER 1078, 59 LGR 32, 95 SJ 333, [1951] 1 TLR 977 .... 10.20; 13.05
Stovin v Wise (Norfolk County Council, third party) [1996] AC 923, [1996]
    3 All ER 801, [1996] 3 WLR 388, 95 LGR 260, [1996] RTR 354, [1996]
    35 LS Gaz R 33, [1996] NLJR 1185, 140 SJLB 201................................. 13.17
Strathclyde Regional Council v Tudhope [1983] JPL 536............................ 14.25
Stuckey v Hooke [1906] 2 KB 20, 75 LJKB 504, 70 JP 393, 4 LGR 815, 54 WR
    509, 50 SJ 463, 94 LT 723, 22 TLR 508 .... 10.23
Sturges v Bridgman (1879) 11 Ch D 852, 48 LJ Ch 785, 43 JP 716, 28 WR 200,
    41 LT 219.. 13.06
Sutradhar v Natural Environment Research Council [2006] UKHL 33, [2006]
    4 All ER 490, [2007] Env LR 10, [2006] PNLR 36, (2006) 150 SJLB
    922 .... 13.48
Sutton v Temple, 152 ER 1108, (1843) 12 M & W 52, Ex Ct 10.37
Swain v Law Society [1983] 1 AC 598, [1982] 2 All ER 827, [1982] 3 WLR 261,
    126 SJ 464 .... 14.72
Sweet v Secretary of State for the Environment & Nature Conservancy Council
    [1989] 2 PLR 14, [1989] JPL 927 .... 19.24
Swindon Waterworks Co v Wilts & Berks Canal Navigation Co (1875) LR 7
    HL 697, 45 LJ Ch 638, 40 JP 117, 40 JP 804, 24 WR 284, 33 LT 513 ...... 17.23

T

Taylor v Hamer [2002] EWCA Civ 1130, [2003] 1 EGLR 103, [2003] 03 EG
127, [2002] 33 EG 96 (CS), [2003] 1 P & CR DG6 .... 2.17
Taylor v Walsall & District Property & Investment Co Ltd (1998) 30 HLR
1062, [1998] Env LR 600, [1998] 06 LS Gaz R 24, 142 SJLB 75 .... 14.71
Taylor Woodrow Property Management Ltd v National Rivers Authority (1994)
158 JP 1101, [1995] Env LR 52, (1994) 158 JPN 787 .... 10.03; 17.43,
17.65
Tesco Stores Ltd v Secretary of State for the Environment [1995] 2 All ER 636,
[1995] 1 WLR 759, 70 P & CR 184, [1995] 2 EGLR 147, [1995] 27 EG
154, [1995] 24 LS Gaz R 39, [1995] NLJR 724 .... 18.25
Tetley v Chitty [1986] 1 All ER 663 .... 13.21
Thames Waste Management Ltd v Surrey County Council [1997] Env LR
148 .... 16.24
Thames Water Authority v Blue & White Launderettes Ltd [1980] 1 WLR 700,
78 LGR 237, [1980] RVR 96, 124 SJ 100 .... 17.108
Thomas v Countryside Council for Wales [1994] 4 All ER 853, [1994] 1 EGLR
17, [1994] 04 EG 138, [1994] RVR 66 .... 19.41
Thomas v Nokes (1894) 58 JP 672 .... 14.25
Thompson v Gibson (1841) 10 LJ Ex 330, [1835–42] All ER Rep 623, 7 M &
W 456 .... 13.20
Thompson v Smiths Shiprepairers (North Shields) Ltd [1984] QB 405, [1984]
1 All ER 881, [1984] 2 WLR 522, [1984] ICR 236, [1984] IRLR 93, 128
SJ 225, [1984] LS Gaz R 741 .... 13.48
Thorpe v Abbotts [2015] EWHC 2142 (Ch) 3.12
Three Rivers DC v Bank of England (Disclosure) (No 3) [2003] EWCA Civ
474, [2003] QB 1556, [2003] 3 WLR 667, [2003] CPLR 349, (2003)
100(23) LSG 37 .... 8.11
Three Rivers DC v Bank of England (Disclosure) (No 4) [2004] UKHL 48,
[2005] 1 AC 610, [2004] 3 WLR 1274, [2005] 4 All ER 948, (2004)
101(46) LSG 34, (2004) 154 NLJ 1727, (2004) 148 SJLB 1369 .... 4.20; 8.11
Titanium Dioxide Directive, Re: EC Commission v EC Council *see* EC Com-
mission v EC Council
T-Mobile (UK) Ltd v First Secretary of State; Hutchison 3G UK Ltd v First
Secretary of State; Orange Personal Communications Services Ltd v First
Secretary of State [2004] EWCA Civ 1763, [2005] Env LR 18, [2005]
1 PLR 97 .... 1.30
Tod-Heatly v Benham (1888) 40 Ch D 80, [1886–90] All ER Rep Ext 1537, 58
LJ Ch 83, 37 WR 38, 60 LT 241, 5 TLR 9 .... 10.20
Tollbench Ltd v Plymouth City Council (1988) 56 P & CR 194, [1988] 1 EGLR
79, [1988] 23 EG 132 .... 10.16
Tombesi *see* Criminal Proceedings against Tombesi (C304/94)
Topfell Ltd v Galley Properties Ltd [1979] 2 All ER 388, [1979] 1 WLR 446, 38
P & CR 70, 249 EG 341, 123 SJ 81 .... 2.33
Total Transport Corpn v Arcardia Petroleum (The Eurus) [1998] 1 Lloyd's Rep
351, [1998] CLC 90, (1998) 95 (1) LSG 24 .... 9.08, 9.10
Transco Plc v Stockport MBC; *sub nom* British Gas Plc v Stockport MBC;
Stockport MBC v British Gas Plc; Stockport MBC v Reddish Vale Golf
Club [2003] UKHL 61, [2004] 2 AC 1, [2003] 3 WLR 1467, [2004] 1 All
ER 589, 91 Con LR 28, [2004] Env LR 24, [2003] 48 EG 127 (CS), (2003)
153 NLJ 1791, (2003) 147 SJLB 1367, [2003] NPC 143, [2004] 1 P & CR
DG12 .... 13.24, 13.30

Transocean Drilling UK Ltd v Providence Resources Ltd (The Arctic III) [2014]
    EWHC 4260 (Comm), [2015] 2 All ER (Comm) 557, [2015] BLR 190 .....   9.10
Trevett v Secretary of State for Transport, Local Government & the Regions
    [2002] EWHC 2696 (Admin), [2003] Env LR D10 ....   18.22
Tulk v Moxhay (1848) 2 Ph 774, [1843–60] All ER Rep 9, 18 LJ Ch 83, 1 H &
    Tw 105, 13 Jur 89, 13 LTOS 21 ....   19.17
Tutton v A D Walter Ltd [1986] QB 61, [1985] 3 All ER 757, [1985] 3 WLR
    797, 129 SJ 739, [1985] LS Gaz R 3535 ....   13.48
Twyford Parish Council v Secretary of State for the Environment [1992]
    1 CMLR 276, [1991] COD 210..   18.30

U

United Utilities v Environment Agency [2006] EWCA Civ 633, [2006] Env LR
    42, [2006] 21 EG 131 ....   20.18
Urban Regeneration Agency & English Partnerships (Medway) Ltd v Mott
    Macdonald (2000) 12 Environmental Law & Management 24, 59 Envi-
    ronmental Law Bulletin 24...   13.48

V

Vale of the White Horse District Council v Allen & Partners [1997] Env
    LR 212...   14.22
Valpy v St Leonard's Wharf Co Ltd (1903) 67 JP 402, 1 LGR 305...................   14.48
Vella v Lambeth LBC *see* R (on the application of Vella) v Lambeth LBC
Vernon Knights Associates v Crnwall Council [2013] EWCA Civ 950, [2013]
    BLR 519, [2014] Env LR 6 ....   13.19
Victoria Laundry (Windsor) v Newman Industries [1949] 2 KB 528, [1949]
    1 All ER 997, 65 TLR 274, (1949) 93 SJ 371..   9.10
Villenex Co Ltd v Courtney Hotel Ltd (1969) 20 P & CR 575 ....   10.09, 10.24

W

WE Black Ltd v Secretary of State for the Environment & Harrow London
    Borough Council [1997] Env LR 1, [1997] JPL 37............................   15.15; 18.05
WWF (UK) v Secretary of State for Scotland 1998 GWD 37-1936, [1999]
    1 CMLR 1021 ....   19.43, 19.46, 19.47
Wagon Mound (No 2), The *see* Overseas Tankship (UK) Ltd v Miller Steamship
    Co Pty, The Wagon Mound (No 2)
Walker & Son (Hauliers) Ltd v Environment Agency [2014] EWCA Crim 100,
    [2014] 4 All ER 825, [2014] PTSR 929..   17.49, 17.57
Walton v Sedgefield BC [1999] JPL 541, (1998) 95(45) LSG 42......................   19.34
Wandsworth LBC v Railtrack Plc; *sub nom* Railtrack Plc v Wandsworth LBC
    [2001] EWCA Civ 1236, [2002] QB 756, [2002] 2 WLR512, [2002] Env
    LR 9, [2002] EHLR 5, [2001] BLGR 544, [2001] 32 EG 88 (CS), (2001)
    98(37) LSG 38, (2001) 145 SJLB 219, [2001] NPC 131 ....   13.15
Warriner, Re; *sub nom* Brayshaw v Ninnis [1903] 2 Ch 367 ....   10.08
Warwick Rural DC v Miller-Mead; *sub nom* Miller-Mead v Warwick Rural DC
    [1962] Ch 441, [1962] 2 WLR 284, [1962] 1 All ER 212, (1962) 126 JP
    143, 60 LGR 29, (1961) 105 SJ 1124 ....   14.21
Waste Incineration Services v Dudley Metropolitan Borough Council [1992]
    Env LR 29...   16.24, 16.25

Waste Recycling Group Ltd v Revenue & Customs Commissioners; *sub nom* Revenue & Customs Commissioners v Waste Recycling Group Ltd [2008] EWCA Civ 849, [2008] BTC 8076, [2008] STI 1871; *affirming* [2007] EWHC 3014 (Ch), [2008] STC 1037, [2008] Env LR 19, [2008] BTC 8003, [2008] STI 25 .... 16.31

Watson v Croft Promo-Sport Ltd [2008] EWHC 759 (QB), [2008] 3 All ER 1171, [2008] Env LR 43 .... 13.45, 13.51

Welsh v Greenwich London Borough Council [2000] EGCS 84 .... 10.13

West v Ian Finlay & Associates (a firm) [2014] EWCA Civ 316, [2014] BLR 324, 153 Con LR 1 .... 8.16

West Ham Central Charity Board v East London Waterworks Co [1900] 1 Ch 624, [1900–3] All ER Rep 1011, 69 LJ Ch 257, 48 WR 284, 44 SJ 243, 82 LT 85 .... 10.28

West Midland Probation Committee v Secretary of State for the Environment (1997) 76 P & CR 589, [1997] NPC 157, [1998] JPL 388 .... 18.21

West v Bristol Tramways Co [1908] 2 KB 14, [1908–10] All ER Rep 215, 77 LJKB 684, 72 JP 243, 6 LGR 609, 52 SJ 393, 99 LT 264, 24 TLR 478: 13.27

Western Power Distribution Investments Ltd v Cardiff CC [2011] EWHC 300 (Admin), [2011] NPC 25 .... 19.22

Westley v Hertfordshire CC (1998) 76 P & CR 518, [1998] 2 PLR 72, [1998] JPL 947, [1998] NPC 24 .... 14.04

Westminster City Council v Haymarket Publishing Ltd [1981] 2 All ER 555, [1981] 1 WLR 677, 79 LGR 528, 42 P & CR 29, [1981] RA 147, 258 Estates Gazette 641, 1981] JPL 751, 125 SJ 220 .... 10.50, 10.56; 15.101

Westminster City Council v Zestfair (1989) 153 JP 613, 88 LGR 288, (1989) 153 LG Rev 828; (1989) 133 SJ 1262 .... 14.45

Wettern Electric Ltd v Welsh Development Agency [1983] QB 796, [1983] 2 All ER 629, [1983] 2 WLR 897, 47 P & CR 113, 127 SJ 286 .... 10.37

Wheat v E Lacon & Co Ltd [1966] AC 552, [1966] 1 All ER 582, [1966] 2 WLR 581, [1966] RA 193, [1966] RVR 223, 110 SJ 149 .... 10.53

Wheeler v J J Saunders Ltd [1996] Ch 19, [1995] 2 All ER 697, [1995] 3 WLR 466, [1995] JPL 619, [1995] Env LR 286, [1995] NPC 4 .... 13.43, 13.45; 14.11

Wheeler v Le Marchant (1881) LR 17 Ch D 675 .... 4.20

Whiting's Application, Re (1989) 58 P & CR 321, [1989] EG 3 (CS) 19.18

Whitwham v Westminster Brymbo Coal & Coke Co [1896] 2 Ch 538, 65 LJ Ch 741, 44 WR 698, 40 SJ 620, 74 LT 804, 12 TLR 496 .... 13.53

Wilchick v Marks & Silverstone [1934] 2 KB 56, [1934] All ER Rep 73, 103 LJKB 372, 78 SJ 277, 151 LT 60, 50 TLR 281 .... 10.36

Wilkinson v Collyer (1884) 13 QBD 1, 53 LJQB 278, 48 JP 791, 32 WR 614, 51 LT 299 .... 10.08

Williams v IC & LGO & Sandwell MBC (EA/2012/0083) 4.20

Wilson v Fynn [1948] 2 All ER 40, 64 TLR 395, 92 SJ 324 .... 10.16

Wiltshier Construction (London) Ltd v Westminster City Council [1997] Env LR 321 .... 14.74, 14.75

Wincanton RDC v Parsons [1905] 2 KB 34, 74 LJKB 533, 69 JP 242, 3 LGR 771, 93 LT 13 .... 14.30

Wivenhoe Port Ltd v Colchester Borough Council [1985] JPL 175; *aff'd* [1985] JPL 396 .... 14.55

Wright v Macadam [1949] 2 KB 744, [1949] 2 All ER 565, 93 SJ 646 .... 17.11

Wringe v Cohen [1940] 1 KB 229, [1939] 4 All ER 241, 109 LJKB 227, 161 LT 366, 56 TLR 101, 83 SJ 923 .... 13.20

Wychavon District Council v National Rivers Authority [1993] 2 All ER 440,
[1993] 1 WLR 125, 158 JP 178, 91 LGR 517, [1993] Crim LR 766, [1992]
33 LS Gaz R 39, 136 SJLB 260 .... 17.54, 17.62
Wyre Forest DC v Bostock (Dennis) [1993] Env LR 235.................................. 14.22

Y

Yandle & Sons v Sutton [1922] 2 Ch 199, [1922] All ER Rep 425, 91 LJ Ch
567, 127 LT 783 .... 2.18
Yellowly v Gower (1855) 11 Ex 274, 156 ER 833 .... 10.29
Yorkshire Water Services Ltd v Sun Alliance & London Insurance plc (No 2)
[1998] Env LR 204 .... 9.34
Young (John) & Co v Bankier Distillery Co [1893] AC 691, [1891–94] All ER
Rep 439, 58 JP 100, 69 LT 838.. 17.24

DECISIONS OF THE EUROPEAN COURT OF JUSTICE ARE LISTED BELOW NUMERICALLY. THESE DECISIONS ARE ALSO INCLUDED IN THE PRECEDING ALPHABETICAL LIST.

C-206/88: Vessoso v Ministere Public of Italy [1990] ECR I-1461 .... 16.11
C-57/89: EC Commission v Germany [1991] ECR I-883 .... 19.43, 19.48
C-106/89: Marleasing SA v La Comercial Internacional de Alimentación SA
[1990] ECR I-4135, [1992] 1 CMLR 305, [1993] BCC 421, 135 SJ 15 .... 1.26
C-188/89: Foster v British Gas Plc [1991] 1 QB 405, [1991] 2 WLR 258, [1990]
3 All ER 897, [1990] ECR I-3313, [1990] 2 CMLR 833, [1991] ICR 84,
[1990] IRLR 353 .... 4.06
C-6, 9/90: Francovich & Bonifaci v Italy [1991] ECR I-5357, [1993] 2 CMLR
66, [1995] ICR 722, [1992] IRLR 84 .... 1.26
C-355/90: Commission v Spain [1993] ECR I-4221 .... 19.43, 19.45
C-46/93: Brasserie du Pêcheur SA v Germany [1996] QB 404, [1996] 2 WLR
506, [1996] ECR I-1029, [1996] All ER (EC) 301, [1996] 1 CMLR 889,
[1996] IRLR 267 .... 1.26
C304/94: Criminal Proceedings against Tombesi; Criminal Proceedings against
Santella (C330/94); Criminal Proceedings against Muzi (C342/94); Crimi-
nal Proceedings against Savini (C224/95) [1997] All ER (EC) 639, [1997]
ECR I-3561, [1997] 3 CMLR 673, [1998] Env LR 59 .... 16.11
C-44/95: R v Secretary of State for the Environment, ex p Royal Society for
the Protection of Birds [1997] QB 206, [1997] 2 WLR 123, [1997] ECR
I-3805, [1996] 3 CMLR 411 .... 1.26; 19.43, 19.45
C-72/95: Aannemersbedrijf PK Kraaijeveld BV v Gedeputeerde Staten van
Zuid-Holland [1997] All ER (EC) 134, [1996] ECR I-5403, [1997] Env LR
265 : 18.31
C-321/95P: Stichting Greenpeace (Greenpeace International) v EC Commission
[1998] All ER (EC) 620, [1998] ECR I-1651, [1998] 3 CMLR 1, [1999]
Env LR 181 .... 1.26
C-3/96: EC Commission v Netherlands [1998] ECR I-3031 .... 19.45
C-129/96: Inter-Environnement Wallonie ASBL v Région Wallonie [1998] All
ER (EC) 155, [1997] ECR I-7411, [1998] 1 CMLR 1057, [1998] Env LR
623 .... 16.11
C-321/96: Mecklenburg (Wilhelm) v Kreis Pinneberg–Der Landsrat [1999] All
ER (EC) 166, [1998] ECR I-3809, [1999] 2 CMLR 418, [1998] 34 LS Gaz
R 33 .... 4.09

C-166/97: Commission of the European Communities v France Case [1999]
Env LR 781.. 19.45

C-217/97: EC Commission v Germany [1999] 3 CMLR 277 .... 4.35

C-293/97: R v Secretary of State for the Environment, ex p Standley (National
Farmers' Union intervening) [1999] QB 1279, [1999] All ER (EC) 412,
[1999] 3 WLR 744, [1999] ECR I-2603, [1999] 2 CMLR 902 .... 17.98

C-418/97: ARCO Chemie Nederland Ltd v Minister van Volkshuisvesting,
Ruimtelijke Ordening en Milieubeheer; *sub nom* Epon, Re (C-419/97);
Vereniging Dorpsbelang Hees v Directeur van de dienst Milieu en Water
van de provincie Gelderland (C-419/97) [2002] QB 646, [2002] 2 WLR
1240, [2003] All ER (EC) 237, [2000] ECR I-4475, [2003] Env LR 2,
[2001] Env LR D6 .... 16.11

C-96/98: Commission v France Case (C-96/98) [2000] 2 CMLR 681 .... 19.45

C371/98: R v Secretary of State for the Environment, Transport & the Regions,
ex p First Corporate Shipping Ltd (C371/98); *sub nom* R (on the application of First Corporate Shipping Ltd) v Secretary of State for the Environment, Transport & the Regions [2001] All ER (EC) 177, [2000] ECR
I-9235, [2001] 1 CMLR 19, [2001] Env LR 34, [2001] 4 PLR 1, [2000]
NPC 131 .... 1.24; 19.45, 19.47

C-353/99 P: Council of the European Union v Hautala [2002] 1 WLR 1930,
[2001] ECR I-9565, [2002] 1 CMLR 15, [2002] CEC 127 .... 4.11

C-9/00: Palin Granit Oy v Lounais-Suomen Ymparistokeskus; *sub nom* Palin Granit Oy'sApplication, Re (C-9/00); Palin Granit Oy v Vehmassalon
Kansanterveystyon Kuntayhtyman Hallitus (C-9/00) [2002] 1 WLR 2644,
[2003] All ER (EC) 366, [2002] ECR I-3533, [2002] 2 CMLR 24, [2002]
Env LR 35 .... 16.11

C444/00: R (on the application of Mayer Parry Recycling Ltd) v Environment
Agency; *sub nom* R v Environment Agency, ex p Mayer Parry Recycling
Ltd (C444/00) [2004] 1 WLR 538, [2005] All ER (EC) 647, [2003] ECR
I-6163, [2003] 3 CMLR 8, [2004] Env LR 6 .... 16.11

C127/02: Landelijke Vereniging tot Behoud van de Waddenzee v Staatssecretaris van Landbouw, Natuurbeheer en Visserij [2005] All ER (EC) 353,
[2004] ECR I-7405, [2005] 2 CMLR 31, [2005] Env LR 14, [2004] NPC
136 .... 19.48, 19.53

C1/03: Criminal Proceedings against Van de Walle (C1/03); *sub nom* Ministere
Public v Van de Walle; Van De Walle v Texaco Belgium SA (C1/03); Criminal Proceedings against Texaco Belgium SA (C1/03) [2005] All ER (EC)
1139, [2004] ECR I-7613, [2005] 1 CMLR 8, [2005] Env LR 24, [2004]
NPC 137 .... 2.32; 16.11

C-176/03: Commission of the European Communities v Council of the European Union [2006] All ER (EC) 1, [2005] ECR I-7879, [2005] 3 CMLR 20,
[2006] Env LR 18 .... 1.24

C-305/03: Commission of the European Communities v United Kingdom
[2007] STC 1211, [2006] STI 383 .... 18.32

C161/04: Austria v European Parliament [2006] ECR IA-7183 .... 1.24

PART I
APPROACHING THE TRANSACTION

Chapter 1

Introduction

THE CONVEYANCING CONTEXT OF ENVIRONMENTAL LAW

1.01 Real estate lawyers of the past had their hands full with the intricacies of property law. Although conveyancing procedures have been simplified by the progressive introduction of registered titles since 1897, the underlying property law has continued to grow more complex, as have the other areas of law affecting properties. Consequently the burdens on property lawyers have grown considerably. They are expected to advise their clients not only on matters related to title, but on the whole gamut of issues affecting owners and occupiers of property. These include the tax implications of a property acquisition and the range of questions which may render ownership and occupation more or less onerous or beneficial. Amongst the latter is environmental law, with its raft of unfamiliar terms and potentially serious liabilities.

THE MEANING AND SIGNIFICANCE OF ENVIRONMENTAL LAW

1.02 There is no agreed definition of environmental law. At one extreme it can mean pollution control law; at the other, Einstein would say that it is the law relating to everything that is not me. For most people an acceptable compromise has to be found between these positions. A possible definition which may commend itself is the law relating to the protection of public health and our natural and man-made surroundings. The temptingly distinctive title 'environmental law' suggests the existence of a specialism in law with which most legal practitioners need not necessarily concern themselves: a view confirmed by the increasing number and size of specialist textbooks dedicated to the subject.[1] More recent still are equally impressive titles in respect of particular aspects of environmental law.[2] Yet it is one function of this book to dispel this myth. The boundaries of environmental law may be unclear and perhaps confusing to the initiated and uninitiated alike, but every lawyer with a practice touching on land and its use should be aware of the potential impact of environmental law in this area.

---

1 Eg, Hughes *Environmental Law* (4th edn, 2002) (the first edition of which was the first UK textbook on the subject); Burnett-Hall *Environmental Law* (2nd edn, 2009); Bell, McGillivray and Pedersen *Environmental Law* (8th edn, 2008); Woolley, et al *Environmental Law* (2nd edn).

2 Kiss and Shelton *Manual of European Environmental Law* (2nd edn, 1997); Howarth *Water Pollution Law* (1988); Tromans and Turrell-Clarke *Contaminated Land* (2nd edn, 2008) – to name just a few.

1.03   This book is not a comprehensive compendium of environmental law, but rather a selective analysis of those aspects of environmental law likely to impact most frequently on property transactions. Part I deals with the overlapping areas between property and environmental law and the practical issues that arise in transactions. Part II considers the substantive environmental law issues directly linked to property transactions themselves, and also liabilities associated with the ownership or occupation of land which may impact on those transactions. These may be both direct, such as continuing liabilities for the creation of nuisances or water pollution,[1] or indirect, such as those which could affect land's asset value.[2]

1 Landlords' liabilities in statutory nuisance or cases of water or land pollution, for example: see paras **10.02–10.06**, **14.30–14.35** and **17.61–17.66** respectively.
2 Owners' and occupiers' potential liabilities under the contaminated land regime are the most obvious example: see Ch 15.

1.04   Part II provides some elaboration on, and context to, the particular issues or enquiries set out in Part I. The balance struck is necessarily a matter of judgment, and it will inevitably be the case that in some cases recourse will have to be had to more specific texts. However, this analysis will introduce and explain many of the issues of most concern, and most current controversy in environmental law as a whole. Constraints of this sort, and of space, have led us to omit detailed consideration of some important aspects of the subject of environmental law, not least of them being controls over radioactive substances, some controls over chemicals and hazardous substances and genetically modified organisms. The application of public law remedies such as judicial review in the context of environmental law is also omitted. Equally, very selective treatment is given to some areas, such as civil liabilities at common law, the law of town and country planning, and the environmental permitting system.

THE PARTIES AFFECTED BY ENVIRONMENTAL CONCERNS

1.05   Generally, the parties involved in property transactions fall into one of five broad categories. Each will be concerned to a greater or lesser degree with environmental matters affecting the property. These parties can be described as follows.

1.06   Sellers need to check that the property is marketable and that it can command a reasonable price. Adverse environmental factors cause many potential buyers to walk away from transactions or to demand substantial discounts from the purchase price or other contractual protection. Sellers may also be affected by the risk of environmental liabilities falling on them after completion of a sale and should consider how they can minimise and protect themselves against them.

1.07   Buyers are concerned not only with the converse of those matters which affect sellers but also with others. Specifically buyers should consider whether:

- the property is worth the asking price;
- the property is likely to be an acceptable security to a lender;
- the property is fit for use by the buyer in its current state;
- there are any environmental factors which may adversely affect occupation of the property;
- the property is likely to give rise to liabilities on the buyer in the future;
- the development potential and/or cost of the property is affected by environment-related factors; and
- the property will be marketable in the future.

1.08   Landlords need to ensure that:

- tenants will not cause environmental problems which may damage the property or give rise to long term or short term liabilities on the landlord;
- liabilities are properly allocated between the parties; and
- the rental value and the capital value of the property is maintained and that the tenant does not undermine his ability to pay rent by undertaking activities which may lead to liabilities falling on the tenant.

1.09   Tenants have to consider most or all of the issues which would concern a buyer depending on the nature and length of its lease. In addition, they need to ensure that the allocation of environmental liabilities between landlord and tenant is reasonable.

1.10   Lenders have three classic concerns:

- potential liability on lenders in respect of the environmental condition of the property;
- the value of the property given as security;
- the continuing ability of the borrower to repay the loan if he is affected by environmental liabilities.

1.11   Most of these parties will be concerned with value and liabilities, particularly ongoing liabilities arising from tightening minimum standards for industrial emissions and the financial consequences of compliance with climate change legislation. However, it must be borne in mind that the value of the property cannot necessarily be calculated by subtracting the figure for environmental liabilities from the notional value of the property without environmental problems. The principal reason for this is that public perceptions of environmental risk may have a blighting effect out of all proportion to the real risks involved.

1.12   Environmental considerations should form part of the basis for a strategy in dealing with every property transaction. They will be crucial in some cases and less so in others. However, they should be addressed in every case and should, therefore, be on the checklist of every property professional.

1.13 Concerns about contaminated land (which is probably the area encountered most frequently by environmental lawyers) prompted the Law Society to issue a practice note setting out its view of 'Good Practice' in this area on 18 December 2014, setting out how they should approach the issue in transactions. The Practice Note sets out the following guidance:

> Law Society Contaminated Land Practice Note - dated 18 December 2014
>
> Commercial and industrial activity may result in land becoming contaminated with substances which, if not properly dealt with, could pose a risk to public health or the environment.
>
> Land in England and Wales has a legacy of contaminants in soil, mainly caused by industrial and domestic pollution. Although most soils contain some contaminants, the levels of risk posed are usually very low.
>
> However, some land poses an unacceptable level of risk, especially former landfill or industrial sites. Land is only treated as 'contaminated land' for legal purposes if it poses an unacceptable level of risk.
>
> The Contaminated Land Statutory Guidance 2012 has replaced the previous statutory guidance issued under Part 2A of the Environmental Protection Act 1990, however, the legislation remains unaltered.
>
> The guidance sets out a modified, broadly risk-based approach to contaminated land. The standards also apply to land that is redeveloped.
>
> Land contamination may be a significant issue in a small number of transactions. You should be aware that environmental liabilities may arise and should consider what enquiries and specialist assistance your client should be advised to obtain.
>
> Contaminated land
>
> The contaminated land regime
>
> The contaminated land regime came into effect in England on 1 April 2000, and in Wales on 15 September 2001. The legislation, which is contained in Part 2A of the Environmental Protection Act 1990 and the regulations and statutory guidance issued under it, is retrospective. It covers existing and future contamination and has been modified to cover radioactivity.
>
> The regime applies to all land - whether residential, commercial, industrial or agricultural - and 'controlled waters', that is, surface, ground and coastal waters. It can affect owners, occupiers, developers, and lenders.
>
> Primary responsibility falls on those who caused or knowingly permitted the land to be contaminated.
>
> The legislation requires local authorities to inspect and identify sites at which there is 'contaminated land', that is, land on which there is a 'significant contaminant linkage', consisting of a significant contaminant, a pathway, and a receptor.
>
> Local authorities can issue remediation notices requiring action to remediate contamination, in the absence of a voluntary agreement to do so.

In the case of 'special sites', which tend to be sites with water pollution or more serious contamination, responsibility for enforcement lies with the Environment Agency in England, or Natural Resources Wales.

Radioactive contaminated land

A separate regime applies to radioactive contaminated land. This is set out in:

- The Radioactive Contaminated Land Statutory Guidance of April 2012, which applies to England; and

- The Radioactive Contaminated Land Statutory Guidance for Wales 2012.

Local authorities have the power to determine land as radioactive contaminated land. Once they do so, the land becomes a 'special site' and the Environment Agency or Natural Resources Wales takes over as the regulator and enforcing authority for remediation. The local authority should be your starting point for queries.

Radioactive contaminated land will not be an issue in the vast majority of transactions, but you should be aware of the existence of this regime.

Liability for remediation of contaminated land

Liability to remediate land may arise as a result of substances in the land which give rise to a risk of harm to persons or other 'receptors' in the form of designated ecological areas, controlled waters, or property in the form of crops, animals or buildings.

Liability falls primarily on those who 'cause or knowingly permit' a contaminant to be in, on or under the land. Such a person is known as a 'class A' person.

However, if a class A person of the land cannot be found, the current owner or occupier may be served with a remediation notice requiring them to remediate the land. In this case, the current owner or occupier is known as a 'class B' person. Mortgagees in possession can also be class B persons.

In some situations the buyer may be determined to be a class A person if the buyer knows that land is contaminated and fails to remediate it after a reasonable opportunity to do so.

If a seller (who would otherwise be a class A person) has made a payment to the buyer for remediation purposes (effected, for example, through a price reduction) or the seller has sold the land 'with information' (that is the requirements of Test 3 in section 7(c) of the statutory guidance have been met), the buyer is likely to bear the liability of the seller as well as its own liability for continuing to permit the land to be contaminated.

This is most likely to be relevant in commercial transactions but could occur in residential transactions - the effect is that liability for contamination will run with the land.

Part 2A of the Environmental Protection Act 1990 makes it an offence to fail to remediate contaminated land in accordance with a remediation notice. In this situation, the local authority can carry out the necessary work and recover the costs from the person or entity served with the remediation notice.

There are complex exclusion provisions for transferring liability from one party to another. Some exclusions apply only on the transfer of land, or the grant of a lease. You may need to consider the applicability of any relevant exclusion before your client enters into such transactions.

<u>Conveyancing transactions</u>

Steps to be taken when acting for the buyer, tenant or lender

You should consider whether land contamination is an issue in all conveyancing transactions.

In all purchases, leases or mortgages, you should, unless your buyer, tenant or lender client instructs you otherwise, undertake a CON 29 and LLC1 search to ascertain whether the land has been designated by the local authority as contaminated.

Enquiry 3.13 on CON 29 will reveal:

- contaminated land notices affecting the property;

- entries on a register maintained under section 78R of the Environmental Protection Act 1990; and

- any consultation with the owner or occupier of the property under section 78G(3) of the Environmental Protection Act 1990 before the service of a remediation notice.

If the land has been designated as contaminated, you should make further enquiries of the seller, landlord or borrower, and take instructions from your client as to any further investigations that may need to be made.

A negative reply from the local authority to question 3.13 on CON 29 can mean one of several things:

- there is no contamination;

- the site has not been inspected;

- the level of pollution is not high enough to meet Part 2A definitions; or

- no conclusion about the site has yet been reached, even if a site inspection has finished.

You may need to make more specific enquiries to ascertain the true nature of contamination on a site.

If it appears that contamination is an issue and you are acting for a buyer, tenant and/or lender, you should:

- Advise of the consequences of acquiring interests in contaminated land. These may include the potential liability for contamination and to have to comply with a remediation notice. You should also advise on the steps that can be taken to assess the risks.

- Make further enquiries of the local authority or Environment Agency or Natural Resources Wales to elicit more details. However, if the land has not been formally identified or determined as contaminated, no information will be held on local authority or Environment Agency or Natural Resources Wales registers.

- Make further enquiries of the seller, landlord or borrower. The extent and type of enquiries to be made will depend on whether the land and property to be transferred is for residential or commercial use.

•   Make full searches of any public registers regarding the site and adjacent land.

•   Suggest to your client that an independent site report from a commercial provider is obtained. This may help your client to assess the risks involved and, if applicable, to learn what remedial works might be required. In doing this, you should consider your client's intended use of the land. If it becomes clear that the intended use will not be possible due to contamination, you should advise your client and seek specific instructions as to whether to proceed.

•   Suggest that your client considers obtaining an independent valuation of the property. A reduction in the market value of the property as a result of contamination may lead to the buyer requiring a price reduction. It may also lead to a lender withdrawing from, or imposing additional conditions in, their offer.

•   Consider and advise your client of the use and effect of appropriate contractual protections. For example, by including exclusion and indemnity clauses and apportionments, warranties, or by making the contract conditional upon the seller complying with any remediation notices, to the buyer's reasonable satisfaction, prior to completion.

•   Consider and advise your client of the appropriateness of obtaining an environmental insurance policy. Such policies are widely available to cover the costs of remediation of both undetected and disclosed contamination and related liabilities. However, such policies may contain limitations on what and who they cover. The amount of any premium, the level of excesses and the imposition of certain conditions are important factors to be considered in selecting a policy.

Steps to be taken when acting for the seller or landlord

Although Part 2A contains provisions which may exclude the seller from liability in certain situations, it may not be possible for the seller or landlord to completely free themselves from liability in relation to a site, particularly if the site is a commercial one. For example, a seller may remain liable for any breaches of consents or legislation committed while the seller was the site owner or in possession.

A seller or landlord will be particularly concerned where a buyer's proposed change of use of the land may expose the seller or landlord to liability for contamination that they had caused or knowingly permitted while they owned the land, but which had not been an issue at the time. For example, if contaminated land was used as a car park when owned by the seller, but the buyer wishes to change its use to residential.

If you are acting for a seller or landlord, you should ensure that you obtain any necessary contractual provisions and indemnities in order to minimise your client's liability.

Remediation notices

In some cases the issue of a remediation notice may be contentious, having regard to independent expert reports.

In this situation, you should advise clients of the appeals process and the costs and risks associated with challenging the notice.

You should only act on instructions to challenge a remediation notice if you have the requisite skills and experience to do so.

Unresolved contamination

If matters relating to contamination cannot be resolved, you should consider advising your clients to withdraw from the transaction and make a note of the advice given.

Different clients, including lenders, will have different appetites for risk.

Where your client is fully aware of the contamination but wishes to proceed, or if your client provides instructions to proceed with the transaction, notwithstanding advice to the contrary, you should reiterate the risks to the client in writing, and obtain their instructions to proceed nonetheless - in writing, if possible.

Conveyancing: specific transactions

Leases

Where contamination is a risk in relation to leasehold property, you should consider whether the usual repair, service charge and statutory compliance obligations transfer remediation liability from the landlord to the tenant, and advise accordingly.

You should also advise your client on any specific environmental clauses in the lease and the implications of such clauses.

Mortgages

Sections 5.4.4 of the Council of Mortgage Lenders (CML) Handbook and section D.11. of the Building Societies Association (BSA) Mortgage Instructions require you to advise your lender client of any contaminated land entries revealed by a local authority search.

You should check Part 2 of the CML Handbook, or the specific requirements section of the BSA Mortgage Instructions to find out if your lender client wants to receive environmental or contaminated land reports (as opposed to contaminated land entries revealed in the local authority search).

Where contaminated land entries are revealed in the local authority search, you will need to seek instructions from your lender client on whether they wish to proceed with the transaction.

In enforcement cases, you should consider and advise your lender client whether to appoint receivers rather than risk remediation liability as a class B person, being a mortgagee in possession.

Share sales and asset purchases

You should consider recommending that your client obtains specialist, technical advice on liabilities, indemnities and warranties and make detailed enquiries.

MONEY LAUNDERING OFFENCES

1.14 Many breaches of environmental legislation constitute criminal offences. These can also amount to money laundering offences under the Proceeds of Crime Act 2002 (POCA), as amended.

Money laundering can no longer be thought of as drug dealers seeking to conceal the origin of their funds. The definition of 'money laundering' in POCA is very wide and can be summarised as any concealing, transferring, acquisition, use or possession of criminal property or being concerned in an arrangement which facilitates the acquisition, retention, use etc of criminal property by another.[1]

Property is 'criminal property' if it constitutes or represents a benefit from criminal conduct, in whole or in part and whether directly or indirectly and the alleged offender knows or suspects that it constitutes of represents such a benefit.[2] 'Criminal conduct' is conduct that constitutes an offence in the UK or would constitute an offence in the UK if it occurred there.[3]

It is to be noted that there is no *de minimis* concept and it can readily be seen, therefore, that an offence under environmental legislation will amount to criminal conduct for the purposes of POCA. Conduct abroad that might not be an offence there could still be criminal conduct for the purposes of POCA.[4]

POCA also makes clear that criminal property can be any pecuniary advantage derived from criminal conduct.[5] Therefore, in the case of environmental offences, the benefit can be the cost saving derived, for example, from operating an installation without the required environmental permit, or discharging trade effluent into controlled waters without a discharge consent. The possession, use, etc. of funds representing that benefit can amount to money laundering.

Where money laundering has occurred, or is suspected to have occurred, or where there are reasonable grounds for knowing or suspecting that money laundering has occurred, solicitors and others in the regulated sector[6] have an obligation to report this to the National Crime Agency (NCA), by making a Suspicious Activity report, subject to legal professional privilege and certain other limited defences to non-reporting.[7]

The entity that has committed the offence is also committing an ongoing money laundering offence, and should seek legal advice as to the desirability of reporting the situation to the NCA.

The existence of offences frequently comes to light in the context of due diligence carried out with a view to an acquisition of property or of shares in the company that committed the environmental offence. In such a situation there is a range of possible actions that it might be necessary or desirable for the various parties to take:

(a) Parties and their advisers who are in the regulated sector will have an obligation to report to the NCA their knowledge or suspicion that money laundering has occurred. The exception to this would be that the solicitors for the target company that has committed the offence would not report if the information attracts legal privilege in the hands of those solicitors or benefits from the defence under POCA of their having received the information in 'privileged circumstances'.[8]

(b) Some or all parties involved in the acquisition, whether in the regulated sector or not, might need to make a report to the NCA and to seek consent to continue with the transaction because to proceed without such consent could risk their committing a number of offences. Such consent enables the transaction to proceed without an offence being committed by the entity or entities that obtained such consent.[9] Such consent is likely to be needed both by the parties and by relevant professional advisers. The nature of the offences for which consent is required may differ according to whether the acquisition is by way of purchase of assets or by way of a share deal.

If on an asset deal the buyer is acquiring a piece of real estate or other property of any kind that was acquired wholly or partly with the proceeds of crime, possible offences by the parties or their professional advisers include:

- acquiring criminal property;
- being party to an arrangement that facilitates (i) the acquisition of criminal property by the buyer and (ii) the retention by the seller company of criminal property; in so far as the price paid relates to the criminal property being acquired, the price will itself represent criminal property in the hands of the seller because it represents an indirect benefit from criminal conduct.

Where the nature of the criminal property is value within the business as a result of failure to take the steps necessary to avoid committing the offence in question then if, before completion of the transaction, the business expends whatever is necessary to remedy the failure, the criminal property should no longer exist, in which case it is unnecessary to obtain consent from the NCA as the offences of acquisition or retention of criminal property will not be committed. However, an intention to correct the failure will not excuse those in the regulated sector from promptly reporting the offence.

Should the acquisition be by way of purchase of the shares of the company that owns the real estate or other property, the issues are a little different. No criminal property is being acquired by the buyer as the shares will not normally have been acquired with the proceeds of crime. However, the following possible offences will need to be considered:

- If the amount of criminal property within the target company is sufficiently large to have influenced the amount payable for the shares, then the seller shareholders will in part be receiving a price that represents an indirect benefit from criminal conduct. Therefore the parties and their advisers risk being party to an illegal arrangement.
- If the criminal property is so relatively small in value that it does not affect the amount the buyer is willing to pay for the shares, then the possible problem arises at a later stage. Once the acquisition is complete, the buyer will usually wish to put its nominees on the Board. Those new directors will be taking possession or control of the criminal property within the company and, therefore, might be committing an offence unless prior consent has been obtained from the NCA.

Under the consent regime, the NCA moves fast when it can and tries to be helpful, but this is not always possible and it is entitled to suspend the transaction for a maximum of seven working days, possibly followed by 31 calendar days.[10] As a result there can be situations where an inability to explain to the other party why a transaction has ground to a halt results in severe embarrassment or, in extreme circumstances, might even lead to loss of the deal.

There is one other type of offence that needs to be borne in mind when making reports to the NCA, whether simple reporting or seeking consent to proceed. This is the offence of 'tipping off'. In the regulated sector it is an offence to disclose the fact that a report has been made if such disclosure is likely to prejudice any investigation that might be conducted following the disclosure.[11] It would be unwise even to disclose that such a report is going to be made.

In the unregulated sector a similar offence can be committed by making a disclosure which is 'likely to prejudice an investigation'.[12] Therefore, it is important to ensure that the entity being reported remains unaware that a report has been made.

1 POCA, s 340(11) and ss 327, 328 and 329.
2 POCA, s 340(3).
3 POCA, s 340(2).
4 There is a limited exception for conduct abroad that is not an offence where it occurred. To be excluded, the maximum penalty that would apply if the conduct occurred in the UK must not exceed a relatively low level designated by statutory instrument, currently 12 months' imprisonment.
5 POCA, s 340(6)–(7).
6 Businesses in the regulated sector comprise, in summary, banks and other credit institutions, financial institutions, auditors, accountants, insolvency practitioners, tax advisers, trust or company service providers, lawyers, estate agents, casinos and firms that sell goods for more than €15,000 in cash.
7 POCA, ss 330–332.
8 POCA, s 330(6)(b).
9 POCA, s 328(2)(a). See also POCA, s 335 for details of the consent regime.
10 POCA, s 335(5) & (6).
11 POCA, s 333(1).
12 POCA, s 342(2).

FRAMEWORK OF ENVIRONMENTAL LAW

1.15 It should not be assumed that environmental law is a new-fangled invention which has only recently started to plague property professionals and owners. On the contrary, it was important long before the word 'environment' became fashionable. The law of nuisance has played its role in protecting owners against the worst local environmental problems since the origins of the common law in the twelfth century. During the medieval period and after, the Crown tried to control air pollution in London by limiting imports of 'sea coal'. Shakespeare's father was prosecuted for allowing a dung heap to collect outside his house in Stratford-upon-Avon in the sixteenth century. Of course, in modern times, the ambit of environmental law is much wider – 'from the street corner to the stratosphere', as Christopher Patten, the former Environment Secretary, put it when introducing the government's Environmental Strategy, 'This Common Inheritance', in 1990.

1.16 UK environmental law is dominated by a complex array of legislative provisions. This includes statutes adapted for new environmental purposes,[1] public health measures with environmental protection spin-offs,[2] environment-specific measures introduced expressly to counter newly-recognised environmental threats,[3] and measures introduced to assist the government of the United Kingdom in attaining its reduction of carbon emissions targets.[4] Law relating to the environment therefore has a longer pedigree than might be supposed, although much of what is now regarded as 'environmental law' has its origin in the last thirty to forty years.[5]

1 Eg, the Town and Country Planning Acts.
2 Some aspects of statutory nuisance can be considered in this way.
3 Most obviously, the Environmental Protection Act 1990 and the Environment Act 1995.
4 The Climate Change Act 2008 and the Energy Act 2011.
5 Hughes *Environmental Law* (4th edn, 2002) Ch 1.

1.17 That is not to say, however, that UK environmental law was based on a series or combination of statutory 'codes'. Rather, its piecemeal development has instead led to the application of a judicious mixture of administrative and criminal measures,[1] which co-exist with a complex background of private law.[2] Statutory systems may share certain characteristics,[3] but material differences also arise.[4] Some areas of environmental law are so distinctive as to make such analogies almost impossible.[5] Nonetheless, even allowing for such differences, it can now be said that environmental law has now developed into a coherent subject based on concepts, principles and enforcement mechanisms that apply in most areas of the subject.[6]

1 A Waite 'Criminal and Administrative Sanctions in English Environmental Law' (1989) 1 *Land Management and Environmental Law Report* 38 and 74.
2 Use of private law in an environmental context is considered in Ch 13, along with the particular, and increasingly important, relationship between statutory licences and private law liabilities: see paras **13.37–13.41**.
3 Eg, features of planning licensing can be found in pollution licensing systems as well.
4 Waste management licensing has particular features, for example, including the broad application of a statutory 'duty of care' – enforceable through the criminal law – on all those connected with certain waste: para **16.39**.
5 Eg, the law of nature conservation: Ch 19.
6 A Waite, 'The Quest for Environmental Law Equilibrium' (2005) 7 Env L Rev 34.

1.18 Today's environmental lawyers must consider not only the current United Kingdom law, but also international treaties and EC law as well as policies, guidelines, codes of practice and a growing mountain of literature on the subject. Environmental legislation continues to pour from Brussels and Westminster. International treaties and EC Directives are rapidly translated into domestic legislation. Practitioners must also check constantly for discrepancies between Community directives and the corresponding UK legislation which implements them since in the case of conflict the former will generally prevail. Current policy statements are a vital clue in determining not only the likely future direction of the law but also the approach taken to implementing existing law.

1.19 Even those areas of environmental law which seem remotest from the day-to-day concerns of the property owner may have a considerable impact.

For example, legislation on the protection of the ozone layer will dictate the availability of refrigerants. The availability and cost of suitable replacements may be a matter on which an intending buyer will require reassurance before committing himself to a transaction, particularly following the prohibition on the use of recycled and reclaimed HCFCs from 1 January 2015. The critical area of climate change is also relevant to property transactions, where advice may be required on such diverse matters as energy performance certificates and flooding.

1.20 Whilst few environmental lawyers have a scientific background, at least an acquaintance with the relevant science is important. In practice, lawyers need to work closely with environmental scientists to gain an adequate understanding of the issues facing their clients. The environment is quintessentially a multi-disciplinary subject.

EUROPEAN COMMUNITY ENVIRONMENTAL LAW

1.21 This complex domestic law framework is also increasingly subject to measures derived from the UK's European commitments. Although these can seem esoteric relative to more familiar forms of law, it is important to appreciate their broad impact. The development of EC environmental law has, however, been somewhat 'halting'. Indeed, until the Single European Act of 1987[1] there was no explicit constitutional provision under which the EC could adopt measures for environmental protection. Instead, once the Community had recognised that environmental standards had a role to play in achieving the general aims of the Community to create a commercially and economically integrated Europe, measures were adopted under Article 352 of the EC Treaty (now the Treaty of the Functioning of the European Union ('TFEU')(a general provision allowing action to achieve the objectives of the Treaty where no specific power is provided within the framework of the policies defined by the treaties)[2] and Article 114 (the general harmonisation article).[3]

1 Single European Act, Article 25.
2 Article 352 reads: 'If action by the Union should prove necessary within the framework of the policies defined by the Treaties to attain one of the objectives set out in the Treaties, and the Treaties have not provided the necessary powers, the Council shall, acting unanimously on a proposal from the Commission and after consulting the European Parliament, shall adopt the appropriate measures'.
3 Article 114 reads: 'The European Parliament and the Council shall, acting in accordance with the ordinary legislative procedure and after consulting the Economic and Social Committee, adopt the measures for the approximation of the provisions laid down by law, regulation or administrative action in Member States which have as their object the establishment and functioning of the internal market...'.

1.22 Environmental action is now firmly Treaty-based. The Single European Act of 1987 brought the introduction into the European Treaty framework of specific provisions to assist in the protection and improvement of the environment. These provisions have themselves been reinforced (and renumbered) by the Treaty of Amsterdam, signed on 2 October 1997 and the Treaty of Lisbon, signed on 13 December 2007. Articles 191–194 provide for measures to preserve, protect and improve the quality of the environment, to contribute to the protection of human health, to ensure the prudent and rational utilisation of natural resources, and to promote measures at an international level to deal with regional or worldwide environmental problems, and in particular combating climate change. In addition, Article 115 permits the adoption of measures intended for the creation of the internal market. Procedurally, this article differs in material respects from Articles 191–194 but it may also be used for the adoption of environmental controls. The significance of these procedural differences has declined since the adoption of the Treaty on European Union. However, the main difference between the environmental and internal legal bases now is that, under the internal market base, it is less easy for Member States to adopt stricter requirements than is the case in relation to environmental measures.[1]

1 Article 193 explicitly provides that Member States may adopt national legislation more strict than European norms. Article 114 also explicitly allows Member States to adopt or maintain more stringent national provisions, but there is a strict procedure under which they may do so.

1.23 Additional provisions introduced by the Treaty of Amsterdam and the Treaty of Lisbon do not substantially change the basis for the adoption of environment-related measures. What those recent changes do effect, however, is an entrenchment as principles of constitutional status within the Community both of the need to 'integrate' environmental protection requirements with the whole range of European laws, and of the core principle of 'sustainable development'. This adds to those principles that already appear in Article 191, namely, the precautionary principle, the principle that preventive action should be taken, that environmental damage should as a priority be rectified at source, and that the polluter should pay. The revised Treaties therefore provide a clearer and stronger basis for Community action than has ever been in place previously and a more secure legislative platform for the EU to legislate on areas such as Energy. Article 191, for example, has required since 1987 that 'environmental protection requirements ... be a component of the Community's other policies'. Since its amendment by the Treaty of Amsterdam, and subsequently by the Treaty of Lisbon, Article 6 of the TFEU now requires that: 'Environmental protection requirements must be integrated into the definition and implementation of the Community policies and activities referred to in Article 3, in particular with a view to promoting sustainable development'. This adds both an express obligation to include environmental protection requirements in the whole range of Community *activities*, and furthers the emphasis on sustainable development. Sustainable development also features in an amendment of Article 3 of the Treaty on European Union, (previously Article 2) to include the achievement of 'sustainable development ... and a high level of protection and improvement of the quality of the environment' as a key objective of the European Union.

1.24 While the meaning and implications of sustainable development itself remain controversial,[1] there is little doubt that the modified Treaty provisions are an improvement on the original position of no substantive commitment to pan-European environmental protection, or the previous, and more qualified, concern to pursue 'sustainable and non-inflationary growth respecting the environment'.[2] Quite how proactive the Community will be permitted to become remains a matter of conjecture, of course.[3] However, the Lisbon Treaty did enhance the requirement for Community institutions and EU Member States to act in compliance with environmental protection aims when implementing EU Law by making the Charter of Fundamental Rights of the European Union legally binding.[4] Other indications also suggest that so high-profile a commitment to sustainable development may not prioritise environmental concerns to the extent that some may have anticipated. For example, Advocate General Leger observes that the use of the term 'sustainable development' in the Preamble to the Treaty on European Union does not mean 'that the interests of the environment must necessarily and systematically prevail over the interests defended in the context of the other policies pursued by the Community in accordance with Article 3 of the EC Treaty'. Rather, it indicates an exercise of balancing or reconciling competing interests.[5]

1 Eg, 'It is a pity that the issue which everyone on the planet will have to tackle at some point has acquired this impenetrable title. It is even more problematic that no definition exists which can be understood by everyone and built into their lives': *Down to Earth – A Scottish Perspective on Sustainable Development* Scottish Office, 1999, p 4.

2 The then Article 2 of the Treaty, as amended by the 1992 Treaty on European Union.

3 Bär and Krämer, 'European Environmental Policy After Amsterdam' (1998) 10 Journal of Environmental Law 315.

4 Under Protocol 30 the UK opted out of the legally-binding nature of the Charter of Fundamental Rights of the European Union where the same are inconsistent with UK Law.

5 *R v Secretary of State for the Environment, Transport and the Regions, ex p First Corporate Shipping Ltd* (Case C-371/98), [2000] ECR I-9235 noted at (2000) 64 Environmental Law Bulletin 6. The case has been decided, but the ECJ judgment did not refer to Article 6 EC. However, there have been other cases on Article 6 EC more recently. The judgment in Case C-176/03 *Commission v Council* [2003] OJC 135/21 (para 42) states: '[In] the words of Article 6 EC, "[e]nvironmental protection requirements must be integrated into the definition and implementation of the Community policies and activities", a provision which emphasises the fundamental nature of that objective and its extension across the range of those policies and activities'. The opinion of Advocate General Geelhoed in Case C-161/04 *Austria v Parliament/Council* [2006] ECR I-7183 (para 59) states: 'Although this provision is drafted in imperative terms, contrary to what the Republic of Austria asserts, it cannot be regarded as laying down a standard according to which in defining Community policies environmental protection must always be taken to be the prevalent interest. Such an interpretation would unacceptably restrict the discretionary powers of the Community institutions and the Community legislature. At most it is to be regarded as an obligation on the part of the Community institutions to take due account of ecological interests in policy areas outside that of environmental protection *stricto sensu*. It is only where ecological interests manifestly have not been taken into account or where they have been completely disregarded that Article 6 EC may serve as the standard for reviewing the validity of Community legislation.' The case was withdrawn before it went to final judgment.

1.25 For present purposes this brief introduction serves to illustrate the potential influence of EC measures on UK environmental law.[1] Substantive illustrations are highlighted in later chapters. As will be seen, the impacts of EC environmental law are particularly marked in the context of water pollution,[2] nature conservation,[3] environmental assessment under the planning system,[4] and changes to industrial pollution controls.[5] Implementation of the landfill directive in the UK has also proved complex, and controversial.[6] Two further measures are also likely to have significant effects: the Water Framework Directive,[7] and the Environmental Liability Directive.[8] Unlike its forebears, the Environmental Liability Directive is relatively limited in scope: it establishes a new regime for non-diffuse sources of environmental pollution, with strict liabilities applying to environmental harm caused by dangerous activities regulated by EC law. Unlike extremely controversial early European proposals on environmental liability,[9] the regime is not intended to be retrospective, although it extends to liability for biodiversity damage and natural resource claims, and provides that non-governmental organisations should have wider legal standing than they currently enjoy in many members states.[10] The Directive was transposed in England by the Environmental Damage (Prevention and Remediation) Regulations 2009, SI 2009/153, as amended but implemented later in Wales, Scotland, Northern Ireland and Gibraltar.

1 More generally see Holder (ed) *The Impact of EC Environmental Law in the United Kingdom* (1997).
2 Both statutory controls, and perhaps curiously, common law measures.
3 Where jurisprudence of the European Court of Justice has lead directly to changes in UK law of direct interest to property owners and developers: see Chapter 19.
4 Paras **18.31–18.43**.
5 See the Industrial Emissions Directive 2010/75/EU.
6 Directive 1999/31/EC [1999] OJ L182; para **16.28**.
7 2000/60/EC.
8 2004/35/EC.
9 Eg, proposals for a directive in civil liability for damage caused by waste (COM(89) 282 final and the revised draft published as COM(91) 219 final) and the Green Paper on Restoring Environmental Damage (COM(1993) 47 final, published as Appendix III to *Remedying Environmental Damage* (HL Paper (1993–94) no 10)).
10 V Fogleman, 'The Environmental Liability Directive and its Impacts on English Environmental Law' [2006] JPL 1443; A Waite, 'The Quest for Environmental Law Equilibrium' (2005) 7 Env L Rev 34, 48–54.

1.26 In addition to these instruments, EC law adds a further level of complexity to the implementation and enforcement of the law. This may manifest itself in a number of different ways. The case of *Marleasing*[1] and subsequent ECJ rulings established that national laws must, if at all possible, be construed in accordance with both the wording and the purpose of relevant EC/EU Directives and this is so even if the national law in question existed before the date on which the Directive came into effect. This case establishes the supremacy of EC/EU law over national law.

Not only might the institutions of the Community themselves act against Member States which fail to implement Community legislation and thereby fail to meet their Treaty commitments, but interest groups and individual citizens of the Community are now increasingly active both in seeking to force Member States to implement EC obligations,[2] and in seeking redress for breaches of Community law. The matter may now even include a remedy in damages against a Member State for its breach of Community law,[3] where the state manifestly and gravely disregards the limits of its discretion.[4] Severe practical obstacles remain, however. For example, third parties have been shown to have very limited chances of challenging the Communities' own actions where they have marked environmental impacts,[5] whilst a committee of the House or Lords has again been highly critical of the general level of implementation of, and compliance with, European environmental law.[6] The Committee's conclusions include that Community environmental law is being widely disregarded, and that the Community itself has given insufficient attention to how its policies could be given effect, enforced or evaluated. However, the new 'citizens' initiative' in Aricle 11(4) of the Lisbon Treaty provides an admittedly political rather than legal ability of, if not collective redress, collective redirection of environmental EU obligations.[7]

1 *Marleasing SA v La Comercial Internacional de Alimentacion* (C-106/89) [1991] 1 ECR 4135.
2 Eg, *R v Secretary of State for the Environment, ex p Royal Society for the Protection of Birds* (C-44/95) [1997] ECR I-3805, 139; see para **19.45**.
3 *Francovich and Bonifaci v Italy* (C-6, 9/90) [1991] ECR I-5357.
4 *Brasserie du Pécheur SA v Germany*, joined cases C-46/93 and C-59/93 [1996] ECR I-1029. See Somsen 'Francovich and its Application to EC Environmental Law', in Somsen (ed), *Protecting the European Environment: Enforcing EC Environmental Law* (1996).
5 *Stichting Greenpeace Council (Greenpeace International) v EC Commission* (Case C-321/95P) [1998] All ER (EC) 620, [1999] Env LR 181.
6 House of Lords Select Committee on the European Communities, *Community Environmental Law – Making it Work* (HL Paper (1997–98) no 12).
7 Maria Lee, 'The Environmental Implications of the Lisbon Treaty' (2008) 10 Env L Rev 10 131–138.

UK ENVIRONMENTAL POLICY AND THE EMERGENCE OF PRINCIPLE

1.27 The development of UK environmental policy has continued apace in recent years. The publication in 1990 of the environment White Paper, *This Common Inheritance*,[1] represented a high-profile recognition of the importance of environment policy, both as a distinct sphere of activity and across policy sectors. In 1994, *Sustainable Development: The UK Strategy*[2] placed the notion of 'sustainable development' at the heart of UK policy for the first time. Indeed, the latter is now presented as a strategic goal, assisted by other principles such as the 'polluter pays' and the precautionary principles.[3]

1 Cm 1200, 1990.
2 Cm 2426, 1994.
3 See generally, Hughes, *Environmental Law* (4th edn), pp 20–27; 56–60.

1.28 Since 1994, the concept of 'sustainable development' has become a focal point of policy in the UK.[1] The 1999 revision of sustainable development strategy created a tripartite concept that sought to address social, economic and environmental sustainability.[2] The policy set out four key objectives which underpin the government's view of sustainable development, namely:

(a) social progress which recognises the needs of everyone;

(b) effective protection of the environment – to the government, this means 'acting to limit global environmental threats, such as climate change; to protect human health and safety from hazards such as poor air quality and toxic chemicals; and to protect things which people need or value, such as wildlife, landscapes, and historic buildings';

(c) prudent use of natural resources; and

(d) maintenance of high and stable levels of economic growth and employment.

Consequently, the Department for the Environment, Food and Rural Affairs ('DEFRA') has monitored national progress towards these objectives by measuring a number of sustainable development indicators, which also serve as a means for policy makers to identify more sustainable policy options.[3]

1 See generally, 'Sustainable Development: Opportunities for Change', DETR Consultation Paper on a Revised UK Strategy, February 1998, noted at (1999) 10 Environmental Law & Management 72 and *A Better Quality of Life: A Strategy for Sustainable Development*, Cm 4345, 1999.

2 See generally, Hughes, *Environmental Law* (4th edn), pp 56–60 and Bell, McGillivray and Pedersen, *Environmental Law* (8th edn), pp 59–68.

3 Sustainable Development Indicators. July 2013. www.gov.uk/defra.

1.29 The four key objectives of 1999 have since penetrated a wide range of policy and legislation. Sustainable development was incorporated in the Government's vision for sustainable communities[1], although it has been said that the incorporation of this social dimension to sustainable development represented a dilution of environmental issues in what was originally an environmental concept.[2] Such is the expansive nature of the concept that much legislation still focuses on encouraging contribution to the achievement of sustainable development, rather than setting targets against which progress could be measured.[3]

1 Sustainable Communities – building for the future, ODPM, February 2003.

2 Hughes, *Environment Law* (4th edn), pp 58–60.

3 For example, Water Act 2003, s 39 and Natural Environment and Rural Communities Act 2006, ss 2, 18, 33, 88.

1.30 Often, however, the impact of these principles on law or practice is hard to assess.[1] The few reported cases that have engaged, for example, with the legal implications of the precautionary principle have not promoted it beyond part of the general background of the considerations which must be taken into account in exercising statutory powers.[2] Indeed, in one decision, the Court of Appeal in effect prioritised the need for consistency in applying telecommunications policy, and the undesirability of delay in doing so, above the need for precaution in assessing the health impacts of mobile telephone aerials.[3] The Courts further expressly reiterated this position by ruling that local planning authorities should not, in the absence of more detailed scientific information (than is currently available) be expected to determine health safeguards; this is the responsibility of government.[4]

But at least some of the principles do now appear in statutory contexts. For example, the Environment Act 1995 sets out in unusually explicit (if not necessarily clear) terms the general aim of the Environment Agency:

'It shall be the principal aim of the Agency (subject to and in accordance with the provisions of this Act or any other enactment and taking into account any likely costs) in discharging its functions so to protect or enhance the environment, taken as a whole, as to make the contribution towards attaining the objective of achieving sustainable development [which the Ministers consider is appropriate for the Agency to make].'[5]

1 See Jewell and Steele 'UK Regulatory Reform and the Pursuit of 'Sustainable Development': The Environment Act 1995' (1996) 8 Journal of *Environmental Law* 283.
2 Eg, *R v Secretary of State for Trade and Industry, ex p Duddridge* [1995] Env LR 151, HC.
3 *R v Tandridge District Council and One 2 One Personal Communications Ltd, ex p Fayed* [2000] JPL 604.
4 *T-Mobile UK Ltd (1) Hutchison 3G UK Ltd (2) and Orange Personal Communications Services Ltd (3) v First Secretary of State (1) and Harrogate Borough Council (2) [2004] EWCA Civ 1763.*
5 EA 1995, s 4(1) and (3). A similar duty is imposed on the Scottish Agency: s 31(2). See A Ross, 'Why Legislate for Sustainable Development? An Examination of Sustainable Development Provisions in UK and Scottish Statutes' (2008) 20 JEL 35.

1.31 Whilst the implications of this obligation are again unclear,[1] it does illustrate the new dominance of so-called environmental principles in UK environmental law, and the length of their reach. They also should be read in conjunction with a further obligation on the Agency in considering whether or not to exercise any power, or in deciding the manner in which to exercise a power, to take into account the likely costs and benefits of the exercise or non-exercise of the power or its exercise in the manner in question.[2] This general 'cost-benefit' test is likely to be of considerable practical importance.

1 See, however, DoE *The Environment Agency and Sustainable Development* (November 1996), which incorporates the statutory guidance referred to in s 4 itself.
2 EA 1995, s 39(1). This obligation is qualified in some circumstances by the same provision.

1.32 A number of other policy trends also seem likely to influence the development of environmental law in the coming years. The first of these is a government commitment to so-called 'economic instruments'. This found most prominent expression in *This Common Inheritance*, where the perceived advantages of such mechanisms were explained.[1] More recently, this commitment has been amplified into a 'presumption in favour' of economic instruments.[2] The advantages of economic instruments revolve around the desirability of giving consumers and industries clear signals about the true environmental costs of using environmental resources, and thus enable those groups, rather than regulators, to decide how best to meet environmental needs. *This Common Inheritance* also contrasted economic instruments with traditional forms of 'direct' regulation, and suggested that the total economic burden of achieving a given environmental target by direct regulation is 'generally likely to be higher than if a successful market-based instrument can be devised'.[3] The presumed advantages of economic instruments were also considered in the UK in a later report of the Royal Commission on Environmental Pollution.[4] Whilst economic instruments have been slow to emerge in practice,[5] a general preference to avoid new environmental regulation is very clear in respect of contaminated land, where new controls demonstrate the perceived importance of not harming the property market.[6]

1 Cm 1200, 1990, Annex A.
2 *This Common Inheritance: Second Year Report*, Cm 2068 (1992) at 35. Later governments have taken a similar view.
3 Ibid, para A4.
4 Royal Commission on Environmental Pollution, Sixteenth Report, *Freshwater Quality*, Cm 1966, (1992) Ch 8. More generally see: Tietenberg 'Economic Instruments for Environmental Regulation' in Helm (ed) *Economic Policy Towards the Environment* (1991).
5 But see paras **16.29–16.31** in respect of the landfill tax. The CRC Energy Efficiency Scheme Order 2010, SI 2010/768 establishes an emissions trading scheme.
6 Paras **15.07–15.09**.

1.33 The second set of developments is towards a greater reliance on voluntarism or self-regulation.[1] These too confirm government's reluctance to 'over-regulate', but they also have important implications for how regulation will be exercised. In particular, co-operative approaches are to be preferred (in appropriate circumstances) to an emphasis on confrontation or litigation. Two illustrations will suffice. First, this enforcement culture is implicit in the Environment Agency's *Code of Practice on Enforcement and Prosecution*.[2] Even when prosecutions are launched and are successful, there remains considerable scope to mitigate in respect of penalties by reference to factors including co-operation with the relevant regulator.[3] Secondly, even where statutory frameworks are in place, the Agency has sought in some cases to provide non-statutory mechanisms to ensure compliance, thus reducing the regulatory burden on affected businesses. One illustration of this is in respect of obligations on producers of packaging-related waste to recycle a proportion of it.[4] In that case, administrative mechanisms have been introduced to simplify compliance and increase the range of non-criminal 'enforcement' options.[5]

1 Eg, Regulation for an Eco-Management and Audit Scheme (1836/93/EC), Department of the Environment Circular 2/91 (noted at (1995) 7 *Environmental Law & Management* 111), and *British Standard on Environment Management Systems* (BS 7750, see also ISO 14001); and Department of the Environment, *Guide to Risk Assessment and Risk Management for Environmental Protection* (1995).
2 In force from 1 November 1998, and available via the Agency's website: www.environment-agency.gov.uk/epns/epp.html.
3 For an insight into how this works in practice see de Prez (1998) 10 *Environmental Law & Management* 187, considering *Environment Agency v ICI Chemicals and Polymers Ltd* (1998) unreported.
4 Producer Responsibility Obligations (Packaging Waste) Regulations 2007, SI 2007/871, as amended.
5 Jewell, 'Voluntary Accreditation of Reprocessors of Packaging Waste' (1998) 10 *Environmental Law & Management* 268.

1.34 The Macrory Review has examined in considerable depth the effectiveness of sanctioning regimes and penalty powers, and underlined the need for 'a more flexible sanctioning toolkit'.[1] In particular, Professor Macrory emphasised the need for the Government to initiate a review of the drafting and formulation of criminal offences relating to regulatory non-compliance, with more appropriate sanctioning regimes focusing on 'Six Penalties Principles'.[2] Further, in designing more appropriate sanctions, regulators should: publish an enforcement policy; measure outcomes not just outputs; justify their choice of enforcement actions year-on-year to stakeholders, Ministers and Parliament; follow up enforcement actions where appropriate; enforce in a transparent manner; be transparent in the way which they apply and determine administrative penalties; and avoid perverse incentives that might influence the choice of sanctioning response. The recommendations also included the introduction of fixed and variable monetary administrative penalties and enforceable undertakings, an improved system of statutory notices, the piloting of Restorative Justice techniques, and the introduction of different sentencing options in criminal courts. Macrory envisaged expanding and enhancing the disciplinary mechanisms available to regulators, whilst encouraging transparency and accountability through the publication of enforcement activities and the sharing of best practice amongst regulators.[3]

1 See generally Grekos, 'Review of civil and administrative penalties for environmental offences: background and development update paper' (2008) 4 Journal of Planning and Environment Law 463.
2 Macrory recommended that sanctions should: aim to change the behaviour of the offender; aim to eliminate any financial gain or benefit from non-compliance; be responsive and consider what is appropriate for the particular offender and regulatory issue (including punishment and the public stigma associated with a criminal conviction); be proportionate to the nature of the offence and harm caused; aim to restore the harm cause by regulatory non-compliance; and aim to deter future non-compliance.
3 Macrory, 'Regulatory Justice: Making Sanctions Effective', November 2006.

1.35 Many of the recommendations in the Macrory Review featured in the Regulatory Enforcement and Sanctions Bill. On 21 July 2008, the Regulatory Enforcement and Sanctions Act gained Royal Assent. Part 1 establishes the Local Better Regulation Office (LBRO), which will have the function of giving guidance to local authorities in England and Wales, and improving co-ordination with central Government. Part 2 establishes a scheme of 'Primary Authorities' that will give advice and guidance to other local authorities to ensure a consistency of enforcement action. Part 3 addresses civil sanctions, and provides for fixed monetary penalties, discretionary requirements (including variable monetary penalties, compliance and restoration notices, and provision for voluntary undertakings), stop notices, and enforcement undertakings.[1] Part 4 requires regulatory bodies to review the exercise of their functions. Whilst the Act may go some way towards establishing consistency and transparency in the use of sanctioning and penalty powers, it should be noted that Part 1 of the Act is only applicable in England and Wales, whilst Parts 2, 3 and 4 are also applicable in Scotland and Northern Ireland. The LBRO may therefore give guidance to local authorities in England and Wales as to how to exercise their functions, but there is still scope for inconsistency amongst local authorities across the UK.[2]

1 The First-tier Tribunal (Environment) (General Regulatory Chamber); the 'Environmental Tribunal' was established in 2010 to hear appeals against sanctions imposed by s 4 of the Act.
2 Regulatory Enforcement and Sanctions Act 2008.

The potential effects of the Human Rights Act 1998

1.36 The explicit legal recognition of human rights in UK law by the Human Rights Act 1998 (HRA 1998 – 'the Act'), which came into force on 2 October

2000,[1] created an important new dimension to environmental law. Given the recent emergence of environmental issues as central concerns to European and national policy, it is not surprising that environmental rights are not expressly included in the catalogue of rights under the European Convention on Human Rights which are now to be protected in the United Kingdom. Nevertheless, environmental law is affected, although a period of uncertainty and reorientation may be expected for some time.[2] Although some reports concentrate on the breadth of potential impacts under the Act, rights seem most likely to be claimed to secure protection against harm to life or property caused by environmental damage in only extreme cases. On the other hand, there are also possibilities of using the rights to thwart the impact of protective measures, especially by claiming that regulatory measures are an undue interference with property rights. From either side there may be criticisms that decision-making procedures do not secure a fair and public hearing before an independent and impartial tribunal.

1 Human Rights Act 1998 (Commencement No 2) Order 2000, SI 2000/1851.
2 See, eg: Upton, 'The European Convention on Human Rights and Environment Law' [1998] JPL 315; Corner, 'Planning, Environment and the European Convention on Human Rights' [1998] JPL 301; Hart, 'The Impact of the European Convention on Human Rights on Planning & Environmental Law' [2000] JPL 117; Holt & Batts (2000) 37 EG 149; Short (2000) 38 EG 192.

1.37 The general provisions of the HRA 1998 Act are well known. More elaborate consideration of those provisions, and the technicalities of their operation, can be found elsewhere.[1] In summary, however, the Act provides that:

(a) so far as is possible, primary and secondary legislation, whenever it was passed, must be read and given effect in a way which is compatible with the Convention;[2]

(b) public authorities have a duty to comply with convention rights, a duty which extends to the courts.[3] Although courts have no power to quash legislation on the basis of its incompatibility with Convention rights, they may declare it to be incompatible, thus shifting the onus to the government and Parliament to consider making modifications through an accelerated Parliamentary process;[4]

(c) the courts are not strictly bound by, but must have regard to, the jurisprudence of the European Court of Human Rights in Strasbourg.[5]

In essence it is unlawful for a 'public authority' such as a court, tribunal or local planning authority, to act in breach of a Convention right, unless it is necessary to do so to 'give effect to legislation' – that is to say that by obeying the Convention, they would be in breach of another law. Such a breach may be justified on the grounds that it protects the amenity of the community.

A victim of such an act has a right of action or a defence where the public authority is acting unlawfully. Where the authority is acting in breach of a Convention right, but is giving effect to legislation, the victim can seek a declaration from the courts that the legislation is incompatible with the ECHR.

However, the European Convention contains a number of different rights. Some of these are absolute and permit no derogation. Those which are most relevant to the environment are qualified and allow derogations where that is necessary for the legitimate benefit of others and the community as a whole. An interference with a qualified right may be justified if it is in accordance with the law and is necessary to a democratic society. Several cases considered by the European Court of Human Rights have provided the following conditions under which an interference may be justified: (1) there is some specific, accessible and precise legal rule justifying the interference; (2) the interference serves one of the aims set out in the qualification to the relevant article; (3) the interference is necessary in a democratic society – namely that there is a pressing social need for the interference and the interference is proportionate to the aim pursued. It is for the public authority in question to justify any interference in all the above respects and the burden of proof is on the public authority once interference has been established. It is worth noting here that the qualified nature of these rights has led to the development by the European Court of Human Rights of the doctrine of 'margin of appreciation', whereby states have considerable discretion as to the extent to which these Convention rights are applied, provided that any restrictions are justified by a competing public interest.

Public authorities are prohibited from acting in a way which is incompatible with any of the human rights described by the Convention (s 6(1)), unless legislation makes this unavoidable. If a public authority acts in a way which is incompatible, then separate proceedings can be brought against it under s 7(1). Therefore the Act creates new rights of action and grounds of appeal whether civil or criminal by a 'victim' of the unlawful act. The rights defined by the ECHR are set out in Sch 1 to the 1998 Act.

1 Eg, Lester, Pannick and Herberg, *Human Rights Law and Practice* 3rd ed (2009); Jacobs, White and Ovey, The *European Convention on Human Rights* 6th ed, (2014); Reid, *A Practitioner's Guide to the European Convention on Human Rights* (1998) and Boyle and Anderson, *Human Rights Approaches to Environmental Protection* 5th ed (2015); Hancock, *Environmental Human Rights* (2005).
2 HRA 1998, s 3.
3 Ibid, s 6(3).
4 Ibid, s 4.
5 Ibid, s 2.

1.38 What is much less clear is the extent to which the Act confers an ability on individuals to rely on the rights 'horizontally', that is, against other individuals. Judicial and academic opinion on this matter has been divided since the HRA 1998 received Royal Assent.[1] Although a fuller appreciation of the significance of the Act for environmental law in property transactions remains to develop, in light of judicial experience with the Act, a number of potentially significant rights can be identified. Those substantive and procedural rights which are likely to be of most relevance include:

(a) The right to life (Article 2 of the Convention).
(b) The right to a fair trial (Article 6(1)). A British case held that the appeal procedure in town and country planning legislation provides an 'independent and impartial tribunal',[2] a case which takes on extra significance in light of the decision of the Outer House of the Court of

Session that the decision to call in an application for listed building consent had deprived the petitioner of its right to have the application determined by an independent and impartial tribunal, since neither the respondents nor the reporter appointed to conduct the public inquiry were independent of the executive agency which was an objector to the application.[3] Similarly, the decision of the Divisional Court in *Alconbury* at first indicated that Article 6 would require drastic changes to the procedures for determining planning applications and appeals. The High Court decided that the Secretary of State's role as both policy-maker and decision-taker in relation to certain development proposals is not compatible with Article 6(1) of the European Convention on Human Rights, which gives the right to a fair hearing by an independent and impartial tribunal. However, the decision of the House of Lords on appeal[4] made it clear that, apart from the need to give reasons, at the most Article 6 means that the courts have the potential to look more closely at the fairness of decision-making by planning authorities. The ability to seek judicial review of the Secretary of State's decision is sufficient to meet the requirement for a fair hearing. A further environmental illustration of the potential for challenge here is in a House of Lords decision concluding that pre-1998 Act 'rights' against self-incrimination were not unlawfully compromised by the scope of the Environment Agency's powers in investigating alleged waste offences.[5]

(c) The right to privacy and home life (Article 8). Recent cases considering the application of this provision have included a challenge to the scheme for regulating night flights at the main London airports[6] and a claim by a house owner for compensation in respect of flooding of his premises by foul water and sewage from Thames Water's sewers.[7] In *Hatton*, the challenge to the scheme for regulating night flights failed because the European Court of Human Rights found that the authorities had not failed to strike a fair balance between the economic interests of the public and the environmental problems faced by the applicant. The authorities were entitled to give the economic considerations greater weight, even though no exhaustive studies had been carried out. In the case of *Marcic*, the House of Lords rejected the house owner's compensation claim. The powers and duties of sewerage undertakers are contained in the Water Industry Act 1991, the duties being enforceable by the statutory regulator – the Director General of Water Services. The House of Lords applied the long-standing principle that a statutory remedy provided for breach of a statutory duty is the only remedy available. No claim could be brought under the law of nuisance, and as Mr Marcic had not persuaded the Director General of Water Services to issue an enforcement order, he had no remedy under domestic law. Fortified by *Hatton*, the House of Lords had no hesitation in taking a similar approach to Mr Marcic's claim under Article 8 and Article 1 of the First Protocol. The statutory scheme under the Water Industry Act 1991 represented a reasonable balance between the interests of those whose houses were prone to sewer flooding, on the one hand, and the company's customers whose properties were drained through the company's sewers, on the other. The scheme therefore fell within the margin of appreciation and so Mr Marcic's human rights claim also failed.

26

However, the Court of Appeal later stated in *Dobson*[8] that *Marcic* does not prevent a claim in nuisance resulting from negligence where determining the same is neither inconsistent with, nor conflicts with the statutory process. Therefore, even in cases where there exist schemes for enforcing statutory undertakers' obligations, statutory undertakers can still be liable to members of the public for nuisance caused by negligence. A further point to note from *Dobson* is that in the assessment of damages, where an infringement of an Article 8 right has been successfully argued, the Court would take into account any other relief or remedy granted to the claimant, supporting the fundamental point that the award of damages at common law to a property owner for an act of negligence would normally constitute just satisfaction for the purposes of an interference with Article 8 of the Act.

(d) The right to an effective remedy (Article 13).

(e) The right to property (Article 1 of Protocol 1). One illustration here is whether designation of a nature reserve may be a breach of the landowner's right to peaceful enjoyment of his possessions.[9]

1 See the analysis provided by Loveland, *Constitutional Law, Administrative Law and Human Rights: A Critical Introduction* (4th edn, 2006).
2 *Bryan v United Kingdom* (1995) 21 EHRR 342.
3 *County Properties Ltd v Scottish Ministers* [2000] SLT 965.
4 [2001] 2 All ER 929; [2001] 2 WLR 1389.
5 *R v Hertfordshire County Council, ex p Green Environmental Industries Ltd and Moynihan* [2000] 2 AC 412, [2000] 1 All ER 773, HL; Scanlan and Monnick [2000] 144 SJ 152.
6 *Hatton v UK* (2003) 37 EHRR 28.
7 *Marcic v Thames Water Utilities* [2004] 1 All ER 135.
8 *Dobson v Thames Water Utilities* [2009] EWCA Civ 28.
9 *Matos Silva Lda v Portugal* (1996) 24 EHRR 573.

1.39 Of greater importance in the environmental context are procedural rights. The most notable instrument containing these rights is the Aarhus Convention on Access to Information, Public Participation in Decision-Making and Access to Justice in Environmental Matters of 1998. These three 'pillars' are briefly highlighted below. The first two have been implemented by EC Directives.

Access to environmental information:[1] Article 4 provides a broad right for the public,[2] without having to state an interest, to require the provision of environmental information[3] from public authorities.[4] The definitions of 'public', 'environmental information' and 'public authority' are wide. The Convention provides that a request for environmental information may be refused if the public authority does not hold it, if the request is manifestly unreasonable or formulated too generally, or if it relates to material in the course of completion or to the internal communications of public authorities.[5] There are also a number of other exceptions.[6] Environmental information must be provided, or a refusal given in writing as soon as possible and at the latest within one month, unless the complexity of the information justifies an extension up to two months after the request.[7] In addition to the duty to provide environmental information on request, Convention parties must ensure that public authorities collect and disseminate environmental information.[8]

Public participation: Article 6 provides a right for the public to participate in decisions on whether to permit proposed activities listed in Annex I, which are broadly those covered by the Environmental Impact Assessment Directive[9] and the Industrial Emissions Directive.[10] The public must be informed by public notice or individually, as appropriate, early in the decision-making procedure, of the proposed activity and the application made, full details of the proposed procedure and the opportunities for the public to participate, the public authority making the decision and the nature of possible decisions or the draft decision, an indication of the relevant environmental information available, and whether the activity is subject to an environmental impact assessment procedure.[11] Convention parties are required to provide for early public participation, when all options are open and effective participation can take place,[12] access to relevant information,[13] and an opportunity for the public to submit in writing or, as appropriate, at a public hearing or inquiry, any comments, information, analyses or opinions that it considers relevant to the proposed activity.[14] The decision by the public authority must take due account of the outcome of the public participation.[15] Public participation procedures must also be in place when permits are reconsidered or their conditions updated,[16] as well as in relation to the preparation of plans, programmes and policies relating to the environment[17] and executive regulations and other generally applicable legally binding rules that may have a significant effect on the environment.[18]

Access to justice: Those whose requests for environmental information have not been dealt with satisfactorily should be given access to a review procedure before a court of law or other independent and impartial body established by law. Where review by a court of law is provided, there should also be access to an expeditious procedure that is free of charge or inexpensive for reconsideration by a public authority or review by an independent and impartial body other than a court of law. Final decisions by any such body are to bind the public authority holding the information. Reasons for a decision must be given in writing, at least in cases of refusal of access to information.[19] Members of the public should also be given access to a review procedure before a court of law and/or another independent and impartial body established by law to challenge the substantive and procedural legality of any decision, act or omission which is covered by the public participation requirements under Article 6.[20] That applies where they can demonstrate a sufficient interest or impairment of a right (where required by national administrative law).[21] In addition, subject to meeting any criteria laid down by national law, members of the public must be given access to administrative or judicial procedures to challenge acts and omissions by private persons and public authorities which contravene national environmental law.[22] The access to justice procedures referred to must provide adequate and effective remedies, including injunctive relief as appropriate, and must be fair, equitable, timely and not prohibitively expensive.[23] Convention parties must also consider establishing appropriate assistance mechanisms to remove or reduce financial and other barriers to access to justice.[24]

1 See Chapter 4.
2 'The public' means one or more natural or legal persons, and, in accordance with national legislation or practice, their associations, organisations or groups: Article 2.4.

3 'Environmental information' means any information in written, visual, aural, electronic or any other material form on: (a) the state of the elements of the environment, such as air and atmosphere water, soil, land, landscape and natural sites, biological diversity and its components, including genetically modified organisms, and the interaction among these elements; (b) factors, such as substances, energy, noise and radiation, and activities or measures, including administrative measures, environmental agreements, policies, legislation, plans and programmes, affecting or likely to affect the elements of the environment within the scope of subpara (a) above, and cost-benefit and other economic analyses and assumptions used in environmental decision-making; (c) the state of human health and safety, conditions of human life, cultural sites and built structures, inasmuch as they are or may be affected by the state of the elements of the environment or, through these elements, by the factors, activities or measures referred to in subpara (b) above: Article 2.3.

4 'Public authority' means: (a) government at national, regional and other level; (b) natural or legal persons performing public administrative functions under national law, including specific duties, activities or services in relation to the environment; (c) any other natural or legal persons having public responsibilities or functions, or providing public services, in relation to the environment, under the control of a body or person falling within subparas (a) or (b) above; (d) the institutions of any regional economic integration organisation referred to in Article 17 which is a party to this Convention. This definition does not include bodies or institutions acting in a judicial or legislative capacity: Article 2.2.

5 Article 4.3. In the case of incomplete material and the internal communications of public authorities, the public interest served by disclosure must be taken into account.

6 Under Article 4.4, a request for environmental information may also be refused if disclosure would adversely affect any of the following interests: (a) the confidentiality of the proceedings of public authorities; (b) international relations, national defence or public security; (c) the course of justice, a person's ability to receive a fair trial, or a public authority's ability to conduct a criminal or disciplinary enquiry; (d) the confidentiality of commercial and industrial information, where protected by law to protect a legitimate economic interest. However, this excludes information on emissions relevant for the protection of the environment; (e) intellectual property rights; (f) the confidentiality of personal data or files relating to a natural person who has not consented to disclosure; (g) the interests of a third party who has supplied the information without being under or capable of being put under a legal obligation to do so and who has not consented to its release; (h) the environment, such as the breeding sites of rare species. However, it is provided that these grounds of refusal should be interpreted restrictively taking into account both the public interest served by disclosure, and whether the information relates to emissions to the environment.

7 Articles 4.2 and 4.7.

8 Article 5.

9 85/337/EEC, as amended.

10 2010/75/EU.

11 Article 6.2.

12 Article 6.4.

13 Article 6.6. This is without prejudice to Article 4.

14 Article 6.7.

15 Article 6.8.

16 Article 6.10.

17 Article 7.

18 Article 8.

19 Article 9.1.

20 Article 9.2. These requirements shall not exclude the possibility of a preliminary review procedure before an administrative authority or affect the requirement of exhaustion of administrative review procedures prior to judicial review where there is such a requirement under national law.

21 The requirements of 'sufficient interest' and 'impairment of right' are to be determined in accordance with those of national law and consistently with the objective of giving the public concerned wide access to justice within the scope of the Convention. Any NGO which promotes environmental protection and meets any requirements under national law is to be deemed to have such an interest and to have rights capable of being impaired.

22 Article 9.3.
23 Article 9.4. Decisions must be in writing. Decisions of courts, and wherever possible of other bodies, must be accessible to the public.
24 Article 9.5.

Implementing the Aarhus Convention

1.40 The Aarhus Convention promises to be effective, at least in the European Union. It has been ratified, approved or accepted by the European Union and most of the Member States, including the United Kingdom.[1] The first two 'pillars' of access to environmental information and public participation have been implemented by Directives.[2]

Apart from the specific requirements of the Convention, there has been a long tradition of public participation in environmental matters in England and Wales. For example, the public must be informed of applications for environmental permits.[3]

The Public Participation Directive amends the Environmental Assessment and IPPC Directives to require the public to be given early and effective opportunities to participate in environmental decision-making and permitting procedures.[4]

The proposed Directive on access to justice in environmental matters followed the Convention in providing for legal standing of 'qualified entities'.[5] Qualified entities were to have 'access to environmental proceedings, including interim relief, without having a sufficient interest or maintaining the impairment of a right', if the matter of review falls within the ambit of their 'statutory activities' and their geographical area of activity. Specific criteria[6] as well as a requirement for a procedure[7] for recognition of qualified entities, were prescribed by the proposed Directive.

However, the proposed Directive was withdrawn on 21 May 2014.

Long before the Aarhus Convention, the English courts had developed the judicial review procedure from the old prerogative remedies. An applicant for judicial review who has 'a sufficient interest in the subject matter to which the application relates'[8] may challenge any illegality, irrationality or procedural impropriety in any act, omission or decision of a public body in relation to it.[9]

Following, and even before the *Inland Revenue Commissioners* case,[10] the rules on standing have become very relaxed. In that case, the House of Lords held that the question of sufficient interest could not be considered in isolation. Rather, 'the test is whether the applicant can show a strong enough case on the merits, judged in relation to his own concern with it'.[11] It follows that the House of Lords has practically abolished any requirement of standing distinct from the merits of the case. According to Wade and Forsyth, 'the real question is whether the applicant can show some substantial default or abuse, and not whether his personal rights or interests are involved. In effect, therefore, a citizen's action, or *actio popularis*, is in principle allowable in suitable cases.'[12]

This goes beyond the requirements of the Aarhus Convention.

The relaxed approach to standing has benefited a number of environmental organisations who have thereby been enabled to bring proceedings for judicial review. For example, Greenpeace had standing to challenge the grant of an authorisation for a nuclear generator,[13] and Friends of the Earth was entitled to proceed against a government department, claiming that water standards should be properly enforced.[14]

The most notable departure from the modern trend on standing is the *Rose Theatre* case,[15] where the judge refused to allow standing to a company established to preserve the archaeological remains of the old Rose Theatre in Southwark. The company sought to challenge the refusal of the Secretary of State to list the remains as an ancient monument. The judge first decided against the company on the merits of the case. Having done so, he held that it had no standing. This approach has not been followed in later cases and may be regarded as an aberration. Wade and Forsyth suggest that it is best regarded as a case where an arguable issue was not shown.[16]

In summary, the liberal rules on standing for judicial review should be sufficient to satisfy the requirements of the Aarhus Convention. However, it will be recalled that the Convention also requires that court procedures must not be 'prohibitively expensive'.[17] The issue as to whether this requirement is being met, particularly in view of the long tradition that the losing party pays the winner's costs in litigation, has been discussed in a number of recent cases; *Corner House,*[18] *Morgan & Baker,*[19] and *Coedbach.*[20]

As a general rule, the allocation of the burden of costs incurred in bringing an action lies within the discretion of the court. Although the *Corner House* case did not relate to an environmental issue (covering judicial applications generally), the Court of Appeal formulated certain principles to be applied in determining whether a Protective Costs Order (PCO), which extinguishes or limits the liability of the losing party to pay the winner's costs, may be made. The court held[21] that a PCO may be made at any time in the proceedings, although normally an application would be made at the time of the initial claim.[22]

Carnwath LJ in *Morgan & Baker*, went further in discussing the application of the Convention with regards to the cost of judicial review relating to an environmental issue, noting that:[23]

(a) The Convention requirement that costs should not be 'prohibitively expensive' should apply to the total potential liability of claimants, including the threat of adverse costs orders.
(b) The rules of the CPR relating to the award of costs remain effective, including the ordinary 'loser pays' rule and the principles governing the court's discretion to depart from it; the principles of the Convention being at most a matter to which the court may have regard in exercising its discretion.
(c) However, as the proposed Directive (noted above) has not yet been implemented, the principle of access to justice under the Convention does

not have direct effect in domestic law and therefore the court's discretion may not be regarded as adequate implementation of the rule against prohibitive costs.

(d) The principles governing the grant of PCOs apply alike to environmental and other public interest cases. The *Corner House* statement of those principles must be regarded as settled, but is to be applied 'flexibly'. Further development or refinement is a matter for legislation or the Rules Committee.

(e) The Jackson review provides an opportunity for considering the Aarhus principles in the context of the system for costs as a whole. Modifications of the present rules in the light of that report are likely to be matters for Parliament or the Civil Procedure Rules Committee.

(f) Apart from the issues of costs, the Convention requires remedies to be 'adequate and effective' and 'fair, equitable, timely'. The variety and lack of coherence of jurisdictional routes currently available to potential litigants may arguably be seen as additional obstacles in the way of achieving these objectives.

Sullivan LJ's Report of the Working Group on Access to Environmental Justice,[24] updated in August 2010 following the Jackson Review,[25] concluded that the UK government was currently relying on judicial review as a means of satisfying the Aarhus Convention requirements but that the existing principles concerning costs and the potential exposure to costs in judicial review proceedings inhibit compliance with the Convention. The Report further concluded that judicial discretion would not satisfy the Commission as to compliance with Aarhus and that the Courts themselves (following *Garner*[26]) were of the view that compliance with Aarhus needed to be secured through changes to the Rules rather than further development of Judge-made law.

The Report referred to above and Carnwath LJ's statement that 'the courts' discretion may not be regarded as adequate implementation of the rule against prohibitive costs' reflected the Commission's stance on the point. In 2007 the Commission issued an initial warning letter, setting out its concerns that legal proceedings in the UK were too costly for NGOs and individuals to risk bringing cases against public bodies, particularly in cases where an interim injunction is sought and cross-undertakings in damages are required. A 'Reasoned Opinion' dated 18 March 2010 concluded that the UK was still failing to comply with the Convention. In reply, the UK did agree to amend its domestic legislation. Following the publication of the Jackson Report on the funding of civil litigation, the Government addressed complaints of improper implementation of the Convention, not by introducing one-way costs shifting (as Jackson had recommended) but, in April 2013, introducing a Practice Direction providing for the maximum amount of costs that the court can order a party to pay in all judicial reviews (environmental and non-environmental) to counter the 'chilling' effect of costs order in cases which have merit.[27]

1 The EU signed and approved the Convention on 12 February 2005. The following Member States have ratified the Convention: Austria (17/01/2005); Belgium (21/01/2003); Cyprus (19/09/2003); Czech Republic (06/07/2004); Estonia (02/02/2001); Hungary (03/07/2001); Italy (13/06/2001); Latvia (14/06/2002; Lithuania (28/01/2002); Malta (23/04/2002);

Poland (15/02/2002); Portugal (09/06/2003); Slovenia (29/07/2004); Spain (29/12/2004); UK (23/02/2005); Sweden (20/05/2005); Luxembourg (25/10/2005); Greece (27/01/06); Germany (15/01/07). The following Member States have approved the Convention: Denmark (29/09/2000); France (08/07/2002). The following Member States have accepted the Convention: Finland (01/09/2004); Netherlands (29/12/2004). Slovakia has acceded to the Convention (5/12/2005).

2 The Directive on public access to environmental information (2003/4/EC) which repealed the earlier Directive 90/313/EEC on the same subject; the Directive on public participation in certain environmental matters (2003/35/EC); and the proposed Directive on access to justice in environmental matters – COM(2003) 624 final. The environmental information Directive has been implemented in England, Wales and Northern Ireland by the Environmental Information Regulations 2004, SI 2004/3391. The Public Participation Directive has been transposed in the UK by a number of Regulations, including the Pollution Prevention and Control (Public Participation) (England and Wales) Regulations 2005, SI 2005/1448. There is also a notable procedure for public participation and access to justice in the Environment Liability Directive 2004/35/CE.

3 Sch 5, paras 5–6 of the Environmental Permitting (England and Wales) Regulations 2010, SI 2010/675.

4 2003/35/EC, Articles 3.4 and 4.3.

5 COM (2003) 624 final, Article 5. The proposed directive was withdrawn on 21 May 2014. It did not progress beyond the draft stage.

6 Article 8.

7 Article 9.

8 Senior Courts Act 1981, s 31(3).

9 See Lord Diplock's statement on judicial review in *Council of Civil Service Unions v Minister for the Civil Service* [1985] AC 374 at 408 ff.

10 *R v Inland Revenue Commissioners, ex p National Federation of Self Employed and Small Businesses Ltd* [1982] AC 617.

11 Wade and Forsyth, *Administrative Law*, Oxford, p 587 (11th edn 2014).

12 Wade and Forsyth, op cit, pp 588-589.

13 *R v Inspectorate of Pollution, ex p Greenpeace Ltd (No 2)* [1994] 4 All ER 329.

14 *R v Secretary of State for the Environment ex p Friends of the Earth Ltd* (1994) 7 Admin L R 26.

15 *R v Secretary of State for the Environment, ex p Rose Theatre Trust Company* [1990] 1 QB 504.

16 Wade and Forsyth, op cit, p 593.

17 Article 9.4.

18 *R (Corner House Research) v Secretary of State for Trade and Industry* [2005] EWCA Civ 192.

19 *Morgan & Baker v Hinton Organics (Wessex) Ltd* [2009] EWCA Civ 107

20 *Coedbach Action Team Ltd v Secretary of State for Energy and Climate Change and Ors* [2010] EWHC 2312 (Admin).

21 A PCO would be made on the basis of five principles: (1) the case raises issues of general public importance; (2) those issues should be resolved in the public interest; (3) the applicant has no private interest in the matter; (4) it is fair and just to make the order considering the financial resources of the parties and the amount of costs likely to be at stake; (5) in the absence of a PCO, the applicant is likely to discontinue proceedings. See also *R (England) v LB Tower Hamlets* [2006] EWCA Civ 1742.

22 Much of the material in this paragraph and the preceding paragraph, as well as para 1.38 is drawn from two articles by A Waite, 'Sunlight through the Trees – a Perspective on Environmental Rights and Human Rights' in *Mélanges en l'honneur de Michel Prieur, Dalloz* (2007), and 'A New Garden of Eden: Stimuli to Enforcement and Compliance in Environmental Law' (2007) 24 PACE Environmental Law Review 343.

23 *Morgan & Baker v Hinton Organics (Wessex) Ltd* [2009] EWCA Civ 107 para 47

24 Sullivan J 'Ensuring access to environmental justice in England and Wales' May 2008, updated August 2010.

25 http://www.judiciary.gov.uk/about_judiciary/cost-review/jan2010/final-report-140110.pdf

26 *R (Garner) v Elbridge Borough Council* [2010] EWCA Civ 1006

27 See also http://www.dojni.gov.uk/index/public-consultations/archive-consultations/cost-protection-for-litigants-summary-of-responses.pdf

STATUTORY REGULATORS

1.41 The day-to-day implementation and enforcement of environmental law and policy lie in the hands of a variety of regulatory bodies. The main bodies are the Environment Agency, the local authorities, water and sewerage undertakers and Natural England.

1.42 The Environment Act 1995 created an Environment Agency for England and Wales ('the Agency') and a separate Scottish Environment Protection Agency ('SEPA'). A range of pre-existing pollution control and environmental protection functions were brought under these agencies' jurisdiction, with the intention of better co-ordinating otherwise disparate functions.[1] In particular, the functions of certain other bodies were transferred to the Agencies, including those of the National Rivers Authority, waste regulation and disposal authorities, Her Majesty's Inspectorate of Pollution, and certain functions of the Secretary of State.[2] The agencies are therefore the first general environmental regulators the UK has known. The Natural Resources Body Wales (generally known as Natural Resources Wales) took over the functions of the Environment Agency in Wales from 1 April 2013.[3]

1 EA 1995, Part I. This book is generally concerned with the position in England and Wales, and references to 'the Agency' hereafter should be interpreted accordingly.
2 EA 1995, s 2.
3 SI 2013/755, Art 4(2), Sch 4 paras 246, 247(a).

1.43 The principal functions of the Agency concern pollution control, although even there they are not solely responsible for the exercise of all relevant powers. Local authorities in various guises retain important controls over, for example, statutory nuisance and noise,[1] aspects of waste regulation,[2] most instances of atmospheric pollution,[3] some aspects of environmental permitting and a central role in the remediation of contaminated land.[4] Local authorities also retain their planning jurisdiction.[5]

Some privatised water companies act as sewerage undertakers, controlling discharges to sewers through the grant of trade effluent consents.

Natural England is a public body having the function of conserving and enhancing the natural environment. It was formed by bringing together English Nature, the landscape, access and recreation elements of the Countryside Agency and the environmental land management functions of the Rural Development Service. Natural England is the Government's statutory adviser on landscape, with responsibility for landscape designations such as National Parks, Areas of Outstanding Natural Beauty and Heritage Coasts. Natural England is also concerned with England's future landscapes, with involvement in planning policy and a range of environmental land management projects. Natural England has responsibilities for conserving and enhancing the marine and coastal environment, and for promoting its sustainable use and opportunities for public enjoyment. Its work includes monitoring marine protected areas and creating new ones, and working to improve coastal and marine biodiversity.[6]

Despite the centralising effects of the creation of the Environment Agency, in practice there will often be a complex web of institutional relationships to be bridged in resolving an individual environmental problem which arises in connection with a property transaction. The particular powers of each regulator are set out in context in later chapters.

1 Ch 14.
2 Ch 16.
3 Ch 20.
4 Ch 15.
5 Ch 18.
6 For a discussion, see paras **19.06–19.12**.

Chapter 2

Dealing with information – the caveat emptor rule and environmental issues

PROTECTING THE PARTIES

2.01   Certainty is better than uncertainty. As a rule of thumb, parties are generally best advised to approach a transaction armed with relevant information on environmental problems. This enables them to evaluate actual and potential liabilities and to formulate an appropriate strategy in negotiations. It can be dangerous for both sellers and buyers to ignore these issues. Sellers may find that awkward questions are raised at a late stage in negotiations which can only be resolved by substantial reductions in price or by conceding onerous indemnities. Buyers risk inheriting liabilities of which they were unaware and for which they have no redress on account of the caveat emptor rule.

2.02   It is, of course, always possible to allocate risk between the parties contractually. However, indemnities are only as good as the party who gives them. It is not unknown for individuals to disappear and for companies to go into liquidation. In any event, the possibilities of unpleasant surprises and of liabilities unlimited in time and amount lead most parties to concede indemnities only if they are strictly limited. The real protection given may therefore not be all that is required.

2.03   For these reasons, the parties should consider investigating environmental matters at an early stage of the transaction. The extent of the investigations will inevitably depend on factors such as local knowledge of contamination and other environmental matters, as well as the value of the transaction. However, it must be appreciated that liabilities, particularly in respect of contamination, are not necessarily limited to the amount of the purchase price. In some cases they could be very much higher.

2.04   Nonetheless, it should not be assumed automatically that the existence of environmental problems need prove fatal to a transaction, or that liabilities will always be serious. Armed with appropriate knowledge, informed decisions can be made by all parties concerned. With goodwill and common sense, solutions can generally be found to the seemingly most intractable environmental problems. In practice, that may enable many transactions to proceed.

2.05   Information can be gathered from a number of sources including:

- preliminary enquiries addressed to the seller or lessor;
- local authority enquiries;
- public registers;
- requests for information from regulatory authorities and other public bodies; and
- environmental surveys.

Prior to discussing these, it is important to consider the effect of the caveat emptor rule, which provides the legal background to the need for environmental information in dealing with property transactions. An outline is also given of the difficult areas of misdescription, misrepresentation, fraudulent concealment, the duty of disclosure, negligent workmanship by the seller, liability for defective building operations and standard contractual terms. For a discussion of these topics outside the particular context of environmental law reference should be made to the standard works on conveyancing and contract.

THE *CAVEAT EMPTOR* (BUYER BEWARE) RULE

2.06 The general rule is that a seller gives no warranty as to the physical condition of the property or as to its suitability for any purpose.[1] Accordingly, it is the responsibility of the buyer to establish, for example, whether the ground is contaminated or whether the building is adequately insulated to prevent the transmission of noise. The buyer must also check for himself that all necessary permits under environmental legislation have been obtained. The seller is not generally obliged to disclose information as to any such matter even if he is aware of it. The *caveat emptor* rule has been subjected to much criticism[2] but so far has not been altered. There seems little immediate prospect that it will be changed. The *caveat emptor* rule is, however, subject to a number of exceptions which are discussed in the following paragraphs. There are also legal requirements on sellers to provide information to prospective buyers, eg energy performance certificates and recommendation reports.[3] The proposed EU Soil Directive also contains a requirement, where a property is to be sold, for the owner or prospective buyer to make a soil status report available to the competent authority and to any other party in the transaction.[4]

1 *Edler v Auerbach* [1950] 1 KB 359; *Hill v Harris* [1965] 2 QB 601.
2 See eg the HC Environment Committee, 1st Report, *Contaminated Land* (1989–1990) paras 89–95. After initially favouring abolition, the Law Commission Standing Committee on conveyancing eventually recommended the retention of the *caveat emptor* rule: *Let the Buyer be well informed* (December 1989).
3 Energy Performance of Buildings (England and Wales) Regulations 2012, SI 2012/3118.
4 Proposal for a directive establishing a framework for the protection of soil, art 12.1, Brussels, COM(2006) 232 final, 2006/0086(COD). However, In October 2013, the Commission adopted a Communication as part of its smart regulation policy, Regulatory Fitness and Performance (REFIT), which indicated that it would withdraw its existing proposal for a Soil Framework Directive because it has been stalled for eight years. However, the Commission also indicated that this could open the way for it to make an alternative proposal.

MISDESCRIPTION

2.07   If the contract misdescribes the property in a material and substantial way, which would deprive the buyer of what he contracted to buy and would have affected the buyer's decision to purchase the property, the buyer may rescind the contract. Contractual attempts to restrict the buyer to the remedy of compensation only in such cases are ineffective.[1] However, where the misdescription is not substantial and is made innocently, the contract remains enforceable against the buyer who is only entitled to an abatement of the purchase price. The buyer's remedies appear to survive completion.[2] Problems over misdescription are most likely to arise where property is auctioned, since the advertised particulars of sale form part of the contract. However, mistakes of this kind can arise where land is sold privately. Misdescription is a breach of contract and should be distinguished from a misrepresentation which induces the buyer to enter into the contract.[3]

1 *Flight v Booth* (1834) 1 Bing NC 370.
2 Emmet on Title, para 4-1018
3 *Barnsley's Conveyancing Law and Practice* (4th edn) pp 636ff; See ibid, pp 640–641 as to how
   to determine whether a misdescription is substantial; *Emmet on Title* volume 1, Ch 4, Pt 2.

2.08   Representations about the state or condition of the land may amount to misdescriptions. In *Re Puckett and Smith's Contract*[1] the particulars of sale claimed that the land had 'a valuable prospective building element'. In fact, the land was crossed by an underground culvert, which posed substantial problems for using the land for construction purposes. This misdescription was held to be sufficient to enable the buyer to rescind the contract.

1 [1902] 2 Ch 258.

2.09   In *Sakkas v Donford Ltd*[1] the description of the house and the conditions of sale stated falsely that to the knowledge of the seller the property was not subject to any planning matter. In fact, it was effectively 'zoned' for public open space. The buyer was therefore held to be entitled to refuse to purchase the house and to rescind the contract.

1 (1983) 46 P & CR 290.

2.10   Clearly it is possible that misdescriptions to the effect that property is free from contamination or that it is suitable for immediate housing development when it is heavily contaminated could give rise to the remedy of rescission. The same applies to statements on other environmental matters such as the presence of asbestos or the existence of noise insulation in the building. Whether such misdescriptions are held to be substantial or otherwise will determine whether the buyer is entitled to rescind the contract or is only entitled to compensation.

MISREPRESENTATION

2.11 Misrepresentation of a material fact by the seller in relation to the property which induces the buyer to enter into the contract gives the buyer a right of action for damages and/or rescission of the contract.[1] This applies where answers to preliminary enquiries are false or misleading. Since the seller is not obliged to answer any questions or to volunteer any information, he is well advised not to answer any questions or make any statements which may give rise to liability.[2]

1 *Barnsley* (above), pp 193–197, 630–632, 660–661; *Emmet on Title* volume 1, Ch 4, Pt 1. *Chitty on Contracts*, 32nd ed (2015), chapter 7. The buyer's remedies continue after completion – see in relation to recission Misrepresentation Act 1967, s 1.
2 But note that a seller who provides the buyer with information as to the nature and extent of contamination on the property may be freed from liability under Part IIA of the EPA 1990. That liability will effectively be assumed by the buyer. See Ch 9 and para **15.90**.

2.12 Representations which could give rise to remedies for misdescription if included in the contract may, of course, amount to actionable misrepresentations where they only induce the buyer to enter into the contract. In *Nottingham Patent Brick and Tile Co v Butler*[1] the seller's statement that he was unaware of any restrictive covenants was actionable, because although the statement was true in one sense, it was also misleading, as no check of the deeds had been undertaken. Again, the dangers of ill-judged responses to enquiries about the presence of ground contamination or other environmental problems on the property are clear. It is better for the seller to reply that 'The buyer must rely on his own investigations' than to state: 'Not so far as the seller is aware'. The latter response implies a representation that the seller has taken reasonable steps to investigate the matter in question.[2]

1 (1886) 16 QBD 778. See also *Rignall Developments Ltd v Halil* [1988] Ch 190.
2 *William Sindall plc v Cambridgeshire County Council* [1994] 1 WLR 1016, 1024–1034, CA.

2.13 An example of liability for an inaccurate reply to preliminary enquiries is *Dodd v Crown Estate Comrs*.[1] The issue related to the drainage of foul water from the property. One of the preliminary enquiries was: 'Does the property have drainage, water, electricity? Which of them are connected to the mains?' The reply was given: 'Please see the agent's particulars of sale'. A plan was annexed to the draft contract which showed the drain leading to the main sewer. In fact, no main sewer served the property and the sellers had no rights of drainage to a main sewer which they could grant. It was held that an innocent misrepresentation was established. On the basis that the buyer had entered into the contract in reliance on the misrepresentation, he was entitled to damages for his losses resulting from the misrepresentation.

1 [1995] NPC 29, [1995] EGCS 35.

2.14 A different conclusion on the facts was reached by the Technology and Construction Court (TCC) in *Lambson Fine Chemicals Ltd v Merlion Capital Housing Ltd*[1] concerning a claim for misrepresentation relating to contamination. Lambson sold the site to Merlion for redevelopment. During the negotiations, it was agreed that Lambson would commission a report on contamination on the property from environmental consultants URS. The URS report indicated the necessity of removing 'Blue Billy'[2] contamination which had been stockpiled following excavation during earlier works. The URS report did not emphasise the advice in earlier reports by another consultant dated 1993 that Blue Billy was likely to be widespread across the central part of the site, nor did URS test for Blue Billy elsewhere or recommend its removal.

Prior to exchange of contracts, the director of Lambson (at the request of Merlion) signed a letter drafted by Merlion's solicitors stating that he had no knowledge of further contamination on the site other than that specifically identified in the URS report. Following completion of the sale, Merlion discovered further Blue Billy in the central part of the site which it had to remove at a cost of £425,000 under a planning condition.

Merlion's claim for damages on the basis of alleged fraudulent misrepresentation in the letter was dismissed. The TCC held that there was no misrepresentation, fraudulent or otherwise. The URS report did set out some limited borehole test results showing high levels of cyanide. It also referred to the 1993 reports which identified the presence of further Blue Billy contamination in the central area of the site. Lambson's director had no additional knowledge.

1 [2008] Env LR 37.
2 'Blue Billy' is a cyanide compound derived from the manufacture of town gas. It had been used on the site as feed for the production of sulphuric acid.

2.15   In principle, the measure of damages for misrepresentation is that for tort, ie the claimant is entitled to be placed in the same position as if the misrepresentation had not been made.[1] In *Lambson Fine Chemicals Ltd v Merlion Capital Housing Ltd*[2] the TCC pointed out that if there had been an actionable misrepresentation, the measure of damages would not necessarily have been the cost of removing the additional contamination. The question was what difference the information would have made to the negotiations between the parties. On the facts, the TCC considered that at most a small discount might have been offered from the purchase price.

However, in cases of fraudulent misrepresentation (including deliberately misleading replies to enquiries before contract), the House of Lords has confirmed in *Smith New Court Securities Ltd v Scrimgeour Vickers (Asset Management) Ltd*[3] that the measure of damages is compensation for all the actual loss, including consequential loss, directly flowing from the transaction induced by the deceit of the wrongdoer. The rules on remoteness of damage applicable in negligence cases do not apply. Accordingly, if the reply given in *Dodd* had been given in the knowledge that it was untrue and it subsequently appeared that unknown to the parties the land concerned had been so grossly contaminated that its value was only half of the purchase price, the buyer would be entitled to recover not only any loss caused by the fraudulent misrepresentation but also the loss in value due to the contamination. However, the buyer would be obliged to mitigate his losses and to give credit for any benefit received from the transaction, for example any increase in price in excess of the true market value obtained on a resale.

It has been held that the measure of damages applicable in fraudulent misrepresentation cases also applies to negligent misrepresentation under s 2(1) of the Misrepresentation Act 1967.[4] Under s 1(b) of the Misrepresentation Act 1967 the buyer's remedy of recission is not lost when the contract is completed.[5]

1 *Barnsley* (above), p 660.
2 [2008] Env LR 37, paras 145–148.
3 [1996] 4 All ER 769. A fraudulent representation is a false representation by the seller which induces the buyer to enter into the contract but which is made knowingly, or without belief in its truth, or recklessly, not caring whether it is true or false: *Barnsley*, (above), p 687.
4 *Royscot Trust Ltd v Rogerson* [1991] 3 All ER 294, CA. However, this case has been criticised and Lords Browne-Wilkinson and Steyn declined to give any opinion on its correctness in *Smith New Court Securities*.
5 Emmet on Title, para 4.013.

2.16   Misrepresentation as to the presence or absence if contamination on a property or any other environmental issue may amount to a criminal offence[1] although that is subject to a due diligence defence.[2]

1 The Business Projection from Misleading Marketing Regulations 2008, SI 2008/1276, reg 3; Consumer Trading from Unfair Trading Regulations 2008, SI 2008/1277, reg 4.
2 Ibid, reg 11 and reg 16 respectively.

FRAUDULENT CONCEALMENT

2.17   If the seller actively conceals defects he is guilty of fraud in respect of which the buyer also has an action for damages and rescission of the contract.[1] Deliberate concealment of structural defects or tell-tale signs of contamination could amount to fraud for this purpose.

1 See, eg, *Ridge v Crawley* (1959) 173 Estates Gazette 959 (cracks indicating settlement concealed); *Gordon v Selico Co Ltd* [1986] 1 EGLR 71 (dry rot concealed); *Taylor v Hamer* [2003] 03 I EGLR 103 (removal of flagstones from garden before contract without informing buyer).

DUTY OF DISCLOSURE

2.18   A seller is under a duty to disclose to an intending buyer latent (as opposed to patent) defects in title of which the seller is aware or has the means of knowledge.[1] Defects in this sense refer to encumbrances affecting the property which will continue to do so after completion of the transaction. This includes 'all outstanding … burdens derogating from absolute ownership of the estate'.[2] A defect is latent if it could not have been discovered by a reasonable inspection of the property. Latent defects include public sewers and sewers vested in local authorities[3] and private sewers in respect of which there are easements to pass sewage.[4] Patent defects (which are not disclosable) are those which a buyer could discover on inspection of the property such as a public footpath[5] or an obvious right of way.[6]

1 *Barnsley's Conveyancing Law and Practice* (4th edn), pp 153–155; *Emmet on Title* vol 1, Ch 4 Pt 3; Silverman *Standard Conditions of Sale* (8th edn, 2013), Ch 5; *Rignall Developments v Halil* [1988] Ch 190; *William Sindall plc v Cambridgeshire County Council* [1994] 1 WLR 1016.

2 *Barnsley* (above), p 153.
3 *Re Brewer and Hankins's Contract* (1899) 80 LT 127; *Re Belcham and Gawley's Contract* [1930] 1 Ch 56.
4 *William Sindall plc v Cambridgeshire County Council.* In that case there was no liability as the sellers did not have knowledge or the means of knowledge of the defect in title. See also *Re Brewer and Hankins's Contract* where it appears that the seller had the means of knowledge.
5 *Bowles v Round* (1800) 5 Ves 508.
6 *Yandle & Sons v Sutton* [1922] 2 Ch 199.

2.19   The duty of disclosure cannot be circumvented by contractual conditions designed to force the buyer to accept a title subject to latent defects of which the seller knows but which he fails to disclose in the contract.[1] However, contractual conditions can provide protection for the buyer if there are latent defects in title of which he has no knowledge, nor the means of knowledge.

1 *Nottingham Patent Brick and Tile Co v Butler* (1885) 15 QBD 261 at 271, per Wills J; affirmed on other grounds by the Court of Appeal (1886) 16 QBD 778; *Rignall Developments v Halil* (above).

2.20   Failure to disclose when there is an obligation to do so entitles the buyer to the appropriate remedy against the seller: rescission of the contract, return of deposit, reduction in the purchase price or to a defence to an action for specific performance.[1] The buyer will only be entitled to rescind or to resist an action for specific performance if the defect is substantial, that is, if in effect he has not obtained what he contracted for.[2] If the defect is not substantial the contract is enforceable but the buyer is entitled to compensation by way of reduction of the purchase price. The buyer can only seek a remedy before completion[3] except that If non-disclosure is fraudulent, the court may set aside the conveyance after completion.[4]

1 *Barnsley* (above), p 155.
2 *Emmet on Title*, 4–027; *Barnsley* (above), pp 640–641 (on the question of substantiality).
3 Emmet on Title, 4-028.
4 *Barnsley* (above), p 155; *Hart v Swaine* (1877) 7 ChD 42.

2.21   In cases where the matter constituting a defect in title is registered as a local land charge, it has been held that it is an incumbrance, registration of which under the Land Charges Act provides actual notice 'to all persons and for all purposes connected with the land affected'.[1] On that basis, a buyer who was unaware of the registered land charge (a town planning scheme) was unable to avoid the contract on the basis of non-disclosure.[2] For that reason, conveyancing practice since 1927 has been to search the Land Charges Register before contract. However, the rule in *Re Forsey and Hollebone's Contract* has been much criticised and in *Rignall Developments Ltd v Halil*,[3] Millett J refused to follow it. He held that a potential liability to repay a grant registered as a local land charge of which the seller had knowledge was subject to the duty of disclosure. In his view, s 198 of the Law of Property Act 1925 is concerned only with notice in relation to the enforcement of third party rights. It has nothing to do with knowledge for the purpose of the duty of disclosure between seller and buyer.[4]

Although Millett J declined to decide whether *Re Forsey and Hollebone's Contract* was correctly decided, he distinguished it on the basis that in that case the incumbrance was irremovable, whereas in the case before him the incumbrance could be removed by repaying the grant if necessary.[5]

It follows that the better view is that although registration gives constructive notice of the local land charge to third parties under s 198 of the Law of Property Act 1925, it does not operate to provide knowledge to the buyer for the purpose of relieving the seller of the duty to disclose.[6]

1 Law of Property Act 1925, s 198.
2 *Re Forsey and Hollebone's Contract* [1927] 2 Ch 379 (decision of Eve J at 386–387, affirmed on other grounds by the Court of Appeal at 388).
3 [1988] Ch 190. See also *Caballero v Henty* (1873–74) LR 9 Ch App 447 (CA).
4 Note that the Law of Property Act 1969, s 24 does not apply to local land charges.
5 According to Millett J, 'the reasoning of the decision [*Re Forsey and Hollebone's Contract*] is too unsound to permit of any extension, however logical, to a situation not directly covered by it': ibid at 203.
6 *Rignall Developments v Halil* (above).

2.22 It appears that the planning and regulatory status of the property is not a matter of title although the point is uncertain.[1] The absence of planning permission or of a consent to discharge to controlled waters under the Water Resources Act 1991 does not, therefore, have to be disclosed by the seller. On the same basis, planning permissions and environmental licences, consents, permits and authorisations are probably not required to be disclosed, even if they are subject to onerous conditions. The same applies to notices revoking or suspending a permit.[2]

1 *Mitchell v Beacon Estates (Finsbury Park) Ltd* (1949–51) 1 P & CR 32; *Gosling v Anderson* (1971) 223 Estates Gazette 1743. *Sakkas v Donford Ltd* (1983) 46 P & CR 290 which is to the contrary, is probably wrongly decided. See *Barnsley* (above) pp 160–161.
2 Eg under the Environmental Permitting (England and Wales) Regulations 2010, SI 2010/675, regs 22 and 37 respectively.

2.23 Potential liabilities arising from the condition of the land or buildings, such as contaminated soil do not have to be disclosed as that would effectively overturn the *caveat emptor* rule.

However, if the liabilities become the subject of statutory action by the regulatory authorities or of disputes with third parties who serve notices under statutory or private law powers, they should be disclosed, assuming that the liability is not purely personal to the seller but will affect any owner.[1]

1 *Carlish v Salt* [1906] 1 Ch 335 (party wall notice and award); *Beyfus v Lodge* [1925] Ch 350 (notice requiring tenant to repair); *Re Englefield Holdings Ltd and Sinclair's Contract* [1962] 1 WLR 1119 (certificate of disrepair); *Citytowns Ltd v Bohemian Properties Ltd* [1986] 2 EGLR 258 (dangerous structure notice served by local authority).

2.24 It follows that the whole range of notices which may be served by the authorities are disclosable, provided that they would affect the position of the buyer as owner of the property if not dealt with satisfactorily. For example, in some cases the buyer may be at risk that in the event of non-compliance with the notice by the seller, the authority may undertake the necessary works in default and recover their expenses from the current owner who by that time may be the buyer.[1] On the other hand, the mere risk that if the seller does not comply with a notice the authority might subsequently serve another notice on the buyer after completion, does not appear to be sufficient to render the original notice disclosable. In such a case, there is no direct link between the seller's liability and any liability on the buyer as owner of the property. A prosecution for non-compliance with environmental law only affects the seller and so is not disclosable.[2]

1 Eg, under the EPA 1990, ss 81(4) (statutory nuisance) and 78N(3)(c), 78P(3) and (4) (contaminated land). See paras **14.61–14.62** and **15.97–15.101** respectively.

2 See eg enforcement notices under the Environmental Permitting (England and Wales) Regulations 2010, SI 2010/675, reg 36.

2.25   This area of the law is not entirely clear cut, however, and so the best practice is to disclose where there is any doubt. In many cases, these matters will be the subject of pre-contract enquiries in respect of which inaccurate or misleading replies could give rise to claims for misrepresentation. The following list of environmental matters indicates whether or not they are disclosable. The list is not exhaustive.

Item	Legislation	Disclosable	Public Register by reference to which disclosure can be made
Species Control Agreements/Orders.	Wildlife and Countryside Act 1981, s 14(4A) and Schedule 9A.	No, because these affect only the owner with whom the environmental authority enters into or offers to enter into a species control agreement.	No.
SSSI.	Wildlife and Countryside Act 1981, ss 28–28R.	Yes, as Local Land Charge.	Yes, Local Land Charges Register.
Management Scheme for SSSI.	Wildlife and Countryside Act 1981, s 28J.	Yes, because a management notice requiring the carrying out of work may be served by Natural England on an owner or occupier who is not giving effect to a management scheme. In default of compliance with a management notice, Natural England may do the work itself and recover any reasonable expenses from the owner or occupier on whom the notice was served: s 28K.	No.

Item	Legislation	Disclosable	Public Register by reference to which disclosure can be made
Limestone Pavement Order.	Wildlife and Countryside Act 1981, s 34.	Yes, because the restrictions imposed affect any owner or occupier of the property.	No.
European site and special nature conservation order.	Birds Directive 79/409/EEC or Habitats Directive 92/43/EEC; Conservation (Natural Habitats &c) Regulations 2010, SI 2010/490.	Yes, because the restrictions imposed affect any owner or occupier of the property.	Yes, register of European sites under the Conservation (Natural Habitats &c) Regulations 1994, SI 1994/2716.
Ramsar Site.	Ramsar Convention.	Probably no, because these designations are only effective through the SSSI system. However, they are disclosable as SSSIs – see above.	No, other than as an SSSI under the Local Land Charges Register.
Waste removal notice.	EPA 1990, s 59ZA.	No, because if not complied with, the Environment Agency may take the required action in default and recover their reasonable expenses only from the person on whom the notice was served. There is no power to make those expenses a charge on the property. However, since it is likely that in the event of non-compliance with the notice, a further notice is likely to be served by the EA, the safer practice is to disclose.	Yes, the Contaminated Land (England) Regulations 2006, Schedule 3, paragraph 15 require enforcing authorities to place details on the register of action taken under s 59.
Abatement Notice.	EPA 1990, s 80 (Statutory Nuisance).	Yes, because in the absence of compliance, the local authority may undertake the work in default and recover their reasonable expenses from the current owner, (ie the buyer), after completion.	No.

Item	Legislation	Disclosable	Public Register by reference to which disclosure can be made
Liability for the local authority's expenses in carrying out any preventive/abatement work.	EPA 1990, s 81(4).	Yes.	No.
Local authority's expenses which become a charge on the premises.	EPA 1990, s 81A.	Yes.	Yes, Local Land Charges Register.
Notice from local authority identifying land as contaminated.	EPA, 1990, s 78B (inserted by EA 1995, s 57).	Probably no, since this affects the regulatory status of the premises rather than imposing any direct obligations. However, since the authority is bound to take further action, disclosure is the safer policy.	The Contaminated Land (England) Regulations 2006, require particulars of the contaminated land to appear in the registers under EPA 1990, s 78R.
Notice designating contaminated land as a 'special site'.	EPA 1990, s 78C (inserted by EA 1995, s 57).	Probably no, since this affects the regulatory status of the premises rather than imposing any direct obligations. However, since the authority is bound to take further action, disclosure is the safer policy.	Yes, registers under EPA 1990, s 78R.
Remediation Notice.	EPA 1990, s 78E (inserted by EA 1995, s 57).	Yes, if it relates to the premises to be sold rather than to work off site in respect of pollutant migration which has already occurred. The enforcing authority has power to carry out work in default of compliance and to charge the cost and interest on the premises if the seller caused or knowingly permitted the presence of the pollutants: EPA 1990, ss 78N(3)(c), 78P(3) and (4).	Yes, registers under EPA 1990, s 78R.

47

Item	Legislation	Disclosable	Public Register by reference to which disclosure can be made
Remediation Statement (setting out work done or to be done by 'appropriate person').	EPA 1990, s 78H(7) (inserted by EA 1995 s 57).	No, since even if not complied with, the liability will not directly affect the buyer. However, the safer practice is to disclose, since if the work is not carried out or is not done properly, liability could fall on the buyer.	Yes, registers under EPA 1990, s 78R.
Enforcing authority's expenses of carrying out remediation under certain conditions in respect of which a charging notice is served.	EPA 1990, s 78P.	Yes.	Yes, Local Land Charge Register when local authority is the enforcing authority.
Works Notice.	Water Resources Act 1991, s 161A.	No, because in the event of default, the Environment Agency may carry out the necessary work, but may only recover their expenses from the party who fails to comply with the notice.	N/A, but there are registers under Water Resources Act 1991, s 190.
Expenses incurred by Environment Agency in cases of default in compliance with works notice.	Water Resources Act 1991, s 161D.	No, because the expenses are only recoverable from the party who fails to comply with the works notice.	No.
Expenses incurred by Environment Agency in carrying out anti-pollution works in certain cases.	Water Resources Act 1991, s 161.	No, because the expenses are only recoverable from the party who caused or knowingly permitted the poisonous, noxious or polluting matter to be in or near controlled waters.	No.
Designation of structure/feature affecting flood risk/ coastal erosion risk.	Flood and Water Management Act 2010, s 30 and Schedule 1.	Yes, as a local land charge.	Yes, Local Land Charges Register.
Local Land Charges (see Chapter 5).	Various and Local Land Charges Act 1975.	Yes.	Yes, Local Land Charges Register.

2.26 Where the disclosable matter is contained in a public register, disclosure can be achieved by reference to the public register, provided that the disclosure is adequate. To be safe the seller should supply to the buyer a copy of the relevant entry in the public register or of the document to which the entry refers.

NEGLIGENT WORKMANSHIP BY THE SELLER

2.27 It has been held that a seller who personally carries out repairs or improvements on the property owes a duty of care to the buyer to take reasonable care to avoid damage to the buyer through faulty workmanship.[1] This principle may also apply to remedial works carried out by the seller to deal with contamination, which create or exacerbate a hazard. However, it is suggested that the principle does not apply to works which have simply proved ineffective in that they have failed to remediate land which is contaminated on account of material which should have been dealt with in the course of the works.

1 *Hone v Benson* (1978) 248 Estates Gazette 1013.

LIABILITY FOR DEFECTIVE BUILDING OPERATIONS

2.28 Under s 1 of the Defective Premises Act 1972 developers, builders, sub-contractors, architects, surveyors and suppliers of purpose-built components are under a duty as from 1 January 1974 to see that building work on new houses is undertaken in a workmanlike manner and with proper materials so that the dwelling is fit for human habitation when it is completed. The duty is owed to the original buyer and to any person who acquires a legal or equitable interest in the dwelling. It cannot be excluded or restricted[1] but does not apply to commercial or industrial buildings.

Statutory liability is excluded where the dwelling is sold with the benefit of the approved NHBC scheme.[2] In that case the builder is bound by the terms of an NHBC Agreement which imposes obligations equivalent to those under the Defective Premises Act.

1 Defective Premises Act 1972, s 6(3).
2 Ibid, s 2.

2.29 Whilst these obligations are aimed primarily at structural defects, such as subsidence, they may also provide a remedy to deal with certain environmental problems provided that they render the dwelling unfit for human habitation. These might include inadequate insulation (for conserving heat and against noise) and the use of building materials which are not resistant to ground contamination or which are prohibited, such as asbestos.

2.30   Builders are also under duties at common law to ensure that their work does not cause damage to third parties, including buyers. However, liability does not extend to pure economic loss and so it has been held that there is no liability in tort for the cost of putting right work carried out negligently. Liability exists, therefore, only for damage to persons or property other than the buildings being constructed.[1]

1 *D & F Estates Ltd v Church Comrs for England* [1989] AC 177, HL; *Murphy v Brentwood District Council* [1991] 1 AC 398; *Bellefield Computer Services Ltd v E Turner & Sons Ltd* [2000] BLR 97.

2.31   It must be remembered that the liabilities described in the preceding three paragraphs only apply to sellers to the extent that they are also the developers, builders etc. to whom the liability specifically applies. Generally, these liabilities are useful because they provide a source of compensation other than the seller. However, because of the limitation of the Act to residential property, buyers of commercial and industrial property often require collateral warranties to be given by the contractor who carries out the work or by the architect or (in the case of remediation work) by the environmental consultant.

LEAVING WASTE ON THE PREMISES

2.32   Leaving waste on a property after another person becomes entitled to possession constitutes an actionable trespass.[1] It follows that a seller (or landlord) who leaves waste on a property at completion of the sale (or commencement of the lease) commits a trespass against the buyer (or tenant). This applies for example to drums of waste chemicals or waste fuel left behind in drums or underground storage tanks on the sale of industrial premises. However, it would not apply to substances which have contaminated the soil and effectively become part of it. In that case, the *caveat emptor* rule applies. On the other hand, if substances such as 'free phase' hydrocarbons beneath the surface which are not part of the soil (for example, because they are floating on groundwater), are capable of being pumped out, in principle it is an actionable trespass for the seller to leave them in situ on completion of the sale.[2] The seller can avoid this problem altogether by including in the contract a provision to the effect that the hazardous substances will be conveyed to the buyer with the property to the extent that they are not part of it.

1 *Hudson v Nicholson* [1839] 5 M & W 437; *Konskier v B Goodman Ltd* [1928] 1 KB 421.
2 It is possible that some courts may ignore principle and take a 'robust' view that such 'free phase' substances are effectively part of the ground. In any case, if the sale agreement provides specifically for liabilities relating to contaminants present under the surface of the ground at completion it should follow that there is an implied licence for them to remain in situ following completion. It is notable that the CJEU held that spilled hydrocarbons were waste in the *Van de Walle case* [2004] ECRI-7613. However, neither that case (which turns on the meaning of waste in an earlier version of the Waste Framework Directive) nor the Waste Framework Directive 2008/98/EC which partly overturns it are strictly germane to the present point which is not concerned with the European law of waste.

2.33   Usually, there is an express provision in the contract that the seller will give vacant possession on completion.[1] There is an implied obligation to that effect under an open contract.[2] The meaning of the term 'vacant possession' may vary depending on the context.[3] In *Cumberland Consolidated Holdings v Ireland*[4] the Court of Appeal held that 'the right to actual unimpeded physical enjoyment is comprised in the right to vacant possession'. However, the right is not breached by every physical impediment. 'It must be an impediment which substantially prevents or interferes with the right of possession of a substantial part of the property'.[5] In that case, vacant possession was not given where the cellars, forming part of a warehouse sold to the buyer, were unusable due to the presence of rubbish including many sacks of hardened cement.[6] On the other hand, the opposite conclusion has been reached in the case of garden rubbish which merges into and becomes part of the surrounding earth.[7] The ease with which waste can be removed is a factor in determining whether vacant possession has been given.[8] Although mere knowledge by the buyer of the presence of such an impediment to vacant possession should not be relevant,[9] waiver or acceptance of the position by the buyer may defeat a claim.[10]

1 See eg *Standard Conditions of Sale* (5th edn), Special Condition 4; *Standard Commercial Property Conditions of Sale* (2nd edn), Special Condition 2.
2 *Cook v Taylor* [1942] 2 All ER 85 at 87; *Midland Bank Ltd v Farmpride Hatcheries Ltd* [1981] 2 EGLR 147 at 151. See generally, *Megarry & Wade: The Law of Real Property* (8th edn, 2012) paras 15–089–15–091.
3 *Topfell Ltd v Galley Properties Ltd* [1979] 1 WLR 446 at 449.
4 [1946] KB 264.
5 [1946] KB 264 at 271. It is unlikely that the free phase hydrocarbons discussed in para **2.32** would normally cause substantial interference with the right of possession of a substantial part of the property, except possibly where soil had to be moved in the course of a redevelopment.
6 *Cumberland Consolidated Holdings Ltd v Ireland* [1946] KB 264.
7 *Hynes v Vaughan* (1985) 50 P & CR 444.
8 Ibid at 458. Presumably the cost of disposal is also a factor.
9 See *Megarry & Wade, op cit* para 15-089.
10 *Cumberland Consolidated Holdings Ltd v Ireland* (supra) at 271.

THE EFFECT OF THE TRANSFER OF PROPERTY ON ENVIRONMENTAL LIABILITIES – THE LIMITS OF *CAVEAT EMPTOR*

2.34   The *caveat emptor* rule only affects the contractual position between seller and buyer. It does not affect the liabilities of either seller or buyer to third parties. It follows that after the transfer of the property to the buyer, the seller remains liable to third parties in respect of any environmental matter for which he was liable before the transfer. For example, if the seller caused contamination on the property which after the sale to the buyer escapes to neighbouring land and causes damage, the seller is liable to the neighbouring owner.[1]

1 Following the principle in *Roswell v Prior* (1706) 12 Mod Rep 635.

2.35   Accordingly, the transfer does not operate to transfer liabilities from the seller to the buyer nor to relieve the seller of liability. The reason is that in principle a person liable (the obligee) to another (the obligor) cannot by some arrangement with a third party relieve himself of liability to the obligor without the latter's consent. The obligor remains entitled to his remedy against the obligee. Nor can this position be altered by a purported transfer of liabilities from seller to buyer in the contract, for exactly the same reason. Otherwise it would be easy for sellers to avoid their environmental liabilities by transferring them to men of straw.

2.36   However, after the property transfer the buyer will be an additional target for liabilities, because he may acquire his own liabilities as owner of the property; liabilities will run in tandem with those of the seller arising prior to the transfer. In the example referred to above, if the buyer buys the property and either becomes aware or should be aware that contamination on the property is threatening to damage neighbouring land, he may be liable for continuing the nuisance.[1] The seller remains liable for causing the nuisance. The neighbour whose property is damaged could sue the seller, the buyer or both. If either party is sued and found liable, that party can ask the court to apportion the damages with the other party (if also liable) on a just and equitable basis.[2]

1 *Sedleigh-Denfield v O'Callaghan* [1940] AC 880. More generally see Chs 13 and 14.
2 Civil Liability (Contribution) Act 1978. See paras **2.45**, **9.03** and **15.76–15.96** in relation to the exclusion of the seller from liability under EPA 1990, Part IIA.

STANDARD CONTRACTUAL TERMS RELATING TO THE *CAVEAT EMPTOR* RULE

2.37   The *caveat emptor* rule may be altered in relation to an individual sale by the terms of the contract between the parties. Several provisions of the standard contractual terms are relevant. Condition 3.2.1 of the Standard Conditions of Sale,[1] for example, provides that:

> 'The buyer accepts the property in the physical state it is in at the date of the contract, unless the seller is building or converting it.'

1 5th edn. Condition 3.2.1 of the Standard Commercial Property Conditions (2nd edn) is identical.

2.38   Terms of this type, which give contractual effect to the *caveat emptor* rule, apply to the physical condition of the land. Accordingly, buyers cannot complain if the soil is found to be contaminated. Although the buyer is not obliged to accept the property in a state which is unusable due to materials left on it[1] the clause does apply where rubbish left on the property now forms part of the soil.[2]

1 *Cumberland Consolidated Holdings Ltd v Ireland* [1946] KB 264. See generally para **2.33**.
2 *Hynes v Vaughan* (1985) 50 P & CR 444.

2.39 On the other hand, the standard contractual terms also make provision regarding the encumbrances and liabilities to which the sale is subject. The Standard Conditions of Sale state that the property is sold free from encumbrances other than those in certain categories subject to which the property is sold, namely:

(a) those specified in the contract;
(b) those discoverable by inspection of the property before the date of the contract;
(c) those the seller does not and could not reasonably know about;
(d) those, other than mortgages, which the buyer knows about;
(e) entries made before the date of the contract on any public register except those maintained by the Land Registry or its Land Charges Department or by Companies House;
(f) public requirements.[1]

1 Clauses 3.1.1 and 3.1.2. The equivalent clauses 3.1.1 and 3.1.2 of the Standard Commercial Property Conditions (second edition) use different wording in part.

2.40 The main effect of these clauses from an environmental perspective is that the buyer has no right of action against the seller in respect of any environmental matters affecting the property which are recorded on public registers or in respect of any public requirements relating to such matters. These clauses do not avoid the duty of disclosure under the general law which is referred to above.[1] The sting in the tail is in clause 3.1.4 which provides that:

> 'The buyer is to bear the cost of complying with any outstanding public requirement and is to indemnify the seller against any liability resulting from a public requirement.'[2]

Accordingly, if the seller is liable to undertake remedial work on the property pursuant to a remediation notice served under Part 2A of the EPA 1990[3] or to undertake works pursuant to an abatement notice served under s 80 of the EPA 1990, the buyer is bound to indemnify the seller in respect of his expenses.[4]

1 Paras **2.18–2.26**.
2 Condition 3.1.4 of the Standard Commercial Property Conditions (second edition) is in identical form.
3 Introduced by the EA 1995, s 57; see paras **15.34–15.104**.
4 There is a wider indemnity in Standard Condition 4.6.4 in relation to continuing obligations affecting the property. This could include liabilities other than public requirements.

2.41 Standard Condition 3.1.4 extends to public requirements outstanding at the date of the contract, not to public requirements made after the date of the contract, even if they relate to the condition of the property at and before the date of contract. It follows that under the Standard Conditions and the Standard Commercial Property Conditions, the buyer would not be obliged to indemnify the seller in respect of compliance with an abatement notice served under s 80 of the EPA 1990 or a remediation notice served under s 57 of the Environment Act 1995, after the date of the contract.[1]

1 See paras **14.12–14.57** and **15.60** et seq respectively.

2.42 In *Lambson Fine Chemicals Ltd v Merlion Capital Housing Ltd*[1] (the 'Blue Billy' contamination case), the judge commented on several provisions of the sale contract:

> '9. MATTERS AFFECTING THE PROPERTY
>
> The Property is sold subject to such of the following matters as relate to it:
>
> ...
>
> 9.5 All matters recorded in any registers open to public inspection or revealed by searches and enquiries that the Buyer has made or a prudent buyer ought to have made;
>
> 9.6 All matters which would be evident on an inspection or survey of the Property
>
> ...
>
> 15.1 The Buyer acknowledges that prior to the date of this agreement it has been given permission and an adequate opportunity to carry out its own investigation into the physical condition of the Property and the extent to which the Property is affected by the presence of substances and has been provided by [sic] all information necessary to assess the state and condition of the Property and the implications of any presence and as such has deemed to purchase with full knowledge thereof.'

The judge concluded that the effect of those clauses was to assign the risk of unforeseen ground conditions fairly and squarely on the buyer.[2]

1 [2008] Env LR 37. See para **2.14** above.
2 ibid, paras 135–138. The letter signed by Lambson's director which is referred to in para **2.14** above was annexed to and formed part of the contract. The judge commented that the letter had, if possible, to be construed in a way not inconsistent with the contract terms. In his view, its effect was to pass part of the risk to the seller, but only to the extent that the director knew of further contamination in the central area of the site which was not identified in the URS report.

ENVIRONMENTAL INFORMATION – THE POSITION OF THE SELLER

2.43 It has been noted above that, as an exception to the *caveat emptor* rule, the seller may be required to reveal certain information on environmental matters to the buyer. The contract (standard form or otherwise) may also require such information to be provided. However, quite apart from these cases, the seller should consider gathering environmental information about the property before he begins negotiations with the buyer.

Once the seller has the full picture of the nature and extent of contamination on the property he will be in a position to develop an effective sale strategy. He will be forewarned of any issues which the buyer may raise and will be able to deal with them.

2.44 In certain cases it may be prudent to disclose the information at an early stage, particularly if the buyer is likely to discover the matters concerned through his own investigations. Otherwise, the seller risks being confronted with the problems at a late stage of the negotiations and facing demands either for a stringent indemnity or for a reduction in the purchase price. At worst, the deal may fall through altogether.

2.45   Under certain circumstances, if the seller ensures that the buyer has sufficient information as to the presence and broad measure of contamination on the property, he will be relieved from liability under Part 2A of the EPA 1990. That liability will be assumed by the buyer.[1] For that reason, the seller has another incentive to provide information on contamination to the buyer.

1 See Test 3, paras 7.46–7.50 of the Part 2A Contaminated Land Statutory Guidance (April 2012). See further Ch 9 and para **15.88**.

Chapter 3

Preliminary enquiries

INFORMATION FROM THE SELLER

3.01 The seller of any property (and/or his advisers) is likely to have access to a considerable amount of information concerning the property, not least about environmental matters. The seller is not bound to provide this information except in the case of the limited duty of disclosure under the general law[1] or as provided by the contract.[2] However, he may conclude that it is better to be helpful where this is possible in order to assist the smooth progress of the transaction. In addition, disclosure may enable the seller to transfer liability relating to contaminated land under Part 2A of the Environmental Protection Act 1990 to the buyer.[3]

1 See Ch 2.
2 Ibid.
3 See Chs 2, 9 and 15.

3.02 Nonetheless, the danger is that the seller, in trying to be helpful or to be seen to be helpful, provides information which is incorrect or misleading. *Dodd v Crown Estate Comrs*[1] is a classic example of a seller providing a plan of the drainage system which incorrectly showed that the drains from the property led to the main sewer. The buyer was held to be entitled to damages for misrepresentation.

1 [1995] NPC 29, [1995] EGCS 35. Discussed in para **2.13**.

3.03 The risks inherent in replying to preliminary enquiries have resulted in a marked reluctance to give answers in relation to environmental questions, particularly where standard form enquiries are used. This highlights the need for some preliminary research on environmental matters by the buyer, so that enquiries directed to the seller can be focused on actual or likely problems. Sellers will find it much more difficult to avoid replying to preliminary enquiries under those circumstances.

3.04 Inevitably, however, preliminary enquiries cannot always be targeted specifically in that way, and so standard form enquiries continue to be necessary. As environmental issues have increasingly become an accepted part of the property equation, sellers and their advisers are providing more informative replies than had previously been the norm. One reason for the shift is the potential for a buyer's solicitor to be found to be negligent for failing to seek environmental information from sellers. In this respect, the Law Society's warning card on contaminated land, issued in June 2001, states, among other things, that '[i]n every transaction [solicitors] must consider whether contamination is an issue'.

3.05 Many of the published standard form preliminary enquiries contain individual enquiries which deal with environmental concerns.[1] These relate to such matters as:

- drainage;
- the metering of water supplies;
- licences to abstract water;
- disputes with neighbours over matters such as noise, rubbish or other pollution;
- flooding; and
- reclaimed land.

Many solicitors' firms have adopted their own standard form enquiries on environmental matters. The Commercial Property Standard Enquiries have been developed by lawyers from the London Property Lawyers Support Group. These enquiries, which include environmental enquiries, are sponsored by the British Property Federation and published by PLC Publishing.[2] The enquiries are intended to represent a fair position between seller and buyer so as to encourage sellers' solicitors to produce more useful replies.

The CPSE includes enquiries relating to environmental issues which are referred to briefly but not set out in full in the following sections.

1 Eg *Encyclopaedia of Forms and Precedents* (5th edn), Form 26 – Pre-contract enquiries relating to a freehold or leasehold commercial property with or without a residential element, subject or not to tenancies, section M, 'Environmental Matters'; ibid, Form 28 – Environmental pre-contract and due diligence enquiries. The enquiries first appeared in a supplement to the Encyclopaedia.
2 Section 15 of General pre-contract enquiries for all commercial property transactions, CPSE.1 (version 3.5) sets out environmental enquiries but some other sections are also relevant. Section 11 of the General short form pre-contract enquiries for all property transactions, CPSE.7 (version 1.0) sets out shorter environmental enquiries.

3.06

8.   PHYSICAL CONDITION
8.1(e) flooding[1]
8.2   Green Deal Plan[2]
8.3   presence of asbestos[3]
8.4   asbestos surveys/assessments[4]
8.5   asbestos management plans
8.6   other hazardous substances used in structures
8.7   asbestos or other hazardous substances removed from property
8.10(b) conduits, fixtures, plant and equipment requiring significant expenditure within next three years [relevant to asbestos removal and/ or replacement of ozone depleting substances]

1 This may affect the availability of insurance and may not be revealed by a survey.
2 Energy Act 2011.

3 Asbestos (and asbestos containing materials) can cause asbestosis, mesothelioma and other diseases when particles are inhaled. Its manufacture, marketing and use are strictly controlled, as is its discharge into air, water and land. Health and safety aspects are regulated by the Control of Asbestos Regulations 2012, SI 2012/632. The use of asbestos in buildings has been banned since 1999. See also *Margereson and Hancock v JW Robers* [1996] Env. LR 304. The Health and Safety Executive have published information and guidance on surveying and managing asbestos on its website (www.hse.gov.uk).

4 Control of Asbestos Regulations 2012, SI 2012/632, reg 4.

3.07

10　　UTILITIES AND SERVICES

10.1(b) and (c)　name of the individual within seller responsible for energy supplies who may be contacted for information about implementation of the Carbon Reduction Commitment Energy Efficiency Scheme (CRC Scheme)[1] in relation to the property

10.2　details of utility supply

10.3　half-hourly metre [relevant to qualification for CRC Scheme]

10.4　supply contracts and other relevant documents [including water abstraction licences]

1 CRC Energy Efficiency Scheme Order 2013, S1 2013/1119.

3.08

12　　PLANNNING AND BUILDING REGULATIONS[1]

12.1　copies of planning permissions and other planning related approvals and consents

12.2　which are still valid?

12.3　copies of certificates under planning legislation

12.4　authorisation of existing buildings by other means

12.5　authorisation of existing use by other means

12.6　existing use of the property

12.7　(non listed buildings and conservation areas) confirmation that necessary planning consents have been obtained for buildings/engineering works in last 10 years

12.8　(listed buildings and conservation areas) details of listing, works undertaken and confirmation that all necessary consents have been obtained

12.9　breaches of planning conditions

12.10 legal challenges (actual or expected) to any planning consent

12.11 details of planning applications not decided, refused or withdrawn or subject to appeal

12.12 planning conditions which need to be satisfied for development to proceed and steps taken

12.13 letters/notices under planning legislation

12.14 possibility of planning enforcement order due to apparent breaches of planning control deliberately concealed

12.15 possibility of listing in local authority's list of assets of community value

1 See generally Ch 18.

3.09

13   STATUTORY AGREEMENTS AND INFRASTRUCTURE
      (eg highway agreements under s 38 of the Highway Act 1980, sewer
      agreements under s 104 of the Water Industry Act 1991 and planning
      agreements under s 106 of the Town and Country Planning Act 1990)[1]
13.1 provide details of these and of related breaches and outstanding
      obligations
13.2 requirement to enter into agreement/obligation with public authority or
      utility provider
13.3 proposals relating to planning, compulsory purchase powers
      infrastructure or environmental health affecting present use of property[2]
13.4 matters registerable (but not registered) on local land charges register[2]
13.5 charges/notices not complied with
13.6 grants made or claimed and circumstances in which they are repayable
13.7 compensation paid or claimed under planning legislation or following
      compulsory purchase

1 See generally Chs 17 and 18.
2 See generally Ch 5.

3.10

14   STATUTORY AND OTHER REQUIREMENTS
14.1 breaches alleged breaches or claims under statutory requirements or
      byelaws affecting the property current use or storage of substances[1]
14.2 details of notices requiring works to property under statute or otherwise[2]
14.3 licences or consents required for current activities[3]
14.6 Energy Performance Certificate (EPC) supplied?[4]
14.7 if not where can EPC be inspected or why is it not needed?
14.8 latest inspection report for air-conditioning system[5]

1 This wide enquiry deals amongst other things with legislation on waste management – see
  Ch 16, and hazardous substances, eg the Planning (Hazardous Substances) Act 1990 and the
  Planning (Hazardous Substances) Regulations 2015, SI 2015/627.
2 This enquiry includes notices requiring works under the Building Act 1984 and the statutory
  nuisance provisions in Part 3 of the Environmental Protection Act 1990.
3 eg under the Environmental Permitting (England and Wales) Regulations 2010, SI 2010/675
  as amended (for certain industrial activities, waste operations and water discharges), Part 2 of
  the Water Resources Act 1991 (water abstraction) and s 118 of the Water Industry Act 1991
  (discharges to sewers).
4 Energy Performance of Buildings (England and Wales) Regulations 2012, SI 2010/3118.
5 Inspections of air-conditioning systems are required every five years under the Energy
  Performance of Buildings (England and Wales) Regulations, reg 18 to promote the energy
  performance improvement of buildings.

3.11

15   ENVIRONMENTAL
15.1 copies of environmental reports
15.2 licences and authorisations given under environmental law and
      confirmation of compliance[1]
15.3 authorisations required under environmental law[2]

15. 4   past and present uses and activities, presence of hazardous substances, present past storage areas for hazardous or radioactive substances, existing or former storage tanks, present or past landfills[3]

15.5   details of notices, correspondence, legal proceedings, disputes or complaints relating to environmental problems within last ten years

15.6   disposal of waste or effluent including consents, agreements and correspondence

15.7   actual, alleged or potential breaches of environmental law, licences or authorisations and other environmental problems affecting the property or nearby land which may affect the property

15.8   environmental insurance policies

1 See para **3.10** fn 3.

2 This enquiry is focused exclusively on environmental law – see para **3.10** fn 3.

3 This enquiry deals with potentially contaminative use of the property. See the contaminated land legislation in the EPA 1990, Part 2A (Ch 15) as well as the waste control provisions of the EPA 1990 (particularly s 59), the Water Resources Act 1991, ss 161 and 161A–D: see Ch 17. Claims against the owner or occupier of contaminated land may also be brought in nuisance and under the Occupiers Liability Acts 1957 and 1984. Conditions attached to planning permissions should also be examined to see if any require investigation or remediation of contamination. If so, further enquiries should be raised as to the nature and extent of any work carried out to comply with those conditions.
Storage tanks, in particular underground storage tanks, tend to corrode and leak after a period of time, causing contamination to the ground and/or groundwater. There are statutory requirements relating to some storage tanks on land which contain hazardous substances. See the Planning (Hazardous Substances) Act 1990 and the Planning (Hazardous Substances) Regulations 2015, SI 2015/627 and in relation to the storage of silage, slurry or fuel oil on farms, see the Water Resources (Control of Pollution) (Silage, Slurry and Agricultural Fuel Oil) (England) Regulations 2010, SI 2010/639. See also Protecting our Water, Soil and Air, A Code of Good Agricultural Practice for farmers, growers and land managers, issued by DEFRA in 2009, parts of which form a statutory code under the Water Resources Act 1991, s 97. In the case of agricultural land a specific enquiry as to compliance with the legislation and the Code of Practice may be relevant. Planning conditions may also be relevant. Further, local petroleum licensing authorities regulate the installation, operation, decommissioning and removal of underground storage tanks which store petroleum spirit: Petroleum (Consolidation) Regulations 2014, SI 2014/1637. A person who has custody or control of an above ground storage tank must ensure that that the tank has secondary containment: Control of Pollution (Oil Storage) (England) Regulations 2001, SI 2001/2954. The regulations exempt certain containers: reg 2(2). A failure to do so may result in an unlimited fine: reg 9.

3.12

27   NOTICES

27.1   notices and related correspondence affecting the property or neighbouring property[1]

27.2   notices expected

1 This enquiry has been the subject of a recent High Court decision in *Thorp v Abbotts* [2015] EWHC 2142. The court held that 'affecting the property' refers to effects on the property itself, or the use or enjoyment of it. Possible effects on the value or desirability of the property are insufficient. However, the effect need not be a direct physical interference. A material increase in noise or smell, or an adverse effect on the view, could 'affect' the property. The requirement to disclose applies to notices (which have legal effect) and communications (which are less formal) but in either case they must indicate a sufficient degree of likelihood that an event will happen. A notice or communication must be sent by a person who proposes to take an action (for example a letter from a neighbour informing the seller that he intends to apply for planning permission

for a development), or from some regulatory body responsible for authorising or permitting that action, but not from other persons. So pamphlets from a local protest group objecting to a nearby development are not within this category.

3.13

28   DISPUTES
28.1   other disputes, claims, actions, demands or complaints

3.14   The following sections set out additional environmental enquiries. They do not claim to be comprehensive.

Ozone depleting substances[1]

3.15

- Are any ozone depleting substances (ODS) used or contained in any equipment on the property?
- If so, please specify the type and quantity of the substance in question, the equipment in which it is used or contained and whether any contracts have been entered into to substitute another substance.

1 These substances are being phased out progressively under the Montreal Protocol 1987 and resulting EU legislation, currently Regulation (EC) No 1005/2009. The current position is summarised in the Table below. The main issue in practice is that equipment containing ODSs such as refrigerators, air-conditioning units and fire extinguishers need to have the ODSs replaced or topped up periodically due to leakages. Whilst it is not unlawful to have equipment which contains an ODS after it has been phased out, it is unlawful to replace or top up that ODS after its use has been banned. Under those circumstances, either the equipment will need to be retrofitted so that it can take a lawful replacement to the banned ODS, or the equipment itself may have to be replaced altogether.

Controlled Substances	Common Use	EU Legislation	Status
Chlorofluorocarbons (CFCs) eg: CFC-11 (R11), CFC-12 (R12), CFC-114 (R114)	refrigerants	Regulation (EC) No 1005/2009	Production, placing on market and use* prohibited
Halons 1211, 1301, 2402	fire extinguishants fire protection systems	Regulation (EC) No 1005/2009	Production, placing on market and use* prohibited except for certain critical uses specified in Annex VI of the Regulation, provided that halons must not be used for such critical uses after the applicable End Date by which date the fire extinguishers or fire protection systems containing halons must be decommissioned

Controlled Substances	Common Use	EU Legislation	Status
Hydrochlorofluorocarbons (HCFCs) eg: HCFC-22 (R22), HCFC-123 (R123), HCFC-1416b (R1416b)	air conditioning systems refrigerants	Regulation (EC) No 1005/2009	Unrestricted production of virgin HCFCs prohibited after 31 December 2009. Thereafter they are being phased out up to 31 December 2019. Up until then they may be placed on the market and used if the Commission grants a time limited exemption for a particular use if technically feasible alternative substances are not available or cannot be used Use* of recycled/ reclaimed HCFCs prohibited for maintenance or servicing of existing refrigeration, air conditioning and heat pump equipment after 31 December 2014

* 'Use' means the utilisation of controlled substances ... in the ... maintenance or servicing, including refilling, of products or equipment ...

Legionella[1]

3.16

- Are there any cooling towers or evaporative condensers on the property within the meaning of the Notification of Cooling Towers and Evaporative Condensers Regulations 1992?[2]
- If so, are they notifiable devices and have they been notified to the local authority in accordance with the Regulations?
- Please give details of all steps taken to maintain them.

1 There are general controls under the Health and Safety at Work etc Act 1974, ss 2–4 and the EPA 1990, Pt III (ss 79–84). Claims in public and private nuisance and under the Occupiers' Liability Acts 1957 and 1984 are also possible.
2 SI 1992/2225.

Sick building syndrome[1]

3.17

- Have any buildings or plant on the property ever been associated with sick building illnesses? If so, please supply details.

1 This area has been little explored, but see the Sixth Report of the House of Commons Environment Committee on Indoor Pollution (1991). Relevant general controls are the Health and Safety at Work etc Act 1974, ss 2–4 and EPA 1990, Pt III (ss 79–84).

Radon gas[1]

3.18

• Is the property located in an area which has been identified as being affected by radon?[2]
• If so, has the property been tested for radon and, if so, when and what were the results?[3]
• What action has been taken in consequence of the test results, and has any further testing been carried out and what were the results?

1 See commentary at paras **6.19–6.21**.
2 The buyer should have the information but the response to local authority enquiry 3.13 in Ch 6 should also confirm the position.
3 The action level of radon gas is 200 Bq/m3 above which precautions are necessary. Defra and the Health Protection Agency have information about the effects of radon and radon-affected areas in the UK available on their websites (www.hpa.org.uk/radiation/radon/publications/htm and www.defra.gov.uk/environment/radioactivity/background/radon.htm).

Noise[1]

3.19

• Have there been any complaints about noise in relation to the property or any part of it? If so, please supply full details.
• Have there been any complaints about noise by occupiers of the property in relation to neighbouring properties? If so, please supply full details.

1 See the Noise Act 2006, the Control of Pollution Act 1974, Pt III (ss 60–74), the EPA 1990, Pt III (ss 79–84) and the common law relating to private and public nuisance. Aircraft noise is generally exempt from action in nuisance: see eg the Civil Aviation Act 1982, s 76.

ADDITIONAL ENVIRONMENTAL ENQUIRIES: INDUSTRIAL PROPERTIES AND/OR HEAVILY CONTAMINATED LAND

Deposits and discharges[1]

3.20

• Except as already answered, is any waste deposited, kept or treated on the property?[2]
• Are there any discharges of effluent from the property to inland or coastal waters?[3]

- Are there any discharges of trade effluent into public sewers?[4]
- Are any emissions made into the air?[5]
- Are any waste disposal contracts in operation with respect to the property?[6]
- Are any hazardous substances kept on-site?[7]

1 The Environmental Permitting (England and Wales) Regulations 2010, SI 2010/675 (EPR 2010) and see Schs 9, 9A and 10. Those Regulations replace earlier legislation, including the Pollution Prevention and Control (England and Wales) Regulations 2000, SI 2000/1973, which were phased in to replace controls under EPA 1990, Pt I (ss 1–28) and the Environmental Protection (Prescribed Processes and Substances) Regulations 1991, SI 1991/472 (as amended).
2 Landfill sites, waste transfer stations and waste treatment stations must be permitted: EPR 2010. If the site is closed, the permit may be surrendered: reg 25 (see Ch 16). Any deposit of waste, or waste disposal or recovery operation must be permitted unless it is exempt. If exempt, it must generally be registered by the Environment Agency: Sch 2, para 3.
3 See the EPR 20, reg 38(1), Schs 21 and 22; Water Resources Act 1991, ss 161 and 161A–D.
4 See the Water Industry Act 1991, s 118 and the Trade Effluents (Prescribed Processes and Substances) Regulations 1989, SI 1989/1156.
5 See the EPR 2010 (see Ch 20) and the Clean Air Act 1993.
6 Such contracts are not binding on the buyer. However, he may wish to take them over from the seller in which case he will have to consider their provisions and the practical arrangements from the viewpoint of the duty of care under EPA 1990, s 34: (see Ch 16).
7 See the Dangerous Substances (Notification and Marking of Sites) Regulations 1990, SI 1990/304, the Planning (Hazardous Substances) Act 1990 and the Planning (Hazardous Substances) Regulations 2015, SI 2015/627 and the Control of Major Accident Hazards Regulations 2015, SI 2015/483.

Water abstraction[1]

3.21

- Is any water abstracted for the benefit of the property?
- If so, please indicate (by reference to a plan) the abstraction point and state the quantities of water abstracted per day and the purpose for which it is used.

1 See the Water Resources Act 1991, ss 24–72 and the Water Resources (Abstraction and Impounding) Regulations 2006, SI 2006/641; Ch 17.

Polychlorinated biphenyls (PCBs) and polychlorinated terphenyls (PCTs)[1]

3.22

- Are there (or have there been) any PCBs or PCTs in electrical transformers, capacitors or other equipment at the property?
- If so, please specify the uses of the PCBs and/or PCTs at the property, their quantity, whether they are contained and/or enclosed, their precise location and (if applicable) when they were removed from the property

1 PCBs and PCTs were widely used in electrical apparatus but are persistent organic pollutants and carcinogens. The EU Directive on the disposal of polychlorinated biphenyls and polychlorinated terphenyls (96/59/EC) has been implemented by the Environmental Protection (Disposal of

Polychlorinated Biphenyls and Other Dangerous Substances) (England and Wales) Regulations 2000, SI 2000/1043 which ban the holding of PCBs, PCTs, other specified dangerous substances and equipment contaminated by them from 1 January 2001 subject to exceptions.

Radioactive substances[1]

3.23

- Are there or have there been any radioactive substances or radioactive wastes present on the property?
- If so, please specify their type, quantity, location and (if applicable) when they were removed from the property.

1 See the EPR 2010 and particularly Sch 23.

Explosives[1]

3.24

- Are there or have there been explosives manufactured, used or stored on the property?
- If so, please specify the substances used, the quantities, their location and when they were used or stored on the property.

1 See the Explosives Act 1875 and the Explosives Regulations 2014, SI 2014/1638.

Chapter 4

Freedom of access to environmental information

INTRODUCTION

4.01   The Freedom of Information Act 2000 ('FOIA 2000') attracted much media publicity. It has domestic origins, being a product of the then New Labour Government. But it is the Environmental Information Regulations 2004 ('EIR 2004'), which also came into force on 1 January 2005 – a product of the international obligations of the Aarhus Convention on Access to Information, Public Participation in Decision-making and Access to Justice in Environmental Matters ('Aarhus Convention') and an EU directive – that has proven to have the greatest impact for those involved in the property transactions process. This is because in respect of environmental information, the EIR 2004 effectively takes precedence over the FOIA 2000. Where the EIR 2004 differ from the FOIA 2000, they do so in ways which favour disclosure. Both the UK and the European Union are signatories to the Treaty. The consequence of this is that the UK is obliged to implement the terms under international law as a signatory to the Convention, but also as a result of the obligations imposed upon it by the EC under Directive 2003/4/EC. Accordingly, when one looks for the correct interpretation of the EIR 2004, one needs to look also at the terms of the Aarhus Convention as well as the requirement of Directive 2003/4/EC. The Directive and the EIR 2004 should be interpreted with regard to the UN Implementation Guide.[1] It is highly authoritative in assisting in the interpretation of the Convention, and '[w]hile this Guide does not purport to be an official interpretation of the Convention, it can serve as an invaluable tool in the hands of governments and parliaments engaged in that task.'[2] The usefulness of the Implementation Guide for the purposes of interpretation has been resounded by the European Court of Justice ('ECJ') in *Solvay v Region Wallone* (C-182/10) [2012] 1 Info LR 456 [at 28], in which the ECJ interpreted the Aarhus Convention by reference to the Convention's Implementation Guide, albeit noting that the Guide is not binding.

It would be a mistake, however, to assume that the new Directive is simply an Aarhus product. The EC had already adopted Council Directive 90/313/EEC on 7 June 1990 on the freedom of access to information on the environment.[3] That directive is repealed. In 'the interest of increased transparency', a decision was taken to replace the Directive rather than to amend it, 'so as to provide interested parties with a single, clear and cogent legislative text.'[4] The case law on the previous directive will provide some assistance in the interpretation of the Directive.

1 This can be found at http://www.unece.org/en/pp/acig.pdf.
2 Foreword to the UN Implementation Guide, at p v.
3 Implemented in England and Wales by Environmental Information Regulations 1992 (as amended in 1998). For a discussion of the impact of the 2004 Regulations, see McCracken, Jones and Pereira, *Statutory Nuisance* (3rd edn, Bloomsbury Professional, 2012).
4 See para (6) of the preamble to Directive 2003/4/EC. This approach is a welcome contrast to that adopted for the amendment of the EIA Directive 85/337 by 91/11/EC.

Relationship between the EIR 2004 and the FOIA 2000

4.02   Section 1(1) of the FOIA 2000 states:

> 'Any person making a request for information to a public authority is entitled–
> (a)   to be informed in writing by the public authority whether it holds information of that description specified in the request, and
> (b)   if that is the case, to have that information communicated to him.'

This right is not confined to any particular subject matter, any particular person or a showing a recognised need to know. However, the rights contained in s 1(1) are subject to s 2. In respect of the right to communication of information, s 2 disapplies the right in relation to any information that is 'exempt information' by virtue of either an 'absolute exemption' (listed at s 2(3)) or an exemption that is not absolute, provided that in all the circumstances the public interest in maintaining the exemption outweighs the public interest in disclosing the information.[1]

The classes of 'exempt information' are listed in Pt II (ss 22–44) of the FOIA 2000. Some refer to a class other require that disclosure should have a likelihood of causing a specific harm. Section 39 deals with 'environmental information.'

Regulation 20 of the EIR 2004 replaces 'Regulations under s. 74' with 'environmental information Regulations'.[2] This reflects the fact that the EIR 2004 are made under s 2(2) of the ECA 1972, rather than s 74 FOIA 2000. The subordination of the FOIA 2000 is not quite comprehensive: s 39 is not an absolute exemption (see s 2(3)). This means that 'environmental information' could be retrieved from a public authority:

(a)   under the EIR 2004; and
(b)   whether or not exempted from disclosure by the EIR 2004, under the FOIA 2000, unless in all the circumstances of the case the public interest in maintaining the s 39 exemption 'outweighs the public interest in disclosing the information'.

The exceptions under the EIR 2004 are generally narrower than the exemptions given under the FOIA 2000. It is difficult to think of examples where a request under the EIR 2004 for environmental information could be refused but granted under the FOIA 2000. Put simply, this means that for any request for information relating to the environment, the more extensive EIR 2004 trumps the FOIA 2000.

It is however an indication of the widespread ignorance about the EIR 2004 that both applicants and public authorities often rely upon the FOIA 2000 when the information in question is 'environmental information'. Indeed, the

Information Tribunal has often been faced with cases relating to environmental information which started their lives as complaints under the FOIA rather than the EIR.

1 Section 2(2).
2 It is questionable whether a statutory instrument can amend an act of Parliament in the absence of a so-called Henry VIII clause. Presumably the justification is s 2(2) of the ECA 1972.

ENVIRONMENTAL INFORMATION REGULATIONS 2004

Code of Practice

4.03   Reg 16 of the EIR 2004 provides that the Secretary of State may issue a:

'... a Code of Practice providing guidance to public authorities as to the practices which it would, in the Secretary of State's opinion, be desirable for them to follow in connection with the discharge of their functions under the [EIR 2004].'

The Secretary of State in February 2005 issued a 'Code of Practice on the discharge of the obligations of public authorities under the Environmental Information Regulations 2004'. The Foreword to the Code (which is not part of the Code) states at paragraph 1 that the Code:

'... provides guidance to public authorities as to the practice it would be desirable for them to follow in connection with the discharge of their functions under the EIR. However, if public authorities do not follow the Code's recommendations it will be difficult for them to meet their obligations under the Regulations.'

Defra Guidance to the Environmental Information Regulations 2004[1]

4.04   Defra has also published guidance (March 2005) ('Defra Guidance'). Described as a 'living document',[2] it has already been subject to updates.

'... It is not legally binding, but is intended to help organisations to comply with their legal obligations under the EIR. It is a statement on the approach public authorities will be expected to follow when applying the EIR.[3]

The 2005 Guidance has been supplemented by various Defra Guidance publications, together principally intended to inform public authorities as to how they may best discharge their duties under the EIR and also finance satisfying particular EIR requests.[4,5,6.]

Following the publication by Defra of the "Smarter Environmental Regulation Review; Phase 1 report: Guidance and Information Obligations" (16 May 2013) the department is also consulting upon plans to reform further environmental guidance to be issued, in conjunction with other Government proposals for making reporting environmental information a simpler exercise and as part of the wider "Smarter Guidance and Data" drive.'[7]

1 See further: ICO Guide to the Environmental Information Regulations (30 October 2015) v. 2.4.3.
2 Para 1.8 of the Defra Guidance.
3 Para 1.7 of the Defra Guidance.
4 'Handling Requests for Environmental Information' (June 2010).
5 'Records Management and Offences' (June 2010).
6 'Charging for Environmental Information under the Environmental Information Regulations 2004' (July 2010).
7 Defra consultation on plans to reform environmental guidance and proposals to make reporting environmental information simpler (consultation ending on 31 March 2015). This forms part of the 'Red Tape Challenge', the Government's attempt at making it '...easier, quicker and clearer to understand what environmental rules apply and simpler to report essential environmental data'.

Guidance from the Information Commissioner's Office

4.05   New, non-statutory guidance on the EIR has been published in February 2014 by the Information Commissioner's Office following the date when the EIR 2004 were laid before Parliament (October 2004) and the date when the EIR 2004 came into force (January 2005). It follows earlier non-statutory guidance that pre-dated the publication of the Code of Practice (February 2005) and the Guidance (March 2005 onwards).

In at least one respect the guidance published by the Information Commissioner's Office appears to take a different approach to the Defra Guidance (in respect of legal privilege and the exception at reg 12(5)(b) in relation to 'the course of justice' – see further below).

'Public authorities'

4.06   The EIR 2004 applies only to 'public authorities'. Under reg 2(2), 'Public authority' is given a broad definition:

'(2)   Subject to paragraph (3), "public authority" means–

(a)   government departments;

(b)   any other public authority as defined in section 3(1) of the Act, disregarding for this purpose the exceptions in paragraph 6 of Schedule 1 to the Act, but excluding–
   (i)   any body or office-holder listed in Schedule 1 to the Act only in relation to information of a specified description; or
   (ii)   any person designated by Order under section 5 of the Act;

(c)   any other body or other person, that carries out functions of public administration; or

(d)   any other body or other person, that is under the control of a person falling within sub-paragraphs (a), (b) or (c) and–
   (i)   has public responsibilities relating to the environment;
   (ii)   exercises functions of a public nature relating to the environment; or
   (iii)   provides public services relating to the environment.

(3)   Except as provided by Regulation 12(10) a Scottish public authority is not a "public authority" for the purpose of these Regulations.'

The first limb of the definition is relatively straight forward and designates 'government departments' and 'other public authorities' as defined in s 3(1) of the FOIA 2000 – save that the definition is slightly different due to the exclusion of certain limiting words from that definition and exclusion of authorities designated under s 5 of the FOIA 2000.[1] It also adds some other bodies not included within the FOIA 2000 definition.

Included are every publicly owned company (s 6 of the FOIA 2000), local authorities and their emanations, the NHS and its accreditations, maintained schools and other educational institutions, and the police. Schedule 1 of the FOIA 2000 also lists hundreds of agencies, commissions, council, boards etc. which are subject to the definition. In particular, the Environment Agency, Defra, local authorities, the Greater London Authority (comprising the Mayor of London and London Assembly), waste disposal authorities, National Park England (and UK), Canal and River Trust, and Natural England are all amongst the bodies included.

The EIR 2004 has wide provisions so as to include persons or body 'that carries out functions of public administration,'[2] or any other body or person under the control of a public body and 'has public responsibilities relating to the environment',[3] 'exercises functions of a public nature relating to the environment' or 'provides public services relating to the environment.'

The main area where debate is likely to arise is in respect of where certain private companies carry out public or semi public functions. Some indication of the government's view are contained in the Defra Guidance on 'public authorities':

'2.2   In addition some bodies outside the scope of FOIA 2000 must comply.

The EIR also covers:

- any other body or person that carries out functions of public administration (other than a Scottish public authority)

- any other body or person (except a Scottish Public authority) under the control of any of the above bodies and organisations that has public responsibilities, exercises functions of a public nature, or provides public services in relation to the environment

2.3   Functions is taken to include the provision of services.

2.4   Control is taken to mean a relationship constituted by statute, Regulations, rights, licence, contracts or other means which either separately or jointly confer the possibility of directly or indirectly exercising a decisive influence on a body. In accordance with this definition any private company that is sufficiently associated with the activities of the government that they owe similar obligations with regard to the environment have responsibilities under the EIR. Control may relate not only to the body but also to control of the services provided by the body. It covers financial, regulatory and administrative control. Examples of bodies covered by EIR are private companies or Public Private Partnerships with obvious environmental functions such as waste disposal,

> water, energy, transport companies (such as the Civil Aviation Authority and port authorities), and environmental consultants. Public utilities, for example, are involved in the supply of essential public services such as water, sewerage, electricity and gas and fall within the scope of the EIRs.[4] Other bodies covered include the Ambulance Service.'

The definition of 'public authority' (and discretionary derogation under Article 2(2) of Directive 2003/4/EC on public access to environmental information) was discussed by the ECJ in *Flachglas Torgau GmbH v Federal Republic of Germany* (C-204/09) [2013] QB 212 [at 38]-[40], [43] and [56] in which the ECJ upheld the refusal by Germany's Federal Ministry for the Environment to provide information concerning a legislative process.

In 2013 the ECJ ruled on the approach to determining whether water companies are public authorities for the purposes of the Directive, in *Fish Legal v The Information Commissioner and Others* (C-279/12). The judgment followed a request for a preliminary ruling from the Upper Tribunal (Administrative Appeals Chamber). The ECJ held that in order to determine whether water company entities may be classified as legal persons which perform 'public administrative functions' under national law, within the meaning of Article 2(2)(b) of Directive 2003/4/EC, it should be examined whether those entities are vested, under the national law with special powers beyond those arising from private law-based 'normal rules' applicable in relations between persons. The water company entities, which provided public services relating to the environment were found to be under the control of a body or person falling within Article 2(2)(a) or (b) of the Directive, and were therefore to be classified as 'public authorities' by virtue of Article 2(2)(c), if they '...do not determine in a genuinely autonomous manner the way in which they provide those services...' It was found that a public authority falling within Article 2(2)(a) or (b) would be one in a position to '...exert decisive influence on their action in the environmental field...'.

The ECJ held that Article 2(2)(b) was to be interpreted as meaning that a person falling within that provision constitutes a public authority in respect of all of the environmental information it holds. Commercial companies, such as the subject water companies, which were capable of being a public authority by virtue of Article 2(2)(c) only insofar as, when they provide public services in the environmental field, they are under the control of a person falling within Article 2(2)(a) or (b), are not required to provide environmental information if it is beyond dispute that the information does not relate to the provision of public services.

The definition of public authority for the purposes of reg 2(2) received some attention in *Montford v IC and BBC* (EA/2009/0114), which concerned information sought from the BBC on expenditure in connection with a seminar programme that involved debating environmental issues. The BBC being a public authority within Schedule 1 of FOIA only within prescribed parameters of journalism, art and literature, the question considered was, given the specific information sought, whether the BBC was a public authority within the meaning of reg 2 of the EIR. The Tribunal concluded that the BBC was not a public authority under the EIR. In any event, the requested information was not 'environmental information' for the purposes of reg 2(1) of the EIR.

As the Defra Guidance indicates, some assistance can be gained from case decided in respect of what is emanation of the state for the purposes of the direct effect of EC law. However, it is submitted that it is, nonetheless, important to recognise that the approach to the question what is an emanation of the state for the purposes of direct effect may be different from the test to be applied as to what is a public body under the EIR 2004.

Case law on the scope of s 6 of the Human Rights Act 1998 ('HRA 1998') may also provide some more limited assistance but should also be treated with some degree of caution.[5] When interpreting these limbs it will be necessary to have regard to the objectives of the Directive in amending the scope of public authority from that covered by the previous directive. In this respect, it is instructive to note that the original Commission proposal for the Directive[6] noted that:

> 'Increasingly, through privitization and new methods of service delivery, services of general interest in relation to the environment traditionally performed by public authorities are being carried out by bodies which do not form part of the public sector. These services include those such as gas, electricity, water and transport...Provision to ensure that bodies now in the private sector grant access to environmental information on the same basis as public authorities carrying court similar services is justified.'

Paragraph 2.5 of the Defra Guidance which states that:

> '... where a contract does bring a private company or organisation under the control of a public authority, the extent of its information that comes under the Regulations should be limited by the extent of the control brought about by the contract.'[7]

1 This is to ensure that the definition in the EIR 2004 accords with Article 2(2) of the Directive. See also recital (11) of the Directive and Article 2.2 of the Convention.
2 Reg 2(2)(c).
3 Reg 2(2)(d).
4 See *Griffin v South West Water Services Ltd* [1995] IRLR, and *Foster v British Gas plc* Case C-188/89, [1990] 2 CMLR 833.
5 See further Lord Kingsland QC and Gregory Jones, 'Public Bodies', *Current Issues in Judicial Review*, Francis Taylor Seminar Papers (2003), p 21.
6 COM (2000) 402 Final June 2000.
7 The Information Tribunal has had to grapple with the issue of what is a public body: see *Port of London Authority v Information Commissioner and John Hibbert* (unreported, 31 May 2007) and *Network Rail Ltd v IC and Network Rail Infrastructure Ltd* (unreported, 17 July 2007).

Judicial or legislative capacity

4.07   The EIR 2004 do not apply to any public authority to the extent that it is acting in a judicial or legislative capacity.[1] Court or Tribunals are, however, within the scope of the EIR 2004 to the extent that they are carrying out other functions such as estates management operations, purchasing and record keeping.[2]

1 Reg 3(3).
2 Para 7.42 of the Defra Guidance.

The holding requirement

4.08   A public authority is obliged only to disclose environmental information that it 'holds' (regs 4(1) and 5(1) of the EIR 2004; see also Articles 1(a) and 3.1 of the Directive). Information held by a public authority is defined to extend to information held by third parties of that public authority.[1]

By contrast to the holding obligation under s 3(2) of the FOIA 2000, under the EIR 2004, information held by a public authority includes information held on behalf of any other person. The Defra Guidance at para 7.7 states:

> 'Hold is to be interpreted widely here. Any information in the possession of the public authority or which is stored elsewhere and is held by a natural or legal person on behalf of, or solely in connection with, services provided to a public authority is "held" by it.'

1 Reg 2(3) of the EIR 2004; see also recital (12) and Articles 2.3, 2.4 and 3.1 of the Directive.

ENVIRONMENTAL INFORMATION

4.09   The EIR 2004 cover only 'environmental information'.[1] Reg 2 faithfully reproduces the definition of 'environmental information' given in Article 2(1) of the Directive. Its derivation is Article 2.3 of the Aarhus Convention. The definition of 'environmental information' is very broad:

> '"environmental information" has the same meaning as in Article 2(1) of the Directive, namely any information in written, visual, aural, electronic or any other material form on–
>
> (a)   the state of the elements of the environment, such as air and atmosphere, water, soil, land, landscape and natural sites including wetlands, coastal and marine areas, biological diversity and its components, including genetically modified organisms, and the interaction among these elements;
> (b)   factors, such as substances, energy, noise, radiation or waste, including radioactive waste, emissions, discharges and other releases into the environment, affecting or likely to affect the elements of the environment referred to in (a);
> (c)   measures (including administrative measures), such as policies, legislation, plans, programmes, environmental agreements, and activities affecting or likely to affect the elements and factors referred to in (a) and (b) as well as measures or activities designed to protect those elements;
> (d)   reports on the implementation of environmental legislation;

(e)   cost-benefit and other economic analyses and assumptions used within the framework of the measures and activities referred to in (c); and

(f)   the state of human health and safety, including the contamination of the food chain, where relevant, conditions of human life, cultural sites and built structures inasmuch as they are or may be affected by the state of the elements of the environment referred to in (a) or, through those elements, by any of the matters referred to in (b) and (c).'

Sub-paragraphs (a) and (b) are wider than the equivalent provisions under the 1992 Regulations. Reg 2(2)(a) of the 1992 Regulations referred only to the 'state of any water or air, the state of any flora or fauna, the state of any soil or the state of any natural site or other land.'

The inclusions of cost-benefit and other economic analyses and assumptions that are used within the framework of policy, legislation, plans, programmes, agreements and activities affecting or likely to affect or designed to protect the environment. Environmental campaigners rightly see this addition as 'essential for members of the public and NGOs wanting to influence policy and decision making, but is precisely the type of information which, in the past, has proved extremely difficult to obtain.'[2]

The Defra Guidance explains that:

'3.7 Environmental information does not, however, include non-existent information that could be created by manipulating existing information, though a digest or summary of this information may be created from existing data. Nor does it include information that does not exist until further research has been carried out. Similarly, it does not include information destroyed in accordance with established records management procedures (but see guidance on Regulation 19 below concerning the offence of altering records to avoid disclosure).'

Another different aspect is the definition of 'State of human health and safety ... in as much as they are or may be affected by' environmental matters. Case law on the old 1992 Regulations provides some assistance. The English courts have held in:

• *R v British Coal Corp ex p Ibstock Building Products Ltd*[3] that the name of an informant who had given British Coal information about by the state of the land was 'environmental information' because such information was necessary in order to assess the credibility of other environmental information concerning the state of the land. This decision would need to be reassessed against the requirement of Data Protection.

• *R v Secretary of State for the Environment, Transport and the Regulations and Midland Expressway Ltd ex p Alliance Against the Birmingham Northern Relief Road and Others*[4] that the content of a concession agreement relating to the construction of a motorway consisted of environmental information. The court also held that whether particular information was 'environmental information' was an objective question for determination by the court.

75

The ECJ has held:

- In Case C-321/96 *Wilhelm Mecklenburg v Kreis Pinneberg-Der Landrat*[5] that an expression of opinion from a countryside protection authority that might impact on the outcome of development consent proceedings was environmental information.

Legal advice has been held to be 'environmental information' (see further the discussion below in respect of 'the course of justice' exception contained in reg 12(5)(b)).

1 Reg 26.
2 Phil Michaels, 'A Guide to the Environmental Information Regulations' 16 (2004) ELM 5.
3 [1995] JPL 836.
4 [1999] Env LR 447.
5 [1998] ECR I-3809.

Historical records

4.10 'Historical records' are given by reg 17 of the EIR 2004 the same meaning as contained in s 6 of the FOIA 2000. A record becomes an historic record at the end of 30 years beginning with the year following that in which it was created. The EIR 2004 requires the public authority holding the information to consult certain bodies as to whether it is in the public interest to maintain the public exception. Unlike the FOIA 2000 the EIR does not provide for the exceptions to fall away with age (see s 63 of the FOIA 2000).

EXCEPTIONS[1]

Categories of exception

4.11 Environmental information must be disclosed on request unless one of the exceptions applies and 'in all the circumstances of the case the public interest in maintaining the exception outweighs the public interesting disclosing the information.'[2] In contrast to the FOIA 2000, where arguably there are absolute exemptions, there are no absolute exceptions under the EIR 2004. An authority considering refusal must satisfy itself as to the balance of the public interest.

Moreover, in accordance with Article 4 of the Directive, exceptions must be interpreted in a restrictive way.[3] The Defra Guidance, however, may be putting it too highly when it states that:

> '[t]his means that a narrow view must be taken of the scope of each exception. If it is credibly arguable that a certain type of information, or a particular piece of information, does not fall within the scope of an exception then it is likely that it is not covered.'[4]

In any event, the public interest requirement derived from the Directive is made stronger by the inclusion in reg 12(1) of an explicit requirement to 'apply a presumption in favour of disclosure.'

As stated above in respect of the structure of FOIA 2000 exemptions, the structure of reg 12 provides for two types of exceptions: stand-alone exceptions[5] and adverse effect exceptions.[6]

1 The FOIA 2000 refers to 'exemptions'. The EIR refers to 'exceptions'.
2 Save for the personal data exception (reg 13) all the exceptions fall under reg 12.
3 This accords with the approach adopted by the European Court of Justice in *Hautala v European Council of the European Union* (Case C-353/99P) [2002] 1 WLR 1930; [2001] ECR I-956.
4 Para 7.2 of the Defra Guidance.
5 Reg 12(4).
6 Reg 12(5).

Exceptions to the duty to disclose environmental Information

4.12 Subject to satisfying the public interest test a public authority may refuse to disclose environmental information requested if–

(a) it does not hold that information when an applicant's request is received;
(b) the request for information is manifestly unreasonable;
(c) the request for information is formulated in too general a manner and the public authority has complied with its duty to assist the applicant to reformulate the request (see reg 9);
(d) the request relates to material which is still in the course of completion, to unfinished documents or to incomplete data; or
(e) the request involves the disclosure of internal communications.

Subject to satisfying the public interest test a public authority may refuse to disclose information to the extent that its disclosure would adversely affect (reg 12(5)):[1]

(a) international relations, defence, national security or public safety;
(b) the course of justice, the ability of a person to receive a fair trial or the ability of a public authority to conduct an inquiry of a criminal or disciplinary nature;
(c) intellectual property rights;
(d) the confidentiality of the proceedings of that or any other public authority where such confidentiality is provided by law;
(e) the confidentiality of commercial or industrial information where such confidentiality is provided by law to protect a legitimate economic interest;
(f) the interests of the person who provided the information where that person:
    (i) was not under, and could not have been put under, any legal obligation to supply it to that or any other public authority;
    (ii) did not supply it in circumstances such that that or any other public authority is entitled apart from these Regulations to disclose it; and
    (iii) has not consented to its disclosure; or

(g) the protection of the environment to which the information relates.

Where one of the seven adverse affect exceptions applies, a local authority may choose to withhold information only where it is satisfied that disclosing the information would 'adversely affect' the interested protected, and where it is satisfied that the public interest in maintaining the exception outweighs public interest in disclosing the information.

In *Ofcom v IC & Others* [2011] 2 Info LR 1 the ECJ decided that a public authority may, when weighing the public interests served by disclosure against the competing interests served by a refusal to disclose in assessing a request for information to be made available, take into account cumulatively multiple grounds for refusal set out in that provision. The public authority may take such multiple grounds together, but would not be required to do so.

1 Public authorities are not entitled to rely on the exceptions listed in items (d) to (g) to refuse to disclose environmental information on emissions.

Separating out

4.13 Reg 12(11) provides that whenever possible refused information must be separated out or 'redacted' from the remaining part of any environmental information. The Defra Guidance expects that, 'In practice refused information will rarely be incapable of being separated from other information for the purpose of making the latter available.'[1] The test does not relate to the resources available to the public authority. The public authority is expected to be able to manage its records to ensure that facilitates disclosure.[2]

It should also be noted that the wording of the exceptions themselves states that the information is expected 'to the extent that' the circumstances described in the exception apply.[3]

1 Para 7.112 of the Defra Guidance.
2 Para 7.113 of the Defra Guidance.
3 Para 7.6 of the Defra Guidance.

Stand-alone exceptions

Not holding documents

4.14 Reg 12(4)(a) provides an exception where the authority does not hold the information requested. The holding requirement has been discussed above. The Defra Guidance states that:

> 'It follows that this exception only applies if the body receiving the request does not hold the information or make use of the services of another body or person to hold this information on its behalf and would therefore have no option but to provide advice and assistance and ask the applicant if they would like the request to be transferred.'[1]

The Code of Practice gives guidance upon the approach that a public authority should follow in transferring a request for information to the appropriate public authority holding the information.[2]

The Information Commissioner warns that although it appears that the exception appears to provide for the refusal of a request if information is received or recorded after a request has been submitted,

> '... public authorities should be mindful of the reputational damage that may arise if it subsequently emerges that it came into possession of the information requested while it was still in the process of dealing with a requester. In any event, they must consider the public interest in providing such information.'

1 Para 7.8 of the Defra Guidance.
2 Paras 31–39, and see also the potted guidance given by the Information Commissioner in *Making a Request for Environmental Information – A Guide for Applicants*, at para 9.

Manifestly unreasonable

4.15   Reg 12(4)(b) provides that requests that are 'manifestly unreasonable' may be refused. The Regulations do not define the term 'manifestly unreasonable'. The wording is to be contrasted with the corresponding s 14 of the FOIA 2000 which refers to requests that are 'repeated or vexatious' being exempted. The Information Commissioner has published advice on vexatious requests under the FOIA, 'Awareness Guidance 22'. It is the Commissioner's view that that Guidance 'will largely be applicable to requests under the EIR.' This guidance is helpful for the EIR 2004 but it must be treated with caution. It is important to note that the reference to 'manifestly unreasonable', or in the case of the FOIA 2000, 'vexatious', does not refer to the person making the request.

The Defra Guidance suggests that the request may be 'manifestly unreasonable' where the request places 'a substantial and unreasonable burden on the resources of a public authority.'[1] However, it should be noted that the UN Implementation Guidance states that:

> 'Although the Convention does not give direct guidance on how to define 'manifestly unreasonable', it does hold it as a higher standard than the volume and complexity referred to in Article 4, paragraph 2. Under the paragraph, the volume and complexity of an information request may justify an extension of the one-month time limit to two months. This implies that volume and complexity alone do not make a request "manifestly unreasonable" as envisioned in paragraph 3 (b).'

Repeated requests for the same information would be 'manifestly unreasonable'.

1 Para 7.9 of the Defra Guidance.

Request formulated in too general a manner

4.16   A public authority may refuse on this ground only where it has already complied with its duty under reg 9 (and see para 6.12 of the Code of Practice) to provide advice and assistance so as to clarify the request.[1]

1 In the Ukraine, the Lviv Oblast Commercial court, by a judgment dated 9 November 2001, rejected submissions by the state-run water supplying company 'Brodyvodocanal' that a request for information regarding the sanitary state of the water facility and the measures needed to ensure the quality of the water supplied and the condition of water supply sources was manifestly unreasonable, being formulated in too general a manner; see http://www.epl.org. ua/a__cases _brodyvodokanal.htm.

Incomplete documentation

4.17 In respect of uncompleted documents, authorities will be able to withhold drafts.[1] However, there may well be a strong public interest in being able to see a draft document, particularly when there is an ongoing public debate.[2] Merely marking a document as a 'draft' will not automatically permit it to enjoy the benefit of the exception.[3]

The Defra Guidance draws an important distinction between the release of documents and of information:

> 'Vital environmental information may be included within an unfinished document. It may be possible to separate out the environmental information and supply this, even though the document as a whole is incomplete, unless this could clearly lead to misunderstanding and not therefore be in the public interest.'[4]

1 Reg 12(4)(d).
2 In *R v Lichfield District Council ex p Lichfield Securities Ltd* [2001] EWCA Civ 304; (2001) EGCS 32, the Court of Appeal relying simply upon the principles of common law fairness held that fairness demanded that a third party developer with a financial interest in the outcome should see a draft of a s 106 agreement in order that he might make informed representations about its contents. Giving the judgment of the Court, Sedley LJ suggested *obiter* that this right would also extend to members of the public.
3 Para 7.15 of the Defra Guidance.
4 Para 7.17 of the Defra Guidance.

Internal communications

4.18 Again, subject to the public interest test, internal communications may be withheld. The purpose of this exemption is to allow the authority to think things through. 'Bodies must be allowed to make decisions in a self-contained space.'[1] The UN Interpretation Guide states that, '...once particular information has been disclosed by the public authority to a third party, it cannot be said to be an "internal communication"'.[2] This exception does not apply to communications between public authorities. It should be noted that the final version of the EIR 2004 has introduced an exception relating to communications between government departments.[3] Some have already suggested that this exception is contrary to Article 4(2) of the Directive, which requires exceptions to be interpreted in a restrictive way and may be challenged in the courts.[4]

Reg 12(4)(e) states that 'a public authority may refuse to disclose information to the extent that the request involves the disclosure of internal communications'. In *Lord Baker v Information Commissioner and the Department for Communities and Local Government*[5] this exception was considered in some depth. The

Deputy Prime Minister decided to grant planning permission for the construction of a residential tower near Vauxhall Bridge in London. There had earlier been a public inquiry, following which the Inspector had recommended that planning permission be refused. Before deciding to grant planning permission against the Inspector's recommendations, the Deputy Prime Minister had received the submissions of two of his officials and some advice. The appellant requested that these documents be made available, pursuant to the EIR. The Office of the Deputy Prime Minister, which by this stage had changed its name to the Department for Communities and Local Government, refused, invoking the exemption under reg 12(4)(e). The Information Commissioner decided that the submissions should have been disclosed, but that the advice should have been redacted and not disclosed. The Tribunal drew a distinction between the situation where a civil servant advises a minister on general policy, and one where a civil servant advises them specifically on a particular administrative decision, such as whether planning permission should be granted in a particular case. In the latter case the advice might well have a more immediate impact on the lives of those affected by it and in controversial cases this might even result in more direct, possibly virulent, criticism of his or her contribution to the decision. However the Tribunal were more persuaded by the contrary arguments. It referred to evidence led during the hearing in which it had been stated that the risk of disclosure of their advice would make civil servants more aware of the need to 'get it right'. While fear of publicity may lead civil servants to alter the manner of their advice, it would not ultimately change the content of it. The Tribunal was of the view that, should a requirement to disclose advice to a Minister generate a tendency to adopt bad practice in the way that advice is given or recorded, effective management guidance should deal with the problem in the same way that it appears to have done at local authority level. Further, the fact that advice between civil servants and ministers would be minuted by the minister's private office provided further protection against the outcome which the Department feared.

The Tribunal ordered that the Department disclose to the appellant an unredacted version of each of the submissions.[6]

1 Para 7.25 of the Defra Guidance.
2 At p 58.
3 Reg 12(8).
4 See Michaels, ELM 16 (2004) 5 at 258.
5 Unreported, 1 June 2007.
6 See also *Exports Credits Guarantee Department v Friends of the Earth* [2008] EWHC 638 (Admin) (2008) Env LR 40.

Adverse effect exceptions

International relations, defence, national security or public security

4.19 The FOIA 2000 provides for exemptions from disclosure if 'disclosure under this Act would or would be likely to prejudice' the interest listed, whereas under the EIR 2004 it uses the words 'adversely affect'. The Regulations themselves give no guidance as to the meaning of these terms. According to the Defra Guidance the exception covers international relations that may compromise confidential information obtained from or relating to a foreign state, an international organisation, or overseas territories where disclosure might compromise future co-operation with the UK.[1] The Commissioner also suggests that this includes relationships between the UK and the EU. This exception may be used by utilities concerned that disclosure of the location of certain facilities might provide succour to terrorists. Reg 15 provides a procedure for Ministerial Certification in support of a decision to a claim of exception under reg 12(5)(a). A certificate is not necessary in order to claim the exception, but where it has been it is likely to strengthen the position. It has another consequence also. The appeal against refusal of disclosure goes directly to the Tribunal, who review the question on a judicial review basis.

1 Para 7.33 of the Defra Guidance; see also ss 2.1 to 3.10 of the guidance on FOIA 2000, s 27.

The course of justice

4.20 Reg 12(5)(b) applies where disclosure would adversely affect 'the course of justice, the ability of a person to receive a fair trial or the ability of a public authority to conduct an enquiry of a criminal or disciplinary nature...' It is immediately apparent that unlike the FOIA 2000, there is no express mention of a legal professional privilege as an exception. The Defra Guidance states:

> 'This exception may relate to actual or likely proceedings. It may include information whose disclosure could prejudice the enforcement or proper administration of the law, including the prevention, investigation or detection of crime, or the apprehension or prosecution of offenders, or proceedings of a coroner's court.'[1]

It goes on to state that whilst every case must be treated on its own facts withholding information once the proceedings have concluded is likely to be more difficult to justify.[2] The Information Commissioner's guidance on this exception however states *inter alia* that:

> '[t]he exception will cover information which is covered by legal professional privilege, particularly where a public authority is or is likely to be involved in litigation.'

But if that were so, it seems somewhat surprising that it was not expressly stated. The basis for the Commissioner's view may be that the course of justice would inevitably be impaired in the absence of legal professional privilege.[3] Lord Taylor remarked that legal professional privilege was a 'fundamental condition upon which the administration of justice as a whole rests.'[4] The UN Interpretation Guide certainly expresses the exception to be in more circumspect terms:

> 'The course of justice refers to active proceedings within the courts. The term "in the course of" implies that an active judicial procedure capable of being prejudiced

must be under way. This exception does not apply to material; simply because at one time it was part of a court case. Public authorities can also refuse to release information if it would adversely affect the ability of a person to receive a fair trial. This provision should be interpreted in the context of the law pertaining to the rights of the accused.

Public authorities can also refuse to release information if it would adversely affect the ability of a public authority to conduct criminal or disciplinary investigations...The Convention clearly does not include all investigations in this exception, but limits it to criminal or disciplinary ones only. Thus, information about a civil or administrative investigation would not necessarily be covered.'

Some matters which are subject to legal professional privilege would be covered even on the restricted interpretation suggestion in the UN interpretation Guide, but far from all matters traditionally regarded as enjoying legal professional privilege would be covered.[5] This suggests that it would be more likely that some aspects of litigation legal privilege[6] would be included within this exception rather than advisory legal privilege. It is to be noted that legal advice given by a lawyer employed in-house would also likely qualify as internal communication and therefore come with that exception. This would create an oddity that advice that was outsourced might be disclosable, whereas the same advice given by an in-house lawyer would not be. Unless legal professional privilege can be made to fit under one of the express exceptions, it is highly doubtful that a local authority could rely upon the common law of legal professional privilege as a free-standing exception not specified in the EIR 2004. For it is to be recalled that reg 5(6) provides that 'Any enactment or rule of law that would prevent disclosure of information in accordance with these Regulations shall not apply'.

The question of the disclosure of legal advice has arisen in at least two recent cases. In *Kirkaldie v Information Commissioner,*[7] Mr Kircaldie made a request to a council asking for access to view the legal advice which the council sought regarding the night-flying policy at Kent International Airport. The legal advice was in relation to the proposed variation of a s 106 agreement under the Town and Country Planning Act 1990 between the council and the owners of the airport. The Tribunal held that the s 106 agreement fell within the meaning of 'environmental agreement' under reg 2(c) of the EIR, and that entering into and extending such an agreement was the sort of measure envisaged by the rule which was likely to affect the matters in reg 2(a) and (b). It followed that the request for legal advice was covered by the EIR. Further, the Tribunal held that the request made by Mr Kircaldie was valid even though it was made before the council 'held' the legal advice for the purposes of reg 5(1). The important factor was that the council 'held' the advice *at the time of responding to the request.*

In *Burgess v IC and Stafford Borough Council,*[8] an enforcement notice was served by the council on the appellant's neighbour, requiring him to reduce the height of a fence he had erected. The neighbour's appeal against the notice was refused by the planning inspector. The appellant entered into correspondence with the council about the appeal decision. The council told the appellant that it was seeking legal advice from a barrister in relation to it. The appellant sought disclosure of the advice. The Tribunal held that the barrister's report came within the definition of 'environmental information' under reg 2(1)(a) and (c).

The Tribunal has also dealt with requests concerning the law which a public body is applying in making a decision. In *Perrins v Information Commissioner*,[9] the appellant was a tenant of a property, 'No 11', owned by the council. The appellant's neighbour, who lived at No 15, had exercised a right to buy from the council. At the time of sale, and by agreement between the council and the new owner of No 15, the council had decided to realign the boundary of No 15. The result was that the appellant's garden, at No 11, was reduced in size. Concerned about possible favourable treatment of the owner of No 15 by the council, the appellant sought certain information from it relating to the decision to realign the boundary of No 15. The appellant also wished to know what criteria and statutory law would be applied at the time of his request. The Tribunal held that the appellant could not require the disclosure of the criteria and statutory law to be applied at the time of his request, since this did not fall within the meaning of 'environmental information' under reg 2(1).

The reg 12(5)(b) exception is that 'a public authority can refuse to disclose information to the extent that its disclosure would adversely affect the course of justice, the ability of a person to receive a fair trial, or the ability of a public authority to conduct an inquiry of a criminal or disciplinary nature'. The Tribunal and Commissioner have held that this exception may be relied on in cases where part of the environmental information sought is legal advice (see also reg 12(5)(d) below). For example, in *Burgess v IC and Stafford Borough Council*, referred to above, an enforcement notice was served by the Council on the appellant's neighbour, requiring him to reduce the height of a fence he had erected. The neighbour's appeal against the notice was refused by the planning inspector. The appellant entered into correspondence with the council about the appeal decision. The council told the appellant that it was seeking legal advice from a barrister in relation to it. Mr Burgess sought a copy of the barrister's advice and the brief served by the council. The council refused. A complaint having been made to him, the Commissioner stated that the information sought by Mr Burgess was subject to legal professional privilege and the privilege had not been waived, that the exception in EIR reg 12(5)(b) covered legal professional privilege and that the public interest in favour of maintaining the exception outweighed the public interest in favour of disclosure. The appellant appealed to the Tribunal claiming that privilege had been waived, as firstly the advice had been seen by a councillor and secondly because in July 2005 the same councillor had offered the barrister's report to Mrs Burgess, the appellant's wife, and that in any event the document should have been disclosed.

On the waiver of privilege point, the Tribunal concluded that the council took careful steps to maintain privilege as it was only disclosed to those elected members of the council who required sight of it for the purpose of performing their statutory duties. Thus the fact that the advice was given to the councillor did not amount to a waiver. The Tribunal did not have sufficient evidence to decide whether the councillor offered a copy of the legal advice to Mrs Burgess. What was clear, however, was that any such offer must have been declined by Mrs Burgess, so in any event there could have been no waiver. The Tribunal held that a disclosure would in this case prejudice the council's ability to maintain the position that it takes in subsequent enforcement proceedings. This was a 'real adverse effect', so reg 12(5) was engaged.

The next question was whether the disclosure should in fact take place on the public interest test, and in light of the presumption in favour of disclosure. In favour of disclosure, the Tribunal considered the general interest in accountability and transparency of decision-making, the need for reasons for a decision to be available, that the council should be seen to be acting appropriately and with probity on the issues before it, and that the particular issue of enforcement in the instant case was no longer a live one. In favour of maintaining the exception, the Tribunal stated that there was a strong public interest in maintaining legal professional privilege, that public authorities should be able to obtain free and frank advice and to be able to give full information to their legal advisors, including matters that would otherwise affect the public authority's position, that the council's position on future cases would be undermined as the advice considered the council's legal rights and liabilities, and that not enough time had elapsed to make the advice 'stale' and the council was entitled to a 'level playing field' in any future litigation. In the circumstances of the case, the Tribunal preferred the latter set of considerations. This decision goes to show that the presumption in favour of disclosure can still be rebutted with sufficiently persuasive argument.

In *DCLG v IC and Robinson* [2012] UKUT 103 (AAC) [2012] 2 Info LR 43, the Upper Tribunal addressed the question of the significance of legal professional privilege in the context of the exception under reg 12(5)(b), and further, the approach to deciding the weight to be attached legal professional privilege when applying the public interest balance. Disclosure had been sought under the EIR from the Planning Inspectorate of internal legal advice given on the question of the appropriate appeal procedure. The Inspectorate had refused disclosure under reg 12(5)(b). The Upper Tribunal had stated that in respect of reg 12(5)(b) it was material to consider the general effect which disclosure would have in weakening confidence in legal professional privilege, as well as on the particular circumstances of the case [at 50]–[51]. The exception would apply only if an adverse effect on the administration of justice was probable. It was significant in this case that the applicant had mooted the possibility of a judicial review challenge at the time of the internal advice so that disclosure would have had an adverse effect, and that it would have been unfair for the Inspectorate to disclose the internal advice.

In *Williams v IC & LGO & Sandwell MBC* (EA/2012/0083) the Upper Tribunal found that legal advice (concerning the application of the Clean Air Act 1993 and Environmental Protection Act 1990) that had been disclosed by a local authority to the Local Government Ombudsman, but not to the requesting party, was subject to legal professional privilege and therefore could properly be withheld under reg 12(5)(b). It was held that the exemption did include legal professional privilege, which had not been waived in the circumstances of the case. As regards weighing the public interest, it was found that the presumption in favour of disclosure had been considered and applied, but that due weight needed to be attributed to legal professional privilege in exercising the public interest balance [at 45]–[46], [51]–[52].

In *McCullough v IC & NI Water* (EA/2012/0082) the Information Commissioner found that the disclosure of technical information concerning noise vibration in the context of sewerage upgrading had been properly refused pursuant to reg 12(5)(b), on the basis that although it was not the subject of legal professional privilege, it was nonetheless expert information likely to be relied upon for litigation purposes and that the public interest required that the exemption be engaged.

1 Para 7.44 of the Defra Guidance.
2 Para 7.45 of the Defra Guidance.
3 The scope and rationale of legal professional privilege as a matter of common law has recently undergone a thorough examination by the House of Lords in *Three Rivers District Council (No 6)* [2004] 3 WLR 1274.
4 *R v Derbyshire Magistrates' Court ex p B* [1996] 1 AC 487 at 507.
5 This also appears to be the view expressed by Edite Ligere in 'FOI in the EU & UK', a paper delivered to Lincoln's Inn, 26 October 2005, in which she states at para 63: '...unlike FOIA, EIR does not provide the exemptions in respect of ...legal privilege (to the same extent as the FOIA)...'.
6 Litigation privilege is 'essentially a creature of adversarial proceedings', and cannot therefore exist in a non-adversarial context, see *Re L* [1997] AC 16. Litigation privilege is broader in scope than legal advice privilege which applies to 'client-lawyer' communications (*Wheeler v Le Marchant* (1881) 17 Ch D 675).
7 Unreported, 4 July 2006.
8 Unreported, 7 June 2007.
9 Unreported, 9 January 2007.

Intellectual property rights

4.21 Reg 12(5) (c) permits the refusal of a request where the disclosure would adversely affect intellectual property rights. The Defra Guidance suggests the example of the constituents of a chemical which has yet to be marketed.[1] The Commissioner's guidance is more restrictive in tone. He expresses the view that this exception:

> '... should only be applied, where there is a real risk that the disclosure (or further dissemination after disclosure) would seriously undermine the rights concerned. If the information would enjoy protection, even after disclosure, from the Copyright Designs and Patents Act, for instance, the case against disclosure would be considerably weakened.'

1 Para 7.46 of the Defra Guidance. See also paras 16–17 of the Foreword to the Code of Practice. See also *R (OffComm v Information Commissioner) v Information Commission* [2008] EWHC 1445 (Admin); [2009] Env LR 1.

Non-applicability with regard to emissions

4.22   It should be noted that the following exceptions (regs 12(5)(d)–(g)) do not apply if the information requested relates to emissions in the environment. Emissions include discharges and other releases into the environment, and should be taken to include:

> '... the direct release of substances, gases, vibrations, light or noise from individual or diffuse sources into or onto air, water or land. It will include any trade or effluent information or information on emissions from aerials that may be held by a public authority. It will also include any residues from veterinary medicines if these are released into the environment.'[1]

The significance of this provision is apparent. This means for example that any emissions data supplied to regulatory authorities is disclosable even if it had been provided on a confidential basis.

1 Para 7.32 of the Defra Guidance.

Confidentiality of proceedings

4.23   Reg 12(5)(d) relates to 'the confidentiality of the proceedings of that or any other public authority where such confidentiality is provided by law ...'. Part VII of the Local Government Act 1972 (inserted by the Local Government (Access to Information) Act 1985) provides for public and press rights of access to meetings and access to documents connected with those meetings. The Local Authorities (Executive Arrangements) (Meetings and Access to Information) (England) Regulations 2012 provide for public and press access to meetings and papers where key executive and executive decisions are made. There are exceptions for information which is 'confidential', so that the effect of reg 5(6) of the EIR 2004 is to provide that the exemptions under the Local Government Act do not apply with respect to environmental information.[1] If the information requested relates to emissions into the environment then, in accordance with reg 12(9), this exception is not available and the information should be released unless some other exception applies.[2]

Under reg 12(5)(d), 'a public authority may refuse to disclose information to the extent that its disclosure would adversely affect the confidentiality of the proceedings of that or any other public authority where such confidentiality is provided by law'. This provision therefore directly contemplates a public authority being able to rely on legal professional privilege. The *Burgess* case, in which legal professional privilege arguments were used in reliance on reg 12(5) (a), is discussed above. In the *Kircaldie* case, in contrast, reliance was placed on reg 12(5)(d). The Tribunal first had to consider a question of waiver of privilege, however. It stated that:

> 'The test for waiver is whether the contents of the document in question are being relied on. A mere reference to a privileged document is not enough, but if the contents are quoted or summarised, there is waiver (*Dunlop Slazenger International Ltd v Joe Bloggs Sports Ltd* [2003] EWCA Civ 901). Publication

of privileged information to the general public will deprive the information of any privilege which previously existed. So, for example, any press release which makes use of privileged information will almost certainly result in a waiver of that privilege (*Chandler Lines v Wilson & Horton Ltd* [1981] 2 NZLR 600).'[3]

Applying this test, the Tribunal held that the council had in fact waived its privilege, so the public interest test did not therefore need to be considered. The case highlights that the issue of waiver is one to which practitioners, faced with privilege arguments in the EIR context, should be alive.

1 Para 7.50 of the Defra Guidance.
2 Para 7.33 of the Defra Guidance.
3 Para 26 of the judgment.

Commercial or industrial confidentiality[1]

4.24 Disclosure may only be refused where the commercial confidentiality would actually be adversely affected. This would mean demonstrating that release of the information would result in real commercial/competitive disadvantage to the person whose interests were to be protected.[2] Public authorities are encouraged to minimise the use of 'confidentiality' in the agreements they enter into.'[3] The Code of Practice advising that when entering into contracts 'public authorities should refuse to include contractual terms that purport to restrict the disclosure of environmental information.'[4] From 1 December 2005, all central government departments and their executive agencies in England have been obliged to have an environmental purchasing policy. This has required authorities to consider the environmental impacts and implications of all government contracts. Once this is carried out the public authority will be readily able to determine to what extent the information it holds is environmental. For local authorities, the National Procurement Strategy for Local Government 2014 sets out the most recently prescribed approach to strategic procurement implementation.

The case of *Jones v IC & Environment Agency* [2012] 2 Info LR 129 relating to reg 12(5)(e) of the EIR concerned a landfill operator that had obtained a permit from the Environment Agency to operate a landfill site. A financial guarantee had been obtained in the form of a bonded sum to be paid to the Environment Agency in the event of environmental accident. The disclosure of information relating to this guarantee had been requested from the Environment Agency. In answering the request, a redacted performance agreement and redacted bond were disclosed, relying on reg 12(5)(e) to justify redacting information concerned with the quantum of the bonded sum required to be secured per annum during the period of operation of the landfill site as well as for a specified period post-operation. The Upper Tribunal held that the information redacted did not amount to commercially sensitive and confidential information covered by reg 12(5)(e). First, the redacted information was not subject to confidentiality provided by law, given that the landfill operator had not actually applied, as had been possible, for the information to be excluded from the public register on confidentiality grounds. Secondly, the information could not be said to be confidential at common law since the information had not been provided in circumstances that gave rise to an obligation of confidence but rather had been created by both the Environment Agency and the landfill operator in negotiation. It was held also that even had reg 12(5)(e) applied, the public interest would have militated in favour of disclosure.

1 Reg 12(5)(e).
2 See the *Amway Corporation v Eurway International Limited and the Birmingham Relief Road* case ([1999] Env LR 447) decided under the 1992 Regulations which were somewhat narrower in the scope of the exception. Whether something was confidential was an 'objective' question for the court.
3 Para 7.56 of the Defra Guidance.
4 Para 46 of the Code of Practice.

Voluntary supply by third party

4.25 Another area that is very likely to be the cause of future dispute concerns the exception relating to the voluntary supply of information.[1] Under this exception an authority may refuse to disclosure information where disclosure would adversely affect the interests of the person who supplied it, where that person was not, and could not be put, under any legal obligation to supply it and has not consented to its disclosure. This raises the prospects that confidential material supplied by a third party may be disclosed to the public against the wishes and interests of the person who supplied the information on a voluntary basis.[2] An area where this issue is likely to arise is in respect of pre-application discussions. The Planning Officers Society advises its members that:

> 'If an authority were to receive a request for the information contained within pre-application consultation they would have to consider disclosing the information unless they could show that its satisfies the criteria necessary for engaging one of the exceptions...An authority would need to consider requests on a case by case basis as it is not possible to apply exemptions in a blanket fashion.'[3]

Reg 5(6) provides for the disapplication of any 'enactment or rule of law that would prevent the disclosure of information in accordance with these Regulations shall not apply.' This is in contrast to s 44 of the FOIA 2000, which prevents disclosure which would if it is 'prohibited by or under any enactment.' This would also have the effect of preventing a general refusal on the basis of 'breach of confidence' permitted under s 41 of the FOIA 2000. Another area of future dispute concerns the ability of local planning authorities to make enforcement decisions based upon material which is not disclosed. A decision by the Information Commissioner[4] concerning Bridgnorth District Council considered this issue. The applicant requested the right to inspect information contained in an enforcement file relating to a piece of land he owned. The Commissioner considered the information to be 'environmental information' subject to the EIR 2004. Having previously considered the request under the FOI Act, the Council subsequently refused to supply the information, citing regs 12(5)(f) (information supplied voluntarily and whose disclosure would adversely affect the interests of the supplier) and 12(5)(b) (investigations of a criminal nature). The Commissioner found that reg 12(5)(b) did not apply, as the investigation could not be construed as being an enquiry of a criminal nature. However, in so far as the information identified the original complainant, the Commissioner was satisfied that reg 12(5)(f) had been correctly applied and considered the public interest to favour non-disclosure. The Commissioner had regard to both the public interest in protecting individuals from malicious complaints and the deterrent effect that identifying complainants may have on the free flow of information which would hinder the activities of the planning authority. The council was ordered to allow the complainant to view the remainder of the file.[5]

In *Dainton v IC and Lincolnshire County Council*,[6] Mrs Dainton asked for copies of statements obtained by Lincolnshire CC concerning an application to modify the definitive map obtained by the council. Under the Wildlife and Countryside Act 1981, certain local authorities, such as the council, are required to keep such a definitive map recording rights of way. Where a right of way is not shown on the definitive map or there is an error in the route or the type of right of way, the Wildlife and Countryside Act provides a mechanism to amend the definitive map. There was an application for such a 'Modification Order'. Mrs Dainton's request concerned the statements that had been obtained by the local authority from various individuals concerning a potential right of way in South Somercotes over a property which she occupied. The request was for the statements made by people to the council in respect of their use of the route. The Commissioner found that reg 12(5)(f) of the EIR 2004 was engaged, as the individuals who supplied the information were (i) under no legal obligation to provide it; (ii) did not supply it in circumstances such that that or any other public authority was entitled (apart from under the Regulations) to disclose it; and (iii) they had not consented to the disclosure of the information. The Commissioner decided under reg 12 that the public interest in maintaining the exception outweighed the public interest in disclosure. The appellant appealed to the Tribunal on the grounds that there was nothing in the WCA 1981 which prohibited the council from making the information available, that it was a breach of natural justice not to make the statements available, and that the statements were provided in the knowledge that they would be disclosed and therefore the Commissioner was incorrect to rely upon the exemption in reg 12(5)(f). The council replied to these grounds by relying on the reg 12(5)(f) exemption. The council also relied on an argument that they were obliged not to disclose the information because it was personal data within the meaning of the Data Protection Act (which is protected by reg 13).

The key definition was s 1(1) of the Data Protection Act, which defines personal data as:

> 'data which relate to a living individual who can be identified –
>
> (a)   from those data, or
> (b)   from those data and other information which is in the possession of, or is likely to come into the possession of, the data controller,
> (c)   and includes any expression of opinion about the individual and any indication of the intentions of the data controller or any other person in respect of the individual.'

The Tribunal concluded that the information provided by individuals on the questionnaire forms provided to the council did count as personal data within the meaning of the Act (and the case law). The only exception to this was section B of the form, which requested a description of the route or path/way in question. In relation to section B, would disclosure of this amount to a breach of any of the data protection principles? The key factor here was whether the individuals who provided the information were aware of the purpose for which they provided it. The council argued that members of the public offering information under the questionnaire procedure would not understand themselves to be authorising disclosure to members of the public in advance of the date of disclosure required under the statutory scheme under which the council was acting. Such a scheme required disclosure of the documents only after the date that a Modification Order was made (which would not always necessarily be the case). Mrs Dainton argued that the information was not confidential and that given that there was a statement on the evidence forms about the information being made available for inspection or produced at court, the individuals completing the forms would anticipate their production. The Tribunal held that in the absence of positive evidence as to individuals' consent to disclosure, it was only fair to assume that they would not have consented except insofar as the information would have become available after the making of a modification order. The information was therefore covered by reg 13.

In light of the above, it was only necessary for the Tribunal to consider the reg 12(5)(f) exemption in respect of section B on the forms. The council argued that there may be adverse effect through disclosure of the evidence forms for example by exposing the makers of the statement to the risk of recrimination by Mrs Dainton. Mrs Dainton argued that the council could produce no evidence to substantiate these submissions. The Tribunal upheld the view that there was insufficient evidence to see how the route of the path/way could amount to something that would adversely affect those individuals' interests, and required the information to be disclosed.

1 Reg 12(5)(f).
2 In *Knaufmann v Credit Lyonnais Bank* (1995) CLC 300 it was held that the general duty of the FSA's predecessor, the Securities and Futures Authority, to keep information confidential was overridden by its duty to disclose information in order to properly discharge its public functions. In that case, the court rejected a public policy argument that regulated entities should be encouraged to be as open as possible with regulators and that this is more likely where entities have confidence in the information they provide will be kept confidential. By contrast, see *Burmah Oil v Bank of England* [1970] 1 WLR 473, which supports the proposition that preserving confidentiality in information provided to a regulator is in the public interest because it encourages cooperation by regulated entities.
3 Environmental Information Regulations 2004: Implications for Local Planning Authorities. 23–02–2005, http://www.planningofficers.org.uk/article.cp/articleid/24.
4 FS50062329, 12 July 2005.
5 The advice of the Planning Officer's Society is that 'It is understood that a request for information relating to an enforcement complaint would not be exempt from public disclosure, unless an authority can demonstrate, on a case by case basis, that there is a suitable exception and that it would not be in the public interest to disclose the information.'
6 Unreported, 10 September 2007.

The environment to which the information relates

4.26   A public authority may refuse to supply the information in order to protect the environment to which it relates.[1] For example, information about the location of nesting sites, rare habitats, vulnerable archaeological sites or endangered species may need to be withheld to avoid possible damage.[2] Indeed, it is difficult to think of examples where the public interest would overcome this exception, for as the Information Commissioner states in his guidance:

> 'The ultimate aim of the EIR, and the EU Directive and the Aarhus Convention upon which it is based, is to increase the protection of the environment by ensuring greater access to environmental information. It would clearly be contradictory if disclosure of information would lead to damage to the environment.'

1 Reg 12(5)(g).
2 See paras 7.75–7.76 of the Defra Guidance.

Personal data

4.27   Should the environmental information include 'personal data', then:

(a) If the applicant is the data subject of that personal data, the applicant has no right to that information;[1]
(b) If the applicant is not the data subject of that personal data, the public authority must refuse to disclose that data in certain circumstances.[2]

Where information is identified as constituting 'personal data' of which the applicant is not the data subject, disclosure is governed by reg 13 of the EIR 2004.

1 Reg 5(3). The applicant will have a right to the information pursuant to s 7 of the DPA 1998 subject to the exemptions contained therein.
2 Some are of the view that this is an absolute exception; see e.g. Coppel [2005] JPL 12 at 30. That may be a correct view in the light of the wording of reg 13, but it is questionable whether it is compatible with the relevant provision of the Convention, which is subject to the same qualification that it 'shall be interpreted in a restrictive way, taking into account the public interest served by disclosure...' (Article 4(4)).

The public interest test

4.28   An authority may only refuse to disclose where one of the exceptions applies *and* the public interest test is satisfied. This means that for example in respect of the adverse effect exceptions it is possible that disclosure could be required, notwithstanding that it would have an adverse effect on a legitimate interest of an individual or public authority. The function of applying the public interest test involves a structured and considered examination of the competing public interests. On one side is the public interest in 'maintaining' the exception. This requires the identification of the public interest which is represented by the exception. On the other side is the 'public interest' in 'disclosing the information'. This involves an examination of the purposes of the Regulations and in turn the purposes of the Directive and the Convention along with any particular benefits to the public interest flowing from disclosure.

The required degree of prejudice is that 'disclosure would adversely affect' any one of the matters protected by reg 12(5).[1] The Information Commissioner has published guidance on 'The Public Interest Test' under the FOIA 2000.[2] It identifies features that would encourage the disclosure of information:

- further understanding of and participation in the public debate of issues of the day;
- promoting accountability and transparency by public authorities for decision taken by them;
- promoting accountability and transparency in the spending of public money;
- allowing individuals and companies to understand decisions made by public authorities affecting their lives and, in some cases, assisting individuals to challenge those decisions;
- bringing to light information affecting public health and public safety.

As mentioned above, the provisions and recitals of the Directive and the Convention are also highly relevant. Reference should also be made to the Aarhus UN Implementation Guide.

1 See Article 4.2 of the Directive and Article 4.4 of the Convention. This is to be contrasted with the prejudice based exemptions in the FOIA 2000 which use the formula 'disclosure would, or would be likely to, prejudice' any of the protected matters in ss 26(1), 27(1), 29(1), 31(1), 33(1), 36(2), 38(1), 43(1) and (2). The requirement under the EIR 2004 that disclosure 'would' rather than just likelihood as under the FOIA 2000 is another example of how the EIR 2004 leads to greater discloser. See also *R (OffComm v Information Commissioner) v Information Commission* [2008] EWHC 1445 (Admin); [2009] Env LR 1.
2 http://www.infomrationcommissioner.gov.uk/cms/DocumentUploads/AG%20320-Pub%20 reform.pdf.

Quality of information

4.29   Reg 5(4) imposes an obligation on the public authority to ensure that where the information to be released has been compiled either by or for the public authority then, so far as it is reasonable, it ensures it is 'up to date, accurate and comparable'. This obligation did not exist under the 1992 Regulations. It does not exist under the FOIA 2000.

Request

4.30   Requests under the FOIA 2000 must be in writing.[1] A request is required under the EIR 2004 but requests under the EIR 2004 need not be in writing. The Commissioner wisely advises that if the request is not made in writing, a written note of the request should be made. Save to the extent that it may be relevant to a consideration of public interest, the motives of the person for making a request are irrelevant to the decision to disclose.[2] The EIR 2004 refer to an applicant being a 'person'.[3] This will no doubt also include legal persons. Views differ upon whether a person living outwith the jurisdiction could make a request. The Aarhus Convention at Article 3.9 suggests that the right may be exercisable by any person, irrespective of citizenship, nationality or domicile. This wording does not appear in the Directive or the EIR 2004. The Information Commissioner in 'Making a Request for Environmental Information – A Guide for Applicants' states:

> '... The right [to make a request for environmental information] is not restricted: any person in the world can request environmental information (this includes organisations as well as individual'.

The Defra Guidance takes a similarly robust view stating at Chapter 6:

> 'Anyone or any organisation can request environmental information, and that request can come from anywhere in the world. No interest needs to be shown or provided, no reasons need be given for the request and no reference to the Regulations needs to be made.'

It is also interesting to note that on the adoption of the Directive, the Commission Press Release stated:

> 'The Directive provides that every natural or legal person, regardless of citizenship, nationality or domicile, has a right of access to environmental information held by or produced by public authorities....'[4]

The point is likely, in most cases to be arid, since in most cases a person would be able to travel or else get a friend situated within the EU to make the request for him in any event.

1 Section 8(1).
2 See Recital (8) of the Directive and Article 4.1 of the Aarhus Convention.
3 Reg 2(1).
4 DN: IP/02/1641 Commission welcomes adoption of directive on public access to environmental information, 8 November 2002.

TIME LIMITS

4.31   Requested information must be provided 'as soon as possible'.[1] The backstop requirement is within 20 working days of the request, although in cases where it is justified by complexity and volume, it is possible to extend the 'backstop' period from 20 to 40 working days.[2] In contrast to the FOIA 2000, it is never permissible to extend time for responding to a request beyond 40 days.

1 Reg 5(2).
2 Reg 7.

Refusal notice

4.32   Where a public authority reuses to supply the information for whatever reason it must issue a 'refusal notice' that complies with the requirements of the EIA 2004.[1] The EIR 2004 set out the reasons that are required in a refusal notice.[2] The refusal notice must also inform the applicant of his right of representations and appeal.[3] If neither a refusal notice nor the information is supplied within the 20-day time limit (unless one of the exceptions described above applies), then:

(a) the applicant has 40 days within which to make representations to the public authority in relation to its failure to comply with its obligations;[4] and
(b) if, within 40 working days of receipt of the representations, the public authority either gives no response or gives a response with which the applicant is not satisfied, this will constitute a possible non compliance with Part II of the EIR 2004, enabling the applicant to make a complaint to the Information Commissioner who will look at the matter afresh.[5]

1 Reg 14(1), derived from recital (14) and Articles 3.4 and 8.2 of the Directive and Article 4.1 of the Convention.
2 Reg 14(2).
3 Reg 14(5).
4 Reg 11(1)–(2).
5 Reg 11(4), 18(1), (3), (4), (6) and FOIA 2000, s 50.

Neither confirm nor deny

4.33   Reg 12(6) allows a public authority to respond to a request by 'neither confirming nor denying' that the information exists. The Directive does not provide for such a response, so that it is at least questionable whether this provision is compatible with the Directive. This is to deal with a very specific request for information which is subject to an exception. The mere acknowledge of the existence of such information may be enough to prejudice an interest supposedly protected by the exception.

Form and content of information provided

4.34   Pursuant to reg 6, a public authority must make the information requested available in the particular form or format requested, unless either:

'(a) it is reasonable for it to make the information available in another form or format; or
(b) the information is already publicly available and easily accessible to the applicant in another form or format.'

Whether it is reasonable to make it available in another format is a matter of fact depending upon the circumstances. It should be noted that the obligation also appears to require the public authority to have regard to the applicant's circumstances when considering whether to rely upon the provision permitting release in another format. In *The Office of Communications v Information Commissioner and T Mobile*[1] the Tribunal held that, there having been a duty to disclose the information requested (that is, that none of the exceptions could successfully be relied upon by OFCOM for non-disclosure), there also arose a duty to disclose the information in either text file, csv file, Access database or Excel spreadsheet, as had been requested. OFCOM could not rely on the exception provided under reg 6(1)(b), since the Information Manager's request as to format was reasonable. It remains to be seen in further cases how far the Tribunal will be prepared to extend the meaning of information 'reasonably requested' in a specific form or format.

1 Unreported, 4 September 2007.

Charging

4.35 Authorities may charge as long as the charge 'does not exceed an amount which a public authority is satisfied is a reasonable amount' (reg 8(3)). They are prohibited from making any charge for allowing an applicant to access any public register or list of 'environmental information' to examine the information requested at the place which the public authority makes available for that purpose.

Where a public authority requires advance payment of a charge, this has the effect of freezing the time for compliance with the request.[1] If the amount is not received within 60 working days of a notification of advance payment, the request effectively lapses.[2]

An applicant can appeal to the Information Commissioner against the amount of fees sought to be imposed.[3]

Despite the apparently subjective wording, the question as to what is a 'reasonable' charge is likely to be regarded as an objective one for the court. Indeed, the ECJ in Case C-217/97 *Commission v Germany* held in the context of the earlier Directive 90/313/EEC that any interpretation of 'a reasonable cost' which may dissuade people from accessing information is impermissible, and the term 'reasonable' means that authorities are not entitled to pass on to those seeking information the entire amount of the costs incurred by the authority.

This issue was addressed directly in *Markinson v the Information Commissioner*[4] Mr Markinson wished to take away from the council's office certain documents relating to planning permissions for his home, but found that he could not afford to pay the cost imposed by the council. He complained to the Information Commissioner. The Commissioner decided that the council had acted in accordance with reg 8(3), which imposes a 'reasonableness' test for the making of charges for taking documents away. The Commissioner made that decision on the basis that the 'reasonableness' test is purely subjective; ie it was sufficient that the council satisfied *itself* that the charge payable was reasonable, irrespective of what the Commissioner himself thought. The issue before the Tribunal was whether the Commissioner had applied the correct test.

The Tribunal considered the requirements of the European Directive 2003/4/EC on public access to environmental information, which 2004 Regulations implement. In particular it concluded that Article 5 of the Directive, which was implemented by reg 8, did not require the Commissioner to decide for himself whether the charge was 'reasonable'. Such a task would be burdensome and disproportionate. However the Tribunal held that reg 8(3) had required the Commissioner to apply a two-stage test:

(a) did the council honestly believe that the charge structure it had set out did not exceed a reasonable one; and

(b) was that a belief which a reasonable authority, properly directing itself as to the relevant law and facts, could hold.

On the facts, the Tribunal held that the Commissioner had not given sufficient consideration, *inter alia*, to the relevant guidance provided to councils by government on the making of charges. The Commissioner had therefore erred in law by not striking down the council's decision.

1 Reg 8(5)–(7). There is no comparable provision in the Directive. This may be a subject of challenge in due course.
2 Reg 8(3).
3 Regs 18(3), (4)(a), (6) and FOIA 2000, s 50(1).
4 Unreported, 28 March 2006.

CRIMINAL OFFENCES

4.36   It is a criminal offence under reg 19 to alter, deface, block, erase, destroy or conceal any record held by a public authority following a request for access to environmental information to which the applicant would have been entitled. The offences apply to the authority, its employees and officers.

Enforcement

4.37   The EIR 2004 similarly apply the enforcement provisions of the FOIA 2000. By Sch 3 of the FOIA 2000 the Information Commissioner may apply for a warrant to enter, search and seize material if it appears that a public authority is not complying with any of the requirements under the FOIA 2000.

REMEDIES

Internal reviews

4.38   An applicant has the right to require an internal review by the public authority of an information decision with which he disagrees.[1] This is a new right. Moreover an authority must make an applicant aware of this right whenever it refuses to disclose a piece of information.[2] The review must be free of charge.

1 Reg 11.
2 Reg 14.

The Information Commissioner and the Information Tribunal

4.39 The enforcement and appeal procedures of the FOIA 2000 have been incorporated into the EIR 2004[1] so that following the internal review, dissatisfied applicants can apply to the Information Commissioner on the same basis as the FOIA 2000.[2] The Tribunal's powers are laid down in s 58 of the FOIA, which provides:

'(1) If on an appeal under section 57 the Tribunal considers—

(a) that the notice against which the appeal is brought is not in accordance with the law, or

(b) to the extent that the notice involved an exercise of discretion by the Commissioner, that he ought to have exercised his discretion differently,

the Tribunal shall allow the appeal or substitute such other notice as could have been served by the Commissioner; and in any other case the Tribunal shall dismiss the appeal.

(2) On such an appeal, the Tribunal may review any finding of fact on which the notice in question was based.'

What exactly is the extent of the Tribunal's jurisdiction under this section? Analysis of the limitations to the Tribunal's jurisdiction was provided in *Bromley v IC and The Environment Agency*.[3] The appellants lived near to the River Avon in Warwick. They had reason to believe that planning permission for the development of the area was made conditional on the erection of a formal flood defence between the houses and the river, although no such defence had been constructed. However there had for some time been an informal flood defence in the form of a strip of raised ground. This informal defence had recently been reduced in height by a bulldozer undertaking development. Concerned about being flooded, and believing they were entitled to have their flood bank reinstated, the appellants wished to obtain certain information from the Environment Agency about the flood defence. They were refused it. They suspected that the possibility of litigation had caused the Environment Agency to be reticent in disclosing their files, which contained crucial evidence which they needed to be successful in their planning proceedings against the council, the aim of which was to object to the bulldozing of the informal defence. The Tribunal noted that it was faced with arguments relating to matters beyond their jurisdiction; it could only consider, in light of the scope, quality, thoroughness and results of the council's searches, whether or not the Environment Agency held further information falling within the scope of the original request. On the facts the Tribunal decided that the council did not hold the requested information.

1 Reg 18.
2 The appeal process is discussed in more detail in the Francis Taylor Seminar Paper by Lewis and Edwards, 'Decisions of the Information Commissioner and appeals to the Information Tribunal.'
3 31 August 2007.

DUTY TO ORGANISE AND DISSEMINATE ENVIRONMENTAL INFORMATION

4.40   The EIR 2004 introduce important new obligations for authorities to organise and disseminate the environmental information they hold. These obligations go further than the FOIA 2000 Act. Under reg 4 there is:

- a 'dissemination obligation', to publish progressively environmental information which the authority holds by easily accessible electronic means;
- an 'organisation obligation', to take reasonable steps to organise the information relevant to the authority's functions with a view to publication.

Chapter 5

Local land charges search

INTRODUCTION

5.01 In practice, the local land charges search may yield a considerable amount of information on environmental matters affecting the property.[1] Local land charges comprise:

- charges on a property in order to secure payment of money due to certain authorities under specified legislation;
- certain prohibitions or restrictions (imposed or enforceable by central or local government) on activities which may be carried out on the property;
- certain positive obligations enforceable by central or local government which bind successive landowners; and
- any matter made a local land charge under legislation other than the Local Land Charges Act 1975.[2]

1 See *Garner's Local Land Charges* (14th edn, 2010); Silverman and Hewitson *Conveyancing Searches and Enquiries* (4th edn, 2011) Part II.
2 Local Land Charges Act 1975, s 1. See s 2 for matters which are not local land charges.

5.02 Local land charges should be registered in the Local Land Charges Register.[1] Registrations are made and the registers kept by registering authorities, that is, district councils, London Borough Councils, the Common Council of the City of London and unitary authorities.[2]

1 Local Land Charges Act 1975, s 5 and the Local Land Charges Rules 1977, SI 1977/985, as amended.
2 Local Land Charges Act 1975, s 3.

5.03 The local land charges register may be kept in documentary or computerised form. A personal search may be made or alternatively an official search can be requested by completing Form LLC1, the Requisition for search and official certificate of search and submitting it to the relevant Local Authority by post or electronically via one of the online search providers. The use of personal searches has increased due to the growth of personal search businesses acting on behalf of solicitors, conveyancers and their clients.[1]

Fees for local land charge services, with the exception of personal searches, are set by the registering authorities, which must have regard to any guidance from the Lord Chancellor.[2]

The Infrastructure Act 2015 provides for the Land Registry to take over responsibility of the Local Land Charges Register and the Land Registry will be responsible for maintaining a single local land charges register in electronic format. It will deal with local land charges searches and provide facilities for personal searches.[3]

1 See Office of the Deputy Prime Minister, Personal Searches of the Local Land Charges Register and Inspection of Other Records Open for Public Inspection Held by Local Authorities; Guidance for Local Authorities and Personal Searchers (February 2005); Department of Communities and Local Government, Personal searches of the local land charges register and other records held by local authorities; Good practice guidance for local authorities and personal searchers (January 2008).
2 Local Land Charges Act 1975, ss 13A(7), (9), as amended by Constitutional Reform Act 2005, s 15(1), Sch 4, pt 1, paras 82, 83.
3 Infrastructure Act 2015, ss 34–36 and Sch 5.

5.04   A local land charge is enforceable against successive owners of a property irrespective of registration. Nonetheless, if a buyer suffers loss due to non-registration, or because in the case of a personal search a computerised registration has not been made available for inspection in visible and legible form or because an official search fails to reveal the existence of a local land charge, the buyer is generally entitled to compensation.[1]

1 Local Land Charges Act 1975, s 10.

THE LOCAL LAND CHARGES REGISTER

5.05   The register is divided into 12 parts,[1] including:

- Part 1: General Financial Charges
- Part 2: Specific Financial Charges
- Part 3: Planning Charges
- Part 4: Miscellaneous Charges
- Part 10: Listed Building Charges
- Part 12: Drainage Scheme Charges

Some of the 'environmental' local land charges are considered as follows.

1 Local Land Charges Rules 1977, SI 1977/985, r 3.

Part 1: General Financial Charges

5.06   General financial charges[1] fall into two categories:

- general charges against premises, without specifying any amount and before a specific charge comes into existence.[2] Examples are certain charges under Local Acts in respect of the provision of sewers in a public street at the expense of frontage owners; and
- charges under the Coast Protection Act 1949 in respect of certain works schemes and maintenance schemes for the purpose of coastal protection which indicate the land in relation to which the charges are payable but not the persons liable to pay them.[3]

1 Local Land Charges Rules 1977, SI 1977/985, r 2(2) – definition of 'general financial charge'.
2 Local Land Charges Act 1975, s 6(2).
3 Coast Protection Act 1949, ss 8(8) and 13(6).

Part 2: Specific Financial Charges

5.07   Specific financial charges[1] fall into two categories:

- charges acquired by local authorities, water authorities,[2] sewerage undertakers or new town development corporations under the Public Health Act 1936, the Public Health (Drainage of Trade Premises) Act 1937, the Public Health Act 1961,[3] the Highways Act 1980 (or any Act repealed by that Act) or the Building Act 1984 or any similar charge acquired by a local authority under any other Act. Such charges must be binding on successive owners of the affected land. However, it makes no difference when the charge was created (either before or after the Local Land Charges Act 1975 was passed);[4] and
- works schemes and maintenance schemes for the purpose of coastal protection which state the parties by whom coast protection charges are payable.[5]

1 Local Land Charges Rules 1977, SI 1977/985, r 2(2) – definition of 'specific financial charge'.
2 On 1 September 1989 the functions of water authorities were transferred to the National Rivers Authority (now the Environment Agency), water undertakers and sewage undertakers under the Water Act 1989, s 4 and the Water Act (Transfer of Functions) (Appointed Day) Order 1989, SI 1989/1530. It appears that the reference to 'water authorities' now includes water undertakers appointed under the Water Act 1989 and its successor the Water Industry Act 1991.
3 The repeal of much of this legislation under the Water Consolidation (Consequential Provisions) Act 1991, s 3 and Sch 3 and its replacement by the Water Industry Act 1991 indicates that local land changes under that Act should also be included: see Interpretation Act 1978, s 17(2).
4 Local Land Charges Act 1975, s 1(1)(a).
5 Coast Protection 1949, ss 8(8) and 13(6).

5.08   Charges in the first category arise where expenses (and interest) incurred for certain purposes by the relevant authority are recoverable from the owner of premises either by statute or by agreement and are stipulated to be a charge on the premises. The standard provisions in the Public Health Act 1936, s 291 and the Building Act 1984, s 107, which have been incorporated by reference into a number of other statutes, govern the creation of many specific financial charges.

5.09   Charges in this category can only be created as against owners where money is recoverable from successive owners and occupiers[1] and generally arise where the authorities carry out works in default of compliance by the person responsible. Many provisions stipulate that requirements may be imposed on owners or occupiers and in some cases only against occupiers. Accordingly, where requirements have been placed on an occupier (in his capacity as occupier) who fails to comply and the authority undertakes works in default, no charge arises.

1 Local Land Charges Act 1975, s 1(2).

Different types of specific financial charge

5.10   The following 'environmental' charges can be created.

5.11   Sewers, drains and cesspools

- The outstanding costs incurred by a local authority or sewerage undertaker in connecting a private drain or sewer with a public sewer at the request of the owner of the relevant property.[1]
- The cost of works undertaken by a local authority which are necessary to prevent the overflowing or leaking of a cesspool where the person responsible has failed to comply with a notice requiring the works to be undertaken.[2]
- Expenses of repairing or unblocking stopped up drains where the owner has failed to do so after being required to undertake the work.[3]
- The local authority's expenses of constructing a private sewer for the drainage of buildings in combination.[4]
- The local authority's expenses in making satisfactory provision for the drainage of a building, where the owner has failed to comply with a notice requiring him to do so.[5]
- A local authority's expenses in renewing, repairing, cleansing, filling up, removing or otherwise rendering innocuous any cesspool, private sewer, drain, soil pipe, rain water pipe, spout, sink or other necessary appliance, where the owner or occupier has failed to comply with a notice requiring him to do so.[6]
- A local authority's expenses in carrying out works of paving and drainage to yards and passages where the owner has failed to comply with a notice requiring him to do so.[7]

1 Public Health Act 1936, s 36. This provision was repealed by the Water Consolidation (Consequential Provisions) Act 1991 and replaced by the Water Industry Act 1991, s 107. However, any charges registered under s 36 continue to have effect by virtue of the Water Consolidation (Consequential Provisions) Act 1991, Sch 2, paras 1(1) and (2). These charges were not registerable from 1 April 1974 until 31 July 1977 because during that period charges were only registerable in respect of expenses incurred by local authorities, whereas any expenses under s 36 would have been incurred by the water authorities.
2 Public Health Act 1936, s 50.
3 Public Health Act 1961, s 17 (as substituted by the Local Government (Miscellaneous Provisions) Act 1982.
4 Building Act 1984, s 22; formerly Public Health Act 1936, s 38.
5 Ibid, ss 59(1)(a) and (2); formerly Public Health Act 1936, s 39.
6 Ibid, ss 59(1)(b), (c), (d) and (2); formerly Public Health Act 1936, s 39.
7 Ibid, s 84; formerly Public Health Act 1936, s 56.

5.12   Closets

- The local authority's expenses incurred in executing works to put a defective closet into a satisfactory condition, where the person responsible has failed to comply with a notice requiring the work to be carried out.[1]
- A local authority's expenses in providing a building with closets, additional closets or substituted closets where the owner has failed to comply with a notice requiring him to do so.[2]

- A local authority's expenses in altering existing sanitary conveniences and providing additional sanitary conveniences in the workplace where the owner or occupier has failed to comply with a notice requiring him to do so.[3]
- Half of the local authority's expenses in replacing earth closets with water closets, where the local authority has elected to do the work or the owner has failed to comply with a notice requiring him to do so.[4]

1 Public Health Act 1936, s 45.
2 Building Act 1984, s 64; formerly Public Health Act 1936, s 44.
3 Ibid, s 65; formerly Public Health Act 1936, s 46.
4 Ibid, s 66; formerly Public Health Act 1936, s 47.

5.13   Watercourses, ditches and culverts

- The expenses of a local authority in repairing, maintaining and cleansing any culvert where the owner of the land in question has failed to comply with a notice requiring him to do so.[1]

1 Public Health Act 1936, s 264.

5.14   Water supply

- The expenses of a water undertaker in providing or repairing a cistern where the consumer fails to comply with a notice requiring him to do so.[1]
- The expenses of a local authority in carrying out works to supply wholesome water to domestic premises where the owner or occupier has failed to comply with a notice requiring him to do so.[2]

1 Water Industry Act 1991, s 66.
2 Ibid, s 82.

5.15   Coast protection

- Coastal protection charges under a works scheme which are recoverable from the holder of a particular interest in land.[1]
- Expenses of carrying out repair or maintenance work on private property to protect the coast, where the person responsible has failed to comply with a notice requiring him to undertake the work.[2]
- Works schemes and maintenance schemes which state the parties by whom coast protection charges are payable.[3]

1 Coast Protection Act 1949, s 10.
2 Ibid, ss 12 and 13.
3 Ibid, ss 8(8) and 13(6) and the Local Land Charges Rules 1977, SI 1977/985, r 2(2) – definition of 'specific financial charge'.

Local land charges search

5.16   Pests and verminous premises

- Expenses of a local authority in taking steps to destroy rats and mice on premises or to keep land free from such creatures, where the person responsible has failed to take the required steps to do so.[1]

- The local authority's expenses of cleaning unwholesome and verminous premises where the party responsible has failed to comply with a notice requiring the work to be carried out.[2]

1 Prevention of Damage by Pests Act 1949, s 7.
2 Public Health Act 1936, s 83, as amended by the Public Health Act 1961, s 35.

5.17 Adaptation of premises in smoke control area

- Expenses of a local authority in undertaking adaptations to premises in a smoke control area to avoid contraventions of the prohibition on smoke emissions in smoke control areas, where the person responsible has failed to comply with a notice requiring the work to be done.[1]

1 Clean Air Act 1993, s 24. See para **20.17**.

5.18 Petrol tanks and containers

- Expenses incurred in undertaking work on a derelict petrol tank or other fixed container, where the party responsible has failed to comply with a notice requiring the work to be done.[1]

1 Public Health Act 1961, s 73.

5.19 Statutory nuisances – Part III of the EPA 1990

- Expenses incurred by a local authority in abating or preventing the recurrence of a statutory nuisance where the owner of the premises has failed to comply with a notice requiring him to do so.[1]

1 EPA 1990, ss 81(3), (4) and 81A; formerly the Public Health Act 1936, ss 95 and 96.

5.20 Contaminated land – Part 2A of the EPA 1990

- Expenses incurred by a local authority in carrying out remediation under certain conditions and in respect of which a charging notice is served.[1]

1 EPA 1990, s 78P. Para **15.103**.

5.21 Miscellaneous

- Expenses incurred by a local authority in carrying out any work which is the responsibility of the owner of premises under the provisions of the Public Health Act 1936, where the local authority has agreed with the owner to carry out the work on his behalf, subject to payment of the authority's expenses.[1]

1 Public Health Act 1936, s 275. This applies eg to the repair and cleansing of culverts, ditches and watercourses under ss 259 and 265.

Enforcement

5.22 Specific financial charges (other than those created under the Coast Protection Act 1949, ss 8(8) or 13(6)) are, when registered, enforceable in the same way as if created by a deed of charge by way of legal mortgage.[1] In other words, the chargee is able to employ all the remedies available to a legal mortgagee to enforce the charge, ie:

* foreclosure;
* sale;
* taking possession;
* appointment of a receiver; or
* an action for the money due.[2]

However, these remedies are 'without prejudice to the priority of the charge'.[3] This qualification appears to mean that although local land charges are only enforceable as charges by way of legal mortgage when they are registered, priority dates from the date of creation rather than registration.

Section 55 of the Land Registration Act 2002 provides that where the local land charge secures the payment of money it must be registered at the Land Registry against the registered title before the security can be realised.

1 Local Land Charges Act 1975, s 7; Law of Property Act 1925, s 85.
2 See Megarry & Wade: The Law of Real Property (8th edn, 2012) paras 25–002–25–070; Cheshire and Burn's Modern Law of Real Property (18th edn, 2011) pp 845–873.
3 Local Land Charges Act 1975, s 7.

Part 3: Planning Charges

5.23   Only 'planning charges' are registerable in Part 3. For present purposes, 'planning charges' can be defined as charges which impose a prohibition of or restriction or condition on the use of land under any statutory provision relating to town and country planning, but excluding those relating to the list of buildings of special architectural or historic interest published under the Planning (Listed Buildings and Conservation Areas) Act 1990, s 2 which should be registered in Part 10 of the Register.[1]

1 Local Land Charges Rules 1977, SI 1977/985, r 2(2) – definition of 'planning charge'; ibid r 3.

5.24   This section considers briefly planning charges which are 'environmental' in character.

* Listed Building Enforcement Notices served by the local planning authority if it considers that works have been carried out to a listed building without first obtaining listed building consent or which are in breach of a condition attached to the consent. The notice must specify the alleged contravention and require steps to be taken for restoration of the building or, if that is not reasonably practicable or would be undesirable, for the alleviation of the effect of the works carried out.[1]
* Conditions attached to a Listed Building Consent.[2]
* Building Preservation Notices served by a local planning authority to protect buildings which are of architectural or historic interest, although not listed, which are thought to be in danger of demolition or alteration. A

Notice has effect for six months during which the Secretary of State may decide to list the building.[3]

- Tree Preservation Orders made by a local planning authority which prohibit the cutting down, topping, lopping, uprooting, wilful damage or wilful destruction of trees except with the consent of the local planning authority.[4] Tree Preservation Orders may be made in respect of individual trees, groups of trees or woodlands.[5] They are frequently encountered in relation to new developments, although this is not always the case. Contravention of an order is an offence, for which the penalty is a fine. Tree Preservation Orders do not apply to operations on trees which are dying or dead or have become dangerous or in order to comply with obligations imposed by statute or which are necessary to prevent or abate a nuisance.[6]

- Waste Land Notices requiring the owner to remedy the condition of land which is adversely affecting the amenity of the area.[7]

- Designations of Conservation Areas which are areas of special architectural or historic interest, the character or appearance of which it is desirable to preserve or enhance.[8]

- Conditions attached to a Hazardous Substances Consent when such consent is required for hazardous substances to be present on, over or under land.[9]

- Hazardous substances contravention notices issued in respect of alleged contraventions of hazardous substances control which require steps to be taken to remedy the contravention.[10]

- Directions by the Secretary of State or the appropriate local planning authority restricting any permitted development under the General Permitted Development Order unless planning permission is granted for it on an application.[11] An example is a direction given to restrict permitted agricultural operations under the General Permitted Development Order.[12]

- Planning obligations[13] which may contain provisions relating to environmental matters.

- Conditions attached to a planning permission,[14] eg which require investigation of contamination on the site, and a scheme for dealing with it to be agreed with the planning authority prior to development.

1 Planning (Listed Buildings and Conservation Areas) Act 1990, s 38.
2 Ibid, s 17.
3 Ibid, s 3.
4 Town and Country Planning Act 1990, s 198(3).
5 Ibid, s 198(1).
6 Ibid, s 198(6).
7 Ibid, s 215.
8 Planning (Listed Buildings and Conservation Areas) Act 1990, s 69. See also para **6.10**.
9 Planning (Hazardous Substances) Act 1990, s 10. A condition attached to a deemed hazardous substances consent under the Planning (Hazardous Substances) Act 1990, s 11 is not a local land charge: Local Land Charges Act 1975, s 2(e).
10 Planning (Hazardous Substances) Act 1990, s 24.
11 Town and Country Planning (General Permitted Development) Order 1995, SI 1995/418, _art 4.
12 Ibid, Sch 2, Part 6.
13 Town and Country Planning Act 1990, s 106.
14 Ibid, s 70.

5.25 It should be noted that conditions attached to planning permissions granted prior to the commencement of the Local Land Charges Act 1975 (ie 1 August 1977) or deemed to be granted (at any time) under any statutory provision relating to town and country planning are not local land charges.[1]

1 Local Land Charges Act 1975, s 2(e).

Part 4: Miscellaneous Charges

5.26 Any local land charges not registerable in any other part of the register should be registered in Part 4 which acts as a 'catch-all'.[1]

1 Local Land Charges Rules 1977, SI 1977/985, r 3.

Different types of miscellaneous charges

5.27 'Environmental' local land charges in Part 4 include the following:

5.28 Nature conservation, amenities and access to the countryside

- Restrictions on the use of land in agreements between local authorities and landowners establishing local authority nature reserves, access agreements and access orders.[1]
- Notifications by Natural England (previously English Nature) that an area of land is of special scientific interest.[2]
- Management agreements between local authorities and landowners intended to preserve or enhance the natural beauty or amenity of particular areas of land. The agreements are enforceable against subsequent owners of the land unless the agreement provides otherwise.[3]
- Agreements between landowners and the Secretary of State relating to the management of agricultural land in Environmentally Sensitive Areas. An agreement is enforceable against successive owners of the land unless it provides otherwise.[4]
- Entries in the register relating to a European site.[5]

1 National Parks and Access to the Countryside Act 1949, ss 21, 64, 65 and 66.
2 Wildlife and Countryside Act 1981, s 28(9). Ch 19.
3 Ibid, s 39.
4 Agriculture Act 1986, s 18.
5 Conservation (Natural Habitats &c) Regulations 1994, SI 1994/2716, reg 14. See Ch 19.

5.29 Smoke control areas

- Smoke control areas declared by local authorities which have the effect of prohibiting the emission of smoke from premises subject to certain exemptions.[1]

- Conditions attached to approvals for the height of chimneys attached to furnaces granted by local authorities.[2]

1 Clean Air Act 1993, s 18. See para **20.17**.
2 Clean Air Act 1993, ss 14 and 15.

5.30   Building over sewers

- Conditions attached to a consent for building over a sewer.[1]

1 Building (Amendment) Regulations 2001, SI 2001/3335, Sch 1, H4.

5.31   Archaeological monuments and areas

- The entry in the Schedule of Ancient Monuments of any monument in England and Wales.[1]
- Conditions attached to a scheduled monument consent which authorise the execution of certain works in respect of a scheduled monument.[2]
- Notices as to compensation given under the Ancient Monuments and Archaeological Areas Act 1979, s 7 in respect of the refusal of scheduled monument consent or the granting of consent subject to conditions.[3] Some or all of the compensation may be repayable if the Secretary of State subsequently grants consent or modifies the conditions.
- A guardianship deed placing an ancient monument in the guardianship of the Secretary of State, English Heritage, Welsh Historic Monuments (called Cadw) or the local authority.[4]
- The acquisition of easements by the Secretary of State, English Heritage, Cadw or the local authority for the benefit of any monument or land under their guardianship over adjoining land or land in the vicinity.[5]
- Designation orders of areas of archaeological importance.[6]

1 Ancient Monuments and Archaeological Areas Act 1979, s 1(2) and (9).
2 Ibid, s 2(3) and Sch 1, para 1(2).
3 Ibid, ss 8(2)(b), (2A) and (6).
4 Ibid, ss 12(1), (1A), (2) and (7).
5 Ibid, ss 16(4) and (8).
6 Ibid, s 33.

5.32   Flood risk or coastal erosion risk

- Designation of structures or features the existence or location of which affects flood risk or coastal erosion risk.[1]

1 Flood and Water Management Act 2010, Sch 1, para 5.

Part 10: Listed Building Charges

5.33   Lists of buildings of special architectural or historic interest which are compiled or approved by the Secretary of State.[1] Buildings included in the list are not necessarily 'ancient monuments' under the Ancient Monuments and Archaeological Areas Act 1979. It is unlawful to demolish, alter or extend a listed building so as to affect its character as a building of special architectural or historic interest unless the local authority has granted a listed building consent authorising the works.[2]

1 Planning (Listed Buildings and Conservation Areas) Act 1990, s 2.
2 Ibid, s 7.

Part 12: Drainage Scheme Charges

5.34 Land drainage schemes made by local authorities for the drainage of areas of land capable of improvement by drainage works but in relation to which is would be impractical to establish an internal drainage board due to the small size of the land affected.[1]

1 Land Drainage Act 1991, s 18(1).

Chapter 6

Local authority and water company enquiries

INTRODUCTION

6.01 Enquiries should be made of the local authority, in addition to making the local land charges search, for two reasons. First, the enquiries are broader in scope than the limited range of information available on the registers. Second, the search reveals only the state of the register at the time when the search is made. Accordingly, information as to the authority's proposals for the future will be revealed only through enquiries. This chapter focuses on those local authority enquiries which are 'environmental' in character. In addition, it discusses drainage and water enquiries which should be made to the relevant water service company.

Local authority enquiries should be submitted to the relevant local authority on the standard form CON 29, the latest edition of which is CON 29 (2015).[1] CON 29 has two parts. CON 29R (formerly Part I) contains standard enquiries that are usually always submitted to local authorities. CON 29O (formerly Part II) contains optional enquiries that may be submitted to local authorities in particular cases.

Water service company enquiries should be submitted on the standard CON 29DW form, the current version of which is CON 29DW (2013).

Additional enquiries may be submitted to local authorities and any other public authority under the Environmental Information Regulations.[2] The Regulations are aligned with but have a wider scope in some respects than, the Freedom of Information Act 2000. See Chapter 4.

The standard CON 29 enquiries which concern environmental matters are set out below, together with a brief commentary.[3] The enquiries do not apply to any matters which are entered on the registers of local land charges.

1 CON 29 (2015) came into operation on 4 July 2016.
2 Environmental Information Regulations 2004, SI 2004/3391. The Regulations replaced the Environmental Information Regulations 1992, SI 1992/3240 on 1 January 2005, the same date on which the Freedom of Information Act 2000 entered into effect.
3 For further reference see Pugsley *Enquiries of Local Authorities, A Practical Guide* (5th edn, 2007). Silverman and Hewitson, *Conveyancing Searches and Enquiries*, (4th edn, 2011), Chs 7 and 8.

RIGHTS OF WAY

6.02

2.2 Is any public right of way which abuts in or crosses the property shown in a definitive map or revised definitive map?

2.3 If so please attach a plan showing the approximate route.

2.4 Are there any pending applications to record a public right of way that abuts or crosses the property on the Register?

2.5 Are there any legal orders to stop up, divert, alter or create a public right which abuts or crosses the property not yet implemented or shown on a definitive map?

6.03   These enquiries relates to public rights of way over land which is otherwise privately owned. For example:
- a *footpath* is a highway over which members of the public have a right of way on foot only;
- a *bridleway* is a highway over which members of the public have a right of way on foot alone or on horseback but it may include a right to drive other animals along the bridleway; and
- a *byway open to all traffic* is a highway over which members of the public have a right of way with vehicles as well as other forms of traffic.

6.04   Part IV of the National Parks and Access to the Countryside Act 1949 directed county councils and former county borough councils to undertake a survey of footpaths and bridleways in their areas. Following the surveys, draft maps were prepared showing the routes of such public highways and after a consultation exercise provisional maps were prepared.

A public right of way which is shown on the definitive map is conclusive evidence of its existence.[1]

1 Wildlife and Countryside Act 1981, s 56.

6.05   Part III of the Wildlife and Countryside Act 1981 replaced the provisions of the 1949 Act in the above respect. Part III imposes a duty on the surveying authority (generally county councils and London borough councils) to keep the definitive map under review and to make modifications where necessary, for example to add new rights which have come into existence, or to record the extinguishment or modification of any rights.[1] The definitive map and all modification orders must be available for public inspection free of charge in each district covered by the map.[2] It is usually kept at the offices of the local authority for the district.

Some public rights of way are maintainable at the public expense whilst others are maintainable by the landowner.

1 Wildlife and Countryside Act 1981, s 53.
2 Ibid, s 57.

6.06 These enquiries will normally be raised in the case of rural properties, particularly in the case of open fields or large sites intended for development. Purchasers will normally prefer a negative answer so that their use of the property will not be restricted. Farmers will note that an occupier whose field is traversed by a public right of way may not keep bulls at large in the field. This restriction is inapplicable in the case of bulls aged ten months or less or if the bull is not a recognised dairy breed (ie Ayrshire, British Friesian, British Holsten, Dairy Shorthorn, Guernsey, Jersey or Kerry) if it is accompanied by cows or heifers.[1] Developers will need to make sure that their proposed developments are not likely to obstruct any public right of way.

1 Wildlife and Countryside Act 1981, s 59.

DRAINAGE MATTERS

6.07

3.3 Drainage matters
(a) Is the property served by a SuDs which is adopted by the SuDs Approval Body (SAB) for which there will be a surface water drainage charge?
(b) Are there adopted SuDs features within the boundary of the Property
(c) If the property benefits from a SuDs who bills the property for the surface water drainage charge?

6.08 Construction work which has drainage implications (ie if it will affect the ability of the ground to absorb rain water) may not be commenced unless a drainage system has been approved by the approving body (unitary authority or county council).[1] Approval must be granted if the approving body is satisfied that the drainage system if constructed as proposed will comply with national standards for sustainable drainage; otherwise, approval must be refused. Approval may be subject to conditions including the requirement for a non-performance bond.[2] Applications can be made separately or in combination with a planning application[3] and are subject to consultation.[4] Approving bodies must adopt drainage systems which comply with the conditions for adoption.[5] The right to connect to a public sewer under s 106 of the Water Industry Act 1991 is subject to approval being obtained under those provisions.[6]

1 Flood and Water Management Act, Sch 3, para 7.
2 Paras 11 and 12.
3 Paras 9 and 10.
4 Para 11(3).
5 Para 17.
6 Para 16.

OUTSTANDING NOTICES

6.09

3.7 Do any statutory notices which relate to the following matters subsist in relation to the property other than those revealed in a response to any other enquiry in this form?

(b) environment;
(c) health and safety;
(g) flood and coastal risk management.

6.10 This enquiry deals, in respect of environmental and health and safety legislation, with a variety of notices. The precise significance of any notice revealed should be considered in the light of the relevant legislative provision. Examples of environmental notices include those:

- requiring works to remedy an overflowing cesspool (Public Health Act 1936, s 50);
- requiring the owner to remedy the condition of filthy or verminous premises (Public Health Act 1936, s 83);
- requiring the abatement of a statutory nuisance (EPA 1990, s 80)[1]; and
- designating structures or natural or manmade features which affect flood risk or coastal erosion risk. A designated structure or feature may not be altered, removed or replaced without the consent of the responsible authority. A designation is a local land charge: Flood and Water Management Act 2010, Sch 1.

1 See Ch 5 for local land charges which can be acquired by local authorities in relation to these notices where the owner fails to comply and the authority carries out works in default.

TREE PRESERVATION ORDER

6.11

3.9 Do any of the following subsist in relation to the property, or has a local authority decided to issue, serve, make or commence any of the following?
(m) a tree preservation order.

6.12 Tree preservation orders under s 198 of the Town and Country Planning Act 1990 prohibit the cutting down, lopping, topping, uprooting or wilful destruction of any trees specified by the order. Existing orders are revealed as local land charges.[1] This enquiry should elicit details of proposals for tree preservation orders.

1 See paras 5.23–5.25.

CONSERVATION AREA

6.13

3.11 Do any of the following apply in relation to the property?

(a) the making of the area a conservation area before 31 August 1974;
(b) an unimplemented resolution to designate the area a conservation area.

6.14 Local authorities may designate an area as a conservation area in order to preserve or enhance its character or appearance if they consider that the area is of special architectural or historic interest. This enquiry does not apply to conservation areas which have been designated on or after 1 September 1974 because they are local land charges.[1] Special procedures apply in relation to planning applications and permissions within a conservation area. In general, planning permission to demolish or alter a building within an area may prove difficult to obtain.

1 See paras **5.23–5.25**.

CONTAMINATED LAND

6.15

3.12 Do any of the following apply (including any relating to land adjacent to or adjoining the property which has been identified as contaminated land because it is in such a condition that harm or pollution of controlled waters might be caused on the property)?

(a) a contaminated land notice;
(b) in relation to a register maintained under section 78R of the Environmental Protection Act 1990:
   (i) a decision to make an entry;
   (ii) an entry.
(c) consultation with the owner or occupier of the property conducted under section 78G(3) of the Environmental Protection Act 1990 before the service of a remediation notice.

6.16   The purpose of enquiry 3.12(a) is to identify land which the local authority has determined to be 'contaminated land' under Part 2A of the Environmental Protection Act 1990, but for which a remediation notice, statement or declaration has not been entered on the register.[1] The CON 29 questions do not include the term 'significant harm or significant possibility of significant harm', as in Part 2A, see paras **15.50–15.52**, although this appears to be intended.

1 This legislation is dealt with fully in Ch 15.

6.17   Registers which are maintained under s 78R of the Environmental Protection Act 1990 are discussed in Chapter 15.

6.18   The purpose of enquiry 3.12(c) is to identify land which adjoins or is adjacent to 'contaminated land' under Part IIA for which the owner or occupier has granted, or will grant, rights to enable the contamination to be remediated.

RADON GAS PRECAUTIONS

6.19

3.13 Do records indicate that the property is in a 'Radon Affected Area' as identified by the Public Health England or Public Health Wales?

6.20 Radon gas, which is a decay product of uranium-238, occurs naturally in certain areas of the country where there are significant outcrops of granite. The gas is colourless and odourless but is considered to cause lung cancer. Where it occurs, adequate ventilation is required in buildings to avoid any undue build-up of the gas. New houses in parts of Devon, Cornwall, Somerset, Derbyshire and Northamptonshire must have radon protection measures installed. In the area of highest risk (the primary zone), houses require a radon proof barrier in addition to other measures which can be activated in the event of high radon levels. In areas of lower risk (the secondary zone), only precautionary measures are required.[1]

1 Building Regulations 2010, SI 2010/2214, Sch 1 (as amended); Office of the Deputy Prime Minister, Approved Document C, Site preparation and resistance to contaminants and moisture paras 2.39–2.41 (2004, amended 2010 and 2013).

6.21 The National Radiological Protection Board (NRPB) has recommended that the 'action level' is 200 becquerels per cubic metre,[1] although there are no mandatory requirements for existing dwellings. Discretionary house renovation grants may be available from the local authority for undertaking appropriate preventive measures.

1 See Health & Safety Executive website (www.hse.gov.uk/radiation/ionising/radon.htm). For further information contact the Health Protection Agency, Chilton, Didcot, Oxon 0X11 0RQ. Tel 01235 822 622; e-mail: radon@hpa.org.uk and the Radon Council, P.O. Box 39, Shepperton, Middlesex TW17 8AD. Tel 01932 221 212; e-mail: radoncouncil@radon-uk.demon.co.uk. See also para **3.18**.

PARKS AND COUNTRYSIDE

Areas of Outstanding Natural Beauty

6.22

8.1 Has any order under s 82 of the Countryside and Rights of Way Act 2000 been made?

National Parks

6.23

8.2 Is the property within a National Park designated under s 7 of the National Parks and Access to the Countryside Act 1949?

6.24 The Countryside Commission was previously authorised to make orders under s 87 of the National Parks and Access to the Countryside Act 1949 (repealed). Section 87 provided for the designation of Areas of Outstanding Natural Beauty (AONBs) which were considered to deserve preservation. Prior to making such orders, a consultation process provided an opportunity for the public to make representations or objections. The order had to be confirmed by the Secretary of State for the Environment. After the order had been confirmed:

- the local planning authority consulted with the Countryside Commission in connection with the preparation of the development plan;
- the local authority had the power to preserve and enhance the natural beauty of the area designated;
- the local authority had the power to make by-laws governing the use of land which it owned within the area; and
- the range of development permitted under the General Permitted Development Order could be restricted.

The 1949 Act, however, provided no duties on the authorities in relation to AONBs.

Part IV of the Countryside and Rights of Way Act 2000 essentially re-enacted s 87 (and s 88) of the 1949 Act. It also placed a duty on the relevant authorities in exercising their functions in relation to land in an AONB to have regard to the purpose of conserving and enhancing the natural beauty of the AONB.[1]

1 Countryside and Rights of Way Act 2000, s 85.

6.25   It is more difficult to obtain planning permission for new development or altering existing buildings in an AONB. Purchasers of existing residential property will therefore generally prefer an affirmative reply to question 8.1. On the other hand, commercial developers will prefer a negative reply.

6.26   Similarly, planning permission is extremely difficult to obtain within a National Park. The preferences of residential purchasers and commercial developers will therefore be the same for National Parks as for AONBs.

NOISE ABATEMENT

Noise abatement zone

6.27

11.1 Have the Council made, or resolved to make, any noise abatement zone order under s 63 of the Control of Pollution Act 1974 for the area?

Entries in register

6.28

11.2 Has any entry been recorded in the noise level register kept pursuant to s 64 of the Control of Pollution Act 1974?

11.3 If there is any entry, how can copies be obtained and where can that register be inspected?

6.29   This legislation (ss 63–67 of the Control of Pollution Act 1974) was little used and has now been repealed by the Deregulation Act 2015, s 59 and Sch 13, Part 5 as from 1 October 2015.

The local authority could until the repeal make a noise abatement order which designated all or part of its area as a noise abatement zone.[1] An order specified the classes of premises to which it applied. Section 64 required the local authority to measure noise levels from all premises covered by the order. The recorded measurements had to be entered in the noise level register which was open to inspection by the public free of charge. Copies of the recorded measurements had to be served on the owner and occupier of each premises concerned. Following registration, the noise level for each premises was not permitted to exceed the registered level except with the written consent of the local authority.[2]

1 Control of Pollution Act 1974, s 63.
2 Ibid, s 65.

6.30 If new buildings of a class specified in the order are to be built within the zone or if a building is to be converted to a specified class of building, the owner or proposed purchaser may request the local authority to determine the acceptable noise level.[1] The local authority has power to serve a noise reduction notice in respect of premises covered by the order if existing noise levels are unacceptable.[2]

Relatively few noise abatement zones have been created but intending purchasers will be concerned to ensure that there are no undue restrictions on noise levels which their activities may create.

1 Control of Pollution Act 1974, s 67.
2 Ibid, s 66.

HAZARDOUS SUBSTANCE CONSENTS

6.31

18.1 Please list any entries in the register kept pursuant to s 28 of the Planning (Hazardous Substances) Act 1990.

18.2 If there are any entries:

(a) how can copies of the entries be obtained?
(b) where can the Register be inspected?

6.32 A consent from the local planning authority is required to keep a hazardous substance on, over or under land. The authority is required to keep a public register of applications, consents, modifications and directions made under the legislation.[1] The term 'hazardous substance' is defined more closely in the Regulations.[2]

1 Planning (Hazardous Substances) Regulations 2015, SI 2015/627, reg 20.
2 Ibid, reg 3, Sch 1.

ENVIRONMENTAL AND POLLUTION NOTICES

6.33

19. What outstanding statutory notices or informal notices have been issued by the Council under the Environmental Protection Act 1990 or the Control of Pollution Act 1974?[1]

(This enquiry does not cover notices under Part 2A or Part 3 of the EPA, to which enquiries 3.12 and 3.7 apply.)

1 See, eg, EPA 1990, ss 34A, 47ZA, 59.

6.34   Notices covered by this enquiry include:

*   enforcement notices served by local authorities under local authority air pollution control legislation;[1]
*   notices requiring the removal of waste by local authorities in their role as waste collection authorities;[2]
*   construction site noise notices which may control the hours during which it is possible to work and therefore may have an impact on a building development programme;[3] and
*   noise reduction notices in respect of premises in noise abatement zones.[4]

1 See generally **chap.20** discussing the Environmental Permitting (England and Wales) Regulations 2010, SI 2010/675.
2 EPA 1990, s 59.
3 Control of Pollution Act 1974, s 60. See paras **14.73–14.76**.
4 Control of Pollution Act 1974, s 66.

HEDGEROW NOTICES

6.35

21.1 Please list any entries in the record maintained under reg 10 of the Hedgerows Regulations 1997.

21.2 If there are any entries:

(a) how can copies of the matters entered be obtained?
(b) where can the record be inspected?

6.36   Records maintained under reg 10 include hedgerow removal notices received, and hedgerow retention notices issued, by the local planning authority.[1]

The Regulations do not protect all hedgerows. Rather, they apply to 'important' hedgerows, the criteria for which include:

*   the location of the hedgerow, that is, the hedgerow must grow in, or adjacent to, common land, a village green, a site of special scientific interest and/or a local nature reserve, or land which is used for agriculture, forestry or the breeding or keeping of horses, ponies or donkeys;

- the hedgerow must have existed for at least 30 years; and
- it must be at least 20 metres long or form part of another hedgerow.

1 Hedgerow Regulations 1997, SI 1997/1160, reg 10.

6.37 The owner of a hedgerow may submit a proposal to remove a hedgerow to the relevant local planning authority (a hedgerow removal notice).[1] If the planning authority considers that the hedgerow should not be removed, it issues a hedgerow retention notice to prohibit the proposed works being carried out.[2]

1 Hedgerow Regulations 1997, SI 1997/1160, reg 5(1).
2 Ibid, reg 5(2)–(9).

FLOOD DEFENCE AND LAND DRAINAGE CONSENTS

6.38

22. Has any flood defence or land drainage consent relating to the property been given or refused of (if applicable) is the subject of a pending application?[1]

1 See para **7.13**.

STANDARD DRAINAGE AND WATER ENQUIRIES

6.39

The Law Society introduced CON 29DW in Summer 2002. The current version is CON 29DW (2016). Enquiries related to water and sewerage assets under and around properties may be made directly to water companies or through a data service provider.

Standard CON 29DW enquiries which concern environmental matters are set out below, together with a brief commentary.

FOUL AND SURFACE DRAINAGE

6.40

2.1 Does foul water from the property drain to a public sewer?

2.2 Does surface water from the property drain to a public sewer?

6.41 It is important to understand the terminology concerning the above enquiries:

- A *private drain* and/or *water supply pipe* serves a single building or property.

- A *sewer* conveys effluent from more than one property.
- A *public sewer* is vested in the sewerage undertaker which is the privatised successor company of the former regional water authority. The sewerage undertaker is not responsible for the maintenance of private drains and private sewers connected to the public sewerage system. The maintenance costs therefore fall upon the owner or owners of the relevant property or properties.
- *Foul drainage* is effluent produced within the property itself, as opposed to *surface water drainage* which comprises rain water.

6.42 Foul drainage which enters the public sewerage system goes to the sewage treatment works for treatment. For that reason, buyers will prefer an affirmative reply to enquiry 2.1. A negative answer will indicate that drainage leads directly to a cesspool or sceptic tank, which will need to be emptied periodically as well as maintained at the cost of the owner. Whilst the owner does not pay the sewage element of the water bill for the property, he or she is responsible for the cost of operating and maintaining the alternative treatment process. In addition, the owner is responsible for establishing and maintaining the connection to the nearest appropriate public sewer if the cesspool or other private plant becomes difficult, unpleasant or too expensive to operate.

6.43 From a buyer's perspective, a positive answer to enquiry 2.2 is preferable because, as noted above, the maintenance of private sewers may be expensive and shared expenditure of this type can give rise to disputes between the owners affected.

Replies to the above two questions and to the next two questions are based on the statutory sewer map which the water and sewerage undertaker hold.

ADOPTION AGREEMENT

6.44

2.6 Are any sewers or lateral drains serving or which are proposed to serve the property the subject of an existing adoption agreement or an application for such an agreement?

6.45 Section 104 of the Water Industry Act 1991 provides for agreements to be made between developers and water service companies in relation to the construction and maintenance of new sewers. The s 104 agreement, which is generally supported by a bond, only requires the sewerage undertaker to adopt the sewer when the developer has complied with his obligations under the agreement. If the adoption or vesting has not already taken place, enquiries should be made as to whether there has been compliance with the agreement. After adoption, the undertaker assumes responsibility for maintenance of the sewer. Until that time it is a private sewer for the repair of which the owners of the properties it serves are responsible.

6.46   An affirmative reply is to be expected in the case of property on a new estate. However, if the response is negative, an enquiry should be made of the sewerage undertaker as to whether such an agreement exists under s 18 of the Public Health Act 1936 (the predecessor of s 104 of the Water Industry Act 1991). Although it may be difficult to obtain a satisfactory reply, enquiries should be made as to the adequacy of the bond. As a general rule, the sewerage undertaker adopts the sewer and sewage pumping station only when they have been shown to be adequate and the development is near completion. Until the undertaker has adopted the sewer and sewage pumping station serving a new estate, the developer is responsible for them.

SEWERS WITHIN THE PROPERTY

6.47

2.4 Does the public sewer map indicate any public sewer, disposal main or lateral drain within the boundaries of the property?

6.48   Sewerage undertakers are under a duty to keep records of the locations and other details of all sewers vested in them including the details requested in this question.[1] The local authority as well as the sewerage undertaker keeps copies of the sewer maps. Both authorities are required to make them available for inspection to the public free of charge. The practical importance of this question is that generally no new buildings are permitted to be constructed over any sewer or drain shown on the sewer map unless the sewerage undertaker consents.[2]

1 Water Industry Act 1991, s 199.
2 Building Regulations 2010, SI 2010/2214, reg 15(3)(b).

NEARBY SEWERS

6.49

2.5 Does the public sewer map indicate any public sewer within 30.48 metres (100 feet) of any buildings within the property?

2.7 Has a sewerage undertaker approved or been consulted about any plans to erect a building or extension on the property over or in the vicinity of a public sewer, disposal main or drain?

6.50   Where a site is bought for development, the proposed purchaser will be concerned to know whether the local authority is likely to require the property to be connected to the public sewer. The authority may not require such a connection unless the public sewer is within 100 feet of the site of the building or in the case of an extension, the site either of the extension or of the original building. In addition, the building must be at a level which makes it reasonably practicable to construct a drain to communicate with the public sewer. Provided that the same conditions are satisfied, the authority may require a connection with a private sewer provided that the site owner is entitled to use it. In either case, the local authority can only require a connection to the sewer if a landowner is entitled to construct a drain through the intervening land. If the sewer to which the connection is to be made is more than 100 feet from the building, the authority must undertake to bear the excess costs.[1]

1 Building Act 1984, ss 21(4) and (5).

6.51 Paragraph H4 of Sch 1 of the Building Regulations 2010[1] prohibits building works, including underpinning, over a drain, sewer or disposal main shown on a map of sewers[2] unless the works are shown not to be detrimental to the continued use and maintenance of the drain, sewer or disposal main. When a local authority receives a proposal for such works, it notifies the sewerage undertaker and must have regard to any views expressed by the undertaker.[3] The purpose of the notification requirement is to ensure that a building or extension is not constructed so as to overload or damage the drain, sewer or disposal main and to allow access to it for any repairs or, if necessary, its diversion.

1 SI 2010/2214.
2 The map of sewers refers to any records which are kept by a sewerage undertaker under s 199 of the Water Industry Act 1991.
3 Building Regulations 2010, SI 2010/2214, reg 15(3).

Chapter 7

Other sources of information

INTRODUCTION

7.01 Local authorities and water service companies do not hold all the environmental information which may be sought about a property. Thus, whilst standard enquiries and searches reveal useful information, it is frequently necessary to contact other authorities in order to obtain a more complete picture of the environmental condition of the property.

When considering whether to approach such authorities about a specific property, the buyer should be aware of any sensitivities on the part of the seller. In appropriate cases, the buyer may wish to commission an investigation by environmental consultants or to obtain a site investigation report rather than to contact the authorities directly. This chapter describes some of the additional investigations which may be made in order to obtain the fullest information on the environmental issues affecting a property.

PUBLIC REGISTERS

7.02 A number of registers are kept by the environmental regulatory authorities which can be inspected free of charge by members of the public. Copies of entries on the registers can be obtained on payment of reasonable charges.

A guide to accessing public registers held by the Environment Agency is available on https://www.gov.uk/access-the-public-register-for-environmental-information.

The principal registers which are likely to contain information which is of interest to property owners and potential buyers are listed below.

Type of Information	Statute/Regulations	Authority Keeping Information
Local Land Charges – many of these relate to environmental matters (see Ch 5)	Local Land Charges Act 1975 and various environmental legislation	Local Authority
Environmental permits (including former waste management licences discharge consents – controlled waters including groundwater, registrations and authorisations relating to radioactive substances), applications, modifications, revocations, suspensions	Environmental Permitting (England and Wales) Regulations 2010, SI 2010/675, Sch 24	Environment Agency Natural Resources Wales Local Authority (Part A2 and Part B activities)

Type of Information	Statute/Regulations	Authority Keeping Information
Register of activities exempt from environmental permitting	Environmental Permitting (England and Wales) Regulations 2010, SI 2010/675, Sch 2, para 7	Environment Agency Natural Resources Wales
Contaminated land: remediation notices, statements, declarations, designations of special sites	Environmental Protection Act 1990, s 78R; Contaminated Land (England) Regulations 2006, SI 2006/1380, r 13 and Sch 3	Local Authority Environment Agency/Natural Resources Wales (for special sites)
Litter control areas; litter control notices	Environmental Protection Act 1990, s 95	Local Authority
Licences for abstracting, impounding water, applications, variations, revocations	Water Resources Act 1991, s 189; Water Resources (Abstraction and Impounding) Regulations 2006, SI 2006/641, r 34	Environment Agency Natural Resources Wales
Maps of main rivers	Water Resources Act 1991, ss 193, 193A–193E.	Environment Agency Natural Resources Wales
Flow, level and volume of water in inland waters and aquifers	Water Resources Act 1991, s 197	Environment Agency Natural Resources Wales
Trade effluent consents, trade effluent agreements	Water Industry Act 1991, s 196	Sewerage Undertaker
Drainage hereditaments	Land Drainage Act 1991, s 52; Registers of Drainage Boards Regulations 1968, SI 1968/1672	Internal Drainage District
Large raised reservoirs	Reservoirs Act 1975, s 2(2)(b)	Environment Agency Natural Resources Wales
Consents, applications and enforcement notices relating to the storage of hazardous substances	Planning (Hazardous Substances) Act 1990, s 28; Planning (Hazardous Substances) Regulations 2015, SI 2015/627	Hazardous Substances Authority (generally the Local Authority)
Registered noise levels, noise reduction notices in noise abatement zones	Control of Pollution Act 1974, ss 64, 66; Control of Noise (Measurement and Registers) Regulations 1976, SI 1976/37	Local Authority
End-of-Life Vehicles authorised treatment facilities	End-of-Life Vehicles Regulations 2003, SI 2003/2635	Environment Agency Natural Resources Wales
Genetically modified organisms notices, applications, offences, directions	Environmental Protection Act 1990, s 122	Environment Agency Natural Resources Wales
Litter control orders and notices	Environmental Protection Act 1990, s 95	Local Authority

POLLUTION INVENTORY

7.03   The Environment Agency compiles and maintains a non-statutory Pollution Inventory which includes data on annual emissions of over 150 substances, including greenhouse gases, into the environment from over 2,000 industrial facilities. Facilities which must report annual emissions to air, water and land, off-site transfers of waste and specified substances in waste water are those regulated by the Environment Agency under various regimes including the Environmental Permitting (England and Wales) Regulations 2010 and specified sewage treatment works.

The Environment Agency reports data from the Pollution Inventory to the National Atmospheric Emissions Inventory and the European Pollutant Release and Transfer Register.[1]

1 The European Pollutant Release and Transfer Register was established under. Regulation (EC) No 166/2006 of the European Parliament and of the Council concerning the establishment of a European Pollutant Release and Transfer Register and amending Council Directives 91/689/ EEC and 96/61/EC, OJ L 33/1 (4 February 2006). It superseded the earlier European Pollutant Emission Register.

ENQUIRIES OF OTHER AUTHORITIES

Environment Agency and Natural Resources Wales

7.04   The functions of the Environment Agency, which came into existence on 1 April 1996,[1] include regulating the following matters which were previously dealt with by other authorities:

- water abstraction under Part II of the Water Resources Act 1991;
- water quality under Part III of the Water Resources Act 1991;
- flood defence under Part IV of the Water Resources Act 1991 and the Land Drainage Act 1991;
- fisheries under Part V of the Water Resources Act 1991 and the Salmon and Freshwater Fisheries Act 1975;
- waste management under the Environmental Permitting (England and Wales) Regulations 2010, SI 2010/675;
- radioactive substances under the Environmental Permitting (England and Wales) Regulations 2010, SI 2010/675; and
- pollution prevention and control under the Pollution Prevention and Control Act 1999 and the Environmental Permitting (England and Wales) Regulations 2010, SI 2010/675.

In addition the Environment Agency has functions in relation to contaminated land under Part 2A of the Environmental Protection Act 1990.[2]

1 Environment Act 1995, s 2; Environment Act 1995 (Commencement No 5) Order 1996, SI 1996/186, s 3. Natural Resources Body Wales (NRBW) generally known as Natural Resources Wales (NRW) became responsible for the Environment Agency's functions in Wales from 1 April 2013: SI 2013/755, Art 4(2), Sch 4, paras 246, 247(a).
2 Environmental Protection Act 1990, Part 2A (inserted by the Environment Act 1995, s 57).

Environment Agency property search reports

7.05   In 2003, the Environment Agency introduced standardised property search reports for specified sites at a fixed charge. An additional charge for further information was based on the time spent by the Agency in answering further enquiries.

The Agency terminated the property search reports on 30 March 2007. In doing so, the Agency noted that the information could be obtained from other sources.

Commercial property search providers

7.06   The following companies provide reports that contain information from the Environment Agency and other sources including the Ordnance Survey, Her Majesty's Land Registry, the Health and Safety Executive, the Coal Authority, trade directories, historical mapping and their own data bases.

Charges for the reports vary depending on the type of report required and the residential or industrial nature of the specified site.

7.07   Argyll Environmental provides the following environmental reports:

* SiteSolutions (range of commercial, estate and residential reports);
* Envirosearch (residential);
* Plansearch (commercial); and
* Plansearch Plus (residential).
* Flood Solutions.

7.08   GroundSure Limited provides the following environmental reports:

* Homebuyers (residential);
* Screening (commercial);
* Review (commercial);
* SiteGuard (commercial);
* Developer (commercial); and
* Data (commercial).
* Flood View.

7.09   Landmark Information Group provides the following environmental reports:

* Homecheck Professional (range of residential reports);
* Envirosearch (residential);
* Envirocheck (commercial);
* Sitecheck (range of commercial reports);
* Historical data; and
* Enviroscreen.

Sitescope Limited also provides a commercial environmental report.

Typical information in commercial property search reports

7.10 The following lists information which tends to be included in reports from commercial search providers. The client may also instruct an environmental consultant to produce a report containing further information on these matters. The consultant will provide the client with a more detailed evaluation of the environmental risks posed by the data in the report and, as instructed by the client, carry out other investigations.

7.11

1 Water Abstraction[1]
1.1 Current licence to abstract or impound water which relates to the property.[2]
1.2 Any proposals to revoke or modify the licence.[3]
1.3 Revocation or modification of the licence together with the reason for revocation or modification.[4]
1.4 Any refusal to issue a licence relating to the property together with the reason for the refusal.[5]
1.5 Consent by the owner of the property to the grant of a licence by the Environment Agency which derogates from any protected rights[6] relating to the property.
1.6 Any works agreement made under s 158 of the Water Resources Act 1991, which affects the property.[7]
1.7 Any breach of Part II of the Water Resources Act 1991 in relation to the property together with any proposed or actual action by the Environment Agency such as criminal proceedings and, if so, their outcome.
1.8 All entries relating to the property in the register kept pursuant to s 189 of the Water Resources Act 1991.

1 These enquiries are relevant only if the proposed buyer intends to abstract or impound water for use on the property. The relevant statutory provisions are in the Water Resources Act 1991, Part II: see Ch 17.
2 If there is a licence, close attention must be paid to the statutory provisions relating to the transfer of licences in abstraction: Water Resources Act 1991, ss 59A–D, to ensure that the buyer does not lose the benefit of the licence: see para **17.41** and Ch 12. Successors in title do not automatically take the benefit of an impounding licence, it must be transferred. Water Resources Act 1991, s 59A.
3 See Water Resources Act 1991, ss 51–56, 59.
4 The reasons behind a positive answer to this question should be examined to discover whether there is a continuing problem with regard to the licence which could result in further action by the Environment Agency even though none is currently contemplated.
5 The Environment Agency may refuse to grant a licence if it considers it necessary or expedient to do so. Water Resources Act 1991, s 38(2)(b). In reaching a decision, the Agency must have regard to existing abstraction and impounding rights (s 39) and the minimum acceptable flow of the waters affected (s 40). Any past refusal of a licence may suggest difficulties in obtaining a licence in the future.
6 See para **17.34**.
7 Under this section the Environment Agency may by agreement arrange for works (or the maintenance of works) in respect of its water resource functions to be undertaken by a water or sewerage undertaker, a local authority or the owner or occupier of any land. Agreements between the Agency and a landowner are registerable as Class D(iii) land charges, or in the case of registered land should be protected by means of notice under the Land Registration Act 2002, ss 58–59. Water Resources Act 1991, ss 158(3) and (4).

7.12

2 Water Pollution[1]

2.1 Any unconsented discharge or entry of any substance from the property into controlled waters together with any action by the Agency (including service of a works notice or prohibition notice).[2]

2.2 Any current environmental permit to discharge into controlled waters which relates to the property.[3]

2.3 Details of any failure to comply with conditions attached to such a consent and any action taken or proposed by the Environment Agency (including service of enforcement notices).[4]

2.4 The last date on which any discharge consent relating to the property was reviewed and any indication by the Agency to review, revoke or vary any discharge consent which relates to the property or whether the Agency has received a direction from the Secretary of State to carry out such a review.[5]

2.5 Sensitivity to pollution of the water resources in the area.

2.6 Any statutory or non-statutory designation relating to water pollution.[6]

2.7 Service of any notice in relation to the property under reg 7 of the Water Resources (Control of Pollution) (Silage, Slurry and Agricultural Fuel Oil) Regulations 2010 and indication of any action to deal with the matter complained of.[7]

2.8 Details of entries relating to the property in the register kept pursuant to s 190 of the Water Resources Act 1991.

1 These enquiries are relevant if discharges from the property enter 'controlled waters', defined in the Water Resources Act 1991, s 104; para **17.43**.

2 This enquiry is designed to ascertain any action taken by the Environment Agency under water pollution legislation. In the event of a positive answer, the buyer should seek to negotiate that the seller undertakes or pays for sufficient measures to alleviate the concerns of the Agency. The relevant offences are considered in paras **17.44–17.68**; the Agency's powers to issue a works notice requiring preventive or remedial work to be undertaken are considered in paras **17.86–17.93**.

3 An environmental permit (formerly a discharge consent) is a defence to certain water pollution offences under the Environmental Permitting (England and Wales) Regulations 2010, SI 2010/675, reg 38(1). See paras **17.69–17.78**, For transfer of permits, see Ch 12.

4 Failure to comply with permit conditions is an offence. Environmental Permitting (England and Wales) Regulations 2010, SI 2010/675, reg 38(2). An enforcement notice may be served under reg 36. See para **20.28**.

5 Review of permits is considered in para **17.74**. Individual legislation provides for conditions under which permits etc may or must be reviewed including whether a permits etc should be affirmed, modified or revoked. An example is the effect of a permits on a Special Protection Area under the Birds Directive or a candidate or designated Special Conservation Area under the Habitats Directive. Conservation (Natural Habitats &c) Regulations 2010, SI 2010/490, reg 63.

6 Statutory and non-statutory designations, including water protection zones and groundwater source protection zones are considered in detail in paras **17.94–17.102**.

7 Crops being made into silage, silage slurry and fuel oil kept for running a farm must be stored in containers in accordance with the requirements of the Water Resources (Control of Pollution) (Silage, Slurry and Agricultural Fuel Oil) (England) Regulations 2010, SI 2010/639, Schs 1, 2 or 3 respectively. An exemption from these requirements may apply if the structure was in use or constructed before 1 March 1991 or if a construction contract had been entered into or it was under construction before that date and the work completed before 1 September 1991: reg 6. However, the Environment Agency may serve a notice under reg 7 specifying the works or other steps required to reduce any significant risk of pollution to a minimum. The notice must be served on the person having custody or control of the substance in question. Notices are subject to a right of appeal to the Secretary of State under reg 8.

7.13

3 Land Drainage and Flood Defence

3.1 Location of the property within a flood risk contour shown on the indicative flood plain maps.

3.2 Any effects from flooding during the past 100 years.[1]

3.3 Location of any watercourse on or adjoining the property which is a main river for the purposes of s 193 of the Water Resources Act 1991.[2]

3.4 Application of any land drainage or flood defence byelaws[3] in relation to the property.

3.5 Any environmental permits for flood risk activities granted (or applied for) in relation to the property under the Environmental Permitting (England and Wales) Regulations 2010 (formerly consents under s 109 of the Water Resources Act 1991),[4] s 23 of the Land Drainage Act 1991[5] or any applicable land drainage or flood defence byelaws.

3.6 Details of any breaches of the legislation referred to in the previous enquiry in respect of the property and any action taken or proposed by the Environment Agency (including service of notices and criminal proceedings) and the outcome of such action including the steps taken (if any) to rectify the position.

3.7 Responsibility, if any, of the Environment Agency for maintaining any watercourse on or adjoining the property.[6]

3.8 Any interest in the property by the Environment Agency.[7]

1 See the Law Society's Flood Risk Practice Note 2014.
2 The Environment Agency publishes a flood map for England and Wales on its website. www. environment-agency.gov.uk Because of their importance in connection with drainage, the Agency exercises most functions in connection with main rivers, their banks and related drainage works. Those functions are exercised by drainage boards in relation to other watercourses. Water Resources Act 1991, s 107.
3 The Environment Agency has power to make byelaws to ensure the efficient working of the drainage system and sea defences in any locality. Water Resources Act 1991, s 210, Sch 25, para 5. An internal drainage board has power to make byelaws to regulate drainage within its district. Land Drainage Act 1991, s 66. Drainage byelaws regulate matters such as the operation of sluices, the removal of obstructions, the control of vermin and the use of watercourse banks. See eg Model Drainage Byelaws (1987), byelaw 27. If positive action is required eg the repair of a structure over a minor watercourse or on its banks, the drainage authority may serve a notice on the person responsible requiring the work to be carried out: Land Drainage Act 1991, s 71. See generally John Bates, *Water and Drainage Law*, Ch 12 (Sweet & Maxwell, looseleaf).
4 EP Regulations 2010, reg 12 and Sch 23ZA.
5 Similar restrictions apply in relation to other watercourses, in which case consent must be obtained from the relevant drainage board: Land Drainage Act 1991, s 23.
6 See fn 1 above. The Environment Agency may be made the drainage board for a district: Land Drainage Act 1991, s 4.
7 The Environment Agency has power to acquire property under the Environment Act 1995, s 37. The Agency owns river banks in some cases which would otherwise belong to the riparian owner. This will affect liability for maintenance of the river bank.

7.14

4 Waste Management[1]

4.1 Existence of any environmental permit for a landfill in relation to the property.[2]

4.2 Any breaches of permit conditions and, if so, any action taken or proposed by the Agency.[3]

4.3 Details of any inspections of the permitted site at the property by the Environment Agency and copies of relevant inspection reports.[4]

4.4 Exemption of any activities carried on at the property from the requirement of an environmental permit.[5]

4.5 Any current concerns by the Environment Agency regarding operations on the permitted landfill site at the property.

4.6 Any fly-tipping or other nonpermitted deposit of waste at the property noted by the Environment Agency together with details.[6]

4.7 Details of all entries relating to the property in the register of exempt activities kept pursuant to Environmental Permitting (England and Wales) Regulations 2010, SI 2010/675, Sch 2, para 7.

1 Environmental Permitting (England and Wales) Regulations 2010, SI 2010/675. See generally Ch 16.

2 An environmental permit is required in order to deposit 'controlled waste' on land or to carry out any disposal or recovery operation on it. Environmental Permitting (England and Wales) Regulations 2010, SI 2010/675, reg 12 and Sch 10. Otherwise subject to certain defences an offence is committed. Ibid, s 38; Environmental Protection Act 1990, s 33. For further details, see Ch 20. For transfer of permits see Ch 12.

3 A breach of permit conditions is an offence. Environmental Protection Act 1990, s 33(6); Environmental Permitting (England and Wales) Regulations 2010, SI 2010/675, reg 38. Recent breaches of permit conditions may indicate problems with the operation of the site which a buyer should investigate before applying for a transfer of the permit.

4 Compliance Assessment Reports should reveal any concerns which the Environment Agency has or had in relation to the management of the site, which may result in enforcement action.

5 Certain waste management activities listed in the Environmental Permitting (England and Wales) Regulations 2010, SI 2010/675, Sch 3 are exempt from the requirement of a permit provided they meet specified requirements. Ibid, reg 5; see para **16.22**. Failure to register an exempt activity is an offence.

6 The Environment Agency has the power to serve a notice on the owner or occupier of land requiring the removal of any waste which has been unlawfully deposited: Environmental Protection Act 1990, ss 59–59A.

7.15

5 **Contamination**[1]

5.1 Any concerns by the Environment Agency about contamination on the property which may give rise to environmental pollution together with details and steps taken or proposed by the Agency to deal with the problem.[2]

5.2 Any landfill site or other waste management or other industrial facility on or within 500 metres of the property. If the response is affirmative, enquiries may be made regarding:

5.2.1 the site(s) in relation to the property by reference to a map;

5.2.2 the dates at which the site(s) was operative; and

5.2.3 whether each site was engineered or is of the dilute and disperse variety.[3]

5.3 The nature and extent of any restoration or remedial measures which have been carried out.

5.4 Details of any environmental permit relating to the property and the area within 500 metres of the property which have been surrendered, including, in particular, the types of waste permitted to be deposited at the site and the date of surrender of the permit(s).[4]

5.5 Details of any activities listed in the Environmental Permitting (England and Wales) Regulations 2007, SI 2007/3538, Sch 1, Part I which are or have been carried out at or within 500 metres from the property.

5.6 Whether the Environment Agency has any concern about contamination originating from the sites outside the property identified under this enquiry and, if so, details and steps taken or proposed by the Agency to take to deal with the problem.[5]

5.7 Proposed or actual designation of part or all of the property as a special site under s 78C of the Environmental Protection Act 1990.

5.8 Proposed or actual service by the Environment Agency of a remediation notice on any person under s 78E of the Environmental Protection Act 1990 in respect of the property and, if so, whether the notice has been complied with or appealed.

5.9 Details of all entries relating to the property in the register kept pursuant to s 78R of the Environmental Protection Act 1990.

1 See generally Ch 15.
2 For the powers of the Environment Agency to deal with water pollution problems, see paras **17.83–17.85**. Part 2A is enforced primarily by local authorities although the Environment Agency exercises jurisdiction over special sites and has the power to issue site specific guidance to local authorities: Environmental Protection Act 1990, ss 78C–78E and 78V respectively. See paras **15.53–15.54**.
3 The traditional landfill in the UK was the dilute and disperse type which operated on the principle that pollutants dissolve in rainwater passing through the site forming leachate which gradually becomes diluted in the groundwater and is rendered less harmful as it disperses. Modern landfills must be contained generally with clay or synthetic linings to prevent the egress of contaminants which when dissolved in water are collected and drained into the main sewers in accordance with a trade effluent consent issued by the sewerage undertaker.
4 Prior to 1 May 1994, waste disposal licences granted under the Control of Pollution Act 1974, Part 2 could be surrendered to the waste regulation authority at will. For the different position in respect of environmental permits, see para **20.23**.
5 See fn 2 above in relation to water pollution and also para **7.14**, fn 6 in relation to unlawfully deposited waste.

7.16

6 Invasive Species
6.1 The presence of any invasive species, such as Japanese Knotweed, on the property.[1]

6.2 Any species control agreement or species control order in effect in relation to the property.[2]

1 Wildlife and Countryside Act 1981, s 14.
2 Ibid, s 14(4A) and Sch 9A. See Ch 2.

7.17

6 Radioactive Substances[1]
6.1 The presence of any radioactive material or radioactive waste on the property.

6.2 Any environmental permit in respect of the keeping or use of radioactive material on the property, the disposal of radioactive waste on or from the property or the accumulation of such waste on the property.[2]

6.3 Any revocation or variation of such an environmental permit.[3]

6.4 Any proposal to cancel or vary any such registration or to revoke or vary such an authorisation.

6.5 Details of any breaches of the conditions of any such registration or authorisation and any action taken or proposed by the Environment Agency.

6.6 Details of all documents and records relating to radioactive substances activities at the property kept pursuant to the Environmental Permitting (England and Wales) Regulations 2010, SI 2010/675, Sch 24.

1 This enquiry is appropriate in the case of any property on which radioactive substances may be present, such as large stores with luminous signs. The legislation is contained in the Environmental Permitting (England and Wales) Regulations 2010, SI 2010/675, Sch 23.
2 Any of these activities is an offence unless an exemption applies: Environmental Permitting (England and Wales) Regulations 2010, SI 2010/675, regs 12(1) and 38(1) and Sch 23.
3 There are wide powers to vary or revoke a permit: Environmental Permitting (England and Wales) Regulations 2010, SI 2010/675, regs 20 and 22.

7.18

7   Industrial Activities, Installations and Mobile Plant[1]

7.1 Any installation controlled under the Environmental Permitting (England and Wales) Regulations 2010, SI 2010/675, Sch 1, Part 2.[2]

7.2 Details of any breaches of the conditions of a permit and any action taken or proposed by the Environment Agency in relation to such breaches including the service of statutory notices.[3]

7.3 Details of any proposed or actual variation or revocation of such a permit.[4]

7.4 Details of all entries relating to the property in the register kept pursuant to the Environmental Permitting (England and Wales) Regulations 2010, SI 2010/675, Sch 24.

1 This enquiry is appropriate in the case of many industrial facilities. Much of the information, however, should be obtainable from the seller.
   Local authorities regulate Part A(2) and Part B activities under the regime. These activities, which relate to multi-media regulation (Part A(2)) and air regulation only (Part B), tend to be less polluting than Part A(1) activities. The relevant local authority should be contacted in respect of information on these activities.
2 It is an offence to operate an installation covered by Sch 1 without an environmental permit or in breach of the permit: Environmental Permitting (England and Wales) Regulations 2010, SI 2010/675, reg 38.
3 In the event of a breach of condition, the Environment Agency may serve an enforcement notice. Environmental Permitting (England and Wales) Regulations 2010, SI 2010/675, reg 36. In the event of an imminent risk of serious pollution, the Environment Agency may serve a suspension notice. Ibid, reg 37.
4 There are wide powers to revoke a permit in whole or in part by serving a revocation notice. Ibid, reg 22.

7.19

8   Fisheries

8.1 Any fisheries byelaws which affect the property.[1]

1 The Environment Agency has the power to make fisheries byelaws under the Water Resources Act 1991, s 210 and Sch 25, para 6, as amended.

7.20

9   Navigation

9.1 Whether the Environment Agency is the navigation authority[1] for any watercourse which is on or adjacent to the property together with a copy of any applicable navigation byelaws.

9.2 Any licence issued by the Environment Agency under applicable navigation legislation in relation to the property together with a copy and indication of whether the licence is transferable to successors in title.

9.3 Any statutory notice which has been served in relation to the property under applicable navigation legislation and, if so, any proposed or actual action.

9.4 Details of any breaches of any applicable navigation legislation in relation to the property and, if so, any proposed or actual action to deal with the matter.

1 The navigation authority is any person who has a duty or power under any legislation to work, maintain, conserve, improve or control any canal or other inland navigation, navigable river, estuary, harbour or dock. Water Resources Act 1991, s 221. The Environment Agency's function varies from area to area depending on the local legislation in force.

Environment Agency regional and area offices

7.21   The Environment Agency is divided into regions, each of which has area offices which cover groups of counties. Enquiries should be sent by the environmental search provider to the Planning Liaison Officer at the appropriate area office.

Sewerage undertakers

7.22   Sewerage undertakers are the privatised successors of the former water authorities. The consent of the relevant sewerage undertaker is required for the discharge of any trade effluent into the public sewers belonging to the undertakers, otherwise an offence is committed.[1] Consent may be given subject to conditions.[2] The consent may be varied by the undertaker from time to time,[3] although subject to certain exceptions[4] no variation may be made within two years of the consent or the last variation.[5] Applications for consent to discharge 'special category effluent' must be referred to the Environment Agency for decision.[6] Appeals may be made to Ofwat, the Water Services Regulation Authority, against decisions of the sewerage undertaker.[7]

The sewerage undertaker may enter into a trade effluent agreement with the discharger instead of giving a consent.[8] Each undertaker must keep a public register containing (inter alia) copies of trade effluent consents, variations, trade effluent agreements and notices served by the Environment Agency in relation to special category effluent. The public is entitled to inspect the registers free of charge at all reasonable times and to obtain copies or extracts of items on the register on payment of a reasonable charge.[9] CON 29DW (2013) deals with drainage and water enquiries. The enquiries should be addressed to the relevant sewerage undertaker.[10]

1 Water Industry Act 1991, s 118. See generally Ch 17.
2 Water Industry Act 1991, s 121.
3 Ibid, s 124(1).
4 Ibid, ss 124(3), (4) and 125.
5 Ibid, s 124(2).
6 Ibid, s 120. 'Special category effluent' is defined in s 138, as amended by Environmental Permitting (England and Wales) Regulations 2010, SI 2010/675, Sch 21. It comprises effluent containing or deriving from processes using prescribed substances listed in the Trade Effluents (Prescribed Processes and Substances) Regulations 1989, SI 1989/1156, as amended by the Trade Effluents (Prescribed Processes and Substances) (Amendment) Regulations 1990, SI 1990/1629, which are known as 'red list' substances. See paras **17.116–17.119**.
7 Water Industry Act 1991, ss 122, 126, as amended by the Water Act 2003, s 36.
8 Ibid, ss 129–131.
9 Ibid, s 196.
10 See Ch 6.

Model enquiries of the sewerage undertaker – trade effluent[1]

7.23

1   Any trade effluent consent or a trade effluent agreement relating to the property.[2]
2   Any direction to vary such a consent together with any proposal for a varation.[3]
3   Any breaches of a trade effluent consent or agreement together with any necessary action to remedy the breach and, if appropriate, any proposed action by the sewerage undertaker.[4]
4   Any unauthorised discharges of trade effluent to public sewers from the property.

1 For documents required to be kept on public registers see para **17.125** and the Water Industry Act 1991, s 196. However, under s 206, subject to specified exceptions, no other information relating to a business (or individual in respect of a business) which has been obtained by virtue of the provisions of the Water Industry Act 1991 may be disclosed except with the consent of the person carrying on the business (or the individual concerned) or for the purpose of certain public functions. The Environmental Information Regulations 2004, SI 2004/3391, restrict the limitation: see Ch 4. Even though water service companies are private sector bodies, they are 'public authorities' and are, thus, subject to the regulations. Environmental Information Regulations 2004, SI 2004/3391, s 2(2).
2 See Water Industry Act 1991, s 118. It is not clear whether a trade effluent consent is transferable from seller to buyer, whether it 'runs with the land' so that any occupier can take the benefit of it, or whether a fresh application for a consent must be made by each new occupier. The problems associated with this are considered in para **17.122**. In particular, a number of sewerage undertakers take the view that an application for a new trade effluent consent must be made by each occupier. Nevertheless the same view does not necessarily prevail across the board within each sewerage undertaker. Accordingly, the view of the officer concerned should be checked on each occasion.

3 Sewerage undertakers vary trade effluent consents by means of a direction: Water Industry Act 1991, s 124.
4 The most likely form of action is prosecution, although in extreme cases the sewerage undertaker could apply for an injunction either on its own account on the basis that the breach of criminal law is harming its interests, or use the relator action procedure.

Model enquiries of sewerage undertakers – charges and sewers

7.24

1 Details of water, trade effluent and sewerage charges levied during the past three years together with the projected levels of increase during the next five years.[1]
2 Location of any sewers which serve the property.[2]

1 The question requests details of water charges in addition to sewerage and trade effluent charges on the assumption that the same undertaker deals with all these functions. However, that is not always the case as water is sometimes provided by water companies. Charges are made in accordance with a scheme under Water Industry Act 1991, s 143 as amended by the Water Industry Act 1999, s 4 or under an agreement under Sch 8 to the Water Industry Act 1991. Variation of charges is considered in Ch 17.
2 This enquiry should be used where insufficient information is forthcoming in response to the local authority enquiries: see Ch 6.

Offices of sewerage undertakers

7.25   Enquiries should be sent to the following sewerage undertakers. Addresses of water companies which do not provide sewerage services are not listed. The buyer should be able to provide the relevant details. A reasonable charge may be made but replies are often free if not a great deal of work is involved.

	Head Office
United Utilities Water plc (formerly North West Water Ltd)	Stephens Way Goose Green Wigan WN3 6PJ Tel: 0870 751 0101 Property.searches@uuplc.co.uk
Welsh Water – Dŵr Cymru Cyfyngedig	P.O. Box 10 Treharris CF46 6XZ Tel: 01443 331 087 searches@.dwrcymru.com
Northumbrian Water Ltd	Abbey Road Pity Me Durham DH1 5FJ Tel: 0870 241 7408 propertysolutions@nwl.co.uk
Yorkshire Water Services Ltd	Western House Halifax Road Bradford BD6 2LZ Tel: 0845 1 24 24 24 www.yorkshirewater.com

	Head Office
Anglian Water Services Ltd	Property Information Centre P.O. Box 770 Lincoln LN5 7WX Tel: 08457 145 145 www.anglianwater.co.uk
Thames Water Utilities Ltd	Clearwater Court Vastern Road Reading Berkshire RG1 8DB Tel: 0118 925 1504 www.thameswater.co.uk
Southern Water Services Ltd	LandSearches Southern House Capstone Road Chatham Kent ME5 7QA Tel: 0845 270 0212 searches@southernwater.co.uk
South West Water Ltd	Conveyancing Services Peninsula House Rydon Lane Exeter EX2 7HR Tel: 01392 443 115 www.southwestwater.co.uk
Wessex Water Services Ltd	Developers Group Operations Centre Claverton Down Bath BA2 7WW Tel: 01225 526 000 www.wessexwater.co.uk
Severn Trent Water Ltd	Severn Trent Searches P.O. Box 6187 Nottingham NG5 1LE Tel: 0115 962 7269 enquiries@severntrentsearches.co.uk

Natural England and Natural Resources Wales

7.26 These authorities are responsible for nature conservation functions and will be able to advise on whether any nature conservation designations apply to the property. The principal designations likely to give rise to concern are:

- sites of special scientific interest (SSSIs);[1]
- European sites under the Birds Directive[2] or the Habitats Directive;[3] and
- sites designated under the Ramsar Convention.[4]

1 Wildlife and Countryside Act 1981, s 28. See generally Ch 19.
2 79/409/EEC.
3 92/43/EEC; see Conservation of Habitats and Species Regulations 2010, SI 2010/490, regs 25–29, (special nature conservation orders for land within European sites).
4 Convention on Wetlands of International Importance, Ramsar, Iran, 2 February 1971.

7.27   If the property falls within any of these types of area, planning permission for development will generally be more difficult to obtain. This is particularly the case with European sites in which development may only be permitted if 'it will not adversely affect the integrity of the site concerned' unless there are 'imperative reasons of overriding public interest, including those of a social or economic nature'.[1]

1 92/43/EEC arts 6(3) and (4), considered in detail in paras **19.52–19.57**.

7.28   The existence of an SSSI should be revealed by the Local Land Charges Search.[1] The seller (lessor) has a final duty in relation to an SSSI: to send notice to National England of the disposal of any interest in land included in the SSSI or of any change of occupation of which the owner is aware within 28 days of the disposal or becoming aware of the change of occupation.[2] Failure to comply without reasonable excuse is an offence.[3]

Almost invariably the other designations listed above are also SSSIs. If an SSSI is revealed, the buyer will wish to know:

- whether there is a management scheme and/or management notice affecting the site;[4]
- any other nature conservation designations affecting the property; and
- the extent to which an SSSI or other designation would prevent or impede a proposed development project.

1 See para **5.28**.
2 Wildlife and Countryside Act 1981, s 28Q(1)–(3).
3 Ibid, s 28Q(4).
4 Ibid, ss 28J and 28K.

7.29   The latter point is likely to be one of great sensitivity and is better dealt with in discussions with the officer concerned, before any formal planning permission is made. This will often facilitate the planning process.[1]

1 Natural England is a statutory consultee in respect of all planning applications affecting SSSIs in England: The Town and Country Planning (Development Management Procedure) (England) Order 2015, SI 2015/595, Art 18(1), Table Sch 4 (w). The Natural Resources Body for Wales (generally known as Natural Resources Wales) is a statutory consultee in respect of all planning applications (Development Management Procedure) (Wales) Order 2012, SI 2012/801, Art 14(1), Table Sch 4(q) as amended by the Natural Resources Body for Wales (Functions) Order 2013, SI 2013/755, Art 4(2), Sch 5, para 80(1).

7.30   Suitable enquiries can be sent to Natural England or Natural Resources Wales at their regional offices. Enquiries are dealt with by telephone as well as by letter. There is no charge.

Other enquiries

7.31   Enquiries should be made in certain parts of the country in relation to mineral extraction, eg coal, tin, clay, brine and limestone. These searches are generally made because of the risk of subsidence.[1] The owner of land on which there is an abandoned mine may be liable at common law for pollution caused by contaminated water from the mine which causes pollution off site.[2] Further, the defence to any prosecution for polluting controlled waters under s 85 of the Water Resources Act 1991 was removed in relation to mines abandoned after 31 December 1999.[3] If there is an abandoned mine under the property, further investigation will be necessary to ascertain whether contaminated water from the mine has caused or is likely to cause pollution. The organisation to whom the original enquiry is addressed may have relevant information.

1 For full details see Hewitson and Silverman, Conveyancing Searches and Enquiries (3rd edn, 2006).
2 *Sedleigh-Denfield v O'Callaghan* [1940] AC 880.
3 Environmental Permitting (England & Wales) Regulations 2010, SI 2010/675, regs 40(2) and (3).

7.32 Where the property is adjacent to or near to a canal, enquiries should be made of the Canal and River Trust as to:

- whether the Board claims any rights over the property;
- the existence of any liabilities on the owner for maintenance and repairs of riverbanks;
- notices of disrepair; and
- details of past flooding.

Chapter 8

Environmental survey

IMPORTANCE OF AN ENVIRONMENTAL SURVEY

8.01 Although a considerable amount of information can be obtained from replies to the enquiries suggested in the previous chapters, there is no substitute for an environmental survey carried out by an environmental consultant. It is likely to be the only way in which all available information can be considered by an expert and the real environmental risks assessed. The lawyer advising his client on potential environmental liabilities can only advise properly on the basis of a competent environmental report.

TYPES OF ENVIRONMENTAL SURVEY

8.02 There are broadly two types of environmental survey: compliance surveys and those which deal with the condition of the property. The former normally covers any process carried on at the property which will be continued by the buyer and which may require expenditure to ensure compliance with environmental law. The appropriate survey is a Phase I environmental survey.[1] Environmental surveys dealing with the condition of the property may be commissioned for two different purposes: (a) to ascertain the presence of contamination in the ground which may prove an impediment to, or increase the cost of, development; or (b) in order to assess the risk of environmental liabilities which may fall on the owner and the likely costs involved in minimising those liabilities. Although much of the investigation undertaken by an environmental consultant would be the same for both of these latter types of report, it would not be identical in each case. In the case of a 'development' environmental survey, much more emphasis would be placed on the potential impact of the development on the surrounding area. For example, piling through impermeable strata may allow contaminants to migrate to an aquifer beneath. In addition, the survey may consider the likely remediation requirements of the authorities pursuant to a planning condition and an indication of the range of costs. In practice, of course, a survey may seek to achieve both goals (a) and (b).

1 See para **8.06**.

8.03 Other matters which may feature in a report include:

* flood risk;
* adverse effects of noise on or from the property;

143

- the proximity of overhead power lines which may give rise to harmful electro-magnetic fields;
- the presence of asbestos or other substances harmful to humans or the environment;
- the presence of any protected flora or fauna on the property which may impede development;
- the energy performance of any buildings; and
- sustainability criteria.

Environmental surveys may be undertaken at three levels which are generally stages in a cumulative investigative process. These are: a desk top assessment; a 'Phase I' environmental survey; and a 'Phase II' survey.[1]

1 Taylor, 'Environmental due diligence for commercial property', SJ 145(7), 152–154, 156 (23 February 2001).

Desk top assessment

8.04   This involves a documentary investigation of:

- present and past uses of the site (including environmental licences/permits currently or previously in force in relation to the site and/or other nearby property);
- likely contamination of the site;
- underlying geology, hydrology and hydrogeology of the site and surrounding area;
- present and past uses of the immediately surrounding area; and
- sensitive uses of the surrounding areas (ie those which may suffer particular damage if pollution were to migrate from the site).

The consultant may also obtain information from regulators such as the Environmental Health and Planning departments at the Local Authority, the Environment Agency, Petroleum Licensing Officer and the Sewerage Undertaker. This may provide valuable confirmation of the consultant's conclusions particularly if the regulators' responses are in writing.

From this information, an environmental consultant is able to form an opinion as to whether the site is one which is likely to give rise to difficulties from the point of view of development, and whether potential environmental liabilities are likely to be significant.

8.05   Full desktop assessments may be undertaken although a number of companies provide rapid risk screening reports. These are generally available in a few days and provide factual information about a site (such as past uses, and past and current licences and consents), combined with a simple risk and liability assessment. This type of report is similar to but with much less explanation than a full desktop assessment and provides most of the data upon which more traditional desk top assessments are based, the main difference being that no direct enquiries are made to regulators.

Phase I environmental survey

8.06 This involves the desk top assessment described above and a physical inspection of the site by the consultant. The site inspection will enable the environmental consultant to identify any physical features on the site which are likely to give rise to liabilities or difficulty from a development perspective. Features such as leaking oil drums and dying plants can be identified which indicate ground contamination as well as processes which may give rise to pollution. Also, a consultant will be able to inspect the surrounding area and identify more clearly any land or activities which may affect or be affected by the property.

A Phase I survey may concentrate either on compliance issues or soil and groundwater issues, or sometimes both. For example, if a business is acquired as an ongoing concern it is necessary to assess the effectiveness of environmental controls (including the company's environmental policy and any environmental management systems). This might include issues such as packaging wastes and ozone depleting substances. However if the land and buildings alone are purchased the Phase I survey would concentrate largely on current or past operations that might have affected the condition of the land.

It is worth noting that there are several standards governing Phase I surveys. The oldest and most well known is the Association for the Testing of Materials (ASTM) E 1527–05 Phase I Standard developed in the United States over 10 years ago and updated regularly since. This is widely used internationally, particularly for due diligence work. Additionally one should also consider the various International Standards developed in conjunction with the Institute of Environmental Management and Assessment (IEMA) in the UK. These standards are intended to guide organisations, auditors and their clients on the general principles common to the conduct of environmental audits. The standards provide definitions on environmental auditing, the related terms and the general principles of environmental auditing. A key standard is EN ISO 14015: 2010 Environmental assessment of sites and organisations. CLR 11 (model Procedures for the management of Land Contamination) and the RICS guidance on Contamination, the Environment and Sustainability: Implications for Chartered Surveyors and Their Clients (3rd edition) are also widely used by environmental consultants.

Phase II environmental survey

8.07 This involves a full investigation of the whole or part of the site including digging trial pits, drilling boreholes and taking samples. The results of the Phase II survey should give a much clearer picture of the nature and extent of contamination on the site. However, sampling can never reveal all contamination present. For that reason, it is important that the sampling strategy is planned carefully to maximise the effectiveness of the study. Sampling is sometimes undertaken from boreholes arranged in a grid, herringbone or other random pattern, or more commonly targeted to Potential Areas of Concern (PAOCs) indicated by a desk top assessment or Phase I survey. However, time and cost constraints mean it is seldom possible to look at all areas of a site and so it can never be guaranteed that hot spots of contamination do not exist in those areas of the ground which have not been sampled. This must always be borne in mind when considering how much reliance can be placed on an environmental survey report, no matter how competently the survey is carried out.

8.08   The environmental consultant must ensure that the samples are properly taken and stored in order to avoid the intrusion of extraneous material which may affect the test results. It is well known that the results of the laboratory analysis of samples can vary considerably and so it is important that the consultant chooses a good laboratory with the best technology to undertake the testing. Laboratories which are accredited for specific tests provide confidence as to the likely accuracy of a test. Accreditation is provided mainly by UKAS and NAMAS. The UKAS accreditation is granted by the United Kingdom Accreditation Service and is the formal recognition that a laboratory and its staff are technically competent to carry out specific types of calibration. NAMAS is an acronym for National Accreditation of Measurement and Sampling. Laboratories and test houses which perform environmental testing to this level have to meet international standards and demonstrate quality assurance of their work. A newer standard MCERTS (Monitoring Certification Scheme) has been established by the Environment Agency and is necessary when regulatory approval is required.

Finally it is worth noting that increasing use is made of new in-situ technologies in the Phase II market, many of which are gaining increasing credibility with regulators as helpful field techniques, even though they are not appropriate substitutes for laboratory analysis. These include XRF (X-ray fluorescence) guns, in-situ testing kits and mobile laboratories. Whilst these are often less accurate than traditional laboratory tests, they are faster, more cost effective and allow more samples to be taken thus increasing the consultant's level of confidence in results obtained from laboratory tests.

WHO SHOULD COMMISSION THE SURVEY?

8.09   A wise buyer will wish to obtain a satisfactory environmental survey before deciding to purchase the property. The results of the survey will facilitate a decision on whether or not to proceed with the purchase and if so on what terms. However, many sellers commission an environmental survey before offering a property for sale. This enables them to understand the potential problems in advance and to formulate a strategy for dealing with questions from buyers.

8.10   It may be appropriate for the seller to hand over the survey report to the buyer prior to exchange of contracts. This will avoid difficulties arising at a late stage in negotiations if the buyer suddenly discovers that the site is affected by environmental problems. Also, under the statutory guidance issued under the contaminated land legislation, liability should fall on the buyer (and the seller should be excluded) under the 'exclusion' tests if the buyer enters into the contract having information which would reasonably allow him to be aware of the nature and extent of the contamination on the property.[1] However, a report prepared for a seller which is intended for use by potential buyers should provide simple interpretation which gives comfort to buyers if appropriate but does not risk being either dismissed as being pro-seller or, at the other extreme, over-cautious and unnecessarily detrimental to the position of the seller.

1 EPA 1990, s 78F(6); Part 2A Contaminated Land Statutory Guidance April 2012, paras 7.46–7.50 (test 3). This is considered in detail in para **15.88**.

DISADVANTAGES OF A SURVEY

8.11 The main disadvantages of an environmental report are that it, or at least parts of it, may get into the public domain, be the subject of discovery in the course of litigation, or have to be produced to a regulatory authority acting under statutory authority. It is important to consider the circumstances in which the 'privacy' of a document can be preserved.

If the report has been provided to a regulatory authority, the authority will generally be under a duty to provide a copy to any person who requests it. However, there are important exceptions.[1]

Documents which are relevant to an opponent's case in litigation are, in principle, subject to the process of discovery, ie copies must be produced to the opponent. However, documents do not have to be disclosed if they are the subject of privilege. Most important for present purposes is legal professional privilege of which there are two types: litigation privilege and legal advice privilege. The former is broader than the latter.

An environmental survey report is privileged from production in subsequent litigation if the report is produced 'for the sole or dominant purpose of either giving or getting advice in regard to ... litigation or collecting evidence for use in ... litigation' which is in prospect or pending.[2] However, a report obtained for the purpose of enabling a client to seek legal advice where litigation is not in prospect is not privileged.[3] Legal advice privilege extends only to communications between lawyer and client.[4] Material in reports may also have to be revealed to the regulatory authorities when exercising certain statutory powers.[5]

1 See generally Chapter 4.
2 *Phipson on Evidence* (18th edn, 2013), para 18.
3 *Phipson on Evidence* ibid; *Three Rivers DC v Bank of England (No 5)* [2003] QB 1556 (CA); *Three Rivers DC v Bank of England (No 6)* [2005] 1 AC 610 (HL).
4 Legal advice privilege extends to communications and documents created in the course of providing legal advice, such as memoranda to update a client on the status of an investigation and notes of meetings between clients and their legal advisers: *Property Alliance Group Ltd v Royal Bank of Scotland Plc* [2015] EWHC 3187 (Ch).

5 Eg under the EA 1995, s 108(4)(k). However, the power to require the production of 'records' may only extend to test results which are reported rather than interpretive material: *R v Tirado* (1974) 59 Cr App Rep 80; *H v Schering Chemicals Ltd* [1983] 1 WLR 143. Cf *R v Jones (Benjamin)* [1978] 1 WLR 195, which gives a broader interpretation of 'report'. See *R v Hertfordshire CC, ex p Green Environmental Industries Ltd* [2002] 2 AC 412 (HL) on the question of requests for information under the EPA 1990, s 71.

SELECTING THE RIGHT CONSULTANT

8.12   Any party commissioning an environmental survey needs to ensure that the right consultant is engaged for the purpose. Environmental consultancies tend to have in-depth strength in a limited number of fields. The selection process must therefore ensure that the candidate selected has the appropriate skills. The identity of the individual or individuals who will form the project team are obviously crucial. If the main focus of the report is contaminated land, appropriate skills and experience in this field should be demonstrated by the environmental consultant. In addition, the selected consultant should have a good commercial sense and be accustomed to writing clear reports for clients with little or no scientific background. However, the key to obtaining a good report is providing clear instructions to the consultant as to the purpose of the report and any particular requirement of the client.

8.13   If a buyer requires to undertake intrusive investigation on the seller's land, the seller is likely to insist that the arrangement is subject to a formal licence which imposes conditions as to the siting of boreholes, access to the results, confidentiality and a restriction on access to the regulatory authorities without the sellers' consent.[1] The buyer will need to ensure that any such restrictions do not devalue the report.

1 The seller is likely to require an indemnity from the buyer in respect of liabilities for environmental damage caused by the buyer's consultant in the course of drilling boreholes as well as for damage to the seller's property.

8.14   The consultant should also have adequate professional indemnity insurance. The consultant should be asked to provide evidence of available cover including financial limits and any exclusions which might result in the survey and report not being covered. Professional indemnity insurance cover for environment consultants is generally limited to an aggregate amount per annum. In such a case, it is important to check whether there are any actual or potential claims against the policy which might mean that there is reduced cover available for further claims. Provisions on insurance should be included in the appointment.[1]

1 See para **8.16**.

The appointment

8.15   Although formal appointments are not always used when instructing environmental consultants, it is advisable to do so in order to ensure that the obligations of each party are clarified. It is better to draw up a specific appointment for the purpose and not to rely on standard form agreements produced by the consultant, which are likely to be one-sided. If the appointment is in the form of a deed, the parties will be able to claim in respect of any breach at any time up to 12 years from the date of the breach, whereas the period will be limited to six years if the appointment is a simple contract.

8.16   The appointment should contain terms which, at the very least, deal with the following matters:

- **Specification of work** This should cover not only the work to be undertaken but the purpose of the report. The environmental consultant can be asked to draft his own specification, provided that he has clear instructions as to the client's objectives.
- **Standard of work** The standard should be that resulting from the level of skill, care and diligence to be expected of an appropriately qualified environmental consultant with experience of dealing with projects of the nature and size of that for which he has been engaged.
- **Price** A fixed price or means for calculating the price should be spelled out clearly including the means for calculating the payment for any additional work which may be requested as a result of the investigations. If the appointment is a construction contract within the meaning of the Housing Grants, Construction and Regeneration Act 1996, Part II, specific provisions apply in relation to payment.[1] A party to a construction contract is entitled to payment by instalments, stage payments or other periodic payments unless it is specified in the contract that the duration of the works is to be less than 45 days or it is agreed between the parties that the duration of the works is estimated to be less than 45 days. The parties may agree the amount of the payments and the intervals at which or the circumstances in which they become due. However, the contract must include certain minimum requirements,[2] in default of which the relevant provisions of the Statutory Scheme[3] apply.
- **Insurance** The environmental consultant should be obliged to maintain professional indemnity insurance with reputable insurers carrying on business in the European Union to cover liabilities relating to the services provided. The amount of cover should be in line with market practice for the type of work in question. It is normal to provide that the obligation only applies where such insurance continues to remain available to environmental consultants in the European Union market at reasonable commercial rates. Insurance cover for environmental matters is generally provided for each and every claim and in the aggregate, and it should be subject only to such conditions, excesses and exclusions as are usual in the market at the time. The consultant should be required to produce documentary evidence of the insurance cover if requested to do so and should be prohibited from settling or waiving any insurance claim without the client's consent. The obligation to maintain insurance cover should last for six or 12 years depending on whether the appointment is under a simple contract or a deed.

149

- **Assignability, collateral warranties and third party rights** The benefit of the appointment is assignable by the client without the consultant's consent unless there is an absolute or qualified prohibition against assignment. However, it is common to clarify the position. In cases where the party commissioning the report intends to sell the land in separate parcels, an obligation should be imposed on the consultant to provide collateral warranties for at least a limited number of buyers of sub-plots. Collateral warranties may also be required by funders and lenders. In addition, under the Contracts (Rights of Third Parties) Act 1999, s 1 a third party may enforce the contract if it purports to confer a benefit on him provided that he is expressly identified in the contract by name, or as a member of a class or as answering a particular description. However, third party rights can be negated in the contract.[4] The parties should consider whether third party benefits should be conferred under the Act so that particular persons or categories of person can rely on reports produced, instead of taking the benefit of collateral warranties.[5] If the number of persons who may rely on the warranties is intended to be strictly limited, the obligation to provide collateral warranties may be the easiest mechanism, if the categories of potential beneficiary are not yet clarified. If it is intended that third parties should not be able to enforce provisions of the appointment directly or that that right is to be restricted to particular persons or categories of person, the appointment should say so explicitly.
- **Confidentiality** An obligation should be imposed on the environmental consultant to keep confidential all matters learned relating to the client, the client's business and the property surveyed. The existence of contamination or any other environmental problem may be particularly sensitive.
- **Intellectual property rights** The appointment should provide that any technical information provided by the client to the consultant remains the property of the client and may not be used by the consultant for any other purpose. In addition, any technical 'know how' evolved by the consultant for the purposes of the investigation should either belong to the client or alternatively the client should have a non-revocable, non-exclusive and royalty-free licence to use it for any purpose in connection with the property. The client should also be free to grant sub-licences. This may be crucial if the client wishes to use the report in connection with a remediation programme but prefers to use another consultant or engineer for that part of the work.
- **Adjudication** In the case of appointments which are construction contracts under the Housing Grants, Construction and Regeneration Act 1996, Part II, an adjudication procedure must be included which meets the minimum requirements of the Act.[6] In default the provisions of the Statutory Scheme[7] apply automatically. In practice, the Statutory Scheme is normally the preferred option.
- **Termination** The appointment should provide a right for the client to terminate the appointment at will, eg on seven days' notice with the proviso that the client will only be liable for the payment of costs reasonably incurred up to the date of termination and excluding loss of profits or any other losses. The consultant may also wish to have the right to terminate

in the event of serious breaches of the client's obligations, particularly failure to pay scheduled payments after an appropriate period has elapsed following the due date.

Environmental consultants often seek to introduce clauses into appointments which would seriously weaken the contractual protection available to the client. Amongst these are the following:

- **Liability cap** Although undesirable from the client's perspective, liability caps are increasingly common. It is important to ensure that they are sufficiently high to cover all foreseeable losses and should be at least at the level of the available insurance cover. However, any cap on liability should not be linked specifically to the level of insurance cover actually held by the consultant. Otherwise, if the consultant (for whatever reason) does not have insurance cover, the liability cap would be zero.

- **Exclusion of economic losses** Consultants often seek to exclude all losses except the cost of remediation. This should be resisted. If the consultant has advised negligently that the contamination is different in type or extent from that subsequently found on the property, the losses might well include loss of profit (if the business has to close during remediation), or loss of a sale (if the report is prepared for the seller).

- **Net contribution clause** In some cases, the negligence or breach of contract of more than one consultant or contractor causes or contributes to the loss suffered by the client. A person whose breach of contract causes a loss to the promisee is liable for the full loss even if another wrongdoer has independently caused or contributed to that loss under the principle of joint and several liability.[8] However, any liable defendant can claim a contribution from any other person liable in respect of the same damage under the Civil Liability (Contribution) Act 1978.[9] The net contribution clause limits the liability of the consultant to its proportionate share of liability on the basis that all other consultants and contractors appointed by the client have paid their fair share of the total liability. The effect of such a clause is that the claimant has to establish the extent of each defendant's liability before any damages can be recovered. It also puts the claimant at risk of the insolvency of any defendant.[10]

1 Housing Grants, Construction and Regeneration Act 1996, ss 109–113 as amended by the Local Democracy, Economic Development and Construction Act 2009. A 'construction contract' includes a contract for the carrying out of construction operations and arranging for the carrying out of construction by others. It includes civil engineering contracts: s 105. Section 104(2)(b) states that references to a construction contact include an agreement 'to provide advice on building, engineering, interior or exterior decoration or on the laying out of Landscape in relation to construction operations'. It is suggested that contracts for Phase I and Phase II environmental surveys are included in the definition if they are carried out in preparation for a remediation programme whether or not it is part of a development. For specific exclusions from the definition of construction contract see ss 105(2) and 106 and the Construction Contract (England and Wales) Exclusion Order 1998, SI 1998/648.

2 The minimum requirements relate, to, inter alia, having an adequate mechanism for payment, the timing of payment and the various notices that have to be given between the parties, particularly where the payer wants to pay less than any amount stated as due in a payment notice.

3 Scheme for Construction Contracts (England and Wales) Regulations 1998, SI 1998/649.

4 Contracts (Rights of Third Parties) Act 1999, s 1(2). The intention of the parties must be deduced from 'a proper construction of the contract'.
5 See para **9.07**.
6 Housing Grants, Construction and Regeneration Act 1996, s 108. The minimum requirements of the Act relate to the ability to refer a dispute to adjudication, the appointment of an adjudicator, the referral of a dispute to him, and the decision making process. For the definition of 'construction contract' see footnote 1 above.
7 Scheme for Construction Contracts (England and Wales) Regulations 1998, SI 1998/649.
8 *Chitty on Contracts* 32nd edn (2015) para 17–004.
9 *Chitty op. cit.* paras 17–004 and 17–029 – 17–035.
10 See *West v Ian Finlay & Associates (a firm)* [2014] BLR 324 (CA) where a net contribution clause in a building contract was upheld.

THE BUYER AND EXISTING REPORTS

8.17 Buyers should be wary of relying on existing environmental reports commissioned by the seller or a third party. However, in some cases pressures of time or otherwise suggest that this should be done. If so, buyers need to ensure that the report was prepared for their required purpose, for example to assess potential liabilities and constraints created by environmental factors. This should be apparent from reading the report provided that the reader is sufficiently experienced. However, it is better to have a copy of the instructions to the consultant which may be set out in the report itself. A buyer also needs to be able to sue the environment consultant who prepared the report if he suffers loss as a result of the latter's negligence. For that purpose the buyer needs either a suitable collateral warranty or a reliance letter[1] from the environmental consultant or an assignment of the benefit of the contract by the seller (having first checked that it is assignable). If the collateral warranty (as is usually the case) stipulates that the beneficiary of the warranty is to have no greater rights against the consultant than the original client, the terms of the deed of appointment should be checked to see what limitations apply. Some consultants now have more flexible terms and conditions for desktop and Phase I assessments that allow automatic reliance by all parties involved in a transaction (seller, buyer, their funders and any professional advisors).[2]

1 Unless the reliance letter is framed as a contract, the consultant may be liable for negligent advice (provided that all the relevant requirements are established), on the principles in *Hedley Byrne & Co Ltd v Heller & Partners Ltd* [1964] AC 456 (HL).
2 However, the full terms of the contract should be considered to assess the extent of the rights conferred and any limitations. See paras **8.15** and **8.16**. As to the right to rely on a contract to which the buyer is not a party, see paras **8.16** and **9.07**.

Chapter 9

Assessing and managing environmental risk: contractual protection and environmental insurance

ANALYSING THE INFORMATION – ASSESSING THE RISK

9.01 Having gathered the information, both the buyer and the seller should assess the real risk of liability. Adverse information on environmental matters needs to be taken seriously. However, it is important to emphasise that it does not necessarily indicate potential disaster. For example, the mere existence of contamination on land does not, of itself, give rise to liability. Liability will only arise if the contamination causes, or is likely to cause, damage to people, property or the environment on the site or in the surrounding area. Liabilities are particularly likely to arise if contaminants can easily enter groundwater which is used for abstracting drinking water. It follows that if contamination is immobile and is unlikely to enter potable drinking supplies or affect human health, property or any protected areas or species, the real risk of liability is small. However, it must be recognised that contamination which is immobile may subsequently be mobilised, for example by development on or near to the property. In addition, if the property is to be developed, the planning authorities may require remediation work to be carried out which could not have been required in the absence of development.[1]

Other considerations which the parties may need to address include asbestos and other hazardous substances in buildings, the presence of Japanese Knotweed, and permits, the benefit of which is to be taken by the buyer.[2]

1 See Ch 15.
2 See Ch 12.

EFFECT OF ENVIRONMENTAL LIABILITIES ON THE TRANSACTION

9.02 If the buyer considers that there are significant environmental problems on the site he has a number of options. He may:

- decide not to proceed with the transaction;
- negotiate a price reduction;

- agree a retention from the purchase price to cover the cost of remediation;[1]
- enter into a contract which is conditional on the seller carrying out or paying for an agreed remediation programme;
- enter into a contract which is conditional on the buyer obtaining funding to meet all or part of the remediation costs; or
- insist on warranties and/or indemnities from the seller.[2]

If there has been insufficient time to carry out adequate investigations, the buyer may enter into a contract which is conditional on obtaining a satisfactory environmental survey report.[3]

Sellers generally wish to sell without retaining any liabilities. For that reason they may seek to tailor the contract so as to channel liabilities to their buyers and may even seek an indemnity from them.

1 Such a solution may prove to be unnecessarily costly because the buyer will be unable to claim contaminated land tax relief if the remediation work is funded by the seller or any other party: Corporation Tax Act 2009, ss 1144 and 1177.
2 On warranties and indemnities see the discussion in S Payne (ed) *Commercial Environmental Law and Liability* (Longman), para C2.84ff.
3 Care needs to be taken in drafting to avoid uncertainty which could render the contract void. However, the courts are reluctant to find contracts void if some reasonable interpretation can be given. In particular, if the vague provision is for the benefit of one party only, that party may waive it: see *Barnsley's Conveyancing Law and Practice* (4th edn), pp 138–139.

DEALING WITH LIABILITIES IN THE CONTRACT

9.03   The contract may be used to document facts and agreements which channel liabilities under private and/or public law to one party or the other. This is likely to be done mainly in relation to contaminated land. For this purpose, it is important to understand who can be liable in respect of contaminated land under the various applicable legal rules and for what damage. The liabilities discussed in this section are third party liabilities. They are not concerned with and do not affect the *caveat emptor* principle discussed in Chapter 2. However, third party liabilities do affect relations between seller and buyer because those liabilities will have to be allocated between them.

Liabilities:

- under the contaminated land legislation (Part 2A of the Environmental Protection Act 1990) fall primarily on 'causers' and 'knowing permitters' and if none are found, on owners and/or occupiers;[1]
- under water pollution legislation fall only on 'causers' and 'knowing permitters';[2]
- under common law fall on causers and on owners who know or ought to know of the problem, for failure to take whatever steps are reasonable under all the circumstances to resolve it.[3]

A buyer may be a knowing permitter/owner (or occupier) with knowledge if the buyer has:

- adequate information;
- power/opportunity to deal with the contamination and it is reasonable to expect the buyer to remediate it, where under all the circumstances it needs to be remediated.[4]

These liabilities are set out in the following diagram:

Part IIA EPA	WRA	*Nuisance/Rylands v Fletcher*
Causers		Wrongdoer
Knowing permitters		Owners/occupiers who know or ought to know of the problem
If none found 'Innocent' owners/occupiers	No liability for 'innocent' owners/occupiers	

In the context of a real estate transaction, liabilities (actual or potential) for contamination other than new contamination caused by the buyer after completion fall into four categories:

1 Damage caused before completion by contamination on the property.
2 Damage caused by contamination migrating from the property before completion, irrespective of whether the damage arises before or after completion.
3 Damage caused after completion by contamination present on the property at completion.
4 Damage caused by contamination migrating from the property after completion which was present on the property at completion.

Under the general law, the seller alone can be liable for damage in categories 1 and 2, but will retain that liability after completion only if the seller caused or knowingly permitted the contamination (or was an owner/occupier with knowledge for the purpose of the law of nuisance). The buyer cannot be liable. If the seller is giving an indemnity it need not therefore extend to those circumstances.[5] On the other hand, the seller and the buyer may both be liable in respect of damage in categories 3 and 4. If the seller has caused or is a knowing permitter/owner (or occupier) with knowledge of the contamination which is on site at the date of completion, and if the buyer is also a knowing permitter/owner (or occupier) with knowledge, the seller and the buyer will share liability according to their degree of responsibility for creating or continuing the risk (unless in the case of the contaminated land legislation there has been an agreement on liabilities or one of the 'exclusion tests' in the statutory guidance applies).[6] If the buyer is not a knowing permitter/owner (or occupier) with knowledge etc, liability falls only on the seller, unless the seller also is not a knowing permitter/owner (or occupier) with knowledge etc in which case neither party may be liable.[7]

These liabilities can be illustrated as follows where both parties are causers or knowing permitters/owners with knowledge:

	CONTAMINATION ON SITE AT COMPLETION DATE	MIGRATION OFF SITE
Before completion	Seller liability only	Seller liability only
After completion	Buyer assumes responsibility and shares liability with seller after completion (subject to Part 2A liability transfer)	Seller and buyer liability (subject to Part 2A liability transfer)

If contamination remains on site which may give rise to liabilities for future harm or threatened harm, a seller who wishes to pass those liabilities to the buyer should ensure that:

- the buyer has adequate information;
- the buyer acknowledges receipt of information in the contract;
- evidence of these matters (correspondence, reports etc) are kept safely.

Those steps will provide evidence (in favour of the seller) that the buyer satisfies the knowledge element of the 'knowing permitter' requirement.

According to the statutory guidance liability under the contaminated land legislation may be channelled to the buyer alone if the buyer as well as the seller is a causer or knowing permitter and:

- there is an agreement between the seller and the buyer as to the allocation of remediation costs;[8] or
- one of the 'exclusion' tests[9] applies under which the seller is excluded from liability, eg Test 3 – the seller will be excluded if before the sale became binding the buyer had sufficient information to be aware of the 'broad measure' of the presence of the contamination.[10]

The seller should therefore include in the contract:

- an agreement allocating remediation costs to the buyer;[11]
- an acknowledgement by the buyer that the buyer has had permission from the seller to carry out its own investigations on the site prior to the sale becoming binding. This will normally establish sufficient information under Test 3 in the case of a sale to a large company after 1990. Nonetheless, acknowledgements by the buyer should also be included as to the buyer's knowledge of the presence and extent of contamination on and under the property.

However, it can never be guaranteed that these steps will be sufficient to exclude the seller from liability in every transaction. In any case, the possibility of excluding the seller from liability only applies in the case of the contaminated land legislation and not water pollution legislation or the common law. In the latter two cases, liability may be allocated between the parties.

If the buyer agrees to assume all the seller's liabilities relating to contamination, the agreement should reflect that position, but state that it is also an agreement for the purpose of the statutory guidance[12] Such a wide agreement should be valid between the parties even if the criteria for an agreement to allocate liabilities under the statutory guidance are not met.[13]

1   EPA 1990, s 78F. See Ch 15.
2   Water Resources Act 1991, ss, 161, 161A–D; Environmental Permitting (England and Wales) Regulations 2010, SI 2010/675, regs12(1)(b) and 38(1)(a). See paras **17.44–17.66**.
3   See Ch 13.
4   See Tromans and Turrall-Clarke, *Contaminated Land* (2nd edn), (Sweet & Maxwell, 2008), para 5.45 (EPA 1990, Part IIA) and *Sedleigh-Denfield v O'Callaghan* [1940] AC 880 (continuance of nuisance).
5   However, the difficulty lies in proving when the migration took place. See para **9.20**.
6   EPA 1990, s 78F(6); Part 2A Contaminated Land Statutory Guidance, April 2012, paras 7.29–7.61. For the rules on apportionment where the exclusion tests do not apply, see paras D.73–D.97. See also paras **15.93–15.96**.
7   In that case, the original causer and/or knowing permitters/owners (or occupiers) with knowledge etc alone would be liable.
8   Part 2A, Contaminated Land Statutory Guidance April 2012, paras 7.29–7.30.
9   See note 4. The exclusion tests apply only if both seller and buyer are causers and/or knowing permitters.
10 Part 2A Contaminated Land Statutory Guidance, April 2012 paras 7.46–7.50. Note that the sale must be at arms' length and the seller must not retain any interest in the land or rights to occupy it (subject to certain exceptions) after the date of the sale. See para **15.88**.
11 For the agreement to be effective, a copy must be provided to the enforcing authority and none of the parties to the agreement must challenge its application. For that reason, the agreement should contain a provision by which each party agrees not to challenge its application nor to take any step which could lead to liability falling on any other party. Note also that if one of the parties is a man of straw, the agreement will be ineffective if liability is to be taken by that party, so that the real burden would fall on the enforcing authority. See Part 2A Contaminated Land Statutory Guidance, April 2012 paras 7.29–730.
12 See text to fn 8.
13 See fn 8. Much of the text on Indemnities in para **9.06**ff is relevant to such agreements. For a discussion of the Hazardous Substances which should be the subject of such an agreement, see para **9.12**.

9.04   If it is agreed that the seller is to pay for the cost of remediating the property, the seller may be excluded from liability under the contaminated land legislation in accordance with Test 2 of the exclusion tests, provided that certain conditions are met.[1] For that purpose, there must be a payment or a reduction in the purchase price explicitly stated in the contract to be made for the purpose of paying for the remediation.

It may be dangerous for a seller to place exclusive reliance on this means of escape from liability because:

- there may be argument over whether the payment was in fact sufficient to pay for remediation which would remove the land from the status of 'contaminated land' under the contaminated land legislation;
- such a payment will not necessarily exclude the seller's liability under the other regimes (eg water pollution legislation and common law) although it may reduce it.

Buyers should resist the Test 2 exclusion because a landowner who accepts funding from a third party to carry out remediation work will be unable to claim contaminated land tax relief.[2]

1   EPA 1990, s 78F(6); Part 2A Contaminated Land Statutory Guidance, April 2012, paras 7.40–745 (Test 2). The conditions relate, inter alia, to the sufficiency of the payment, and the absence of control by the seller over the condition of the land after the payment, subject to certain exceptions. See para **15.87**.
2   Corporation Tax Act 2009, ss 1144 and 1177.

WARRANTIES

9.05   Warranties are contractually binding statements as to particular matters relating to the property, which are of importance to either of the parties. Many of these may have been raised in preliminary enquiries. In corporate transactions, they are often used to obtain disclosure of desired information, since the warranties are generally made subject to disclosures. A disclosure mechanism is unusual in property transactions unless they form part of a corporate sale or acquisition and so warranties given in the absence of disclosures must be accurate.

Warranties from the seller may be appropriate in certain property transactions. Examples are warranties that:

- the seller has not undertaken any activity on the site which is likely to cause or exacerbate contamination;
- the seller has remediated the site to a given standard;
- there are no circumstances which will or may give rise to liabilities under environmental law;
- there are no circumstances which are likely to lead to the revocation, suspension, modification of or refusal to transfer or grant to the buyer any environmental permit.

One problem with warranties is that the measure of damages is generally the difference between the purchase price and the amount which would have been paid if proper disclosure of the true position had been made. If the property being sold has been remediated, the seller may be required to procure for the buyer suitable warranties from the contractor and environmental consultant.

INDEMNITIES

9.06   Indemnities are the best means of allocating risk between the parties and may be appropriate in view of the uncertainty surrounding the statutory methods of transferring liability under the contaminated land legislation. They are particularly useful if it has not been possible to evaluate the precise extent of the risk. In negotiating indemnities, it is important to relate them to the real risks on the site. If it is understood that the only major problem on site is heavy metal contamination, there may be little real value in insisting on a wider indemnity.

The allocation of risk between seller and buyer depends largely on the strength of bargaining position of each of the parties and the degree of importance which they attach to environmental issues. Obviously, sellers prefer to walk away from the property after the sale without being affected by residual liabilities and so may seek an indemnity from their buyers. Buyers on the other hand, may be reluctant to enter into a contract unless they have adequate protection by way of an indemnity from their sellers. Environmental indemnities are often required in property transactions where the seller desires a clean break.

It must always be remembered that indemnities are not a panacea and, in any event, are only as good as the financial strength of the party who gives them ('the indemnitor'). They may be of little value in the event of the death or liquidation of that party.

If the financial status of the indemnitor is in doubt, it is worth seeking an indemnity or a guarantee from a more credit-worthy parent company or a bank respectively. In cases where it is likely that claims will be made within a reasonably short time, it may be appropriate to place a sum of money in an escrow account under the control of both parties to cover those liabilities. The balance of the fund can be repaid to the indemnitor at the end of an agreed period or in tranches so as to reduce the sum in the account gradually.

9.07 A further question is who takes the benefit of the indemnity? It may be drafted so as to benefit only the other party to the contract (buyer or seller). However, some indemnities are expressed to be also for the benefit of the indemnitee's directors, officers, employees and agents and/or successors in title.

There is now a statutory presumption that where a contract purports to confer a benefit on a third party, that person may enforce the relevant provision, (even though not a party to the contract) unless a proper construction of the contract shows that the parties to it did not intend to confer a right of direct enforcement on the third party.[1] If it is intended that third parties should not be able to enforce the indemnity, a clear statement to that effect should be set out in the agreement which negatives the statutory presumption.

1 Contracts (Rights of Third Parties) Act 1999. The Act came into full force on 11 May 2000. Between 11 November 1999 and 11 May 2000, the Act applied only if expressly invoked by the contract. For the enforcement of third party rights in cases where the Act does not apply see *Chitty on Contracts* 32nd edn (2015) paras 18–045ff.

9.08 It has been held that the term indemnity can have two meanings: damages for breach of contract and loss attributable to a particular cause whether or not contemplated by the parties.[1] The term indemnity is used in the latter sense in this chapter.

There are significant differences between claims for damages and indemnities, which include the following:

- in claims for damages the claimant must establish that he has suffered loss. An indemnity gives rise to a debt when a specified condition or event has occurred;
- remoteness of damage is relevant in claims for damages but not under an indemnity;
- the requirement to mitigate loss arises in claims for damages for breach of contract but not under an indemnity.[2]

Some common forms of wording may not affect the nature of the indemnity clause, but it is worth understanding their effect.

The words 'and hold harmless' sometimes appear in indemnity wording, but have little practical effect.

Other common wording is 'and keep indemnified' which does not (as may be intended) extend the benefit of an indemnity beyond the termination of an agreement. If the parties wish to extend an indemnity in that way, it should be done specifically in a survival clause.

The word 'defend' in the phrase 'indemnify, defend and hold harmless' has been held not to impose a requirement on the indemnitee to hand over the defence of any claim to the indemnitor. Rather it is used in general sense of 'protect from'. At most it may give the indemnitee the right to request the indemnitor to take over the defence of proceedings brought against it:[3]

1 *Total Transport Corporation v Arcadia Petroleum, the Eurus* [1998] 1 Lloyd's Rep 351 (CA).
2 However, a requirement to mitigate loss and the rules on remoteness of damage can be imposed contractually. See paras **9.10** and **9.16**.
3 *Codemasters Software Co Ltd v Automobile Club de L'Ouest* [2010] FSR 12 (Arnold J).

Extent of indemnity cover

9.09 When negotiating an indemnity, it is important to agree precisely which risks are to be borne by the seller and which by the buyer. An indemnity can cover the risk of liabilities from any one or more of the following:

- all environmental matters (which can be broadly defined);
- all contaminating substances;[1]
- specified substances only;
- known contamination caused by carrying on the seller's business;
- unknown contamination caused by carrying on the seller's business;
- known historic contamination not caused by the seller;
- unknown historic contamination not caused by the seller;
- contamination caused or exacerbated by the activities of the buyer after completion;[2]
- hazardous substances in the built environment such as asbestos;[3] and
- invasive species such as Japanese Knotweed.[4]

1 In this context the definition of 'Hazardous Substances' is important. See para **9.12**.
2 The seller cannot in principle be liable for contamination caused by the buyer after completion. However, that contamination could be a concern for the seller if it reacts with contamination already in the ground and creates a new substance which gives rise to damage for which the seller could be liable. In relation to Part 2A of the Environmental Protection Act 1990, see s 78F(9) and exclusion Test 4, Part 2A Contaminated Land Statutory Guidance, April 2012, paras 7.51–7.53.
3 Owners or (in the case of leaseholds) tenants who have an obligation to maintain or repair have important duties to assess and manage asbestos in non-domestic property under reg 4 of the Control of Asbestos Regulations 2012, SI 2012/632. These duties are in addition to duties under the Occupiers Liability Acts 1957 and 1984 and under the law of nuisance. For the sake of clarity, it is better to state expressly if the indemnity is to relate to hazardous substances in the built environment.
4 Liabilities relating to invasive species are to be found in the Wildlife and Countryside Act 1981, s 14(2) (causing to grow in the wild any plant which is included in Part II of Sch 9) and the common law of nuisance: see *Sedleigh-Denfield v O'Callaghan* [1940] AC 880 (in relation to continuance of a nuisance). See also the EU Invasive Alien Species Regulation, (1143/2014) and the Infrastructure Act 2015, Part 4 Environmental Control of Animal and Plant Species.

9.10   Indemnities normally extend to one or more of the following:

- the cost of remedial work required by the regulatory authorities on site;
- the cost of remedial work required by the regulatory authorities off site occasioned by the migration of contamination from the site;
- economic/business loss caused by contamination or the remediation of contamination;
- breach of contract by the indemnitors;
- claims for compensation by third parties;
- costs and expenses (including the cost of legal and other professional advice) in dealing with claims and requirements which are the subject of the indemnity. The indemnitee should insist that where there is a requirement to mitigate losses which are the subject of the indemnity, the expenses incurred in mitigating any such losses are also covered.[1]

A common formula used in indemnities to cover these matters is 'all and any actions, claims, losses, damages, liabilities, judgments, charges, costs (including without limitation legal and consultancy fees) and expenses ... (including without limitation the expenses incurred in mitigating any such losses) ...'. A specific head of management time can also be added although this may be included within 'costs' or 'expenses'.

The list of matters in the formula should be comprehensive to avoid the danger that the courts will construe the indemnity in its narrower meaning: damages for breach of contract.[2] This is most likely to be an issue where the indemnity covers the indemnitor's breach of contract rather than in cases where it is restricted to liabilities falling on the indemnitee. For the same reason indemnitees are well advised to avoid references in the main part of the indemnity to concepts which are redolent of remoteness of damage or mitigation of damage (both of which apply to breach of contract claims but not debt). The former include direct, indirect and consequential loss. Therefore, if the parties wish to exclude economic or other forms of loss from the indemnity or impose an obligation to mitigate loss or restrict costs to those which are reasonable that should be expressed in a separate limitations clause.[3]

The indemnitor will usually wish to avoid giving an indemnity which enables the indemnitee to undertake remedial work at the indemnitor's expense if contamination is discovered. In that case, the indemnitor should ensure that the terms 'costs' and 'expenses' are limited to those related to dealing with claims etc covered by the indemnity. However, such wider costs and expenses indemnities are sometimes given in circumstances where, if the work were not done, liabilities would be likely to arise.

The parties should consider whether liabilities to be covered by the indemnity are purely environmental[4] or whether harm to health, health and safety issues and interference with amenity are also included. Depending on the context, these may be included by relating liabilities to the definition of Environment since damage to the Environment is an invariable precondition of the other forms of harm. However, clarity is more likely to be achieved by excluding or including them specifically. This can be done in the context of one or other of the definitions of Environment or Environmental Law discussed in the following paragraphs.

Some indemnities are limited to liabilities under a particular regime, such as the contaminated land legislation, although this is unusual.

Before deciding on the scope of the indemnity, the parties need to be aware of which liabilities can and which cannot fall on each of them. An indemnity should only be requested/given in respect of liabilities which may fall on the indemnified party under the general law or contract.

It is becoming increasingly common for sellers to require an indemnity from buyers in respect of all residual seller liabilities. Sellers will argue that the sale includes all liabilities relating to the property (including those relating to the pre-completion off-site migration of contamination) and will point to the difficulty in distinguishing between pre- and post-completion migrations. However, a buyer may legitimately object to giving an indemnity in relation to hazardous substances which have migrated from the property before completion and over which it has never had control.

Some indemnities purport to extend to fines imposed for criminal offences. The general rule is that such an indemnity is illegal and unenforceable on the ground of being contrary to public policy.[5] However, there is an exception where the indemnitee shows that the offence was committed without criminal intent or negligence on his part and that the fault was that of the indemnitor.[6]

It follows that an indemnity against fines for future offences would be contrary to public policy unless these related to circumstances solely attributable to the acts or omissions of the indemnitor. A possible example is a water pollution offence due to the continued use by the seller/indemnitor of a sewer on the buyer's newly acquired land.

Indemnities often contain exclusion clauses designed to restrict the scope of the losses recoverable. Although exclusion clauses are construed according to the ordinary rules of construction, courts seek to construe them in accordance with the true intention of parties and to avoid interpretations which would render contractual promises (including the benefit of an indemnity) illusory.[7] In the case of any ambiguity, courts tend to construe such exclusion clauses restrictively in accordance with the *contra proferentem* rule. In a similar vein, courts lean against construing an indemnity as applying to loss caused by the indemnitee's own negligence. However, if the indemnity expressly or on a true construction of the wording covers negligence, the court will give effect to the parties' intention.[8] Words such as 'all liability' or 'howsoever arising' are wide enough to cover negligence but they may be limited by their factual context and in that case may not apply to the indemnitee's negligent act.[9]

Environmental indemnities commonly exclude 'consequential losses'. The courts have held in several cases that in the context of an exclusion clause, this term does not encompass loss of profits. The reason is that 'consequential losses' refers only to losses recoverable under the second limb of the rule in *Hadley v Baxendale*,[10] ie those losses which ought to have been reasonably contemplated by the defendant at the time of the contract due to special circumstances known to the defendant which were beyond the 'ordinary course of things'. Losses recoverable under the first limb of the rule are those which arise in the 'ordinary course of things', ie the type of losses which any reasonable person in the position of the defendant would have foreseen at the time of the contract. Loss of ordinary profits has been held to fall within the first limb of the rule in a number of cases and so does not constitute a 'consequential loss'.[11] Of course, the rule in *Hadley v Baxendale* applies to claims for damages not to claims in debt including indemnity claims. However, the restricted interpretation of 'consequential losses' which has been suggested by the courts should apply to claims and liabilities which are covered by indemnities.[12] In order to avoid these difficult issues, exclusions should be drawn precisely. If loss of profits is to be excluded, that should be stated expressly.

Loss of profits and other economic losses[13] may form part of a third party claim covered by the indemnity as well as a loss suffered directly by the indemnitee. The drafting should state clearly which of these falls within the scope of the indemnity.

Since the rules on remoteness of damage do not apply to indemnities, the indemnitor may wish to limit his liability by applying the rule in *Hadley v Baxendale*[14] expressly.

1 In *BAL 1996 Ltd v British Alcan Aluminium Plc* [2006] Env LR 26, a clause in the environmental deed provided that 'subject to [the defendant] indemnifying' the buyer against 'any and all Liabilities … costs, damages, fees, expenses, claims or demands which may reasonably be suffered or incurred by [the buyer] in so doing, [the buyer] shall take such steps as are reasonably practicable in mitigating the Liability in relation to such claim.' The Technology and Construction Court held that the purpose of the clause was to enable the defendant if it wished to require the buyer to take steps to mitigate any liability on giving an indemnity. It did not entitle the buyer to make a claim except under the indemnity given under that clause. The use of the words 'subject to' indicated that the giving of the indemnity was a condition precedent to the obligation to mitigate, not a correlative obligation. In practice, the parties to an indemnity may consider that the obligation to mitigate should not be subject to a pre-condition. See para **9.16**.

2 *Total Transport Corporation v Arcadia Petroleum, the Eurus* [1998] 1 Lloyd's Rep. 351 (CA). Any settlement of a claim must be reasonable if it is to be covered by an indemnity: *Biggins & Co Ltd v Permanite Ltd* [1951] 2 KB 314 (CA); *Codemasters Software Co Ltd v Automobile Club de L' Ouest (No 2)* [2010] FSR 13 (Warren J). The Court of Appeal has held that an indemnity 'against all proceedings, claims and demands' in respect of liabilities includes a reasonable settlement of a claim by the indemnitee: *Rust Consulting v PB Ltd* [2012] BLR 427 (CA).

3 See the discussion post and para **9.16**.

4 See definition of 'Environment': para **9.11**.

5 The public policy is expressed in the maxim *ex turpi causa non oritur actio*. *R Leslie v Reliable Advertising etc Agency Ltd* [1915] 1 KB 652 at 658–659 per Rowlatt J; *Askey v Golden Wine* [1948] 2 All ER 35 at 38 per Denning J; *Gray v Thames Trains* [2009] AC 1339; *Safeway Stores Ltd v Twigger* [2011] Bus LR 1629 (CA). The position is discussed by O Lomas [1989] JEL 48 at 54ff in the context of insurance against marine pollution fines.

6 *Cointat v Myham & Son* [1913] 2 KB 220; *Osman v J Ralph Moss Ltd* [1970] Lloyd's Rep 313 at 316 per Sachs LJ. In *Safeway Stores Ltd v Twigger* [2011] Bus LR 1629 at 1642 Pill LJ after citing *Osman* said 'It is not easy to provide a single, simple rule which applies to the wide range of situations in which civil claims may follow a conviction or quasi-conviction. The principle is one of law but its application will vary with the circumstances. Findings in this case or by the House of Lords in *Gray's* case do not in my judgement necessarily have the effect of

overruling cases cited where the principle has not been applied'. However, Longmore LJ (with whose judgment Lloyd LJ agreed) said 'It has not been expressly decided whether the maxim applies where the criminal act is one of strict liability and the claimant may not have been at fault at all'.

7 See *Chitty on Contracts* 32nd edn (2015) para 15-011.
8 See *Chitty*, op.cit. para 15-018; *Canada Steamship Lines Ltd v R* [1952] AC 192 (PC); *Smith v South Wales Switchgear Co Ltd* [1978] 1 WLR 165 (CA); *Lictor Anstalt v MIR Steel UK Ltd* [2013] 2 All ER (Comm) 54 (CA) (deliberate acts).
9 *Chitty*, op.cit. para 15-014. However, in *Persimmon Homes v Ove Arup* [2015] EWHC 3573 (TCC) an exclusion of all liability for any asbestos claim from a warranty (by environmental consultants who provided professional services relating to the development of a site) was held to be unqualified and therefore applied so as to exclude liability for negligence.
10 (1854) 9 Ex 341. See also *Victoria Laundry (Windsor) Ltd v Newman Industries Ltd* [1949] 2 KB 528.
11 *British Sugar v NEI Power Projects Ltd* (1998) 87 BLR 42; *Deepak v ICI* [1999] 1 Lloyd's Rep 387; *BHP Petroleum Ltd v British Steel plc* [1999] 2 Lloyd's Rep 583 (affirmed in part [2000] 2 Lloyd's Rep 277); *Hotel Services Ltd v Hilton International Hotels (UK) Ltd* [2000] BLR 235; *Pegler Ltd v Wang (UK) Ltd (No 1)* [2000] BLR 218. However, in *Caledonia North Sea Ltd v BT Plc* [2002] 1 Lloyd's Rep 553, Lord Hoffmann reserved his position on this point. Note that in certain circumstances loss of profit can fall under the second limb of the rule in *Hadley v Baxendale* and is therefore not recoverable where consequential losses are excluded: *Elvanite Full Circle Ltd v AMEC Earth & Environmental (UK) Ltd* [2013] EWHC 1191 (TCC).
12 In *Transocean Drilling UK Ltd v Providence Resources Ltd*, the Arctic III [2014] EWHC 4260 (Comm), Popplewell J accepted that the rule in *Hadley v Baxendale* applied to an indemnity which operated to exclude recovery of a claim for costs falling within the definition of consequential loss. However, it appears that in that case the term indemnity refers to the satisfaction of a claim for damages for breach of contract rather than the meaning used in this chapter which is the obligation to reimburse loss attributable to a particular cause whether or not contemplated by the parties. See para **9.08**.
13 Economic losses can be greater than claims for remediating physical damage caused by contamination: see *Blue Circle Industries plc v Ministry of Defence* [1999] 2 WLR 295 (CA). Economic losses can include loss of sale of the property and disturbance to a business caused by the presence of contamination or the need to clean it up.
14 (1854) 9 Ex 341 and see the discussion of consequential loss above. If that rule is applied expressly, it will affect the construction of the term 'consequential loss' which then could not be as suggested in the cases referred to, and text thereto. The reason is that if the second limb of the rule in *Hadley v Baxendale* is applied expressly, it would not be excluded by the term 'consequential losses'. Equally, the term would still not apply to loss of profits if they are included in the first limb of the rule. In that case, it is arguable that 'consequential losses' could refer to those losses which would fall outside both limbs of the rule in *Hadley v Baxendale*, ie. losses which are unforeseeable even to the defendant.. On the other hand, if loss of profits is expressly excluded from the scope of the indemnity, it is likely to be construed as an exception to the rule in *Hadley v Baxendale*, if that rule is applied expressly.

Definitions

9.11   As indicated above some definitions have an important bearing on the scope of the indemnity. Three require explanation: 'Environment'; 'Hazardous (Dangerous) Substances' and 'Environmental Law'.

The definition of 'Environment' generally refers to the media of land, water and air. The best practice (assuming that a broad definition is required) is to add clarifications to each of these. 'Land' should include buildings and structures attached to or in the land. 'Water' should include all surface, coastal and groundwater. It is better to avoid the more limited definition of 'controlled waters' in the Water Resources Act 1991, s 104 because that excludes water in lakes or ponds which does not ultimately flow into the sea, and water in public and private sewers and drains. 'Air' should include air inside natural or man-made structures. Some definitions also include all living organisms (including man) and their ecosystems (including, in the case of man, property).

9.12 'Hazardous Substances' may be defined in relation to their propensity to harm the environment or human health. In some cases the definition is so wide as to cover almost any substance. If so, it should be checked that the indemnity does not cover unintended risks, such as injuries caused by rusty nails on the ground or people drowning in water tanks. Two further issues to consider are:

- Should the definition cover substances which *can/may/could* cause harm or only those which are *likely* to do so? The latter formulation can unduly restrict the effect of an indemnity because at the date the indemnity is given the substances may be immobile and therefore unlikely to cause harm. They may not be caught by the indemnity if subsequent events, eg development, render them mobile so that they migrate and cause harm. Whether the indemnity applies will depend on the context in which the definition is used and particularly on whether the substances must be hazardous substances (as defined) at the date of completion or whether the definition can apply at a later date. A hazard based definition (*can/may/could*) is likely to be more effective in that respect than a risk based one (*likely*).
- Some definitions cover substances 'which alone or in combination with others' can cause harm. This can have the following effect. An innocuous substance ('substance A') is in the ground at the date of completion. Apart from the 'alone or in combination' formula it would not be within the scope of the definition of 'Hazardous Substance'. After completion, a further substance ('substance B') is introduced by the activities of a third party which when combined with substance A reacts to form a harmful substance ('substance C'). The 'alone or in combination' formula ensures that substance A is included in the definition. An indemnitor will argue that he should have no responsibility for the effects of substance B or substance C if he will have no control of the property after completion. Under these circumstances the indemnitor will, no doubt, point to the effect of the Statutory Guidance which is to exclude from liability under the contaminated land legislation, the party responsible for substance A.[1]

An alternative approach to defining 'Hazardous Substances' (which is not widely used in practice) is to refer to all substances covered by specified legislation, such as the Notification of Installations Handling Hazardous Substances Regulations 1982, the Planning (Hazardous Substances) Regulations 1992, the Control of Substances Hazardous to Health Regulations 2002 (as amended), or the EU Regulation on Classification, Labelling and Packaging of Substances and Mixtures (1272/2008).

If the indemnity is to be given in respect of contaminants from a particular industry, reference can be made to substances listed in various technical documents relating to contaminants usually found on land used for that industrial process. Examples are the Guidance Notes published by the Inter-departmental Committee on the Redevelopment of Contaminated Land (ICRCL), which have now been superseded, the Contaminated Land Research Programme Reports (CLR),[2] and by the Construction Industry Research and Information Association (CIRIA) on the investigation and remediation of contaminated land. The weakness of this approach is that the list of contaminants may not be comprehensive and therefore may not include all the hazardous substances on the site. A more comprehensive list of contaminants is contained in the Dutch Guidelines produced by VROM, the Ministry of Housing, Physical Planning & Environment in 1995 and the *Handbook of Environmental Contaminants: A Guide for Site Assessment*.[3]

If asbestos and asbestos-containing materials in buildings are to be included, it is better to do so expressly for the sake of clarity at least by referring to hazardous substances in buildings.

It is doubtful whether invasive species such as Japanese Knotweed would be 'substances' for the purpose of the definition of Hazardous Substances. Although the word 'substance' can have a broad meaning, ie the matter of which a physical thing exists, in the context of contaminated land its more natural meaning is something of a definite chemical composition.[4] Perhaps more significantly, there is a distinction between a substance, the physical or chemical properties of which may have external impacts, and a living organism. The key feature of the latter is that it is alive and, most significantly in the case of Japanese Knotweed, has the capacity to grow. Accordingly, if it is intended that the indemnity should cover invasive species, the definition of Hazardous Substances should include them expressly or the indemnity should be framed to cover them separately.

1 Part 2A Contaminated Land Statutory Guidance April 2012, paras 7.51–7.53
2 Published by DEFRA and the Environment Agency.
3 By Chris L Shineldecker (Lewis Publishers, 1992). The Department of Environment (now DEFRA) Industry Profiles provide information on the processes, materials and wastes associated with many industries and are still widely used.
4 See the definition of 'substance' in EPA 1990, s 78A(9).

9.13 Some important issues arise with regard to the definition of 'Environmental Law'. The breadth of the legal regime to be covered by the indemnity must be considered here. It could be limited to liabilities for regulatory requirements under specified legislation or it could extend to all legislation and the common law. Reference should also be made to European law as well as by-laws if appropriate.

A particular concern of indemnitors is that the indemnity should not extend beyond known liabilities under existing law. Otherwise the extent of their liability under the indemnity becomes uncertain. On the other hand indemnitees will wish all liabilities to be covered, if they are not responsible for the source of the liability.

The question is whether the indemnity should be restricted to laws in force at the date of completion or should future laws be included? It is important to consider that in some cases there is a considerable gap between the passing of legislation and its coming into force.[1] For that reason, it is usual to include laws enacted but not yet in force even if future laws in general are not included.

Re-enactments and consolidations of legislation should normally be included in the definition, at least to the extent that they do not bring about substantive changes to the law.

Some definitions list particular pieces of legislation. The best practice is to give these as examples to be included 'without limitation' in a wider definition. The danger of relying exclusively on a list is that key liabilities may be excluded inadvertently.

It is common to include a reference to guidance, codes of practice and circulars, whose requirements may be much more detailed than those of the law itself. In some cases, such as the contaminated land legislation, the guidance is part of the statutory regime. In other cases, codes of practice may be published by private bodies with no official sanction. Indemnitors can reasonably object to the latter. A compromise solution is to include guidance, codes of practice and circulars to the extent that they have the force of law.

In cases where there is a narrow definition of 'Environment', some definitions of 'Environmental Law' include the law relating to human health alone, or human health and safety.

1 This was the case with the contaminated land legislation in EPA 1990, Part 2A, which was passed as s 57 of EA 1995 and came into force in England in April 2000.

Trigger event

9.14 It is important to define the event or events which will 'trigger' the indemnity to avoid arguments over when liability under the indemnity crystallises. Possible 'triggers' include:

- service of a statutory notice by a regulatory authority;
- any demands, claims, actions or proceedings;[1]
- a serious threat of proceedings;[2]
- judgment by a court against the indemnitee;
- remedial work is reasonably necessary to avoid liabilities under environmental law;
- remedial work is reasonably necessary to avoid harm to the environment or human health;
- remedial work is reasonably required to enable the buyer to develop the property for a particular use;
- remedial work is reasonably required to avoid disruption to the business of the buyer.

Awaiting a statutory notice or court judgment to trigger the indemnity may be too late from the perspective of both parties because considerable damage may have been caused which could have been avoided if an earlier trigger were provided. On the other hand a seller will be unwilling to allow the buyer a free hand to carry out remedial work at the seller's expense. A sensible compromise approach is to allow voluntary work to be carried out with the consent of the indemnitor or, in the absence of consent, if an independent expert states that the trigger condition has been met.

1 See the *Eastern Counties Leather* case, paras **9.22ff**.
2 In *BAL 1996 Ltd v British Alcan Aluminium Plc* [2006] Env LR 26, the indemnity claim related to an on-site landfill and radioactive contamination which came to light after completion of the sale and purchase agreement containing the indemnity. The trigger for a claim was 'a serious threat of proceedings from a Third Party' which was distinguished from 'a notice or communication received from or intimated by a Third Party (in either case falling short of proceedings)'. The Environment Agency had sent a number of letters to the buyer about the landfill with an implied but no explicit threat of proceedings. On the defendant's application to strike out, the court held that it could not be said that the claimant had no reasonable prospect of persuading a court that the test was whether a properly informed reader would have understood from the letters that, unless appropriate action was taken, legal proceedings were likely and that no express threat was necessary.

Standard of remedial work

9.15 Sellers and buyers (indemnitors and indemnitees) are likely to have different views as to the appropriate standard for remedial work. Indemnitors will generally prefer the lowest cost solution which will avoid further liabilities or any other indemnity 'trigger'. Indemnitees (particularly buyers) will prefer a 'Rolls-Royce' solution, since somebody else is paying for it. In most cases, the first approach is more likely to be acceptable to both parties. Possible drafting formulae include:

- to the standard which would be required by any reasonable owner [or funder] of the property;
- to the standard which would be required by any reasonable occupier of the property with the interest of the buyer carrying on the business of [   ]
- to the [minimum] standard required to ensure that there is no [material/significant] risk of [material/significant] harm to the environment [and/or any living organism including man];
- to the [minimum] standard required to ensure that no owner or occupier of the property is likely to be subject to liabilities under environmental law due to the presence of hazardous substances in on or under the property;
- to [the standard required by] [the minimum standard necessary to satisfy the requirements of] a competent regulatory authority acting within its statutory powers or duties;
- to the standard which is likely to be required by any competent regulatory authority acting reasonably.

Of these alternatives, the first considers the point of view of a buyer indemnitee, taking account of regulatory liabilities, potential compensation claims and the needs of the owner in respect of protection of health and comfort and maintenance of property value. It should also be appropriate to the needs of a seller indemnitee whose concern is to avoid further liabilities. The reference to funders has been added as an option because sometimes funders have concerns above those of most reasonable owners. The second alternative may be appropriate for tenants with a limited period of occupation but with a concern to avoid business disruption. The third and fourth alternatives may be preferable to the first in providing a clearer concept of what the standard should achieve. They can be used in tandem and, if appropriate, the other concerns of an owner under the first alternative can be referred to expressly. The fifth alternative presupposes a statutory notice trigger, whilst the sixth involves a decision as to a 'reasonable' regulatory authority requirement. Neither the fifth nor sixth alternatives are ideal from the indemnitee's viewpoint, because they focus only on the concerns of the authorities which may not address all liabilities, eg potential claims by adjacent landowners for damage to their property. In the case of all the alternatives, a mechanism is required for an independent expert to determine the standard in the event of disagreement between the parties.

Limitations on the indemnity

9.16   An indemnitor (particularly a seller) will be concerned to prevent the indemnitee from carrying out actions which are likely to lead to liability under the indemnity. For that reason indemnities may be limited so as not to apply in the following situations:

- *Where the buyer indemnitee develops the site.* Disturbance of the ground may result in contamination migrating and causing harm. In that case it should be specified that the burden of proving whether the development was the cause of the harm falls on one party or the other. Alternatively, the indemnity may be disapplied in the event of any development on the property or of specified areas of the property. The same problem could arise through disturbance of the ground by third parties whether authorised by the buyer or not. In addition, development of adjacent land may result in the migration of contamination from the property. The parties should consider whether any or all of those circumstances should exclude the application of the indemnity.
- *Where liability arises following 'whistle blowing' by the indemnitee.* The indemnity may be expressed to be conditional on the indemnitee not contacting any competent regulatory authority in relation to the condition of the property. In order to allow such contact to be made where it is reasonable, the restriction should not apply if the indemnitor consents, such consent not to be unreasonably refused or delayed.[1]
- *Where the buyer indemnitee carries out investigations.* The indemnitor will not wish the indemnitee to carry out investigations which may lead to the discovery of previously unknown contamination. For that reason, an indemnity may be expressed to be conditional on the indemnitee not carrying out any investigations, at least until after a liability trigger event has occurred. Alternatively, the indemnity may be disapplied in the case of liabilities arising as a result of the discovery of contamination in the course of investigations by or on behalf of the indemnitee.

- *Where liability is due to any act or omission after completion.* This is a broad limitation, which buyer indemnitees should seek to restrict in several ways. First, 'omissions' should specifically exclude any failure to carry out remediation work. Second, 'acts or omissions' should only be those of the buyer or its employees or agents. Third, 'acts' should only be those outside the normal business activity of the buyer indemnitee.
- *Where there has been a change of use of the property.* Indemnitors will be concerned that a change of use may make liabilities more likely, even if there is no disturbance of the soil, for example if existing industrial buildings are converted to residential use. For that reason, an indemnitor will usually insist that the indemnity should not apply in the event of a change of use. However, a buyer should resist such a restriction in the event that a change of use of the property is planned.
- *Double recovery.* An indemnitor will wish to avoid an obligation to pay under the indemnity, where the indemnitee has recovered or has the right to recover from another party. For that reason, the terms of the indemnity may require the indemnitee to exhaust its remedies against all other parties before making a claim under the indemnity. That is likely to be unacceptable to an indemnitee in particular because it may result in a claim being out of time in cases where time limits apply. An alternative which is likely to be more acceptable is a requirement (which is not a pre-condition) on the indemnitee to use all reasonable endeavours to claim against third parties and to refund to the indemnitor all sums received relating to the subject matter of the indemnity which have been paid or are payable by the indemnitor under the indemnity.

It is also important to require the indemnitee to mitigate its loss. Such a requirement is not implied automatically in a contract of indemnity. The requirement to mitigate can be in the form of a covenant by the indemnitee or as a limitation to the right to recover under the indemnity.[2] Certain types of loss such as economic loss may also be excluded specifically[3] and if costs are to be limited to those which are reasonable that should be included in the limitations provisions.

The suggested limitations are clearly less appropriate where the indemnity is given by the buyer to the seller. The seller will normally have no further control or interest in the property and therefore little opportunity to influence the occurrence of events likely to lead to liabilities.

1 See paras **9.27** and **9.28**.
2 See para **9.10** fn 1 and text thereto.
3 See the discussion in para **9.10**.

Time limits

9.17 Environmental liabilities may be 'long tailed', that is, they can arise many years after the occurrence which gave rise to the problem. For example, landfill gas and leachates are often produced many years after waste is deposited in a landfill site. It may take many more years before leachate escapes from the landfill site and pollutes groundwater or surface water. As is demonstrated by *Cambridge Water Co v Eastern Counties Leather plc*[1] and *Blue Circle Industries plc v Ministry of Defence*,[2] the actual loss may not occur for a considerable time after the claimant's land or water supply is polluted. In *Cambridge* Water this occurred when the slightly contaminated water supply failed the strict standards subsequently imposed. In *Blue Circle* actionable damage only occurred when the sale of the claimant's land was aborted due to the discovery by the prospective buyers that the property had been polluted at an earlier time by contamination from the defendant's neighbouring site. For that reason, buyers should negotiate an indemnity which is unlimited in time or one which is effective for as long a period as possible. Conversely, the seller will seek to minimise the indemnity period.

On the other hand, if it is agreed that the buyer is to assume all liabilities, it is common for an indemnity given by the buyer to the seller to be unlimited in time. The reason is that the indemnity is generally designed to give the seller a clean break from liability as far as possible and, therefore, it makes little sense to terminate it after a period of years.

A distinction must be made between the time within which a right to indemnification can arise which is regulated by agreement,[3] and the limitation period for bringing an action to enforce the right to indemnification after it arises. The latter period of six years (or twelve years under a deed) stipulated by the Limitation Act 1980 generally runs from the date the indemnified party's liability has been ascertained.[4] However, that type of limitation period can also be regulated by contract.[5]

1 [1994] 2 AC 264, HL. See paras **13.25–13.29**.
2 [1999] Ch 289 (CA). See paras **13.54.13.56**.
3 Notification of the claim to the indemnitor is usually also required to be made within that period.
4 *Chitty on Contracts* 32nd ed (2015) vol 1, 28-049. The words 'on demand' in an indemnity provision appear to support that approach.
5 *Chitty*, op.cit. 28-107, 28-109, 28-111, 28-113, 28-114.

Caps on liability

9.18 When considering caps on liability, it should be remembered that environmental liabilities can be very high and may exceed the purchase price of the transaction. From the indemnitee's point of view, any cap on the amount of the indemnity should, therefore, not be too low and ideally should be unlimited. The indemnitor, on the other hand, will be anxious to limit the amount of the indemnity as much as possible.

Counter indemnities

9.19 If the parties agree on a clear division of environmental liabilities, this can be achieved neatly by the indemnitee giving a counter indemnity in respect of all liabilities not covered by the indemnity he receives.[1] For example, a counter indemnity may be given to the indemnitor in respect of:

- all contamination related liabilities affecting the site which are not covered by the indemnity;
- liabilities in excess of the cap and/or crystallising beyond the time limit agreed for the indemnity.

The counter indemnity is also a useful way for a seller to obtain protection against liabilities which would not have arisen but for the activities of a buyer indemnitee, eg in developing the property. In this respect, the counter indemnity may cover the same ground as that discussed under Limitations on the Indemnity above.[2]

1 Both in public and private law the original polluter and even previous owners as well as the current owner may be liable for damage caused by ground contamination.
2 Para **9.16**.

Problems of proof

9.20 One of the main difficulties which may be faced by an indemnitee who seeks to enforce an indemnity is to establish that the liabilities relate to contamination which is covered by the indemnity. The problem is most likely to occur where the property continues to be used for the same industrial process as before the sale, so that contamination could have been caused by either the buyer or seller. The same point may arise in relation to a sale from an earlier owner to the seller, if the seller's indemnity is only given in respect of contamination he has caused. Obviously, this problem may not be significant if only one party, eg the seller, could have caused the contamination, because only he has operated the industrial process which gave rise to it.

There are several means of dealing with the problem of proof:

- *Baseline survey.* Provision may be made in the indemnity for a Phase II (intrusive) survey to be carried out as near as possible to the time of completion. This will provide good evidence as to the condition of the ground and the nature and extent of contaminants in it at that time. The parties may agree that the baseline survey is to be conclusive evidence of its contents or that there is a rebuttable presumption that it is accurate. However, in view of the fact that no such survey can be complete (and may be imperfect) the parties may prefer the normal rules of evidence to apply.
- *Presumptions.* The indemnity may provide that if specified contaminants are found on the property, they shall be deemed to have been caused by the indemnitor. Alternatively, there may be a rebuttable presumption to that effect.
- *Sliding scale indemnity.* Under this model, risk is allocated between the parties on the basis of proportions which vary over time. By this means the risk is generally shifted gradually from seller to buyer. For example, in the first year the seller takes 100% of the risk of any liability arising from

contamination. In the second year, the seller is liable for 90% of the amount and the buyer's share is 10%. The seller's share of any liability decreases by 10% each year whilst the buyer's share increases by a corresponding amount. In the eleventh year, the seller's liability will have ended and the buyer takes full responsibility for any contamination related liability.

Regime for claims

9.21 A special regime for making claims may be advisable to ensure that the many sensitive issues referred to above are dealt with properly. Points to consider include:

- The maximum period between the trigger event and notification of the indemnitor.
- Should the right to an indemnity depend on whether the notification to the indemnitor provides specified details?
- Is the indemnitee required to take action in the courts within a prescribed period from the date of giving notice to the indemnitor or should the limitation period of six years allowed under the general law apply?
- Which party should have conduct of any litigation which is the subject matter of the indemnity? Similarly, if the indemnitee is required by a regulatory authority to undertake remediation work, which party is to take charge of the work? It should normally be provided that the party having conduct of litigation or control of the work must consult with and comply with the reasonable requirements of the other. Indemnitors may wish to exercise conduct or control in order to ensure that recoverable expenses are minimised. However, seller indemnitees should consider that by taking control of remediation work they may increase their liability, if they decide in the course of the remedial work that some contamination should be left in the ground or the contamination spreads as a result of the work and causes damage.[1] Additionally they would deprive themselves of the opportunity of taking advantage of exclusion Test 2 in the Statutory Guidance under the contaminated land legislation.[2]
- The need for an effective dispute resolution procedure, generally by means of arbitration, neutral experts or other means of alternative dispute resolution.

1 Eg the seller could be liable respectively as a knowing permitter or a causer: EPA 1990, s 78F(2).
2 Part 2A Contaminated Land Statutory Guidance, April 2012, paras 7.40–7.45 (Test 2 – payments made for remediation). Test 2 cannot be satisfied if the party (seeking exclusion from liability) who makes a payment to the other for the purposes of enabling the recipient to carry out remediation, retains any control over the condition of the land. Holding contractual rights to ensure the proper carrying out of the remediation work does not amount to control for that purpose. However, the right to carry out the remediation work goes further than the contractual rights referred to. For those reasons, seller indemnitees may prefer to have the more limited rights to inspect the work whilst it is being carried out and following its completion and to receive a full report as to what has been done including a photographic record. (Note the disadvantage to buyers of allowing sellers to rely on Test 2 – see para **9.04**, text to fn 2). Test 3 – sold with information paras 7.46–7.50, should not be affected. Test 3 will not exclude a seller from liability, if after the date of sale he retained any interest in the land or any rights to

occupy or use it. It is unlikely that a seller who merely retains a right to carry out remediation work would be excluded from the benefit of Test 3 under those circumstances. A right to carry out remedial work is not an interest in land, but rather a contractual right. Nor is it a right to occupy, which implies a long term connection with the land. Nor is it a right to use the land which suggests obtaining a benefit from it. See generally para15.88.

The *Eastern Counties Leather* case[1]

9.22   This is the fullest decision on environmental indemnities and therefore merits detailed consideration. The background to this case is the claim for compensation in *Cambridge Water Company v Eastern Counties Leather plc.*[2] It will be recalled that the claim by the Cambridge Water Company failed because the pollution of the water supply by a chemical known as PCE used in Eastern Counties' tannery business was not foreseeable at the relevant time. The House of Lords held that foreseeability of damage was necessary for a successful claim both in nuisance and under the rule in *Rylands v Fletcher*.

However, that was not the end of the matter because the regulatory authority (initially the National Rivers Authority (NRA), but subsequently the Environment Agency (EA)) required the groundwater to be cleaned up. The agreed clean-up method was for the polluted groundwater to be pumped out pursuant to the claimant company's (PLC's) abstraction licence. It was then used in the tannery process, which had the effect of stripping out much of the PCE. The waste water was then discharged to foul sewer. Pumping out the groundwater did not achieve the desired reduction in the levels of PCE. The EA, therefore, obtained government funding to carry out the necessary work itself, the cost of this work being recoverable from PLC.[3]

However, before the work could be carried out, the law changed so that the EA was no longer empowered to do the work itself but could only require PLC to carry it out by means of a works notice[4]. The EA, therefore, wrote to PLC on 1 March 2000 ('the March letter') setting out a broad outline of the work required. The letter continued:

> 'I would be grateful therefore if you would prepare a statement outlining your proposals for carrying out the work necessary to improve groundwater quality to an acceptable level. This statement must be presented to the EA by 1ˢᵗ May 2000.
>
> Should an adequate plan, including a realistic and acceptable timetable, not be received by that date, a works notice requiring certain work from you will be issued pursuant to Section 161A of the Water Resources Act 1991 and The Anti-Pollution Works Notices Regulations 1999.'

1 *Eastern Counties Leather plc v Eastern Counties Leather Group Ltd* [2002] Env LR 34; [2003] Env LR 13 (CA); S Payne [2003] JEL 202.
2 [1994] 2 AC 264 (HL).
3 Under s 161 of the Water Resources Act 1991 (WRA) as it was in 1994, the NRA (later the EA) was empowered to carry out preventive or remedial works to deal with poisonous, noxious or polluting matter in or likely to enter controlled waters and to recover their reasonable expenses for doing so from any person who caused or knowingly permitted the presence of such matter.
4 New ss 161A–D were added to the WRA from 29 April 1999 to enable the EA (which by then had replaced the NRA) to serve a works notice requiring any person who caused or knowingly

permitted the presence of any poisonous, noxious or polluting matter which is in or likely to enter controlled waters to undertake appropriate preventive or remedial works. Section 161 remains in force but in amended form, empowering the EA to investigate the source of the matter and the identity of the polluter. The EA's power to carry out works and operations and to recover the cost is limited to cases where it is considered necessary to carry out preventive or remedial work forthwith or where it appears after reasonable enquiry that no person can be found on whom to serve a works notice under s 161A.

The Pollution Indemnity Agreement (PIA)

9.23   In the meantime, on 30 March 1994, the ownership of PLC was transferred from the Moore family to the Byrne family under the terms of a share sale agreement. Due to uncertainty about the possibility of claims by the NRA under s 161 of the Water Resources Act 1991, the PIA was entered into between the defendant company ('Group') and PLC.

The relevant provisions of the PIA as set out in the judgment are as follows:

'2.1   Subject to the following provisions of this Deed [Group] covenants with PLC to indemnify PLC against:

2.1.1 any Pollution Claim

2.1.2 any settlement of any Pollution Claim

2.1.3 any costs (including but not limited to legal and environmental consultant's costs) expenses and fines incurred by PLC or any of the Company's officers directly in relation to any Pollution Claim

2.1.4 any costs incurred by PLC in obtaining or maintaining in force any Consents

2.1.5 any liability incurred by the Company to the NRA or any other regulatory body pursuant to any Consent.

3.1   The indemnity contained in clause 2.1 shall not apply:

3.1.1 unless PLC has given written notice of any claim specifying in reasonable detail (so far as practicable) particulars of the claim prior to the Expiry Date.

3.2   The maximum liability of [Group] in respect of all claims under this Deed shall not exceed £980,000.'

Clause 4, which is headed 'The Works', provided as follows:

'4.1   PLC undertakes to [Group] that subject to obtaining the Consents it will carry out the Works in accordance with the NRA's requirements insofar as those requirements relate to the Boreholes or any substituted borehole or boreholes as may be required from time to time by the NRA and shall ensure that the water is pumped therefrom in accordance with the requirements of the NRA but not further or otherwise.

4.2   The indemnity contained in clause 2 is conditional upon PLC complying with clause 4.1 but for the avoidance of doubt PLC shall not be regarded as being in breach of that clause by reason only that the pumping operations by PLC have not at the relevant time (being the date on which any claim is made by PLC pursuant to clause 2) achieved a reduction in PCE to the levels mentioned in the Letter.'

Clause 5.1 required PLC to:

'Notify [Group] in writing of any Pollution Claim which comes to its notice from which it appears that [Group] is, or may become, liable to indemnify PLC under this Deed. Such notification shall be made within fifty six days after the date on which the Pollution Claim comes to PLC's notice.'

Clause 1 contained definitions of expressions used in the PIA. 'Pollution Claim' was defined as meaning 'any demands, claims, actions or proceedings made or commenced by the NRA against PLC arising out of or in connection with the Pollution Incident'. The expression 'Pollution Incident' was defined as 'the alleged spillage by PLC of PCE on the Site or the dumping by PLC of waste contaminated by PCE in either case prior to 1976.'

PLC's solicitors sent a copy of the March letter to Group under cover of a letter asserting that it constituted a Pollution Claim under the PIA and that a copy was enclosed by way of notification under clause 5.1 of the PIA.

Group resisted the claim on a number of grounds:

(i)   no relevant Pollution Claim within the meaning of clause 1 of the PIA was made ('the claim issue');
(ii) if such a Pollution Claim was made, notification of it by PLC to Group was too late ('the notification issue');
(iii) if such a Pollution Claim was made and PLC gave due notice of it to Group, the condition precedent to Group's liability contained in clause 4.2 was not fulfilled by reason of PLC's non-compliance with clause 4.1 ('the clause 4.1 issue');
(iv) in any event PLC was in breach of an implied term of the PIA that PLC would do nothing to incite or encourage the EA to make a Pollution Claim with the result that either PLC was disabled from claiming an indemnity or was liable to pay damages to Group in an amount equal to the amount of the indemnity ('the implied term issue'); and
(v)   Group was not entitled to any security for any Pollution Claim against which PLC is entitled to be indemnified ('the security issue').

The last issue will not be discussed here.

The claim issue

9.24   The judge, Blackburne J, held that the March letter amounted to a 'claim' within the definition of 'Pollution Claim' in the PIA.[1] An assertion that 'we are going to hold you liable' was capable of amounting to a 'claim', and it was not necessary for the EA to have served a works notice nor for the March letter to be quantifiable in terms of money either when made or by the expiry date (30 March 2000) referred to in the PIA. In reaching that conclusion, the judge was influenced by a memorandum agreed shortly before the PIA was entered into which made it clear that before the NRA carried out any remediation work, water abstraction would be carried out for a fairly lengthy period in an attempt to resolve the problem. In addition, any work carried out by the NRA would probably have extended over a period of years so that at least some of the costs could probably not be quantified until incurred.[2]

1 The judge considered that the order of words in the definition 'demands', 'claims', 'actions' did not imply any ascending order of severity.

2 The judge rejected an alternative submission on behalf of PLC that only a single Pollution Claim could be made under the PIA. He pointed out that the definition referred to 'any demands, claims, actions or proceedings ...', which clearly implied the possibility of more than one demand or claim. PLC had sought to argue that an earlier letter submitted by the EA, accompanied by an invoice, amounted to the whole Pollution Claim. The invoice related to the cost of assessment work carried out by the EA, for which reimbursement was sought under the original version of s 161 of the Water Resources Act 1991. Group accepted that that invoice amounted to a Pollution Claim (but subject to the issue of whether the cost of assessment work was recoverable under the original form of s 161). However, in the accompanying letter the EA indicated that they might seek to recover their costs of carrying out remediation works. The judge held that that letter was insufficient to amount to a Pollution Claim in relation to the cost of such works.

The notification issue

9.25   Clause 5.1 of the PIA required PLC to inform Group in writing of any Pollution Claim within 56 days of the claim coming to PLC's notice. Blackburne J rejected a submission by Group that an earlier letter from the EA which covered the same ground as the March letter amounted to a Pollution Claim, because the letter did no more than invite PLC to submit remediation proposals without any threat of sanctions.

However, even if that letter had constituted a Pollution Claim, the judge considered that failure to comply with the notification requirement did not involve the loss of the right to be indemnified. At most it would give rise to a claim for damages. The reason for this was that clause 5.1 did not set out any express consequence for failure to observe the 56-day notification requirement. In particular, it was not referred to in the list of indemnity exclusions in clause 3.1, where it would be expected if non-compliance was intended to result in disentitlement to the right to be indemnified.

The clause 4.1 issue

9.26   Clause 4.1 imposed on PLC an obligation to carry out certain works and, if it failed to meet that obligation, PLC was to be deprived of the benefit of the indemnity by clause 4.2. Clauses 4.1 and 4.2 are set out above. There were three relevant definitions in clause 1:

'Consents' was defined as 'any licence consent or permission necessary in order that PLC may undertake the Works'.

'Works' was defined as 'the steps to be taken by PLC and as requested by the NRA (provided that such steps are generally in accordance with the Letters) in an attempt to remedy the pollution allegedly caused by the Pollution Incident as described in the Letters.'

'Letters' referred to two letters (one from Messrs Berrymans, the solicitors then acting for PLC, to the NRA dated 25 February 1994 and the other, a letter in reply from the NRA, dated 22 March 1994) and a so-called 'memorandum of understanding', copies of which were annexed to the PIA.

The memorandum of understanding ('the memorandum') attached to the PIA, was as follows:

> 'ELC [ie PLC] will provide the groundwater abstraction pump (or pumps), the electricity and the pipework from the borehole designed by the NRA on the company's property at Sawston to the factory. ELC [ie PLC] will extract water up to the amount allowed by the existing effluent discharge agreement and will continue the works until such time as further pumping will no longer achieve a significant reduction in PCE or to a level of not more than 100 microgrammes per litre for six consecutive months.
>
> It is recognised between the parties that further boreholes may be required in the future. Should any further boreholes be required these will not be funded at the NRA's expense, however the NRA will continue to carry out additional monitoring at the site should this be necessary in pursuance of its statutory functions.'

The letter of 25 February stated that it should be treated as setting out the agreed action to be taken but without creating any enforceable obligation.

The judge found (although that finding was challenged) that PLC was entitled to abstract a lower volume of water under its abstraction licence than it was entitled to discharge under the effluent discharge agreement. In addition, under the abstraction licence PLC could not lawfully extract water in excess of what it was able to use in its tanning process.

Even when the plant was operating at maximum capacity it did not abstract the maximum volumes of water permitted. In 1998, PLC changed from the production of chamois leather to sheepskins. Since the latter required relatively little water, the quantities of water abstracted dropped. The EA complained that 'water is no longer being pumped at the agreed rate'. PLC therefore increased its abstraction even though much of the water was not needed in the new production process. Once it emerged that the abstracted water was being discharged to sewer without the PCE being stripped out in the course of the tanning process, the EA requested PLC not to abstract in excess of its actual needs.

Against that background, Group asserted that PLC was not entitled to claim under the indemnity because it had failed to comply with its obligations under clause 4.1 of the PIA. They argued that reading the memorandum as part of the 'Works' which PLC was obliged to undertake, PLC was bound to abstract at the maximum rate permitted by the abstraction licence, bearing in mind that the 'Works' were to be carried out subject to obtaining the 'Consents'.

That construction was rejected both by Blackburne J and the Court of Appeal.[1] Bearing in mind the factual position at the date of the PIA, Group's approach would have had such a draconian outcome that it was unlikely to have represented the intention of the parties. Blackburne J and the Court of Appeal concluded that the obligation on PLC was simply to undertake the Works in accordance with the NRA's requirements. The reference in clause 4.1 to steps being taken 'generally in accordance with the Letters' (including the memorandum) merely placed a ceiling on the obligations of PLC.

In the Court of Appeal, Buxton LJ drew support for this conclusion from the fact that the memorandum was expressed to be non-binding. Accordingly, even when incorporated by reference into clause 4.1, the meaning of the memorandum had to be construed in the context of a non-binding agreement.

The remaining question was whether the Works had been undertaken in accordance with the NRA's requirements. Both Blackburne J and the Court of Appeal concluded that Group had failed to establish a breach of the requirements. Buxton LJ's reasoning was as follows:

(1) The EA's witness was not asked what the 'agreed rates' were. Since the burden was on Group to establish a breach of the requirements, proper evidence had to be given of what those requirements were.

(2) The EA's complaint was retrospective. A requirement not formally notified to PLC but only perceived afterwards should not count as a requirement for the purpose of the PIA.

(3) The assumption throughout was that the extraction would be for the purpose of the tannery business, until PLC was told otherwise, and that that was sufficient to meet the requirements of the NRA/EA.

1 [2003] Env LR 13. The only issue before the Court of Appeal was whether PLC had failed to comply with the requirements of clause 4.1.

The implied term issue

9.27 Group argued that there was an implied term in the PIA to the effect that PLC would do nothing to promote or incite the making of a Pollution Claim. They suggested that that term had been broken through statements made by PLC's solicitors in various letters and meetings.

Blackburne J (despite a concession on the point by PLC's counsel) questioned 'whether ... a duty of the kind alleged can properly be implied into the PIA. I do not see why, once it becomes likely that a Pollution Claim will be made, PLC should be compelled to stand silently and altruistically by and lose its chance of indemnification because the Expiry Date is fast approaching. I have difficulty in seeing why, in order to give business efficacy to the PIA, it is necessary to imply such a vow of silence on PLC's part'.

In any event, the judge held that even if there was such an implied term, there had been no breach. The statements made by PLC's solicitors amounted to no more than continuing a dialogue with the EA on matters which they had raised and making them aware of Group's interest in the case through the PIA.

Lessons from *Eastern Counties Leather*

9.28 A number of significant issues arise from this case which are worth highlighting:

(1) The terms of an indemnity (like any other contract) will be construed in the light of the factual background to the agreement.[1]

(2) The word 'claim' in an indemnity is likely to be construed as including a statement of intention to serve a formal notice or compensation claim. The claim need not be quantifiable at that stage. If the parties intend to restrict claims to those which are either quantified or capable of quantification by a certain date, express wording to that effect should be included. On the other hand, a mere invitation by the regulatory authority to submit remediation proposals without any threat of legal action if the proposals are not submitted is unlikely to constitute a claim.

(3) Indemnities often contain provisions specifying various requirements imposed on the indemnified party. If those requirements are intended to be preconditions to making a claim under the indemnity, that should be stated expressly. Otherwise, a breach of such a requirement may only give rise to a claim for damages by the indemnifying party. Depending on the construction of the particular clause, it may not involve a loss of the right to be indemnified.

(4) Even if certain requirements are a precondition of the right to claim under an indemnity, those requirements must be clear if breaches are to negate the indemnified party's right to claim.

(5) If other documents are to be incorporated by reference into the indemnity agreement, the nature of those agreements, the context in which they were made, and whether they are binding or non-binding should be considered. Those issues will affect the construction of those documents even when incorporated in the indemnity. To avoid uncertainty, it may be simpler to set out the desired wording in full in the indemnity, rather than rely on incorporation by reference.

(6) It is unlikely that courts will imply terms into detailed indemnity agreements.[2] For that reason, if a 'no whistleblowing' provision is intended, it should be included expressly. The parties also need to consider the intended effect of a breach of such a requirement and provide for it.[3] It has been suggested that a 'no whistleblowing' provision which interferes with how the indemnified party responds to enquiries or notices from a regulator may be void on public policy grounds.[4] In order to avoid any such arguments, a 'no whistleblowing' requirement can exclude cases where there is a legal requirement on the indemnified party to provide the information, or perhaps even where information is requested by a regulatory authority.

1 *Chitty on Contracts* 32nd edn (2015) para 13-121.
2 *Chitty on Contracts* 32nd edn (2015). Ch 14; Payne [2003] JEL 202, 234–235.
3 See para **9.16**.
4 Payne [2003] JEL 202, 235.

Standard conditions

9.29 Standard conditions are often incorporated into property sale agreements. Some of these which deal with contaminated land (even though not explicitly) have been discussed earlier.[1] Where they apply, it should be ensured that in the event that specific clauses cover contamination, those clauses should prevail in the event of any conflict with the standard conditions.

1 See Ch 2.

Subject to planning

9.30 Some contracts are expressed to be subject to the grant of planning permission. Where that is so, planning permission may be granted subject to conditions relating to the investigation and/or remediation of contamination.[1] In such cases, the parties need to agree on how the related expenses are to be shared between them. They could be shared in accordance with agreed proportions. Alternatively, one party could be responsible for all such expenses up to an agreed figure, and the other party for expenses above that figure. In all such cases, it may be appropriate to include provisions avoiding gold plating and requiring certification of work by an approved environmental consultant. Dispute resolution clauses should also be included.

1 See Ch 15.

Covenants and easements

9.31 If the seller sells part of its contaminated land, it may wish to impose covenants on the buyer for the protection of the retained land. These may be positive covenants requiring the buyer to remediate the land acquired. Alternatively, the seller may impose restrictive covenants prohibiting certain activities which may exacerbate the condition of the seller's retained land. The rules as to when such covenants bind successors in title of the seller and buyer are in the standard land law text books.[1]

It is now firmly established that easements to emit noise (or other forms of pollution) which affect neighbouring property can be acquired expressly as well as by prescription.[2] An easement to pollute will operate as a defence to a common law nuisance action, but it is no defence to statutory nuisance whether action is taken by the local authority under s 80 of the EPA 1990 or by an aggrieved person under s 82. The reason is that the only defences to a statutory nuisance action are those set out in the EPA 1990 and these do not include an easement to pollute – see s 80. It is unlikely that this difficulty could be overcome by seeking a covenant from the grantor of the easement (the servient owner) that that party will make no complaint of any pollution from the dominant tenement to any regulatory authority nor take any action in respect of it in any court or tribunal. The reason is that this would probably amount to a waiver of statutory rights which extend beyond a purely personal benefit (which can be waived) to those serving the public purpose of protecting public health and the environment (which cannot be waived).[3]

1 Eg: *Megarry and Wade, The Law of Real Property* (8th edn, 2012), Ch 32; *Cheshire and Burn's Modern Law of Real Property*, 18th edn (2011) Ch 19.

2 *Lawrence v Fen Tigers Ltd* [2014] AC 822, paras 28–46, Lord Neuberger PSC. See generally Megarry and Wade, op.cit. Chs 28–30; Cheshire and Burn, op.cit. Ch 18.
3 *Chitty on Contracts*, 32nd edn (2015) 16-025.

Certificates of title

9.32 In some property transactions, particularly those associated with corporate mergers and acquisitions, certificates of title are provided in lieu of the buyer's solicitors investigating title. The City of London Law Society (CLLS) Land Law Committee 'Long Form' Certificate of Title is now the industry standard being widely known and commonly used in these transactions. The latest, seventh edition, of this Certificate takes the view that it should be for the recipient of the Certificate to consider what investigations it wishes to make in relation to the environmental condition of the property. Accordingly, this form of Certificate clearly includes a statement that no environmental or flood assessments, audits, surveys or other reports on the environmental condition of the property have been considered. The only information which this form of Certificate does contain on environmental matters are certain statements made by the property owning company itself which render the information of very limited value unless supported by contractual warranties elsewhere in the transactional documentation.

ENVIRONMENTAL INSURANCE

9.33 As an addition or alternative to the indemnities or other contractual provisions referred to above, the parties to a property sale and purchase may contemplate purchasing an environmental insurance policy to cover the seller, buyer or both as well as additional insureds such as lenders. An environmental insurance policy may, subject to its terms and conditions, directly cover environmental liabilities, including liabilities under the Environmental Liability Directive,[1] which may fall upon an insured, or alternatively pay on behalf of the insured liabilities arising under, or exceeding, an indemnity.

1 Directive 2004/35/CE on environmental liability with regard to the prevention and remedying of environmental damage (2004) OJ L143/56.

9.34 The environmental insurance market has developed since the early 1990s to fill an ever-increasing gap in cover for environmental liabilities under public liability policies. In particular, virtually all public liability policies issued or renewed since 1990 have excluded cover for gradual pollution. Even when public liability policies provide cover for environmental liabilities, not only is the extent of such coverage far from clear,[1] but they are liability policies; they do not provide cover for damage to an insured's own site.[2]

1 *Bartoline Ltd v Royal & Sun Alliance plc and Heath Lambert Ltd* [2007] All ER (D) 59 (QBD) (public liability policy provides cover only for tort liabilities not statutory liability for cost of cleaning up water pollution). The case was appealed but settled out of court.
2 *Yorkshire Water Services Ltd v Sun Alliance and London Insurance plc* [1998] Env LR 204.

9.35 As the environmental insurance market evolved, policies became increasingly less restrictive and are now a common means by which the risk of future liabilities can be transferred from seller or buyer to an insurer. Several major insurance companies offer environmental cover, and a constantly increasing volume of business is being transacted. Most of the large firms of brokers have a specialist group dealing with environmental issues.

As with any insurance policy, the risk transfer is not absolute. The policies have an excess/deductible or a self-insured retention as well as a limit of indemnity for each and every loss and an aggregate limit of indemnity. The policies also contain exclusions. For example, they will not provide cover for criminal fines imposed by enforcing authorities because it is against public policy to insure them. The policies will also not cover claims by employees for exposure to pollutants; such cover is not necessary because it is included in mandatory employees' liability insurance policies.

9.36 Environmental insurance does not remove the need for conventional public or products liability insurance; it is an additional coverage available for specific risks. Apart from cover in respect of pure property transactions, environmental insurance is also available, among other things, to cover potential liabilities under business sale agreements, where warranties and indemnities are often required on environmental issues. Warranty and indemnity insurance for such transactions, although an expanding market in itself, usually excludes cover for environmental claims.

Types and extent of environmental insurance policies

9.37 Environmental insurance policies are, with the exception of occurrence-based contractors pollution liability policies, written on a claims-made-and-reported basis. That is, a claim must be made against the insured, and the insured must report the claim to the insurer within the policy period. Depending on the type of policy and the insurer, the policy period may be extended for up to three years beyond the termination date by means of an extended reporting period, on payment of an additional premium.

9.38 There are two main types of policies which apply to property transactions: policies for pre-existing contamination and policies for operational risks. Both types are site-specific. That is, they provide cover in respect of sites which are listed in the policy. Sites may be added to, or deleted from, the policy during the policy period as the insured acquires or disposes of them, respectively. In addition, they frequently provide cover for losses from covered operations, transportation, business interruption and non-owned disposal sites.

Insurers offer property transfer policies for periods of up to ten years and operational risk policies for periods of up to three years. Operational risk policies are also offered on an annual basis.

'Environmental-lite' policies that provide more limited cover are also available from some environmental insurers, as are endorsements to public liability policies to provide cover, among other things, for the cost of remediating pollution and other environmental damage.

9.39   The insurance policy for pre-existing contamination, known as a property transfer policy, provides cover for liabilities which arise from contamination on, or migrating from, the insured's site. In order for the risk of liability to be covered, the insured must not have known about the contamination, or must have disclosed the contamination to the insurer, prior to inception of the policy. In many cases, insurers will provide cover for disclosed contamination on the basis that they are willing to take the risk of liabilities arising from it during the policy period. Factors influencing the level of risk include a low level of contamination and the absence of receptors which could be harmed by it. The insurer may exclude cover for known contamination which is being remediated on part of a site until the remediation is complete; providing cover only for losses arising from contamination that migrates off site during that period.

The existence of a property transfer policy does not necessarily mean that the insured can remediate contamination or other environmental damage at the site in the absence of involvement by an enforcing authority and then claim the costs of doing so against the policy. Policies do not, however, require the enforcing authority to have served a remediation, works, or other notice on the insured in order for cover to be triggered. For example, a notification of contaminated land under Part 2A of the EPA 1990, a request by the Environment Agency or Natural Resources Wales to remediate water pollution under the WRA 1991, or the discovery of an imminent threat of, or actual, environmental damage is generally sufficient. Some policies also have a discovery trigger according to which insurers cover the costs of remediating a pollution condition or other environmental damage discovered during the policy period. Further, some policies provide cover for emergency remedial measures or preventive measures under the Environmental Liability Directive (as well as cover for remedial measures under it).

Risks covered by a property transfer policy include third-party bodily injury and property damage and the cost of remediating on-site and off-site contamination from pollution conditions, or other environmental damage, which originate on an insured site, personal liability of directors and officers for the above risks and defence costs. Depending on the insurer, a policy may also provide cover for business interruption costs, diminution in the value of first-party or third-party property, loss of rental income and relocation costs resulting from contamination and other environmental damage and its remediation.

In addition, the policies may be drafted specifically to cover risks arising under a specified environmental indemnity or other contractual provisions.

9.40   Policies for operational risks provide cover for losses which arise from a pollution incident or other environmental damage which occurs at the insured's site and in some policies also the location of specified operations carried out by or on behalf of the insured, during transportation, and/or at a non-owned disposal site during the policy period. Risks which are covered include third-party bodily injury and property damage and on-site and off-site remediation costs arising from a pollution incident or environmental damage under the Environmental Liability Directive, as well as defence costs. A policy may also include business interruption, loss in rental income, diminution in value of third-party property, and relocation costs arising from the contamination or other environmental damage.

Conditions and limits

9.41 Environmental insurance policies contain terms and conditions which are similar to, or the same as, other types of policies. For instance, a policy may, as in other insurance policies, contain provisions requiring an insured to notify the insurer of actual or potential claims as well as specifying that the insured may not admit liability without the prior approval of the insurer.

The policies also include claims co-operation provisions. Such provisions may, among other things, specify measures to be taken by an insured to keep the insurer informed of developments in remediating contamination and handling the claim if the insurer is not handling the claim on behalf of the insured. Other co-operation provisions apply regardless of whether the insured or the insurer is handling the claim.

Placing a policy

9.42 If a client decides to purchase, or to consider purchasing, an environmental insurance policy, the client or its solicitor on its behalf should contact a broker with experience in placing such policies. The broker will ask for information concerning the type of cover being sought, the number of sites, required limits and deductibles / self-insured retentions and information about the environmental condition of, and polluting operations at, the sites to be covered.

The broker will contact insurers who may be interested in providing a quotation and will then present the insured with the quotations and a comparison of the cover being offered by each insurer. At the prospective insured's request, each insurer generally provides a range of quotations based on different deductibles / self-insured retentions, policy periods and limits of indemnity.

Before providing information concerning a site, the prospective insured or its solicitor may wish to ensure that confidentiality agreements are in place between the client and the broker and between the client and each insurer to which environmental information is provided.

As negotiations for placing the policy proceed, the broker, on behalf of the prospective insured, will narrow down the number of potential insurers. Finally, the wording of the policy may be negotiated and the insured will receive the final policy wording and schedule and pay the premium for it.

Insurers which offer environmental insurance policies tend to have a specimen policy which is set out in a menu-type format to allow a prospective insured to select the types of cover it wishes to purchase. Standard, and as appropriate bespoke, endorsements may be added to the specimen policy to vary its terms and conditions in order to tailor it for the particular insured.

Property transfer policies are also available on an annual basis. Sites covered by such policies are generally considered to have a low risk of contamination. In addition, policies are available to cover the risk of Part 2A liabilities in respect of residences. Both of these types of policies tend not to be negotiated.

Further, as indicated in para **9.38** above, an insured may purchase an 'environmental-lite' policy that offers more limited cover, or an endorsement to a public liability policy to cover, in particular, clean-up costs.

Duty of fair presentation

9.43   Under the Insurance Act 2015, which applies to commercial insurance policies entered into on or after 12 August 2016, a prospective insured has a duty of fair presentation. The duty clarifies information that a business must provide to an insurer and information that the insurer ought to know.

In the context of an environmental insurance policy, the insured should disclose, at the very least, the following information concerning the site or sites to be insured:

- environmental assessments and other environmental reports known to, or commissioned by, the insured;
- correspondence with the Environment Agency/Natural Resources Wales or any similar body;
- any correspondence with third parties concerning actual or potential environmental claims; and
- any information suggesting that there may be claims in the future.

The duty of fair presentation does not mean that the prospective insured must commission an environmental assessment or other report for a site. Insurers may, among other things, acquire information of the environmental condition of, and environmental operations at, a prospective insured's sites by visiting one or more of the sites or by telephone calls with site managers. The more environmental information an insured provides about a site(s), the better able the insurer to quote a premium which reflects the risks associated with the site.

In addition to requesting environmental information about a site, the insurer will also request the prospective insured to complete a proposal form. As with other information, a prospective business insured must disclose and not misrepresent information on the proposal form.

The parties and their advisors, including the broker acting for the insured, will frequently list the documents which the insured has provided to the insurer on a disclosure schedule in order to avoid any future questions regarding the information which the insured has provided.

The Insurance Act 2015 applies only to business policies. Under the Consumer Insurance (Disclosure and Representations) Act 2012, the applicant for a consumer policy must generally also answer questions in a proposal form; the consumer must not misrepresent answers to those questions; non-disclosure does not apply.

The Insurance Act 2015 and the Consumer Insurance (Disclosure and Representations) Act 2012 also include other reforms to insurance law. Insurers may contract out of the former but not the latter. An insurer may not, however, include a basis of the contract clause, under which the contents of a proposal are incorporated into and form the basis of a policy, thus transferring the answers into warranties. Basis of the contract clauses are prohibited by both Acts.

9.44   Particular points which need to be considered for an environmental policy on a case-by-case basis are as follows.

*   *Sites.* Each site to be covered should be listed on the policy. Note, however, that some operational risk policies also provide cover for operations specified in the schedule, transportation, and non-owned disposal sites.
*   *The limit of indemnity and the deductible.* Clean-up and legal liability costs can be substantial. Different limits of indemnity may apply for each type of cover, and this should be assessed, as well as the agreed level of deductible or self-insured retention. Deductibles/self-insured retentions are likely to be on an aggregate as well as an each and every claim basis.
*   *The term of the policy.* As discussed above, property transfer policies are normally written for a period of up to ten years and operational risk policies are normally written for up to three years and, for some policies, on an annual basis. An environmental insurance policy will virtually always cover legislative changes during the policy period.
*   It is important to remember that environmental insurance should be treated as part of an overall insurance package with other policies covering motor, employers' liability claims, etc.

Policies for a seller's or buyer's advisors and contractors

9.45   The seller or buyer in a property sale and purchase often instructs environmental consultants and may also instruct general and/or remediation contractors. Insurers offer policies specifically designed to cover environmental risks faced by such advisors and contractors.

The environmental insurance policy for environmental consultants, which is issued on a claims-made-and-reported basis, covers liabilities arising from their advice and errors and omissions in carrying out works. Policies issued on a blanket basis – which is the case for most policies – have an aggregate limit of indemnity. Policies may also be issued for specific projects, in which case the limit of indemnity applies only to the specific project.

Contractors' pollution liability policies are issued on a claims-made-and-reported basis as well as an occurrence basis, the latter for a higher premium. The policies provide cover for environmental liabilities arising from the contractor's errors and omissions in carrying out works. Policies may be issued on a blanket basis as well as for specific projects. Blanket basis policies have an aggregate limit of indemnity. So-called 'wrap-around' policies may also be issued to provide cover for subcontractors on a project as well as the main contractor.

Chapter 10

Particular transactions – leases, lending and securitisation

LEASES

Introduction

10.01 Environmental provisions in a lease have two broad functions:

- to preserve the value and amenity of the property;
- to reduce the liabilities of the covenantee by imposing them on the covenantor.

A lease can regulate the environmental rights and duties between landlord and tenant, although it cannot directly affect the obligations of either to third parties. However, the obligations on one party may assist the other, in turn, to fulfil his obligations to neighbours. For example, a covenant by a tenant to ensure that the property does not give rise to a nuisance does not relieve the landlord of any obligations he may have in nuisance to third parties.[1] Nonetheless, if the tenant complies with his covenant, the landlord has no problem. On the other hand, if the tenant fails to comply, the landlord is entitled to damages for his losses including any liability of the landlord to a third party.

1 *Brew Bros Ltd v Snax (Ross) Ltd* [1970] 1 QB 612.

Liabilities to third parties

10.02 The respective liabilities of landlords and tenants under private law to third parties caused by the condition of the property or activities on it are dealt with in a later chapter.[1] However, the terms of the lease may impact on the landlord's liability to third parties in nuisance. In *Coventry v Lawrence (No 2)*,[2] the Supreme Court held that a landlord may be liable for nuisance caused by the tenant if the landlord: (1) authorises, or (2) participates in it. A nuisance is authorised by the landlord if it is the inevitable or nearly certain consequence of the letting.[3] In the *Coventry* case, the noise nuisance was not authorised by the landlords because it was clear that the motor racing activities could be and indeed had been operated in the past without causing a nuisance.[4] Nonetheless, there may be cases where there is doubt about the inevitably of a nuisance. In order to avoid any doubt, the lease should be drafted to permit a particular user 'unless it causes a nuisance' or 'to the extent that it does not cause a nuisance'. However, the existence in the lease of a 'no nuisance' covenant or its (non) enforcement by the landlord does not affect the latter's liability either way.[5]

1 Ch 13.
2 [2014] UKSC 46; [2014] 3 WLR 555. However, see *Cocking v Eacott* [2016] EWCA Civ 140 where a licensor was held liable for nuisances committed by a licensee, because the licensor retained control and possession of the property.
3 Ibid, paras 11–15 (Lord Neuberger PSC).
4 Ibid, para 15.
5 Ibid, para 17.

10.03 The offence of causing or knowingly permitting any poisonous, noxious or polluting matter or any solid waste matter to enter any controlled waters[1] may be committed by both landlords and tenants either or both of whom may be prosecuted. In cases where tenants on an estate with a common landlord discharge into a common drainage system under the control of the landlord, the landlord may be liable for causing any substance discharged into the drains by the tenant, to enter controlled waters. The basis of this view is that:

- the courts have confirmed that an offence of causing can be committed by more than one person even when they carry out different acts;[2] and
- a party who sets up a system for collecting discharges which are then carried into controlled waters may be guilty of 'causing'.[3]

In the circumstances outlined above, the landlord may also be liable under reg 38(2) of the Environmental Permitting (England and Wales) Regulations 2010 as amended for breach of a consent condition which is due solely to the action of one of the tenants.[4]

1 Environmental Permitting (England and Wales) Regulations 2010, SI 2010/675 as amended, reg 38(1)(a).
2 *A-G's Reference (No 1 of 1994)* [1995] 2 All ER 1007; *Environment Agency (formerly National Rivers Authority) v Empress Car Co (Abertillery) Ltd* [1999] 2 AC 22 [1998] Env LR 396.
3 *National Rivers Authority v Yorkshire Water Services Ltd* [1995] 1 AC 444. These cases, and others, are considered in detail in paras **17.47–17.66**.
4 *Taylor Woodrow Property Management Ltd v National Rivers Authority* [1995] Env LR 52.

10.04 Since the offence of 'causing' is a strict liability offence[1] there is little that a landlord can do to prevent liability arising if the act of a tenant results in poisonous, noxious or polluting matter entering controlled waters via the landlord's drainage system. The same applies in relation to breaches of consent conditions caused by the activities of a tenant. However, landlords can usefully take the following steps to reduce the risk:

- install oil interceptors in the drains and consult the Environment Agency as to any other desirable measures;
- ensure that the tenants are informed of the existence of the consent and its conditions;
- ensure that each lease contains a covenant by the tenant to comply with statute and an indemnity against losses caused by any breach of covenant.[2]

Essentially the same considerations apply in cases where the Environment Agency serves a works notice on the causer or knowing permitter in water pollution cases[3] or undertakes preventive or remedial works itself and charges the cost to the causer or knowing permitter.[4]

1 *Alphacell Ltd v Woodward* [1972] 2 All ER 475. See para **17.48**.
2 Although, in general, indemnities do not cover criminal liability as a matter of public policy, there is an exception, see para **9.10**.
3 WRA 1991, ss 161A-D. It should be noted that neither this procedure (except in the event of failure to comply with a works notice: s 161D(1) and (2)) nor the procedure referred to in the text to fn 4 involves a breach of criminal law. It follows that an indemnity may cover any resulting expenditure and that the doubt expressed in fn 2 as to the applicability of indemnities to breaches of criminal law do not apply in those cases. See paras **17.86–17.93**.
4 WRA 1991, s 161 (as amended by the EA 1995, Sch 22).

10.05 Either or both of landlords and tenants may be responsible for dealing with contaminated land under the contaminated land legislation on the ground that they have caused or knowingly permitted the substances by reason of which the land is contaminated land to be present.[1] If they are not 'causers' or 'knowing permitters' they may be liable as owners or occupiers.[2]

1 EPA 1990, s 78F(2) (inserted by EA 1995, s 57). Where two or more persons would be 'appropriate persons', ie responsible under this legislation, guidance issued under the Act may indicate whether any such person is to be treated as not being an appropriate person: s 78F(6). See the Statutory Guidance, Part 2A Contaminated Land Statutory Guidance, DEFRA, April 2012, and paras **15.84–15.96**.
2 EPA 1990, s 78F(4).

10.06 Landlords and/or tenants may be liable for statutory nuisances under the EPA 1990, Part III.[1] Liability (enforced initially through service of an abatement notice) generally falls on the 'person responsible' who is defined as 'the person to whose act, default or sufferance the nuisance is attributable'.[2] If the person responsible cannot be found, liability falls on the owner or occupier of the premises.[3] It appears that if more than one person is a 'person responsible', an abatement notice could be served on all those responsible, although this point is not dealt with specifically in the legislation.[4] However, in cases where the nuisance arises from defects of a structural character, the owner of the premises is liable in the first instance.[5] The term 'owner' is not defined in the legislation, but it is clearly apt to cover long leaseholders as well as freeholders. Under these provisions, a landlord may be liable even though he has no obligation under the lease or under statute to do the work in question.[6] If an abatement notice is not complied with, the local authority may undertake the work required themselves, and recover their reasonable expenses from the party by whose act or default the nuisance was caused. If that person is the owner of the premises, recovery may be made from the owner for the time being. The court has power to apportion the costs between those by whose acts or defaults the nuisance is caused in such manner as the court considers fair and reasonable.[7]

1 Paras **14.30–14.35**.
2 EPA 1990, s 79(7).
3 EPA 1990, s 80(2)(c).
4 The general principle should apply that the singular includes the plural: Interpretation Act 1978, s 6. This contention is supported by the Statutory Nuisance (Appeals) Regulations 1995, SI 1995/2644, which provide that an appeal against an abatement notice may be made on the

ground that the notice might lawfully have been served on some person in addition to the appellant: reg 2(2)(j).

5 Ibid, s 80(2)(b).
6 *Birmingham District Council v Kelly* (1985) 17 HLR 572; *R v Highbury Corner Magistrates' Court, ex p Edwards* [1994] Env LR 215.
7 EPA 1990, s 81(3) and (4). See paras **14.47–14.49**.

Tenants' liabilities under the lease

10.07 Standard leases contain a number of provisions which may regulate environmental liabilities as between landlord and tenant. The principal covenants and other provisions are considered in this section.

1   Covenant to pay all existing and future … outgoings … payable in respect of the Demised Premises … whether by the owner or occupier

10.08 This covenant to pay 'outgoings' appears wide enough to cover any expenses incurred by the landlord pursuant to any statutory notice served by the regulatory authorities,[1] such as abatement notices under the statutory nuisance legislation,[2] remediation notices under the contaminated land legislation,[3] and works notices under the Water Resources Act 1991.[4] However, the covenant must be read in conjunction with the other covenants of the lease. If specific covenants clearly impose on the landlord an obligation to carry out work which is the subject of the statutory notice, the matter will not be covered by a covenant to pay outgoings.[5] If the covenant is merely to pay rates, taxes and assessments without any reference to the wider terms such as 'outgoings', 'duties', 'burdens' or 'impositions', it is unlikely to cover the subject matter of a statutory notice.[6] The word 'impositions' in a tenant's covenant to pay rates, taxes and other impositions, has been held not to oblige the tenant to pay the landlord's expenses in abating a statutory nuisance following receipt of a notice under the Public Health Act 1875,[7] whilst the reverse was true in the case of the expenses of removing a privy and replacing it with a water-closet under London County Council by-laws[8] and the expenses involved in reconstructing drains.[9]

1 This was the opinion of Darling J in *Horner v Franklin* [1904] 2 KB 877, whose judgment was affirmed by the Court of Appeal [1905] 1 KB 479, although the CA expressed no opinion on that particular point. See also *Stockdale v Ascherberg* [1904] 1 KB 447 (reconstruction of drainage system).
2 EPA 1990, s 80.
3 EPA 1990, s 78E.
4 WRA 1991, s 161A: paras **17.86–17.93**.
5 *Howe v Botwood* [1913] 2 KB 387
6 *Bird v Elwes* (1868) LR 3 Exch 225; *Wilkinson v Collyer* (1884) 13 QBD 1; *Baylis v Jiggens* [1898] 2 QB 315.
7 *Rawlins v Briggs* (1878) 3 CPD 368.
8 *Foulger v Arding* [1902] 1 KB 700.
9 *Re Warriner* [1903] 2 Ch 367.

10.09 The term 'duties' in this context has been defined by the courts to mean 'sums payable pursuant to some duty imposed by Act of Parliament',[1] including expenses of a non-recurring type.[2] Accordingly, 'duties' has been held to cover the expenses of abating a statutory nuisance[3] as well as re-laying defective drains.[4]

1 *Farlow v Stevenson* [1900] 1 Ch 128, 138 per Lindley LJ.
2 *Villenex Co v Courtney Hotel* (1969) 20 P & CR 575.
3 *Budd v Marshall* (1880) 5 CPD 481.
4 *Brett v Rogers* [1897] 1 QB 525.

2 Covenant to undertake all works on the Demised Premises as are required under or by virtue of any Act of Parliament whether by the landlord or the tenant

10.10 This type of covenant is far stronger than that referred to in section 1 above for the purpose of placing responsibility for statutory obligations firmly on the tenant.[1] It should cover a remediation notice served on either party under the contaminated legislation[2] requiring remediation of contamination whether caused before or after the commencement of the lease.

1 It is possible that depending on the precise wording such a covenant may be held to confer a benefit on the various statutory authorities for the purposes of the Contracts (Rights of Third Parties) Act 1999. If such a result is not desired the statutory presumption should be negatived expressly. See also paras **8.16** and **9.07**.
2 Part 2A of the Environmental Protection Act 1990.

3 Covenant to keep the Demised Premises in good and substantial repair [and condition]

10.11 Although a repairing covenant must be construed in the context of the lease as a whole, it is questionable whether a covenant to repair alone would be held to apply to the remediation of contamination. The concept of repair seems inappropriate to deal with such a matter, a conclusion which is fortified by two factors. First, most of the decided cases refer to the repair of buildings or other man-made structures.[1] Second, a covenant to keep premises in repair has been held not to include an obligation to remove an accumulation of mud (which was causing a nuisance) from a 'piece of ornamental water' on the premises. Such a covenant could at most require that the landlord carry out such repairs as might be required to prevent the sluices from bursting, and the water from overflowing its banks and flooding neighbouring fields.[2] Although unrelated to contaminated land, the case suggests that at least in the nineteenth century ordinary repairing covenants would not generally be held to apply other than to built structures. However, the New Zealand High Court[3] appears to have assumed that a statutory implied condition to 'keep ... the demised premises in good and tenantable repair, having regard to their condition at the commencement of the said lease ... fair wear and tear ... excepted' could require a tenant to remediate contamination. In particular, the term 'premises' refers to land as well as buildings.[4] In that case, the implied condition was excluded because the parties had inserted an express condition in different terms.[5] Even if the implied condition had not been excluded, the judge indicated that under the circumstances it would probably not have afforded an effective remedy to the landlords because:

- The land was already heavily contaminated at the date of the latest renewal of the lease, which was known to the landlords. The remediation sought by the landlord arguably went 'beyond making good the damage to requiring renewal of the subject matter of the demise. Normally a covenant to repair will not go that far.'[6]
- BP (the tenant) could argue that 'the contamination was the result of fair wear and tear in the sense that it was the inevitable result of BP's reasonable authorised use.'[7]

The actual repair clause was in terms confined to buildings, structures, fixtures, fences and drains. The judge held that contamination caused by BP's failure to repair and maintain storage tanks and ancillary equipment could give rise to a claim for consequential loss.[8]

1   *Woodfall: Landlord & Tenant* 13–024ff.
2   *Bird v Elwes* (1868) LR 3 Exch 225.
3   *BP Oil New Zealand Ltd v Ports of Auckland Ltd* [2004] NZLR 208 (Rodney Hansen J), paragraphs 44–60.
4   Ibid paras 46–48.
5   Ibid paras 49–55.
6   Ibid para 59.
7   Ibid para 60.
8   Ibid paras 24–31. However the damages claim failed in relation to the earlier contamination due to the expiry of the limitation period (see paras 90–114) and in relation to the later contamination because, by the time it occurred, the extent of prior contamination was such that full remediation was required, and so it caused no loss (see paras 124–133).

10.12   However, if contamination in the ground attacks the foundations, a covenant to keep in repair requires the tenant to repair them, even if the damage occurred prior to the commencement of the tenancy.[1] For the obligation under the covenant to arise, the foundations (or other part of the building) must have deteriorated from their original condition.[2] Nonetheless, a covenant to repair has been held to include preventive measures to avoid damage, particularly if damage is imminent.[3] Where damage has occurred, works to prevent recurrence are also required.[4] On that basis, removal or treatment of contamination which poses an imminent threat to foundations, service ducts or other structures is within the repair covenant. The same applies where repairs are being carried out if removal or treatment of contamination is necessary to prevent a recurrence of damage.

1   *Proudfoot v Hart* (1890) 25 QBD 42.
2   *Post Office v Aquarius Properties* [1987] 1 All ER 1055, CA; *Quick v Taff-Ely Borough Council* [1986] QB 809.
3   *London and North Eastern Rly Co v Berriman* [1946] AC 278; *Day v Harland & Wolff* [1953] 1 WLR 906.
4   *Stent v Monmouth District Council* [1987] 1 EGLR 59; *Holding & Management v Property Holding & Investment Trust* [1989] 1 WLR 1313; *Greetings Oxford Koala Hotel Property v Oxford Square Investments Property* (1989) 18 NSWLR 33.

10.13 On the other hand, a covenant to keep in good condition, goes beyond mere repair[1] and, it is suggested, may involve the obligation of remediating contaminated soil within the property, even if the contamination was present at the date of the lease. Certainly, the language appears broad enough for that purpose, although the decided cases only deal with buildings. The standard of remediation is that necessary to put the property into the condition contemplated by the parties at the date of the lease.[2]

In accordance with general principles, relevant factors in determining the intention of the parties include the character of the premises at the beginning of the lease, the condition of the premises (ie nature and extent of contamination) which would be required by a reasonably-minded tenant of the class likely to take them (rather than the actual condition of the premises at the date of the lease) and the nature and cost of the remedial work required.[3]

It is probable that in the case of leases entered into before the end of 1990, most landlords and tenants would not have considered the question of contamination at all. However, since that time contamination has been an issue.[4] Discerning landlords and tenants would be likely to contemplate that the condition of the ground should be such that:

- it is at least safe for people working at, living in or visiting the property for the purpose of the permitted use, and
- pollutants are not likely to migrate from the property so as to give rise to liabilities on the owners and/or occupiers.

Accordingly, it is suggested that covenants to keep in good condition in leases entered into after 1990 may include an obligation to carry out remedial work to contaminated land so as to achieve that standard even if that requires the removal and replacement of contaminated soil. However, it cannot be stated with certainty that the courts would require that standard, which in any event may vary in accordance with the circumstances of each lease, as indicated above. Accordingly, if the intention is that one party should remediate all historic contamination present at the beginning of the lease that obligation should be stated expressly.[5]

The measure of damages for breach of the tenant's repairing covenant both during and at the termination of a lease is limited by s 18 of the Landlord and Tenant Act 1927 to the amount by which the value of the reversion is diminished as a result of the breach of covenant.[6] However, that limit does not apply to a claim in debt such as for the recovery of the landlord's costs under a right to enter and repair and charge the cost to the tenant.[7]

1 *Crédit Suisse v Beegas Nominees Ltd* [1994] 4 All ER 803; *Welsh v Greenwich LBC* (2001) 81 P & CR 12. Woodfall, Landlord and Tenant, para 13-034. A tenant's covenant to maintain all pleasure grounds in good and proper order and condition included an obligation to remove sufficient mud from an ornamental lake to maintain the fishery. Such cleansing did not fall within the landlord's covenant to carry out structural repairs: *Horlick v Scully* [1927] 2 Ch 150.
2 *Smedley v Chumley & Hawkes Ltd* (1981) 44 P & CR 50; *Crédit Suisse v Beegas Nominees Ltd* (above); *Welsh v Greenwich LBC* (above).
3 *Proudfoot v Hart* (1890) 25 QBD 42; *Anstruther-Gough-Calthorpe v McOscar* [1924] 1 K.B. 716; Megarry & Wade, *Law of Real Property*, 8th edn, 19-112; Cheshire & Burn, *The Modern Law of Real Property*, 18th edn, 246-248.

4 For example, EPA 1990, s 143 (repealed by EA 1995, Sch 24) provided for registers of land which may be contaminated. Section 143 was never brought into force and has been repealed. EPA 1990 was passed on 1 November 1990.
5 See para **10.36**.
6 See generally Woodfall, *Landlord and Tenant*, paras 13.081–13.088.
7 *Jervis v Harris* [1996] Ch 195.

4   Covenant to keep the Demised Premises in a clean and tidy condition

10.14 Although at first sight a covenant such as this might appear to apply to contamination of the soil, it is most unlikely that the courts would construe it in that way. The purpose of the covenant appears to be to protect the appearance of the property rather than its condition.

5   Prohibition against assignment or underletting

10.15 This type of covenant is useful to protect the landlord against the risk of an assignee of the tenant or a sub-tenant with a poor environmental record who may cause contamination of the property. Some covenants are absolute, others are qualified by words such as 'without the consent of the landlord, such consent not to be unreasonably withheld'.[1]

1 In the case of covenants against alienation 'without the consent of the landlord', the added qualification to the effect that the consent is not to be unreasonably withheld is implied by the Landlord and Tenant Act 1927, s 19(1).

10.16 The courts have held that consent may be refused reasonably in order 'to protect the landlord from having his premises used or occupied in an undesirable way, or by an undesirable tenant or assignee'.[1] A landlord may generally refuse consent if he reasonably objects to the proposed use of the property by the intended assignee, even if that use would not contravene any provision of the lease or the general law.[2] However, that does not normally apply if the proposed use is within the sole use permitted by the lease.[3] On that basis, a landlord should be able to object to an intended assignee with a track record of poor environmental practices or if the proposed use is likely to result in ground contamination affecting the property or pollution affecting the landlord's other tenants or where the surrounding area would be affected.[4] Despite the qualification referred to concerning a single use lease, if the sole permitted use is for industrial purposes and the intended use is an industrial process which is necessarily far more polluting than most, it is arguable that the landlord may nevertheless reasonably refuse consent.

1 *International Drilling Fluids v Louisville Investments (Uxbridge)* [1986] Ch 513, CA; *Roux Restaurants v Jaison Property Development Co* (1997) 74 P & CR 357.
2 *Premier Confectionery (London) Co v London Commercial Sale Rooms* [1933] Ch 904; *Wilson v Fynn* [1948] 2 All ER 40; *Creery v Summersell and Flowerdew & Co* [1949] Ch 751; *Packaging Centre v Poland Street Estate* (1961) 178 Estates Gazette 189; *Tollbench v Plymouth City Council* (1988) 56 P & CR 194.

3 *International Drilling Fluids v Louisville Investments* (Uxbridge) (above).
4 The landlord may reasonably wish to maintain the character of the area which would affect his rental income as well as (possibly) the capital value of the property. He may also wish to protect himself against nuisance claims by neighbours such as in *Coventry v Lawrence (No2)* [2014] UKSC 46; [2014] 3 WLR 555.

10.17 In the case of new leases under the Landlord and Tenant (Covenants) Act 1995 (other than residential leases), the matter can be put beyond doubt. If the lease spells out the circumstances in which the landlord may withhold his licence or consent to the assignment of the whole or part of the demised premises, or any conditions to which the licence or consent may be subject, the landlord will not be regarded as unreasonably withholding his licence or consent if he acts in accordance with those provisions.[1] It follows that new leases can safely be drafted to accommodate the landlord's environmental concerns in the event of a proposed assignment, although care needs to be taken to avoid an adverse impact on rental income at rent reviews.

1 Landlord and Tenant (Covenants) Act 1995, s 22 (adding s 19(1A) to the Landlord and Tenant Act 1927). Note that the provisions regulating licence or consent to an assignment may be contained either in the lease or in a separate agreement entered into at any time prior to the application for the landlord's licence or consent; s 19(1A) does not apply to sub-letting.

6 Covenant to use only for permitted purpose or not to use for specified purposes

10.18 The user covenant is one of the most significant means by which the landlord can avoid contamination on the property or polluting activities which may affect a wider area. However, it must be remembered that restrictions on permitted use have an adverse impact on rental income, particularly at rent reviews. As mentioned above, a landlord may also avoid liability to third parties for authorising the tenant's nuisance, by specifically excluding any nuisance element from the permitted user.[1]

1 See para **10.02**.

7 Covenant not to commit, permit or suffer any act or thing which may be or become a nuisance or annoyance to the landlord or the tenants or occupiers of adjoining properties

10.19 The term 'nuisance' refers to nuisance as understood at common law.[1] The covenant against nuisance is wide enough to include not only the creation of nuisances eg by ground contamination, water pollution, smells or noise (for example), but also nuisances which the tenant continues, in the sense that he fails to take reasonable steps to end them when he knows or ought to know of their existence.[2] Accordingly, under the terms of such a covenant the tenant could be liable for contamination present on the property at the date of the lease if it migrates or is likely to migrate to neighbouring properties. That applies whether the contamination was caused by the landlord or by some previous owner or occupier. However, care must be taken with 'nuisance' covenants. Some are limited to acts of commission and so do not apply to passive failure to remedy nuisances created by others.[3]

1 *Hampstead v Suburban Properties v Diomedous* [1969] 1 Ch 248.
2 *Sedleigh-Denfield v O'Callaghan* [1940] AC 880.
3 For the possible impact of the Contracts (Rights of Third Parties) Act 1999, see para **10.10**, fn 1.

10.20 'Annoyance' is a wider concept. 'If you find a thing which reasonably troubles the mind and pleasure, not of a fanciful person or of a skilled person who knows the truth, but of the ordinary sensible English inhabitant of a house – if ... there is anything which disturbs his reasonable peace of mind, that [is] an annoyance, although it may not amount to physical detriment to comfort'.[1] One noisy, all night party or an occasional smutty bonfire, which may not qualify as a nuisance, since it does not represent a continuous state of affairs,[2] may nevertheless be an annoyance under the covenant. Breach of the covenant will be easier to prove since the criteria of nuisance do not have to be established.

1 *Tod-Heatly v Benham* (1888) 40 Ch D 80; *Chorley Borough Council v Ribble Motor Services* (1997) 74 P & CR 182.
2 *Stone v Bolton* [1950] 1 KB 201. However, on whether a single incident can amount to a nuisance see *Crown River Cruises v Kimbolton Fireworks* [1996] 2 Lloyd's Rep 533 and paras **13.05–13.08**.

8   Covenant not to operate a noisy, noxious or offensive trade or business on the premises

10.21 In deciding whether a trade or business is a noisy, noxious or offensive trade or business it has been held that the matters to have regard to are: (1) the nature of the business, (2) the locality in which it is situated, and (3) the manner in which it is carried on.[1] On that basis, a fried fish business which led to neighbours losing lodgers and nearby houses being unlet was held to be an offensive business.[1] Similarly a private hospital may be an offensive trade[2] but not a well run hospital for tuberculosis.[3]

The inclusion of the word 'noxious' before 'offensive' in the covenant also suggests that this covenant has a restricted meaning, ie only a high level of polluting emissions would render the operation 'offensive'.[4]

Many types of industrial operations are controlled under the Environmental Permitting (England and Wales) Regulations 2010[5] as amended (the EPR). Operators are required to hold a permit,[6] the conditions of which limit polluting emissions in accordance with the applicable schedule of the EPR. The schedules which set out the detailed regulatory requirements, apply the provisions of relevant EU directives. The schedules include:

	EPR Schedule	EU Directive
Part A Installations (Schedule 1)	7A	Industrial Emissions Directive (2010/75/EU) (IED) article 11 – all appropriate preventive measures – best available techniques – no significant pollution
Part B Installations (air pollution only) (Schedule 1)	8 – appropriate preventive measures – no significant pollution – best available techniques	Not applicable
Waste Operations	9	Waste Framework Directive, Article 13: waste management must be carried out without endangering human health, without harming the environment and in particular...without causing a nuisance through noise or odours.
Landfill	10	Landfill Directive (1999/31/EC), Annex 1, para 5: measures must be taken to minimise nuisances and hazards through emissions of odours and dust, ... noise and traffic

On that basis, there seems to be no basis for suggesting that the operation of a facility is an offensive trade provided that it is regulated under the EPR and that it complies with the permit conditions. One purpose of the IED/EPR regime is to ensure that industrial activities which may be 'offensive' if left unregulated, are not 'offensive' when operated in accordance with the conditions of an environmental permit whose conditions comply with the principles of the IED and EPR. Conversely, if the facility is operated in breach of the conditions of its environmental permit, depending on the nature and extent of the breach, it may become an offensive trade.

1 *Duke of Devonshire v Brookside* [1899] 81 LT 83.
2 *Earl of Pembroke v Warren* [1896] 1 IR 76.
3 *Frost v King Edward VII Welsh et Association* [1918] 2 Ch 180.
4 *Earl of Pembroke v Warren* [1896] I IR 76, 117.
5 SI 2010/675.
6 Reg 12.

9   Covenant to allow the Landlord to inspect the Premises

10.22 The courts have held in *Heronslea (Mill Hill) Ltd Kwik Fit Properties Limited*[1] that the traditional right for a landlord to inspect premises does not extend to a right to carry out intrusive environmental investigations. If a landlord considers that it may wish to undertake such investigations during the course of the lease, a specific right should be included. However, under those circumstances a tenant is likely to seek a suspension of rent or other compensation where an exercise of such rights causes disruption of the tenant's use of the Property.

1 [2009] Env LR 28.

Effect of statutory appeal provisions

10.23 A landlord may face a difficulty if a regulatory authority requires him to comply with a statutory notice, compliance with which is the responsibility of the tenant under the terms of the lease. A choice must be made as to whether to comply with the notice and claim for the cost under the tenant's covenant or to appeal against the notice (or the allocation of responsibility under it) in accordance with the relevant legislation. If the landlord sues under the covenant but the statutory appeal is held to be an exclusive remedy, the landlord may find that it is too late to appeal since the usual time limit is 21 days.

The question of whether the statutory appeal is the only means of obtaining a reallocation of responsibility is one of statutory construction.[1] Since the answer is generally not spelled out in the legislation, it is a matter of inference from the terms of the statute whether Parliament intended the statutory appeal to be an exclusive procedure or not. In the absence of a judicial decision on the particular statutory wording, the process of interpretation may not be easy. However, the desirability of avoiding two appeal routes leading to different results, may favour a decision that the statutory appeal is an exclusive remedy.[2]

It is clear that if the statutory procedure is held to be the only means of transferring responsibility to the tenant, the landlord cannot by-pass it by claiming under the covenant in the lease.[3] However, if the lease contains an indemnity by the tenant which covers liability incurred by the landlord under a statutory notice, that indemnity should apply despite any failure to use the applicable appeal mechanism. The reason is that an indemnity (unlike the covenants discussed above) operates to reallocate liabilities after the primary legal process for allocating liabilities has run its course.[4] On the other hand, the covenants would (if the statutory appeal were not an exclusive remedy), operate as an alternative to the primary allocation process for those liabilities.

The question of exclusivity of the statutory procedure has been litigated in relation to notices served by the sanitary authority under the Factory and Workshop Act 1891 (now repealed), requiring the owner of a factory to provide a fire escape. Section 7(2) of the Act provided (inter alia) 'that, if the owner alleges that the occupier ought to bear or contribute to the expenses of complying with the requirement, he may apply to the county court, and thereupon that court, after hearing the occupier, may make such order as appears to the Court just and equitable under all the circumstances'. It has been held that this provision excluded the jurisdiction of the High Court to hear a claim by a landlord suing under a covenant in the lease claiming the expenses of complying with the statutory requirement. Any such claim had to be made by application to the county court in accordance with the statutory procedure.[5] The reasoning of the Court of Appeal in *Horner v Franklin* was that Parliament would wish to avoid two regimes leading to different outcomes, one decided on the words of the covenant, the other under statute, giving a wide discretion to do what is 'just and equitable under all the circumstances of the case'.[6]

1 *Century National Merchant Bank and Trust Co Ltd v Davies* [1998] 2 WLR 779 at 786 (PC); Wade & Forsyth *Administrative* Law (11th edn 2014) pp 605-608. For differing applications of the basic principle see *Barraclough v Brown* [1897] AC 615 (HL); *Pyx Granite Co Ltd v Ministry of Housing and Local Government* [1960] AC 260 (HL).
2 This was the approach taken in *Horner v Franklin* [1905] 1 KB 479 (see post); Woodfall *Landlord & Tenant* 12.075 ff; Hill & Redman *Law of Landlord & Tenant*, paras **A [7165]**–**[7168]**.
3 *Horner v Franklin* [1905] 1 KB 479.
4 The indemnity operates as a contractual obligation to pay a 'debt', ie the cost of compliance by the landlord.
5 *Horner v Franklin* [1905] 1 KB 479; *Stuckey v Hooke* [1906] 2 KB 20. In such cases, the court was obliged to take into account the terms of the lease, and follow it where it clearly covers the case: *Monro v Lord Burghclere* [1918] 1 KB 291 (covenant to execute all such works as are or may under or in pursuance of any Act or Acts of Parliament already passed or hereafter to be passed be directed or required by any local or public authority to be executed at any time during the said term upon or in respect of the said premises whether by the landlord or the tenant thereof). This case concerned the London Building Acts (Amendment) Act 1905 under which 'the court may make such order concerning such expenses or their apportionment ... as appears to the court to be just and equitable in the circumstances of the case regard being had to the terms of any lease or contract affecting such building' (s 20). However, in the case of a covenant to pay 'outgoings', the court is not bound to follow the terms of the lease slavishly: *Monk v Arnold* [1902] 1 KB 761; *Horner v Franklin* [1905] 1 KB 479 (CA).
6 *Horner v Franklin* [1905] 1 KB 479 at 486–487 (Vaughan Williams LJ), 488–489 (Romer LJ) and 489–490 (Stirling LJ). So far this reasoning has not been applied judicially to other legislation. However, it was applied by the Bloomsbury and Marylebone County Court to a landlord's claim for the full cost of installing a fire escape. The lease contained a covenant by the tenant to pay for all works on the property necessitated by Acts of Parliament. The judge held that ss 33, 35 and 107 of the London Buildings Acts (Amendment) Act 1939 required the court to consider what was just and equitable, which was to be determined not only by the terms of the lease but by what the parties contemplated. The court awarded the landlord a contribution of about 27% of the total cost claimed on the basis that the full cost seemed to fall outside the tenant's contemplation: *Duke of Bedford v University College Medical School* [1974] CLY 2063.

10.24 It is not easy to determine whether these principles apply to appeals against statutory notices under modern environmental legislation.

Appeals may be brought against abatement notices under statutory nuisance legislation on a number of grounds[1] including the ground that the notice should have been served on another person.[2] Such appeals must be made to the magistrates' court, which may allocate or apportion the cost of works to be undertaken and expenses recoverable by the local authority 'as it thinks fit'.[3] In exercising those powers, 'the court shall have regard, as between an owner and an occupier, to the terms and conditions, whether contractual or statutory, of any relevant tenancy and to the nature of the works required'.[4]

There is a difference between s 7(2) of the Factory and Workshop Act 1891[5] and the statutory nuisance legislation because the former involves only an allocation of expenses between owner and occupier whereas the latter concerns an appeal against an abatement notice involving the local authority which served it. However, crucially, the appeal provisions relating to abatement notices do provide for an allocation of the cost of works between the parties. In common with the 1891 Act, the court is required to have regard to factors other than the terms of the tenancy, a point relied on heavily in the judgments in *Horner v Franklin*. For that reason it seems possible that a similar approach would be adopted under statutory nuisance legislation to that taken under the 1891 Act. The right to challenge liability under an abatement notice may, therefore, only be exercisable by means of the statutory appeal remedy.[6]

The conclusion reached on this matter in relation to abatement notices under the statutory nuisance legislation is also likely to apply to other notices which may be served under the Public Health Acts 1936–61 and other legislation with similar appeal provisions. The notices affected include the following:

Notice	Legislation	Appeal
Notice requiring works to prevent leaking/overflowing cesspool	PHA 1936, s 50	PHA 1936, s 290
Notice requiring owner to repair/ unblock stopped-up drains	PHA 1961, s 17	PHA 1936, s 290
Notice requiring owner to make satisfactory provision for the drainage of a building	Building Act 1984, s 59(1)(a)	Building Act 1984, s 102
Notice requiring owner or occupier to renew, repair, cleanse etc any cesspool, private sewer, drain etc	Building Act 1984, s 59(1) (b), (c), (d)	Building Act 1984, s 102
Notice requiring owner to carry out paving and drainage to yards and passages	Building Act 1984, s 84	Building Act 1984, s 102
Notice requiring works to put defective closet into satisfactory condition	PHA 1936, s 45	PHA 1936, s 290
Notice requiring owner to provide a building with closets	Building Act 1984, s 64	Building Act 1984, s 102
Notice requiring owner or occupier to alter or provide additional sanitary conveniences in the workplace	Building Act 1984, s 65	Building Act 1984, s 102
Notice requiring landowner to maintain or cleanse a culvert	PHA 1936, s 264	PHA 1936, s 290
Notice requiring person responsible to undertake adaptations to premises in smoke control area to avoid contraventions of prohibition on smoke emissions in that area	Clean Air Act 1993, s 24	PHA 1936, s 290
Notice requiring responsible party to undertake work on a derelict petrol tank or other container	PHA 1961, s 73	PHA 1936, s 290

1 EPA 1990, s 80(3); Statutory Nuisance (Appeals) Regulations 1995, SI 1995/2644, reg 2.
2 Statutory Nuisance (Appeals) Regulations 1995, SI 1995/2644, reg 2(i) and (j).
3 Ibid, reg 2(6).

4 Ibid, reg 2(7).

5 Discussed in *Horner v Franklin*, (above).

6 However, *Villenex Co Ltd v Courtney Hotel Ltd* (1969) 20 P&CR concerned a notice served on the landlord under the Public Health Act 1936. Willis J held that the tenant's covenant to pay 'duties … imposed or charged on the premises' covered the landlord's expenses in complying with the notice. Although the judge referred to s 290 which deals with appeals, neither counsel nor the judge referred to the exclusive remedy principle. This is despite the fact that s 290 provides for the court to allocate expenses between the parties and, as in the 1891 Act, requires the court to have regard to other factors as well as the terms of the tenancy. The omission may be considered as a clear indication that the court did not consider the exclusive remedy principle to be applicable. However, in the absence of any discussion of *Horner v Franklin*, it may be that the case was decided *per incuriam*.

10.25 The contaminated land legislation provides a different method for allocating liabilities. The allocation process is undertaken by the enforcing authority in accordance with statutory guidance.[1] If the enforcing authority fails to act in accordance with the guidance, that provides a ground of appeal.[2] The statutory guidance provides that agreements between two or more 'appropriate persons' should generally be followed by the enforcing authority provided that 'none of the parties to the agreement informs the authority that it challenges the application of the agreement'.[3] In the event of a challenge, the exclusion and apportionment tests[4] apply which do not require the authorities to take into account the terms of leasehold covenants. It seems unlikely that Parliament intended the agreement of the parties to prevail if there is no challenge to it but that in the event of a challenge it should not apply even to the parties' rights and obligations *inter se*. It seems more likely that the intention was to allow the parties' agreement to regulate the matter unless there is a challenge. In that case, the enforcing authority should apply the tests and serve a remediation notice, leaving the parties to enforce their private law rights thereafter.[5]

The works notice procedure relating to water pollution[6] provides for an appeal against a notice[7] but does not specify any grounds of appeal,[8] although there is a clear indication that appeals can be made on the basis that the notice should have been served on some other person.[9] The legislative provisions are broad enough to enable an allocation of expenses to be undertaken. However, although much of the reasoning in *Horner v Franklin* applies, it is less likely that the courts would hold that the legislature intended to deprive the parties of any remedy available to them under a lease in the absence of a specific procedure for allocating liability such as exists in the statutory nuisance legislation[10] and the Factory and Workshop Act 1891.

1 Part IIA of the Environmental Protection Act 1990, see Ch 15.

2 Contaminated Land (England) Regulations 2006, SI 2006/1380, reg 7.

3 Part 2A Contaminated Land Statutory Guidance, DEFRA, April 2012, para 7.29.

4 Ibid, Parts 5–8, D.40–D.97. See paras **15.84–15.96**.

5 See L Coates 'Tenant's Liability for Contaminated Land' (2002) 11 E-Law 4–6, which points to differences between the legislation underlying the old case law and Part IIA of the Environmental Protection Act 1990 and suggests that the terms of the lease would ultimately govern liabilities as between landlord and tenant. On the other hand it can be argued that the reasoning in *Horner v Franklin* is applicable, since the application of the exclusion and apportionment tests could lead to a different result from the agreement.

6 WRA 1991, ss 161A–161D. See paras **17.86–17.93**.

7 WRA 1991, s 161C.

8 Ibid; Anti-Pollution Works Regulations 1999, SI 1999/1006, reg 3.
9 Anti-Pollution Works Regulations 1999, SI 1999/1006, reg 3(4).
10 Statutory Nuisance (Appeals) Regulations 1995, SI 1995/2644, reg 2(6) and (7).

10.26 In cases where statutory appeal procedures are used, the appeal must be brought within the specified time limit.[1] Otherwise, the right to appeal is lost. Provided that the statutory appeal is not an exclusive remedy, it is possible to appeal against the notice and then claim under the covenants in the lease in respect of any expenditure or liability which remains allocated to the claimant (generally the landlord) after the appeal.[2] Alternatively, a claim can be made solely under the covenants. If there is any doubt as to whether the statutory appeal is an exclusive remedy, it is advisable to appeal. Even if the statutory appeal is not exclusive, such an appeal will be an effective demonstration of mitigation of loss[3] in the event of a claim under the leasehold covenants.

1 Generally, the time limit is 21 days beginning with the date of service of the notice. See, eg, EPA 1990 s 80(3).
2 *Horner v Franklin* [1905] 1 KB 479 at 486 (Vaughan Williams LJ).
3 Assuming that the appeal can also be made on substantive grounds, eg that the work required by the local authority is unreasonable or unnecessary: Statutory Nuisance (Appeals) Regulations 1995, SI 1995/2644, reg 2(2)(c).

Intimation notices

10.27 Frequently, the regulatory authorities request a party responsible to undertake the necessary work by means of a letter or informal 'intimation notice'. However, therein lies a trap for landlords. The covenants applicable to liability under statutory notices do not apply until a formal statutory notice has been served.[1] It follows that if the landlord carries out the work in response to an informal intimation notice and before a statutory notice has been served, he will be unable to recover his expenses from the tenant under the terms of the covenant.[2] Any expenditure incurred under those circumstances is incurred voluntarily and so is not an 'outgoing', 'duty' or 'imposition' nor is it required under any Act of Parliament. This approach should also apply to remediation carried out voluntarily by a landlord after the identification of the land as contaminated land under Part 2A of the Environmental Protection Act 1990 but before a remediation notice has been served.[3]

1 See paras **10.08–10.10**. The same applies even if a letter or intimation notice is sent to a responsible party under the statutory umbrella of the Environmental Protection Act 1990, s 80(2A)(b). Such a letter or notice is only persuasive, not compulsory.
2 *Harris v Hickman* [1904] 1 KB 13.
3 See Ch 15.

Waste

10.28 In cases where the lease contains no express or implied provision concerning environmental degradation of the property, the tort of waste may be important. Waste includes acts or omissions by tenants which cause damage to the landlord's reversion. The liability of tenants for voluntary waste, that is positive acts, is clearly established.[1] So, for example, acts which permanently change the nature of the property are waste, such as depositing rubbish on the land so that future development is made more difficult.[2] The same is also likely to apply to ground contamination caused by the activities of the tenant. The doctrine of waste does not extend to damage resulting from the reasonable use of land, as determined by the nature of the demised premises and the use ordinarily expected of the premises.[3] In the case of contamination, this depends on best practice at the relevant time in terms of plant and equipment used and associated operating practices. The question also arises whether the extent of contamination is consistent with reasonable use over the period of the lease.[4]

1 Statute of Marlborough 1267, s 2; *Marsden v Heyes Ltd* [1927] 2 KB 1.
2 *West Ham Central Charity Board v East London Waterworks Co* [1900] 1 Ch 624.
3 *The Manchester Bonded Warehouse Company Ltd v Carr* (1880) 5 CPD 507 at 512 (Lord Coleridge CJ); *BP Oil New Zealand Ltd v Ports of Auckland Ltd* [2004] 2 NZLR 208, paras 71 and 72.
4 *BP Oil New Zealand Ltd v Ports of Auckland Ltd* [2004] 2 NZLR 208, paras 178 and 179.

10.29 However, despite a doubt as to the liability of tenants for permissive waste, that is omissions which lead to the deterioration of the property,[1] it has been decided that such liability does exist.[2] On the basis of the old cases, it can be suggested tentatively that:

• Failure to remediate contamination on the premises which was present at the beginning of the lease is not permissive waste.

• Failure to remediate contamination caused by a third party without the tenant's knowledge or consent is not permissive waste.

• Failure to prevent further damage to the demised premises resulting from contamination caused during the lease without the tenant's knowledge or consent is permissive waste.

• Failure to prevent the spread of contamination on the demised premises which the tenant is aware of and has the power to prevent is permissive waste.

1 *Woodfall: Landlord and Tenant*, para 13.124.
2 *Yellowly v Gower* (1855) 11 Ex 274; *Dayani v Bromley LBC* [1999] 3 EGLR 144. The latter case contains an extensive review of the earlier authorities by Judge Havery QC in the Technology and Construction Court beginning with a Year Book case of 1293.

10.30 Under the terms of the Statute of Marlborough, the duty not to commit waste can be excluded.[1] However, it must be shown that the parties, either expressly or by necessary implication, agreed that the doctrine of waste will not apply.[2] A mere omission to provide for the matter in the lease covenants is insufficient for that purpose. The covenants must effectively negative the law of waste.[3] In cases where covenants achieve the same result as the law of waste, there are conflicting decisions as to whether landlords may choose whether to sue on the covenant or under the tort of waste.[4] However, since the landmark case of *Henderson v Merrett Syndicates Ltd*,[5] it is suggested that there is concurrent liability in tort and under the covenants in the lease. The measure of damages for waste is the diminution in the value of the reversion, subject to a discount for immediate payment.[6]

1 By 'special licence had by writing of covenant': Statute of Marlborough, s 2.
2 *Marlborough Properties Ltd v Marlborough Fibreglass Ltd* [1981] 1 NZLR 464, 466 (Cooke P), 469 (Richardson J), 475 (McMullind J).
3 Ibid; *BP Oil New Zealand Ltd v Ports of Auckland Ltd* [2004] 2 NZLR 208, paras 72–75.
4 *Jones v Hill* (1817) 7 Taunt 392; *Marker v Kenrick* (1835) 13 CB 188; *Mancetter Developments v Garmanson* [1986] QB 1212 (CA).
5 [1995] 2 AC 145.
6 See generally *Woodfall: Landlord and Tenant*, para 13.128.

CRC Energy Efficiency Scheme

10.31 Under the CRC Energy Efficiency Scheme[1] groups of companies which consume more than 6000 MWh of electricity in the qualifying year[2] measured on half hourly meters[3] are obliged to participate in and comply with the scheme.[4] Participants must surrender a number of allowances equivalent to the number of tonnes of carbon dioxide emitted in the production of the electricity and gas they consume in each year.[5]

Under the so called landlord and tenant rule landlords who supply electricity and /or gas to their tenants are obliged to aggregate that energy to that consumed by their company group even through it is not consumed by the landlord.[6] The reasoning behind this rule is that landlords should be able to influence the energy consumption of their tenants.

Landlords who incur costs of participating in the scheme in relation to the supply of energy to their tenants may pass on the appropriate proportion of the costs to each tenant provided that it is permitted under the lease through specific provisions or sufficiently broad wording in the service charge.

1 CRC Energy Efficiency Scheme Order 2013, SI 2013/1119.
2 Article 3.
3 Article 3.
4 Article 5.
5 Article 36.
6 Schedule 1, paras 14(3) and 16(1) and (2). There is an exception in the case of construction Leases: Schedule 1, para 16(3)(b).

Energy Performance Certificates

10.32 A prospective landlord must make available to a prospective tenant of a building an energy performance certificate (EPC)[1] free of charge.[2] An EPC must be entered on the register maintained by the Secretary of State[3] and is valid for 10 years form the date of entry on the register.[4]

Obtaining an EPC can be costly. A landlord can pass on the cost of obtaining an EPC provided that the tenant is not charged for an EPC which must be made available under the EPB Regulations. This can be done if the landlord commissions a new EPC during the period of a tenancy and charges the cost to the current tenant provided that the cost can be passed to the tenant under the service charge provisions in the lease. It should be noted that the EPC is not obtained for the purpose of compliance with the EPB Regulations in such a case and so reliance could not be placed on a 'compliance with legislation' provision in the service charge.

1 The Energy Performance Certificate must comply with the Energy Performance of Buildings (England and Wales) Regulations 2012, SI 2012/3118, (EPB Regs), reg 9(1). It shows the energy rating of a building measured on a scale from A–F.
2 EPB Regs, reg 6.
3 EPB Regs, reg 27.
4 EPB Regs, reg 9(2).

Covenant for quiet enjoyment

10.33 A covenant for quiet enjoyment is implied in every lease unless expressed. 'The covenant is that the lessor is entitled to grant some tenancy and that the lessee will enjoy quiet possession without interruption by him or through the lawful acts of anyone claiming through or under him'.[1] The covenant is given in this qualified form if implied. If express it may be qualified or absolute. In the latter case, the covenant covers the same ground as the qualified form except that it also extends to interruptions through the lawful act of any person claiming by title paramount. The effect of the implied covenant (from the environmental perspective) is that the tenant shall not be disturbed by the landlord or those deriving title under the landlord exercising adverse rights over the property or the landlord's neighbouring property.[2] Although the covenant does not guarantee freedom from undue noise[3] it may be infringed by the noisy activities of the landlord or those claiming under him on adjacent land. 'If the landlord blows a trumpet for hours every day outside the tenement, that would normally amount to a breach of the covenant of quiet enjoyment. Not because there is a lack of quiet, but because the quality of enjoyment of possession that the tenant contracted with the landlord to obtain has been interfered with by the landlord'.[4]

It used to be said that the covenant applies to the landlord's acts whether rightful or wrongful but only to the rightful acts of those claiming under him.[5] However, more recently the courts have been prepared to hold landlords liable for failure to control the activities of other tenants where they have power to do so.[6] It seems unlikely that that approach will survive the Supreme Court's decision in *Coventry v Lawrence (No 2)*.[7]

It was once understood that a landlord was liable for any unreasonable interference due to the normal use of adjoining premises let by the same landlord.[8] However, this approach has been overturned by the House of Lords in *Southwark London Borough Council v Mills*.[9] In that case, tenants of individual flats in a multi-occupied building were disturbed by the noises of everyday living by their neighbours in adjacent flats. The cause of the problem was inadequate sound insulation which predated the commencement of the tenancy. The House of Lords held that there was no breach of the covenant for quiet enjoyment on two main grounds. First, the covenant is prospective in nature. It 'does not apply to things done before the grant of the tenancy, even though they may have continuing consequences for the tenant'.[10] Secondly, 'the tenant takes the property not only in the physical condition in which he finds it but also subject to the uses which the parties must have contemplated would be made of the parts retained by the landlord'.[11] The covenant cannot be used to create an obligation on the landlord to repair or improve the premises which does not otherwise exist.

It follows that the covenant for quiet enjoyment may be breached (inter alia) by:

- undue noise made by the landlord which disturbs the tenant's occupation of his premises;
- noise by an occupier of adjoining premises which due to reduced noise insulation (eg due to conversion of the premises) after the beginning of the lease unduly disturbs the tenant, both parties having the same landlord;
- the migration of contaminants through the soil from the landlord's adjacent premises to the tenant's land if it is sufficient to disturb the tenant's use of his property, but only if the polluting act occurred after the grant of the lease.

1 *Hill and Redman's Law of Landlord & Tenant*, para A[6801].
2 *Hudson v Cripps* [1896] 1 Ch 265 at 268.
3 *Jenkins v Jackson* (1888) 40 Ch D 71.
4 *Southwark London Borough Council v Mills* (1998) 45 EG 151 per Schiemann LJ; see also [1999] 3 WLR 939 at 945–6 (Lord Hoffmann), ibid 957 (Lord Millett). See also paras **13.06** and **14.09**.
5 In the case of wrongful acts by eg other tenants of the landlord, the tort of nuisance applies.
6 *Megarry and Wade: The Law of Real Property* (8th edn, 2012), para 19–016; *Hilton v James Smith & Sons (Norwood) Ltd* [1979] 2 EGLR 44.
7 [2014] UKSC 46; [2014] 3 WLR 555.
8 *Sampson v Hodson-Pressinger* [1981] 3 All ER 710. *Baxter v Camden London Borough (No 1)* (1998) 22 EG 150, [1998] Env LR 270.
9 [1999] 3 WLR 939.
10 *Southwark LBC v Mills* [1999] 3 WLR 939 at 946, per Lord Hoffmann. Lord Hoffmann approved *Sampson v Hodson-Pressinger* [1981] All ER 710, CA on the basis that the alterations complained of had been carried out after the grant of the plaintiff's lease. In that case, the landlord carried out alterations to the upstairs flat, including the construction of a tiled terrace over the plaintiff's living room. The tiles were not laid properly and consequently the plaintiff was seriously disturbed in his living room by the noise of people walking on the terrace. This was held to be a breach of the covenant for quiet enjoyment as well as a nuisance.
11 *Southwark LBC v Mills* [1999] 3 WLR 939 at 946.

Obligation not to derogate from grant

10.34 Landlords are obliged not to 'derogate from the grant' to their tenants. The principle which is of wider application than the field of landlord and tenant means that the landlord 'having given a thing with one hand is not to take away the means of enjoying it with the other'.[1] In other words 'if the ... demise be made for a particular purpose, the ... lessor comes under an obligation not to use the land retained by him in such a way as to render the land ... demised unfit or materially less fit for the particular purpose for which the ... demise was made'.[2] The obligation falls not only on the landlord but on those claiming under him.

It is clear that the obligation may be broken by the landlord even if no nuisance is committed in law. For example, if land is let for the purpose of a timber merchant's business, the landlord may not build on adjacent land which he has retained so as to interrupt the flow of air to the tenant's sheds used for drying timber.[3] Similarly, the landlord may not use his retained land to cause vibrations on the land let to the tenant, even though the vibrations would not amount to a nuisance.[4] The same applies to undue noise caused by alterations to adjoining flats in the same building and their subsequent use for commercial purposes.[5] Where land is let for the storage of explosives, the landlord and those claiming under him may not use the adjoining land for a purpose which would render the necessary statutory licence subject to revocation.[6] The same approach should apply to leases for the purpose of other activities which require statutory licences, eg environmental permits under the Environmental Permitting (England and Wales) Regulations 2010.[7] More recently the landlord of a shopping mall was held liable to the tenant of a shop within it because the landlord had failed to prevent another tenant from conducting his business in a manner that caused nuisance to other tenants in the mall. The grant to the tenants depended on proper management by the landlord.[8] However, the Supreme Court has cast some doubt on that approach in *Coventry v Lawrence (No 2)*.[9] It seems that the landlord may only be liable for disturbance created by tenants in the common parts which the landlord controls directly.

The extent of the obligation is measured by the parties understanding of the purpose of the lease at the time it was granted. Accordingly, the landlord will not be liable for interference with the tenant's business due to an abnormal sensitivity which was not known to the landlord at the date of the lease.[10]

1 *Birmingham, Dudley and District Banking Co v Ross* (1888) 38 Ch D 295 at 313 per Bowen LJ.
2 *Browne v Flower* [1911] 1 Ch D 219 at 226 per Parker J. In *Southwark LBC v Mills* [1999] 3 WLR 939 at 957–958 Lord Millett expressed the view that there is little if any difference between the covenant for quiet enjoyment and the obligation not to derogate from a grant.
3 *Aldin v Latimer Clark, Muirhead & Co* [1894] 2 ChD 437.
4 *Grosvenor Hotel Co v Hamilton* [1894] 2 QB 836.
5 *Newman v Real Estate Debenture Corporation Ltd* [1940] 1 All ER 131.
6 *Harmer v Jumbil (Nigeria) Tin Areas Ltd* [1921] 1 Ch 200.
7 See the Environmental Permitting (England and Wales) Regulations 2010, SI 2010/675 as amended.
8 *Chartered Trust plc v Davies* (1997) 49 EG 135. See also *Petra Investments Ltd v Jeffrey Rogers plc* [2000] NPC 61.
9 [2014] UKSC 46, para 14; [2014] 3 WLR 555
10 *Robinson v Kilvert* (1889) 41 Ch D 88.

New leases

10.35 Although the traditional provisions in leases often deal adequately with environmental matters, this may not always be so. In particular, where the site is known to be contaminated, or the tenant is likely to carry out activities on the demised property which may give rise to environmental problems, provisions may be necessary to protect the position of one or other party.

The landlord's viewpoint

10.36 The landlord may wish to include the following provisions in the lease:

1   A covenant that the tenant obtains and maintains all the licences, consents, authorisations and permits necessary to carry out the envisaged operations. At the termination of the lease the tenant should be required to ensure that all such licences which are transferable are duly transferred to the landlord or to any other person at his direction. This may be particularly important where new licences are difficult to obtain on the same terms (eg water abstraction licences). Alternatively, in cases where the licence is likely to be onerous and will not be required by future occupiers, the tenant should be required to procure its surrender if the landlord so directs. This may apply to environmental permits if the operations concerned will not outlast the tenant's occupation.

2   A covenant to comply with good industrial practice including relevant codes of practice.

3   A covenant to obtain a report from an environmental consultant before commencing any undertaking on the property and to comply with the recommendations.

4   A covenant to notify the landlord of any proceedings against the tenant relating to environmental matters.

5   A covenant to obtain a report from the consultant at the end of the lease as to the steps required to put the property and any facility on it into good environmental condition and to comply with the recommendations.

6   A covenant to allow the landlord to enter to inspect the environmental condition of the property, to take samples, to carry out any necessary remedial work and to recover the cost from the tenant. However, the existence of such a covenant could render the landlord liable in nuisance for any environmental problems created by the tenant after the commencement of the lease, since the landlord would have the power to remedy the situation.[1]

7   A covenant to remediate all contamination on the premises, including that present at the date of the lease. In its strongest form, the covenant may require the tenant to keep the premises free from contamination at all times. A much less demanding obligation is a covenant to ensure that the property is no more contaminated at the end of the lease than at the beginning. Such a covenant can only be enforced properly if it is supported by evidence of the contamination on the property at the beginning and end of the lease in the form of reports of full environmental surveys with complete sampling results. Although that expenditure may not be commercially viable in many cases, the covenant is worth taking, since it may be possible to demonstrate that any contamination is only likely to

have resulted from the tenant's activities and not from pre-lease activities. It should be noted that a covenant in the form suggested would render the tenant liable to deal with any contamination which migrates to the property from elsewhere during the tenancy.

8   A covenant to use all reasonable endeavours to agree with the landlord (and then to comply with) an energy management plan to facilitate the sustainable use of resources at the Premises and on the Landlord's estate.[2]

9   Use all reasonable endeavours to reduce, reuse or recycle waste from the Premises and to comply with the Landlord's reasonable requirements for the deposit, storage and removal of waste on the Premises [and the Common Parts].[2]

A disadvantage of provisions of this type is that they may prevent the landlord taking the benefit of exclusion tests 2 and 3 in the Statutory Guidance under the contaminated land legislation.[3] The difficulty has been explored above in relation to freehold transactions.[4] Although test 3 applies to grants or assignments of long leases (over 21 years)[5] as well as freeholds, there is a slight difference with regard to the grant of leaseholds. Whilst the landlord (if he is to take the benefit of test 3) must not retain any interest in the land or any rights to occupy or use it, the landlord's reversion on expiry or termination of the lease is to be disregarded for that purpose.[6] Leasehold covenants are interests in land because, subject to certain conditions, the benefit and burden are capable of running with the reversion and the lease.[7] The benefit of restrictive covenants is also to be disregarded for the purpose of test 3.[8] The question is whether the benefit of positive covenants by the tenant are to be disregarded on the basis that they are part of the reversionary interest. The wording of paragraph 7.48(e)(iii) of the Statutory Guidance suggests that the 'reversion' refers only to the landlord's right to possession on the termination of the lease, rather than the whole of the landlord's interest (including the benefit of leasehold covenants) after granting the lease. On that basis the existence in the lease of positive covenants by the tenant (which are almost invariably present) would prevent the landlord taking the benefit of test 3. However, the better view is possibly that the benefit of positive leasehold covenants are part of the reversionary interest for this purpose, because otherwise landlords could in practice never take the benefit of test 3, a result which is plainly not intended by the Statutory Guidance.

1 *Payne v Rogers* (1794) 2 Hy Bl 350; *Heap v Ind Coope and Allsopp Ltd* [1940] 2 KB 476; *Wilchick v Marks* [1934] 2 KB 56; *Mint v Good* [1951] 1 KB 517. In such cases, the landlord's liability is not for the actions of the tenant, but rather for the condition of the land over which the landlord retains a sufficient measure of control. Cf *Coventry v Lawrence (No 2)* [2014] UKSC 46.; [2014] 3 WLR 555.
2 These provisions will be most appropriate in leases of part of a multi-occupied building, shopping mall or industrial or commercial estate.
3 EPA 1990, s 78F(6); Part 2A Statutory Guidance (April 2012) paras 7.40–7.45 (test 2 – payments made for remediation), paras 7.46–7.50 (test 3 – sold with information). See paras **15.87–15.88**.
4 Para **9.21**, fn 2.
5 Part 2A Statutory Guidance (April 2012) para 7.48(a). The lessee must satisfy the definition of 'owner' in EPA 1990, s 78A(9).
6 Part 2A Statutory Guidance (April 2012) paras 7.47(d) and 7.48(e)(iii).
7 See *Megarry & Wade: The Law of Real Property* 2012 (8th edn), Ch 20.
8 Part 2A Statutory Guidance (April 2012) para 7.48(e)(iv).

The tenant's viewpoint

10.37 The main environmental concerns of tenants are likely to be that existing contamination on the property may render it unfit for the tenant's intended purpose and could result in liabilities falling on the tenant both to third parties and under the lease. It has long been settled that in the absence of a specific warranty, a lease does not include any implied agreement that the property is fit for the tenant's intended purpose. Accordingly, a tenant was obliged to continue paying rent for a pasture, even though some of his cattle died as a result of contamination of the land through poisonous paint flakes which had been mixed with manure.[1]

1 *Sutton v Temple* (1843) 12 M&W 52. For the different rule in relation to licences, see *Wettern Electric Ltd v Welsh National Development Agency* [1983] QB 796.

10.38 For that reason well advised tenants should obtain a report from environmental consultants in respect of the property before taking a lease.[1] If the report reveals the existence or likely presence of contamination, the tenant may wish to consider: (a) taking only a 'pie crust' lease; and/or (b) insisting on appropriate protection in the lease. That protection should have three aims: (i) to minimise the risk that the tenant will be liable under the general law in respect of pre-lease contamination at the property;[2] (ii) to ensure that the landlord assumes any liability for such contamination which may fall on the tenant; and (iii) to ensure that any provisions in the lease are disapplied which might otherwise impose liability on the tenant for such contamination.

1 See Ch 8.
2 See paras **10.1–10.5**.

10.39 Under a 'pie crust' lease, the property demised includes only the top uncontaminated layer of soil or may be limited to the space from ground level upwards. By that means, the tenant will not occupy any contaminated soil below ground level and should thereby avoid liability for any such contamination unless he causes it. This type of lease is more likely to be appropriate for short rather than long leases. In the case of the latter, there are problems in that the lessee may be unable to develop the site unless appropriate rights to dig foundations etc are provided.

10.40 Tenants may prefer to negotiate the following type of provisions in new leases:

1   A covenant by the landlord to remediate any contamination existing on the demised premises at the commencement of the lease. To be effective a full environmental survey should be undertaken at that time. However, even without such a precaution it may be possible to differentiate between pre and post commencement date contamination if the property has been subject to different uses prior to the lease. The advice of an environmental consultant should be taken on that point.
2   A provision which gives the landlord exclusive control[1] over pre-lease hazardous substances in the property so that liability in respect of them should fall on the landlord rather than the tenant.[2]

3   An agreement by the landlord to assume any liability for pre-lease contamination which might fall on the tenant.[2]
4   A provision which specifically disapplies the operation of any tenant covenants relating to pre-lease contamination at the property.[2]
5   An indemnity from the landlord in respect of any liability for environmental matters caused prior to the commencement of the lease. Again an environmental survey is advisable to provide the necessary evidence.
6   A suspension of rent during any period in which remedial works carried out on the property in respect of pre-lease contamination cause unreasonable disruption to the tenant.
7   Break clauses enabling the tenant to surrender the lease if pre-lease contamination is discovered on the property which is likely to give rise to material liabilities on the tenant or to give rise to unreasonable disturbance to his business or home life on the property.
8   A rent review which does not exclude from the disregard for improvements any environmental work undertaken pursuant to a statutory notice or other obligation. Otherwise, the tenant may suffer an upwards review of rent in respect of work which he is obliged to carry out.

1 This type of provision should not be used except in the case of lease where the tenant will not need to disturb the ground.
2 See para **10.38**.

LENDER LIABILITY ISSUES

Introduction

10.41 As indicated in Chapter 1, lenders have three major concerns:
*   the borrower's ability to repay the loan if he has onerous environmental liabilities;
*   adverse impact on the value of the property due to its environmental condition; and
*   liability falling on the lender in respect of the condition of the property or activities taking place on it.

Much has been written on the subject of lender liability in environmental law.[1] It will suffice in this section to summarise the position and to indicate the steps which lenders can take to protect their position.

1 Eg, Jarvis and Fordham *Lender Liability* (1993).

Borrower's environmental liabilities

10.42 It is self-evident that if the borrower faces onerous environmental liabilities his ability to repay the loan may be adversely affected. Lenders generally wish to avoid that situation even if the loan is secured. For that reason, the lender will wish to assess the environmental position of the borrower.

10.43 In the case of contaminated land, owners may be liable as 'knowing permitters' or as owners/occupiers under the new contaminated land legislation[1] and as 'knowing permitters' under the Water Resources Act 1991.[2]

1 EPA 1990, Part IIA (inserted by the EA 1995, s 57). See Ch 15.
2 WRA 1991, ss 161 and 161A-D (the latter inserted by the EA 1995, Sch 22, para 162.

Environmental impacts on the value of the security

10.44 It is perhaps equally clear that environmental liabilities which could affect any owner or occupier of the land will have an adverse impact on the value of the property which is the security for the loan. This will be the case with contaminated land and with industrial plant on the property which needs to be upgraded to meet new environmental standards.[1]

1 Eg, under the Environmental Permitting (England and Wales) Regulations 2010, SI 2010/675 as amended.

Direct liability on lenders

10.45 Lenders are only liable for environmental matters to the extent that they fall within one or more of the categories of person whose liability is prescribed by statute or common law. In general, liability arises through control over the operations which cause environmental damage or through ownership or occupation of the property. It follows that lenders have to walk the tightrope between obtaining adequate information to protect their interests and avoiding the degree of involvement which may result in liabilities. A few of the main trigger categories for environmental liability will be mentioned. These are dealt with in more detail in Part II of this book.

Causing

10.46 This arises in the context of water pollution offences[1] and contaminated land.[2] There are numerous cases on water pollution[3] which demonstrate that liability is strict. If the lender actively controls the borrower's activities, he may be liable for any pollution caused. The position is less clear if the lender:

- supports the borrower financially knowing that his operations are causing pollution; or
- withdraws financial support when it would be used to undertake pollution prevention work.

It is suggested that such actions would not amount to causing unless the lender controls the borrower's operations, as opposed to his money supply.

1 Environmental Permitting (England and Wales) Regulations 2010, SI 2010/675 as amended, reg 38(1)(a).
2 EPA 1990, Part IIA.

3 Eg *Alphacell Ltd v Woodward* [1972] AC 824; *National Rivers Authority v Yorkshire Water Services Ltd* [1995] 1 AC 444; *Empress Car Company (Abertillery) Ltd v National Rivers Authority* [1999] 2 AC 22. For more detail, see paras **17.47–17.66**.

Knowingly permitting

10.47 This term also arises in water pollution and contaminated land legislation as an alternative to causing. In *Alphacell Ltd v Woodward*,[1] Lord Wilberforce indicated that 'knowingly permitting … involves a failure to prevent the pollution … accompanied by knowledge'. This approach has been followed by dicta in later cases[2]. If this approach were followed literally, it could be asserted that a lender who takes a covenant from the borrower to comply with statute and who knows that the borrower is failing to prevent water pollution from the mortgaged premises, knowingly permits that pollution to occur. However, it is suggested that the courts should not follow such an approach. The reason is that it ignores the reason for the covenant, which is to protect the position of the lender, rather than to give him control over the borrower's activities. On the other hand knowingly permitting could be much easier to establish if the lender was, in fact, exercising control over the operations of the borrower.[3]

1 [1972] AC. 824 See paras **17.50–17.51**.
2 *Price v Cromack* [1975] 1 WLR 988. The case was criticised by Lord Hoffmann in the *Empress Car* case but in relation to 'causing' rather than 'knowingly permitting'. For some of the difficulties concerning 'knowingly permitting' in the context of the contaminated land legislation, see *Circular Facilities (London) Ltd v Sevenoaks DC* [2005] Env LR 35.
3 In case a lender were found to be a knowing permitter solely by reason of making a loan (secured or otherwise), he would be excluded from liability under the contaminated land regime by Test 1 provided that other causers or knowing permitters had been found: Part 2A Contaminated Land Statutory Guidance, (April 2012, para 7.39(a)(ii). See **15.86**.

Person responsible

10.48 This term arises in statutory nuisance legislation and is defined as 'the person to whose act, default or sufferance the nuisance is attributable'.[1] In this context it has been held that 'default' does not mean failing to do something except where there is an obligation under the legislation to do it.[2] 'Sufferance' appears to have a similar meaning to 'knowingly permitting'.[3] Mortgagees in possession and lenders exercising control over the activities of their borrowers risk falling within the definition of 'person responsible'. It is unlikely that lenders would do so otherwise.

1 EPA 1990, s 79(7). See para **14.30**.
2 *Neath RDC v Williams* [1951] 1 KB 115.
3 *R v Staines Local Board* (1888) 60 LT 261.

Owner

10.49 The term is not defined in statutory nuisance legislation[1] except in relation to the recovery of a local authority's expenses, where it is defined as follows:

'"owner" in relation to any premises, means a person (other than a mortgagee not in possession) who, whether in his own right or as trustee for any other person, is entitled to receive the rack rent of the premises or, where the premises are not let at a rack rent, would be so entitled if they were so let.'[2]

The definition of 'owner' in the contaminated land legislation is essentially the same.[3]

1 *Camden LBC v Gunby* [2000] 1 WLR 465 which applied the definition used in the predecessor legislation. See para **14.34**.
2 EPA 1990, s 81A(9) (inserted by the Noise and Statutory Nuisance Act 1993, s 10(2)).
3 Ibid, s 78A(9) (inserted by the EA 1995, s 57).

10.50 Although a mortgagee of land generally has an interest in property,[1] it does not necessarily follow that he is *the* owner for the purpose of the legislation. The definitions of owner referred to above clearly refer to the owner who is immediately concerned with management of the property. On that basis, a mortgagee not in possession is not an owner for this purpose.[2] However, a mortgagee in possession seems to fulfil the criteria and so would be an owner, a result achieved in other statutory contexts.[3]

1 A mortgage of land can only be created by way of a lease for a term of years (but not, following the Land Registration Act 2002, s 23, over registered land) or by way of charge by way of legal mortgage. The latter has the same effect, in practice, as the former: Law of Property Act 1925, ss 85–87.
2 *Midland Bank v Conway* [1965] 1 WLR 1165 in which the mortgagee/bank was held not to be an 'owner' under the Public Health Act 1936 where rent was paid into the landlord's bank account – note the wider definition of 'owner' under s 343 where receipt includes receipt as agent. The definition in the EPA 1990 is narrower.
3 *Westminster City Council v Haymarket Publishing Ltd* [1981] 1 WLR 677; *Maguire v Leigh-on-Sea UDC* (1906) 95 LT 319.

10.51 The meaning of 'owner' is wider in the legislation on sites of special scientific interest, which requires that every owner of land be served with a notification of that fact.[1] Any owner so served is then prohibited from carrying out activities on the land specified in the notification.[2] This formula suggests that any person with an ownership interest may be served including a mortgagee not in possession. However, a lender is only likely to be affected to the extent that the SSSI designation devalues the land.

1 Wildlife and Countryside Act 1981, s 28(1)(b).
2 Wildlife and Countryside Act 1981, ss 28E and 28P. More generally, see Ch 19.

Occupier

10.52 This term is used but not defined in the legislation on sites of special scientific interest,[1] waste removal notices,[2] contaminated land[3] and statutory nuisance.[4]

In all of these categories except waste removal notices, 'occupier' is an alternative to 'owner', either or both being affected by the legislation. It seems that the terms are overlapping, with occupation also including a relationship with land that falls short of ownership.

1 Wildlife and Countryside Act 1981, s 28.
2 EPA 1990, s 59.
3 Ibid, s 78F (inserted by the EA 1995, s 57).
4 Ibid, s 80.

10.53 In *Southern Water Authority v Nature Conservancy Council*,[1] a case on SSSIs, Lord Mustill said that an occupier is:

> 'someone who, although lacking the title of an owner, nevertheless stands in such a comprehensive and stable relationship with the land as to be, in company with the actual owner, someone to whom the mechanisms can sensibly be made to apply.'[2]

In the context of the Occupiers' Liability Act 1957, *Wheat v Lacon*[3] suggests that occupation involves control over property. Although Lord Mustill in the *Southern Water Authority* case warned against transposing definitions of 'occupier' from one statutory context to another, it appears that the concepts in both of these cases may be appropriate in the interpretation of the term 'occupier' in the three statutory regimes in the EPA 1990 which are referred to above.

1 [1992] 1 WLR 775.
2 Ibid at 782. This case is considered in more detail in paras **19.35–19.38**.
3 [1966] AC 552.

10.54 A mortgagee in possession is likely to fulfil the necessary conditions of an occupier. On the other hand, a mortgagee not in possession will probably not do so unless in practice he exerts a considerable degree of control over the land and the activities which take place on it. There is at least one instance of a waste removal notice being served on a lender in possession.[1]

1 (1995) 7 *Environmental Law & Management* 105.

Lender liability for the acts of receivers and administrators

10.55 In principle, a receiver or administrator is the agent of the borrowing company rather than the lender.[1] For that reason no liability for the activities of the receiver or administrator should fall on the lender. However, that assumption may be displaced in cases where the lender has interfered in the activities of the receiver or administrator.[2] Receivers formerly required an indemnity from the appointing lender before they would act. This is no longer the general practice with most banks. However, where an indemnity is given, the lender can take comfort from the limitation on the liability of receivers and administrators under the contaminated land legislation.[3]

1 Law of Property Act 1925, s 109(2) in the case of LPA receivers whose task is to deal with the real estate assets charged by the mortgage or charge; Insolvency Act 1986, s 44(1)(a) in the case of administrative receivers appointed under a debenture created prior to 15 September 2003 which creates a floating charge over all the assets of the company. Due to changes made by the Enterprise Act 2002, administrative receivers can only be appointed in narrowly defined circumstances, where the floating charge was created on or after 15 September 2003. The appointment of an administrator is therefore much more common after that date. Administrators

act as agent of the (borrower) company by virtue of the Insolvency Act 1986, Sch B1, para 69. Note that receivers and administrators generally have little or no knowledge of the real estate of which they are disposing and so will not provide meaningful replies to pre-contract enquiries on disposal.

2 *Standard Chartered Bank v Walker* [1982] 1 WLR 1410; *American Express v Hurley* [1985] 3 All ER 564.

3 EPA 1990, s 78X(3) provides in effect that receivers and administrators (and liquidators who are not agents of the borrower) will not be personally liable unless the presence of the contamination results from any unreasonable act or omission on their part.

Priority of rights

10.56 Lenders need to know whether their security will take priority over any claim by a regulatory authority for their expenses in carrying out work on the property after the date of the mortgage or legal charge. The answer is that if the expenses are made a charge on the premises, as is the case under the contaminated land legislation[1] and statutory nuisance legislation,[2] that charge will rank in priority above a lender's mortgage or legal charge even if the latter took effect before the regulatory authority's expenses were incurred.[3] On the other hand, if the expenses are merely recoverable from a designated person such as the 'causer' or 'knowing permitter',[4] it appears that they are recoverable only as a simple debt and do not affect the priority of a lender's security.

1 EPA 1990, s 78P (inserted by EA 1995, s 57).
2 Ibid, s 81A (inserted by the Noise and Statutory Nuisance Act 1993, s 10(2)).
3 *Westminster City Council v Haymarket Publishing Ltd* [1981] 1 WLR 677 (a case on the General Rate Act 1967).
4 Eg WRA 1991, ss 161, 161D.

Protecting the lender's position

10.57 The best protection for lenders is adequate information which can be used as a basis for an assessment of the real environmental risks presented by the proposed loan. Inevitably, the cost of the information gathering and risk assessment exercise must be taken into account to avoid loans becoming uncommercial for lenders and borrowers alike.[1] The two principal areas which will give rise to concern are:

- the possibility of historic contamination of the property; and
- the potential for the borrower's activities to give rise to environmental liability.

1 Lenders will also need to avoid the degree of involvement with the borrower's business that could result in liability falling on the lenders themselves. See above.

10.58 Generally, lenders wish to minimise the expense of gathering environmental information. In some cases, the valuation report will indicate features or circumstances suggesting that environmental problems may exist. Invariably, lenders will also rely on environmental information received by way of due diligence. Environmental due diligence will usually be undertaken unless it is clear that environmental considerations pose a very low risk.

10.59 In cases where preliminary information suggests that there may be an unacceptable environmental problem associated with the site or the proposed activity, the intending borrower is usually required to obtain a report from an environmental consultant. The report should be addressed to the lender as well as the borrower so that the former can place reliance on it. Alternatively, the lender can seek a collateral warranty from the environmental consultant. In either case, the lender will be concerned with the issues which affect all third parties in these circumstances, eg the identity of the party on whom reliance is placed, limits on liability, and insurance cover.[1]

1 See Ch 8.

10.60 The Environmental report should deal with risks posed by contaminated land as well as risks arising from the borrower's intended operations on the site. Appropriate measures to ensure compliance with good environmental practice and to minimise the risk of liability should be set out in the report. The report should also cover the environmental consents and licences required by the borrower and as far as possible details of the borrower's history of compliance with environmental law.

10.61 Having obtained information on environmental factors, the lender has to assess the risk. If a site specific report is obtained from an environmental consultant, his assessment of the risk will be important. Whilst the risk assessment exercise is essentially similar to that for other property transactions, it must be remembered that the risks faced by lenders are different to those encountered by purchasers or tenants. If the environmental report contains recommendations, eg to carry out further investigations, undertake remedial work or take out environmental insurance, that will usually be made a condition precedent of drawing down the loan. Alternatively, where less critical to making the loan, these actions can be made a condition subsequent to drawdown. Failure to comply within the requisite timescales will then constitute an event of default under the loan. In any case, loan facility agreements usually include standard warranties and covenants from the borrower as well as conditions precedent or subsequent in respect of environmental matters.

Environmental provisions in loan documentation

10.62 Usual environmental provisions in loan facility agreements include:

1. warranties that:
    *   the borrower is, and has been for the last [three] years, in compliance with all applicable environmental law and with all necessary environmental permits;
    *   there is no claim or investigation under environmental law (current, threatened or pending) against the borrower or in respect of the charged property;

219

- there are no past or present circumstances which could give rise to such a claim or investigation which might result in a material adverse effect or any liability being payable by the lender;
2. covenants/undertakings to:
    - comply with applicable environmental law and maintain all necessary environmental permits and take all reasonable steps in anticipation of known/expected changes thereunder;
    - implement promptly all steps recommended by any environmental report (to the extent required to comply with law or which are in the interests of good estate management) and notify the lender's representative;
    - inform the lender's representative as soon as reasonably practicable of any claim, proceeding or investigation under environmental law or of any contamination or matter which might result in a claim, proceeding or investigation which has been threatened (in any case where the claim, if adversely determined, might reasonably be expected to have a material adverse effect);
    - indemnify the lender against any loss or liability resulting from any actual or alleged breach of environmental law by any person in relation to the charged property;
3. a condition precedent to the first drawdown to obtain an environmental report in relation to the property addressed to the lender.

In addition, lenders may wish to include the following provisions in the loan documentation in order to protect their position:

- A covenant to provide to the lender on request all information relating to the borrower's compliance with environmental law including compliance with conditions attached to any environmental licence, consent or other permit.
- A covenant to maintain environmental insurance provided that such insurance is obtainable on reasonable terms.
- A covenant to comply with environmental best practice.
- A covenant to ensure that the property is kept materially free from hazardous substances (excluding any such substances which are required for the carrying on of the borrower's business, provided that they are kept strictly in accordance with all applicable environmental law).
- A provision for early repayment in the event of any material breach of environmental law or of any covenant by the borrower.
- A provision for early repayment in the case of any change in environmental law which gives rise to a material risk of loss to the lender in respect of the property or the business of the borrower, or any event or situation which may cause the rights of any third party to rank ahead of those of the lender.

Protection for the lender when considering enforcing the security

10.63 Prior to taking any step to enforce the security, for example, by appointing a receiver or taking possession, the lender should undertake further investigations to ascertain whether he is likely to incur environmental liabilities in so doing. It must be remembered that when the lender takes possession of mortgaged property, the risk of incurring environmental liability whether as owner, occupier or by carrying on the business is considerably increased. For that reason, it is extremely rare for lenders to take possession.

Securitisation

10.64 The concept of securitisation is shown in the following diagram:

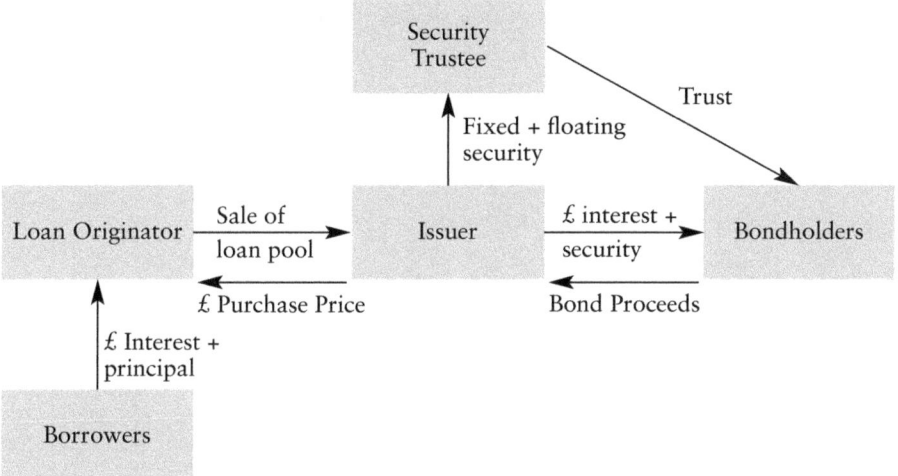

Securitisations enable finance providers to fund specific assets or portfolios of assets. Investors rely on the credit risk of the assets. Almost any assets, including freehold and leasehold property, can be securitised.

Some securitisations relate to NNN leases (so-called 'triple net leases') which provide that the tenant will pay the full rent reserved under the lease and accept all liabilities (including environmental liabilities) for the premises for the full contractual term of the lease in all eventualities. An absolute environmental indemnity is the simplest way to ensure that the tenant remains responsible for all environmental liabilities.

Loan originators, ie the lending banks, undertake due diligence to identify all risks, including environmental risks. Appropriate environmental warranties by the borrower are given under the loan agreement to all finance parties, a term which should be defined to include the loan originator as well as the issuer and security trustee.

Reliance is placed primarily on environmental reports and warranties from the borrower. In the case of securitisations of existing loans, no new due diligence is undertaken. It is therefore important to obtain a deed of collateral warranty or a suitable reliance letter from the environmental consultant who prepared the report in favour of the Issuer and the security trustee (who acts on behalf of the bondholders) in addition to the loan originator. For that reason, the environmental consultant's deed of appointment should include a requirement to issue a sufficient number of collateral warranties or reliance letters on request.[1]

In the case of securitisations of new loans, due diligence is undertaken prior to the close of the loan. The environmental consultant should be required to address the environmental report to the issuer and the security trustee as well as the loan originator.

Environmental reports will also need to be disclosed (but not addressed) to the rating agency giving the risk rating (ie default probability) in respect of the loan which is to be securitised.

1 See Ch 8.

Chapter 11

Agreements for remedial works

REMEDIAL WORKS

11.01 Property transactions sometimes provide that one of the parties will undertake remediation works either independently or as part of a development scheme. In the latter case it is not uncommon to provide a simple obligation to the effect that the developing party shall undertake any remedial work necessary for the purposes of the development. However, that approach is not ideal, because as a rule, both parties, whether vendor and purchaser or landlord and tenant, have an interest in ensuring that remediation is carried out to an appropriate standard. The reason is that both parties may have potential liabilities in relation to any contamination remaining on the property after the remedial work has been completed.[1]

1 Those liabilities are explained in Chs 9 and 15.

Viewpoint of the party taking the benefit of the obligation ('beneficiary')

11.02 The beneficiary will wish to ensure that:

- the remedial work planned is sufficient for the purpose of avoiding liabilities in the future. If that party is going to develop the property, the remedial work should be sufficient to enable the development to proceed without the need for further remediation;
- the regulatory authorities are given the opportunity to comment on and approve the plans for the remedial work;
- any necessary consents are obtained from the regulatory authorities;
- the remedial work is properly carried out;
- there is an appropriate verification that the remedial work has been completed;
- a full record of the work is provided which will assist both parties in resisting liabilities in the future;
- warranties are provided by the environmental consultant, the environmental engineer and the remediation contractor engaged on the project that they have used all reasonable skill in carrying out their work, unless the beneficiary is able to take the benefit of the Contracts (Rights of Third Parties) Act 1999.[1]

1 Para **8.16**.

Viewpoint of the party carrying out the work ('remediator')

11.03 The remediator will share the interests of the other party to a large extent because both may have potential liabilities relating to the condition of the land in the future. However, if the remediator is also paying for it, he will be concerned to minimise:

- costs, by ensuring that no more work is required than is reasonably necessary for the purpose;
- interference by the other party in carrying out the work.

The remediation contract

11.04 The remediation contract should be drafted bearing those considerations in mind. Sometimes it forms part of the body of the sale agreement, but if, as is often the case, it is a complex arrangement, it may be appropriate to place it in a schedule or even in a separate environmental deed. The various components of the remediation contract will now be examined in detail.

Dramatis personae

11.05 The remediator and the beneficiary will have duties and rights under the contract. However, there are at least two and possibly three other parties who are critical to the work:

- the environmental consultant, whose function is to investigate the extent of the contamination and the risk it presents, and usually to prepare the remediation method statement outlining the work to be carried out and the methodology;
- the environmental engineer, who will supervise the carrying out of the work, and certify to all parties that it has been completed in accordance with the remediation method statement. The environmental consultant usually acts as the environmental engineer;
- the remediation contractor, who carries out the remedial work.

Each of these parties should be referred to in the remediation contract. In some cases, the parties will have already chosen a consultant or contractor to fill one or more of these roles, in which case that party can be identified by name. It is more usual, however, to provide that each of the environmental consultant, environmental engineer and remediation contractor shall be appointed by the remediator (sometimes with the approval of the beneficiary,[1] depending on the degree of involvement the beneficiary is to have in the project).

The remediation contract should specify that each of these parties is to be properly qualified and experienced in undertaking work of the type and scale required. Even if a named party has been appointed, it is advisable to provide for the appointment of a replacement in case the named party drops out.

1 If approval is required, it should be provided that the approval is not to be unreasonably withheld or delayed.

Investigating site condition and assessing the problem

11.06 If it has not already been done, the remediation contract should require the remediator to engage an environmental consultant (with appropriate qualifications and experience) to:

- investigate the presence and extent of contamination on the property;
- assess the risks to the environment and human health posed by the contamination on the property;
- assess the liability risks arising from the presence of the contamination;
- based on that information (and the proposed end use of the property) assess the need for and extent of remedial work required.

REMEDIATION METHOD STATEMENT

11.07 On the basis of the investigation and assessment, the remediator (in practice, the environmental consultant who has carried out the investigation and assessment) should be required to prepare the remediation method statement, which will set out the proposed method and extent of remediation works.

An important issue is the extent of the beneficiary's involvement in the preparation of the remediation method statement. It is not uncommon to provide that the document is subject to some level of approval or comment by the beneficiary. This may be achieved by one of the following methods:

- approval by the beneficiary (such approval not be unreasonably withheld or delayed);
- approval by the beneficiary within a stipulated time, provided that in the event of an objection which is not resolved, the draft remediation statement is to be referred to an independent expert for a binding opinion either as expert or arbitrator;
- the beneficiary may submit comments to the remediator which the latter shall take into account or shall follow insofar as they are reasonable and in accordance with the remediation contract.

The agreed approach will depend on reconciling the remediator's wish to carry out the work unfettered by the beneficiary and the extent of the beneficiary's desire to become involved in the project. In this respect the beneficiary faces something of a dilemma. The more control the beneficiary has over the remediation method statement, the greater will be his confidence that the remedial work will be carried out so as to avoid future liabilities and costs. On the other hand, the disadvantage of such control is that it increases the likelihood of liability falling on the beneficiary in the future if residual contamination on the property causes harm at a later time.

The remediation contract should also stipulate that the remediation method statement is to be submitted for comment and approval to the environmental health department of the local authority and the Environment Agency, and modified in accordance with their reasonable comments. The purpose of this procedure is to minimise the chance of the regulatory authorities deciding at a later time that more work should have been done and possibly even determining the site as contaminated land under Part IIA of the Environmental Protection Act 1990.[1]

In any event, planning conditions generally require any proposed remedial works to be approved in advance by the local planning authority, who normally consult their environmental health department and the Environment Agency.

Difficulties can arise if the environmental authorities suggest amendments to the remediation method statement which one or both of the parties considers to be unreasonable. Ideally, that should be resolved through negotiations with the authority concerned. In the absence of agreement with the authority, the remediation contract should require the parties to agree between themselves any appropriate amendments to the remediation method statement. If they cannot agree, the matter may be resolved by an independent arbitrator or expert.

1 See Ch 15.

Remediation standard

11.08 It is important that the parties agree the standard to which remedial work is to be carried out. That will depend largely on the intended future use of the property. Remediation standards have been considered above in the context of indemnities.[1] The different options explained apply equally in the case of remediation contracts.

1 Para 9.15.

Carrying out the remediation works

11.09 The remediator should have a duty to the beneficiary to carry out the remedial works. Some provision should be made as to the timing of the works. It may not be wise to stipulate a precise time frame on account of probable uncertainties as to the extent of the work needed, the requirements of the authorities and difficulties associated with the site. For that reason, the best solution may often be to require the works to be completed as soon as reasonably practicable after the date of the remediation contract.

The remediator should be under a duty to ensure that the works are carried out under the supervision of the environmental engineer, who will be required to use all the skill, care and diligence as may reasonably be expected of a properly qualified and competent environmental engineer experienced in supervising remediation works of a similar size, scope, nature and complexity to the remedial works. It is often provided that the deed of appointment is to be subject to the approval (not to be unreasonably withheld or delayed) of the beneficiary. That is important if the beneficiary wishes to check the adequacy of the contractual benefits which he hopes to obtain.

The remediator should likewise be obliged to ensure that the remedial work is carried out by the remediation contractor and similar considerations apply to the skill, care and diligence to be used by the contractor and to the approval of his contract by the beneficiary.

The remediation contract should also provide that:

- on completion of the remedial works, the remediation standard[1] shall have been achieved;
- the remediator shall ensure that all legal requirements and all reasonable requirements (whether compulsory or not) of the regulatory authorities[2] are complied with in connection with the remedial works;
- the remediator shall ensure that the remedial works are completed to the reasonable satisfaction of the regulatory authorities;
- on completion of the remedial works the remediator shall produce to the beneficiary evidence of compliance with its contractual obligations in relation to the works.

1 See para **9.15**.
2 Primarily, the Environment Agency and the Environmental Health Department of the local authority.

Completion certificate

11.10 It is advisable for the remediation contract to provide a mechanism for 'signing off' the remedial works to demonstrate to all concerned that they have been carried out properly. This is usually achieved by means of a completion certificate signed by a competent environmental consultant stating that the remedial works have been completed in accordance with the remediation contract.

The completion certificate can be signed by the remediator's environmental consultant, in which case the beneficiary should be able to rely on it contractually and/or under the rule in *Hedley Byrne & Partners Ltd v Heller & Co Ltd*.[1] However, if the beneficiary requires independent certification, the following options may be considered:

- completion certificate to be signed by the beneficiary's environmental consultant;
- completion certificate to be signed by a third party independent environmental consultant;
- draft completion certificate prepared by the remediator's environmental consultant to be sent to the beneficiary for agreement. In the absence of agreement, an independent expert is to determine whether the remedial

works have been completed in accordance with the remediation contract. If he decides that they have so completed the remedial works, the completion certificate is deemed to be issued. If not, the independent expert should be required to prescribe the additional work to be carried out following which the completion certificate procedure should be repeated.

It is useful to provide which party is to be responsible for any further remedial work if it is required after the issue of the completion certificate. In order to clarify the position as to which party is to be responsible for liabilities in relation to any residual contamination, the simplest approach will be for the responsible party to indemnify the other.[2]

1 [1965] AC 465.
2 Ch 9.

Meetings, information and records

11.11 The beneficiary may wish to ensure that the work is proceeding in accordance with the remediation contract. For that purpose it is desirable to provide that:

*   the remediator shall attend regular meetings with the beneficiary to discuss the progress of the remedial works;
*   the beneficiary shall be entitled to attend meetings with the regulatory authorities;
*   the beneficiary shall be entitled to inspect the remedial works as they are carried out;
*   the remediator is to provide on request full details in writing of the remedial works carried out to date.

These provisions may be contentious as the remediator will be concerned to proceed with the project without undue interference and without being coerced into any 'gold-plating' through additional requirements of the regulatory authorities following prompting by the beneficiary.

One of the most important matters from the beneficiary's perspective is to provide that after completion of the remedial works, he receives from the remediator a full record of all the works carried out. This should include:

*   reports of the condition of the site prior to carrying out the remedial works;
*   the remediation method statement;
*   a full record of all steps taken in carrying out the remedial works including a written description, diagrams, plans and photographs;
*   a copy of the completion certificate;
*   copies of all monitoring data, before during and after completion of the remedial works;
*   copies of all necessary permits and consents in relation to the remedial works;

- copies of all correspondence with the regulatory authorities relating to the condition of the site, the remediation method statement and the remedial works.

The importance of these records is that they provide good evidence as to the condition of the site which should give a substantial measure of comfort to regulatory authorities, future buyers, tenants, lenders and funders of the property. It should therefore reduce potential liabilities and enhance the marketability and value of the property. With regard to liabilities, the regulatory authorities should be less likely to require additional work to be undertaken if it is clear that the site has been remediated to a satisfactory standard. Additionally, the records should be sufficient for the purpose of excluding the beneficiary from liability under the contaminated land legislation[1] if he later sells the property.

1 Exclusion test 3, Part 2A Contaminated Land Statutory Guidance April 2012, paras 7.46–7.50.

Collateral warranties

11.12 The remediation contract should require the remediator to procure warranties in favour of the beneficiary from the environmental consultant, the environmental engineer and the remediation contractor. It is advisable from the beneficiary's viewpoint to agree the form of each warranty and to provide that the warranty shall be in that form subject only to such amendments as may reasonably be required by the party giving the warranty provided that the amendments do not materially diminish the position of the beneficiary.

The remediator should ensure that the warrantor has agreed to provide a warranty in that form. If there is any doubt on the matter, the remediator should undertake only to use reasonable endeavours to procure a warranty:

- in the form in the schedule; or
- in a form and in substance satisfactory to the beneficiary acting reasonably.

Warranties usually provide that the beneficiary is to have no greater rights against the warrantor than the original client. For that reason, the beneficiary should require a copy of the original appointment to ensure that there are no limitations in the appointment which unduly restrict his rights.

The provisions of contracts appointing consultants are discussed in Chapter 8. As an alternative to collateral warranties the beneficiary may be able to rely on the original appointment under the Contracts (Rights of Third Parties) Act 1999.[1]

1 Para **8.16**.

Step-in rights

11.13 If the remediator fails to carry out the remediation work at all within the stipulated period or fails to undertake it in accordance with the remediation contract, the beneficiary will have a right to claim damages under the contract. However, the beneficiary may wish to provide for step-in rights which entitle the beneficiary to take over the remediation work at the remediator's reasonable cost in appropriate cases.

Other

11.14 If the remedial work is to be carried on as part of or in preparation to construction operations, the provisions of the Part II Housing Grants, Construction and Regeneration Act 1996)[1] relating to adjudication and payments will apply.

1 Ss 104–113, as amended by the Local Democracy, Economic Development and Construction Act 2009. See para **8.16**.

Chapter 12

Transferring permits

12.01 When the property is transferred, it is essential that all environmental licences, consents, authorisations and other permits ('permits') which are transferable are duly transferred to the buyer and that any statutory requirements, for example, as to notification of the regulatory authorities, are complied with. An appropriate provision should be included in the contract requiring the seller to transfer any such permit to the buyer and to undertake any other step required by the applicable legislation in order to effect a transfer. In cases where a fee is payable, the contract should provide for the allocation of the payment between the parties.

12.02 In cases where the buyer has to apply for a new permit, the contract should contain a covenant by the seller to provide the buyer with all information and to undertake all reasonable steps necessary to enable the buyer to make the application. In the case of permits which 'run with the land', nothing need be done. Unfortunately, in some instances,[1] it is not clear whether a permit runs with the land or not. In such cases, it is advisable to take account of the view of the regulatory authorities before deciding how to proceed.

1 Eg trade effluent consents.

12.03 Permits are governed by a number of different statutes and the regimes for transferring them from seller to buyer can vary considerably. It is important to be aware that generally permits are not transferred automatically and steps have to be taken by the seller and the buyer.

ENVIRONMENTAL PERMITS

12.04 Several different types of permit have been brought within the environmental permitting regime under the Environmental Permitting (England and Wales) Regulations 2010 ('the EP Regulations'). The following types of permit (amongst others) are included in this regime:

- permits for 'dirty' industrial activities;
- permits for waste operations;
- permits for water discharge activities;
- permits for discharges to groundwater;
- permits for flood risk activities; and
- permits for radioactive substance activities.[1]

These permits need to be transferred to the buyer. If this is not done at completion, both parties may commit an offence: in the case of the buyer, operating a regulated facility without a permit; in the case of the seller, (depending on the facts) knowingly causing or knowingly permitting the offence by the buyer.[2]

The following transfer procedures in respect of a permit or any part of a permit apply under the EP Regulations:

- for permits for stand-alone water discharge activities, groundwater activities and flood risk activities, both seller and buyer must jointly notify the Environment Agency (EA) or Natural Resources Wales (NRW) on form D1, and the EA may transfer the permit on the date specified in the notification which must be at least 20 working days after the date on which the notification is given;[3]
- in the case of all other permits covered by the environmental permitting regime, a joint application by the seller and buyer must be made to the regulator to transfer the permit.[4] The regulator has two months to decide whether or not to transfer the permit but that period can be extended by agreement.[5] The regulator must refuse to transfer the permit if it considers that the transferee will not be the operator or that it will not operate the facility in accordance with the environmental permit.[6] The parties can appeal to the Secretary of State if the application is refused;[7]
- registrations of exemptions are not transferable so the buyer must make an application for a new registration.[8]

1 EP Regulations, SI 2010/675, reg 8.
2 EP Regulations, SI 2010/675, reg 38(1).
3 EP Regulations, SI 2010/675, reg 21(4). Note that the EA can also transfer permits if the sole individual operator, or one of two or more individuals who comprise the operator cannot be found. In that case, the notification must be made respectively by the proposed transferee or by the individual transferor(s) who can be found and the proposed transferee jointly: reg 21(4)(a), (b) and (c).
4 EP Regulations, SI 2010/675, reg 21(1)(c). Similar provisions apply in the case of sole individual operators who cannot be found as in the case of permits for water discharge activities, groundwater activities and flood risk activities except that an application has to be made to the regulator instead of a notification: reg 21(1)(a) and (b). See fn 2 above. In the event of the death of a sole operator, the permit ceases to have effect six months after the operator's death, unless the permit has been transferred under reg 21 or a transfer application has been made by the deceased operator's personal representatives and the application has not been withdrawn or finally determined: reg 67A.
5 EP Regulations, SI 2010/675, Sch 5, para 15.
6 EP Regulations, SI 2010/675, Sch 5, para 13.
7 EP Regulations, SI 2010/675, reg 31. Strangely, possibly due to legislative oversight, the appeal provision does not apply in terms if the EA fails to transfer the permit where a notification rather than an application has to be made.
8 EP Regulations, SI 2010/675, Sch 2, paras 3(1)(b)(ii), 4(b) and 5(b); Sch 3 (Parts 1, 2 and 3).

PETROL STORAGE CERTIFICATES AND LICENSES

12.05 Petrol storage certificates for the storage of petrol on dispensing premises run with the land but outgoing and incoming occupiers must notify the petroleum enforcement of the proposed change in occupation at least 28 days and no more than six months before it occurs.[1] Licences for the storage of petrol on land for private use are personal to the licensee and not transferable.[2]

1 Petroleum (Consolidation) Regulations 2014, SI 2014/1637, regs 9 and 10.
2 Petroleum (Consolidation) Regulations 2014, SI 2014/1637, reg 14(8).

HAZARDOUS SUBSTANCES CONSENT

12.06 A hazardous substances consent, runs with the land unless the consent states otherwise.[1] Accordingly, it is not transferable.

1 Planning (Hazardous Substances) Act 1990, s 6.

Trade effluent consents

12.07 Trade effluent consents probably run with the land, and so do not need to be transferred but some sewerage undertakers disagree.[1] If the consent is considered by the sewerage undertaker not to run with the land, an application for a new trade effluent consent should be made. A trade effluent agreement is probably transferable, subject to the terms of the agreement, but the legislation does not clarify the position.[2]

1 See para **17.122**.
2. See Water Industry Act 1991, s 129.

Water abstraction licences

12.08 In the case of water abstraction licences, the licence holder and the proposed transferee must give notice (with prescribed information) of their agreement that the licence should be transferred ('transfer notice') to the EA (or NRW). The EA (or NRW) must then amend the licence by substituting the name of the transferee as licence holder.[1] If a licence holder wishes to transfer part of its entitlement to abstract to a third party transferee or to transfer the whole entitlement to more than one party, both or all parties must give an apportionment notice to the EA (or NRW), which must then revoke the existing licence, and grant a new licence to each successor party who will carry out part of the licensed abstraction.[2]

1 Water Resources Act 1991, s 59A. See para **17.41**.
2 Water Resources Act 1991, s 59C.

Consent to works in ordinary watercourses

12.09 Consents to erect an obstruction or erect or alter a culvert in ordinary watercourses appear to be personal to the applicant. However, the internal drainage board or lead local flood authority may give the benefit to third parties if the consent conditions (which must be reasonable) are expressed to be binding on successors in title of the applicant and owners/occupiers of the land on which the works are situated.[1]

1 Land Drainage Act 1991, s 23.

12.10 A greenhouse gas permit is required for specified industrial operations which produce significant amounts of carbon dioxide.[1] Those processes which require a permit are then included in a 'cap and trade' scheme under which in each year operators have to surrender the number of allowances equivalent to the tonnes of carbon dioxide emitted in the previous calendar year.[2]

A greenhouse gas permit must be transferred by the EA or NRW on the joint application of the permit holder and proposed transferee if the EA/NRW is satisfied that the proposed transferee will operate the installation and will be capable of monitoring and reporting its emissions in accordance with the requirements of the permit. Otherwise, the transfer must be refused.[3]

1 Greenhouse Gas Emissions Trading Scheme Regulations 2012, SI 2012/3038, reg 9. See also Directive 2003/87/EC.
2 Greenhouse Gas Emissions Trading Scheme Regulations 2012, regs 16 and 41.
3 Ibid, reg 12.

Marine licences

12.11 Marine licences may be transferred by the Marine Management Organisation to another person on the application of the licensee.[1]

1 Marine and Coastal Access Act 2009, s 72(7) and (8).

Hazardous waste notification

12.12 Premises at which hazardous waste is produced or from which it is collected or removed must be notified to the Environment Agency (or Natural Resources Wales) unless the premises are exempt.[1] From 1 April 2016 this requirement no longer applies in England but continues to apply in Wales.[2] The notification is valid for 12 months[3] and does not need to be repeated within that period if there is a change in ownership or occupation of the premises.[4]

1 Hazardous Waste (England and Wales) Regulations 2005, SI 2005/894, reg 21(1). The conditions for exemption are that waste is only removed by a registered or exempt carrier and is less than 500 kg in total in any twelve months period: regs 23 and 30.
2 Hazardous Waste (England and Wales) (Amendment) Regulations 2016, SI 2016/336, reg 2(3).
3 Ibid, reg 21(2).
4 Ibid, reg 21(3).

THE DELAYED TRANSFER PROBLEM

12.13 When a permit has to be transferred from the seller to the buyer, it is advisable to request the regulatory authority to effect the transfer on the date of completion. If this does not happen the buyer may be carrying out an activity without a required permit and (depending on the facts) the seller may be knowingly permitting this to happen. In that case, both the seller and buyer would be committing an offence under the EP Regulations. The position is similar under most other permitting regimes. It is unlikely that the regulatory authority would prosecute if the parties have taken all the steps required of them and the delay was due to the authority itself. However, it is better practice to avoid the commission of offences altogether and many corporate bodies have policies that require them to comply with the law. In order to deal with the possibility that permits may be transferred after completion, it is recommended that the following clauses should be used:

> 1. *Transfer of Environmental Permits*
> '(a)   The Buyer and the Seller shall take all reasonable steps to ensure that the Environmental Permit is transferred from the Seller to the Buyer at Completion (or in default as soon as possible thereafter) including without limitation signing any application or other document which is required by law for that purpose and providing any information and or documentation which is reasonably required by the competent regulatory authority.
>
> (b)   During the Period, the Seller at the cost of the Buyer shall continue to operate the Activity as agent for and for the benefit of the Buyer in accordance with the Buyer's wishes to the extent that they are consistent with the Seller's continued operation of the Activity provided always that the Buyer shall grant to the Seller all rights necessary to enable the Seller to exercise control over the Activity. During the Period, the Seller shall appoint the Buyer to carry out and the Buyer shall carry out on behalf of the Seller and at the cost of the Buyer all actions necessary to operate the Activity which shall remain under the control of the Seller.
>
> (c)   The Buyer undertakes to indemnify and hold harmless the Seller (for itself and as trustee for each member of the Seller's Group) in respect of all liabilities which fall on the Seller solely in its capacity as operator of the Activity due to any acts or omissions of the Buyer during the Period.
>
> 2.   The following definitions shall apply:
> (a)   "Environmental Permit" means [give reference and date of permit etc]
> (b)   "Activity" means the activity regulated under the Environmental Permit.
> (c)   "Period" means the period from Completion until such time as the Environmental Permit has been transferred to the Buyer.'

Clause 1(a) requires the parties to take all reasonable steps to have the permit transferred at Completion (or as soon as possible thereafter).

In order to avoid problems where there is a delay between Completion and the transfer of the permit, clause 1(b) employs a 'double agency' solution, under which during the period between Completion and the date when the permit is transferred the seller continues to be the operator of the permitted activity as agent for the buyer. The buyer in turn carries out the day to day activity but under the control of the seller. The object of the exercise is to ensure that the seller remains the operator under the permit until the transfer is effected, whilst the buyer is able to carry on business at the Property.

The indemnity in clause 1(c) is designed to protect the seller against liabilities falling on it as operator after Completion where these are due to the acts or omissions of the buyer.

In cases, where the transfer is not automatic, such as an environmental permit, it is wise to check that the proposed transferee is acceptable to the regulator.

If there is any doubt the sale agreement should contain default provisions in case the permit transfer is refused. Possibilities include a reversal of the sale or a long term 'double agency' agreement.

12.14 The following table sets out in outline the provisions governing the transfer of the most common permits discussed above. Those no longer in force (but which governed past permit transfers) are shown in italics.[1]

Type of permit	Legislation	Regulatory authority	Transferable	Other requirements
Storage certificate (for storage of petrol on dispensing premises) (from 1 October 2014)	Petroleum (Consolidation) Regulations 2014, regs 9 and 10	Petroleum enforcement authority: fire and rescue authority in Greater London or metropolitan county; elsewhere usually county council	No, it runs with the land	Notification to petroleum enforcement authority required by outgoing and incoming occupier (a maximum of 6 months and a minimum of 28 days before the change in occupation)
Storage Licence (for storage of petrol for private use – not including sale) (from 1 October 2014)	Petroleum (Consolidation) Regulations 2014, reg 14(8)	Petroleum enforcement authority: fire and rescue authority in Greater London or metropolitan county; elsewhere usually county council	No, it is personal to the licensee and not transferable	An application has to be made by the buyer for a new licence
Petroleum Licence. (before 1 October 2014)	*Petroleum (Transfer of Licences) Act 1936, s 1*	*Local Authority*	*Yes*	*The Local Authority could transfer the licence by endorsement of the licence or otherwise*
Hazardous Substances Consent	P(HS)A 1990, ss 6 and 17	Hazardous substances authority (generally district councils, London Borough councils and Welsh counties or county boroughs	No, it runs with the land unless the consent states otherwise	NB: An HSC is revoked if there is a change in the person in control of part of the land to which it relates, unless an application for the continuation of the consent has previously been made to the hazardous substances authority

Type of permit	Legislation	Regulatory authority	Transferable	Other requirements
Trade Effluent Consent	WIA 1991, s 118	Sewerage Undertaker	Probably runs with the land, but some sewerage undertakers disagree	If the consent is considered not to run with the land an application for a new trade effluent consent must be made
Trade Effluent Agreement	WIA 1991, s 129	Sewerage Undertaker	Probably yes depending on the terms of the Agreement	If the benefit of the Agreement is not assignable, a new agreement must be negotiated with the sewerage undertaker.
Water Abstraction Licence (before 1 April 2006)	*WRA 1991, s 49*	*EA*	*Yes, automatic transfer if buyer occupied the whole of the land in the licence) on which abstracted water was to be used*	*The successor (buyer) had to notify the EA of the change of occupation within 15 months beginning with the date on which he became occupier. Otherwise, the licence ceased to have effect*
Water Abstraction Licence (before 1 April 2006)	*WRA 1991, s 50; WR(SL)R 1969, reg 4*	*EA*	*Yes, automatic transfer if the buyer occupied the whole of the land previously occupied by the seller, but the land was only part of that which could benefit under the licence in the absence of agreement that the seller would continue to hold the licence*	*The successor (buyer) had to notify the EA within one month beginning with the date on which he became occupier. Otherwise, the licence ceased to have effect. If it was agreed that the seller would continue to hold the licence, notice to that effect had to be given by seller and buyer to the EA*

Type of permit	Legislation	Regulatory authority	Transferable	Other requirements
Water Abstraction Licence (before 1 April 2006)	*WRA 1991, s 50 Water WR(SL)R 1969, regs 5–7*	*EA*	*No, if buyer occupied only part of the land occupied by previous licence holder and on which abstracted water was to be used*	*If the seller sold part of the land Licence benefited by the licence, the buyer was entitled to a new licence if he applied within one month beginning with the date he became occupier, provided that the seller (or other occupier of the retained land) applied for a new licence or revocation/ variation of the original licence. In effect, the benefits of the original licence were split. If the deadline was missed, the entitlement to a new licence was lost*
Water Abstraction Licence (before 1 April 2006)	*WRA 1991*	*EA*	*No, if no land was specified on which the water is to be used*	*The buyer could take the benefit of the licence indirectly, by abstracting water as agent for the seller under an agreement whereby the seller continued to occupy the borehole and was obliged to supply water to the buyer pending the buyer obtaining his own licence*
Water Abstraction Licence (from 1 April 2006)	WRA 1991, s 59A	EA (NRW)	Yes	The licence holder and the proposed transferee must give notice of their agreement that the licence should be transferred ('transfer notice') containing required information to the EA. The EA must then amend the licence by substituting the name of the transferee as licence holder

Type of permit	Legislation	Regulatory authority	Transferable	Other requirements
Water Abstraction Licence (from 1 April 2006)	WRA 1991, s 59C	EA (NRW)	Yes	The licence holder and any person proposing to carry on part of a licensed abstraction must give notice of their agreement to the division and transfer (apportionment notice) containing required information to the EA. The apportionment notice must be accompanied by an application by the holder of the existing licence for its revocation. The EA must then revoke the existing licence and grant to each person who will carry on part of the licensed abstraction (including the existing licence holder if appropriate) a licence relating to that part of the abstraction
Consent to erect alter or repair structure in main river (before 6 April 2016)	*Ss 109 and 110*	*EA (NRW)*	*No. The consent appeared to be personal to the applicant*	*A consent could be given subject to any reasonable condition as to the time at which and the manner in which any work was to be carried out: WRA 1991, s110(2)(c). The EA usually included a condition requiring the person to whom consent was given to notify them if the subject land was to be transferred. The EA then had discretion as to whether the benefit of the consent was given to the transferee of the land*

Type of permit	Legislation	Regulatory authority	Transferable	Other requirements
Consent to erect obstruction to flow of ordinary watercourse	LDA 1991, s 23	Internal drainage board or lead local flood authority	No. The consent appears to be personal to the applicant (but see note in next column)	A consent may be subject to reasonable conditions: LDA 1991, s 23(1A) Some conditions are expressed to be binding on successors in title of the applicant and owners/occupiers of the land on which the works are situated
Waste Management Licence (up to 5 April 2008)	*EPA 1990, s 40*	*EA*	*Yes*	*The current holder and the proposed transferee had to apply jointly to the EA who could only effect the transfer if they were satisfied that the proposed transferee was a 'fit and proper' person*
Discharge Consent/ Groundwater Authorisation (before 1 October 2004)	*WRA 1991, Sch 10 para 11. GWR 1998 reg 18*	*EA*	*Yes*	*The transferor (seller) had to notify the EA not later than the end of 21 days beginning with the date of the transfer.*
				NB Any discharge consent in force on 31 March 1996 lapsed unless notice was given to the EA by 30 September 1996 by any person intending to rely on the consent thereafter of his intention to do so

Type of permit	Legislation	Regulatory authority	Transferable	Other requirements
Discharge Consent/ Groundwater Authorisation (from 1 October 2004 to 5 April 2010)	*WRA 1991, Sch 10, para 11. GWR 1998, reg 18*	*EA*	*Yes*	*The proposed transferor (seller) and transferee (buyer) had to notify the EA of the proposed transfer in a joint notice containing any information prescribed within 21 days beginning with the date of receipt of the notice. The EA was then required to amend the consent substituting the name of the transferee as holder and notify the transferor and transferee that the amendment had been made*
Registration of User of Radioactive Material (before 6 April 2008)	*RSA 1993, s 7*	*EA*	*No*	*An application had to be made by the buyer for a new registration*
Authorisation for disposal/ accumulation of radioactive waste. (before 6 April 2008)²	*RSA 1993, ss 13, 14 and 16*	*EA*	*No*	*An application had to be made by the buyer for a new authorisation*
IPC/LAAPC Authorisation	*EPA 1990, s 9*	*EA/local authority*	*Yes*	*Transferee had to notify the EA/Local Authority of the transfer within 21 days beginning with the date of transfer*
PPC permit	*PPC (E&W) Regs 2000, reg 18*	*EA/local authority*		*The operator and the proposed transferee had to make a joint application to the regulator to transfer the permit in whole or in part to the proposed transferee*

Type of permit	Legislation	Regulatory authority	Transferable	Other requirements
Environmental permit (former PPC permits and waste management licences – from 6 April 2008; for radioactive substances activities, water discharge activities and groundwater activities from 6 April 2010 and flood risk activities from 6 April 2016)	EP (E&W) Regs 2010, reg 21 (from 6 April 2010). EP (E&W) Regs 2007 reg 21 (before 6 April 2010)	EA (NRW)/ local authority	Yes	The operator and the proposed transferee make a joint application (or joint notification in the case of environmental permits authorising stand-alone water-discharge, groundwater or flood risk activities) to the regulator to transfer the environmental permit in whole or in part to the proposed transferee. The regulator may then transfer the permit. In cases where an application is required, the regulator must refuse to transfer the permit, if it considers that the transferee would not be the operator or would not operate the facility in accordance with the environmental permit. From 6 April 2012 if the operator is an individual who cannot be found (or two or more individuals, one or more of whom cannot be found) the transfer may proceed on the joint application of the remaining individual(s) and the transferee
Registration of exemptions for waste, water discharge activities, and groundwater activities	EP (EW) Regs 2010, Schedule 2, paras 3(1) (b)(ii), 4(b) and 5(b); Schedule 3 (Parts 1, 2 and 3)	EA (LA for waste operations T3 and T7 carried on by mobile plant)	No	An application has to be made by the buyer for a new registration

Type of permit	Legislation	Regulatory authority	Transferable	Other requirements
Greenhouse Gas Permit	GHGETS Regs 2012	EA (or NRW)	Yes	The permit holder and proposed transferee make a joint application to the regulator which must grant the application if it is satisfied that the proposed transferee will be the operator and will be capable of monitoring and reporting emissions from the installation in accordance with the permit
Marine Licence	M&CAA 2009 72(7) and (8)	Secretary of State (DEFRA) whose functions are delegated to the Marine Management Organisation	Yes	The licensee makes an application to the licensing authority which granted the licence. That authority may then transfer the licence from the licensee to another person and if so must vary the licence accordingly. Note that a licence authorising the construction, alteration or improvement of any works within the UK marine licensing area either (a) in or over the sea bed or (b) on or under the sea bed, may provide that the conditions attached to it are to bind any other person who for the time being owns occupies or enjoys the use of the works in question (whether or not the licence is transferred to that other person): M&CAA 2009, s71(5)

243

Type of permit	Legislation	Regulatory authority	Transferable	Other requirements
Hazardous Waste Notification	Hazardous Waste (England and Wales) Regulations 2005, reg 21 (repealed in England only from 1 April 2016 by the Hazardous Waste (England and Wales) (Amendment) Regulations 2016). The notification requirement remains in force in Wales.	EA (or NRW)	No, it runs with the land	The notification is valid for 12 months

Abbreviations used in table above:

EPA 1990 – Environmental Protection Act 1990

EP (E&W) Regs 2007 – Environmental Permitting (England and Wales) Regulations 2007; SI 2007/3538

EP (E&W) Regs 2010 – Environmental Permitting (England and Wales) Regulations 2010 as amended; SI 2010/675

GHGETS Regs 2012 – Greenhouse Gas Emissions Trading Scheme Regulations 2012, SI 2012/3038

GWR 1998 – Groundwater Regulations 1998; SI 1998/2746

HSC – Hazardous Substances Consent

LDA – Land Drainage Act 1991

M&CAA 2009 – Marine and Coastal Access Act 2009

P(HS)A 1990 – Planning (Hazardous Substances) Act 1990

PPC (E&W) Regs 2000 – Pollution Prevention and Control (England and Wales) Regulations 2000; SI 2000/1973

RSA 1993 – Radioactive Substances Act 1993

WIA 1991 – Water Industry Act 1991

WRA 1991 – Water Resources Act 1991

WR(SL)R 1969 – Water Resources (Succession to Licences) Regulations 1969; SI 1969/976

1 The former regimes shown in italics do not now apply even if the permit was originally granted when a former regime was in force.

2 In the case of authorisations for the disposal of radioactive waste on or from premises on a nuclear site, from 27 July 2004 an application for a transfer had to be made to the EA jointly by the transferor and proposed transferee. Following consultations, the EA could only grant the application if satisfied that the transferee would have operational control over the disposals and was able and willing to comply with the limitations and conditions of the authorisation, and that there were no other grounds on which it would be reasonable to refuse the application: RSA 1993, s 16A.

PART II
THE BROADER CONTEXT

Chapter 13

Civil liability

INTRODUCTION

13.01 The phrase 'civil liability' is a broad one. In the context of this book, however, it is considered selectively. This chapter sets out aspects of the principal torts relevant to property transactions – nuisance, *Rylands v Fletcher*, trespass and negligence – which arise at common law. At a practical level, equally significant civil liabilities may exist under statute in some contexts. These include certain liabilities in respect of emissions of radiation,[1] as well as civil liabilities under statute relating to the costs of avoiding or remedying some other forms of pollution. These are considered elsewhere in this book.[2] The main focus here, then is on private civil liabilities.

1 Nuclear Installations Act 1965, particularly ss 7–9; see paras **13.54–13.56**.
2 On the remediation of contaminated land see Ch 15; on statutory nuisances, paras **14.25–14.26**.

13.02 While the subservience of private law remedies to public law is often assumed, both in the general emphasis given to statutory environmental law and in the particular assumption that private law rights are 'extinguished' by public law interventions,[1] private land retains distinctive features which explain its enduring importance. These largely originate in private law's ancient basis in property rights.[2] This enables private liabilities to play a continuing role in resolving conflicts between neighbouring owners or users of land. The emergence of public law systems of environmental regulation, especially since the 1990s, may even have contributed to boosting the role of private law, in defining notions of environmental damage for example,[3] and suggest complementary roles for private and public law.

1 For example, under the defence of statutory authority: see paras **13.41–13.46**.
2 Although this may present an impediment to the more creative adaptation of tort for contemporary environmental purposes more generally: Steele 'Private Law and the Environment: Nuisance in Context' (1995) 15 *Journal of Legal Studies* 236.
3 *Cambridge Water Co v Eastern Counties Leather plc* [1994] 2 AC 264; see paras **13.24–13.33**.

13.03 It is important to appreciate the features and relative importance to property transactions of different forms of civil liability. This book is concerned in large part with enabling those involved in property transactions to make informed decisions as to the allocation of environmental risk, and therefore of associated liabilities. One purpose of the enquiries and pre-transaction stages set out above[1] is to ensure that the information necessary to make these decisions is available. This is no less true of private law liabilities than those arising under public law. What is equally clear, however, is that those liabilities may operate differently between parties to a given transaction. A general appreciation of civil liabilities arising at common law is therefore necessary.

1 Chs 1–9.

NUISANCE

13.04 Nuisance is the most obvious environment-related tort, and this is reflected in the emphasis given to it here. Three types of nuisance are generally actionable: private, public and statutory. The practical advantages of statutory nuisance, not least the duty on local authorities to detect and abate them,[1] may make it an attractive remedy in some cases. Statutory nuisance is the subject of Chapter 14. The emphasis there is on abatement, however, with the prospect of compensation being less likely than in a private (or even public) nuisance claim.[2] Public nuisance – a crime at common law[3] – is considered below.[4] An explanation of private nuisance is required first, in that one class of public nuisance is that which amounts to a private nuisance, but which affects a larger number of people.[5] The other class relates to interference with the safety or convenience of members of the public generally, but where there is no direct interference with a person's enjoyment of land.[6]

1 EPA 1990, ss 79(1) and 80(1); and see Ch 14.
2 Although conviction for an offence under, eg, EPA 1990, s 82, will enable a magistrates' court to make an award of compensation under the Powers of Criminal Courts (Sentencing) Act 2000, s 130: see paras **14.70–14.72**.
3 *R v Madden* [1975] 3 All ER 155, CA.
4 Paras **13.34–13.36**.
5 *A-G v PYA Quarries Ltd* [1957] 2 QB 169.
6 *Shillito v Thompson* (1875) 1 QBD 12.

Private nuisance

13.05 Although the authorities are complex, nuisance may generally be defined as an unlawful interference with a person's use or enjoyment of land or some right over or in connection with it. It will often be the case that such interference arises from a continuing state of affairs on land not belonging to the claimant, although the damage suffered need not be continuing.[1] There is no rule that nuisances can arise only from a continuing state of affairs, as a one-off occurrence clearly may be actionable in certain circumstances.[2] A defendant is liable for an isolated escape, however, only if 'the case can be brought within the scope of the rule in *Rylands v Fletcher*'.[3]

Not every interference will constitute an actionable nuisance, and so, for example, interference with television reception is not actionable.[4] Activities that may lead a neighbour to be fearful but do not actually pose a danger are not actionable.[5] The law of nuisance seeks to balance the right of the owners or occupiers of land to do what they like on that land against the right of owners of 'neighbouring' land[6] to be free from interference.[7] A use of land must therefore be 'unreasonable' for it to give rise to an actionable nuisance.[8] This does not mean that the use of land must be reasonable only for the user's purpose, but rather that it is reasonable by reference also to his neighbours: 'The governing principle is good neighbourliness, and this involves reciprocity'.[9] This notion is, of course, extremely fluid and its applicability has been the subject of some confusion.[10]

1 *Stone v Bolton* [1950] 1 KB 201.
2 *British Celanese Ltd v A H Hunt (Capacitors) Ltd* [1969] 1 WLR 959; *Crown River Cruises v Kimbolton Fireworks* [1996] 2 Lloyd's Rep 533.
3 *Northumbrian Water Limited v Sir Robert McAlpine Limited* [2014] EWCA Civ 685, [18].
4 *Hunter v Canary Wharf Ltd* [1997] 2 All ER 426.
5 *Birmingham Development Company Limited v Tyler* [2008] EWCA Civ 859.
6 Although it need not be immediately adjacent: *British Celanese Ltd v A H Hunt (Capacitors) Ltd* [1969] 1 WLR 959, at 964D.
7 It should be noted that in some circumstances a person may be liable in nuisance despite not being an owner or occupier of land from which a nuisance emanates. This may have implications for vendors: see paras **13.20–13.23**.
8 *Cambridge Water Co Ltd v Eastern Counties Leather plc* [1994] 2 AC 264, per Lord Goff at 299.
9 Per Lord Millett, *Southwark London Borough Council v Mills* [1999] 3 WLR 939, at 954H.
10 Caused, in part, by the relationship between nuisance and negligence: C Gearty, 'The Place of Private Nuisance in a Modern Law of Torts' (1989) 48 CLJ 214. On 'reasonable user' see also *Graham v Rechem* [1996] Env LR 158.

13.06 In determining whether the user of land is reasonable it is first necessary to consider whether the effects of the alleged nuisance amount (on one hand) to interference with the use of premises or natural rights incidental to ownership ('amenity nuisance'), or (on the other) to actual physical damage. The basis for this is that it has been suggested that the 'reasonableness' test is not applicable where physical damage to property is caused.[1] Although this is now generally considered not to be the case,[2] different factors will apply in assessing 'reasonable user' as between cases of amenity nuisance and cases of physical damage. In particular, the nature of the locality will be considered in cases of amenity nuisance,[3] but not in cases of property damage.[4] The dividing line may be difficult to draw, however, particularly where the *value* of property is affected by a nuisance to the extent that it may be considered to be property damage.[5] The UK Supreme Court has held that a defendant can contend that the activities alleged to be a nuisance are part of the character of the area but only inasmuch as the activities are not a nuisance.[6]

Despite the 'locality' rule, if a nuisance is established, it is no defence to say that the nuisance existed first and that the claimant came to the nuisance. In 2014, however, the UK Supreme Court added the proviso that if a claimant builds on, or changes the use of, the land, it may be a defence if, among other things, the defendant's activity is lawful and was not a nuisance before the building works or change of use of the claimant's land and the nuisance is not greater than before them.[7] As Maria Lee remarked, whilst the UK Supreme Court confirmed 'the orthodoxy that coming to a nuisance is no defence, [it] simultaneously create[d] an exception (through the locality/character of the neighbourhood principle) so great that it almost overwhelms the rule. Coming to the nuisance is no defence, but in *precisely* the most challenging cases (change of use) 'locality' allows the courts to protect defendants'.[8] For example, building a house on previously unoccupied land is within the exception.[9]

Other factors which will be considered in determining 'reasonable user' include the nature and duration of the interference,[10] but not the sensitivity of the claimant (an abnormally sensitive claimant or use of land will not provide grounds for an action in nuisance where a claimant or user without that sensitivity would not succeed).[11] It should also be noted that potential claimants are expected to be more tolerant of transient building or demolition operations, with the burden instead being on the defendant to show absence of negligence in carrying them out.[12]

1 Ogus and Richardson 'Economics and the Environment: A Study of Private Nuisance' (1977) 36 CLJ 284.
2 Steele 'Private Law and the Environment: Nuisance in Context' (1995) 15 *Legal Studies* 236, at 252.
3 *Sturges v Bridgman* (1879) 11 Ch D 852, per Thesiger LJ at 857; *Gillingham Borough Council v Medway (Chatham) Dock Co Ltd* [1993] QB 343.
4 *St Helens Smelting Co v Tipping* (1865) 11 HL Cas 642.
5 The distinction actually drawn in *Tipping* was between interferences with comfort and enjoyment, and 'sensible injury to the value of property': (1865) 11 HL Cas 642, at 650–51.
6 *Coventry v Lawrence* [2014] UKSC 13, [2014] AC 822 845 (per Lord Neuberger).
7 *Coventry v Lawrence* [2014] UKSC 13, [2014] AC 822, 841-42 (per Lord Neuberger).
8 Maria Lee 'Private Nuisance in the Supreme Court: *Coventry v Lawrence*' (2014) 7 *Journal of Planning & Environment Law* 705, 711.
9 David Hart 'Supreme Court brings private nuisance into the 21st century' (2013) 6 *Environmental Liability* 226, 226.
10 *Crown River Cruises v Kimbolton Fireworks* [1996] 2 Lloyd's Rep 533.
11 *Robinson v Kilvert* (1889) 41 Ch D 88; *Heath v Brighton Corpn* (1908) 98 LT 718; *Bridlington Relay Ltd v Yorkshire Electricity Board* [1965] Ch 436.
12 *Andreae v Selfridge & Co* [1938] Ch 1.

13.07 An important example of the application of these principles can be seen in a case involving Victorian residential premises that had been converted in 1972 and re-let in 1992.[1] In issue was whether the absence of sound insulation could give rise to a nuisance actionable by the tenants: all the normal noise of domestic activity could be heard between the flats, causing tension and distress. The then House of Lords concluded that the ordinary and reasonable use of the premises by the tenant was not in itself an actionable nuisance, and that the landlord could not be liable for having authorised any nuisance if it was such an ordinary and reasonable use. As Lord Hoffmann put it: '... I do not think that the normal use of a residential flat can possibly be a nuisance to the neighbours. If it were, we would have the absurd position that each behaving normally and reasonably, was a nuisance to the other'.[2] Earlier authorities were distinguished on the basis that they did not involve normal or ordinary user.[3] As the Court also concluded that the landlord's covenant for quiet enjoyment had not been broken either, essentially on the basis of caveat lessee, the claimants were left with no legal remedy.[4]

1 *Southwark London Borough Council v Mills; Baxter v Camden London Borough Council* [1999] 3 WLR 939.
2 Ibid, at 950C-D.

3 Eg, *Sampson v Hodson-Pressinger* [1981] 3 All ER 710, considered in *Southwark v Mills*, at 950G-951A.
4 See Murdoch, (1999) 9946 EG 186; Madge, (2000) 97 LSGaz 37; and Mills & Joss (2000) 144 SJ 269.

13.08 Where the user is held to be reasonable, the defendant will not be liable for consequent harm to its neighbour's enjoyment of land, or to property. Conversely, where the user is not reasonable, then liability in nuisance is strict to the extent that the defendant will normally be liable for harm which is reasonably foreseeable, even though the defendant may have exercised reasonable care and skill to avoid that harm.[1] It may be that compliance with good industrial practice provides powerful evidence that it has not been foreseen that damage would result from activities carried on for some time, but each use will nonetheless be approached on its merits.[2] Once a nuisance is established, this extends to damage to sensitive activities,[3] although that sensitivity will not be relevant in determining the existence of the nuisance in the first place.[4]

1 *Cambridge Water Co v Eastern Counties Leather plc* [1994] 2 AC 264, HL, per Lord Goff at 74D-E.
2 *Savage v Fairclough* [2000] Env LR 183, CA.
3 *McKinnon Industries v Walker* (1951) 3 DLR 577, PC.
4 Para **13.06**.

13.09 The conclusion that liability in nuisance extends only to damage which the defendant could reasonably foresee was confirmed by the then House of Lords in *Cambridge Water Co v Eastern Counties Leather plc.*[1] Although generally concerned with the rule in *Rylands v Fletcher,*[2] that case also considered nuisance and its relationship with both *Rylands* and negligence. Lord Goff, for example, noted that:

> '... if a [claimant] is in ordinary circumstances only able to claim damages in respect of personal injuries where he can prove [reasonable] foreseeability on the part of the defendant, it is difficult to see why, in common justice, he should be in a stronger position to claim damages for interference with the enjoyment of his land where the defendant was unable to foresee such damage.'[3]

1 [1994] 2 AC 264.
2 (1868) LR 3 HL 330; see paras **13.24–13.33**.
3 [1994] 2 AC 264, applying *Overseas Tankship (UK) Ltd v Miller Co Pty The Wagon Mound (No 2)* [1967] 1 AC 617.

13.10 As a footnote to this, it can added that liability for damage which is reasonably foreseeable extends to both natural[1] and man-made hazards occurring on land. A landowner or occupier is under a duty at common law to take such steps as are reasonable to prevent or minimise the risk of injury or damage to a neighbour or to their property of which they knew or ought to have known.[2] Whilst this principle emerged in the context of duties owed to 'downhill' neighbours affected by landslides, it has subsequently been established that it applies 'uphill' as well.[3] The extent of this duty may not be as large as it may first appear to be, however: as it depends on foreseeability, then liability may not arise if the nature or extent of the potential problem could only have been gauged with expert assistance.[4] Analogies can be drawn here with those cases in which a subsequent owner or occupier of land may be found liable for nuisances which he did not create, but has allowed to continue.[5]

1 See para **13.19**.
2 *Leakey v National Trust* [1980] QB 485, CA. See also *Arscott v The Coal Authority* [2004] EWCA (Civ) 892, [2005] Env LR 6, CA (flood damage to properties not reasonably foreseeable when infilling of neighbouring property occurred).
3 *Holbeck Hall Hotel Ltd v Scarborough Borough Council* [2000] 2 WLR 1396, CA.
4 The Court of Appeal differed with the judge at first instance (reported at [1997] 2 EELR 213) in the *Holbeck Hall Hotel* case, ibid, concluding that there was no liability in that case.
5 See paras **13.14–13.23**. The distribution of liabilities between 'owners' and 'occupiers' is also considered in these paras.

Entitlement to sue in private nuisance

13.11 Nuisance is a tort directed at the claimant's enjoyment of rights over land. Actions will therefore usually be brought by freeholders or tenants, or by licensees with exclusive possession.[1] It was long accepted that, in law, a person who has no rights in land affected by an alleged nuisance cannot sue in private nuisance.[2] However, this may leave open the question of precisely what sort of rights will in practice suffice. What was seen as a considerable liberalisation in the courts' approach to this question was introduced by the Court of Appeal in *Khorasandjian v Bush*.[3] In that case, a resident daughter without any formal interest in the property in question was nonetheless considered to have sufficient connection with the land to ground an action in private nuisance. In light of this and at the level of principle, a unanimous Court of Appeal subsequently held in *Hunter v Canary Wharf Ltd*[4] that a 'substantial link between the person enjoying the use and the land on which he or she is enjoying it' is sufficient to confer upon that person that capacity to sue in private nuisance.[5] This decision was overruled.[6]

1 *Newcastle-under-Lyme Corpn v Wolstanton Ltd* [1947] Ch 92, cited with approval in *Hunter v Canary Wharf Ltd; Hunter v London Docklands Development Corpn* [1997] 2 All ER 426, HL, per Lord Goff at 692A-B.
2 *Malone v Laskey* [1907] 2 KB 141, CA.
3 [1993] QB 727, [1993] 3 All ER 669, CA.
4 [1996] 1 All ER 482.
5 Eg, per Pill LJ, at p 498b-c.
6 [1997] 2 All ER 426; see Steele, 'Being There is Not Enough – The House of Lords puts the Brakes on Nuisance in the Home' (1997) 9 JEL 345.

13.12 Following *Hunter* in the then House of Lords, a person affected by an alleged nuisance must have a legal right to exclusive possession in order to bring an action in private nuisance.[1] Mere presence without exclusive possession, or 'substantial occupation' which falls short of exclusive possession, is not sufficient. The application of this principle to cases of shared premises may be complex. For example, where a number of related companies occupy a single building, but the area of each company's occupation is fluid in response to shifts in their activity, then none of the companies may have the exclusive occupation necessary to maintain a nuisance action.[2] It seems, however, that a tolerated trespasser may still retain exclusive occupation and thus the right to bring a nuisance claim.[3] An alternative for other persons affected in such cases may be negligence,[4] although reliance of that tort on fault and the fact that actionable forms of damage are not necessarily synonymous with 'interferences' actionable in nuisance appears to limit the prospect of this.[5]

1 [1997] 2 WLR 684, Lord Cooke of Thorndon dissenting.
2 *Butcher Robinson & Staples Ltd v London Regional Transport* (2000) 79 P & CR 523.
3 *Pemberton v Southwark London Borough Council* [2000] 3 All ER 924.
4 Per Lord Hoffmann at 710A.
5 Eg, see Steele (1997) 9 *Journal of Environmental Law* 345, at 381.

Identifying a defendant

13.13 In *statutory* nuisance, the EPA 1990 provides that the person liable to abatement proceedings is the person to whose act, default, or sufferance the nuisance is attributable.[1] In private nuisance, complex authorities lead to a similar conclusion.[2] The starting point is that responsibility rests on the person in possession and control of the land from which the nuisance originates.[3] Thus, a vendor who created a nuisance but who subsequently dispensed of his interest in the land from which it proceeds remains liable for the damage resulting from his action.[4] An occupier may be liable under these general principles for nuisance created by his agents, servants or even independent contractors.[5]

1 EPA 1990, ss 80(2) and 79(7); paras **14.30–14.35**.
2 See generally *Sedleigh-Denfield v O'Callaghan* [1940] AC 880.
3 Ibid, per Lord Wright, at 903.
4 *Roswell v Prior* (1701) 12 Mod Rep 635; but see further paras **13.20–13.23**.
5 *Bower v Peate* (1876) 1 QBD 321; *Matania v National Provincial Bank* [1936] 2 All ER 633. The latter can be distinguished with the general position in negligence: *Rivers v Cutting* [1982] 1 WLR 1146.

13.14 An occupier of land is also liable for nuisances which he continues or adopts. In *Sedleigh-Denfield v O'Callaghan*,[1] for example, it was held that an occupier of land 'continues' a nuisance if, with knowledge or presumed knowledge of its existence, he fails to take reasonable means to bring it to an end, when he has ample time to do so; and he 'adopts' it if he makes use of the thing that constitutes the nuisance. In that case Lord Wright said that:

> '[The defendant] may have taken over the nuisance, ready made as it were, when he acquired the property, or the nuisance may be due to a latent defect or to the act of a trespasser, or stranger. Then he is not liable unless he continued or adopted the nuisance or, more accurately, did not without undue delay remedy it when he became aware of it, or with ordinary and reasonable care should have become aware of it.'[2]

1 [1940] AC 880, HL.
2 At 904–05. See also *Goldman v Hargrave* [1967] 1 AC 645, PC.

13.15 Railtrack was accordingly found liable for costs incurred by a local authority in cleaning up fouling by pigeons under a railway bridge, a public nuisance, after Railtrack had failed to remediate the nuisance, having had a reasonable time to do so and when it had the means to control and prevent the pigeons from roosting under its bridge. Railtrack's liability for the costs ceased when it offered the local authority access to the bridge to re-install netting to stop the pigeons nesting and, when doing so, fouling the pavement.[1]

1 *Wandsworth London Borough Council v Railtrack plc* [2002] QB 756, [2002] 2 WLR 512, CA.

13.16 Liability for the failure to act does not mean that a defendant must carry out extensive investigations to discover the potential harm from a nuisance. The duty of care owed by the defendant exists only if there is foreseeability and proximity as well as it being fair, just and reasonable to owe the duty. Thus, Scarborough Borough Council was not liable for the loss of a hotel that had begun to slip into the sea following a massive land slip on the council's land. The council had commissioned a report that noted the potential for a deep-seated slip to exist on its land, but had failed to follow recommendations in the report for further investigations. Stuart-Smith LJ concluded that the council's duty was limited to an obligation to avoid harm to the hotel, provided that the council could have foreseen the harm without further geological investigation.[1]

1 *Holbeck Hall Hotel Ltd v Scarborough Borough Council* [2000] QB 836, [2000] WLR 1396, CA; see para **13.19**.

13.17 Statutory or local authorities may also 'adopt' or 'continue' nuisances occurring on their land. However, this must be considered in light of their statutory functions. For example, on the privatisation of the water industry, statutory water undertakers took on certain functions in respect of the prevention of flooding. Whilst these include a power to undertake works, the effect of which could have been abatement of the nuisance, mere failure to exercise that power does not amount to the adoption or continuance of a nuisance.[1] There is no common law duty on such bodies to exercise their power. Equally, they may choose *not* to do so without being negligent.[2]

1 *Dear v Thames Water* (1992) 33 Con LR 43.
2 See also *Stovin v Wise* [1996] AC 923.

13.18 The existence of a statutory scheme may act as a bar to an action in nuisance. In particular, s 94(1)(a) of the Water Industry Act 1991 imposes a duty on a sewerage undertaker 'to provide, improve and extend ... a system of public sewers ... as to ensure that [its] area is and continues to be effectually drained'. The then House of Lords concluded that an individual whose property was flooded by a sewer whilst waiting for the water company to carry out flood alleviation works did not have a remedy in nuisance because the claimant was, in essence, attempting to enforce a duty which arose under the statutory scheme. The appropriate course, therefore, was for the individual to make a claim to the Director General of Water Services following the water company's failure to comply with its statutory duty.[1]

1 *Marcic v Thames Water Utilities Ltd* [2004] 2 AC 42, [2003] 3 WLR 1603, HL.

Natural nuisances

13.19 Landowners may be liable for failing to prevent harm from natural nuisances on their land, that is, 'nuisances which are caused by the operation of nature rather than any act of the landowner'.[1] Thus, a landowner or occupier may be liable for failing to prevent an escape of water[2] or fire[3] if measures to prevent the escape were reasonable in respect of the owner or occupier. The Court of Appeal concluded that the National Trust was liable for failing to stop soil and rubble from a large mound on its land falling onto its neighbour's land because it was reasonable for the Trust to stop the nuisance.[4] Conversely, as indicated above, the Court of Appeal concluded that Scarborough Borough Council was not liable to the owner of a hotel that had had to be demolished after it became unsafe when its lawn and seaward wing slipped into the sea due to a massive landslide. The Court of Appeal concluded that, whilst the council had a report indicating that there may be a deep slip on its land, it did not have a duty to carry out further investigations before preparing remedial measures because this was not within the council's measured duty of care to prevent danger to neighbouring land.[5]

Two recent cases illustrate a governmental authority's liability in respect of flooding. In *Lambert v Barratt Homes Ltd*, Rochdale Borough Council was not liable for not having constructed drainage ditches and a catchpit to stop flooding. Rochdale had sold the lower part of some playing fields to Barratt Homes and had retained the higher part. During its development of houses on the lower part, Barratt had filled in a water course and culvert resulting in rainwater from Rochdale's retained land flooding nearby houses. The Court of Appeal concluded that Rochdale's measured duty of care did not extend to carrying out works to prevent flooding. Instead, its duty was limited to allowing others access to its land, co-operating with any works that were carried out on it and, possibly, carrying out some limited measures. The court noted that even though the council had available finances, it was not reasonable to expect Rochdale to spend them on extensive flood prevention measures because doing so would have meant that the money was not available for other purposes.[6]

In *Vernon Knights Associates v Cornwall Council*, the Court of Appeal concluded that a council was liable to a holiday village which had been flooded during heavy rainfall in November 2006 and September 2008. The council had installed a series of drains, gullies and a catchpit in a dip in the road to prevent flooding but had failed to remove leaves and other debris from the gratings to keep the infrastructure functioning properly.[7] The court stated that the council's measured duty of care required it to take reasonable measures to keep the drainage installation functioning properly. In contrast to *Lambert*, the council had concluded that the risk of flooding had warranted installation of the infrastructure.[8]

1 *Vernon Knights Associates v Cornwall Council* [2013] EWCA Civ 950 [36], CA.
2 *Sedleigh-Denfield v O'Callaghan* [1940] AC 880, 912 (occupier was liable for damage to neighbour caused when a culvert created by a trespasser was choked by l eaves when occupier had continued to use the culvert to drain his fields; '[a]ll that it was necessary to do was to provide a grid that would prevent the rubbish that fell into the ditch from passing into the culvert').

3 *Goldman v Hargrave* [1967] 1 AC 645, [1966] 3 WLR 513, 633-34 (PC) (occupier could easily have put out a fire caused by a lightning strike by spraying it with water).
4 *Leakey v National Trust for Places of Historic Interest or Natural Beauty* [1980] 1 QB 485, 526.
5 *Holbeck Hall Hotel Ltd v Scarborough Borough Council* [2000] 2 WLR 1396, CA.
6 [2010] EWCA Civ 681 [15]-[19].
7 [2013] EWCA Civ 950 [58]-[59].
8 Other remedies may be available in some cases to persons who have suffered flooding. In *Robert Lindley Ltd v East Riding of Yorkshire Council* [2016] UKUT 6 (LC), 2016 WL 2355, the Upper Tribunal concluded that the council was liable to compensate a family farming company for damage from flooding under s 14A(11) of the Land Drainage Act 1991. The council, which was the lead flood authority for the area, and the Environment Agency, had decided to pump floodwater from a village, resulting in the claimant suffering the loss of its carrot crop in a downstream field due to the additional flooding as a result of the decision. Section 14(5) of the Land Drainage Act 1991 provides that a local authority (or drainage board) is 'liable to make full compensation to the injured person' when that person is injured by the exercise of their powers under s 14. Section 14A(11) provides that 'section 14(5) and (6) applies in relation to the exercise by any authority of powers under this section as to the exercise of their powers under section 14'.

Landlords and tenants

13.20 Particular variations of the principles of adopting or continuing a nuisance apply in the case of landlords and tenants. First, if land is held by a tenant, then the tenant may be liable as an occupier, either for creating or for continuing a nuisance. He does not escape liability on the ground that the landlord is also liable, as the landlord may be if the nuisance arises from breach of his covenant to repair.[1] However, where the landlord is liable in respect of a nuisance under the terms of a lease, it may be possible for a tenant to recover under the landlord's covenant.[2] A landlord will continue to be liable after letting for nuisances which he created, or of which he knew or ought to have known before letting, even if the damage occurs after letting;[3] neither is he relieved from liability simply because the tenant has covenanted to repair or otherwise rectify the problem under the terms of the lease.[4] Nevertheless, the landlord may be able to recoup losses under the lease itself. Where a nuisance is caused by a trespasser or by a 'secret and unobservable operation of nature' neither landlord nor tenant is liable unless, with actual or constructive knowledge, he allows the nuisance to continue.[5] A landlord who created the nuisance may also be liable for it despite the fact that he may no longer have power to abate it, or may be unable to abate it without breaking the terms of a lease.[6]

1 *Payne v Rogers* (1794) 2 Hy Bl 350; *St Anne's Well Brewery Co v Roberts* (1928) 140 LT 1.
2 On the limitations of covenants to repair generally, however, see *Quick v Taff-Ely Borough Council* [1986] QB 809, CA.
3 *Spicer v Smee* [1946] 1 All ER 489; *Sampson v Hodson-Pressinger* [1981] 3 All ER 710.
4 *Brew Bros Ltd v Snax (Ross) Ltd* [1970] 1 QB 612.
5 *Wringe v Cohen* [1940] 1 KB 229. See also para **13.13**.
6 *Thompson v Gibson* (1841) 7 M & W 456; *Spicer v Smee* [1946] 1 All ER 489.

13.21 A second situation is where a tenant or licensee creates a nuisance. In such cases, not only might the tenant be liable but so too might the landlord in particular circumstances. Landlords' duties to repair have been mentioned,[1] but landlords may also be liable in respect of nuisances for which express or implied consent has been given. This would include letting or licensing land for a purpose the 'natural and necessary consequence' of which is the creation of a nuisance.[2] It is important to note that this would require an effect on third parties to be a 'necessary consequence', and so activities *potentially* amounting to a nuisance which were properly confined (perhaps by covenants in the lease itself) could not necessarily be deemed to have been authorised.

1 Para **13.20**.
2 *Harris v James* (1876) 45 LJQB 545; *Tetley v Chitty* [1986] 1 All ER 663.

13.22 The liability in nuisance of the owner or occupier of land for the actions of its tenants or licensees may extend beyond these situations, however. In particular, two cases have considered whether an owner or occupier may be liable for tenants' or licensees' actions when they are not even on the land in question. *Hussain v Lancaster City Council*[1] concerned a nuisance action brought by shopkeepers against the local authority as landlord of tenants who had damaged the claimants' property and harassed them. The Court of Appeal concluded that the Master had been correct to strike out the claim on the basis that the acts complained of did not involve the tenants' use of their land and so fell outside the scope of the tort of nuisance.[2] The Court went on to observe that the council could not be liable for acts of nuisance committed by its tenants unless it had specifically authorised or adopted these acts.[3] In light of earlier authorities,[4] this conclusion is no real surprise. What is surprising, perhaps,[5] is the application of these principles in the subsequent case of *Lippiatt v South Gloucestershire Council*,[6] decided by a differently constituted Court of Appeal just two weeks later. The claimant farmer had been affected by travellers who had occupied for four years a strip of land owned by the defendant council, land adjacent to the claimant's farm. Distinguishing *Hussain* on its facts, the Court of Appeal concluded that there was no rule that an owner or occupant can never be liable in nuisance for the actions of his licensees for occurrences away from his land.[7] The action should not have been struck out, as it could be argued that this is a case where such liability could be established, because the nuisance consisted of repeated acts committed on the victim's land, to the council's knowledge, and which interfered with the victim's use and enjoyment of his land. What appears to have distinguished this case from *Hussain* was that: the acts complained of in that case were a public nuisance for which the individual perpetrators could be held liable;[8] the conduct there was not in any sense linked to, nor did it emanate from, the homes where they lived;[9] whilst in *Lippiatt* the presence of the travellers was known to the council and they had been allowed to remain despite complaints; that presence therefore amounted to a 'continuing and potentially injurious state of affairs on the council's land'.[10]

1 [2000] 1 QB 1, CA.
2 Per Hirst LJ, at 23G.
3 Ibid, at 23C-24F.
4 Para **13.14**.
5 Eg, Hunter, 'One Law for Farmers another for Residents on Housing Estates' (1999) 2 *Journal of Housing Law* 85.
6 [2000] 1 QB 51, CA.

7 Per Evans LJ, at 58H-59A.
8 This was not so here, as the travellers had finally been moved on, and were untraced.
9 Per Evans LJ, at 61C.
10 Per Mummery LJ, at 64C-D.

13.23 In *Coventry v Lawrence (No 2)*,[1] the issue arose as to whether the landlord's knowledge of the intended use of premises was sufficient to make the landlord liable if that use did, in fact, result in a nuisance. In a 3:2 split, the UK Supreme Court concluded that the following measures by the landlord did not amount to the landlord's active participation in the nuisance: doing nothing to stop or discourage the tenant from causing a nuisance; trying to mitigate the nuisance; and taking a lead role in defending the nuisance claims. The Court stated, however, that if the nuisance had been certain or inevitable the landlord would have been liable. However, covenants in the lease that the tenant would not cause a nuisance would not have affected whether the landlord was liable for a nuisance nor would the enforcement or lack of enforcement of such covenants.[2]

1 [2014] UKSC 46, [2015] AC 106.
2 Ibid 112-18 (per Lord Neuberger). For the different position in the case of a licensor's liability for nuisances committed by a licensee see *Cocking v Eacott* [2016] EWCA Civ 140.

The rule in Rylands v Fletcher

13.24 Whilst for many years liability under the so-called 'rule in *Rylands v Fletcher*'[1] has been regarded as a distinctive head of liability – perhaps even one developing towards a form of common law strict liability relating to ultra-hazardous activities, as in some other jurisdictions[2] – it was subject to authoritative retrenchment in the House of Lords[3] together, subsequently, with an explicit statement by the Court that the rule should not be abolished.[4] The Court concluded that even though the law of negligence had developed and expanded since *Rylands v Fletcher* had been decided (including a holding by the High Court of Australia that the principles of negligence had absorbed the rule[5]), and even though difficulties in interpreting the rule existed:

- it is just to impose strict liability in a small category of cases;
- abolition of the rule could significantly modify rights that Parliament had assumed would continue to exist;
- a more principled and better controlled application of the rule is preferable to 'stop-go' legal development; and
- even though replacement of the rule with a fault-based rule would assimilate the law of England and Wales with the law of Scotland, it would result in an increased disparity with the law of France and Germany.[6]

It will be remembered[7] that, under the rule, a person who brings on to his land or collects and keeps there something which is likely to cause damage if it escapes, is under a duty to prevent an escape. If he fails in that duty, he is strictly liable to any person suffering loss or damage as a natural consequence of the escape. The rule is limited by the requirement that a defendant is only liable if the keeping of the substance on the land is a 'non-natural use'.[8]

1 (1866) LR 1 Exch 265.
2 Eg, some of the United States: Weir '*Rylands v Fletcher* Reconsidered' (1994) 53 CLJ 216.
3 *Cambridge Water Co v Eastern Counties Leather plc* [1994] 2 AC 264, [1994] 2 WLR 53, HL; Waite, Deconstructing the Rule in *Rylands v Fletcher*, (2006) 18 Journal of Environmental Law 423.
4 *Transco plc v Stockport Metropolitan Borough Council* [2004] 2 AC 1, [2003] 3 WLR 1467 (HL).
5 *Burnie Port Authority v General Jones Property Ltd* (1994) 120 ALR 42 (Australian High Court), cited in *Transco plc v Stockport Metropolitan Borough Council* [2004] 2 AC 1, 4, [2003] 3 WLR 1467, HL.
6 *Transco plc v Stockport Metropolitan Borough Council* [2004] 2 AC 1, 9, [2003] 3 WLR 1467, HL.
7 For a fuller account, see Buckley *The Law of Nuisance* (2nd edn, 1996), pp 51–62.
8 See paras **13.28–13.31**.

13.25 Controversy as to the relationship between liability under *Rylands v Fletcher* and nuisance or negligence, the meaning of 'non-natural use', and whether or not liability under *Rylands* is limited only to damage which is reasonably foreseeable came to the fore in *Cambridge Water Co v Eastern Counties Leather plc*.[1] The defendants in *Cambridge Water* operated a tannery and, over a period of many years, had inadvertently caused quantities of a solvent (perchloroethane – 'PCE') to be spilled on their property. Having percolated both through a concrete surface and underground aquifers, quantities of PCE were subsequently detected in water drawn from a borehole owned and operated by the claimant water company. The levels of PCE detected in the water made it 'unwholesome' for the purposes of public supply after 1 September 1989, when certain European obligations on the UK government were given effect.[2] It was the fact that the water company was statutorily prohibited thereafter from supplying the water, and its consequences, that constituted the damage complained of. At no time was it reasonably foreseeable that PCE would percolate through the underground chalk and affect users of the groundwater.[3] The 'damage' having been done, the water company was forced to re-site its borehole, at a cost of almost £1 million.

1 [1994] 2 AC 264, [1994] 2 WLR 53, HL.
2 Directive 80/778/EEC; SI 1989/1147; current versions at Directive 98/83/EC (consolidated version including Commission Directive (EU) 2015/1787); SI 2000/3184, as amended.
3 [1994] 2 AC 264, 307.

13.26 The claimant's claims in nuisance and negligence were dismissed at first instance on the basis that damage of the relevant type was not reasonably foreseeable, whilst the company's claim in *Rylands* was dismissed on the basis that the activities complained of were not a non-natural use of its land. However, the finding of liability was reversed in the Court of Appeal,[1] on the basis that the claimant had a right to abstract water percolating beneath his land, and the defendant had no right to contaminate the groundwater to which the claimant was entitled.[2] The Court of Appeal's decision was strongly criticised,[3] and then roundly reversed in the then House of Lords.[4] The Court considered two crucial questions: first, whether foreseeability of damage is a necessary element of liability under *Rylands v Fletcher;* and, secondly, the question of non-natural user of land. In addressing these questions, the House clarified the status of liability under *Rylands* as an extension of the law of nuisance to cases of isolated escape,[5] and firmly resisted pressures to extend *Rylands* liability, for reasons including the emergence of well-informed and carefully structured legislation.[6]

1 Reported along with the House of Lords decision at [1994] 2 AC 264, [1994] 2 WLR 53, HL.
2 On the authority of *Ballard v Tomlinson* (1885) 29 Ch D 115, CA.
3 Eg, Weir 'The Polluter Must Pay – Regardless' (1993) 52 CLJ 17.
4 Above, fn 1.
5 [1994] 2 AC 264, 304 (per Lord Goff).
6 Ibid 307; see para **13.24**.

13.27 Given the emanation of liability under *Rylands v Fletcher* from nuisance (as identified by the House of Lords), the conclusion that foreseeability by the defendant of the relevant type of damage is a prerequisite to *Rylands* liability is no surprise.[1] Lord Goff stated that:

> '… it appears to me to be appropriate now to take the view that foreseeability of damage of the relevant type should be regarded as a prerequisite of liability in damages under the rule. Such a conclusion can … be derived from Blackburn J's original statement of the law; and I can see no good reason why this prerequisite should not be recognised under the rule, as it has been in the case of private nuisance.'[2]

In reaching this conclusion certain earlier authorities were distinguished,[3] and considerable emphasis was placed on earlier limitations to *Rylands* liability introduced by the House of Lords itself.[4] These included the requirement that an escape from land under the control of the defendant is also a prerequisite to liability under *Rylands*.

1 [1994] 2 AC 264, 304-305; applying *Overseas Tankship (UK) Ltd v Miller Co Pty The Wagon Mound (No 2)* [1967] 1 AC 617.
2 [1994] 2 AC 264, 306.
3 Eg, *West v Bristol Tramways Co* [1908] 2 KB 14 and *Rainham Chemical Works Ltd v Belvedere Fish Guano Co Ltd* [1921] 2 AC 465.
4 Eg, *Read v J Lyons & Co Ltd* [1947] AC 156.

13.28 The application in law of the non-natural user test seemed to be rather less problematic, in that it was at least indisputably a constituent of liability. However, Lord Goff explored its development from early exclusion of liability from things 'naturally upon the land', to a more 'modern' application to embrace the 'ordinary use of land'.[1] Quoting an earlier authority, he stated that:

> 'It is not every use to which land is put that brings into play [the] principle. It must be some special use bringing with it increased danger to others, and must not merely be the ordinary use of the land or such a use as is proper for the general benefit of the community.'[2]

1 [1994] 2 AC 264, 308.
2 Ibid, quoting Lord Moulton in *Rickards v Lothian* [1913] AC 263, at 280.

13.29 Without attempting any general redefinition, the Court concluded that the use in *Cambridge Water was* a non-natural use. While taking into account any 'general benefit to the community' provided by the tannery,[1] the Court went so far as to describe the storage of chemicals in substantial quantities and their use in tanning as 'an almost classic case of non-natural use'. Authority from other jurisdictions is confirmed by this approach,[2] but it is not so immediately consistent with those authorities in England and Wales which have considered the storage of explosives,[3] and the storage of light metal strips capable of being blown by the wind[4] not to be non-natural uses of land.[5]

1 Which contributed to persuade the judge at first instance, Ian Kennedy J: he described the area in which the tannery was situated as an 'industrial village', hence not a non-natural use, at 272.
2 Eg, a Canadian court has held a landfill site from which methane gas escaped to be a non-natural use: *Gersten v Municipality of Metropolitan Toronto* (1973) 41 DLR (3d) 646.
3 *Read v J Lyons & Co Ltd* [1947] AC 156.
4 *British Celanese Ltd v A H Hunt (Capacitors) Ltd* [1969] 1 WLR 959.
5 But also see *Smeaton v Ilford Corpn* [1954] Ch 450 where use of land for sewerage purposes was held to be non-natural; cf. *Pride of Derby Angling Association v British Celanese* [1953] Ch 149, per Denning LJ at 189.

13.30 The House of Lords subsequently recognised the uncertainty caused by application of the rule in respect of non-natural user. In *Transco plc v Stockport Metropolitan Borough Council*, Lord Walker stated that the rule should apply when an occupier has brought a substance onto his land that he recognises or should have recognised would lead to an 'extraordinary risk to neighbouring property'.[1] Similarly, Lord Bingham stated that the rule should apply when an occupier has brought onto, or kept on, his land 'an exceptionally dangerous or mischievous thing in extraordinary or unusual circumstances'.[2] The Court reaffirmed that the rule should continue to apply to a case such as *Cambridge Water*. In *Transco*, it concluded that a local authority was not liable for the cost of repairing a high pressure gas main in an easement on a neighbouring embankment. The council had used a large asbestos cement pipe to supply water to tenants of 66 flats in an 11–storey tower block. The pipe had fractured, causing water to leak into a former landfill on which the tower block had been built. Water from the saturated former landfill flowed onto the embankment, causing it to collapse and the gas main to become exposed and unsupported. The Court concluded that the council had simply provided a source of water, rather than bringing a substance onto its land that would cause danger or mischief if it escaped. The Court further concluded that the council's use of its land was ordinary and routine and was, thus, outside the rule in *Rylands v Fletcher*.

1 *Transco plc v Stockport Metropolitan Borough Council* [2004] 2 AC 1, [2003] 3 WLR 1467, HL. Per Lord Walker at 2 AC 38.
2 Ibid, per Lord Bingham at 2 AC 12.

13.31 Subsequently, in *Stannard (trading as Wyvern Tyres) v Gore*,[1] the Court of Appeal concluded that the rule in *Rylands v Fletcher* did not apply to a case involving a company that supplied, fitted and balanced car and van tyres at a light industrial estate. An electrical fire at the business when no-one was there caused approximately 3,000 tyres that were haphazardly stored at the rear of the business to burn, destroying neighbouring businesses. The Recorder at the Worcester County Court had concluded that, although the business had not been negligent regarding the start or spread of the fire, it was liable under the rule in *Rylands v Fletcher* because although tyres are not normally flammable, if a fire develops, they may ignite and, if so, burn rapidly and intensely. The Recorder also concluded that the haphazard storage of a large quantity of tyres for the size of the premises posed an exceptionally high risk of danger and was, thus, a non-natural use of land.[2]

The Court of Appeal disagreed. It concluded that the rule in *Rylands v Fletcher* did not apply to the facts of the case because the business had not brought an exceptionally dangerous thing onto its land that had escaped. Instead, the fire – not the tyres – had escaped; tyres are not exceptionally dangerous.[3] The court further concluded the commercial activity carried on by the business was not a non-natural use of the land but was an ordinary and reasonable activity to be carried on in a light industrial estate.[4]

1 [2012] EWCA Civ 1248, [2014] QB 1.
2 See ibid 9-10.
3 [2014] QB 1, 26 (per Ward LJ); ibid 30-31 (per Etherton LJ).
4 Ibid 31 (per Etherton LJ).

13.32 The person who accumulates or keeps a 'dangerous thing' on land is liable whether he is owner, occupier or licensee. The owner or occupier is liable if he expressly or impliedly authorised the accumulation. There has been doubt as to whether an owner of land would remain liable after he has let the land.[1] Given the affirmation that *Rylands* liability emanates from nuisance,[2] it is likely that the same principles would apply here as apply to nuisance itself.[3]

1 Atkin LJ's view in the Court of Appeal in *Belvedere Fish Guano Co Ltd v Rainham Chemical Works* [1920] 2 KB 487, at 502 that liability would remain with the owner is not consistent with Lord Buckmaster's view in the House of Lords: [1921] 2 AC 465, at 476.
2 In *Cambridge Water:* para **13.25**.
3 See paras **13.13–13.23**.

13.33 Liability under *Rylands v Fletcher* is subject to certain well-established defences, including statutory authority,[1] consent, contributory negligence, and acts of third parties and of God.[2]

1 See paras **13.41–13.46**.
2 See *Gore v Stannard (trading as Wyvern Tyres)* [2012] EWCA Civ 1248, [2013] 3 WLR 623, 636.

Public nuisance

13.34 In a legal context so dominated by statutory and private nuisance it is perhaps a surprise that public nuisance – a crime at common law[1] – survives at all. It differs in certain material respects from both private and statutory nuisance, not least in its far looser association with property rights than other causes of action.[2] A public nuisance is an act unwarranted by law or an omission to discharge a legal duty which materially affects the life,

health, property, morals, or reasonable comfort or convenience of a class of
Her Majesty's subjects who come within the sphere or neighbourhood of its
operation.³ Public nuisance may therefore overlap with private nuisance to
the extent that it satisfies the constituent elements of that tort, but affects a
considerable number of persons; alternatively,⁴ it may involve interference
with the safety or convenience of members of the public generally, but does
not involve interference with an individual's enjoyment of their own land.⁵
In order for a person to be convicted of public nuisance it is not necessary to
prove that he had actual knowledge of the nuisance, but merely that he was
responsible for a nuisance which he knew or ought to have known would be
the consequences of activities on his land.⁶

1 *R v Madden* [1975] 3 All ER 155, per James LJ at 157h.
2 Paras **13.11–13.12** and Ch 14 respectively.
3 *A-G v PYA Quarries Ltd* [1957] 2 QB 169.
4 John Pointing (2011) 13 'Public Nuisance: Beyond Highway 61 Revisited?' Environmental Law
  Review 25, 35 ('dividing line between public and private nuisance is sometimes ambiguous or
  unclear in environmental cases').
5 On the latter see paras **13.06–13.10**.
6 *R v Shorrock* [1993] 3 All ER 917, CA.

13.35 The usual remedy for a public nuisance is an injunction. Due to a public
nuisance being so widespread in its range or indiscriminate in its effect, it would
not be reasonable to expect one person to put a stop to it.¹ A local authority is
entitled to sue in its own name for an injunction on behalf of the inhabitants of
its area, under s 222 of the Local Government Act 1972.²

In addition, where a public nuisance causes a person to suffer 'special damage',
that is, damage over and above that suffered by the general public, that person
too may bring proceedings.³ In such cases damages awarded may relate to
personal injury as well as (in the case of obstruction of the highway) pure
economic loss,⁴ although exemplary damages may not be awarded.⁵

1 Per Denning LJ in *A-G v PYA Quarries Ltd* [1957] 1 All ER 894, CA at 908.
2 Eg, *Gillingham Borough Council v Medway (Chatham) Dock Co Ltd* [1993] QB 343.
3 *Benjamin v Storr* (1874) LR 9 CP 400.
4 See generally Spencer 'Public Nuisance – A Critical Examination' (1989) 48 CLJ 55.
5 *Gibbons v South West Water Services* [1993] QB 507. On the situation in private nuisance see
  para **13.53**.

13.36 The Court of Appeal has confirmed that compensatory damages for
personal injuries may be awarded in a public nuisance action. The action had
been brought by individuals who claimed that deformities of their upper limbs
were due to their mothers having been exposed to toxic materials during Corby
Borough Council's reclamation and remediation of a heavily contaminated
former steelworks site in Northamptonshire. In particular, they claimed that
the council had allowed toxic material to escape into the area where the
mothers had lived and had also allowed vehicles involved in the reclamation
to spread contaminated liquids and toxic sludges on the public highway. The
claimants brought actions in negligence and breach of statutory duty as well
as public nuisance. The council had applied to strike out the public nuisance
claim. Dyson LJ rejected an argument that the House of Lords had impliedly

reversed the principle that damages for personal injury are recoverable in public nuisance, stating that the purpose of public nuisance is 'to protect the public against the consequences of acts or omissions which do endanger their lives, safety or health'.[1] He, therefore, stated that it was not open to the Court of Appeal to conclude that damages for personal injury may not be recovered in a public nuisance action.

Following trial, the Technology and Construction Court held that the local authority was liable to 17 of the 19 claimants in negligence, breach of statutory duty and public nuisance provided that each claimant could establish that the local authority's acts or omissions had caused the harm suffered by them.[2] The case subsequently settled for an undisclosed amount before the further proceedings had commenced.

1 *Corby Group Litigation v Corby Borough Council* [2008] EWCA Civ 463, CA.
2 *Corby Group Litigation v Corby Borough Council* [2009] EWHC 1944 (TCC).

Defences

13.37 Some of the constituents of liability in private nuisance, *Rylands v Fletcher* and public nuisance tend to suggest what would normally be considered to be defences in themselves. In particular, the notions of 'reasonable user' or 'non-natural use' operate in defining liability, rather than excluding it. However, certain other defences may be pleaded in addition.[1] These do not generally include that a nuisance existed first and the claimant came to it,[2] nor that the defendant merely contributed to a nuisance rather than being the sole cause,[3] but it may be possible to plead the existence either of an easement to pollute or statutory authority.

1 On *Rylands v Fletcher* specifically see para **13.24ff**.
2 *Bliss v Hall* (1838) 4 Bing NC 183; *Miller v Jackson* [1977] QB 966; see para **13.06**.
3 *Brew Bros Ltd v Snax (Ross) Ltd* [1970] 1 QB 612; *Lambton v Mellish* [1894] 3 Ch 163. In such cases contributors are liable for their own proportion of the total damage: *Pride of Derby Angling Association Ltd v British Celanese* [1952] 1 All ER 1326.

Prescriptive easements

13.38 It is not easy to establish a prescriptive easement to cause a nuisance. In addition to the hurdles which normally arise in relation to prescription claims, several other obstacles frequently present themselves. For example, an easement by prescription must have a lawful origin: it cannot therefore be created if the user was unlawful during any part of the prescriptive period relied on.[1] When an offence under environmental law is committed during that period, perhaps by the escape of prohibited pollution, an easement could not arise.

1 *Green v Matthews* (1930) 46 TLR 206; *George Legge & Son Ltd v Wenlock Corpn* [1938] 1 All ER 37. For judicial approval of the same principle in relation to prescriptive easements to abstract water, see *Cargill v Gotts* [1981] 1 WLR 441, per Templeman LJ, at 446.

13.39 The easement is also limited to the scale of the nuisance (for example, the amount of pollution) at the beginning of the prescription period,[1] whilst the degree of user must remain certain and uniform. Thus, a progressive increase in a nuisance over time will defeat a claim.[2] The period of prescription does not begin to run until the polluting discharge causes damage,[3] and it is also essential that the claimants or their predecessors in title have knowledge of the nuisance.

1 *Crossley v Lightowler* (1867) 2 Ch App 478; *Scott-Whitehead v National Coal Board (1985)* 53 *P & CR 263.*
2 *Hulley v Silversprings Bleaching and Dyeing Co* [1922] 2 Ch 268.
3 *Liverpool Corpn v H Coghill & Son Ltd* [1918] 1 Ch 307; *Scott-Whitehead v National Coal Board* (1985) 53 P & CR 263.

13.40 It is particularly difficult to establish prescription involving noise, odour or dust, none of which would occur continuously for 20 years but which would tend to be intermittent as well as to vary in intensity during that time period.[1] Although such a nuisance need not be continuous throughout the entire 20-year period, there must be sufficient evidence to show continuity. If, for example, no neighbouring business or residence existed to be affected, or if the noise, odour or dust intensified such that it was not a nuisance during the years at the beginning of the 20-year period, prescription does not apply.[2]

The difficulties are illustrated by *Coventry v Lawrence*, in which the UK Supreme Court concluded that the defendant had not acquired a right by prescription to use its land for speedway, stock car and/or banger racing (and, thus, the right to transmit sound waves (noise) over neighbouring property) because the defendants had not established that they had carried out their activities for at least 20 years.[3] However, the Court confirmed that an easement to pollute can also be created by express grant.[4]

1 See David Hart 'Supreme Court brings private nuisance into the 21st century' (2013) 6 *Environmental Liability* 226, 226.
2 See Maria Lee 'Private Nuisance in the Supreme Court: *Coventry v Lawrence*' (2014) 7 *Journal of Planning & Environment Law* 705, 712.
3 *Coventry v Lawrence* [2014] UKSC 13, [2014] AC 822, 859 (per Lord Neuberger).
4 *Coventry v Lawrence* [2014] UKSC 13, 29, [2014] AC 822.

Statutory authority

13.41 The 'residual' character of actions at private law is perhaps most obvious when their relationship with rights under public law is considered, in particular, when a person has a statutory or quasi-statutory authorisation to cause a nuisance. It is well-established that if a statute expressly or impliedly authorises the commission of a tort, then that authorisation is a defence to a tort action.[1] This defence owes its existence to the presumption that Parliament has considered all conflicting interests when determining the appropriate distribution of powers and duties, and has decided that the benefits of the authorised activity will outweigh any adverse side-effects. Where this defence is pleaded, the terms of the statute in question must be examined to ascertain whether the defence exists, with the burden being on the defendant to establish that the nuisance complained of was the inevitable or unavoidable consequence of that which was authorised.

1 *Allen v Gulf Oil Refining Co* [1981] AC 1001, HL; *Department of Transport v North West Water* [1983] 1 All ER 892; revsd [1983] 3 All ER 273, HL.

13.42 It is important to be aware of the limitations of this defence, especially because of the large number and range of statutory permits in environmental law. Defendants should be aware that holding a statutory permit – a planning permission or water discharge consent for example – will not bring automatic immunity: the test is far more rigorous than that. There are two lines of cases. The first sets out the general principles, is expressly concerned with statutory powers (as opposed to powers delegated under statute to grant permits), and relates to the exercise of those powers by statutory bodies rather than by individuals. A useful summary of the defence in this context is set out by Webster J in *Department of Transport v North West Water,*[1] a case which concerned the defendant's liability in nuisance for damage attributable to the performance of a statutory duty to supply water. In those circumstances – the exercise of statutory powers or duties – four propositions were approved by the then House of Lords:

(a) in the absence of negligence,[2] a body is not liable for a nuisance which is attributable to the exercise by it of a duty imposed on it by statute;

(b) it is not liable in those circumstances even if by statute it is expressly made liable or not exempted from liability for nuisance;

(c) in the absence of negligence, a body is not liable for a nuisance which is attributable to the exercise by it of a power conferred by statute if it is not expressly either made liable or not exempted from liability for nuisance; and

(d) a body is liable for nuisance by it which is attributable to the exercise of a power conferred by statute, even without negligence, if by statute it is expressly made liable, or expressly not exempted from liability for nuisance.[3]

1 [1983] 1 All ER 892, approved by the House of Lords at [1983] 3 All ER 273.
2 'Negligence' has a particular meaning in this context, that is immunity is subject to the condition that work is carried out or operations conducted with all reasonable regard and care for the interests of other persons: per Lord Wilberforce in *Allen v Gulf Oil Refining Ltd* [1981] AC 1001, at 1011.
3 [1983] 1 All ER 892, 895 (per Webster LJ).

Effect of planning permission/permit

13.43 The other line of authorities, that in respect of the exercise by individuals of 'rights' under statutory *permits* – 'delegated powers' – is far less categoric, and suggests that the defence will be difficult to establish. As a starting point, it is clear that a public nuisance, and thus by extension a private nuisance too,[1] can result from a lawful act or activity.[2] The main authorities relate to the relationship between planning permission and nuisance,[3] and whilst planning may have characteristics distinguishing it from other environmental permitting regimes, the reluctance to grant to permit holders the same broad immunities as derive from statutory powers and duties applies outside planning cases. In particular, Peter Gibson LJ stated in *Wheeler v JJ Saunders Ltd* that:

> 'The court should be slow to acquiesce in the extinction of private rights without compensation as a result of administrative decisions which cannot be appealed and are difficult to challenge.'[4]

1 Para **13.34**; see also the speech of Lord Cooke in *Hunter v Canary Wharf Ltd* [1997] 2 WLR 684, at 723H.
2 *Gillingham Borough Council v Medway (Chatham) Dock Co Ltd* [1992] 3 WLR 449, per Buckley J at 458–459.
3 *Gillingham*, above, fn 2; *Wheeler v JJ Saunders Ltd* [1996] Ch 19, CA; *Hunter v Canary Wharf Ltd* [1997] 2 WLR 684, HL.
4 [1995] 3 WLR 466, at 480, cited with approval by Pill LJ in the Court of Appeal in *Hunter v Canary Wharf Ltd* [1996] 2 WLR 348, at 360B-E.

13.44 In respect of planning, the *Gillingham* case concerned a local authority's attempt to restrain through a nuisance action the inevitable effects of a planning permission it had itself granted some years earlier for development of a commercial port on a former naval base.[1] In finding on the facts that no nuisance existed, Buckley J drew an analogy with statutory authority. He concluded that whilst a planning authority has no general jurisdiction to authorise a nuisance, it may through the exercise of its planning powers change the character of the neighbourhood so as to render innocent activities which would otherwise have amounted to a nuisance. The question of nuisance then falls to be decided by reference to the neighbourhood with the relevant development in place, not as it was previously.[2] This conclusion, whilst inventive, would in practice seem to enable planning authorities indirectly to authorise nuisances, at least amenity nuisances.[3] Subsequently, however, the Court of Appeal retreated from so broad a conclusion.

1 *Gillingham Borough Council v Medway (Chatham) Dock Co Ltd* [1993] QB 343. See Steele and Jewell 'Nuisance and Planning' (1993) 56 MLR 568 and Waite 'The Gillingham Case: The Abolition of Nuisance Law by Planning Controls' (1992) 4 *Land Management and Environmental Law Report* 119.
2 [1993] QB 343, 360.
3 Paras **13.05–13.06**.

13.45 In *Wheeler v JJ Saunders Ltd1* the Court of Appeal held that a planning consent for the construction of houses for the rearing of 800 pigs did not provide immunity from a subsequent action in private nuisance, despite that nuisance being both an inevitable and an anticipated consequence of the development permitted. Whilst not unambiguously approving *Gillingham,2* the court nonetheless held that the development did not change the character of the neighbourhood sufficient to render the pig-rearing innocent. The same conclusion was reached in a later case which considered the impacts of a licensed landfill site.[3] There was no suggestion in that case that the planning permission cases did not apply to the combination of a planning permission and a waste management licence. Similarly, the High Court subsequently concluded that the use of land for a motor racing circuit did not change the essentially rural character of the area.[4] Despite some remaining ambiguities, the principle was, therefore, that a planning consent was no licence to commit a nuisance, although it may effect a material change in the character of its neighbourhood.[5]

The UK Supreme Court subsequently resolved the issue of the relationship between planning permission and nuisance in a case involving noise from a speedway.[6] Lord Neuberger stated 'that the mere fact that the activity which is said to give rise to the nuisance has the benefit of a planning permission is normally of no assistance to the defendant in a claim brought by a neighbour who contends that the activity causes a nuisance to her land in the form of noise or other loss of amenity'.[7]

1 [1996] Ch 19.
2 See generally Steele 'Private Rights and Planning Consent' [1995] 2 *Web Journal of Current Legal Issues.*
3 *Blackburn v ARC Ltd* [1998] Env LR 469, HL.
4 *Watson v Croft Promo-Sport Ltd* [2008] EWHC 759, [2008] Env LR 43, QBD.
5 See *Merthyr Tydfil Car Auction Limited v Thomas* [2013] EWCA Civ 815 [30] ('grant of planning permission cannot authorise the commission of a nuisance but it may, following its implementation, change the character of the locality [and if so] the question whether activities constitute a nuisance must be decided against the background of its changed character').
6 *Coventry v Lawrence* [2014] UKSC 13, [2014] AC 822.
7 Ibid 849 (per Lord Neuberger).

13.46 In respect of environmental permits, Carnwath LJ (as he then was) rejected an argument that a person who carries out activities in compliance with an environmental permit has a complete defence to claims in nuisance.[1] The case involved claims for odour nuisance by residents of an area neighbouring a landfill. Carnwath LJ concluded that the landfill operator did not have either express or implied statutory immunity from the common-law nuisance claims by virtue of its environmental permit.[2]

1 *Barr v Biffa Waste Services Limited* [2012] EWCA Civ 312 [93].
2 Ibid [41].

TRESPASS TO LAND

13.47 An action for trespass to land can be brought by a person entitled to possession of the land against a person whose unlawful act caused direct physical interference with it. Whilst trespass does arise in environmental contexts,[1] it has not given rise to the same attention as has nuisance, at least in the context of property transactions. A purchaser or vendor will, however, wish to ensure before entering into a transaction that no trespasses continue, or have caused damage such as to affect that property. Trespass does offer some advantages over nuisance, however. For example, it is actionable without proof of damage,[2] and it is also actionable at the suit of a person in possession of land, that is, the person entitled to immediate and exclusive possession. A 'mere' right to property without actual possession will therefore not enable a person to bring an action in trespass: for example a landlord cannot sue for trespass to land in the occupation of a tenant.[3] The interference must be direct, however, and therefore is rather different to the sort of indirect interferences actionable in nuisance.[4]

1 Eg, solid matter deposited in a stream and carried onto another's land: *Jones v Llanrwst UDC* [1911] 1 Ch 393.
2 *Ashby v White* (1703) 2 Ld Raym 938.
3 *Attersoll v Stevens* (1808) 1 Taunt 183.
4 *Esso Petroleum Co Ltd v Southport Corpn* [1956] AC 218, at 242 and 244.

NEGLIGENCE

13.48 There have been fewer reported cases involving environmental claims in negligence than there has been in nuisance. There have, however, been some notable negligence claims in respect of the failure to warn water consumers or users of the potential effects of water pollution,[1] the failure to take adequate steps to protect employees against excessive noise,[2] spraying pesticide on crops contrary to good practice and thereby harming the claimant's bees,[3] failure to take appropriate steps to safeguard residents in the vicinity of asbestos works from the known associated dangers,[4] civil engineers' negligence in providing advice in respect of the remediation of contaminated land,[5] and breach of a duty to take reasonable care to prevent airborne toxic pollutants from remedial works being deposited on public roads with the result that pregnant women were exposed to them.[6] The Court of Appeal has also concluded that prospective purchasers seeking expert views under an ordinary surveyor's contract on the likely impacts on property of noise are not entitled to damages for disappointment, in addition to these for diminution in value, if the surveyor is negligent.[7] This, at least, should provide some reassurance for property professionals.[8]

1 *Barnes v Irwell Valley Water Board* [1939] 1 KB 21; *Scott-Whitehead v National Coal Board* (1985) 53 P & CR 263. See Pugh and Day *Toxic Torts II* (1995) Ch 12. See also *Sutradhar v Natural Environment Research Council* [2006] UKHL 33, HL (British Geological Survey did not owe duty to people who drank groundwater contaminated by arsenic in Bangladesh by publishing report regarding drinking water resources that did not mention arsenic contamination).
2 *Thompson v Smiths Shiprepairers (North Shields) Ltd* [1984] QB 405.
3 *Tutton v A D Walter Ltd* [1986] QB 61.
4 *Margereson v JW Roberts Ltd and Hancock v JW Roberts Ltd* [1996] Env LR 304, [1996] PIQR P 358, CA.
5 *Urban Regeneration Agency and English Partnerships (Medway) Ltd v Mott Macdonald* (2000) 12 *Environmental Law & Management* 24, noted at (1999) 59 *Environmental Law Bulletin* 24. See also *Lambson Fine Chemicals Ltd v Merlion Housing Limited* [2008] EWHC 168, TCC (letter from director confirming no knowledge of further contamination than that specified in environmental consultant's report did not contain actionable misrepresentation).
6 *Corby Group Litigation v Corby Borough Council* [2009] EWHC 1944 (TCC).
7 *Farley v Skinner* [2000] PNLR 441.
8 On the extremely rare split decision of the two-judge Court of Appeal which first heard this case see Murdoch (2000) 2 EG 116.

13.49 The constituents of negligence liability are well known, in that a claimant must establish a duty of care, a breach of that duty, and foreseeable damage resulting from that breach. The clear position of negligence as a fault-based form of liability can limit its utility in the present context, certainly when compared to nuisance.[1] The affirmation that nuisance, negligence and liability under *Rylands v Fletcher*2 are all subject to the same test as to the foreseeability of damage of the relevant type[3] has reduced any putative difference in that one respect at least. It should be noted, however, that when seeking damages in negligence for personal injury it will be sufficient if the defendant could reasonably foresee some 'personal injury', rather than a particular form of such injury,[4] although this will not overcome the difficulties of establishing causation. Unlike the position in nuisance, defendants to a claim in negligence will not be liable in most cases for the acts of their independent contractors,[5] nor will injunctions be available, nor will economic loss be recoverable.[6] As with nuisance, exemplary damages are not recoverable in an action for negligence.[7]

1 Paras **13.05–13.08**.
2 (1866) LR 1 Exch 265.
3 In *Cambridge Water Co v Eastern Counties Leather plc* [1994] 2 AC 264.
4 *Page v Smith* [1996] AC 155; *Margereson v JW Roberts; Hancock v JW Roberts* [1996] Env LR 304, [1996] PIQR P 358. See Steele and Wikeley 'Dust on the Streets and Liability for Environmental Cancers' (1997) 60 MLR 265.
5 Para **13.13**.
6 *Murphy v Brentwood District Council* [1991] 1 AC 398.
7 *Gibbons v South West Water Services* [1993] QB 507.

LIMITATION OF ACTION AND REMEDIES

13.50 The basic limitation period in tort is six years from the date on which the cause of action arises.[1] In the case of pollution or other environmental damage the cause of action only arises when damage has occurred, rather than on the date of the incident which causes the pollution. So, in *Cambridge Water*2 the limitation period ran not from the date on which the solvent was spilled, but from the date on which the polluted water became 'unwholesome', that is, when it was declared such by changes made under water legislation.[3] In the case of continuing nuisances, such as encroachment by the roots of trees, there is a continuing cause of action.[4] In actions in negligence, but not in nuisance or other torts, an alternative limitation period runs for three years from the date on which the claimant or any person in whom the cause of action was vested before him had both the knowledge required for bringing an action and the right to bring it, if those three years end after the initial six years.[5] There is an absolute long stop of 15 years from the date of the defendant's breach of its duty of care.

1 Limitation Act 1980, s 2.
2 Paras **13.08** and **13.22–13.30**.
3 The fact of its 'unwholesomeness' being the damage complained of: para **13.19**. See also *Blue Circle Industries plc v Ministry of Defence* (1996) 6 P&CR 251, *Environmental Law & Management* 165 where damage was held to accrue on the date of discovery of the contamination. See also para **13.49**.
4 *Delaware Mansions Ltd and Flecksun Ltd v Westminster City Council* [2000] BLR 1.
5 Limitation Act 1980, ss 14A and 14B; Latent Damage Act 1986.

13.51 The foremost remedy for a nuisance, in addition to compensatory damages for past nuisance, is an injunction to restrain the defendant continuing to carry out the nuisance. The defendant has the burden of showing why an injunction should not be granted.[1] If, however, the defendant has been granted planning permission that expressly or inherently authorises it to carry out an activity in such a way that the activity causes a nuisance, the grant of planning permission is a relevant factor in deciding whether an injunction should be granted in respect of its strong support for the contention that the activity benefits the public.[2]

Courts have traditionally been reluctant to grant an injunction, with the notable exceptions of *Dennis v Ministry of Defence*[3] and *Watson v Croft Promo-Sport Ltd*.[4] In *Dennis,* Buckley J concluded that the owner of a country house and a 1,400–acre estate in Cambridgeshire should be awarded £950,000 damages for the past and future loss of the estate and amenity and the loss of the estate's capital value. He concluded that the extreme noise caused by flights over and in the vicinity of the estate by Harrier jet fighters from the nearby Royal Air Force base had caused a nuisance since 1984. He stated, however, that the Royal Air Force was phasing out the Harriers, replacing them with other types of aircraft, perhaps at a different location, and that ordering the fighters to be moved would lead to a nuisance being caused in another location.[5] In *Watson,* the High Court had awarded damages for loss of amenity from a noise nuisance emanating from a motor racing circuit in a rural area.[6]

The approach to the grant of an injunction has changed since the UK Supreme Court's judgment in *Coventry v Lawrence,* in which the Court stated that the power to award damages in lieu of an injunction is unfettered, although the courts can lay down factors which can and cannot be taken into account.[7] In particular, the grant of planning permission may support a contention that an activity is for the public benefit. The Court further stated that another factor to consider is the public interest, such as the loss of jobs if an injunction is granted or, alternatively, other persons who are affected by the nuisance.[8] As Lord Clarke stated, however, the principles for granting an injunction 'must be developed on a case by case basis', with each case dependent 'on the circumstances'.[9]

1 *Coventry v Lawrence* [2014] UKSC 13, [2014] AC 822, 855.
2 Ibid [125].
3 *Dennis v Ministry of Defence* [2003] JPL 1577, [2003] Env LR 741, QBD.
4 *Watson v Croft Promo-Sport Ltd* [2008] EWHC 759, [2008] Env LR 43, QBD.
5 *Dennis v Ministry of Defence* [2003] JPL 1577, [2003] Env LR 741, QBD.
6 *Watson v Croft Promo-Sport Ltd* [2008] EWHC 759, [2008] Env LR 43, QBD. The restrictive tests in *Shelfer v City of London Electric Lighting Co* [1895] 1 Ch 287 were disapproved.
7 *Coventry v Lawrence* [2014] UKSC 13, [2014] AC 822, 852.
8 Ibid 856.
9 Ibid 866.

13.52 Injunctions may be sought in public nuisance generally only by governmental authorities, except where an individual has suffered 'special damage'.[1] This remedy is not available in a negligence action.[2] An interim or interlocutory injunction may be sought,[3] as may a *quia timet* injunction in appropriate circumstances.[4] Courts are generally reluctant to close factories by injunction if the defendant can show a good reason to the contrary.[5]

1 Para **13.31**.
2 *Miller v Jackson* [1977] QB 966.
3 Eg, *American Cyanamid Co v Ethicon Ltd* [1975] AC 396.
4 *Redland Bricks Ltd v Morris* [1970] AC 652.
5 *Pride of Derby Angling Association v British Celanese Ltd* [1953] Ch 149; *Shoreham-By-Sea UDC v Dolphin Canadian Proteins Ltd* (1972) 71 LGR 261.

13.53 Damages are assessed on normal principles of tort law, in particular, the court will seek to ensure that the claimant is placed as far as possible in the position it would have been in had the wrongful act not occurred. This would include damages for personal injury.[1] Exemplary damages are not generally available in nuisance, negligence or under *Rylands v Fletcher*,[2] although they may be in trespass where the (very onerous) conditions are met.[3] Equally, whilst damages for pure economic loss are generally not available in negligence,[4] they may be in public nuisance.[5] As an illustration, where waste has been dumped on land, damages have been awarded in respect of diminution of the value of the land, the cost of removing the waste, and compensation for unauthorised use of the land.[6] Loss of amenity through odours has also been calculated,[7] as has loss to fishing rights,[8] and diminution in the value of a residence on the basis that the threat of a nuisance to future purchasers would continue.[9]

1 Although in the case of nuisance this view may demand reconsideration in light of the *Cambridge Water* case.
2 *Gibbons v South West Water Services* [1993] QB 507.
3 *Rookes v Barnard* [1964] AC 1129.
4 *Murphy v Brentwood District Council* [1991] 1 AC 398.
5 *Harper v GN Haden & Sons* [1933] Ch 298.
6 *Whitwham v Westminster Brymbo Coal and Coke Co* [1896] 2 Ch 538; *Heath v Keys* (1984) Times, 28 May.
7 *Dobson v Thames Water* [2011] EWHC 3253 (TCC) (odours from sewage treatment works); see also *Bond v Seale* [1975] 1 WLR 797.
8 *Marquis of Granby v Bakewell UDC* (1923) 21 LGR 329.
9 *Raymond v Young* [2015] EWCA Civ 456 [38].

13.54 Although generally beyond the scope of this work, civil liability for damage to property or persons by the emission of ionising radiation provides an example of the operation of these principles. The Nuclear Installations Act 1965, as amended, provides a regime of control in respect of installations connected to the creation of nuclear energy or the disposal of nuclear waste. This includes statutory strict liabilities for escapes of radiation.[1] It has been established that the Act does not create liability for pure economic loss,[2] a conclusion influenced by the general position described above. More recently, however, it has been concluded that in some cases contamination can cause damage which is compensable under the 1965 Act.[3]

1 Nuclear Installations Act 1965, ss 7–10. The Nuclear Installations Act is being amended by the Nuclear Installations (Liability for Damage) Order 2016 (which was in draft when this book went to print).
2 *Merlin v British Nuclear Fuels plc* [1990] 2 QB 557, where damages for contamination of a house falling short of physical damage and a *risk* of damage rather than actual damage were held not to be recoverable.
3 *Blue Circle Industries plc v Ministry of Defence* [1999] Ch 289, CA.

13.55 In the *Blue Circle* case, as a result of heavy rain in 1989 water contaminated by radioactive matter from the Aldermaston Atomic Weapons Establishment ('AWE') overflowed onto a small part of the adjacent Aldermaston Court Estate, owned by Blue Circle. The radioactive matter did not pose any threat to health although the quantities were above levels permitted under the Radioactive Substances Act. In 1993, negotiations between Blue Circle and a potential purchaser of the estate were discontinued when the contamination came to light. AWE arranged to remove the contaminated material. Blue Circle claimed compensation for the loss of sale and expenses in connection with the incident. At first instance, Carnwath J (as he then was) held that Blue Circle was entitled to compensation. He awarded damages, calculated on common law principles, comprising 75% of the anticipated proceeds of sale, plus the running costs of the site from the anticipated date of sale to the date of the trial, less the value of the site at trial. The 25% reduction reflected the risk that the sale would not have taken place. To this was added the claimant's own clean-up costs. An appeal against this decision failed.

13.56 The case does not disturb the principle that damages for pure economic loss are not recoverable. However, it does add a gloss to what we understand 'physical damage' to be. In particular, it arises if there is a physical alteration in the characteristics of the property which renders it less useful or less valuable. This will be evident in cases where decontamination requires a major engineering operation, for example, involving the removal of large quantities of earth from the site. Damage to property may also occur if the contamination renders the condition of the land unacceptable to the regulatory authorities, even if the extent of the physical change is small. However, if the contamination does not affect the use of the property, make it less valuable, or lead the regulatory authorities to require remediation, it may be dismissed either as de minimis, or not as physical damage at all. Clearly the dividing line between pure economic loss and damage to property may be fine, and the peculiar features of radioactive contamination (which is quite likely to prompt regulatory intervention) may distinguish it from other airborne contaminants, such as dust.[1] The majority of the Court of Appeal regarded the matter of 'stigma' affecting property values as being soundly based in the ordinary principles of damages: once it was established that there had been physical damage, all losses that were reasonably foreseeable and not too remote were recoverable.[2] However, this is a more liberal interpretation of the notion of physical damage than in earlier cases, and may have corresponding implications for recoverability of damages under the torts considered in this chapter.

1 On which also see *Hunter v Canary Wharf Ltd* [1997] 2 All ER 426.
2 [1999] Ch 289, 302. Chadwick LJ regarded entitlement to these damages not as an issue of foreseeability but of causation: at 314.

LIABILITY FOR THE TORTS OF INDEPENDENT CONTRACTORS

13.57 In general, an employer is not liable for the torts of its independent contractor. However, this rule is subject to an exception where the contractor is employed to carry out extra-hazardous work. To be within the exception the activity must involve some special risk of damage or it must be work which, from its very nature, is likely to cause danger or damage.[1] Work which is likely to cause pollution which could affect neighbouring properties or watercourses may fall into this category.

1 *Alcock v Wraith* (1991) 59 BLR 16, [1991] NPC 135.

CAUSATION AND CONTRIBUTION

13.58 In some cases, damage may be caused by two or more parties acting independently, for example, whose groundwater is contaminated as a result of activities of both the previous owner and present owner of a site. Provided that each one is an effective cause, liability for the whole damage falls on each party responsible.[1] It has been held that if it can be proved on a balance of probabilities that nuisance is caused by a plurality of sources, each polluter is liable even though the amount of pollution caused by him does not amount to a nuisance by itself.[2] However, if it cannot be proved on a balance of probabilities from which of two or more sites the contaminants came then, in principle, no liability should attach to those responsible for any of the suspect sites. However, it may be otherwise if all the sites in question are part of a single business operation and it is established on a balance of probabilities that the contaminants came from one of them.[3] If two sources cause *different damage* to the same claimant, each tortfeasor is liable to the claimant only for the part of the damage for which that tortfeasor is responsible. If evidence is not available to apportion the damages, they are apportioned equally between the tortfeasors.[4]

1 *Clark v Newsam* (1847) 1 Exch 131, 140. The claimant cannot recover in total more than the amount of damages awarded. Special rules apply if an individual develops mesothelioma due to having negligently been exposed to asbestos by more than one person: Compensation Act, s 3.
2 *Blair v Deakin* (1887) 57 LT 522; *Pride of Derby v British Celanese Ltd* [1952] 1 TLR 1013, 1023.
3 *Oliver v Mills* 144 Mo 852 (1926).
4 See, eg, *Rahman v Arearose Ltd* [2001] QB 351, [2000] 3 WLR 1184, CA (liability of each tortfeasor is joint but not joint and several when it is impossible to identify precisely the part of the damage caused by each defendant).

13.59 If the claimant's own negligence has contributed to the harm he has suffered, the court will reduce the damages awarded as it considers 'just and equitable having regard to the claimant's share of responsibility for the damage'.[1] That will depend not only on the extent to which the claimant's negligence was a causative factor, but also on his blameworthiness.[2] If there is more than one defendant, the claimant's contribution is established in relation to that of the defendants as a whole, before the relative liability of each defendant is ascertained. In every case, the claimant is under a duty to minimise his loss and will not recover any loss which he could reasonably have avoided.

1 Law Reform (Contributory Negligence) Act 1945, s 1.
2 *Stapley v Gypsum Mines Ltd* [1953] AC 663, per Lord Reid at 682.

13.60 In the event of an accident or pollution giving rise to liability in tort under these general rules, a person who is liable may be entitled to seek a contribution from another party who is also liable for the *same damage* under the provisions of the Civil Liability (Contribution) Act 1978. Under s 1: 'any person liable in respect of any damage suffered by another person may recover contribution from any other person liable in respect of the same damage (whether jointly with him or otherwise).' The court has power to award a contribution to the extent that it considers just and reasonable having regard to the extent of the other person's responsibility. Such a contribution could amount to a complete indemnity. The 1978 Act does not affect any rights to recover under a contractual indemnity.

13.61 In some – albeit a small minority of – cases, in which it is impossible for a claimant to prove the precise cause of the harm suffered, courts have concluded that the claimant must prove only that the defendant's fault made a material contribution to the risk of the harm; it is not necessary for the claimant to prove that 'but for' the defendant's act or omission the harm would not have occurred. Thus, in *Fairchild v Glenhaven Funeral Services Ltd*, employers who had negligently breached their duty to an employee in exposing him to asbestos fibres were liable even though the claimant could not prove which employer had exposed him to the fibre that led to him developing mesothelioma.[1] Causation was established on the basis that the defendant's negligence had materially increased the risk of the claimant developing the disease. A local authority was subsequently concluded to be liable in negligence to a lady who had developed mesothelioma when the authority had materially contributed to the risk of her doing so by negligently exposing her to asbestos when she had attended school many years before, as was an employer that had exposed an office worker to asbestos as she walked around other parts of the factory.[2] The first case involved 'very slight and short term exposure' whilst the second case involved 'relatively light but long term exposure'.[3] In both cases, however, substitution of the 'but for' test meant that the claims succeeded.[4] Parliament had, in effect, codified the test in *Fairchild* for claims for damages for mesothelioma by s 3 of the Compensation Act 2006 following a retrenchment of the test by the then House of Lords in *Barker v Corus UK Ltd*.[5] The result is that in mesothelioma (but not other) cases, a defendant is liable for payment of the full compensation even though other persons or factors may also have contributed to the risk.

In a recent case involving property damage rather than bodily injury, however, HH Judge Reddihough concluded that the 'material contribution to the risk' test could not be substituted for the 'but for' test in a claim in nuisance and negligence in which the claimants alleged that the neighbouring landowner had caused a reduction in the water level of lakes on their land by excavating lakes on the defendant's land. The judge stated that the factual situation in such a case is very different from that in the disease and clinical negligence cases in which courts have substituted the 'material contribution to the risk' test and that the defendants were not liable because the claimants could not prove that it was more likely than not that, but for the excavation works, the lowering of the water level in the lakes on its land would not have occurred.[6]

1   [2003] 1 AC 32, [61]-[62].
2   *Sienkiewicz v Greif (UK) Ltd* [2011] UKSC 10,
3   Ibid [167] (per Baroness Hale).
4   Ibid.
5   [2006] 2 AC 572. That case held that the defendant can limit its liability to the extent of its contribution to the risk. That position applies to all cases involving the material contribution to risk that other than mesothelioma: *International Energy Group Ltd v Zurich Insurance Plc* [2015] UKSC 33.
6   *Chetwynd v Tunmore* [2016] EWHC 156, [33]-[34] (QB).

Chapter 14

Statutory nuisance

INTRODUCTION

14.01 Statutory nuisance legislation is designed to provide a summary procedure for the remedy of a disparate collection of unacceptable states of affairs, most of which put at risk human health or harm the amenity of neighbours.[1] Summary remedies are provided by local authorities and magistrates' courts. They are intended to be speedy, cheap and readily accessible to ordinary persons, as was said of the statutory nuisance proceedings brought by individuals under Environmental Protection Act 1990 ('EPA 1990'), s 82:

> '... the system should be operable by people who may be neither very sophisticated nor very articulate and who may not in some cases have the benefit of legal advice...the hallmarks of the statutory remedy can be summarised in two words: "simple" and "speedy".'[2]

Unfortunately the law has become complex. In terms of practical impact, practitioners are far more likely to encounter statutory nuisance powers than some of the more 'esoteric' pollution controls. The National Noise Survey 2008, carried out by Ipsos Mori for Environmental Protection UK, found that 17% of participants were bothered, annoyed or disturbed by noise from neighbours inside their homes.[3] Indeed, during an eight-year period, parts of the country have seen an increase in the number of noise complaints of over 40%.[4] There has been a consequential growth in statutory nuisance proceedings[5] – a development suggestive of a greater willingness by local authorities to exercise their powers, and a corresponding willingness to challenge the exercise of those powers. Statutory nuisance may have important consequences for land transactions, because land may be acquired (and priced) on the understanding that it may be used for a particular purpose, only for that use to subsequently be limited by the terms of a statutory nuisance abatement notice or order.

1 For a detailed and authoritative examination of the law of statutory nuisance, see McCracken, Jones and Pereira, *Statutory Nuisance* (3rd edn, 2012, Bloomsbury Publishing).
2 Rose LJ, Vice President of the Court of Appeal, Criminal Division in *Hall v Kingston upon Hull City Council* [1999] 2 All ER 609 at 618.
3 Ipsos Mori, National Noise Survey 2008, Published 4 January 2009, https://www.ipsos-mori. com/Assets/Docs/Polls/poll_national-noise-survey-2008.pdf.
4 Department of the Environment, Northern Ireland. Noise Complaint Statistics 2011/2012. http://www.doeni.gov.uk/noise_complaints_statistics_report_2011_2012.pdf.
5 Legal 500 http://www.legal500.com/developments/3069.

14.02 The origin of statutory nuisance is the seminal *Report on an Enquiry into the Sanitary Conditions of the Labouring Populations of Great Britain* of 1842 by Edwin Chadwick, which led to the adoption of various Public Health Acts for the abatement and suppression of nuisance. The law in this field was consolidated in Part III of the EPA 1990. This was amended by the Noise and Statutory Nuisance Act 1993 and the Clean Neighbourhoods and Environment Act 2005, which added further categories to those activities which might constitute a statutory nuisance, and the Environment Act 1995, which created a new statutory system for the remediation of contaminated land (amongst other things, this excludes the application of Part III of the 1990 Act from contaminated land)[1] and also extended the statutory nuisance regime to Scotland.[2]

The impact of statutory nuisance is more obvious on activities being conducted on land than directly on property transactions themselves. However there will be exceptions. First, statutory nuisances may arise from the general 'state' of premises or from accumulations or deposits on them.[3] Questions arise in relation to potential liabilities being acquired by the purchaser on transfer of ownership. Provision was also made under the Housing Act 1996 in connection with 'nuisance neighbours' but this was more a matter of housing regulation than statutory nuisance under the 1990 Act.[4] Certain amendments have already been made in respect of noise emitted at night, although these apply only where the relevant powers have been adopted by a local authority.[5]

1 EPA 1990, s 79(1A); EA 1995, s 57. Generally see Ch 15.
2 Replacing from 1 April 1996 the relevant parts of the Public Health (Scotland) Act 1897 and Part III of the Control of Pollution Act 1974. See also the Public Health (Scotland) Act 2008 which extends the categories of statutory nuisance.
3 For the classes of statutory nuisances see para **14.04**.
4 See also Tromans and Grant (Eds) *Encyclopaedia of Environmental Law*, paras D21–236 – D33–001 re the Noise Act 1996. NB additional powers to control anti-social behaviour are contained within the Anti-social Behaviour, Crime and Policing Act 2014 (not yet in force at the time of writing). Guidance on the control of anti-social behaviour generally is to be found in guidance published by the Home Office – 'Anti-social Behaviour, Crime and Policing Act 2014: Reform of anti-social behaviour powers Statutory guidance for frontline professionals', July 2014.
5 Noise Act 1996, noted at (1996) 8 *Environmental Law & Management* 152; The Noise Act 1996 (Commencement No 1) Order 1996, SI 1996/2219. See DETR Circular 41/97, *Noise Act 1996*; *Noise and Statutory Nuisance Act 1993* (21 July 1997).

14.03 Secondly, landlords may be liable for the abatement of nuisance arising from defects in the structural character of premises.[1] This has obvious implications for the relationship between a landlord and a tenant, for which appropriate provision should be made.[2] Thirdly, and connected, in certain circumstances costs incurred by a local authority in the exercise of its powers to abate a statutory nuisance may be recoverable from the owner of the relevant premises; costs which may be made a charge on those premises.[3] A broad explanation of the framework provided by the amended 1990 Act is therefore necessary, with elaboration of some of its more particular implications for property transactions and those with interests in property.

1 Where abatement is sought in such cases, it is the owner who must be served with the abatement notice: EPA 1990, s 80(2) (b). However, this is subject to limitations in light of the decision of the House of Lords in *Southwark London Borough Council v Mills; Baxter v London Borough of Camden* [2001] 1 AC 1. See para **14.27**.

2 See generally Ch 10.
3 EPA 1990, s 81A; inserted by s 10(2) of the Noise and Statutory Nuisance Act 1993. This provision does not apply in Scotland: EPA 1990, s 81A(10); EA 1995, Sch 17, para 5. See paras **14.58–14.62.**

THE DEFINITION OF STATUTORY NUISANCES

14.04 Section 79(1) of the EPA 1990 as amended provides that the following categories, listed in s 79(1)(a)–(h), constitute 'statutory nuisances' for the purposes of Part III of that Act:

(a) Any premises in such a state as to be prejudicial to health or a nuisance. 'Premises' is defined under s 79(7) of the EPA 1990 to include 'land'. However, this category does not apply to public sewage systems and sewage treatment works.[1] For those premises not otherwise excluded it is only the unacceptability of the state or condition of such premises, not the use or purpose to which they are put which can bring them within this category.[2] Thus a building which was a nuisance only by reason of being used as a hospital for infectious diseases was not within the meaning of the same words in earlier legislation.[3] However, a house inadequately protected from the elements which becomes damp can be premises prejudicial to the health of its occupants,[4] although the design or layout of a premises of themselves cannot be regarded as rendering the state of the premises prejudicial to health.[5] Furthermore, premises with inadequate sound insulation which fail to prevent the penetration of external noise do not fall within this category.[6] If the nuisance or prejudice to health is caused by premises classified as contaminated land, liability under Part III of the Act is expressly excluded.[7] This category does not include noise from vehicles, machinery and equipment in the street (which is expressly dealt with by category(ga)).[8]

(b) Smoke emitted from premises so as to be prejudicial to health or a nuisance. As defined by EPA 1990, s 79(7), 'smoke' includes soot, ash, grit and gritty particles emitted in smoke. This has been held to include the smell of smoke, despite evidence that the 'smoke' emitted was not visible to the naked eye at ground level.[9] There are many exceptions to, and limitations imposed upon this category.[10]

(c) Fumes or gases emitted from premises so as to be prejudicial to health or a nuisance. This category applies only to private dwellings,[11] in contrast to category (d), below.

(d) Any dust, steam, smell or other effluvia arising on industrial, trade or business premises and being prejudicial to health or a nuisance. This category is confined to *emissions* from property. This category, unlike category (a), applies to sewage treatment works.[12]

(e) Any accumulation or deposits that is prejudicial to health or a nuisance. An accumulation is the result of a series of deposits, whether by man, beast, nature or machine. A deposit is the result of a single instance. It covers piles of refuse, ordure or waste material, whether on the street, on a farm, within premises or on the beach.13 It does not need to be permanent.14 In the absence of a nuisance, a pile of material which included dangerous but inert things such as knives or broken glass would not be prejudicial to health.[15] The defence of 'best practicable means' applies on industrial or trade premises (EPA 1990, s 80(7), (8)(a)). Furthermore, EPA 1990, s 79(10) provides that proceedings may not be initiated by local authorities without the consent of the Government in respect of premises subject to Integrated Pollution Control or Local Authority Air Pollution Control under Part I of the EPA 1990, if proceedings might be taken under that legislation or under the replacement regime of the Pollution Prevention and Control Act 1999 (Pollution Prevention and Control Act 1999, s 6, Sch 2, para 6). Any matters constituting a statutory nuisance to the extent that the nuisance consists of, or is caused by, any land being in a 'contaminated state' are excluded from the definition of statutory nuisance.[16] In some circumstances this provision would exclude accumulations or deposits.[17]

(ea) In Scotland (but *not* in England and Wales), the categories of nuisance include 'any water covering land or land covered with water which is in such a state as to be prejudicial to health or a nuisance.'[18]

(f) Any animal kept in such a place or manner as to be prejudicial to health or a nuisance. Keeping may be for a relatively short time; thus keeping pigs from morning until evening without feeding them amounted to keeping them.19 Traditionally the keeping of pigs within a city was regarded as nuisance in itself.20 It can apply where the animals are kept in a public place. Sheep droppings in a market have been held to be a nuisance.21 There seems to be no reason why it should not apply to noise from animals, as Lord Widgery CJ was inclined to accept;22 such noise was however held not to be a nuisance under this head by a predecessor of his, Lord Goddard CJ.23 It is sensible therefore to rely upon category (g) as well in respect of animal noise.24 The defence of best practicable means is available in respect of industrial, trade or business premises (EPA 1990, s 80(7), (8)(a)).

(fa) Any insects emanating from relevant industrial, trade or business premises and being prejudicial to health or a nuisance.[25] The potentially wide scope and apparent value of this category may in practice be severely limited by the exceptions. These include not only pasture land, woodland, and market gardens, but also agricultural units[26] which have been exempted by the Secretary of State or Welsh Assembly.[27] Insects which may be protected or associated with sites protected under nature conservation legislation are usually excepted.[28] The category does not apply to rivers, watercourses, lakes or ponds or land flooded by them. It does apply to sewers and drains.[29]

(fb) Artificial light emitted from premises so as to be prejudicial to health or a nuisance. This category was added by the Clean Neighbourhoods and Environment Act 2005, s 102. The exceptions provided under EPA 1990, s 79(5B) are extensive. They are airports, harbour premises, railway premises (subject to certain exceptions), tramway premises, bus stations and associated facilities, public service vehicle operating centres, goods vehicle operating centres, lighthouses and prisons. The defence of 'best practicable means' applies to light from both[30] industrial, trade or business premises and from outdoor non-domestic[31] sports facilities designated[32] by the Secretary of State or Welsh Assembly. Proceedings may not be initiated by local authorities without the consent of the Government in respect of premises subject to Integrated Pollution Control or Local Authority Air Pollution Control under Part 1 of EPA 1990 or the replacement regime of the Pollution Prevention and Control Act 1999,[33] if proceedings might be taken under those Acts.[34]

(g) Noise emitted from premises so as to be prejudicial to health or a nuisance. Today it is one of the most important categories. It includes vibration. Premises means a separate unit of occupation; thus loud music emanating from a neighbouring flat or bar in the same building would be caught by the subsection. By contrast, tenants could not use this subsection for noise from a malfunctioning water supply system within their own flat. It can be invoked in respect of noise originating in the open provided that it is possible to define distinct areas from which it is emitted and into which it penetrates. Noise is emitted from premises even if it merely passes through them and is not produced therein.35 The provisions of the Noise Act 1996 and ss 60–61 of the Control of Pollution Act 1974 should be noted in relation to night-time noise from dwellings and licensed premises, and construction activities. Pursuant to EPA 1990, s 80(7), (8)(a) the defence of best practicable means applies to industrial trade and business premises. It is a defence to show that the noise was consistent with the requirements of consent or other notice issued under the Control of Pollution Act 1974.

(ga) Noise that is prejudicial to health or a nuisance and is emitted from or caused by a vehicle, machinery or equipment in a street, or in Scotland, a road. This does not apply to traffic noise (the cumulative noise of vehicles moving or waiting to move along the highway), defence forces or political demonstrations (EPA 1990, s 79(6A)). It applies to individual vehicles, so that noise from refrigerated lorries waiting to deliver goods and noise from noisy car stereo systems is included. The defence of best practicable means applies to industrial, trade and business activities. 'Statutory undertakers' who supply water, gas, and electricity have powers granted by Parliament to carry out certain works. They are not guilty of nuisance in exercising those powers provided that they cause no more collateral harm to the community than is reasonably necessary; Special provisions under EPA 1990, s 80A as to service of notices apply.

(h) Any other matter declared by any enactment to be a statutory nuisance. This includes certain matters in relation to watercourses, and structures used for human habitation that are in such a condition as to be prejudicial to health.[36] The defence of best practicable means does not apply37 to this category.

1 *East Riding of Yorkshire Council v Yorkshire Water Services* [2000] Env LR 113 and *Hounslow LBC v Thames Water Utilities Ltd* [2003] EWHC (Admin); [2004] QB 212 per Scott Baker LJ at [62].
2 *R v Parlby* (1889) 22 QBD 520.
3 *Metropolitan Asylum District Managers v Hill* (1881) 6 App Cas 193.
4 *Issa v London Borough of Hackney* [1997] 1 All ER 999; [1997] Env LR 157, CA. On the many physical states which are capable of supporting a finding that the premises are prejudicial to health see McCracken, Jones and Pereira, *Statutory Nuisance* at para 1.29.

5 *Birmingham City Council v Oakley* [2001] 1 AC 617.

6 *R (Vella) v London Borough of Lambeth* [2005] EWHC 2473 (Admin); [2006] Env LR 33. For a discussion about the conflicting case law which appeared to exist on this point see McCracken, Jones and Pereira, *Statutory Nuisance* at paras 1.31–1.33.

7 EPA 1990, s 79(1A), in force from 1 April 2000: para **15.38**. For a discussion of the contaminated land exception see McCracken, Jones and Pereira, *Statutory Nuisance* at paras 1.91–1.100. For an illustration of the use of nuisance powers in such cases before this exclusion see *Ministerial Planning Appeal Decision Ref T/APP/K1745/A/94/233729/P7*, noted at [1994] JPL 864.

8 *Haringey London Borough Council v Jowett* (1999) 32 HLR 308; [1999] EHLR 410.

9 *Griffiths v Pembrokeshire County Council* [2000] Env LR 622.

10 The following are excluded from the category: smoke from the chimneys of private dwellings within smoke control areas (s 79(3)(i)); dark smoke from industrial or trade premises or from chimneys associated with buildings or fixed plants (s 79(3)(ii) and (iv)); crown defence service property (s 79(2)) and smoke from railway steam engines (s 79(3)(iii)). Where the smoke comes from a chimney and the 'best practicable means' have been used, there shall be a defence (s 80(8)(b)). EPA, s 79(10) provides that proceedings may not be initiated by local authorities without the consent of the Secretary of State in respect of premises subject to Integrated Pollution Control or Local Authority Air Pollution Control if proceedings could be taken under Part I of the EPA 1990 or under the replacement regime of the Pollution Prevention and Control Act 1999. By virtue of EPA 1990, s 79(7), the definition provisions of the Clean Air Act 1993 apply.

11 EPA 1990, s 79(3)(4).

12 *Hounslow LBC v Thames Water Utilities Ltd* [2003] EWHC (Admin); [2004] QB 212 per Scott Baker LJ at [70] and Pitchford J at [54].

13 *R v Carrick District Council, ex p Shelley* [1996] Env LR 273.

14 This was so even under waste control under the Control of Pollution Act 1974: *R v Metropolitan Stipendiary Magistrate, ex p London Waste Regulation Authority* [1993] 3 All ER 113, DC.

15 *Coventry City Council v Cartwright* [1975] 2 All ER 99; [1975] 1 WLR 845.

16 EPA 1990, s 79(1A); EA 1995, Sch 22, para 89.

17 See *Westley v Hertfordshire County Council* [1998] JPL 947, which concerned obstruction of a bridleway by building works.

18 Inserted by s 111 of the Public Health (Scotland) Act 2008. Section 112 provides a power for the Scottish Minister by regulations to add new categories of statutory nuisance and amend the descriptions of existing classes.

19 *Steers v Manton* (1893) 57 JP 584.

20 *R v Wigg* (1705) 2 Salk 460.

21 *Draper v Sperring* (1861) 142 ER 392.

22 *Coventry City Council v Cartwright* [1975] 1 WLR at 850G.

23 *Galer v Morrissey* [1955] 1 WLR 110.

24 In *Budd v Colchester Borough Council* [1999] Env LR 739 the Court of Appeal assumed that the barking of greyhounds could be a nuisance but it is not clear whether they did so based upon (f) or (g). It appears to have been common ground in *Manley v New Forest District Council* [1999] PLR 36; [2000] EHLR 113 that noise from barking dogs could come within s 79(g), and in *Manley v New Forest District Council (No 2)* the Divisional Court noted that that it could come within the categories set out in s 79(1) without specifying which.

25 This category was added by the Clean Neighbourhoods and Environment Act 2005, s 101.

26 Land occupied as a unit for purposes defined as agricultural under s 109 of the Agriculture Act 1947; EPA 1990, s 79(7D).

27 EPA 1990, s 79(7C), (7D) and see for England the Statutory Nuisances (Insects) Regulations 2006, SI 2006/770, which exempt various categories of agricultural units regarded as having particular economic value.

28 EPA 1990 s 79(5A) (insects included in the Wildlife and Countryside Act 1981 Schedule 5, unless included only under s 9(5) of that Act) and s 79(7C)(e) (sites of special scientific interest).

29 EPA 1990, s 79(7C); 'drain' is defined in the Water Resources Act 1991.

30 EPA 1990, ss 80(8)(aza), 82(10)(aza).

31 EPA 1990, ss 80(8C), 82(10A). Domestic premises are those used wholly or mainly as a private dwelling and include for these purposes land enjoyed with a private dwelling.

32 EPA 1990, ss 80(8B), 82(10A) designation may be by inclusion in a list prepared by a specified body (such as Sport England).
33 PPCA 1990, s 6 and Sch 2, para 6.
34 EPA 1990, s 79(10).
35 Network Housing Association v Westminster City Council [1995] Env LR 176.
36 Public Health Act 1936, ss 141 and 259(1); Transport Act 1968, s 108. For further categories see McCracken, Jones and Pereira, *Statutory Nuisance* at paras 1.70–1.77.
37 EPA 1990, s 80(7) and (8).

14.05 A statutory nuisance can be established in two ways: that the matter complained of is either 'prejudicial to health' or it is a nuisance.

'Prejudicial to health'

14.06 'Prejudicial to health' is defined by s 79(7) of the EPA 1990 as 'injurious or likely to cause injury to health'.[1] It is broad enough to apply to that which interferes with the 'vigour and vitality' of the well.[2] It applies to making sick people worse. Guidance from bodies such as the World Health Organisation,[3] the experience of relevant professionals and common sense will all contribute to what is ultimately a judgment.

1 This test is different from 'fitness for habitation': *Salford City Council v McNally* [1976] AC 379 at 389.
2 *Malton Board of Health v Malton Manure Co* (1879) 4 Ex D 302.
3 In *Murdoch v Glacier Metal Co Ltd* [1998] Env LR 732 such material was held to be relevant but not necessarily determinative.

14.07 Injury to the *health* of a person must be likely; likelihood of *personal injury* is not sufficient[1]: '... the underlying conception ... is ... a threat to health in the sense of a threat of disease, vermin or the like'.[2] Risk of injury from broken glass was held not to be prejudicial to health; likewise, a steep and dangerous staircase, liable to cause accidents, has been held not to be prejudicial to health.[3] 'It cries out from the page that the target of the legislation was disease not physical injury.'[4] Interference with comfort is not sufficient to amount to prejudice to health, although it may amount to nuisance.[5] The term has a broad meaning. The effects on health may be indirect. Thus, sleeplessness has been held to be injurious to health.[6] The test however is objective. It depends not on the particular personal circumstances of the individual affected, but on the potential effects on health generally.[7] This type of statutory nuisance protects the health of anyone put at risk by the relevant state of affairs. Thus, it protects the occupants of a house against the conditions of the house; the state of a house can be prejudicial to the health of its occupants.[8] In this respect it is, in England and Wales, different from the second limb, mere nuisance, which only protects neighbours or the nearby community, but not those on the land from which the nuisance originates. Courts are not entitled to form a view without expert evidence or in rejection of unanimous expert evidence, but the relevant professional experience is not confined to the medical profession.[9] The expertise of others such as building inspectors and environmental health officers is recognised by the courts.[10] Courts will disregard the opinions about this of those with no relevant expertise; such people may, of course, give factual evidence of their observations.

1 There are suggestions in some nineteenth-century cases that the equivalent provision of the 1875 Act would apply to premises 'so dilapidated as to be a source of danger to life or limb': see *R v Parlby* (1889) 22 QBD 520. Such premises may well today be regarded as a second limb statutory nuisance if they are hazardous to passers-by.
2 *Coventry City Council v Cartwright* [1975] 1 WLR 845, DC, per Lord Widgery at 849B–C.
3 *R v Bristol City Council, ex p Everett* [1999] 1 WLR 1170, CA.
4 *R v Bristol City Council, ex p Everett* [1999] 1 WLR 1170, CA per Lord Buxton at 1181. Buxton LJ made this remark referring to the Public Health Act 1875, which he regarded as a pointer to the scope of the EPA 1990, Pt III.
5 *Salford City Council v McNally* [1976] AC 379, HL; see Lord Wilberforce at 389E and Lord Edmund Davies at 393G.
6 *Lewisham v Fenner* [1995] 248 ENDS Report 44.
7 *Cunningham v Birmingham City Council* [1998] Env LR 1. A kitchen was harmful to an autistic child. It was otherwise acceptable. The relevant test was not met: *Robb v Dundee* [2002] SC 301. It is not necessary, however, that actual injury has been caused to someone's health.
8 *Salford City Council v McNally* [1976] AC 379, HL, see Lord Wilberforce at 389A.
9 *O'Toole v Knowsley* [1999] Env LR D29; *Patel v Mehtab* (1980) 5 HLR 78. *Southwark London Borough Council v Simpson* [1999] Env LR 553.
10 *Southwark London Borough Council v Simpson* [1999] Env LR 553.

'Nuisance'

14.08 Nuisance is unacceptable interference with the personal comfort or amenity of neighbours or the nearby community. The principle is '[In the] use and occupation of land and houses ... [of] give and take, live and let live'.[1] Lord Millett stated that: 'The governing principle is that of good neighbourliness, and this involves reciprocity. A landowner[2] must show the same consideration for his neighbour as he would expect his neighbour to show for him'.[3]

1 *Bamford v Turnley* (1860) 3 B & s 62 at 83–84: see Ch 13 and *Coventry v Lawrence (No 1)* [2014] AC 822.
2 Or anyone else using land (see Baron Bramwell in *Bamford v Turnley*, above, and *Cambridge Water Co v Eastern Counties Leather plc* [1994] 2 AC 264 at 299: 'the principle of give and take between neighbouring occupiers of land'.
3 *Baxter v London Borough of Camden* [2000] Env LR 112 at 126.

14.09 The fundamental principle said to apply to the second limb, but not applicable to the first limb is that 'a nuisance cannot arise if what has taken place affects only the person or persons occupying the premises where the nuisance is said to have taken place'.1 The principle has, however, been doubted, at least for Scotland, by an Extra Division of the Court of Session.[2]

1 *National Coal Board v Neath Borough Council* [1976] 2 All ER 478 at 482.
2 *Robb v Dundee City Council* [2002] SC 301.

14.10 There are two important differences between common law1 and statutory nuisance. First it has been held that the term has, in one sense, a narrower meaning in the statutory context than it does at common law. The existence of circumstances capable of amounting to a common law nuisance is, in one respect, a necessary but not a sufficient condition for the existence of this first limb of statutory nuisance.2 The development of statutory nuisance in public health legislation3 suggests that statutory nuisance, unlike common law nuisance, does not deal with harm to property unless that causes harm to people's comfort or amenity4: 'The legislature intended to strike at...anything which diminished the comfort of life though not injurious to health [and at anything which would in fact injure health]'.5 Secondly, the test is also wider. There is no need for the victim to have property rights of the kind required (in the majority's opinion in Hunter v Canary Wharf Ltd6) before the common law provides a remedy in private nuisance. Private nuisance at common law protects private property rights; statutory nuisance protects people not property.

1 Common law nuisance may be public or private. There is an interesting discussion of their relationship to each other and statutory nuisance in the Opinion of Lord Bingham of Cornhill in *R v Rimmington* [2005] UKHL 63, [2006] 1 AC 459 [5]–[31]. Public nuisances cause common injury to members of the public by interference with rights enjoyed in common by them. They are crimes punishable on indictment.
2 *National Coal Board v Thorne* [1976] 1 WLR 543, DC.
3 Nuisances Removal Act 1855 and Public Health Acts 1875–1936.
4 *National Coal Board v Thorne* [1976] 1 WLR 543, DC. See also *Robb v Dundee* [2002] SC 301.
5 *Bishop Auckland Local Board v Bishop Auckland Iron and Steel* Co (1880) 10 QB 138 at 141 endorsed by Lord Wilberforce in the House of Lords in *Salford City Council v McNally* [1976] AC 379 at 389E.
6 [1997] AC 655.

14.11 Relevant considerations for assessing whether something amounts to a nuisance include the following: the character of the neighbourhood, the time, duration, frequency, social convention, importance and value to the community of the activity in question, and the difficulty in avoiding external effects of activity.[1] Planning permissions, and potentially other statutory powers or licences, may in certain circumstances affect the 'character of the neighbourhood'.[2] This possibility would apply only to cases of 'amenity' nuisance, rather than physical damage, and has in any event been subject to restrictive interpretation by the courts.[3]

1 For a detailed examination of the various factors see McCracken, Jones and Pereira, *Statutory Nuisance* at paras 1.12–1.20.
2 See *Gillingham Borough Council v Medway (Chatham) Dock Co Ltd* [1993] QB 343; *Wheeler v JJ Saunders Ltd* [1995] 2 All ER 697; *Hunter v Canary Wharf* [1996] 1 All ER 482; *Roper v Tussauds Theme Park Ltd* [2007] EWHC 624, [2007] Env LR 31 and *Coventry (t/a RDC Promotions) v Lawrence* [2014] UKSC 13.
3 *Blackburn v ARC Ltd* [1998] Env LR 469; *London Borough of Camden v London Underground Ltd* [2000] Env LR 369 (by analogy).

Duty to serve an abatement notice

14.12 Section 80(1) of the EPA 1990 provides that:

> '[W]here a local authority is satisfied that a statutory nuisance exists, or is likely to occur or recur, in the area of the authority, the local authority shall serve ... an abatement notice.'

This was interpreted as a duty (in other words 'shall' means 'must' in this context) by Carnwath J in *R v Carrick District Council, ex p Shelley*.[1] In that case, two sewage discharges permitted by consents from the National Rivers Authority (the precursor to the Environment Agency) were perceived nevertheless to be a statutory nuisance by the local authority. Since the consents were being appealed by the water authority, the local authority decided to 'monitor the situation', ie do nothing for the time being. This was held to be in breach of its obligations under s 80(1) of the EPA 1990.

1 [1996] Env LR 273 cited with apparent approval in *The Barns v Newcastle Upon Tyne City Council* [2005] EWCA Civ 1274.

14.13 An earlier case, Nottingham Corpn v Newton,1 held that in a case where another route was available to the local authority the 'shall' did not impose a duty to take the EPA 1990 route. The Divisional Court held that the authority in question could have acted under the Public Health Act 1936 (a predecessor of the 1990 Act) or the Housing Act 1957 to deal with a house that was in a state prejudicial to health. Once it had chosen which route to take, there was a duty to go down that route. In both Ex p Shelley and Nottingham two schemes of enforcement existed that could be employed in order to address the nuisance. However, the situations were distinguishable because in Ex p Shelley only one scheme of enforcement, that of statutory nuisances under the EPA 1990, was open to the local authority; the other scheme was a matter for the Environment Agency over which the local authority would have no control.

1 [1974] 1 WLR 923 at 927A–C. This case was not cited in the Ex p Shelley judgment.

14.14 Section 86 of the Clean Neighbourhoods and Environment Act 2005 subsequently inserted provisions into s 80 of the EPA 1990. The provisions deal only with statutory nuisance falling within paragraph (g) of s 79(1) of the EPA (that is 'noise emitted from premises so as to be prejudicial to health or a nuisance'). The amended s 80 now provides in respect of this particular type of nuisance that, where it is satisfied that a statutory nuisance exists or is likely to occur or recur in its area, a local authority may, as an *alternative* to its duty to serve an abatement notice, 'take such other steps as it thinks appropriate for the purpose of persuading the appropriate person to abate the nuisance or prohibit or restrict its occurrence or recurrence' (sub-s (2A)(b)). Where it does so the Secretary of State advises that a record for its reason for so doing must be kept.1

1 Para 34 of the DEFRA *Guidance on Sections 69 to 81 and Section 86 of the Clean Neighbourhoods and Environment Act 2005*.

14.15 This provision is intended to encompass discussion and negotiations between the local authority and the nuisance-maker with the aim of avoiding the service of an abatement notice. The Secretary of State considers that '[i]n some circumstances an informal approach will engender greater co-operation and a faster resolution of a noise nuisance. Sometimes it can be counterproductive and/or unnecessary to issue an abatement notice – for example, the notice may provoke one party to withdraw from negotiations, actually aggravate a situation, or enable the person responsible to avoid having to abate the problem by, for example, holding a one-off noisy party. The option to defer serving an abatement notice for up to seven days in order to pursue specific steps may support resolution without recourse to a formal abatement notice.'1 A local authority would clearly have to exercise caution before pursuing this 'alternative route' in instances where the 'noise emitted from premises' is prejudicial to health, as opposed to noise which is merely a nuisance. Where the noise nuisance is prejudicial to health, a decision to defer the service of the notice pending discussions or negotiations clearly risks extending the time during which the health of an affected person is prejudiced.

1 Para 36 of the *DEFRA Guidance on Sections 69 to 81 and Section 86 of the Clean Neighbourhoods and Environment Act 2005.*

14.16 If the authority should choose to adopt the alternative course, there is then provision for a 'relevant period' (stated in sub-s (2D) to be 'seven days starting with the day on which the authority was first satisfied that the nuisance existed, or was likely to occur or recur'). The Secretary of State advises local authorities that 'it will usually be appropriate to advise the person responsible for the nuisance in writing that a noise nuisance exists or is likely to occur or recur, and of the decision to defer service of an abatement notice provided the nuisance is dealt with within seven days. The local authority may also inform the noisemaker that if the nuisance continues after seven days of the notification of deferral, an abatement notice will be served. Outlining the consequences of an abatement notice in this initial letter advising of the decision to defer is recommended.'[1]

14.17 After the expiry of the seven-day period, the authority shall then serve the notice on the 'appropriate person' (defined in sub-s (2E) as 'the person on whom the authority would otherwise serve the notice had it chosen to serve straight away') if either of two conditions are satisfied – that 'the authority is satisfied at any time before the end of the relevant period that the steps taken will not be successful in persuading the appropriate person to abate the nuisance or prohibit or restrict its occurrence or recurrence' (sub-s (2C)(a)), or 'the authority is satisfied at the end of the relevant period that the nuisance continues to exist, or continues to the likely to occur or recur, in the area of the authority'(sub-s (2C)(b)). This appears to mean, although it is not entirely clear, that, unless the authority are satisfied that the discussions and/or negotiations are successful at the end of the seven-day period so that the original nuisance has been abated and/or is unlikely to recur, they must then issue the abatement notice; they do not need to do so otherwise. This view appears to be supported by the guidance given by DEFRA.2 However, it is not necessarily true that the nuisance actually has to be abated by the conclusion of the seven-day period. The provision appears to mean that the local authority need only be satisfied that the nuisance will (at some point) be abated in order for the service of a notice to be avoided.

1 Para 37 of the DEFRA *Guidance on Sections 69 to 81 and Section 86 of the Clean Neighbourhoods and Environment Act 2005.*

2 Paras 38–39 of the DEFRA *Guidance on Sections 69 to 81 and Section 86 of the Clean Neighbourhoods and Environment Act 2005.*

14.18 Section 80(1)(a) of the EPA 1990 provides that an abatement notice may seek the abatement, prohibition or restriction of the nuisance. In our view the power to restrict rather than abate should be used only rarely.

14.19 In the case of certain activities within the Environment Agency's jurisdiction, the position is subject to s 79(10) of the EPA 1990. In cases where the nuisance arises from smoke; dust, smell or other effluvia arising on industrial, trade or business premises; accumulations or deposits; artificial light emitted from premises; or noise (or, in Scotland only, noise emitted from a vehicle, machinery or equipment in the street),[1] a local authority's duty to abate a statutory nuisance is subject to the consent of the Secretary of State where enforcement action could be subject to enforcement action under the integrated pollution prevention and control system.[2] This restriction does not apply, however, to enforcement action taken by an individual.[3]

1 Corresponding to the EPA 1990, s 79(1)(b), (d), (e), (fb), (g) and, in Scotland, (ga).
2 EPA 1990, s 79(10), as amended by the EA 1995, Sch 17, para 2(d); Pollution Prevention and Control Act 1999, Sch 2, para 6; The Pollution Prevention and Control (England and Wales) Regulations 2000, SI 2000/1973, Sch 10, para 7.
3 See s 82 of the EPA 1990.

THE POWER TO SEEK INJUNCTIONS

14.20 This power is provided by s 81(5) of the EPA 1990. If the abatement by other means is considered by the local authority to be inadequate, the authority may take proceedings in the High Court (ie seek an injunction). A failure to comply with the terms of a court injunction is a contempt of court, for which the offender may be fined and imprisoned. The defendant is provided with an additional defence, namely that he has a notice or a consent under the Control of Pollution Act 1974. We also consider it likely that the employment of best practicable means by the defendant would often be accepted by the High Court as a reason for not granting an injunction.

14.21 The authority must be of the opinion that criminal proceedings are inadequate. However, if the power to reach such an opinion has been properly delegated, it can be reached by a committee, sub-committee or officer of the council. Note that the decision cannot be made by a single member.[1] The decision ordinarily should be taken before a claim is issued but it has been held to be acceptable to take it a few days afterwards.[2] Any delegation to a committee or officer cannot however be made retrospectively.[3]

1 *R v Secretary of State for the Environment, ex p London Borough of Hillingdon* [1986] 1 WLR 192.
2 *Warwick RDC v Miller-Mead* [1962] 1 All ER 212.
3 *Bowyer, Philpott and Payne Ltd v Mather* [1919] 1 KB 419.

14.22 In the case of Vale of White Horse District Council v Allen & Partners1 it was held that it must be the case that criminal proceedings are considered inadequate, not just that High Court proceedings would be more convenient.2

1 [1997] Env LR 212.
2 It was further held in that case that a local authority's power to seek injunctions generally under Local Government Act 1972, s 222(1), was not free-standing in relation to statutory nuisance. This was despite Court of Appeal observations that the powers were concurrent: see Wyre Forest District Council v Bostock [1993] Env LR 235. Bell J held in Vale of White Horse that s 222(1) was an enabling power to allow an authority to sue under EPA s 81(5) in its own name.

14.23 It is not possible for a local authority to seek an injunctive remedy under s 81(5) unless it has first served an abatement notice under s 80(1). In *The Barns v Newcastle Upon Tyne City Council*,[1] it was held that the provisions in the Act that were intended to be *consecutive* steps when dealing with a statutory nuisance. First the authority should serve the abatement notice; where there was no compliance, there should be either prosecution in the magistrates' court or self-help by the local authority requiring the wrongdoer to compensate the local authority for its expenses; as a last resort, there was action in the High Court for an injunction under s 81(5). Read literally, some of the strictly speaking *obiter* reasoning in *The Barns v Newcastle Upon Tyne City Council* would appear to create a number of quite cumbersome obstacles for local authorities seeking effective enforcement of the statutory nuisance regime. *East Dorset District Council v Eaglebeam Ltd & Ors*[2] is therefore an important decision for local authorities.

1 [2005] EWCA Civ 1274.
2 [2006] EWHC 2375 (QB).

14.24 In *East Dorset District Council v Eaglebeam Ltd & Ors*,[1] the court held that where an abatement notice had been served on a company of which an individual was the owner and director, a local authority was entitled to issue proceedings for injunctive relief pursuant to s 81(5) against the individual notwithstanding that the individual had not been served with an abatement notice in his personal capacity. The rationale being that the underlying principle in *The Barns v Newcastle upon Tyne City Council* was that a person should first be served with an abatement notice in order that an opportunity to abate the nuisance be given. Where, as in the case of a director, the individual has been afforded this opportunity, by virtue of the service of the abatement notice on the company, it was not unfair for the local authority to seek injunctive relief against the individual in circumstances where the service of an abatement notice on the company had failed satisfactorily to abate the nuisance.

The court also rejected the submission that the injunction proceedings were an abuse of process when there was an on-going appeal in the magistrates' court against the abatement notice issued by the local authority. Similarly, the court did not consider that *The Barns v Newcastle upon Tyne City Council* meant that in addition to serving a notice it was necessary for a local authority actually to have prosecuted or attempted self help before it could seek an injunction. Rather it had to demonstrate that such options were not adequate to deal with the problem.

1 [2006] EWHC 2375 (QB) (26 July 2006).

The abatement notice

14.25 An abatement notice may do any or all of the following:

(a) require the abatement of the nuisance or prohibit or restrict its occurrence or recurrence;
(b) require the execution of such works and the taking of such steps as may be necessary for any of these purposes.

An abatement notice must usually specify the time or times within which it must be complied with.[1] This is clearly dependent on, amongst other things, the nature of the nuisance and the particulars of abatement. A reasonable time, depending on the circumstances, must be allowed for abatement.[2] Whilst the failure to provide a reasonable time for compliance could enable a court to vary a notice on appeal, it would not be a proper basis on its own for an adjournment of summary proceedings for breach of the notice.[3] A distinction should also be made between notices requiring abatement and those prohibiting recurrence of a nuisance. Only the latter will clearly be valid if they do not specify a time limit on recurrence – a long-stop.[4]

1 EPA 1990, s 80(1).
2 *Thomas v Nokes* (1894) 58 JP 672; *Bristol Corpn v Sinnott* [1918] 1 Ch 62; *Strathclyde Regional Council v Tudhope* [1983] JPL 536.
3 *R v Dudley Magistrates' Court, ex p Hollis* [1998] JPL 652.
4 *R v Clerk to the Birmingham Justices, ex p Guppy* (1988) 152 JP 159; *R v Tunbridge Wells Justices, ex p Tunbridge Wells Borough Council* (1996) 160 JP 574.

14.26 An abatement notice need not be in any particular form. Perhaps partly as a consequence, there has been considerable recent litigation as to what should – or should not – be included in an abatement notice, or in accompanying documents. The starting point is s 80(1) itself: whether a notice should be single or double-barrelled – requiring simple abatement, works, or both. Although it is clear that an authority has a choice,[1] the real issue is whether the nature of the nuisance is such that the recipient can only be clear of the legal obligations imposed by a notice if works are specified. The guiding principle, despite confusing case law, is that: 'bearing in mind the risk of exposure to penal sanctions for non-compliance, it is essential that the [recipient] should be told clearly what works are to be carried out'.[2] A local authority therefore need not always specify precisely what it requires in order to abate every nuisance. In some cases, a mere requirement to abate will be sufficient. Cases in this 'category' have included barking dogs, in both small and large numbers,[3] appropriate receptacles for the storage of domestic waste[4] and the control of amplified music from licensed premises.[5]

1 *Budd v Colchester Borough Council* [1999] Env LR 739, CA.

2 Per Buckley J in *Network Housing Association Ltd v Westminster City Council* (1994) 93 LGR 280, 27 HLR 189, cited with approval by Swinton Thomas LJ in *Budd*, ibid.
3 *Budd*, ibid, itself concerned one dog; *Manley & Manley v New Forest District Council* [2000] EHLR 113, DC concerned dog breeding; and *Myatt v Teinbridge District Council* (1995) 7 *Environmental Law & Management* 96 concerned a large number of dogs.
4 *Stanley v London Borough of Ealing* [2000] EHLR 172.
5 *SFI Group plc v Gosport Borough Council* [1999] Env LR 750, CA.

14.27 More complex nuisances have created more complex conclusions, however. In particular, two decisions of the Court of Appeal seem at first sight to be hard to reconcile. The first, *SFI Group plc v Gosport Borough Council*[1] concerned amplified music from a bar. The court concluded that a simple notice to abate was sufficient in that case. However, the court went on to say that if a notice *in fact* requires works to be done then it should set out those works. It seems to be the nature of the particular nuisance which determines whether specification of works is required, not the mere fact that the notice is a simple, single-barrelled 'abate' notice. This suggests that an authority cannot avoid specifying works simply by requiring abatement. A more complex nuisance was the subject of *R v Falmouth & Truro Port Health Authority, ex p South-West Water:*[2] an alleged nuisance caused to an estuary by sewage discharges made by a statutory water undertaker in accordance with a discharge consent issued by the Agency. Despite the decisions of the Court of Appeal in *SFI Group plc* and *Budd v Colchester Borough Council*,[3] the court concluded that it was free to decide what it took to be the central issue in that case: whether the local authority had a discretion not to require works in a notice. The conclusion was that the authority did have such a discretion.[4] If, however, an authority did require works, then they must be specified.

1 [1999] Env LR 750, CA decided on 29 March 1999.
2 [2000] 3 All ER 306. First instance decision reported at [1999] Env LR 833.
3 [1999] Env LR 739, considered in para **14.26**, above.
4 On this point, overruling *Kirklees Metropolitan Council v Field* [1998] Env LR 337, a three-judge Divisional Court, in the process.

14.28 The formalistic conclusion in *Falmouth & Truro*[1] will cause problems. It is explicable on the facts: the water company was in a far better technical position to assess how to abate a nuisance than the local authority; it has statutory responsibility for discharging sewage and any modification to its discharging practices will require the consent of the Agency. The local authority's proposed solution, on the other hand, was merely to switch off the discharge pumps: a view described by Harrison J at first instance as 'the most absurd contention that [I have] ever heard'.[2] Assuming the existence of a statutory nuisance, the company was clearly best placed to provide a practical solution. The decision is also broadly consistent with earlier authority suggesting that the person responsible for a nuisance (often an owner or occupier of land) will often have better understanding of the property (for example), the problem and their own abatement resources, than the local authority.[3] Hard-pressed local authorities are likely to welcome the decision, as it suggests that even in the most complex cases they can simply issue an 'abate' notice, which they can then withdraw at any time.[4] It may help to avoid familiar situations where notices have been quashed as being insufficiently precise, for example, in failing to specify the point from which sound levels are to be measured,[5] or merely requiring 'alterations' to a block of flats in order to reduce noise to a specified level.[6]

1 [2000] 3 All ER 306; [2000] 3 WLR 1464.
2 [1999] Env LR 833, 856.
3 *Sterling Homes v Birmingham City Council* [1996] Env LR 121.
4 *R v Bristol City Council, ex p Everett* [1999] 2 All ER 193.
5 *R v Fenny Stratford Justices, ex p Watney Mann (Midlands)* [1976] 1 WLR 1101 but now also see *Sevenoaks District Council v Brands Hatch Leisure Group Ltd* [2001] EHLR 114.
6 *Network Housing Association Ltd v Westminster City Council* (1994) 93 LGR 280.

14.29 The problems remain, however. It is not clear that the decisions are consistent: it is certainly clear that the approach of the court in *SFI Group plc*[1] was different both in principle and in general approach to the differently-constituted court in *Falmouth & Truro*.[2] It is not difficult to imagine cases whose facts are less clear-cut than *Falmouth & Truro,* where it would be unjust or unreasonable for a local authority to fail to specify works required, and therefore inconsistent with the general principles set out in *Budd*.[3] Cases of individual landowners facing the high costs of abating complex nuisances which they did not cause and of which they were unaware do arise.[4] As recipients of simple 'abate' notices in such cases may choose to appeal them on the grounds that they are unreasonable or excessive,[5] local authorities may nonetheless choose to require works at an early stage, to avoid more appeals, liability to costs and the substitution by magistrates of different requirements than the authority would itself have imposed.

1 [1999] Env LR 750.
2 [2000] 3 All ER 306.
3 [1999] Env LR 128.
4 Precisely the circumstances in *Kirklees Metropolitan Council v Field* [1998] Env LR 337.
5 Statutory Nuisance (Appeal) Regulations 1995, reg 2(2)(c).

Identifying the recipient of an abatement notice

14.30 The abatement notice must be served on the 'person responsible' for the nuisance, that is, the person to whose act, default, or sufferance the nuisance is attributable.[1] Where the nuisance arises from any defect of a structural character the owner of the premises must instead be served, as must the owner or occupier of the premises where the person responsible cannot be found or the nuisance has not yet occurred.[2] Where more than one person is responsible for a statutory nuisance, any or all of them may be served with an abatement notice whether or not what any one of them is responsible for would in itself amount to a nuisance.[3] If more than one person is responsible for the nuisance, a person on whom an abatement notice is served cannot avoid responsibility by showing that a third person is also liable for the problem.[4] This would appear to embrace both those cases where more than one person has contributed to a situation which only amounts to a nuisance in combination (accumulations or deposits for example), and those where one person's act creates a nuisance, and another suffers it to continue.

1 EPA 1990, ss 80(2) and 79(7).
2 Ibid, s 80(2)(b) and (c). In the latter case, the local authority serving the notice may choose between the owner and the occupier.
3 Ibid, s 81(1).
4 *Wincanton RDC v Parsons* [1905] 2 KB 34.

14.31 The class of persons suffering a nuisance to continue would include a landlord allowing a nuisance caused by a tenant to continue, despite the landlord having both notice of the nuisance and powers under a lease or tenancy agreement to require its discontinuance. This would be so even though apart from the law of nuisance the landlord is under no *obligation* to remedy it.[1] This would seem to go beyond liability in common law nuisance, although this point has not been directly addressed.[2] Landlords' liabilities in such cases are illustrated by *Network Housing Association Ltd v Westminster City Council*[3] where an abatement notice was served on a landlord in respect of a noise nuisance arising from the 'noise of everyday living': it was the lack of sound insulation that contributed to create the nuisance. The Divisional Court held the landlord Housing Association liable as the 'person responsible' on the basis that it had notice of the nuisance (although, significantly, *not* when it purchased the property) and that it was within the landlord's power to remedy the lack of sound proofing.

1 *Clayton v Sale UDC* [1926] 1 KB 415. This reflects the position in private nuisance: *Sedleigh-Denfield v O'Callaghan* [1940] AC 880, HL. In particular, liabilities in statutory nuisance may extend beyond those enforceable under covenants to repair, see *Birmingham District Council v Kelly* [1986] 2 EGLR 239, QBD; and *R v Highbury Corner Magistrates' Court, ex p Edwards* [1995] Crim LR 65, QBD.
2 *Southwark London Borough v Mills; Baxter v London Borough of Camden* [2000] Env LR 112, per Lord Millett at 134. See further Ch 13.
3 [1995] Env LR 176, and see 27 MLR 189.

14.32 There may be a difficult dividing line in cases where factors external to the property itself change in such a way as to render landlord's nuisance abatement measures inadequate. Where landlords are not responsible for those factors themselves (increases in traffic for example) their responsibility seems likely to be assessed against the construction of the property and abatement measures at the time of construction.[1] However, this has not been determined conclusively. It has more recently been concluded, albeit obiter, that a statutory nuisance could be attributable to any act, default or sufferance by a local authority even though it had kept the premises in its original state.[2] Although here the magistrates were cautioned against too readily holding local authorities as landlords liable for a 'continuous' nuisance in light of their 'wide housing responsibilities and limited resources'.

1 *R v Newham East Magistrates, ex p London Borough of Newham* [1995] Env LR 113.
2 *Haringey London Borough Council v Jowett* (2000) 32 HLR 308; noted at (1999) 11 Environmental Law & Management 197.

14.33 More broadly, the inclusion of 'act' within the definition of 'person responsible' does not necessarily connote a need to establish fault on the part of that person. A person may be responsible in statutory nuisance for an act which he has a legal right to do.[1]

1 *Riddell v Spear* (1879) 43 JP 317. The ratio of this case is not entirely clear, but the principle is supported by *Clayton v Sale UDC* [1926] 1 KB 415, per Lord Hewart CJ.

Identifying an 'owner'

14.34 Although in most cases abatement notices are to be served on the 'person responsible' for the nuisance, in some circumstances this expressly includes the 'owner' of premises.[1] The term 'owner' is not defined in Part III of the 1990 Act however. Predecessor legislation did define the term as: 'the person for the time being receiving the rack rent of the premises ... whether on his own account or as agent or trustee for another person, or who would receive the rack rent if the premises were let at a rack rent',[2] although this can clearly not be directly transposed to the 1990 Act. Whilst omission of this definition may well have been intended to avoid the technicalities arising in consequence of the earlier definition, the High Court has apparently acquiesced in counsel's argument that 'owner' in s 80(2) should be given 'that same well-established, historically-based meaning'.[3]

1 See para **14.31**.
2 Public Health Act 1936, s 343 and Control of Pollution Act 1974, s 105.
3 Per Rose LJ, *Camden London Borough Council v Gunby* [1999] 4 All ER 602, at 608c, adopting submissions at 606a–c. A definition is provided for the purposes of charging expenses on premises: EPA 1990, s 81A.

14.35 There remains no exhaustive definition. However, it is anticipated by regulations made under the Act that there may be more than one owner.[1] The phrase might therefore include: (i) the freeholder, (ii) the person in whom the property is beneficially vested and who has occupation or control (for example, a lessee), (iii) any person who has a recognised property right in the premises, (iv) the person with the most valuable property interest. Indeed, given the flexibility of the appeal system – the fact that there is a chance for a person served as 'owner' to rely in their defence on the fact that the true owner is someone else – a managing agent who received rack rent from premises has been found to be included within the meaning of 'owner'.[2]

1 Statutory Nuisance (Appeals) Regulations 1995, SI 1995/2644, reg 2(2)(j)(ii).
2 *Camden London Borough Council v Gunby* [1999] 4 All ER 602.

Restrictions on service of an abatement notice

14.36 In a nineteenth-century case under predecessor legislation it was held that an abatement notice cannot lawfully be served requiring a person to carry out works on land which that person neither owns nor occupies, and has no right to enter.[1] On the other hand, an abatement notice is valid if it merely prohibits the nuisance under those circumstances.[2] However, it has also been held that where an abatement notice has to be served on the owner of premises, the notice may be served on the landlord, requiring him to carry out works, even though he has no right under the lease to enter for that purpose.[3]

1 *R v Cumberland Justices, ex p Trimble* (1877) 41 JP 454; see also *Scarborough Corpn v Scarborough Sanitary Authority* (1876) 1 Ex D 344. This can be contrasted with the position where a person is required to undertake works or operations in respect of actual or threatened water pollution: WRA 1991, s 161A. In such cases, a third party compensation entitlement will arise. Ibid, s 161B, inserted by the EA 1995, s 120, Sch 22, para 162.
2 The *Scarborough Corpn* case, n 1 above.
3 *Parker v Inge* (1886) 17 QBD 584, considering the Public Health Act 1875, ss 94 and 95.

14.37 The position that a person who neither owns nor occupies land on which a statutory nuisance exists cannot be served with an abatement notice is unsatisfactory for three reasons. First, s 80 provides for mandatory service on the 'person responsible', a requirement which extends to each responsible person.[1] There is no provision for exempting a person from service on account of their having no right to access to the premises in question. Secondly, a person served can assert 'reasonable excuse' in criminal proceedings if denied access, and so there is no question of injustice.[2] Thirdly, it is difficult to see how, strictly speaking, such a person can be made liable for the cost of works in default if a notice cannot be served on him.[3] That person would have had no opportunity of complying with the notice more cheaply, or of appealing against it. These reasons combine to suggest that a different conclusion than that reached in *R v Cumberland Justices, ex p Trimble*[4] could be reached were the point now to be raised under the EPA 1990. A compensation entitlement similar to that under s 161B of the Water Resources Act 1991 would also be desirable.

1 EPA 1990, s 81(1).
2 Paras **14.50–14.51**.
3 EPA 1990, s 81(4), see para **14.58**.
4 (1877) 41 JP 454.

Appeals

14.38 A person on whom an abatement notice is served may appeal against the notice to the magistrates' court within 21 days of its service.[1] A further appeal lies from that decision to the Crown Court.[2] Appeals to the magistrates' court are now provided for by the Statutory Nuisance (Appeals) Regulations 1995.[3] Grounds of appeal against an abatement notice include:

(1) the abatement notice is not justified by s 80;
(2) there is some material informality, defect or error in connection with the notice;
(3) the authority has refused unreasonably to accept compliance with alternative requirements, or the requirements of the abatement notice are otherwise unreasonable in character or extent, or are unnecessary;
(4) the time or times within which the requirements of the notice are to be complied with is or are not reasonably sufficient for the purpose;
(5) that, in certain cases in relation to 'industrial, trade or business premises', the 'best practicable means' were used to prevent, or counteract the effects of, the nuisance;[4]
(6) in respect of noise emitted from premises and noise in the street and in the case of noise emitted from premises in categories (g) or (ga), that the

requirements of the notice are more onerous than the existing controls in relation to the noise under the Control of Pollution Act 1974, ss 60, 61, 65, 66, or 67 as appropriate, or, in the case of noise in the street, the requirements of the notice are more onerous than the requirements of any condition of a consent given under the Noise and Statutory Nuisance Act 1993, Sch 2, para 1 in respect of the same noise for loudspeakers on the street;

(7) the abatement notice should have been served on some person instead of the appellant, being:

(i) the person responsible for the nuisance; or

(ii) the person responsible for the vehicle, machinery, or equipment; or

(iii) in the case of a structural defect, the owner of the premises; or

(iv) in the case where the person responsible for the nuisance cannot be found or the nuisance has not yet occurred, the owner or occupier of the premises;

(8) the abatement notice might have been lawfully served on some person instead of the appellant, being:

(i) in the case where the appellant is the owner of the premises, the occupier of the premises; or

(ii) in the case where the appellant is the occupier of the premises, the owner of the premises;

and that it would have been equitable for him to have been served;

(9) the abatement notice might have been lawfully served on some person in addition to the appellant, being:

(i) a person also responsible for the nuisance;

(ii) a person who is also owner of the premises;

(iii) a person who is also the occupier of the premises;

(iv) a person who is also responsible for the vehicle, machinery, or equipment

and it would have been equitable for him to have been so served.

1 EPA 1990, s 80(3).
2 Ibid, Sch 3, para 1(3).
3 SI 1995/2644, (as amended by the Statutory Nuisance (Appeals) (Amendment) (England) Regulations 2006 for England and as amended by the Statutory Nuisance (Miscellaneous Provisions) (Wales) Regulations 2007 (SI 2007/117) for Wales; the corresponding procedure for Scotland is set out in the Statutory Nuisance (Appeals) (Scotland) Regulations 1996, SI 1996/1976 (as amended by the Public Health etc (Scotland) Act).
4 This ground of appeal applies to nuisances contained in categories (a), (d), (e), (f), (fa) or (g) of s 79 of the EPA 1990, and category (b) where the smoke emitted is from a chimney. It also arises in respect of noise emitted from vehicles etc in the street: (category ga).

Relevant date

14.39 The best practicable means ground of appeal is also a defence.[1] The meaning of this phrase is considered below.[2] It was once thought that the question of whether best practicable means have been used to abate a nuisance must include consideration of all the steps taken right up to the appeal hearing and indeed also that the hearing date was also the relevant date for the determination of the existence of a nuisance.[3] However, this view has been overruled: the relevant date for both purposes is the date on which the notice was served.[4] One consequence is that a local authority will not be deprived of the costs of its abatement notice and success before the magistrates' court on the basis that by the time the matter came to be considered in the Crown Court the nuisance had been abated.[5]

1 EPA 1990, s 80(7); paras **14.54–14.56**.
2 Para **14.47**.
3 *Johnsons News of London v Ealing Borough Council* (1989) 154 JP 33.
4 *SFI Group plc v Gosport Borough Council* [1999] Env LR 750, CA.
5 Ibid, per Stuart-Smith LJ, at 762.

14.40 Abatement notices are not suspended pending appeal to the magistrates unless:[1]

- compliance would involve any person in expenditure on the carrying out of works before the hearing of the appeal; or
- they are based on categories (g) or (ga) and relate to noise necessarily caused in the performance of some duty imposed by law.

1 Statutory Nuisance (Appeals) Regulations 1995, SI 1995/2664, reg 3(1)(b)(i)(ii).

14.41 In such cases abatement notices are generally suspended. The local authority can only prevent them from being suspended if:[1]

- the nuisance is injurious to health;[2] or
- the nuisance is likely to be of limited duration so that suspension would render it of no practical effect;[3] or
- the expenditure on works would not be disproportionate to the public benefit to be expected in the period before the appeal is determined.[4]

The notice must then state (or the notice will be suspended):

- that para 2 of reg 3 of the Statutory Nuisance (Appeals) Regulations 1995 applies;
- that it will have effect, notwithstanding any appeal to the magistrates;
- which of the grounds applies.

1 Statutory Nuisance (Appeals) Regulations 1995, SI 1995/2644, reg 3(2)(a)(b).
2 Reg 3(2)(a)(i).
3 Reg 3(2)(a)(ii).
4 Reg 3(2)(b).

Procedural and evidential Issues

14.42 When hearing an appeal against an abatement notice, magistrates are not confined to considering whether the local authority acted in good faith and had been reasonably satisfied that a statutory nuisance did exist (or was likely to occur or recur) when issuing the notice. Rather, the court should consider whether the underlying facts which constituted the nuisance (or its likely occurrence or recurrence) existed at the date on which the notice was served.[1]

Previous authority to the effect that magistrates should make such a judgment as at the date of the trial, as opposed to the notice, has been overruled.[2]

1 *SFI Group plc v Gosport Borough Council* [1999] Env LR 750, CA.
2 *Johnsons News of London Ltd v Ealing London Borough Council* (1989) 154 JP 33, QBD.

14.43 An appeal is by way of civil complaint. There are no express provisions in the rules enabling the magistrates' court to order, for example, disclosure by the parties, or for the compulsory exchange of evidence before the hearing date. However, it is common and good practice for the court to hold a pre-trial review in more complicated cases in order to address matters in the same way as a directions hearing. The court will expect cooperation between the parties (see *Sovereign Rubber Ltd v Stockport Metropolitan Borough Council* [2000] Env LR 194).

14.44 There is some debate about the extent to which the rules of evidence apply to appeals against abatement notices. Hearsay evidence may be permitted in civil cases before the magistrates' court. The rules relating to the admission of hearsay evidence have been set down in the Magistrates' Court (Hearsay Evidence in Civil Proceedings) Rules 1999.[1] They greatly relax the restrictions previously applying to hearsay evidence in civil cases.

1 SI 1999/681 (made pursuant to Civil Evidence Act 1995, s 12).

14.45 If one accepts that the magistrates are sitting in a regulatory capacity, then the court would not be bound by any rules of evidence. Support for this view can be gained from the Court of Appeal's decisions in Kavanagh v Chief Constable of Devon and Cornwall1 and Westminster City Council v Zestfair Ltd.2

1 [1974] 2 All ER 697.
2 (1989) 153 JP 613.

14.46 Whether or not property is prejudicial to health is a matter requiring expert evidence, although it need not always be medical expertise: a surveyor with relevant expertise may suffice.[1] Equally, in such cases, it is not necessary to call evidence as to the actual health of occupants if other expert evidence going to the state of the premises themselves is properly admitted.[2] The amount and character of such evidence remains, of course, a matter of judgment in each case.

1 *London Borough of Southwark v Simpson* [1999] Env LR 553.
2 *O'Toole v Knowsley Metropolitan Borough Council* [1999] EHLR 420; (1999) 11 *Environmental Law & Management* 197, QBD.

Orders consequent on appeals

14.47 On hearing an appeal the court may quash the notice, vary it (but only in favour of the appellant)[1] or dismiss the appeal.[2] Appeals based on any informality, defect or error in, or in connection with, the notice will be dismissed if that error is not material.[3] The court may make such an order as it thinks fit as to the person who is to carry out works and to the contribution to the cost of these works to be made by any person, or to the proportions in which expenses recoverable by the local authority are to be shared by the appellant and any other person. In exercising these powers, the court is expressly required to have regard, as between owner and occupier, to the terms and conditions, whether contractual or statutory, of any relevant tenancy and the nature of the works required.[4]

1 This may include reducing the area to which the notice relates if that is in fact to the appellant's advantage: Sovereign Rubber Ltd v Stockport Metropolitan Borough Council [2000] Env LR 194; noted at (2000) 12 Environmental Law & Management 27.
2 SI 1995/2644, reg 2(5).
3 Ibid, reg 2(3).
4 Ibid, reg 2(7)(a).

14.48 A further important point arises in respect of the terms of leases or other agreements. A common term in leases, for example, requires the tenant to pay all 'rates, taxes, assessments, and outgoings whatsoever in respect of the premises'. This obligation only relates to outgoings which there is a legal *obligation* to pay.[1] If a landlord is served with an abatement notice and wishes to recover costs from a tenant under the terms of a lease – then he should appeal, and ask the court to order the tenant to carry out the work, or order him to contribute to the costs. The cost of works done in the absence of an appeal and formal order will not be recoverable.

1 See, eg, *Valpy v St Leonards Wharf Co* (1903) 1 LGR 305 and *Harris v Hickman* [1904] 1 KB 13. See further paras **10.08–10.09** and **10.23–10.27**.

14.49 Once an appeal has been made, it should not be withdrawn without reaching a comprehensive agreement with the local authority as to the terms of withdrawal. This should include the question of costs: otherwise the local authority may seek an order for the payment of their costs from the appellant.[1] The court may be asked to make an agreed order that the appeal be withdrawn without a costs order, or alternatively it may agree to an adjournment 'sine die'.[2]

1 Courts Act 1971, s 52 (abandonment of appeals to the magistrates' court); Magistrates' Courts Act 1980, s 109 (abandonment of appeals from the magistrates' court). See further McCracken, Jones and Pereira, *Statutory Nuisance*, ch 7.
2 However, on this point see Dewhurst, 'Costs in Statutory Nuisance Proceedings' (1993) 5 Environmental Law & Management 169.

Summary proceedings: defences

14.50 A person upon whom an abatement notice has been served may present a 'reasonable excuse' for non-compliance[1] and thus escape liability.[2] In establishing whether or not an excuse is 'reasonable' the normal rules of evidence apply. Hence, there is an evidential burden on the recipient of the notice to show that there may have been a reasonable excuse, with a consequential burden on the local authority to satisfy the court that the excuse was not a reasonable one.[3] This position can be contrasted with the express defences provided by the Act. As there is no definition of 'reasonable excuse' in the 1990 Act, it is a question for the court to decide whether an excuse is reasonable. It has been held that mere lack of finance would not suffice,[4] although reasonable excuses have included illness and non-receipt of the notice.[5]

1 Para **14.13**. Strictly, the *actus reus* of the offence is 'without reasonable excuse contravening a requirement of the notice', per O'Connor LJ in *City of London v Bovis Construction Ltd* (1988) 84 LGR 660 at 676 (a case on the similar wording of the Control of Pollution Act 1974, s 60).
2 EPA 1990, s 80(4).
3 *Polychronakis v Richards & Jerrom* [1997] EWHC Admin 885; [1998] Env LR 346; [1998] JPL 588.
4 *Saddleworth UDC v Aggregate and Sand Ltd* (1970) 69 LGR 103.
5 *A Lambert Flat Management Ltd v Lomas* [1981] 2 All ER 280. See also *Butuyuyu v London Borough of Hammersmith & Fulham* [1997] Env LR D13; (1997) 38 Environmental Law Bulletin 35.

14.51 It follows that if an abatement notice is served requiring a person to carry out work on land which he neither owns nor occupies, the recipient of the notice may be able to show a reasonable excuse. Evidence should be presented to show that efforts to obtain permission were undertaken, but that they were unsuccessful. An excuse cannot generally be 'reasonable' if it involves matters which could have been raised on appeal unless such matters arose after the appeal was heard (if there was an appeal), or after the time limit for bringing an appeal has expired.[1] The defence cannot therefore be used to allow the recipient of a notice to have the choice of forum in which to challenge the notice, and in particular to challenge the correctness and justification of the notice where the statutory appeal mechanism was not used. An exception seems not to be ruled out, however, in that an appellant's reasonable excuse may explain the failure to appeal against the abatement notice in the first place.[2]

1 *A Lambert Flat Managment Ltd v Lomas* [1981] 2 All ER 280, per Skinner J at 284 d-e.
2 *Butuyuyu v London Borough of Hammersmith & Fulham Hope* [1997] Env LR D13; (1997) 38 Environmental Law Bulletin 35.

14.52 The general principle, however, is that the validity of a local authority's action *can* be challenged in criminal proceedings where the invalidity argument is crucial to the defence.[1] Crucially, however, this depends on the statutory context.[2] The closest analogy to statutory nuisance on which there is clear authority arises in the context of planning. The House of Lords has held that a planning enforcement notice is one which is issued by a local authority and is formally valid in the sense that it complies with the requirements of the Act and has not been quashed on appeal or by judicial review.[3] Whilst breach of condition notices have now been distinguished from enforcement notices in this respect,[4] abatement notices would seem to have more in common with enforcement notices than with breach of condition notices. Not least amongst these similarities is the appeal machinery itself – an important part of the reasoning in *Dilieto*.[5] On this basis, it seems that abatement notices are probably also an exception to the general principle: in the absence of an appeal, the question for the court will merely be whether or not the notice has been complied with.[6] This may be ameliorated by potential grounds of appeal – that there has been some informality, defect or error in, or in connection with, the abatement notice[7] – but not in every case.

1 *Sterling Homes v Birmingham City Council* [1996] Env LR 121.
2 *Boddington v British Transport Police* [1998] 2 WLR 639, HL.
3 *R v Wicks* [1997] JPL 1049, HL.
4 *Dilieto v London Borough of Ealing* [1998] 2 All ER 885, contrary to the expectations of some commentators, eg, Harwood [1997] JPL 1180.
5 Ibid.
6 This would be consistent with earlier authority: AMEC *Building Ltd and Squibb & Davies Ltd v London Borough of Camden* [1997] Env LR 330, DC.
7 SI 1995/2644, reg 2(2)(b).

14.53 It may also amount to a defence for the person on whom the abatement notice was served to show that they are not the person responsible for the nuisance.[1] This category may be wider than it would at first sight appear to be. For example, if a tenant repeatedly and unreasonably refuses to move to suitable alternative accommodation when their absence would allow the landlord or remedy a statutory nuisance of which the tenant has complained, then the landlord may be found not to be responsible for the nuisance.[2] The tenant's own actions in this case effectively transferred responsibility away from the landlord, even though it is unlikely that that transfer was to the tenant. Equally, the tenant's actions in this case were rather unusual.

1 EPA 1990, s 82(4)(a). See paras **14.30–14.33**
2 *Quigley v Liverpool Housing Trust* [2000] *Env* LR D9.

'Best practicable means'

14.54 It is also a defence in respect of certain proceedings under s 80(4) to show that the best practicable means were used to prevent, or to counteract the effects of, the nuisance.[1] The classes of nuisance to which this defence applies are in general the same as those to which it applies as a ground of appeal against an abatement notice with two additions. These are:

(a) fumes or gases emitted from premises; and
(b) any other matter declared by any enactment to be a statutory nuisance.[2]

1 EPA 1990, s 80(7). On 'best practicable means' as a ground of appeal see para **14.38**.
2 EPA 1990, s 80(8)(c): classes of nuisance corresponding to those in s 79(1)(c) and (h).

14.55 'Best practicable means' is partially defined by the Act.[1] 'Practicable' means reasonably practicable having regard to matters including (but not confined to) local conditions and circumstances, to the current state of technical knowledge and to the financial implications.[2] The means to be employed include the design, construction and maintenance of buildings and structures.[3] Whilst the effect of the costs of required works on the profitability of a company has been held to be relevant in determining practicability, clear evidence of those effects must be presented for the court to be able to assess what is reasonably practicable.[4] What 'best practicable means' does not extend to is relocation of the business or activity which is subject of the complaint.[5] As a matter of law, then, the steps that must be taken to show that the best practicable means have been used are steps in connection with the premises to which the abatement notice relates.

1 EPA 1990, s 79(9).
2 Ibid, sub-s (9)(a).
3 Ibid, sub-s (9)(b).
4 *Wivenhoe Port Ltd v Colchester Borough Council* [1985] JPL 175.
5 *Manley & Manley v New Forest District Council* [2000] EHLR 113.

14.56 Where the alleged nuisance is a noise nuisance then additional codes of practice made under s 71 of the Control of Pollution Act 1974 in respect of noise abatement may apply,[1] as might other specific defences relating to construction site noise, noise abatement zones and orders, and noise from certain new buildings.[2]

1 See, eg, SIs 1984/1992 and 1987/1730, relating to noise from construction and open sites.
2 Under Control of Pollution Act 1974, ss 63–67: EPA 1990, s 80(9). On construction noise, see paras **14.73–14.76**.

Offences

14.57 Commission of a statutory nuisance creates a *potential* criminal liability, in that it is an offence for a person on whom an abatement notice[1] is served, without reasonable excuse, to contravene or fail to comply with any requirement or prohibition imposed by that notice.[2] A person who commits this offence is liable on summary conviction to an unlimited fine [3] together with a further fine of an amount equal to one-tenth of the greater of £5000 or level 4 on the standard scale for each day on which the offence continues after conviction.[4] Where the offence is committed on industrial, trade or business premises an unlimited fine may be imposed.[5] In practical terms service of an abatement notice does of course also give a person served with a notice a period within which to abate the nuisance *before* a consequential criminal liability can arise. If the case does proceed to trial, it is now clear that the date on which the court is to examine the justification for, and validity of, an abatement notice is the date on which it was served, and not the date of the trial.[6] This brings a number of consequences, for example, as to costs and the task of magistrates in determining appeals,[7] but will at least confine exposure to continuing fines to those cases where a subsequently-convicted defendant has failed to comply with an abatement notice by the time of the trial itself.

1 See paras **14.15–14.33**.
2 EPA 1990, s 80(4).
3 See LASPO Act 2012, s 85.
4 EPA 1990, s 80(5).
5 Ibid, s 80(6). Definitions in s 79(7).

6 *SFI Group plc v Gosport Borough Council* [1999] Env LR 750, Court of Appeal, concluding that *Johnsons News of London Ltd v Ealing London Borough Council* (1989) 154 JP 33 was wrongly decided.
7 See paras **14.49** and **14.42** respectively.

Local authorities' abatement expenses

14.58 If an abatement notice is not complied with, irrespective of whether a prosecution is brought, a local authority may abate the nuisance and do whatever may be necessary in the execution of the notice.[1] Any expenses reasonably incurred by a local authority in abating a statutory nuisance may be recovered from the person(s) by whose acts or default the nuisance was caused, and the court may apportion the expenses as it considers fair and reasonable.[2] There is no express provision for the recovery of expenses from a person by whose 'sufferance' a nuisance was caused.[3] However, if a person becomes aware of a nuisance on land and fails to abate it, he is in breach of an obligation to his neighbours for continuing the nuisance. Breach of that obligation places him in default,[4] hence he becomes liable to meet a local authority's expenses. In cases where expenses are recoverable from the owner of premises, they may be recovered from any person who is the owner for the time being.[5]

1 EPA 1990, s 81(3).
2 Ibid, sub-s (4).
3 Cf EPA 1990, ss 79(7) and 80(2).
4 *Nathan v Rouse* [1905] 1 KB 527.
5 EPA 1990, s 81(4).

14.59 In general, and as noted above,[1] the expenses incurred in carrying out the works required by an abatement notice (or recovered from a landowner in default) may be recoverable under a lease or other contract. For example, an obligation on a tenant to pay 'all outgoings payable in respect of the premises' has been held to include compliance with an abatement notice.[2] However, such a provision is subject to any specific obligation to the contrary in the lease. So where the abatement notice requires works to be carried out which fall within the landlord's repairing covenant, the tenant will not be liable despite otherwise being responsible for 'all outgoings'.[3]

1 Para **14.58**.
2 Under predecessor legislation: *Stockdale v Ascherberg* [1904] 1 KB 447.
3 *Howe v Botwood* [1913] 2 KB 387. See also *Foulger v Arding* [1902] 1 KB 700 and *Harris v Hickman* [1904] 1 KB 13. See further paras **10.08–10.09** and **14.48**.

14.60 Conversely, the EPA 1990 does provide express power to apportion costs between persons by whose acts or defaults a nuisance is caused,[1] and early authorities, based on similar statutory wording, have upheld the courts' ability to apportion costs by taking into account the terms of a lease rather than being bound by them.[2] Later authorities suggest a greater judicial reluctance to intervene in the contractual relationship between landlord and tenant, particularly where the tenant had notice of potential statutory obligations before entering into the tenancy.[3] The principle is that the terms of a lease or other contract will not be determinative of apportionment where expenses are recovered under s 81, and this is confirmed by similar statutory provisions in respect of appeals.[4]

1 EPA 1990, s 81(4).
2 *Monk v Arnold* [1902] 1 KB 761 and *Horner v Franklin* [1905] 1 KB 479, especially Vaughan Williams LJ at 487–488: 'No one has suggested that when [the judge] comes to consider what is "just and equitable" he is not to bear in mind the terms of the tenancy … I cannot see that there would be any defeating or nullifying of the terms of the tenancy because the decision of the question of who is ultimately to bear and in what proportions the expenses of fulfilling this statutory obligation is left to the [judge].'
3 Eg, *Monro v Lord Burghclere* [1918] 1 KB 291.
4 SI 1995/2644, reg 2(7)(a); see paras **10.08–10.09, 10.23–10.26** and **14.48**.

Expenses as a charge on premises

14.61 The amendments to the EPA 1990 made by the Noise and Statutory Nuisance Act 1993 include the addition of provisions enabling a local authority to secure recovery of its expenses incurred in abating a statutory nuisance by making the debt a charge on premises.[1] These powers were previously provided by s 291 of the Public Health Act 1936. Where expenses incurred under s 81(4) are recoverable from a person who is the owner of the premises in question then the authority may serve a notice on that person to the effect that those expenses shall carry interest (at a reasonable rate determined by the authority itself), and that both the principal sum and interest shall be a charge on the premises.[2] For the purposes of enforcing that charge, the local authority has all the powers and remedies under the Law of Property Act 1925 and otherwise as if it were a mortgagee by deed having powers of sale and lease, of accepting surrenders of leases, and of appointing a receiver.[3] A person served with a notice under this section has 21 days in which to appeal to the county court.[4]

1 Noise and Statutory Nuisance Act 1993, s 10, inserting EPA 1990, ss 81A and 81B.
2 EPA 1990, s 81A(1). Notice must also be served on all those persons having an interest in the property capable of being affected by the charge: s 81(3).
3 Ibid, sub-s (8).
4 Ibid, sub-ss (4)–(7).

14.62 It has been noted that 'owner' is not defined for the general purposes of Part III of the Act.[1] A specific definition for the purposes of this section alone is given however: 'owner' in relation to any premises, means a person (other than a mortgagee not in possession) who, whether in his own right or as trustee for any other person, is entitled to receive the rack rent of the premises or, where the premises are not let at a rack rent, would be so entitled if they were so let.[2] Additional provision is made in respect of the payment by instalments of expenses which are charged on premises in this way, and the size of those instalments.[3]

1 Paras **14.34–14.35**.
2 EPA 1990, s 81A(9).
3 Ibid, s 81B.

SUMMARY PROCEEDINGS BY A 'PERSON AGGRIEVED'

14.63 A 'person aggrieved' by a statutory nuisance may bring summary proceedings for an abatement order to abate a statutory nuisance instead of relying on the local authority to issue an abatement notice.[1] Indeed, in the past it was often used by tenants of premises which are prejudicial to health where the landlord has been the local authority. In such a case a magistrates' court in addition to making an abatement order may immediately impose an unlimited fine.[2] The magistrates' power pre-1990 to make an award of compensation in favour of a complainant is retained.[3] The standard of proof required to secure a conviction under s 82 is the criminal standard[4] with the civil standard applying to appeal proceedings under s 80.

1 This remedy is provided by the EPA 1990, s 82.
2 EPA 1990, s 82(2).
3 Under the Powers of Criminal Courts (Sentencing) Act 2000, s 130. The exercise of this power may only follow a criminal conviction.
4 See *Botross v London Borough of Hammersmith and Fulham* (1994) 16 Cr App Rep (S) 622, DC and *London Borough of Lewisham v Fenner* (1996) 8 Environmental Law and Management 11. For a full discussion on the s 82 procedure, see McCracken, Jones and Pereira, *Statutory Nuisance*, Ch 6.

14.64 The summary procedure is also set out by which any person 'aggrieved' by the existence of a statutory nuisance may seek an abatement order from the magistrates' court. However, notwithstanding the wording of s 82, the proceedings should be commenced by way of an information.[1] 'Person aggrieved' is not defined by the Act, but in any event must overlap the class of persons able to bring an action in private nuisance.[2] In particular, 'persons aggrieved' must include those who complain of prejudice to their health caused by a statutory nuisance, in addition to those who complain of nuisances causing interference with personal comfort. If the court is satisfied on considering a complaint that the alleged statutory nuisance exists, or (if abated) is likely to recur, then the court is *required* to make an abatement order for purposes similar to those possible in relation to an abatement notice.[3] In addition, and unlike the situation with abatement notices, the court may immediately impose an unlimited fine,[4] whilst contravention of an abatement order without reasonable excuse[5] is also an offence.[6] As with abatement notices, the 'best practicable means' defence is generally applicable in relation to an action brought by a person aggrieved for a breach of an abatement order.[7] It is an open question whether it is available as a defence to the making of an abatement order.

1 EPA 1990, s 82, subject to certain notice requirements: s 82(6) and (7).
2 The significance of this point to statutory nuisance is discussed in paras **14.05–14.11**.
3 Ibid, ss 82(2) and 80(1) respectively. See para **14.25**. Unlike s 80, it is generally considered that an abatement order under s 82 cannot be made in anticipation of a nuisance which has yet to occur at all.
4 EPA 1990, s 82(2); LASPO Act 2012, s 85.
5 Paras **14.50–14.51**.
6 EPA 1990, s 82(8).
7 Ibid, s 82(9) and (10).

14.65 Whilst empirical evidence is sparse, the structure of Part III of the Act (with local authorities under duties to inspect, to respond to complaints, and to abate) suggests that the summary remedy is infrequently used. Its potential utility should not be underestimated however. It can easily give rise to binding criminal obligations, and consequent abatement costs. Statutory nuisance has also provided a powerful weapon against local authorities themselves, for example, in matters of disrepair in housing stock.[1] However, the conviction of a local authority in statutory nuisance will not in itself lead to the additional complication of a further civil liability on the authority.[2]

1 See *R v Newham Justices, ex p Hunt* [1976] 1 All ER 839; *Salford City Council v McNally* [1976] AC 379. For an example where it has been used see *Roper v Tussauds Theme Park Ltd* [2007] *EWHC* 624 (*Admin*); [2007] Env LR 31.
2 *Issa v London Borough of Hackney* [1997] Env LR 157, CA.

14.66 It is not entirely clear whether a local authority can serve an abatement notice on itself: it cannot do so with a notice under housing legislation.[1] Either way, local authorities are very unlikely (and for good reason) to enforce statutory nuisance controls against themselves. Their duties in this respect can be contrasted with those applying in certain health and safety matters, where the Health and Safety Executive has responsibility for regulating on local authority premises matters normally within those authorities' own jurisdiction.[2] Of particular note is the possibility of those in 'transient' occupation of land on which a statutory nuisance has arisen, or land adjacent to it – perhaps those holding a mere licence – who would be able to rely on s 82 in cases of prejudice to health, when a private nuisance action would not be available to them.

1 *R v Cardiff City Council, ex p Cross* [1981] JPL 748. The enactment of the 1990 Act may compromise the application of this case here however.
2 Health and Safety (Enforcing Authority) Regulations 1998, SI 1998/494. See Jewell, 'Statutory Nuisance and the Educational Environment' (1997) 9 Education and the Law 181.

14.67 The Act is even less particular about the degree of specificity required of complaints under s 82 than it is about abatement notices. Taken with certain policy considerations, this results in far more latitude for individuals laying complaints than for local authorities issuing abatement notices.[1] The Act simply requires that a person aggrieved provide notice in writing of their intention to bring proceedings, specifying the matters complained of.[2] The courts have been very reluctant to import any additional requirements, partly because of the deterrent effect of over technical requirements on members of the public with well-founded complaints.[3] The notice must specify the premises in question, and indicate the basis upon which the recipient is said to be obliged to abate the nuisance. The complainant must 'indicate very broadly the nature of the complaint, to draw attention to the matters that are bothering him. It is clearly desirable that a list of defects is given, but any errors or indications that the notice may not be exhaustive cannot conceivably invalidate it'.[4] In that case, the surveyor's report attached to the notice included matters identified as being likely to deteriorate and become a statutory nuisance. Whilst the Act gives an individual no power to anticipate a statutory nuisance in this way,[5] their inclusion was held not to compromise the notice in respect of other matters that did amount to an extant statutory nuisance.

1 On the latter, see paras **14.25–14.29.**
2 EPA 1990, s 82(6).
3 *Staffordshire Borough Council v Fairless* [1999] EHLR 128.
4 *Pearshouse v Birmingham City Council* [1999] JPL 725, QBD, per Collins J.
5 EPA 1990, s 82(2), contrast the position with an abatement notice: para **14.12.**

Service of notice

14.68 Service of notice under s 82 must normally be at the 'proper address' of the recipient: in the case of a body corporate, its registered or principal office.[1] The criminal consequences which can flow from a complaint initially provoked a formal application of this requirement: service by a local authority tenant on his landlord's senior estate manager rather than on the authority's principal office was held not to be valid service.[2] More latitude has subsequently been granted, however. For example, where a local authority had informed tenants that service should be on the technical services manager, the Divisional Court has concluded that magistrates were wrong in holding subsequent service on that manager to be invalid.[3] Provision is made for service on an authority's secretary or clerk,[4] and a person to be served may specify an address other than their 'proper address' for service.[5] This ability to specify an alternative is not confined to the secretary or clerk personally, but extends to the authority itself, for example, by the terms of its tenants' leases.

1 EPA 1990, s 160.
2 *Leeds v Islington Borough Council* [1998] COD 293.
3 *Hall v Kingston-upon-Hull City Council* [1999] 11 Environmental Law & Management 123.
4 EPA 1990, s 160(3).
5 Ibid, sub-s (5).

14.69 An even broader approach to interpretation of the service provisions has been applied to a private company. Where a course of correspondence, ultimately including a s 82 notice, was conducted with a company director at an address other than the company's registered office, but the summons was served at the registered office, the validity of the service of the notice has nonetheless been upheld.[1] The court concluded that the permissive phrasing of s 160 ('any notice ... *may* be served') and the summary procedure designed for use by lay people merited a less rigid approach than (for example) in companies law. In any event, the Justices had erred in dismissing the complaint for want of proper service as there was material before the court upon which it should have found that effective notice had been given.

1 *Hewlings v McLean Homes East Anglia Ltd* [2001] 2 All ER 281.

Recovery of costs by a 'person aggrieved'

14.70 Where a complaint leads to summary proceedings at which it is proved that a statutory nuisance existed at the date of making the complaint then the complainant is entitled as a matter of right to compensation for their expenses properly incurred.[1] This entitlement arises even if there has been insufficient time to abate the nuisance between giving notice and laying a complaint.[2] In the *Hollis* case, a local authority tenant had complained of a nuisance which the authority, as landlord, was in the process of abating, which would take between nine and 14 weeks. Four weeks after giving notice the tenant laid a complaint. The Divisional Court quashed the magistrates' refusal of costs, and their decision to adjourn to allow abatement: the magistrates were not entitled to refuse costs because they considered the local authority to be acting reasonably; nor could the power to adjourn be used to deprive the complainant of rights conferred by the statute. In practice, there is a real possibility that the complainant had in fact incurred expenses in making the initial complaint, such as surveyors' fees.[3] Equally, however reasonable the landlord was being in abating the nuisance, it had in fact arisen in the first place, and without a conviction the complainant would have no opportunity to seek a compensation order under general powers.[4]

1 EPA 1990, s 82(12).
2 *R v Dudley Magistrates' Court, ex p Hollis* [1998] JPL 652.
3 As in *Pearshouse v Birmingham City Council* [1999] JPL 725, QBD. See para **14.58**.
4 Powers of Criminal Courts (Sentencing) Act 2000, s 130 – a discretionary remedy, see eg *R v Daly* [1974] 1 All ER 290, CA.

14.71 A complainant should, as a matter of routine, give advance notice of any claim for costs, and when a substantial amount is claimed the court must take proper steps to investigate how the claim is arrived at.[1] The court in that case also suggested that the respondent should indicate in advance if he accepts the claim, or the basis on which it is challenged, possibly by an appropriate adaptation of a *Calderbank* letter.[2] When awarding costs, the court is under no obligation to give reasons.[3]

1 *Taylor v Walsall and District Property & Investment Company Ltd* [1998] Env LR 600, QBD.
2 Ibid, per Simon-Brown LJ at 606.
3 *London Borough of Camden v London Underground Ltd* [2000] Env LR 369.

14.72 It is important to note that the entitlement to costs only extends to the complainant's costs, properly incurred.[1] Where a complainant employs a solicitor, there is a presumption that the complainant will be personally liable for those costs, such that evidence to that effect need not ordinarily be adduced.[2] If a genuine issue is raised, however, a complainant should be prepared to adduce evidence.[3] Solicitors should also take care in making fee arrangements with clients if they presume that costs will be awarded. Whilst failure to require a retainer on the basis of 'confidence' that costs would be recovered has escaped classification as an unlawful contingency fee arrangement – albeit on evidential, not substantive, grounds[4] – others have been less fortunate. In *Hughes v Kingston-upon-Hull Council*[5] solicitors for an impecunious complainant who was not aware of the costs he might incur and who did not follow the progress of the case were also less than frank that their motivation for supporting the action was its value as a test case. On these facts, the High Court upheld a refusal to award costs under s 82(12), concluding that the arrangement was a conditional fee agreement that was contrary to the Solicitors Practice Rules, and thus unlawful.[6]

1 EPA 1990, s 82(12).
2 *R v Miller; R v Glennie* [1983] 1 WLR 1056.
3 *Hazlett v Sefton Borough Council* [2000] Env LR 416.
4 Ibid.
5 [1999] Env LR 579, considered by Haden (1999) 2(3) Journal of Housing Law 33.
6 Following *Swain v The Law Society* [1983] AC 598; Legal Services Act 1990, s 58.

CONSTRUCTION SITE NOISE

14.73 Although not falling within statutory nuisance controls proper, regulation of construction site noise provides an important statutory addition to other controls on noise nuisance. The particular weaknesses of nuisance in this respect,[1] have led to a special procedure under the Control of Pollution Act 1974. Under that Act, a local authority can serve a notice in respect of premises on which a wide class of construction works are being carried out imposing requirements as to the way those works are to be carried out.[2] In particular, a notice may specify plant or machinery which is, or is not to be, used, permitted hours of working, permitted noise levels from the site or from any specified point on the site or during specified hours.[3]

1 See eg, *Hunter v Canary Wharf Ltd* [1997] 2 All ER 426, HL.
2 CoPA 1974, ss 60–61; Waite 'Statutory Controls on Construction Site Noise' (1990) 6 *Construction Law Journal* 97; Bruce 'Problems of Building Site Noise and How to Avoid them' (1998) 142 (35) SJ 834.
3 CoPA 1974, s 60(3).

14.74 In preparing a notice, an authority must have regard to defined matters, including any relevant codes of practice,[1] the need for ensuring that the 'best practicable means' are used to minimise noise,[2] and the need to protect people in the locality from the noise. A notice may be appealed within 21 days to a magistrates' court, on certain grounds.[3] The grounds are similar to those applying to appeals against statutory nuisance abatement notices,[4] and are set out in regulations.[5]

1 Issued under Part III of CoPA 1974: s 60(4). See, eg, the Control of Noise (Code of Practice for Construction and Open Sites) Order 1987, SI 1987/1730.
2 Defined in s 72 to include consideration of local conditions, the current state of technical knowledge and the financial implications. A requirement that recipients of notice will employ the BPM will often be imposed by a notice: eg, in *Wiltshier Construction Ltd v Westminster City Council* [1997] Env LR 321.
3 Section 60(7).
4 Paras **14.38ff**.
5 Control of Noise (Appeals) Regulations 1975, SI 1975/2116, as amended.

14.75 A s 60 notice must be served on the person who appears to the local authority to be carrying out, or going to carry out, the works and on such other persons appearing to the local authority to be responsible for or to have control over the carrying out of the works.[1] Sub-contractors would be caught by this, even if they commence works after preparation of the notice. Indeed, in one case a conviction for breach of the terms of a notice[2] was upheld even though the *identity* of a particular contractor was not known when that notice was prepared.[3] A strict approach is taken in respect of service of notices, however, which may be invalid if improperly served – even when service is made on a sister company in shared premises.[4]

1 CoPA 1974, s 60(5).
2 Para **14.67**.
3 *Wiltshier Construction Ltd v Westminster City Council* [1997] Env LR 321.
4 *AMEC Building Ltd v Camden London Borough Council* [1997] Env LR 330, DC.

14.76 Contravention of a notice without reasonable excuse[1] is an offence[2] punishable on summary conviction to an unlimited fine, with a continuing fine for each day of non-compliance following conviction.[3] Commission of an offence requires the presence and participation of the defendant, so a principal contractor could not be liable for an offence committed outside permitted hours by a sub-contractor, when the principal contractor was not himself present.[4] In certain circumstances, a person can seek a local authority's consent for activities to which s 60 applies.[5] Carrying out works in accordance with that consent provides a defence to a prosecution under s 60(8).[6]

1 On the meaning of which in the context of statutory nuisance, see paras **14.50–14.51**.
2 CoPA 1974, s 60(8).
3 CoPA 1974, s 74; Legal Aid, Sentencing and Punishment of Offenders Act 2012, s 85.
4 *City of London Corpn v Bovis Construction Ltd* (1988) 86 LGR 660.
5 CoPA 1974, s 61.
6 Ibid, s 61(8).

Chapter 15

Contaminated land

INTRODUCTION

15.01 Legal controls over contaminated land – its remediation, its development, and liabilities for its environmental impacts – are some of the most controversial of all environmental laws. Given that the subject matter is the condition of land itself, these controls are also of central importance to property transactions. But this chapter can be distinguished from others in Part II of this book in that contaminated land is not exclusively catered for by the law considered here: many of the activities more directly regulated by, for example, industrial pollution, water quality regulation or planning controls may give (or have given) rise to 'contamination' of land even if done lawfully. It is the consequences of this which explain in large part why the regulation of contaminated land is so controversial. Complex statutory pollution control systems take account of future contamination risks.[1] The contaminated land powers considered in this chapter are concerned with the identification and clean up of contaminated land in circumstances where other regimes such as the environmental permitting regime[2] or other regulatory regimes do not apply. Much of what follows is therefore concerned with the present or future impacts of past behaviour: rules which require the clean up of contaminated land are thus essentially *retrospective* as well as prospective in that they create potential liability for past (as well as future) actions;[3] controls over proposed lawful pollution are, conversely, essentially *prospective* only.

1 Eg, the environmental permitting regime expressly includes emissions to land: Environmental Permitting (England and Wales) Regulations 2010, SI 2010/675, as amended, reg 2(1).
2 *Environmental Protection Act 1990: Part 2A – Contaminated Land Statutory Guidance*, April 2012 ('Statutory Guidance'), para 1.5.
3 See *R (National Grid Gas plc) v Environment Agency* [2007] UKHL 30, [2007] 1 WLR 1780, 1782 ('It is true that [Part 2A] was retrospective in the sense that it created a potential present liability for acts done in the past. But that is not the same as creating a deemed past liability for those acts. There is nothing in the Act to create retrospectivity in this sense' (per Lord Hoffman)).

15.02 This is not to say that regulatory controls have no application to the particular factual situation of contaminated land.[1] One purpose of prospective regulatory controls is the avoidance of future pollution or contamination of the environment, including land. Some controls can also be used to address the consequences of contaminated or polluted land, in particular the law of statutory nuisance[2] or waste management.[3] Civil liabilities for damage caused by past activities may also arise under the common law,[4] whilst the role of planning law as a mechanism to provide for clean up as part and parcel of development has a crucial – and continuing – everyday role.[5] When assessing the asset value of land or interests in it, the condition of the land itself is a crucial factor. What has emerged is **an** awareness of the potential for contamination of land to have environmental and legal consequences, and thus an inherent concern in any transaction concerning land.

1 See paras **15.34–15.104**.
2 Ch 14, but see para **14.04** on the limitations of statutory nuisance in this context.
3 Eg, waste removal notices under the EPA 1990, s 59.
4 Ch 13.
5 See paras **15.10–15.27**.

THE GENERAL POLICY POSITION

15.03 General policy discussions in this area have been informed by a number of European and UK reports and policy documents, coupled with the powerful influence exercised by the United States' experience of historic contamination and measures to clean it up. The documents include reports from the House of Commons Select Committee on the Environment[1] and the House of Lords Select Committee on the European Communities.[2] Most controversial, however, and resulting in a change to subsequent developments concerning the remediation of contamination and other environmental damage in the UK, is the EU's Environmental Liability Directive ('ELD').[3]

1 *Toxic Waste* (HC Paper (1988–89) no 22) and *Contaminated Land* (HC Paper (1989–90) no 170).
2 *Paying for Pollution* (HL Paper (1989–90) no 84).
3 Directive 2004/35/CE of the European Parliament and of the Council on environmental liability with regard to the prevention and remedying of environmental damage, as amended; see paras **15.105–15.110**.

15.04 The legal framework for cleaning up contaminated land established by the Environment Act 1995[1] is complex. A peculiarity of the framework, which creates a system within which historic contamination may be compulsorily cleaned up (or 'remediated')[2] is the scope it has given Ministers to determine matters of essential detail: from what land is considered to be 'contaminated', through to who is required to remediate it and to pay for that remediation, to the standards of clean up that apply.

1 Introducing a new Part 2A into the EPA 1990: EA 1995, s 57. Considered fully in paras **15.34–15.104**. This chapter refers to Part 2A, rather than Part IIA, because that is the term that is now generally used.
2 EPA 1990, s 78A(7). Part 2A came into force (in England) on 1 April 2000. Environment Act 1995 (Commencement No 16 and Saving Provision) (England) Order 2000, SI 2000/340 (c8). Broadly equivalent regulations came into force in Scotland on 14 July 2000: SI 2000/178, and Wales on 15 September 2001: SI 2001/3211.

15.05 An important point of practical emphasis should be made however. Much has been written about the controls set out in Part 2A of the 1990 Act.[1] The extent of their application, and their relationship with other controls, should be kept in context, however. Most contaminated land in the UK is remediated under the planning regime. In addition, most contaminated land which is remediated under Part 2A is remediated voluntarily, that is, without the service of a notice ordering its remediation. As stated in the Statutory Guidance to Part 2A, '[e]nforcing authorities should seek to use Part 2A only where no appropriate alternative solution exists'.[2]

1 See, eg, S. Tromans and R. Turrall-Clarke, *Contaminated Land* (2nd edn, 2007, Sweet & Maxwell).
2 Statutory Guidance, para 1.5.

15.06 The regulatory controls have had major implications in particular cases. In the vast majority of cases, however, other issues have been at the forefront of practitioners' minds: site investigation, searches, valuation, enquiries, warranties and indemnities, and planning matters being prominent amongst them. Indeed, avoiding liability under Part 2A has probably been the principal concern.

GUIDING PRINCIPLES

15.07 Whilst the complexity of this area of law should not be understated, three 'guiding principles' provide context for the regime. The first of these relates to clean-up standards. The premise on which UK policy is based is that of 'suitability for use'.[1] Remedial action under this approach is only warranted when contamination poses unacceptable actual or potential risks to human health or the environment, and where there are cost-effective means to remediate, taking into account the actual or intended use of the site. This can be contrasted with the approach that was originally adopted in the United States[2] and the Netherlands[3] but which was subsequently abandoned in both jurisdictions. The UK approach seeks to minimise regulatory intervention and compulsory clean up, and thus the impacts of legal liabilities on the property market.[4]

1 See, eg, DoE *Paying for Our Past: The Arrangements for Controlling Contaminated Land and Meeting the Cost of Remedying Damage to the Environment* (March 1994); DoE, *Framework for Contaminated Land* (November 1994). The Framework was the outcome of the policy review initiated by Paying for Our Past, and provided the basis for what has become the EPA 1990, Part 2A.
2 The US Environmental Protection Agency was widely criticised in the 1980s and 1990s for its multi-functionality approach to clean ups under the Comprehensive Environmental Response, Compensation, and Liability Act 1980 ('CERCLA' or 'Superfund'). In 1995, the EPA issued a directive to ensure that future land use is considered in clean ups: Environmental Protection Agency, Land Use in the CERCLA Remedy Selection Process, OSWER Directive No. 9355.7–04 (25 May 1995).
3 The Netherlands also originally adopted a multifunctionality approach, requiring clean up to ensure suitability for any use.
4 Elaboration of this concept has been provided in the context of the regime: Statutory Guidance, paras 1.6, 3.2; see para **15.39**.

15.08 Second, the general view that the polluter should pay applies in the context of contaminated land just as elsewhere.[1] Much of the controversy associated with the drafting of s 57 of the Environment Act 1995, which introduced Part

2A, related to how any new liabilities should be allocated under this principle. In particular, it is the normal practice that responsibility for land, and for the effects of that land on others and the environment shifts with the transfer of ownership. The normal rule applies that the original polluter remains liable unless statute provides otherwise. The 'polluter pays principle' and the owner responsibility rules are not always compatible. In particular, Part 2A shifts liability for remediating contamination on the transfer of ownership of the contaminated land to the new owner or occupier in specified circumstances.[2]

1 In *Remedying Environment Damage*, (HL Paper (1993–94) no 10), Appendix 4, para 3.13. Allocation of liabilities – in accordance with this concept and otherwise – is considered in paras **15.74–15.92**.
2 Eg, limitations on polluters' liability where land is 'sold with information': see para **15.88**.

15.09 Reliance on the operation of the property market is the third guiding principle. Not only should development proposals for suspected or actually contaminated land consider the investigation and remediation of contamination (remediation costs therefore becoming a normal part of calculations of when and how to develop),[1] but in deciding who is responsible for a certain site the terms on which the site was (or is) to be transferred should be considered. Price should – ideally – reflect the condition of the site and the need for remediation. In practice, this depends, of course, on factors such as the date of transfer, the extent of information available or sought, and the discoverability of contamination.[2] Clearly, transfer values do not always accommodate these factors. However, where the price negotiated reflects any residual post-transfer liabilities, the government took the view that liability based on current ownership is still consistent with the polluter pays principle.[3]

1 Related works were exempt from the landfill tax: Finance Act 1996, ss 43A and 43B. The exemption has, however, been abolished. The Landfill Tax (Material from Contaminated Land) (Phasing out of Exemption) Order 2008, SI 2008/2669.
2 In respect of present enquiries, etc, which might be made see Chs 3–7.
3 See, eg, EPA 1990, ss 78F(4), (6); Statutory Guidance, para 8.5(b); paras **15.75–15.79**.

CONTAMINATED LAND AND PLANNING POWERS

15.10 Prospective controls relating to the remediation of contaminated land, as opposed to those concerned with avoiding activities which are actually contaminating, conveniently start with planning powers. The application of the general planning framework to environmental issues is discussed elsewhere in this book,[1] but this is supplemented by specific concerns arising in respect of contaminated land. These can be described broadly as strategic planning, questions of site investigation, mandatory remediation under planning conditions, and the use of planning obligations. Before considering these powers (or indeed any others), it should be added that their application, particularly in serious cases of contamination, will be assisted by an understanding of some of the scientific and practical problems associated with site remediation.

1 See Ch 18.

Strategic issues

15.11 Although land contamination is subject to specific controls,[1] actual or threatened contamination is a material planning consideration and should be taken into account during the preparation of local plans and the determination of planning applications.[2] General planning policy favours the re-use of previously developed **land in** urban areas – 'brownfield' sites – in preference to 'greenfield' sites,[3] and this **tends** to make the development of urban contaminated land a priority. The National Planning Policy Framework lays heavy emphasis on the pursuit of sustainable development through the planning system.[4] Local planning authorities have a key role in seeking to balance a national policy commitment to the maintenance of high and stable levels of economic growth, with the objectives of sustainable development.[5]

1 Eg, paras **15.34–15.104**.
2 See Planning Practice Guidance, Land affected by contamination; http://planningguidance. planningportal.gov.uk/blog/guidance/land-affected-by-contamination/land-affected-by-contamination-guidance/ The courts are the ultimate arbiters of the meaning of 'material considerations', but this clearly includes whether and to what extent land is contaminated, eg: *Cheshire County Council v Secretary of State for the Environment and Rathbone* [1996] JPL 410, QBD.
3 See National Planning Policy Framework, para 111; Planning Practice Guidance, Brownfield land, soils and agricultural land.
4 See National Planning Policy Framework, para 6; see further Ch 18.
5 See National Planning Policy Framework, para 7.

15.12 This is in general conformity with the 'suitable for use' approach described above.[1] In the particular context of contaminated land, the planning purpose of this approach is threefold: to prevent new development from contributing to an unacceptable risk from contamination;[2] to keep or bring back such land into beneficial use; and so to minimise avoidable pressures on greenfield sites.[3]

1 See para **15.07**.
2 See National Planning Policy Framework, paras 109, 120.
3 See ibid, para 17.

15.13 In preparing local plans, planning authorities will therefore take into account the possible effects of contaminated land.[1] This clearly places a premium on information in respect of actual or potential contamination. A general obligation in statutory nuisance law enables a local authority to collect such information,[2] but specific duties on local authorities to inspect land under Part 2A of the 1990 Act[3] **are a** source of information which is useful for planning purposes even if action is not subsequently taken under Part 2A itself. Registers of that information **have been** established **and CON 29 includes questions on contaminated land. In addition,** a general right of access exists where those specific requirements are too narrow in a particular case.[4]

1 See National Planning Policy Framework, paras 120, 121.
2 See EPA 1990, s 79(1) (duty to inspect for statutory nuisances).
3 See paras **15.53–15.57**.
4 See Ch 4.

15.14 Particular interest has focused on previous uses of land, although information here is often incomplete and, in any event, usually indeterminative.1 The responsibility for providing information on whether such land is actually contaminated rests primarily with the developer.[2] In preparing local plans, planning authorities should do the following: consider a strategic, phased approach to dealing with potential contamination if potential contamination is an issue over a wide area; formulate the appropriate strategy by using a sustainability appraisal including appropriate objectives to assess the impact and proposed monitoring; allocate land known to be affected by contamination only for development appropriate to it, including its remediation; take account of the possible effect of the contamination on surrounding areas; and have clear requirements for information on the contamination and its assessment, particularly as concerns the role of developers.[3] The potential for contamination should also be considered in drawing up a neighbourhood plan or in considering a neighbourhood development order.[4]

1 Provisions to require local authorities to compile registers of potentially contaminative uses were repealed for these reasons, amongst others: EPA 1990, s 143 (repealed); see EA 1995, s 120(3), Sch 24. Generally see Lewis 'The Abandonment of Registers of Contaminative Uses' (1993) 5 Environmental Law & Management 26.
2 National Planning Policy Framework, para 120.
3 Planning Practice Guidance, Land affected by contamination, para 5.
4 Ibid, para 6.

Development control

15.15 The principle underlying the use of planning powers for environmental purposes generally, and development control powers in particular, is that they should not be operated so as to duplicate controls which are the statutory responsibility of other bodies.[1] Planning policy, therefore, avoids unnecessary duplication, and encourages co-operation between planning authorities and environmental regulators, especially the Environment Agency. Similarly, the Environment Agency avoids unnecessary duplication with planning in its environmental controls.[2] The existence of specific controls may be a material planning consideration,[3] and planning authorities should assume that those controls will be properly applied and enforced. There may be some overlap between parallel systems however, and a planning condition will not necessarily be invalid if its purpose is one which could also be achieved under other legislation.[4] In the case of contaminated land this overlap is potentially very marked, particularly as contaminated land powers themselves demonstrate a clear preference for site **remediation** in connection with development or on a voluntary basis, rather than through mandatory **remediation** under **Part 2A of the 1990 Act.** For example, mandatory remediation is not required when an 'enforcing authority'[5] is satisfied that appropriate things are being, or will be, done by way of remediation without service of a notice.[6] Issues surrounding the likelihood of implementing planning permission remain,[7] as does the latitude presented by the meaning of 'will be' – within what period, for example – but the preference for other controls is nonetheless evident.

1 Fuller consideration of this is given in Ch 18.
2 See Environment Agency, National Planning Policy Framework – planning and contaminated land (Quick guide 362_12, 12 May 2012); https://www.gov.uk/government/uploads/system/uploads/attachment_data/file/297014/geho0512bupg-e-e.pdf
3 *Gateshead Metropolitan Borough Council v Secretary of State for the Environment and Northumbrian Water Group plc* [1994] JPL 255; affirmed by the Court of Appeal: [1995] JPL 432.
4 *W E Black Ltd v Secretary of State for the Environment and Harrow London Borough Council* [1997] JPL 37, concerning duplication of measures as to drainage and sewerage infrastructure, otherwise possible under the Water Industry Act 1991.
5 EPA 1990, s 78A(9); see para **15.65**.
6 EPA 1990, s 78H(5)(b).
7 See S. Tromans and R. Turrall-Clarke, *Contaminated Land*, para 4.58 (2nd edn, 2007, Sweet & Maxwell).

Planning conditions

15.16   Planning conditions clearly operate within the general planning law and policy framework, which is beyond the scope of this book.[1] Some specific policy considerations arise in respect of contaminated land however.[2] The planning system works alongside Part 2A; it is not a substitute for it, and vice versa.[2]

1 See *Butterworths Planning Law Service* and, for an introduction, Ch 18.
2 See Planning Practice Guidance, Land affected by contamination.

15.17   When a planning authority considers that a site **may** be contaminated, it should seek a risk assessment from the developer 'to determine the existence or otherwise of contamination, its nature and extent, the risks it may pose and to whom/what (the 'receptors') so that these risks can be assessed and satisfactorily reduced to an acceptable level'.[1] It is the developer's responsibility to provide such information.[2] In addition, the risk assessment should 'identify the potential sources, pathways and receptors ('contaminant linkages') and evaluate the risks'.[2]

The planning authority uses this information to determine whether more detailed investigation is required, or whether any remediation proposed by the developer is satisfactory.[3] The planning authority may also require the developer to provide a report of a desk study and site walk-over, typically called a phase I environmental assessment. The use of this information may be adequate to enable the development of 'a conceptual model of the source of contamination, the pathways by which it might reach vulnerable receptors and options to show how the identified contaminant linkages can be broken'.[4] Local authorities have no power to charge developers for undertaking consultations[5] which in any case clearly operate to their own advantage as well as to developers.

Unless the risk assessment described above 'clearly demonstrates that the risk from contamination can be satisfactorily reduced to an acceptable level, further site investigations and risk assessment will be needed before the application can be determined'.[6] Before the authority grants outline planning permission, it must, among other things, be satisfied that:

- it understands the contaminated condition of the site;
- the proposed development is appropriate as a means of remediating it; and
- it has sufficient information to be confident that it will be able to grant permission in full at a later stage bearing in mind the need for the necessary remediation to be viable and practicable.[7]

Some local planning authorities, and associations of such authorities, have published technical advice on carrying out risk assessments.[8]

1 Planning Practice Guidance, Land affected by contamination, para 7.
2 Ibid.
3 Ibid.
4 Ibid.
5 *McCarthy & Stone (Developments) Ltd v Richmond-upon-Thames London Borough Council* [1992] 2 AC 48, [1992] JPL 467, HL.
6 Planning Practice Guidance, Land affected by contamination, para 7.
7 Ibid, para 8.
8 See, eg., Hertfordshire and Bedfordshire Contaminated Land Forum, Development on Potentially Contaminated Land and/or for a Sensitive End Use; Technical Guide for Planning Applicants and Developers 2nd edn, July 2012); http://www.milton-keynes.gov.uk/assets/attach/4402/Contaminated_Land_Planning_Guidance.pdf; Amber Valley Borough Council, Land Contamination; http://www.ambervalley.gov.uk/environment-and-planning/pollution/land-contamination.aspx; Borough Council of King's Lynn and West Norfolk, Contaminated Land Assessment for Planning Applications; http://www.west-norfolk.gov.uk/default.aspx?page=24551.

15.18 If concerns about contamination remain, the planning authority should work with the developer to find ways to move the application forward, for example, granting permission subject to conditions or planning obligations. The authority must, however, be satisfied that a proposed development will be appropriate for its location and will not pose an unacceptable risk.[1]

The Planning Practice Guidance refers to the Statutory Guidance for criteria on identifying and dealing with land that poses an unacceptable risk.[2] In doing so, it refers to 'land that may be affected by contamination' rather than 'contaminated land' as in Part 2A.[3]

Other functions may also be relevant, including those under the Building Regulations 2010.[4]

1 Planning Practice Guidance, Land affected by contamination, para 9; see R *(Technoprint PLC and others) v Leeds City Council* [2010] EWHC 581 (Admin).
2 Planning Practice Guidance, Land affected by contamination, para 9.
3 Ibid, para 2.
4 SI 2010/2214, as amended.

15.19 Planning conditions may be used if relevant criteria are satisfied, to ensure that development, except for development carried out under an approved remediation scheme, does not begin until specified stages of the remediation scheme have been discharged. Such stages, together with factors that planning authorities should consider in formulating appropriate planning conditions, include the following:

- site characterisation – what is required, including what sort of survey, assessment and appraisal, by whom and how the work is to be presented;

- submission of the remediation scheme – what it should include;
- implementation of the approved remediation scheme – notification to the local planning authority of when the works will start, validation that the works have been carried out and reporting of unexpected contamination; and
- monitoring and maintenance – what is required and for how long.[1]

1 Planning Practice Guidance, Land affected by contamination, para 9.
2 Ibid.
3 Ibid.

15.20 In May 2008, the Department for Communities and Local Government issued model conditions for contaminated land.1 In 2012, the National Planning Policy Framework resulted in the replacement of the model conditions by the framework and its accompanying planning practice guidance.[2]

1 Letter to Chief Planning Officers: Model planning conditions for development on land affected by contamination (30 May 2008).
2 National Planning Policy Framework, Annex 3, item 35.

Planning obligations

15.21 It is well established that planning obligations may be used to complement or supplement conditions.[1] In the context of contaminated land they have particular appeal deriving from the opportunity they provide to create continuing obligations going beyond those which might be imposed through conditions. Although the Statutory Guidance provides for monitoring following **remediation,**[2] it only infrequently **extends** to the sort of monitoring possible under planning powers.

Examples of situations in which planning obligations concerning contaminated land may be used are the following:

'to ensure that any necessary offsite treatment works (eg the installation of gas-migration barriers, water treatment or monitoring arrangements) are put in place;

to restrict the development or future use of the land concerned; or

for payments to the local planning authority, for example, for ongoing monitoring, maintenance, or as a bond to cover the contingency of future action triggered by the monitoring'.[3]

1 Town and Country Planning Act (TCPA) 1990, s 106, as amended. For an introduction see paras **18.24–18.27.**
2 Statutory Guidance, para 6.8; see generally para **15.40.**
3 Planning Practice Guidance, Land affected by contamination, para 9.

15.22 A **case** of the development of contaminated land with an associated planning obligation involved Portsmouth City Council. A proposal to redevelop for residential use a former Ministry of Defence site, which was contaminated by military and industrial waste, was ultimately granted on appeal, subject to settlement of a planning obligation.[1] Although the case occurred in the mid-1990s, it is still notable for two reasons. First, because relatively little weight was given to the planning committee's ambitions for long-term decontamination (planning and environmental health officers having recommended a conditional grant in the first instance), as opposed to remediation sufficient to make the site suitable for residential use for thirty years. Secondly, because the planning obligation entered into provided extensive details in respect of, for example:

(a) protection measures required to treat the surface of the site to prevent escape of contaminants and harm to persons or the environment;
(b) appointing an independent consultant to oversee construction;
(c) advising new occupants of activities which will compromise protection methods; and
(d) appointing a groundsman to maintain landscaped areas and to monitor the integrity of protection measures, on a part-time basis, for the lifetime of the site's residential use.

1 Appeal Decision T/APP/K1745/A/94/233729/P7, noted at [1994] JPL 864.

AMENITY NOTICES

15.23 Certain types of contaminated land may also be subject to general planning powers designed to safeguard 'amenity'.[1] Although undefined, 'amenity' is a broad term which may refer to matters affecting the human senses, **for example,** views or unpleasant odours. These powers may be of broad 'environmental' application therefore, and rather narrower in the particular context of contaminated land. They are concerned more with 'tidying up' unsightly land than dealing with the health and environmental threats caused by contamination per se.

1 TCPA 1990, s 215.

15.24 If it appears to a local authority that the amenity of a part of its area is 'adversely affected' by the condition of land then it can serve on the owner *and* occupier of that land an 'amenity notice'.[1] **The** notice shall require specified steps to be carried out to remedy the condition of the land.

1 TCPA 1990, s 215(1).

15.25 Failure to comply with an amenity notice is an offence carrying a maximum fine of level 3 on the standard scale.[1] Continued non-compliance with a notice after conviction is a further offence carrying a fine not exceeding £40 for each day following the first conviction on which any requirement of the notice is not complied with. There are procedures for enabling a person served with a notice who has ceased to be the owner or occupier prior to the end of the compliance period to ensure that the new owner or occupier is brought before the court.[2] If that person is proved to be in default he may be convicted of the offence. The original defendant must be acquitted if he shows that he took all reasonable steps to ensure compliance.[3] A vendor who receives such a notice prior to completion of the sale should disclose it to the purchaser and seek an arrangement to ensure compliance with its terms. If the notice is served before exchange of contracts, the contract should provide for the carrying out of the requisite works by one of the parties.[4] A person served with a notice may appeal against it to a magistrates' court at any time within the period specified in the notice on any of the following grounds:

(a) the condition of the land does not adversely affect the amenity of any part of the local planning authority's area or of any adjoining area;

(b) the condition of the land is attributable to, and ordinarily results from, operations or land use which does not contravene the relevant planning legislation;

(c) the requirements of the notice exceed what is necessary for the purpose; or

(d) the period specified for carrying out the require steps is unreasonably short.[5]

1 TCPA 1990, s 216(2): currently £1,000, Criminal Justice Act 1982, s 37.
2 TCPA 1990, s 216(3) and (4).
3 Ibid, sub-s (5).
4 Clause 3.1.2(e) of the Standard Commercial Property Conditions (2nd edn) provides that the property is sold subject to 'public requirements'. These are defined as any notice, order or proposal given or made (whether before or after the date of the contract) by a body acting on statutory authority. It is unlikely that this in itself would be sufficient to show that a vendor had taken all reasonable steps to ensure compliance with the notice.
5 TCPA 1990, s 217(1) and (2).

15.26 The notice is ineffective pending the final determination or withdrawal of the appeal.[1] The magistrates' court may correct any informality, defect or error in a notice if satisfied that it is not material, otherwise it must determine the appeal.[2] A further appeal against the decision of the magistrates' court lies to the Crown Court.[3] Authority from 1990 would suggest that the issue of ultra vires may be decided on appeal, on prosecution or by way of judicial review.[4] However, the options now **seem** more likely to be confined to appeal and judicial review.[5]

1 TCPA 1990, s 217(3).
2 Ibid, sub-ss (4) and (5).
3 Ibid, s 218.
4 *R v Crown Court at Oxford, ex p Smith* (1990) 154 LGR 458.
5 *Boddington v British Transport Police* [1999] 2 AC 143, HL; *R v Wicks* [1998] AC 92, [1997] JPL 1049, HL.

15.27 If the steps required by the notice are not taken within the period specified or any extended period allowed by the local planning authority, the authority may enter the land, take the steps required and recover any expenses reasonably incurred in so doing from the current owner of the land.[1] Any money expended by the owner or occupier in complying with a notice or by an owner in reimbursing the reasonable expenses of the local planning authority in taking action in default, may be recovered from the person who caused or permitted the land to come to be in the condition it was in when the notice was served.[2]

1 TCPA 1990, s 219(1).
2 Ibid, sub-s (2).

CONTAMINATED LAND AND WASTE MANAGEMENT

15.28 Contamination of land in a broad sense can clearly arise from permitted as well as unpermitted activities, although in many cases, contamination of land is just one part of permitted activities. For example, the potential for contamination of soil is one consideration amongst many under the environmental permitting regime.[1] More obviously, the disposal of waste to landfill involves direct contamination of land itself but, if proper steps are taken, the **potential for** off-site contamination is reduced to a minimum level. Therefore, there may be a close practical link between waste and contamination.

1 See Ch 20.

15.29 The legal starting point is that the contaminated land regime does not apply in relation to any land in respect of which there is for the time being in force **an environmental permit that was formerly** a site licence under **Part 2 of** the EPA **1990** except where the reason for the land being classified as 'contaminated land' is attributable to something *other than* a breach of the conditions of that licence or the carrying on of activities that are licensed.[1] The effect of this complex section is to make breaches of **environmental permits** which cause contamination, or contamination caused by permitted activities, enforceable under the Environmental Permitting Regulations and not under contaminated land controls. Options would then include prosecution[2] or a requirement to remove unlawfully deposited **waste**.[3] Where land becomes classified as 'contaminated **land**' by reason of activities carried on before an environmental permit concerning waste took effect, Part 2A **does**, however, apply to the contamination arising from that activity.

1 EPA 1990, s 78YB(2). Waste management licences automatically became environmental permits on 6 April 2008 when the Environmental Permitting (England and Wales) Regulations 2007, SI 2007/3538, entered into force (now Environmental Permitting (England and Wales) Regulations 2010, SI 2010/675, as amended).
2 See para **20.28**.
3 EPA 1990, s 59.

15.30 The **environmental permitting regime (which includes the former** waste management licensing system) also regulates unpermitted activity. For example, certain waste authorities are empowered to require the removal from land of waste that is unlawfully deposited in certain circumstances.[1] If land becomes contaminated as a result of such a deposit, then the contaminated land powers cannot be used if and to the extent that the powers of the relevant waste authority 'may be exercised'.[2] This prohibition applies whether or not the site is permitted, and so if a waste authority *may* use s 59 to enforce a breach of condition then Part 2A does not apply. The deposits of waste to which s 59 applies became 'unlawful' on 1 April 1992.[3] It follows that s 59 may not apply to deposits before this date, and so Part 2A will apply unless s 16 of the Control of Pollution Act 1974 applies.[4] Equally, the deposit must have been of 'waste' within the (broad) technical definition of that term. If the contaminant was not waste, or derived from the unlawful deposit of such waste, then it too may not be subject to waste powers, and Part 2A will again apply. Further, 'land (in situ) including unexcavated contaminated soil and buildings permanently connected with land' is excluded from the scope of the Waste Framework Directive.[5]

1 EPA 1990, s 59. From 6 April 2008, the Clean Neighbourhoods and Environment Act 2005 extended s 59 to require the owner to remove the waste if there is no occupier of the land or the authority would incur 'unreasonable expense' in finding the occupier. Ibid, s 59ZA.
2 EPA 1990, s 78YB(3).
3 No earlier than 1 April 1992.
4 Although the Control of Pollution Act 1974 has been largely repealed, it remains in force for earlier deposits.
5 Directive 2008/98/EC on waste (2008) OJ L312/3, art 2(1)(b); see Waste (England and Wales) Regulations 2011, SI. 2011/988, art 75(2) (defining 'waste' as 'anything that is waste within the meaning of Article 3(1) of [the Waste Framework Directive]').

15.31 What is an important tactical consequence follows for **owners and** occupiers of land. The obligation on an occupier (**or an owner if there is no** **occupier or the authority would incur 'unreasonable expense' in finding the** **occupier**) to remove unlawfully-deposited waste must be set aside on appeal if the occupier (**or owner**) shows that **he** did not deposit the waste or knowingly cause or knowingly permit its deposit – an 'innocent occupier (**or owner**)' defence.[1] Occupiers **and owners** will not necessarily benefit from the same defence under Part 2A – indeed, that Part expressly provides for some liability to be borne in some cases by owners or occupiers.[2] If an occupier **or owner** can therefore show that an authority's powers under s 59 'may be exercised' – perhaps against a previous owner or occupier not discovered or traced by an authority enforcing the contaminated land regime – then Part 2 and not Part 2A will apply.

1 EPA 1990, s 59(3); see ibid, s 59ZA(5).
2 See paras **15.75–15.79.**

CONTAMINATED LAND AND STATUTORY NUISANCE

15.32 One justification for the creation of the contaminated land regime **was** that it is merely a 'clarification' of liabilities which would otherwise exist in any event under statutory nuisance controls.[1] Whilst there are certain similarities, this is a gross over-simplification – not least because a powerful reason for the introduction of Part 2A was the practical limitations of those other controls. With the implementation of **Part 2A** on 1 April 2000 (in England) the danger of duplication with predecessor statutory nuisance controls **was** addressed by certain consequential amendments. In particular, it was expressly declared that no matter constitutes a statutory nuisance to the extent that it consists of, or is caused by, land being in a contaminated state.[2]

1 Eg, *HL Debates*, col 1054 (20 March 1995), on the Environment Bill's Third Reading in the House of Lords.
2 EPA 1990, s 79(1A), inserted by EA 1995, Sch 22, para 89, also brought into force on 1 April 2000.

15.33 Land is only in a 'contaminated state' if it is in such condition by reason of substances in, on or under the land that harm is being caused or there is a possibility of harm being caused, or pollution of controlled waters is being, or is likely to be, caused.[1] This exclusion is wider than the definition of contaminated land provided for Part 2A itself,[2] in particular, it is not required that the relevant harm, or its possibility, be 'significant'. There is therefore a 'gap' between the two systems. No steps have been taken to meet the suggestion that guidance under the Act should apply to all types of harm that would be 'prejudicial to health or a nuisance',[3] although this does not appear to have been an issue in enforcement of either Part 2A or the statutory nuisance regime.[4] Where deposits or substances on land give rise to offence to human senses which does not amount to 'harm', this may amount to a statutory nuisance.

1 EPA 1990, s 79(1B). 'Controlled waters' are, in essence, surface water courses and other inland waters except for public sewers or sewers or drains that drain into a public sewer, lakes and ponds that discharge directly or indirectly into them, groundwater, coastal waters and territorial waters. WRA 1991, s 104; see para **17.43**.
2 See paras **15.40–15.52**.
3 *Contaminated Land*, (HC Paper (1996–97) no 22), noted at (1997) 9 *Environmental Law & Management* 67.
4 For the meaning of 'harm' see paras **15.40–15.42**.

REMEDIATION OF CONTAMINATED LAND – PART 2A OF THE ENVIRONMENTAL PROTECTION ACT 1990

15.34 Part 2A of the EPA 1990[1] established a statutory regime for remediating contaminated land. The details of the regime are set out in three documents: Part 2A itself, which was inserted into the EPA 1990 by s 57 of the Environment Act 1995; the Statutory Guidance, which contains the details of the regime;[2] and certain other matters of detail and elaboration which are set out in the Contaminated Land (England) Regulations 2006, as amended ('Regulations').[3]

In addition, the Radioactive Contaminated Land (Modification of Enactments) (England) Regulations 2006, as amended ('Modification Regulations'),[4] which came into force on 4 August 2006, extended the regime, with modifications, to radioactive contaminated land other than for circumstances in which the operator of a nuclear installation is liable under the Nuclear Installations Act 1965.

1 Section 78L of the EPA 1990 was amended by the Clean Neighbourhoods and Environment Act 2005. The amendment, which came into force on 4 August 2006, removed appeals of

local authority remediation notices from magistrates' courts to the Secretary of State. Clean Neighbourhoods and Environment Act 2005 (Commencement No 2) (England) Order 2006, SI 2006/1361. See para **15.71**.

2 The Statutory Guidance revoked and replaced Department for the Environment, Food and Rural Affairs Circular 01/2006 ('2006 Guidance'), which, in turn, had revoked and replaced Department of the Environment, Transport and the Regions Circular 01/2000.

3 SI 2006/1380. The Regulations consolidated the Contaminated Land (England) Regulations 2000, SI 2000/227, and the Contaminated Land (England) (Amendment) Regulations 2001, SI 2001/663, which it revoked and replaced, with amendments.

4 SI 2006/1379. The Modification Regulations were made by the Secretary of State pursuant to powers under Part 2A, as modified by the Radioactive Contaminated Land (Enabling Powers) (England) Regulations 2005, SI 2005/3467. The Modification Regulations also transposed Articles 48 and 53 of Council Directive 1996/29/Euratom, which set out basic safety standards for the protection of the health of workers and the general public from dangers arising from ionising radiation.

EPA 1990, Part 2A: history

15.35 The general controversy surrounding contaminated land[1] prompted the publication in 1994 of a wide-ranging consultation paper.[2] This ultimately led to the formulation of a statutory regime for the inspection and remediation of contaminated land.[3] What **Part 2A** in fact does is establish liabilities in respect of past environmental damage, where that damage is quantified in terms of the cost of corrective (or 'remedial') activity. **That is, Part 2A establishes liability for remediating current contamination caused by past pollution incidents when the current contamination is causing an unacceptable risk of harm.** After considerable delay, the regime was brought into force in England on 1 April 2000.[4] **Broadly** similar controls were given effect in Scotland on 14 July 2000[5] **and Wales on 15 September 2001.**[6]

There are separate statutory guidance and regulations for Scotland and Wales. The regime has not been brought into force in Northern Ireland.[7]

1 See paras **15.01–15.06**.

2 Department of the Environment, *Paying for Our Past: The Arrangements for Controlling Contaminated Land and meeting the Cost of Remedying Damage to the Environment* (March 1994).

3 EPA 1990, Pt 2A, inserted by EA 1995, s 57.

4 Environment Act 1995 (Commencement No 16 and Saving Provision) (England) Order 2000, SI 2000/340.

5 Environment Act 1995 (Commencement No 17 and Saving Provision) (Scotland) Order 2000, SI 2000/180.

6 Environment Act 1995 (Commencement No 20 and Saving Provision) (Wales) Order 2001, SI 2001/3211.

7 See the Waste and Contaminated Land (Northern Ireland) Order 1997, SR 1997/2778, part III (not in force). The Radioactive Contaminated Land Regulations (Northern Ireland) 2006/345, as amended, transposed Articles 48 and 53 of Council Directive1996/29/Euratom.

15.36 One reason for the delay in the implementation of the regime **was** the complexity of, and controversy surrounding, the statutory guidance under the Act. The Statutory Guidance sets out essential detail in respect of many of the principal features of the regime, including: definitions; the identification of who will be liable and for what; the allocation of liabilities; and the scale of liabilities themselves. A first round of formal consultation on that guidance took place in 1995,[1] followed by an 'informal' consultation on a subsequent Departmental working paper with 'representatives from a number of bodies having an interest in the contaminated land provisions'.[2] Further formal consultation on revised drafts began in late 1996.[3] The final version of the statutory guidance was published on 20 March 2000 **as Annex 3 of DETR Circular 02/2000.**

1 [Draft] *Guidance on Determination of Whether Land is Contaminated Land under the Provisions of* [Part 2A] *of the Environmental Protection Act 1990*, May 1995.
2 DoE *Contaminated Land*, 20 February 1996.
3 *Consultation on Draft Statutory Guidance on Contaminated Land* September 1996 (two volumes) *('Draft Guidance')*. That guidance was accompanied by draft regulations proposed in connection with the operation of the new regime.

EPA 1990, Part 2A: principal features

15.37 The main features of Part 2A are as follows (see Table 15.1):

(a) The definition of 'contaminated land', including a category of 'special sites' which because of their greater polluting potential is the responsibility of the Environment Agency[1] rather than local authorities: s 78A.
(b) Creation of a 'duty of inspection' on local authorities to identify contaminated land and special sites, and to designate the latter: ss 78B–78D.
(c) Creation of duties on local authorities and the Agency to require the 'remediation' of contaminated land in certain cases and to certain extents, including provision for the service of 'remediation notices': ss 78E, 78H, 78J, and 78K.
(d) Determination of the 'appropriate person' (or persons) to bear responsibility for remediation and for the allocation of liabilities between them, where appropriate: ss 78F and 78K.
(e) Consultation between local authorities and the Agency, and with persons who may be 'appropriate persons' in respect of potential remediation requirements: ss 78H and 78YA.
(f) Offences for contravening Part 2A and procedural matters, including appeals and authorities' powers to act in default: ss 78L–78P.
(g) Compilation of a register in respect of functions carried out under Part 2A: ss 78S–78V.

1 The enforcing authorities for special sites in Wales and Scotland are Natural Resources Wales and the Scottish Environment Protection Agency, respectively.

Table 15.1: Part 2A of the EPA 1990

Section 78	Function
A	Preliminary (definitions, etc)
B	Identification of contaminated land
C	Identification and designation of special sites
D	Referral of special site decisions to the Secretary of State
E	Duty of enforcing authority to require remediation, etc
F	Determination of the appropriate person to bear responsibility for remediation
G	Grant of, and compensation for, rights of entry, etc
H	Restrictions and prohibitions on serving remediation notices
J	Restrictions on liability relating to the pollution of controlled waters
K	Liability in respect of contaminating substances which escape to other land
L	Appeals against remediation notices
M	Offences of not complying with a remediation notice
N	Powers of the enforcing authority to carry out remediation
P	Recovery of, and security for, the cost of remediation by the enforcing authority
Q	Special sites
QA	Land no longer considered to be contaminated
R	Registers
S	Exclusion from registers of information affecting national security
T	Exclusion from registers of certain confidential information
U	Reports on the state of contaminated land
V	Site-specific guidance concerning contaminated land
W	Regard to be had to guidance given by the Secretary of State
X	Supplementary provisions
Y	Application to the Isles of Scilly
YA	Supplementary provisions with respect to the Secretary of State's guidance
YB	Interaction with other enactments
YC	Radioactivity

Statutory Guidance

15.38 In many important respects these framework provisions are supplemented by the Statutory **Guidance**, which is either binding or to be 'had regard to' depending on the context. *Binding* guidance issued by the Secretary of State relates to: whether land is 'contaminated';[1] the inspection of local authorities' areas to identify contaminated land;[2] identifying persons who are *not* to be considered 'appropriate persons';[3] apportionment of liability between two or more appropriate persons;[4] and inspection and review of 'special sites'.[5] Guidance to which local authorities and the Agency must *have regard* relates to: what remediation is required and the standard of remediation;[6] recovery of costs by authorities;[7] and general guidance to the Agency.[8] The Agency may itself issue site-specific guidance to which local authorities must have regard, although the Secretary of State's guidance takes precedence in the case of any inconsistency.[9]

The Department of Environment, Food and Rural Affairs ('Defra') has published three versions of the Statutory Guidance; in 2000, 2006 and 2012. Defra published the 2012 – and current – version following criticism by the UK Government of the 2006 Guidance and its conclusion that there was 'a general need to bring some aspects of [it] up to date in order to reflect some of the hurdles in its application which have been encountered by its users over the years'.[10] The Statutory Guidance that revoked and replaced the 2006 Guidance drastically reduced its length to 69 pages, a reduction that was achieved, in part, by deleting non-statutory guidance that had described the Part 2A regime and the concepts on which it is predicated and publishing the provisions that relate to radioactive contaminated land in separate guidance.

That is, two versions of the statutory guidance under Part 2A were published in April 2012; Defra published updated Statutory Guidance for contaminated land, and the Department of Energy & Climate Change published separate statutory guidance for radioactive contaminated land ('Radioactive Contaminated Land Statutory Guidance'),[11] both in respect of England.

1 EPA 1990, s 78A(2); Statutory Guidance, s 4; see paras **15.40–15.52**.
2 EPA 1990, s 78B(2); Statutory Guidance, s 5; see paras **15.53–15.57**.
3 EPA 1990, s 78F(6); see paras **15.75–15.92**.
4 EPA 1990, s 78F(7); Statutory Guidance, s 7; see paras **15.93–15.96**.
5 EPA 1990, s 78Q(6); Statutory Guidance, paras 2.1, 2.14, 3.35(d), 5.8 and 6.1; see paras **15.51–15.52**.
6 EPA 1990, s 78E(5); Statutory Guidance, s 6.
7 EPA 1990, s 78P(2); Statutory Guidance, s 8; see paras **15.98–15.101**.
8 EPA 1990, s 78W(1).
9 EPA 1990, s 78V(1) and (2).
10 Defra, 'Impact assessment, simplification of the contaminated land regime' (IA No. Defra 11/33, URN 11/1109 ver. 3.0, 6 October 2011) para 11.
11 Department of Energy & Climate Change, Environmental Protection Act 1990: Part IIA Contaminated Land, Radioactive Contaminated Land Statutory Guidance (April 2012); available at https://www.gov.uk/government/uploads/system/uploads/attachment_data/file/48325/4472–draft-statutory-guidance-covering-radioactive-cont.pdf The Welsh and Scottish Governments published the Statutory Guidance and the Radioactive Statutory Guidance for Wales and Scotland, respectively.

15.39 Part 2A created an extended process by which contaminated land is identified, and remediation solutions tailored to individual sites on a cost-benefit basis. Extended negotiation with those likely to be affected is intrinsic to that process, with unusual statutory bars to action put in place to require consultation in respect of authorities' plans,[1] and to prefer voluntary rather than forced clean up.[2] That negotiation is, of course, done in the shadow of the law. Persons likely to be responsible for remediation[3] need to be well-acquainted with matters such as an authority's preferred solution, and the character and extent of remediation it might require. Yet even the Statutory Guidance provides few absolutes.[4]

1 Eg, EPA 1990, s 78H(1) prohibits service of a remediation notice before consultation has been attempted with intended recipients.
2 Ibid, s 78H(5)(b).

3 As to which see paras **15.74–15.92**.
4 The closest it comes in this respect is in defining the categories of 'significant harm' which are to be remedied: EPA 1990, s 78A(5); Statutory Guidance, s 4; see paras **15.47–15.50**.

What is 'contaminated land'?

15.40 'Contaminated land' (**other than radioactive contaminated land**) is any land which appears to the relevant local authority to be in such a condition, by reason of substances in, on or under the land, that either significant harm is being caused or there is a significant possibility of such harm being caused, or significant pollution of controlled waters is being caused or there is a significant possibility of such pollution being caused.[1] 'Harm' means harm to the health of living organisms or other interference with the ecological systems of which they form part, including harm to property[2] – a very broad definition, which is substantially truncated in the Statutory **Guidance.** Determinations of whether harm **or water pollution** is 'significant', or there is a 'significant possibility' of such harm, must be made in accordance with the Secretary of State's guidance.[3]

'Remediation' means anything from site assessment to clean-up operations and post clean-up monitoring.[4] The definition therefore focuses not so much on whether land itself is contaminated, but on its potential to affect other things: it is a definition of contaminating land rather than contaminated land.

In respect of radioactivity, 'contaminated land' is any land which appears to the relevant local authority to be in such a condition, by reason of substances in, on or under the land, that harm is being caused or there is a significant possibility of such harm being caused.[5] 'Harm' means 'lasting exposure to any person resulting from the after-effects of a radiological emergency, past practice or past work activity'.[6] 'Remediation' has a similarly broad meaning to 'remediation' in respect of non-radioactive contaminated land.[7]

1 EPA 1990, s 78A(2).
2 Ibid, s 78A(4).
3 Ibid, s 78A(2) and (5). Section 86 of the Water Act 2003 amended the term 'pollution of controlled waters is being, or is likely to be, caused' in s 78A(2)(b) of the EPA 1990 to 'significant pollution of controlled waters is being caused or there is a significant possibility of such pollution being caused'. The significance threshold came into effect on 6 April 2012. See Water Act 2003 (Commencement No. 11) Order 2012/264; EPA 1990, s 78A(5) (as amended by the Water Act 2003, s 86).
4 EPA 1990, s 78A(7).
5 Modification Regulations, reg 5(1).
6 Ibid, reg 5(4).
7 Ibid, reg 5(6). Other terms, such as 'substance' are also defined so they relate to radioactivity. See ibid, reg 5(8).

15.41 Rather than providing numerical or other environmental standards by way of a definition, the Statutory Guidance provides a definition of contaminated land which is based on 'the principles of risk assessment'.[1]

In respect of radioactive contaminated land, the local authority must have 'reasonable grounds' for believing that the land is contaminated before inspecting it. If it considers that the land is 'contaminated land', it designates the land as a' special site'.[2] Due to such a designation resulting in the Environment Agency being the enforcing authority, the local authority should arrange for the Agency to carry out the risk assessment.[3]

1 See Statutory Guidance, paras 3.33–3.36. In July 2008, Defra published a consultation which included the reasons why the Government chose not to prescribe risk-based numerical thresholds for triggers under Part 2A. Defra, Guidance on the Legal Definition of Contaminated Land, para 5 (July 2008); see paras **15.56–15.59**.
2 Modification Regulations, reg 6; see para **15.52**.
3 Radioactive Contaminated Land Statutory Guidance, para 3.2.

15.42 The Statutory Guidance defines 'risk' as 'the combination of: (a) the likelihood that harm, or pollution of water, will occur as a result of contaminants in, on or under the land; and (b) the scale and seriousness of such harm or pollution if it did occur'.[1] The Statutory Guidance further states that '[r]isk assessments should be based on information which is: (a) scientifically-based; (b) authoritative; (c) relevant to the assessment of risks arising from the presence of contaminants in soil; and (d) appropriate to inform regulatory decisions in accordance with Part 2A and [the Statutory] Guidance'.[2]

Further guidance on the role of scientific and technical assessments is provided in the Statutory Guidance in the context of local authorities' duties of inspection and designation.[3] In general, however, the intention is that this definition should give effect to the 'suitable for use' approach: land will only be contaminated if, in its current use,[4] it presents an actual or likely risk to specified categories of interest.

1 Statutory Guidance, para 3.1.
2 Ibid, para 3.4.
3 Ibid, s 4; see paras **15.53–15.59**.
4 The term 'current use' is defined in para 3.5 of the Statutory Guidance.

Soil guideline values and generic assessment criteria

15.43 The original statutory guidance, published in 2000, stated that a local authority could simplify its risk assessment procedure, when appropriate, by the use of 'authoritative and scientifically based guideline values for concentrations of the potential pollutants in, on or under the land in contaminant linkages of the type concerned'.[1] The non-statutory guideline values envisaged by the original guidance were soil guideline values ('SGVs'), which were first published by Defra and the Environment Agency in March 2002 and were subsequently used by local authorities in determining whether there was a significant possibility of significant harm (referred to by Defra as 'SPOSH') to human health in respect of residential land (with vegetable growing and without), allotments, and commercial/industrial land. SGVs were estimated by using a computer-based model, known as the Contaminated Land Exposure Assessment ('CLEA').[2] Due to only 10 SGVs having been developed, they were supplemented by generic assessment criteria ('GACs') to assess risks to human health for an additional 120 contaminants that had been prepared by organisations such as the Chartered Institute for Environmental Health and the Environmental Industries Commission.[3]

The use of SGVs and GACs by local authorities to identify the point at which land reached a trigger value of significant possibility of significant harm to human health led to problems. Local authorities encountered two main areas of uncertainty in making the determination: uncertainty in determining the degree of contamination that amounted to 'contaminated land' in the absence of a precise legal definition; and how to make a determination in cases when it was not scientifically possible to estimate risks accurately.[4] Meanwhile, the Environment Agency, the Health Protection Agency, the Food Standards Agency and Government expert committees became concerned about the scientific uncertainty in proposals for trigger points linked to estimates of excess lifetime cancer risks. Government lawyers advised against using non-statutory technical guidance to indicate where the Government considered that legal trigger points of significant possibility of significant harm should lie. The lawyers considered that even if the SGVs (and GACs) were scientifically based, a court may take a different view on the relevant trigger.[5]

In July 2008, therefore, Defra announced that the use of SGVs as trigger values would be discontinued.[6] Defra stated, however, that local authorities could use the SGVs, when they had been revised, as screening thresholds in their risk assessments on whether to determine land as 'contaminated land' under Part 2A. Defra's rationale was that if concentrations of contaminants at a site are below the relevant SGV, 'it is very unlikely that a significant possibility of significant harm would exist'.[7] If the concentrations are above the relevant SGV, the contaminant may or may not be a significant possibility of significant harm.[8]

1 Department of the Environment, Transport and the Regions Circular 01/2000, para B.47; see also ibid, paras B.48–B.49.
2 Department for Environment, Food and Rural Affairs, Assessment of Risks to Human Health from Land Contamination: An Overview of the Development of Soil Guideline Values and Related Research (March 2002); Potential Contaminants for the Assessment of Land (March 2002); Contaminants in Soils: Collation of Toxicological Data and Intake Values for Humans (March 2002); the Contaminated Land Exposure Assessment Model (CLEA): Technical basis and algorithms (March 2002). SGVs were subsequently issued for various contaminants including arsenic, cadmium, chromium, ethylbenzene, lead, mercury, nickel, phenol, selenium and toluene.
3 CL:AIRE, Soil Generic Assessment Criteria for Human Health Risk Assessment (January 2010, 2, para 1.
4 See Defra, Guidance on the Legal Definition of Contaminated Land, para 5 (July 2008).
5 Defra, Improvements to Contaminated Land Guidance: Outcome of the 'Way Forward' Exercise on Soil Guideline Values, para 8 (22 July 2008).
6 Ibid, para 7. Defra also announced various measures including the issuance of revised CLEA guidance documents.
7 Defra, Guidance on the Legal Definition of Contaminated Land, para 37 (July 2008).
8 Ibid, paras 38–39.

Category 4 screening levels

15.44 In 2010, the Government announced a review of the use of SGVs and GACs by local authorities due to its view that local authorities were still using them to determine that land was contaminated land under Part 2A when this was not their function.[1] In 2011, a new system was introduced for determining whether land is contaminated land due to a significant possibility of significant harm to human health.[2] Under the new system, called Category 4 screening levels, land for which such a determination is 'clearly acceptable' is placed in category 1; land that is clearly not contaminated land is placed in category 4. Land that is capable of a determination of contaminated land is placed in category 2. Finally, land that does not appear to meet the threshold for such a determination is placed in category 3.[2]

Category 4 screening levels have subsequently been developed for arsenic, benzene, benzo(a)pyrene, cadmium, chromium (VI) and lead.[3]

1 Defra, 'Impact assessment, simplification of the contaminated land regime' (IA No. Defra 11/33, URN 11/1109 ver. 3.0, 6 October 2011), paras 18–19.
2 Statutory Guidance, paras 4.17–4.29; see Defra, 'SP1010, Development of Category 4 Screening Levels (C4lSLs) for assessment of land affected by contamination', Final Project Report (Revision 2) (Contaminated Land: Applications in Real Environments (CL:AIRE), 24 September 2014) ('SP1010'); available at http://randd.defra.gov.uk/Document.aspx?Document=12352_SP1010MainReport.pdf.
3 See SP1010, appendices C-H (provisional).

Significant contaminant linkages

15.45 In applying the risk-based approach to a specific site, the first step is the identification of a particular 'contaminant linkage'. The contaminant linkage is the key physical ingredient whose presence may identify land as being contaminated, and on which remediation activity is subsequently focused. To break a contaminant linkage is to remove one of the elements in it that defines land as contaminated. Each contaminant linkage consists of three elements:

(a) a *contaminant* – 'a substance which is in, on or under the land and which has the potential to cause significant harm to a relevant receptor, or to cause significant pollution of controlled waters';

(b) a *receptor* – 'something that could be adversely affected by a contaminant, for example a person, an organism, an ecosystem, property, or controlled waters'; and

(c) a *pathway* – one or more routes or means 'by which a receptor is or might be affected by a contaminant'.[1]

In respect of non-radioactive contaminated land, the receptors are human beings, ecological systems or specified property.[2]

In respect of radioactive contaminated land, the sole receptor is a human being.[3] A contaminant linkage exists if one or more 'substances' is resulting in, or presenting a significant possibility of, harm to any person in the contaminant linkage.[4] The terms 'contaminant', 'pollutant' and 'substance' refer only to 'substances containing radionuclides which have resulted from the after-effects of a radiological emergency or have been processed as part of a past practice or past work activity'.[5] The Modification Regulations set out the steps to be followed for radioactive contaminated land. These steps differ, as appropriate, from those for non-radioactive contaminated land in order to tailor them to harm caused by the presence of radionuclides.[6]

1 Statutory Guidance, para 3.8.
2 Ibid.
3 Radioactive Contaminated Land Statutory Guidance, para 5.5.
4 Ibid.
5 Ibid, s 8.
6 Modification Regulations, regs 5–17.

15.46 The otherwise very broad definition of contaminated land for non-radioactive contaminated land is significantly truncated by provision in the Statutory Guidance of an *exclusive* list of the categories of receptors which can form part of a contaminant linkage.[1] Unless one of these categories is involved, land cannot be contaminated land for the purposes of the Act. The categories are:

(a) human beings;
(b) any ecological system, or living organism forming part of such a system, which is within a location subject to any of eight statutory or non-statutory conservation designations. These include sites of special scientific interest ('SSSIs'), actual and proposed sites under EU conservation legislation, and nature reserves;[2]
(c) property in the form of crops, produce grown domestically or on allotments for consumption, livestock, other owned or domesticated animals, and wild animals which are the subject of shooting or fishing rights;[3] and
(d) property in the form of buildings.[4]

It is significant that this list does not include harm to land itself. Contamination of land which affects the value of land itself, or even the value of an adjacent site, but which poses no risk of harm to receptors of the type provided in the Statutory Guidance do not fall within the definition, and therefore cannot be made subject to compulsory remediation.

1 Statutory Guidance, s 4.
2 Ibid, Table 1. On these designations, see generally Ch 19.
3 Statutory Guidance, Table 2.
4 Ibid.

15.47 The second step in identifying contaminated land, once a contaminant linkage has been identified, is to determine if the 'harm' to the relevant receptor is 'significant', that is, if 'significant harm is being caused or there is a significant possibility of such harm being caused', or if 'significant pollution of controlled waters is being caused or there is a significant possibility of such pollution being caused'.[1] 'Harm' means 'harm to the health of living organisms or other interference with the ecological systems of which they form part and, in the case of man, includes harm to his property';[2] the question of significance is to be determined in accordance with the Statutory Guidance.[3] A further exclusive list is provided by the Statutory Guidance of harm that is to be regarded as significant harm by type of receptor. Whilst it might be arguable that the limitation of harm by the Statutory Guidance only to certain categories of living **organisms** is outside the power provided by the Act – 'harm' includes on its face *all* living organisms[4] – the definition of significance clearly is for the Statutory Guidance. By way of illustration, 'significant harm' includes:

(a) for people, 'death; life threatening diseases (eg cancers); other diseases likely to have serious impacts on health; serious injury; birth defects; and impairment of reproductive functions' ('human health effects');[5]
(b) for ecological systems, and living organisms forming part of them, in designated areas, 'harm which results in an irreversible adverse change, or in some other substantial adverse change, in the functioning of the ecological system within any substantial part of that location or harm which significantly affects any species of special interest within that location and which endangers the long-term maintenance of the population of that species at that location' ('ecological system effects');[6]
(c) for property in the form of livestock or such like, death, disease or other physical damage, or a substantial diminution in yield (minimum 20%) from such causes ('animal or crop effects');[7] and
(d) for property in the form of buildings, '[s]tructural failure, substantial damage or substantial interference with any rights of occupation' ('building effects').[8]

In respect of human health effects, the Statutory Guidance provides that a local authority may consider a wide range of other health effects to be significant harm, either alone or in combination. They include 'physical injury; gastrointestinal disturbances; respiratory tract effects; cardio-vascular effects; central nervous system effects; skin ailments; effects on organs such as the liver or kidneys; or a wide range of other health impacts'.[9]

1 EPA 1990, s 78A(2).
2 Ibid, sub-s (4).
3 Ibid, sub-s (5).
4 EPA 1990, s 78A(4).
5 Statutory Guidance, para 4.5.
6 Ibid, Table 1.
7 Ibid, Table 2.
8 Ibid.
9 Ibid, para 4.6.

15.48 Where the threat of significant harm is established rather than actual significant harm, for land to be contaminated there must also be a significant possibility of harm arising.[1]

The Statutory Guidance sets out criteria for determining whether a significant possibility of significant harm is present for each receptor. The criteria for human health effects are described in para **15.47** above.

The criteria for ecological system effects are:

'significant harm ... is more likely than not to result from the contaminant linkage in question; or there is a reasonable possibility of [such] significant harm ... being caused, and if that harm were to occur, it would result in such a degree of damage to features of special interest at the location in question that they would be beyond any practicable possibility of restoration'.[2]

In respect of property, a significant possibility of significant harm exists if 'the local authority considers that significant harm is more likely than not to result from the contaminant linkage in question'.[3] Criteria for the local authority to take into account for an animal or crop effect include the ecotoxicological effects of the contaminant.[4] Criteria to take into account for a building effect include the 'expected economic life of the building (or in the case of a scheduled Ancient Monument the foreseeable future)'.[5]

In all cases concerning ecological system effects and building effects, the local authority should take account of 'relevant information', that is, 'information which is: (a) scientifically-based; (b) authoritative; (c) relevant to the assessment of risks arising from the presence of contaminants in soil; and (d) appropriate to inform the determination of whether any land is contaminated land'.[6]

1 EPA 1990, s 78A(2).
2 Statutory Guidance, Table 1.
3 Ibid, Table 2.
4 Ibid.
5 Ibid.
6 Ibid, para 4.32.

15.49 Very little guidance was initially provided on assessing whether pollution of controlled waters was being, or was likely to be, caused.[1] The then DETR considered that the statute did not permit it to provide guidance on what constituted 'pollution of controlled waters',[2] and so there was none. The government recognised that this situation could create difficulties and, therefore, indicated an intention to review the primary legislation with a view to amendment.[3] Section 86 of the Water Act 2003 subsequently amended the definition of contaminated land in respect of the pollution of controlled waters. In effect, s 86 inserted a requirement of 'significance' into the pollution of controlled waters, providing powers to the Secretary of State to issue statutory guidance regarding the significance threshold.[4]

Section 86 also re-defined the term 'ground waters' to exclude waters in the unsaturated zone, that is, waters contained in underground strata above the saturation zone.[5]

1 EPA 1990, s 78A(5).
2 DETR Circular 02/2000, Annex 1, para 2.9; R. Burnett-Hall, 'Beware: Pollution Costs' (2000) 1 *Estates Gazette* 84.
3 DETR Circular 02/2000, Annex 1, para 2.10.
4 See Statutory Guidance, s 4.4.
5 EPA 1990, s 78A(9).

15.50 The Statutory Guidance states that the following types of pollution are significant pollution of controlled waters:

'(a)   Pollution equivalent to "environmental damage" to surface water or groundwater as defined by The Environmental Damage (Prevention and Remediation) Regulations [2015], but which cannot be dealt with under those Regulations.

(b)   Inputs resulting in deterioration of the quality of water abstracted, or intended to be used in the future, for human consumption such that additional treatment would be required to enable that use.

(c)   A breach of a statutory surface water Environment Quality Standard, either directly or via a groundwater pathway.

(d)   Input of a substance into groundwater resulting in a significant and sustained upward trend in concentration of contaminants (as defined in Article 2(3) of the Groundwater Daughter Directive (2006/118/EC))'.[1]

The local authority must be satisfied that the substances that may result in the pollution being significant pollution 'are continuing to enter controlled waters; or that they have already entered the waters and are likely to do so again in such a manner that past and likely future entry in effect constitutes ongoing pollution'.[2] If the substances that the local authority is considering are already present in controlled waters, their entry into such waters from land has ceased, or it is not likely that further entry will take place, Part 2A does not apply.[3]

The term, 'possibility of significant pollution of controlled waters', is defined to mean 'the estimated likelihood that significant pollution of controlled waters might occur'.[4] In making such a determination, the local authority should consider the following:

'(a)   The estimated likelihood that the potential significant pollution of controlled waters would become manifest; the strength of evidence underlying the estimate; and the level of uncertainty underlying the estimate.

(b)   The estimated impact of the potential significant pollution if it did occur. This should include consideration of whether the pollution would be likely to cause a breach of [EU] water legislation, or make a major contribution to such a breach.

(c)   The estimated timescale over which the significant pollution might become manifest.

(d)   The authority's initial estimate of whether remediation is feasible, and if so what it would involve and the extent to which it might provide a solution to the problem; how long it would take; what benefit it would be likely to bring; and whether the benefits would outweigh the costs and any impacts on local society or the environment from taking action'.[5]

As with the other determinations of contaminated land, the local authority should determine which of the four screening level categories into which to place the land.[6]

1 Statutory Guidance, para 4.38. The local authority may also consider that other types of specified pollution, including significant concentrations6 of hazardous substances or non-hazardous pollutants in groundwater, may be significant pollution of controlled waters. Ibid, para 4.39.
2 Ibid, para 4.41.
3 Ibid, para 4.42.
4 Ibid, para 4.43.
5 Ibid, para 4.45.
6 Ibid, para 4.46. The Statutory Guidance sets out criteria for such categorisation.

'Special sites'

15.51 Even though all contaminated land presents a threat of, or is causing actual, significant harm or significant pollution of controlled waters, provision is also made for a category of more seriously contaminated areas – 'special sites'.[1] Unlike other contaminated land, which is the responsibility of local authorities, special sites are the responsibility of the Environment Agency: the term 'enforcing authority' refers to both the Agency and local authorities in their respective capacities.[2] Whilst all special sites must first meet the general description of contaminated land,[3] in order to be 'special' a site must also fall into a category of land prescribed by regulations, and not have had its designation as such terminated.[4] In prescribing categories of land as special sites, the Secretary of State may have regard to whether the land presents a threat of serious harm or serious pollution, or whether the Agency is likely to have expertise in dealing with that pollution.[5]

1 EPA 1990, ss 78C and 78D.
2 Ibid, s 78A(9). The appropriate agencies in Wales and Scotland, respectively, are Natural Resources Wales and the Scottish Environment Protection Agency, respectively.
3 See paras **15.40–15.50**.
4 EPA 1990, s 78Q(4).
5 Ibid, s 78C(10).

15.52 The Regulations prescribe those descriptions of land which are required, if contaminated, to be designated as a special site.[1] **There are four** general categories:

(a) water pollution cases – to ensure that the Agency is the enforcing authority in four cases where contaminated land is affecting controlled waters and their quality, namely, in respect of the wholesomeness of drinking water, surface waters classification criteria, environmental objectives for designation as protected waters under the Water Framework Directive (2000/60/EC), and major aquifers;
(b) industrial cases – where land is, or has been, used for industrial activities that either pose special remediation problems or are subject to other national regulatory systems, such as sites subject to the Industrial Emissions Directive (2010/75/EU),[2] nuclear sites, oil refining and explosives;
(c) defence cases – most cases where contaminated land involves the Ministry of Defence, including cases involving visiting forces; and
(d) radioactivity cases, including cases where there is a mixture of radioactive and non-radioactive pollutants at a site.[3]

1 Contaminated Land (England) Regulations 2006, SI 2006/1380, regs 2 and 3, Sch 1.
2 See Ch 20.
3 Contaminated Land (England) Regulations 2006, SI 2006/1380, reg 2(1)(k). A fifth description of sites is also prescribed, namely, land contaminated by an adjoining or adjacent special site, other than certain water pollution cases: Ibid, reg 2(1)(l).

Inspection and designation

15.53 Every local authority **has a continuing duty** to inspect its area both to identify contaminated land and to consider whether such land is required to be designated as a special site.[1] If an authority identifies any contaminated land it shall notify the Agency, the owner of the land, any apparent occupier, and every person who appears to be an 'appropriate person'.[2] 'Owner' means 'a person (other than a mortgagee not in possession) who, whether in his own right or as a trustee for any other person, is entitled to receive the rack rent of the land, or, where the land is not let at a rack rent, would be so entitled if it were so let'.[3] This is a familiar definition, although one not without controversy, particularly in the case of lenders' potential liability. Authorities have extensive powers of entry and inspection in respect both of this general inspection power and their other functions under Part 2A.[4]

1 EPA 1990, s 78B(1).
2 Ibid, sub-s (3) and (4). The meaning of 'appropriate person' is considered below: paras **15.74**–**15.92**. The appropriate agencies to notify in Wales and Scotland are Natural Resources Wales and the Scottish Environment Protection Agency, respectively.
3 EPA 1990, s 78A(9); a separate definition is provided in the same section for Scotland.
4 EA 1995, s 108.

15.54 The initial responsibility to designate special sites also falls to local authorities, although in considering designation they must consult the Environment Agency.[1] If the local authority considers that the land would meet the description of land required to be designated as a special site, it should consult the Agency and, if the Agency agrees, arrange for the Agency to carry out the intrusive inspection of the land on behalf of the authority.[2] Although the Agency does not itself designate, it may notify a local authority that it considers land to be a special site.[3] In the event of a disagreement between the Agency and a local authority, the local authority is required to refer the decision to the Secretary of State.[4] The same classes of persons must be notified of the designation of special sites, disagreements between authorities, and any decision of the Secretary of State in respect of final designation as must be notified of the identification of contaminated land.[5]

1 EPA 1990, s 78C(3).
2 Statutory Guidance, para 2.14. Local authorities are required to act in accordance with this guidance: EPA 1990, s 78B(2).
3 EPA 1990, s 78C(4).
4 Ibid, s 78D.
5 See para **15.53**; EPA 1990, ss 78C(1), (2) and (5), 78D(3) and (4).

15.55 The Statutory Guidance complements these bare obligations with elaboration of the 'strategic approach' that local authorities **must** adopt in carrying out inspections[1] and the risk assessment approach that they must use.[2] In general terms the approach to be taken by authorities must lead to 'proportionate, clear and accountable decisions'.[3]

1 Statutory Guidance, paras 2.3–2.6.
2 Ibid, s 3.
3 Ibid, p 2.

15.56 Following the culmination of their strategic approaches, local authorities have inspected their areas and made determinations of whether land is contaminated, albeit to only a limited extent.

A report commissioned by Defra stated that by the end of 2013, although 91% of local authorities in England had established a list of potentially contaminated sites (typically established between 2001 and 2007), only 30% were on target to achieve the objectives of their inspection strategies, 17% had not identified any targets, 49% were behind target, and 5% had made no progress.[1]

1 Cranfield University and CL:AIRE, Examination of contaminated land sector activity in England (SP1011 Final Project Report for Defra, 10 June 2014), p 4. Also by the end of 2013, 95% of local authorities in Wales had established a list of potentially contaminated sites, and 47% were behind target in achieving the objectives of their inspection strategies. Cranfield University and CL:AIRE, Examination of contaminated land sector activity in Wales (SP1011 Final Project Report for Defra, 21 June 2014), p 4.

15.57 The Statutory Guidance lists four possible grounds for the determination of land as non-radioactive contaminated land, namely that:

(a) significant harm is being caused to a human or relevant non-human receptor;
(b) there is a significant possibility of such significant harm being caused;
(c) significant pollution of controlled waters is being caused; or
(d) there is a significant possibility of significant pollution of controlled being caused.[1]

The Radioactive Contaminated Land Statutory Guidance lists two possible grounds for the determination of land as radioactive contaminated land:

(a) harm is being caused to a human being; or
(b) there is a significant possibility of such harm being caused.[2]

It is important – but perhaps not surprising – to note that a local authority must make a determination of non-radioactive contaminated land on the balance of probabilities.[3] If a local authority considers, after having carried out a 'robust, appropriate, scientific and technical assessment of all the relevant and available evidence', that conditions for considering land to be contaminated land do not exist, it should not make a determination that the land is contaminated land.[4]

The Statutory Guidance recognises that the risk assessment approach to the assessment of potentially contaminated land involves uncertainty. In this respect, it states that there is 'unlikely to be any single "correct" conclusion on precisely what is the level of risk posed by land'. The local authority should, therefore, 'use its judgement to form a reasonable view of what it considers the risks to be on the basis of a robust assessment of available evidence in line with [the Statutory] Guidance'.[5]

1 Statutory Guidance, para 5.6; see Modification Regulations, reg 7 for the identification and designation of special sites involving radioactive contaminated land.
2 Radioactive Contaminated Land Statutory Guidance, para 5.5.
3 See Statutory Guidance, paras 4.4, 4.19(c).
4 Ibid, para 5.7
5 Ibid, para 3.32.

Risk summaries

15.58 The 2012 Statutory Guidance introduced a new requirement for local authorities to prepare a risk summary before making a determination that an area of land is contaminated land. The risk summary should explain the local authority's understanding of the risks and other relevant factors1 and should be written so that it is understandable to a layperson, including the owners of the land and members of the public who may be affected by the authority's decision.[2]

The risk summary must include at least the following:

'(a) A summary of the authority's understanding of the risks, including a description of: the contaminants involved; the identified contaminant linkage(s), or a summary of such linkages; the potential impact(s); the estimated possibility that the impact(s) may occur; and the timescale over which the risk may become manifest.

(b) A description of the authority's understanding of the uncertainties behind its assessment.

(c) A description of the risks in context, for example by setting the risk in local or national context, or describing the risk from land contamination relative to other risks that receptors might be expected to be exposed to in any case.

...

(d) A description of the authority's initial views on possible remediation. This need not be a detailed appraisal, but it should include a description of broadly what remediation might entail; how long it might take; likely effects of remediation works on local people and businesses; how much difference it might be expected to make to the risks posed by the land; and the authority's initial assessment of whether remediation would be likely to produce a net benefit, having regard to the broad objectives of the [contaminated land] regime ...'.[3]

If the land is likely to be a special site if the authority makes a determination that the land is contaminated land, the authority should seek the views of the Environment Agency and take them into account in its description of possible remediation.[4]

1 Statutory Guidance, para 3.33. Risk summaries are not required for negative determinations. Ibid, para 3.36(a).
2 Ibid, para 3.34.
3 Ibid, para 3.35.
4 Ibid.

Extent of contaminated land

15.59 As part of its approach to apportioning liability for remediating contaminated land between appropriate persons, the Statutory Guidance provides that a local authority may sub-divide the area of land to be determined as contaminated land by issuing separate determinations for smaller areas of land. In deciding whether to do so, the authority should take the following into account:

'(i) the nature of the contamination;
(ii) the degree of risk posed, and whether this varies across the land;
(iii) the nature of the remediation which might be required;
(iv) the ownership of the land; and
(v) the likely identity of those who may bear responsibility for the remediation'.[1]

The above description is worded more flexibly than as stated in the 2006 Guidance, which provided that an area of contaminated land was likely to be the smaller of (a) an area in separate ownership or occupation or which was separately recorded in the Land Registry, and (b) the area of land in which the presence of significant pollutants has been established.[2] As a practical matter, however, the effect appears to be the same.

The approach on subdividing land has led local authorities to determine large numbers of individual residences in housing estates as separate areas of contaminated land rather than determining the entire contaminated section of the estate as a single area of contaminated land.[3]

1 Statutory Guidance, para 5.11.
2 2006 Guidance, para B.34.
3 In one housing estate in Leckworth, Cardiff, 110 determinations of contaminated land were made. ENDS Rep 375, pp 35–39 (April 2006); see para **15.104**.

Duty to require remediation

15.60 Where contaminated land has been identified or a special site designated, the enforcing authority is normally required, **subject to specified restrictions and prohibitions,**[1] to serve a 'remediation notice' on each 'appropriate person' specifying what that person is to do by way of remediation, and within what period.[2] Only such measures may be included in a remediation notice as the enforcing authority considers reasonable having regard to the likely cost and the seriousness of the harm or pollution of controlled waters in question.[3] This may include steps which require consent to be granted by a third party, in which case that consent must be granted.[4] This gives rise to a compensation entitlement on the part of the grantor against the person doing the works.[5] Detailed provision has been made in the Regulations for making applications for compensation, for its calculation, and for the determination of disputes.[6]

It is an offence, without reasonable excuse, to fail to comply with any requirements of a remediation notice,[7] punishable by an unlimited fine[8] and a further fine of up to one-tenth of £5,000 for each day on which failure to comply continues after conviction.[9] Injunctive relief may also be sought where summary proceedings would provide an ineffectual remedy.[10]

1 See paras **15.64–15.67**.
2 EPA 1990, s 78E(1).
3 Ibid, s 78E(4). Modification Regulations, reg 8 restricts the discretion of an enforcing authority in determining the remediation that is 'reasonable' for radioactive contaminated land. Reg 11 prohibits an enforcing authority serving a remediation notice in respect of serious pollution of controlled waters.
4 EPA 1990, s 78G.
5 Ibid, sub-s (5). In respect of radioactive contaminated land, see Modification Regulations, reg 10.
6 SI 2006/1380, reg 6, Sch 2.
7 EPA 1990, s 78M(1).
8 Ibid, s 78M(3), s 78M(4). The £5,000 maximum limit for failure to comply, and the £20,000 limit for industrial, trade or business premises for failure to comply, pursuant to the Criminal Justice Act 1982, s 37, is now unlimited. Legal Aid, Sentencing and Punishment of Offenders Act 2012, s 85.

9 See *Canterbury City Council v Ferris* [1997] Env LR D14 (QBD) (daily fine under EPA 1990, s 80(5) may be less than the amount specified).
10 EPA 1990, s 78M(5).

15.61 Regulations provide further detail of the content of remediation notices.[1] These add little in terms of the real substance of remediation notices – actual standards of remediation, for example[2] – but they do set out certain procedural and practical matters. Not only must notices include details of each relevant **contaminant linkage** and of each appropriate person involved in the remediation, but important obligations are placed on the enforcing authority to set out its reasoning in key respects. These include the reasons for its decisions as to the things by way of remediation required to be done, its reasons for excluding certain persons from bearing remediation responsibilities,[3] and its reasons for allocating remediation costs proportionately between more than one person (where applicable).[4]

1 Contaminated Land (England) Regulations 2006, SI 2006/1380, reg 4.
2 On remediation requirements themselves, see paras **15.68–15.70**.
3 See further paras **15.80–15.92**.
4 SI 2006/1380, reg 4(1)(g), (i) and (j).

15.62 Where there is more than one 'appropriate person'[1] each notice must expressly state the proportion of remediation costs that each recipient is liable to bear. This does not necessarily imply that the *same* notice is served on all appropriate persons. However, the Regulations make it clear that where more than one person is an appropriate person, every remediation notice must include details of every person who appears to be an appropriate person.[2] Different notices may be served on different persons if different things by way of remediation are required to be done.[3]

1 See paras **15.75–15.92**.
2 Contaminated Land (England) Regulations 2006, SI 2006/1380, reg 4(h).
3 EPA 1990, s 78E(2).

15.63 As with the definition of contaminated land itself, the true impact of the duty to require remediation is difficult to assess for two principal reasons. First, there are extensive statutory limitations on the 'duty', and, secondly, decisions made under the Statutory Guidance provide detail in respect of both who may be liable (including exclusions from liability)[1] and what may be required by way of remediation.[2] The latter determines how much remediation will actually cost.[3]

1 EPA 1990, s 78F(6).
2 Statutory Guidance, s 6.
3 See further paras **15.68–15.70**.

Restrictions and prohibitions on serving remediation notices

15.64 The enforcing authority is obliged to 'reasonably endeavour' to consult the intended recipients of a remediation notice concerning what is to be done by way of remediation before issuing that notice.[1] Further, once contaminated land has been identified or a special site designated, a period of three months must elapse before a notice may be served.[2] These restrictions do not apply in urgent cases, that is, those where there is imminent danger of serious harm, or serious pollution of controlled waters is being caused.[3] This built-in three-month delay was introduced at a late stage of the Bill's passage through Parliament,[4] despite objections that it would effectively give notice of prospective enforcement action and thus create the opportunity to evade liability. Having been enacted, however, the reasoning is that it **forces** negotiation in respect of remediation; negotiation which may itself obviate the duty to issue a remediation notice.[5]

1 EPA 1990, s 78H(1).
2 Ibid, s 78H(3).
3 Ibid, s 78H(4).
4 As a Government amendment at the Commons Committee Stage: HC Official Report, SC B, 23 May 1995, col 328.
5 EPA 1990, s 78H(5)(b); see para **15.60**. On the policy underpinning this provision, and its anticipated use, see DETR Circular, Annex 2, paras 6.10–6.13.

15.65 In addition to the limitations set out immediately above, certain more permanent restrictions on the issue of a remediation notice apply. These are of two sorts: those where certain other powers could be used or other powers apply[1] (in particular, where a power to serve a waste removal notice may be exercised under the EPA 1990, s 59);[2] and those which derive from the contaminated land regime itself. The latter are generally not actually permanent in the sense that circumstances may change and a remediation notice may subsequently be required.[3] However, if any of four conditions are met in a particular case a remediation notice shall not be served.[4] Those conditions are that:

(a) nothing by way of remediation could be specified in a notice served on that person, in consequence of applying parts of s 78E;[5]
(b) appropriate things are being, or will be, done without service of a remediation notice on that person;[6]
(c) the authority would itself be the recipient of the notice;[7] or
(d) the authority is satisfied that its own powers to carry out remediation under s 78N are exercisable.[8]

1 EPA 1990, s 78YB; see paras **15.28–15.31**.
2 EPA 1990, s 78YB(3).
3 Ibid, s 78H(10).
4 Ibid, s 78H(5).
5 Ibid, s 78H(5)(a): including what is to be considered reasonable having regard to cost and to the Statutory Guidance. See paras **15.60** and **15.64**.
6 EPA 1990, s 78H(5)(b).
7 Ibid, s 78H(5)(c). See Modification Regulations, reg 14 regarding the powers of local authorities to carry out remediation in respect of radioactive contaminated land.
8 EPA 1990, s 78H(5)(d); see para **15.97**.

15.66 The fourth condition set out above includes the situation where the enforcing authority takes the view that it could recover none or only a portion of its remediation costs, having applied the 'hardship' test in s 78P.[1] Anticipated 'hardship' on the part of the recipient of a notice, if forced to pay the enforcing authority's costs, would therefore preclude the issue of a notice in the first place.

Further limitations apply in some cases in respect of water pollution, where persons liable solely through being an owner or occupier of contaminated land may incur lesser liabilities than other appropriate persons.[2]

In addition, a remediation notice may not be served in respect of radioactive contaminated land if damage to property occurs in breach of specified duties under the Nuclear Installations Act 1965 or in related circumstances.[3]

1 EPA 1990, ss 78H(5)(d), 78N(3)(e) and 78P(2); see para **15.98**.
2 EPA 1990, s 78J; a point considered more fully in para **15.80**.
3 Modification Regulations, reg 17.

15.67 In all of **the above** cases, where an enforcing authority is precluded from specifying any particular thing by way of remediation which it would otherwise have specified, it must issue a 'remediation declaration',[1] setting out those things and the grounds on which issue of a notice was precluded. Examples of remediation declarations include that issued by the Congleton Borough Council for the Malkins Bank Golf Course on 29 September 2011, the same day that the council determined that the site was contaminated land. The council stated that it would be disproportionate to remediate the site in view of the limited benefits because the groundwater pollution was having a minimal impact on the quality of nearby surface waters. The estimated costs of remediating the site, at which industrial uses, including a chemicals works and a hazardous waste disposal facility, had begun in 1864, ranged from £9.7 million to £92.4 million, excluding maintenance costs, depending on the method of remediation.[2] Another example of a remediation declaration is that issued by the Cornwall Council on 27 October 2011 for a site in Falmouth. Pollutants, including polycyclic aromatic hydrocarbons and total petroleum hydrocarbons, were continuing to enter the Fal Estuary (a special area of conservation under the Habitats Directive) through the harbour wall. The estimated cost of remediating the site, a former gasworks that had been re-developed as a car park, ranged from £645,000 to £4.7 million, depending on the method of remediation. The council had determined the site as contaminated land on 14 December 2010 due to the presence of 14 significant contaminant linkages.[3]

If remediation measures *are* to be implemented voluntarily or by the authority itself, then a 'remediation statement' must instead be issued by the person carrying them out or the authority.[4] The statement records the remediation measures done or expected to be done, by whom and within what period. This also makes cases of voluntary action under the regime a matter of public record. If a person fails to carry out such measures (that is, the conditions in s 78H cease to apply),[5] a remediation notice must instead be served[6] – a provision which makes voluntary measures ultimately enforceable. It is less clear how remediation by authorities can be compelled, as the conditions will not cease to apply by reason of an authority's failure to act.

1 EPA 1990, s 78H(6).
2 See V. Fogleman, 'The contaminated land regime: time for a regime that is fit for purpose (Part 2)' (2014) 6 International Journal of Law in the Built Environment 129, 146.
3 See ibid, 147.
4 EPA 1990, s 78H(7) and (8).

5 See para **15.65**.
6 EPA 1990, s 78H(10).

Remediation requirements

15.68 The only things by way of remediation which the enforcing authority may do, or require to be done, under Part 2A are things which it considers to be reasonable, having regard to the cost which is likely to be involved and the seriousness of the harm or pollution of controlled waters in question.[1]

The broad aim of remediation is 'to remove identified significant contaminant linkages, or permanently to disrupt them to ensure they are no longer significant and that risks are reduced to below an unacceptable level; and/or ... to take reasonable measures to remedy harm or pollution that has been caused by a significant contaminant linkage'.[2] This aim does not necessarily mean that the contaminated land must be cleaned up; instead, it means that each significant contaminant linkage must be disrupted so that the significant contaminant does not cause significant harm or a significant possibility of significant harm to an identified receptor or, in the case of controlled waters, significant pollution or a significant possibility of significant pollution.

In respect of the 'reasonableness' of required remediation, an enforcing authority must consider various factors, having regard in particular to '(a) the practicability, effectiveness and durability of remediation; (b) the health and environmental impacts of the chosen remedial options; (c) the financial cost which is likely to be involved; and (d) the benefits of remediation with regard to the seriousness of the harm or pollution of controlled waters in question'.[3] Each of these concepts receives detailed consideration in the Statutory Guidance.[4]

1 EPA 1990, s 78E(4); see also Modification Regulations, reg 8 which, in effect, requires an enforcing authority to balance the benefit of any intervention against the detriment to human health and costs arising from such intervention and to maximise the benefit in respect of radioactive contaminated land.
2 Statutory Guidance, para 6.5.
3 Ibid, para 6.20.
4 See para **15.69**.

15.69 In order to satisfy the requirement of 'reasonableness' of a remediation action, the enforcing authority must be satisfied that its benefits are likely to outweigh its costs.[1]

This cost-benefit approach reflects other general duties on the Environment Agency[2] – although in this case the Statutory Guidance specifically sets out factors to be considered by the enforcing authority. They include the following.

'(a)   The cost of preparing for remediation to take place (eg feasibility studies, design of remedial actions, management costs, and the cost of relevant assessment actions).

(b)   The cost of undertaking the remediation actions and making good afterwards, including any tax payable.

(c) The cost of managing the land after the main remediation action has taken place (eg on-going requirements to manage or maintain the remediation action, and the cost of any monitoring or assessment action).

(d) Relevant disruption costs (eg depreciation in the value of land or other interests, or other loss or damage, which is likely to result from the carrying out of the remediation action in question).

(e) The above costs relative to any estimated increase in the financial value and utility of the land as a result of remediation, and whether such increase in value and utility would accrue to the person(s) bearing the cost of remediation'.[3]

The Statutory Guidance emphasises that the identity or financial standing of any person who may be required to pay for a remediation action are not to be considered as relevant in determining whether the costs of that action are, or are not, reasonable, with the caveat that the costs of remediation may be relevant in deciding whether they can be imposed on such a person.[4] In this respect, therefore, the reasonableness of remediation measures relates to the site and not to the relevant appropriate person(s). A 'hardship' test applies, however, in the event that an enforcing authority seeks to recover from another person the costs of remediation measures which the authority itself has incurred.[5] This also affects the authority's power to serve a remediation notice.[6]

1 Statutory Guidance, para 6.21.
2 EA 1995, s 39.
3 Statutory Guidance, para 6.29.
4 Ibid, para 6.30.
5 EPA 1990, s 78P(2); see para **15.98**.
6 See para **15.65**.

15.70 The steps that may be required to be taken by way of remediation – whether simple 'actions', 'packages' or 'schemes'[1] – may clearly be extremely complex. They may require further assessment of the condition of land before a remediation package can be planned,[2] they may be phased[3] and they may require longer term monitoring action.[4] Whilst these may mean a continuing obligation on an appropriate person beyond an initial physical clean up, it must nonetheless be directly related to the contaminant linkage by reason of which the land was identified as contaminated land, and the land itself in its current use.[5]

1 Statutory Guidance, paras 7.12–7.14; see ibid, paras 6.5–6.9.
2 Ibid, para 6.8.
3 Ibid, paras 6.10–6.12.
4 Ibid, paras 6.27–6.28.
5 Ibid, para 6.9.

Appeals against remediation notices

15.71 A person served with a remediation notice may appeal to the Secretary of State.[1] Very wide discretion is granted to the Secretary to determine the appeals procedure, including the grounds of appeal.[2] The relevant section is more complex and explicit than the statutory nuisance equivalent.[3] An extensive list of grounds of appeal is set out in the Regulations.[4]

1 EPA 1990, s 78L. Section 78L was amended from 4 August 2006 to move appeals of local authority remediation notices in England and Wales from magistrates' courts to the Secretary of State (Clean Neighbourhoods and Environment Act 2005, s 104). An appeal from a remediation notice in Wales is now to the Welsh Assembly. IEPA 1990, s 78L. Only one Part 2A case was heard by a magistrates' court. On appeal, the High Court ordered a retrial. *Circular Facilities (London) Ltd v Sevenoaks District Council* [2005] EWHC 865 (Admin); [2005] Env LR 35, [2005] JPL 1624 (QBD). Sevenoaks District Council appealed the High Court's decision but the case was settled shortly before the appeal was due to be heard; no retrial, therefore, was held.
2 EPA 1990, s 78L(4) and (5).
3 See paras **14.38–14.49**.
4 Contaminated Land (England) Regulations 2006, SI 2006/1380, reg 7.

Grounds of appeal

15.72 The grounds of appeal include familiar 'procedural' grounds (for example, service of a notice on the wrong person and non-compliance with binding guidance), but extend to very much more complex and unfamiliar matters. These include that the enforcing authority 'unreasonably failed to be satisfied' that appropriate things were being done by way of remediation without the service of a remediation notice,[1] or that the authority 'could not reasonably have taken the view' that the land in question was in such a condition that there was an imminent danger of serious harm or serious pollution of controlled waters.[2] These require the Secretary of State to address rather different aspects of authorities' behaviour than they normally have been familiar with. Indeed, it looks more like judicial review than an appeal under statute.

1 SI 2006/1380, reg 7(1)(i); see EPA 1990, s 78H(5) and para **15.65**.
2 SI 2006/1380, reg 7(1)(h); see EPA 1990, s 78N.

15.73 A hearing or local inquiry must be held if the appellant or **enforcing authority** requests it, and may be held otherwise.[1] Certain entitlements to appear at such hearings have been provided, including for persons alleged by the appellant to be an appropriate person but who is not named in the relevant remediation notice.[2] As with statutory nuisance,[3] where an appeal is duly made against a remediation notice, the notice is suspended pending the final determination or abandonment of the appeal.[4] Unlike statutory nuisance, however,[5] there is no mechanism by which an enforcing authority can revoke that suspension in cases (for example) where the nuisance/contamination is injurious to health. This is so even in those cases where there is an imminent danger of serious harm, or serious pollution of controlled waters.[6]

1 SI 2006/1380, reg 9.
2 Ibid, regs 10(2) and 8(2)(a).
3 Statutory Nuisance (Appeals) Regulations 1995, SI 1995/2644, reg 3(1); see paras **14.40–14.41**.
4 SI 2006/1380, reg 12(1).
5 SI 1995/2644, reg 3(2)–(3).
6 EPA 1990, s 78H(4).

Who is liable for remediation?

15.74 The most controversial aspect of Part 2A is the identity of those persons liable to carry out, or rather bear the costs of, remediation: 'appropriate persons'.[1] It is appropriate persons upon whom remediation notices are served.[2] The principal policy concern was avoidance of the joint and several liability approach of the United States' **Superfund** liability system.[3] Equally, however, it has been recognised that in some cases liability may fall on present owners or occupiers, particularly where the value of land when transferred reflects the presence of contamination.[4] In this respect, a hierarchy of appropriate persons is provided by the Act (complemented in considerable detail by the Statutory **Guidance**): from those who caused or knowingly permitted contamination at the top, to present owners and occupiers at the bottom.[5] It should be noted that where liability falls on persons towards the bottom of this hierarchy, in some cases the costs for which they can be made responsible may be less than if they had caused the pollution themselves.[6] It should also be noted, however, that Part 2A is unique in that it provides in some cases for the exclusion from liability of the person who caused the contamination, a concept that does not appear in other liability systems for remediating contaminated land.[7]

1 EPA 1990, s 78F(1).
2 Ibid, s 78E(1); see para **15.60**. Contaminated Land (England) Regulations 2006, SI 2006/1380, reg 4.
3 See V. Fogleman, 'The contaminated land regime: time for a regime that is fit for purpose (Part 2)' (2014) 6 International Journal of Law in the Built Environment 129, 134.
4 See para **15.78**.
5 Statutory Guidance, s 7, 'Liability'.
6 EPA 1990, s 78P. This includes important considerations for those acquiring a freehold or leasehold interest in land, and owner-occupiers of residential property.
7 See V. Fogleman, 'The contaminated land regime: time for a regime that is fit for purpose (Part 1)', (2014) 6 International Journal of Law in the Built Environment 43, 50–52.

Defining 'appropriate persons'

15.75 An appropriate person is defined as any person or persons who caused or knowingly permitted the substances, or any of the substances, by reason of which the contaminated land in question is such land to be in, on or under that land.[1] A further partial definition makes it clear that it is the appropriate person who 'bear[s] responsibility for any thing which is to be done by way of remediation in any particular case'.[2] This only applies in relation to remediation measures which are to any extent referable to substances which that person caused or knowingly permitted to be present in, on or under the land in question.[3] However, if those substances escape to other land then that person will also be taken to have caused or knowingly permitted those substances to be in, on or under that other land.[4] The phrase 'cause or knowingly permit' is familiar from other environmental law contexts, and is considered in depth elsewhere in this book.[5]

1 EPA 1990, s 78F(2).
2 Ibid, s 78A(9).

3 Ibid, s 78F(3). This includes cases where biological processes or chemical reactions take place: sub-s (9). See *Circular Facilities (London) Ltd v Sevenoaks District Council* [2005] EWHC 865 (Admin); [2005] Env LR 35, [2005] JPL 1624 (QBD) (discussed further below). In respect of radioactive contaminated land, it also includes cases where radioactive decay takes place. Modification Regulations, reg 9.

4 EPA 1990, s 78K(1); see further para **15.82**. See also Modification Regulations, reg 13 regarding liability in respect of radioactive contaminating substances that escape to other land.

5 See paras **17.47–17.66**.

15.76 In respect of the word 'caused' in the phrase 'caused or knowingly permit' under Part 2A, the House of Lords ruled, in R *(National Grid Gas Plc, formerly Transco Plc) v Environment Agency*,[1] that National Grid Gas Plc ('National Grid') was not liable because it did not exist when the relevant contamination had been caused. The case arose when the owner of a house that had been built on the site of a former gas works discovered coal tar residues in his garden. The site had been operated by the East Midlands Gas Board and its predecessor companies before its sale to developers in 1965. Both developers had been dissolved. The gas industry, meanwhile, was nationalised by the Gas Act 1948, re-organised by the Gas Act 1972 and privatised by the Gas Act 1986. Each Act provided that the new entity would succeed to the predecessor's liabilities that existed 'immediately before' the statutory transfer date. The then House of Lords concluded that National Grid could not be liable because liabilities under Part 2A were created in 1995 when the Environment Act 1995 amended the EPA 1990. Lord Hoffmann stated that 'It is true that [Part 2A] was retrospective in the sense that it created a potential present liability for acts done in the past. But that is not the same as creating a deemed past liability for those acts. There is nothing in the Act to create retrospectivity in this sense.'[2]

The *National Grid* case does not mean that other privatised companies may not be liable under Part 2A for having caused or knowingly permitted contamination; Lord Neuberger mentioned, in particular, that 'much more explicit words' may have been used such as in para 3 of Sch 2 to the Water Act 1989. The issue, thus, depends on the precise terms used in the transfer legislation. The issue may thus also arise in respect of the transfer of liabilities in contractual documentation involving private companies.

In addition, a person does not necessarily have to introduce a contaminant onto land in order to cause further contamination by the contaminant. This is illustrated by a case involving contamination at the former chemical works at Sandridge, near St Albans, which was owned and operated by Steetley Chemical Company (subsequently taken over by Redland Minerals, owned by Lafarge). In 1983, Redland Minerals had sold the land to Crest Nicholson for development as housing, carrying out some remediation of the contamination caused by Steetley as part of the process. In 2000, Veolia Water Company discovered bromate and bromide pollution in the groundwater when it tested for bromate in respect of a new 10 microgram per litre drinking water standard. Redland and Crest each contended that the other party was responsible for remediating the contamination.

Following lengthy litigation, Sales J concluded that 'Redland had caused all the bromide and bromate to be on the land in the first place and allowed them to filter down to the lower strata during its long period in control of the site. Crest had brought no contaminants onto the site but had accelerated the way in which the contaminants already in the land were flushed down to the lower levels'.[3] He thus apportioned liability between the parties.[4]

1 [2007] UKHL 30.
2 Ibid [4].
3 *R (Redland Minerals) v Secretary of State for Environment, Food and Rural Affairs* [2010] EWHC 913 (Admin) [37].
4 See paras **15.88** and **15.93ff.**

15.77 An owner or occupier may be a 'knowing permitter' even though not himself responsible for the initial (or other) escape or release of a substance to land. This is because primary liability under Part 2A attaches to a 'knowing permitter' as well as the person who caused the contamination.[1] That is, the 'causer or knowing permitter' is the person who bears principal liability for remediation of those significant contaminant linkages for which the person is responsible. The Statutory Guidance refers to these persons as 'Class A persons'[2] as well as 'polluters'.[3]

Newman J provided guidance on the meaning of 'knowingly permit' under Part 2A in *Circular Facilities (London) Ltd v Sevenoaks District Council.*[4] The case involved a developer who had built houses on land that contained decaying organic matter about three metres below ground level. The methane and carbon dioxide generated by the decay resulted in a significant possibility of significant harm to the houses and their residents from explosion and asphyxiation, respectively. A geotechnical report specifying the presence of the matter and the gases generated by it was on the planning register. The magistrates' court had not included a conclusion in its judgment, however, that the controlling mind of the development company had knowledge of the report. Accordingly, Newman J ordered a retrial as to whether the company had the requisite knowledge given that an individual who had been in an 'informal partnership' with the company and who may have acted as its agent, but who had since died, knew of the existence of the report. Newman J stated that a person need only have knowledge of the presence of a substance; knowledge of harm caused by the substance is not required.

1 EPA 1990, s 78F(2).
2 Statutory Guidance, para 7.3(a);.
3 Statutory Guidance, para 8.5(b).
4 [2005] EWHC 865 (Admin); [2005] Env LR 35, [2005] JPL 1624 (QBD).

15.78 If, after reasonable enquiry, a Class A person has not been found for any significant contaminant linkage, the owner or occupier for the time being of the contaminated land in question becomes an appropriate person.[1] Such persons are described in the Statutory Guidance as 'Class B persons'.[2] The rationale is clear: owners and occupiers only become liable in certain circumstances where the 'polluter' cannot be found. A hierarchy of appropriate persons is therefore established, and the operation of the Statutory Guidance is such that as liability moves down that hierarchy then it will, in most cases, reduce. Crucially for transactions involving the disposal of land, however, the term 'polluter' includes, not only the original polluter but an owner or occupier who 'knowingly permits' the land to continue to be contaminated land by having the power to remediate it but failing to do so after having had a reasonable opportunity.[3]

The term 'owner' is itself defined simply,[4] but 'occupier' is not defined.[5] A definition of 'occupier' for other environmental law purposes – the law of nature conservation – suggest that it would not be readily transferable.[6] Much therefore depends on the context in which the word 'occupier' is used,[7] and it is therefore potentially significant that the Statutory Guidance discusses the potential liability of owners of leaseholds, and distinguishes between those with different types of property interest in assessing what might reasonably be expected of Class B persons who may be liable.[8]

1 EPA 1990, s 78F(4) and (5).
2 Statutory Guidance, para 7.3(a).
3 See DETR Circular, annex 2, paras 9.10–9.12; *cf Alphacell Ltd v Woodward* [1972] AC 824, 834 [1972] 2 WLR 1320 (House of Lords) (term 'knowingly permit' [in Rivers (Prevention of Pollution) Act 1951] 'involves a failure to prevent the pollution, which failure, however, must be accompanied by knowledge'); see also Statutory Guidance, para 8.5(b).
4 EPA 1990, s 78A(9); see para **15.53**.
5 Neither is it defined for the purposes of statutory nuisance, although on 'owner' in that context, see paras **14.34–14.35**.
6 See, eg, *Southern Water Authority v Nature Conservancy Council* [1992] 3 All ER 481, [1992] 1 WLR 775, 781–83.
7 See the approach to 'owner' in the context of statutory nuisance: *Camden London Borough Council v Gunby* [1999] 4 All ER 602; see paras **14.34–14.35**.
8 Statutory Guidance, paras 7.76–7.79; see para **15.92**.

15.79 A proposed intermediate class of appropriate persons – those to whom liability has been directly or indirectly transferred – was abandoned in the passage of the Bill. However, liability may be effectively transferred – partially or totally – when land is 'sold with information'.[1] Strictly speaking, it is not possible to transfer a liability unless that transfer is permitted by statute. In this case, the operation of the Statutory Guidance is therefore to exclude certain persons from liability, whilst leaving others included.

1 Statutory Guidance, paras 7.46–7.50; see para **15.88**.

Liability to remediate: statutory exclusions

15.80 The Act itself provides for three classes of exclusion from, or limitations on, liability under Part 2A. First, appropriate persons falling into Class B – owners or occupiers for the time being[1] – cannot be made liable for the remediation of land which is 'contaminated land' by reason of actual or threatened water pollution, or for the remediation of controlled waters in such cases.[2] An exclusion also applies from remediation liability which might attach to any appropriate person permitting water to escape from an abandoned mine.[3] This reflects similar exemptions from liability under the Water Resources Act 1991, although both immunities were withdrawn in the case of abandonment taking place after the end of 1999.[4]

351

1 See para **15.53**.
2 EPA 1990, s 78J(2).
3 Ibid, s 78J(3)–(6).
4 Ibid, s 78J(4); Water Resources Act 1991, ss 91A–91B (inserted by EA 1995, s 58).

15.81 Secondly, a class of persons acting in certain professional capacities ('relevant capacity') is excluded from personal liability under Part 2A in certain circumstances. 'Relevant capacities' include acting as an insolvency practitioner, official receiver or accountant in bankruptcy.[1]

1 EPA 1990, s 78X(3) and (4).

15.82 Thirdly, in some cases liability is limited in respect of contaminating substances that escape to other land.[1] The starting point is that a person in Class A[2] shall also be taken to have caused or knowingly permitted the substances for which they are liable to be in, on or under any other land to which they appear to have escaped.[3] The limitations apply when the owner or occupier of that other land did not itself cause or knowingly permit the substances to be under its land. In such cases, no remediation notice shall require those owners or occupiers to remediate any land or waters contaminated by the polluting substances, other than their own land.[4] This applies to remediation consequent on further land becoming contaminated by the same escaping substances.[5] Finally, where the original Class A person disposes of an interest in contaminated land, then the purchaser of that interest cannot be made liable for the vendor's acts or omissions in relation to off-site remediation unless the purchaser caused or knowingly permitted the escape of the polluting substances from his land to the other land.[6] The vendor may be excluded from liability however.[7]

1 EPA 1990, s 78K.
2 See para **15.75**.
3 EPA 1990, s 78K(1).
4 Ibid, s 78K(3); see Figure 15.1.
5 Statutory Guidance, s 78K(4), see Figure 15.2.
6 Statutory Guidance, s 78K(5).
7 Namely, if the purchaser is a knowing permitter. See para **15.88**.

15.83 Having applied these statutory exclusions, no appropriate person in respect of a particular contaminant linkage may remain. The Statutory Guidance refers to such contaminant linkages as an 'orphan linkage'.[1] Other than in the case of these statutory exclusions, the only other situation in which an orphan linkage should be able to arise is if no Class A or Class B persons at all can be found, although one special site appears to have been determined to be an orphan site due to liability for remediation being 'questionable'.[2]

When an orphan linkage arises, the enforcing authority itself may be responsible for remediation.[3] The Statutory Guidance indicates that the enforcing authority should bear the cost of carrying out any remediation action which is referable to an orphan linkage, and is not referable to any other linkage for which there is a liability group.[4] Where one or more significant contaminant linkages exist along with an orphan linkage, and remediating the former would contribute to or remediate the orphan linkage, the Statutory Guidance makes provision for the apportionment of costs between the enforcing authority and those bearing the other costs.[5]

1 Statutory Guidance, para 7.6(e).
2 Waverley Borough Council, A1 WA/2013/1947, Rural Arisings and Steward Transport Ltd 23/10/2013 (planning application recommendation) ('Part 2A of the Environmental Protection Act 1990 makes provision for compulsory remediation of land in situations where volunteered remediation through development is not possible and the risks to human health or the environment are judged to be high. Remediation, however, is not guaranteed and where liability for remediation is questionable, as in this case [Cranleigh Brick and Tile, Surrey], the contaminated land may become an "orphan" site'); available at https://modgov.waverley.gov. uk/documents/s4857/A1%20WA2013–1947%20Cranleigh%20Brick%20and%20Tile%20 Works%20Knowle%20Lane%20Cranleigh%20GU6%208JP.pdf.
3 EPA 1990, s 78N(3).
4 Statutory Guidance, para 7.15.
5 Ibid, paras 7.92–7.98.

Liability to remediate: non-statutory exclusions

15.84 In addition to the statutory exclusions, the Act allows for liability to be excluded in some cases by guidance. If more than one person within a class is found to be responsible for remedying a particular contaminant linkage, guidance will be determinative in deciding if one or more should be excluded from liability.[1] It should be emphasised, therefore, that exclusions under this section only apply when more than one appropriate person has been found. Equally, they do not apply if they would result in the exclusion of *all* appropriate persons within that class.[2]

1 EPA 1990, s 78F(6).
2 Statutory Guidance, para 7.32(c).

15.85 The exclusions provided by the Statutory Guidance are extensive, but emphasise exclusion from Class A liability groups rather than Class B liability groups. The exclusions from Class A are set out in six 'tests', to be applied sequentially in respect of each individual significant contaminant linkage. Exclusion of a person by the application of the tests to one contaminant linkage does not presuppose exclusion of that person from any further linkage.[1] The general effect of the exclusion tests is to remove from liability persons who fall into Class A through having carried out defined types of action, or whose actions have been affected by other persons. The intended effect of the tests is to allocate liability only to those who really are directly responsible for the contamination or its continued existence.

Crucially for disposals of land, an overall intent is to transfer liability forwards to the most recent 'knowing permitter'. Responsibility is also allocated (that is, the exclusions applied) according to a hierarchy, with those judged to be least responsible being excluded first. Importantly, however, when an exclusion question concerns the relationship between two or more related companies, the tests are modified.[2] Essentially, 'related companies'[3] on the date on which notification was first given of land being contaminated fall or stand together. One company in a group cannot take advantage of the exclusion tests to shift its own liability to another within that group, possibly capping that liability in doing so. The exclusion tests are briefly explained below.

1 Statutory Guidance, para 7.32(a).
2 Ibid, paras 7.35–7.37, guidance which did not appear in earlier drafts.
3 Companies that are members of a group consisting of a holding company and its subsidiaries, within the meaning of the Companies Act 2006, s 1159.

Test 1 – 'Excluded activities'

15.86 The first group who may be excluded are those who have been identified as having caused or knowingly permitted the land to be contaminated solely by reason of having carried out one or more certain specified activities.[1] The specified activities include: providing or withholding certain financial assistance to another person, including grants, loans, guarantees or indemnities; underwriting insurance, including carrying out any action for the purpose of deciding whether to do so; consigning as waste to another person the substance which is now a significant contaminant under a contract under which that other person knowingly took over responsibility for it; creating at any time a tenancy over the land in question in favour of another person who has subsequently caused or knowingly permitted the presence of the significant **contaminant linkage** in question (whether or not the tenant can now be found); as owner of the land, licensing at any time its occupation by another person (other than where the owner operated a waste storage or disposal site); and providing legal, financial, engineering, scientific or technical advice to (or design, contract management or works management services for) another person in certain circumstances, whether or not that other person can now be found. The Statutory Guidance notes that undertaking these activities would not **necessarily** bring a person within Class A in the first place.[2]

1 Statutory Guidance, paras 7.38–7.39.
2 Ibid, para 7.38.

Test 2 – 'Payments made for remediation'

15.87 Those who have, in effect, met their responsibilities by making certain kinds of payment to some other member of the liability group, which would have been sufficient to pay for adequate remediation are excluded by this test.[1] Elaborate conditions must be met for this exclusion to apply, and in any event it only applies to certain types of payment. The latter include payments as part of a contract for the transfer of ownership of the land in question which is either specifically provided for in the contract to meet the cost of carrying out the particular remediation or which consists of a reduction in the contract price explicitly stated in the contract to be for that purpose.[2] Caution should clearly be exercised in making reductions in price attributable to remediation costs. An obvious danger is that insufficient site investigations are conducted before a price reduction is agreed to make accurate allowance for remediation. Although the enforcing authority is required to ensure that the payment should have been sufficient at the date it was made for the remediation in question, this is hardly a precise test. Equally, the elapse of time between the agreement and any remediation subsequently required will necessarily increase the true cost to the payee: an increase that cannot then be passed back to the payor.

1 Statutory Guidance, paras 7.40–7.45.
2 Ibid, para 7.42(c).

Test 3 – 'Sold with information'

15.88 Although persons excluded under this test will have caused or knowingly permitted the presence of a significant contaminant in, on or under land, they can nonetheless be excluded where they have disposed of that land in circumstances where it is 'reasonable' that some other member of the liability group, who has acquired the land from them, should bear the liability for remediation of the land.[1] Only if four quite onerous conditions are met will this exclusion apply: both buyer and seller are members of the Class A liability group; the sale was the transfer of a freehold or long lease (over 21 years) at arm's length (more a question of the terms expected in an open market sale than of the identity of the parties); before the sale was binding, the buyer had information that would reasonably allow that particular person to be aware of the presence of the pollutant in question, and its broad measure, and the seller did nothing material to misrepresent the implications of that presence;[2] and after the date of the sale, the seller did not retain any interest in the land in question or any rights to occupy or use that land.[3]

A distinction is made between buyers with differing resources: in transactions since the beginning of 1990 when the buyer is a 'large commercial organisation or public body', permission from the seller for the buyer to carry out his own investigations of the condition of the land should normally be taken as sufficient indication that the buyer had the necessary information.[4] If, therefore, the buyer is not a large commercial organisation or public body (terms which are not defined), the sold with information test is much less effective to transfer liability.

The difference between application of the test to a buyer that is a large commercial organisation and one that is not such an organisation is illustrated by the case involving groundwater contaminated by bromate and bromide described above.[5] In apportioning liability between the seller and the buyer, Sales J concluded that Crest Homes (the buyer) was liable for the costs of remediating 15% of bromate contamination and 55% of bromide contamination; Redland Minerals (the seller) was liable for the costs of remediating 85% of bromate contamination and 45% of bromide contamination.[6] In reaching his decision, Sales J apportioned liability by partially applying the sold with information exclusion test to the bromide significant contaminant linkage (in addition to the parties' actions concerning the bromide at the site). In doing so, he referred, among other things, to the Secretary of State's conclusion that Crest could not have been aware in 1983, when it purchased the site, 'that there was bromide in the soil, ie the upper part of the site and that it could not reasonably have been aware of the bromide contamination which had already by then penetrated to lower aquifer strata on the land'.[7]

If Sales J had concluded that Crest was a large commercial organisation and had been given permission by the seller to carry out its own intrusive investigations before the sale became binding, Crest would have been liable for the costs of remediating the bromide it knowingly permitted to continue to be at the site regardless of its knowledge of that contamination.

1 Statutory Guidance, paras 7.46–7.50.
2 Note that this is not necessarily the same as 'to materially misrepresent', and that it is limited to implications rather than the presence of the contaminant itself.
3 Not including easements for the benefit of other land where the contaminated land is the servient tenement and equivalent statutory rights; reversions on expiry of a long lease, ie, one of more than 21 years, where the lessee satisfies the definition of owner in EPA 1990, s 78A(2); or the benefit of restrictive covenants or equivalent statutory agreements: Statutory Guidance, para 7.48(e).
4 Statutory Guidance, para 7.48(d).
5 See para **15.76 – 15.77**.
6 *R (Redland Minerals) v Secretary of State for Environment, Food and Rural Affairs* [2010] EWHC 913 (Admin) [30].
7 Ibid.

Test 4 – 'Changes to substances'

15.89 This test provides for the exclusion of a Class A person when a substance introduced by that person results in a significant contaminant linkage only because of its interaction with another substance which was later introduced to the land by another person.[1] Again, this exclusion depends in part on meeting seven conditions.

1 Statutory Guidance, paras 7.51–7.53.

Test 5 – 'Escaped substances'

15.90 Where a Class A person would otherwise be liable for the remediation of land which has become contaminated as a result of the escape of substances from other land, that person can be excluded where it can be shown that another member of the liability group was actually responsible for that escape.[1]

1 Statutory Guidance, paras 7.54–7.56.

Test 6 – 'Introduction of pathways or receptors'

15.91 In the same way that Test 5 excludes from liability those who are responsible solely because of the introduction by another member of the liability of a substance, this test excludes liability where that other Class A person introduced other pathways or receptors in the significant contaminant linkage in question.[1] For example, a company that develops housing on contaminated land without carrying out the necessary remediation may be liable under Part 2A due to having introduced houses and people onto the land; the person who caused the contamination would be excluded.[2]

1 Statutory Guidance, paras 7.57–7.61.
2 See *Circular Facilities (London) Ltd v Sevenoaks District Council* [2005] EWHC 865 (Admin); [2005] Env LR 35, [2005] JPL 1624 (QBD); discussed at para **15.77**.

Figure 15.1: Liability for escapes to other land: I

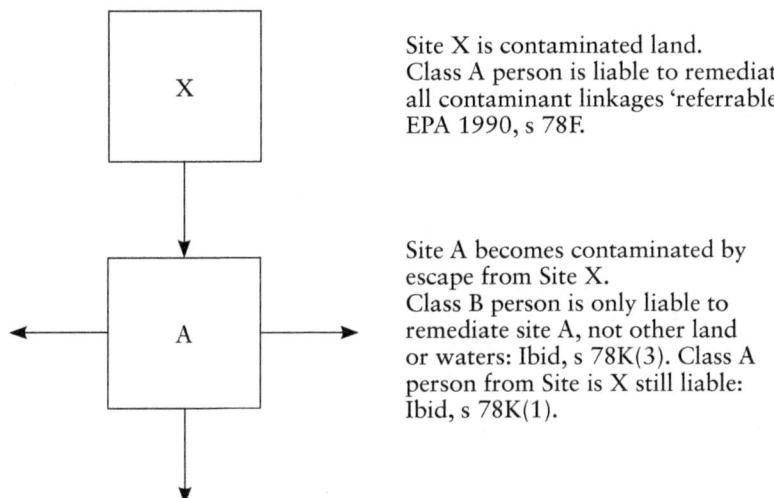

Site X is contaminated land.
Class A person is liable to remediate
all contaminant linkages 'referrable':
EPA 1990, s 78F.

Site A becomes contaminated by
escape from Site X.
Class B person is only liable to
remediate site A, not other land
or waters: Ibid, s 78K(3). Class A
person from Site is X still liable:
Ibid, s 78K(1).

Figure 15.2: Liability for escapes to other land: II

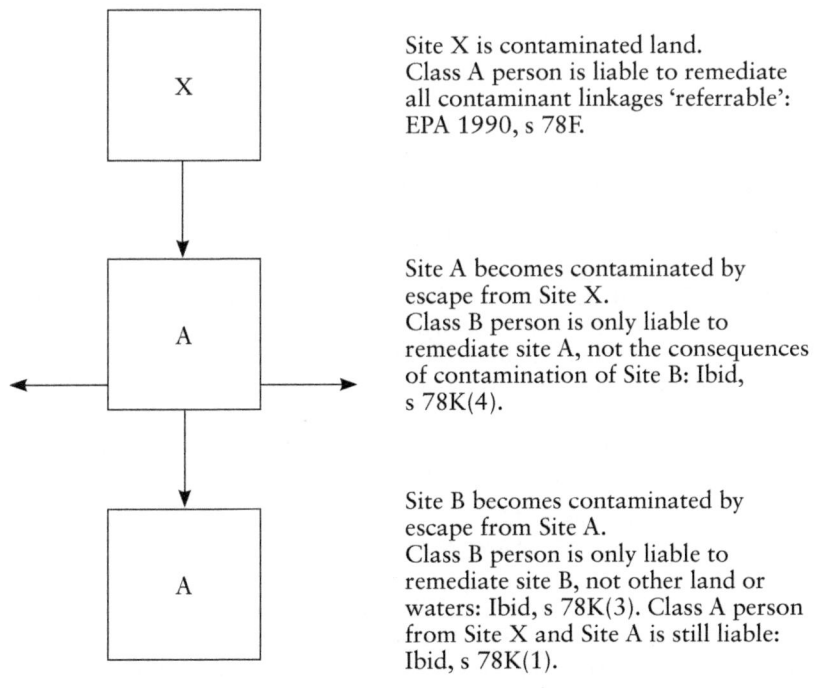

Site X is contaminated land.
Class A person is liable to remediate
all contaminant linkages 'referrable':
EPA 1990, s 78F.

Site A becomes contaminated by
escape from Site X.
Class B person is only liable to
remediate site A, not the consequences
of contamination of Site B: Ibid,
s 78K(4).

Site B becomes contaminated by
escape from Site A.
Class B person is only liable to
remediate site B, not other land or
waters: Ibid, s 78K(3). Class A person
from Site X and Site A is still liable:
Ibid, s 78K(1).

15.92 Exclusions in respect of Class B persons – owners or occupiers for the time being – are much briefer than those for Class A persons. The intention is to exclude from liability those **persons** who do not have an interest in the capital value of the land in question.[1] As with the exclusion of Class A persons, the non-statutory exclusion may apply where there are two or more Class B persons, but should not be applied where the consequence would be exclusion of all those persons. A Class B person may be excluded if either the person:

(a) 'occupies the land under a licence, or other agreement, of a kind which has no marketable value or which he is not legally able to assign or transfer to another person' (the actual market value itself, or the fact that it would not attract a buyer, are irrelevant); or

(b) 'is liable to pay rent which is equivalent to the rack rent for such of the land in question as he occupies and holds no beneficial interest in that land other than any tenancy to which such rent relates' where the rent is subject to periodic review, the rent should be considered to be equivalent to the rack rent if, at the latest review, it was set at the full market rent at that date'.[2]

This exclusion from direct liability under the Act may be wider than a tenant enjoys from his obligation to indemnify a landlord under his lease.[3]

1 Statutory Guidance, para 7.76.
2 Ibid, para 7.78.
3 See Taylor (2000) 4(3) *Landlord & Tenant Review* 70–73.

Liability to remediate: apportionment

15.93 Even when statutory and non-statutory exclusions have been applied, more than one appropriate person may remain. They may both (all) be Class A or B persons, or there may be a combination of the two. The latter situation will only arise where one remediation action is referable to two or more significant **contaminant linkage**s, as in every other case the identification of a Class A person will preclude the identification of a Class B person.[1] If more than one person is an appropriate person in respect of a particular remediation measure, **the Statutory Guidance sets out** the apportionment of liability between them.[2]

1 EPA 1990, s 78F(1)-(5); see para **15.78**.
2 Statutory Guidance, paras 7.80–7.86; see EPA 1990, s 78F(7).

15.94 The principle informing the Statutory Guidance on apportionment between Class A persons is that their relative responsibility for creating or continuing the risk now being caused by the significant **contaminant linkage** should be reflected in their share of remediation costs.[1] That assessment of 'relative responsibility' may be assisted by considering if the circumstances set out in the tests for exclusion might apply, but not to such an extent as to justify exclusion.[2] Where one person caused or knowingly permitted the presence of a substance, and another knowingly permitted its continuing presence, their relative means and opportunity to address the contamination **are** relevant in apportioning remediation costs.[3] The consideration of such criteria does not, however, apply if the person who caused the presence of a substance has been excluded from liability by an exclusion test, in particular, the sold with information test.

Statutory Guidance is also provided to assist in apportionment between two or more persons who have each knowingly permitted the presence of a substance (rather than caused it to be present), when factors such as relative duration and areas of land on which operations were carried out are relevant.[4] Where a company and one or more of its officers remain in the liability group, they should usually be treated as all being a single unit for the purposes of attributing liability to them and to other members of the liability group.[5]

1 Statutory Guidance, para 7.64.
2 Ibid, para 7.66; see paras **15.84–15.92**.
3 Statutory Guidance, para 7.67.
4 Ibid, para 7.73.
5 Ibid, paras 7.74–7.75.

15.95 Apportionment between Class B persons should be done either on the basis of discrete areas of the land in question owned or occupied, or in proportion to capital value of their interest in the land in question.[1] Apportionment between Class A and Class B persons is more complex.[2] In these cases, Class A persons are likely to bear a higher proportion of costs than Class B persons – indeed, sometimes all the costs. Limited provision is made for calculating enforcing authorities' liabilities for orphan linkages.[3]

1 Statutory Guidance, paras 7.83–7.84.
2 Ibid, paras 7.88–7.89.
3 Ibid, paras 7.95, 7.98.

15.96 It may be that different appropriate persons have sought to provide their own solution to the apportionment of liability, which would otherwise fall to be determined under these provisions. Providing the relevant enforcing authority is provided with a copy of any such agreement, and that none of the parties has informed the authority that it challenges the application of the agreement, the authority should generally give effect to that agreement in its attribution and apportionment decisions.[1] The practical effect is that an agreement will take precedence over these tests. The tests on attribution and apportionment should be applied as usual as between those parties and any non-party, however. Equally, if giving effect to the agreement would increase the share of the costs borne by a person otherwise entitled to plead hardship,[2] the enforcing authority should disregard the agreement.[3]

1 Statutory Guidance, para 7.29.
2 Under EPA 1990, s 78P(2); see para **15.98**.
3 Statutory Guidance, para 7.30.

Hardship and cost recovery

15.97 Section 78N provides the enforcing authority with power to do what is appropriate by way of remediation in certain circumstances. Whilst this includes cases of imminent danger of escape and acting in default,[1] it also extends to situations: where a written agreement has been made with the authority to carry out remediation on behalf – and at the cost – of an appropriate person; where the authority is precluded from requiring an appropriate person to do something by way of remediation;[2] where the authority would decide not to recover (all of) the costs of remediation;[3] and where no appropriate person has been found after reasonable inquiry.

1 EPA 1990, s 78N(3)(a) and (c).
2 Ibid,s 78H(5), s 78N(3)(b), s 78J (water pollution) or s 78K (escapes from land); see paras **15.80** and **15.82**.
3 EPA 1990, s 78P(2) – having applied the 'hardship test': see para **15.98**.

15.98 Where an authority exercises its powers to carry out works, it may be entitled to recover its reasonable costs from the relevant appropriate person or persons (if they have been identified).[1] In an unusual limitation, the authority seeking to recover its costs in this way is required to consider not just the Secretary of State's guidance but also the hardship the recovery may cause to the person from whom it is recoverable.[2] This is very different from determining the reasonableness of remediation itself having regard to its cost,[3] where the Statutory Guidance makes clear that the financial standing of any person who may be required to pay for remedial action is not relevant.[4] In making any decision as to the recovery of costs, the enforcing authority must have regard to two general principles: that the overall result should be as fair and equitable as possible to all who may have to meet the costs of remediation, including taxpayers; and the 'polluter pays' principle, by which the authority should consider the degree and nature of responsibility of the appropriate person for the creation, or continued existence, of the circumstances that lead to the land being identified as contaminated land.[5] In general, the Statutory Guidance continues, 'the enforcing authority should seek to recover all of its reasonable costs'.[6]

1 EPA 1990, s 78P.
2 Ibid, s 78P(2).
3 Ibid, s 78E(4).
4 Statutory Guidance, para 6.20; see para **15.60**; see also para **15.64** on limitations on issue of a remediation notice.
5 Statutory Guidance, para 8.5; see generally ibid, s 8, 'Recovery of the costs of remediation'.
6 Ibid, para 8.6.

15.99 The Statutory Guidance extends to factors which enforcing authorities must take into account in applying the cost recovery provisions to Class A persons,[1] Class B persons[2] and to both Class A and B persons.[3] From the point of view of property transactions, important ameliorative guidance is provided in respect of trusts, charities and social housing landlords.[4] Most obvious, however, are those applying to Class B persons, which are of particular relevance to smaller landowners and tenants. Various opportunities are presented for Class B persons to propose a reduction in any costs the local authority may seek against them. In this respect, an authority is advised to consider reducing its costs recovery where a Class B person who is an owner of land demonstrates to the satisfaction of the authority that:

(a) he took such steps prior to acquiring the freehold, or accepting the grant of assignment of a leasehold, as would have been reasonable at that time to establish the presence of any contaminants;

(b) when he acquired the land, or accepted the grant or assignment of the leasehold, he was nonetheless unaware of the presence of the significant contaminant now identified and could not reasonably have been expected to have been aware of its presence; and

(c) it would be reasonable, taking into account the interests of national and local taxpayers, that he should not bear the whole cost of remediation.[5]

1 Statutory Guidance, paras 8.23–8.26.
2 Ibid, paras 8.28–8.34.
3 Ibid, paras 8.12–8.22.
4 Ibid, paras 8.19–8.22, whether they are Class A or Class B persons.
5 Ibid, para 8.31.

15.100 Equally, the safeguards which might reasonably be expected to be taken are different in different types of transaction (commercial as opposed to residential)[1] and between different types of buyer, and the acquisition of commercial as opposed to recreational land.[2] The Statutory Guidance suggests that where a Class B person owns and occupies a dwelling on contaminated land, the enforcing authority should consider waiving or reducing its costs recovery where that person satisfies the authority that at the time of the survey he did not know, and could not reasonably have been expected to know, that the land was adversely affected by the presence of a contaminant.[3] In this respect, pre-purchase contamination surveys for residential property transactions are widely available.

Also in this respect, the report on the state of contaminated land in England and Wales, published by the Environment Agency in 2009, stated that, of the 230 sites that had been identified as contaminated land in England and the 120 such sites in Wales; appropriate persons were expected to pay to remediate only 78 sites in England and eight in Wales.[4] The low percentage was due to two factors. First, local authorities had focused their inspections on significant harm, or a significant possibility of significant harm, to human health,[5] with the result that most sites that had been identified were residential. Second, the authorities had applied the hardship criteria to conclude that the identified

Class B persons should not be required to pay to remediate the contamination at their residences.[6]

1 Statutory Guidance, paras 8.33–8.34.
2 Ibid, para 8.32.
3 Ibid, para 8.33.
4 Environment Agency, Reporting the Evidence; Dealing with contaminated land in England and Wales; A review of progress from 2000 to 2007 with Part 2A of the Environmental Protection Act 1990 (2009), p 19.
5 Ibid, p 21.
6 See E. Lees, 'Interpreting the contaminated land regime: should the 'Polluter' pay?' (2012) 14 Environmental Law Review 98, 102–04.

Charging notices

15.101 Where costs are recoverable from an owner or occupier who is *also* a Class A person,[1] the enforcing authority may issue a 'charging notice'.[2] Having taken effect, this will be a charge on the relevant premises – likely to affect, and take priority over, all existing mortgages, charges, options and other legal or equitable estates or interests in land[3] – which will also carry interest. For the purpose of enforcing that charge an enforcing authority has the same powers and remedies as if it were a mortgagee by deed having powers of sale and lease, of accepting surrenders of leases and of appointing a receiver.[4] Matters of detail in respect of the service of charging notices, including provision for appeals, are set out in the Act.[5]

1 See para **15.75**.
2 EPA 1990, s 78P(3). These provisions do not extend to Scotland: sub-s (14).
3 See *Westminster City Council v Haymarket Publishing Ltd* [1981] 2 All ER 555.
4 EPA 1990, s 78P(11).
5 Ibid, s 78P(5)–(10).

Registers

15.102 As with other environmental regimes, public registers must be maintained by every enforcing authority under Part 2A.[1] These must include details of, for example, remediation notices (and appeals), statements and declarations, designation of special sites, notification by recipients of remediation notices of 'what they claim has been done by them by way of remediation'[2] and such other matters as may be prescribed.[3] The latter include details of convictions for offences under Part 2A, guidance issued by the Environment Agency, and details of cases where the enforcing authority is precluded from serving a remediation notice by virtue of the operation of certain other statutory controls.[4] The Agency, as enforcing authority, must copy entries made on its register to the relevant local authority. What is notably lacking is a formal process by which sites might be 'signed off' as having been adequately remediated, a process that has been introduced in Scotland.[5]

1 EPA 1990, ss 78R–78T; Contaminated Land (England) Regulations 2006, SI 2006/1380, reg 13 and Sch 3.
2 EPA 1990, s 78R(h) and (j).
3 Ibid, s 78R(l).
4 Contaminated Land (England) Regulations 2006, SI 2006/1380, Sch 3, paras 12–16.
5 EPA 1990, s 78TA. Section 78TA also sets out specified procedures for removing such information from registers.

15.103 Information shall be excluded from inclusion in registers if, in the opinion of the Secretary of State, its inclusion, or the inclusion of information of that description, would be contrary to the interests of national security.[1] The Secretary of State has very wide powers to direct enforcing authorities as to what information shall be excluded; powers identical to those applying in respect of water registers.[2] The same applies to exclusion of information on the grounds that it is commercially confidential.[3]

1 EPA 1990, s 78S(1).
2 Ibid, s 78S(2); Water Resources Act 1991, s 191A(2), the latter introduced by EA 1995, s 120, Sch 22, para 170; see paras **17.79–17.80**.
3 EPA 1990, s 78T; WRA 1991, s 191B; see para **17.81**.

Reports

15.104 Part 2A directs the Environment Agency, from time to time (or as directed), to prepare and publish a report on the state of contaminated land.[1] Local authorities are required to co-operate in the supply of information acquired in the exercise of their functions under Part 2A of the Act.[2] Properly speaking, this is a relatively narrow obligation, as authorities may well acquire relevant information other than in the exercise of powers under this part of the Act. In that case, there would be no obligation on them to supply such information to the Agency for this purpose. It would presumably be available under other powers,[3] but on the basis that the making of copies would be subject to payment of a fee.

The Environment Agency has published two reports on the state of contaminated land, in 2002[4] and 2009.[5] The report on the state of contaminated land, published by the Environment Agency in 2009, stated that local authorities had determined 659 sites in England and 122 in Wales, of which 33 and two were special sites, respectively.[6] The total of 781 sites included 110 determinations on a housing estate in Leckworth, Cardiff, and over 100 determinations on a housing estate in Seaton Carew, Hartlepoool.[7]

By the end of December 2013, local authorities in England had determined 511 sites as contaminated land, of which 50 were special sites; 377 of the 461 local authority sites had been fully remediated at a cost of approximately £29.8 million; 31 of the 50 special sites had been fully remediated at a cost of approximately £12.4 million.[8]

The subsequently withdrawn Contaminated Land Capital Grants Programme ('CLCGP')[9] had paid to remediate 85% of the local authority sites and 44% of the special sites, with Class A persons paying to remediate 29% of the special sites and Class B persons paying to remediate 27% of them.[10]

Also by the end of December 2013, local authorities in Wales had determined 177 sites as contaminated land, of which two were special sites; 90 local authority sites had been fully remediated at a cost of £3.7 million; both special sites had also been fully remediated at a cost of approximately £1.2 million.[11] The CLCGP had paid 71% of the costs of remediated the sites, with Class A persons paying 22%.[12]

1 EPA 1990, s 78U. The Environment Agency is now directed to publish such reports only for England, with Natural Resources Wales and the Scottish Environment Protection Agency being directed to publish reports for Wales and Scotland, respectively. Ibid.
2 Ibid, s 78U(2)–(3).
3 Eg, the TCPA 1990 or the Environmental Information Regulations 2004, SI 2004/3391. On the latter see generally chap 4.
4 Environment Agency, Dealing with contaminated land in England, Progress in 2002 with implementing the Part IIA regime (September 2002).
5 Environment Agency, Reporting the Evidence; Dealing with contaminated land in England and Wales; A review of progress from 2000 to 2007 with Part 2A of the Environmental Protection Act 1990 (2009).
6 Ibid, p 8.
7 See 'Tensions mount as land remediation regime stalls' (April 2006) ENDS Rep., No 375, 35.
8 Cranfield University and CL:AIRE, Examination of contaminated land sector activity in England (SP1011 Final Project Report for Defra, 10 June 2014), p 4.
9 Ibid.
10 See Environment Agency, Contaminated Land Capital Grants Notes for Applicants (2014–2015) (September 2014, CL_GN_04); available at https://www.gov.uk/government/uploads/system/uploads/attachment_data/file/350575/LIT_8067.pdf
11 Cranfield University and CL:AIRE, Examination of contaminated land sector activity in Wales (SP1011 Final Project Report for Defra, 21 June 2014), p 4.
12 Ibid.

ENVIRONMENTAL LIABILITY DIRECTIVE

15.105 Environmental damage that has occurred after the deadline for transposing the ELD[1] into domestic law but which has not been remediated, should also be considered in property transactions, particularly pollution or contamination that affects land, EU-protected areas (that is, sites protected under the Birds[2] and Habitats[3] Directives), SSSIs and groundwater. The Environmental Damage (Prevention and Remediation) Regulations 2015 ('ELD Regulations'), the predecessor of which transposed the ELD into English law, entered into force on 1 March 2009.[3] The Court of Justice of the European Union has ruled, however, in two cases concerning sites in Italy, that the relevant date for application of the ELD is 30 April 2007,[4] a date that has been conceded by Welsh Ministers in giving direct effect to the ELD in this respect.[5]

1 Directive 2004/35/CE of the European Parliament and of the Council on environmental liability with regard to the prevention and remedying of environmental damage, as amended.
2 Directive 2009/147 on the conservation of wild birds (codified version) (2010) OJ L20/7.
3 Council Directive 92/43 on the conservation of natural habitats and of wild fauna and flora (consolidated version 1 January 2007).
4 ELD Regulations, SI 2015/810, reg 8(1). The regulations for Wales, Scotland and Northern Ireland, with the dates they came into force, are as follows: Environmental Damage (Prevention and Remediation) (Wales) Regulations, SI 2009/995, as amended (6 May 2009); Environmental Liability (Scotland) Regulations SSI 2009/266 (Scottish SI), as amended (24 June 2009); and Environmental Liability (Prevention and Remediation) Regulations (Northern Ireland) 2009/252, as amended (24 July 2009).
4 Case C–534/13 *Ministero dell'Ambiente e della Tutela del Territorio e del Mare v Fipa Group Srl* (CJEU, 4 March 2015, not yet reported), para 44; [2014] Case C–378/08 *Raffinerie Mediterranee (ERG) SpA v Ministero dello Sviluppo economico* [2010] ECR I–1919, para 38; see V. Fogleman, 'The temporal provisions of the Environmental Liability Directive: the start date, direct effect and retrospectivity' [2014] (4)) Environmental Liability 137, 142–43.
5 See *R (Seiont, Gwyrfai and Llyfni Anglers' Society) v Natural Resources Wales v Dŵr Cymru Cyfyngedig Trading as Dŵr Cymru Welsh Water, First Hydro Company Limited* [2015] EWHC 3578 (Admin), paras 83–85.

15.106 A company or other person may be liable under the ELD Regulations if it is an 'operator'.[1] There are two categories of operator. The operator of an activity carried out under EU legislation listed in Schedule 2 of the ELD Regulations (and Annex III of the ELD) is strictly liable for measures to prevent or remedy damage to land, water (ground, surface, transitional, coastal, and marine waters in the territorial sea and exclusive economic zone), species and natural habitats protected under the Birds and Habitats Directives, and SSSIs.[2] Schedule 2 includes, among other things, sites subject to the Environmental Permitting (England and Wales) Regulations 2010 in respect of the Industrial Emissions Directive (2010/75/EU) and EU waste management legislation.[3] The operator of a non-schedule 2 activity is liable for measures to prevent or remedy damage to protected species and natural habitats and SSSIs provided that the operator is negligent or otherwise at fault.[4] In contrast to Part 2A of the EPA 1990,[5] therefore, the purchaser of land that is contaminated or polluted is not potentially liable under the ELD Regulations. The purchaser could, however, suffer disruptions to its business during any remediation at the site.

1 ELD, arts 2(6), 3(1); ELD Regulations, regs 13, 14, 18.
2 ELD Regulations, reg 5(1), Sch 2; see paras **19.43–19.57** (describing European sites).
3 Environmental Permitting (England and Wales) Regulations 2010, SI 2010/675, reg 3.
4 ELD Regulations, reg 5(2).
5 See paras **15.77–15.78**. The UK government has not identified additional responsible persons as indicated in art 16 of the ELD.

15.107 Environmental damage to land occurs if there is a significant risk of human health being adversely affected by contamination.[1] The operator who damaged the land must remove the significant risk.[2] The threshold for land contamination under the ELD Regulations is roughly equivalent to the threshold under the Statutory Guidance.[3]

1 ELD, art 2(1)(c); ELD Regulations, regs 4(1)(c), (5).
2 ELD, annex II, para 2; ELD Regulations, Sch 4, part 2.
3 *Cf* The Environmental Damage (Prevention and Remediation) Regulations 2009, Guidance for England and Wales (2ⁿᵈ Update, November 2009), para A1.94 *with* Statutory Guidance, paras 4.5–4.6;

15.108 Environmental damage to water occurs if there is a significant adverse effect on the ecological, chemical or quantitative status or the ecological potential of the water.[1] Environmental damage to protected species and natural habitats occurs if there is a significant adverse effect on reaching or maintaining the favourable conservation status of a protected species or habitat.[2] Environmental damage to a SSSI occurs if the damage has 'an adverse effect on the integrity of the site (that is, the coherence of its ecological structure and function, across its whole area, that enables it to sustain the habitat, complex of habitats or the levels of populations of the species affected)'.[3] A schedule 2 operator who damages water, a protected species or natural habitat, or the SSSI is strictly liable for primary, complementary and compensatory remediation;[4] a non-schedule 2 operator who damages a protected species or natural habitat or a SSSI is liable for such remediation if it is negligent or intended the damage.[5]

1 ELD, art 2(1)(b); ELD Regulations, regs 4(1(b), (3), (4).
2 ELD, art 2(1)(a); ELD Regulations, regs 4(1)(a), (2), Sch 1, para 1.
3 ELD Regulations, reg 4(2), Sch 4, part 2.
4 Ibid, reg 5(1).
5 Ibid, reg 5(2).

15.109 Primary remediation is the restoration of the natural resource and services rendered by it to its baseline condition, that is, its condition before it was damaged.[1] Complementary remediation is any remedial measure carried out to compensate for the inability to restore a natural resource to its baseline condition by providing a similar level of natural resources or services at another site.[2] Such remediation is in addition to partial restoration of the damaged natural resource. Compensatory remediation is the provision of improvements and other measures to a natural resource to compensate for 'interim losses', ie, the loss of the natural resource or services rendered by it from the time of the damage to restoration to its baseline condition.[3]

1 ELD, annex II, para 1(a); ELD Regulations, Sch 3, part 1, para 4(2).
2 ELD, annex II, para 1(b); ELD Regulations, Sch 3, part 1, para 4(3).
3 ELD, annex II, paras 1(c)–(d); ELD Regulations, Sch 3, part 1, para 5.

15.110 The ELD Regulations may not be the only liability regime to apply to a single site. For example, Part 2A could apply to the remediation of past contamination, s 161 of the Water Resources Act 1991 could apply to water pollution below the threshold for the ELD Regulations, and the ELD Regulations could apply to water pollution above its threshold after 30 April 2007.[1] Complexities may thus arise, particularly because various exclusions and defences that apply under the ELD Regulations do not exist under Part 2A or s 161 of the Water Resources Act 1991.[2]

1 Article 17 of the ELD provides that 'This Directive shall not apply to: – damage caused by an emission, event or incident that took place before the date referred to in Article 19(1) [30 April 2007, or] damage caused by an emission, event or incident which takes place subsequent to [30 April 2007] when it derives from a specific activity that took place and finished before the said date',
2 See The Environmental Damage (Prevention and Remediation) Regulations 2009, Guidance for England and Wales (2nd Update, November 2009), para 2.32, annex 4.

Chapter 16

Waste

INTRODUCTION

16.01 Waste law and policy have been transformed in recent decades by a growing recognition of the scale of the environmental challenge presented by ever-increasing quantities of waste generated by social and economic activities. Whereas waste law used to focus exclusively on the environmental risks associated with waste disposal, it has developed to concentrate too on wider questions of waste management and waste reduction. The shift, which originated with the European Waste Framework Directive,[1] has seen the extension of regulation and liability to affect the producers and holders of waste as well as those directly responsible for its disposal. Waste is regulated all along the waste chain from production to final disposal. The development of a national waste strategy,[2] environmental permitting schemes,[3] landfill tax[4] and the promotion of alternatives to landfill are part of a substantial and complex regulatory regime which may affect those engaged in development and property transactions.

1. Waste Framework Directive 2008/98/EC (WFD)
2. Department for the Environment, Food and Rural Affairs (Defra), National Waste Management Plan (2013) – https://www.gov.uk/government/uploads/system/uploads/attachment_data/file/265810/pb14100-waste-management-plan-20131213.pdf
3. Environmental Permitting (England and Wales) Regulations 2010
4 Finance Act 1996. Landfill Tax Regulations 1996.

The scale of the problem

16.02 In 2012, the UK generated 200 million tonnes of waste.[1] Half of this was generated by construction, almost a quarter came from commercial and industrial activities, with households responsible for a further 14 per cent. In the past, most waste in the UK was disposed of in landfill, however, the last couple of decades has seen a significant increase in rates of recycling. The revised Waste Framework Directive 2008/98/EC ('WFD') calls for EU member states to 'move closer towards a recycling society' and sets ambitious targets for waste reduction, recycling and recovery.[2] Almost half of the 186.2 million tonnes of total waste that entered final treatment in the UK in 2012 was recovered. The proportion that went to landfill was 26 per cent.

Whilst waste disposal needs are increasingly being met by incineration and alternative reuse or recycling initiatives, it must be recognised that each of these disposal methods has its own environmental drawbacks. The EU target for the UK is to recycle at least 50 per cent of household waste by 2020. By 2014, the UK's domestic recycling rate had reached 44.9 per cent in 2014 compared to 40.4 per cent in 2010.[3]

1 Defra, UK Statistics on Waste, December 2015.
2 Preamble to Directive 2008/98/EC, Recital 28, Article 11(2).
3 Defra, UK Statistics on Waste, December 2015.

Scope of the chapter

16.03 This chapter focuses on those aspects of European and domestic waste law which affect property transactions and on-site development and management. The chapter examines the complicated issue of the legal definition of 'waste' and how this impacts on property owners. It outlines the environmental permitting regime, the interaction between waste law and planning controls and the statutory duties and liabilities that arise in relation to waste management. A key aim of waste management controls is the prevention of the future dereliction of land. Ongoing obligations to monitor or regulate sites used for waste management affect not just the present owners or occupiers of land but future ones too. The distribution of those liabilities may need to be managed in the course of property transactions. The chapter reflects the law as it stands on the date of publication.

Historical development of waste law and policy

16.04 Historically, legal controls on waste were introduced in response to existing pollution or contamination incidents. Preventative controls were only established with the modern planning system under the Town and Country Planning Act 1947, and planning permission remains a prerequisite for environmental permitting.

The Control of Pollution Act 1974 introduced the first comprehensive licensing system for waste disposal. At the same time the influence of European waste legislation and waste management policy begun to be felt. The Waste Framework Directive was originally adopted in 1975 as Directive 75/442/EEC. The focus of the original Directive was on ensuring the safe disposal of waste with all member states adopting their own national definitions of waste. The Directive has since evolved so the aim of waste policy is not simply to address the environmental risks associated with the disposal of waste but to encourage the prevention, recycling and reuse of waste in a strategic way. A greater emphasis on waste management rather than mere disposal was heralded by Part II of the Environmental Protection Act 1990 ('EPA 1990'), which provides 'cradle to the grave' regulation throughout the entirety of the waste cycle, regulating the producers, holders, carriers and disposers of waste.

UK waste law and policy over the past two decades has been characterised by a convergence with European policy. Waste management is increasingly guided by overarching policy objectives transposed from the Waste Framework Directive and reflected in the Waste Management Plan for England published in 2013.[1] The Plan enshrines a 'waste hierarchy' which prioritises waste minimisation, recycling and reuse and makes landfill waste disposal a last resort.

1 This builds the Waste Strategies for England and Wales published in 2000 and 2007.

EUROPEAN WASTE FRAMEWORK DIRECTIVE

16.05 The revised European Waste Framework Directive[1] (WFD) defines the meaning of waste and provides the legislative framework for the collection, transport, recovery and disposal of waste. The WFD requires all member states to take the necessary measures to ensure waste is recovered or disposed of without endangering human health or causing harm to the environment and includes permitting, registration and inspection requirements. The European Commission has published guidance on the interpretation of key provisions of the Directive.[2] The WFD is supplemented by directives for specific waste streams[3] and particular methods of waste treatment.[4] It contains the 'polluter pays' principle (Article 14), provisions on waste management planning (Article 28) and waste prevention programming (Article 29).

At the heart of WFD is the waste hierarchy.[5] Article 4 of the WFD sets out five mandatory steps for dealing with waste ranked according to their environmental impact. Prevention, which offers the best outcome for the environment, is at the top of the priority order followed by reuse, recycling, the recovery of waste, reclamation or other processes which extract secondary raw materials or energy from waste. Safe disposal of waste is at the bottom of the hierarchy.

The revised WFD has been transposed into national law by The Waste (England and Wales) Regulations 2011 (2011 Regulations). The waste hierarchy is enshrined in Regulations 12,15 and 35 of 2011 Regulations.[6]

1 Waste Framework Directive 2008/98/EC.
2 http://ec.europa.eu/environment/waste/framework/pdf/guidance_doc.pdf.
3 Eg Directives dealing with batteries (2006/66/EC), PCBs (96/59/EC) packaging (94/62/EC), electrical equipment (2002/96/EC) and vehicles (2000/53/EC).
4 Eg Directives on Landfill (99/31/EC) and Industrial Emissions (Integrated Pollution Prevention and Control) (2010/75/EU).
5 WFD, Article 4.
6 SI 2011/988.

Waste hierarchy

16.06 Prevention – (Article 9) measures taken before a substance or product has become waste that reduce:

- the quantity of waste, including through the re-use of products or the extension of the life span of products;

- the adverse impacts of the generated waste on the environment and human health; and
- the content of harmful substances in materials and products.

Article 29 of the WFD requires member states to establish waste prevention programmes and set quantitative targets for the reduction of waste.

Re-use – (Article 11) any operation by which products or components that are not waste are used again for the same purpose for which they were conceived.

Preparing for re-use – checking, cleaning or repairing recovery operations, by which products or components of products that have become waste are prepared so that they can be re-used without any other pre-processing.

Recycling – (Article 11) means any recovery operation by which waste materials are reprocessed into products, materials or substances whether for their original or other purposes. A recycling operation is different in nature to other recovery operations in that it will always result in the substance in question ceasing to be waste when it is transformed.[1]

Recovery – (Article 10) means any operation the principal result of which is waste serving a useful purpose by replacing other materials which would otherwise have been used to fulfil a particular function, or waste being prepared to fulfil that function, in the plant or in the wider economy eg energy recovery. Annex II contains a non-exhaustive list of recovery operations.

Disposal – (Article 12) means any operation which is not recovery even where the operation has as a secondary consequence the reclamation of substances or energy. Annex I sets out a non-exhaustive list of safe disposal operations. Landfill should only be used as a last resort.

1 WFD, Article 11 requires the separate collection of paper, metal, plastic and glass. See 2011 Regulations, regs 13,14.

Producer Responsibility Principle

16.07 The producer responsibility principle is integral to the WFD (Article 8). The Directive's preamble articulates its approach to waste management which 'takes into account the whole life-cycle of products and materials and not only the waste phase'. The extension of producer responsibility is aimed at reducing waste production and encouraging recycling. The policy targets producers to assume responsibility for their product once it becomes waste at the end of its life cycle. With specific types of waste, producers must bear the costs for the collection, sorting, treatment, recycling or recovery.[1]

The policy is also incorporated into specific directives on Packaging and Packaging Waste,[2] Waste Electrical and Electronic Equipment (WEEE),[3] End of Life Vehicles (ELV)[4] and Batteries and Accumulators.[5] These directives have been identified as 'priority waste streams' because of growing concern about their impact on the environment.

1 See Section 93 of the Environment Act 1995 which provides for the introduction of regulations to impose obligations on producers of materials or products to recycle, recover or reuse those products.
2 94/62/EC (as amended). Transposed by The Producer Responsibility Obligations (Packaging Waste) Regulations 2007 as amended. Defra has announced plans to consolidate these regulations in the course of 2016.
3 WEEE Directive 2012/19/EU came into force on 13 August 2012 and is transposed by the Waste Electrical and Electronic Equipment (England and Wales) Regulations 2013.
4 2000/53/EC. Transposed by End-of-Life Vehicles Regulations 2005.
5 2006/66/EC. Transposed by Waste Batteries and Accumulators Regulations 2009/890.

The Directive objectives

16.08 The primary objectives of waste management legislation are to protect the environment and human health as well as to improve the impacts and efficiency of resource use.[1] These objectives, which are set out in Article 13 and 16 of the WFD, are transposed in The Waste (England and Wales) Regulations 2011 and the Environmental Permitting (England and Wales) Regulations 2010, Schedule 9. European and domestic legislation must be interpreted with these objectives in mind. The Court of Appeal has held that they create a stand-alone duty on regulatory authorities, such as the Environment Agency and local planning authorities, to ensure that waste is recovered or disposed of without endangering the environment or human health.[2] The mandatory nature and the importance of the Directive objectives, and the need for decision makers to have due regard to the objectives when making decisions, has been consistently emphasised by the domestic courts.[3]

1 WFD, Article 1. The economic dimension of waste was considered in Case C-2/90 *Walloon Waste* at [28]. See also Defra, *Guidance on the legal definition of waste and its application* (2012), 24–30
2 *R v Bolton Metropolitan Borough Council ex parte Kirkman* [1998] Env LR 719
3 *R v Daventry District Council ex parte Thornby Farms; R (Murray) Derbyshire County Council* [2002] Env LR 28, Pill LJ at [53]; *R (Blewett) v Derbyshire County Council* [2005] Env LR 15.

WHAT IS WASTE?

16.09 The application of the WFD and transposing legislation is dependent on the substance in question being defined as 'waste'.[1] This is a complex area of law which concerns those engaged in property transactions since whether something does or does not constitute 'waste' will affect a property owner's liability for its lawful management.

The difficulty with defining 'waste' arises because one man's waste may be another's raw material. There is a stigma associated with waste which can limit its beneficial use. The underlying policy of the WFD is that recycling should be promoted as an economically useful activity and that waste is a valuable resource. The challenge for legislators has been to reconcile competing objectives in waste management policy: on the one hand, a wide definition of waste can lead to overregulation and discourage environmentally useful activities which reduce waste production, such as recycling and reuse. On the other hand, too narrow a definition could mean that recycling and reclamation processes, which themselves may cause environmental harm, will not be properly regulated.[2]

1 National guidance on the definition of waste is contained in Defra, *Guidance on the legal definition of waste and its application*, August 2012.
2 Bell, McGillivray and Pedersen, *Environmental Law* (8th edn) 683; Waite, 'The Quest for Environmental Law Equilibrium', (2005) Env L Rev 34, 37–38.

The definition of Directive waste

16.10 'Waste' is defined in Article 3(1) of the WFD as 'any substance or object which the holder discards or intends or is required to discard'.[1] In domestic legislation reg 2 of the Environmental Permitting (England and Wales) Regulations 2010 defines waste as 'anything that is waste for the purposes of the Waste Framework Directive'. This means that the jurisprudence of the European Court on the interpretation of terms such as 'discard' is directly relevant.

The old Framework Directive 2006/12/EC contained a two-stage test in order to establish whether a substance was waste. This has been removed in the revised WFD, along with the categories of wastes in the old Annex I. However, the central test of whether a substance is waste or not remains, whether the substance has been **discarded**.[2]

Article 7 of the WFD provides for a 'List of Wastes' to be prepared and regularly updated by the European Commission. The purpose of the list is to ensure uniformity in the categorisation of wastes across the EU. The list is neither exhaustive nor determinative of whether something is waste but it does give an idea of the sorts of substances and objects likely to be regarded as waste.[3]

1 See also WFD Preamble, Recital 24 which provides that in order to promote certainty in the definition of waste the Commission may adopt guidelines to specify in certain cases when substances or objects become waste.
2 See para **16.11**.
3 Commission Decision 2014/955/EU.

General principles of European court case law

Meaning of 'discard'

16.11 The key to determining whether something is or is not waste is whether the substance or object has been 'discarded' by its holder. The 'discard' test is applied in a very wide range of circumstances but, in each case, the test must be interpreted so as to give effect to the objectives of the WFD.

A substance or object may be discarded for a range of reasons: intentional or accidental, voluntary or required.[1] The WFD makes clear that a substance or object will be classified as waste if the holder **intends** to discard it. The test relates to the conduct of the holder rather than the intrinsic characteristics of the substance or object. In some cases, this will be obvious. Suppose a person disposes of some usable, but surplus, tiles by placing them in a skip. Despite the fact that the tiles could have been put to a productive use by someone else, the intention to discard them is clear. The European Court has held that the mere fact that a substance is capable of reuse does not remove it from the definition of waste if it has, in fact, been discarded.[2] A holder's intention is to be inferred from his actions in light of the aims of the WFD.

The European Court has developed a broad purposive definition of waste which is not always easy to apply. It has encouraged a case-by-case approach and consistently cautioned member states not to adopt modes of proof, such as statutory presumptions, which would have the effect of restricting the scope of the Directive.[3] The Court's jurisprudence on the meaning of waste addresses three key issues in the application of the 'discard' test: (i) what significance does a recovery or disposal operation have in determining whether a substance has become waste? (ii) what is the difference between by-products and waste? And (iii) when does waste material cease to be waste?

(i) The 'discard' test in the context of recovery and disposal operations

The European Court has explained that 'discard' has an extended meaning in the WFD that includes the recovery of a substance or object as well as its disposal.[4] A person may be regarded as discarding a substance or object if they are carrying out a recovery operation in the course of their business, even though the substance or object has a commercial value to them.[5] It makes no difference whether a disposal or recovery operation is carried out by the person who produced the waste or someone else. In both cases the substance or object will be 'discarded' and will therefore be waste.[6]

An important factor in determining whether a material has been discarded is whether the substance or material has been consigned to a particular waste disposal or recovery operation. Where a substance is consigned to waste disposal, for example by landfill or incineration, there is an obvious intention to discard. Annex I of the WFD lists a series of operations for finally disposing of waste including landfill, deep injection and incineration. However, where a recovery operation is itself an integral part of a larger industrial process, the distinction between the recovery operation and the industrial process may be more difficult to draw.

In *Euro Tombesi and Adino Tombesi*[7] Advocate General Jacobs suggested that 'discard' referred to any object which had or was to be dealt with by means of a 'disposal operation' or 'recovery operation' as set out in Annexes IIA and IIB of WFD. The Court qualified the so called 'Tombesi by-pass' by holding that a substance consigned to a recovery process could be deemed to be discarded but was not necessarily to be treated as such in every case.

The *Tombesi* approach effectively substituted the question of whether a substance had been 'discarded' with a test of whether or not a substance has been consigned to a recovery operation or disposal operation. Initially,

Tombesi was followed in *Inter Environment Wallonie v Region Wallonie*[8] and by the English courts in *Mayer Parry Recycling v Environment Agency.*[9] However, the problem with the *Tombesi* approach was that the listed operations in many cases referred to operations involving material which was not waste. For example, where an industrial by-product is used to fuel a kiln the by-product is being used as part of the normal industrial process and at the same time energy is being recovered from it, therefore it cannot necessarily be regarded as waste.

Mindful of that difficulty the ECJ abandoned the '*Tombesi* by-pass' in the *ARCO/Epon* case.[10] *ARCO/Epon* concerned the use of a by-product from a manufacturing process as fuel in cement manufacture and the use of wood chips originating from the construction sector as fuel in a power station. The ECJ indicated that the test of whether something is waste is solely whether the holder of material discards it or intends to discard it. Whether a material is consigned to a recovery operation is not determinative of whether it is waste, although it may be a relevant factor to suggest that it is. Whether the substance has been discarded must be interpreted in the light of the aims of the Directive and will depend on the particular facts of the case. Following the *ARCO/Epon* decision, the '*Tombesi* by-pass' no longer applies in UK law.[11] However, in practice, substances which are consigned to a specialised recovery operation are likely be treated as waste.

ARCO/Epon was followed by the *Palin Granit* case[12] which concerned the issue of whether leftover stone at a granite quarry was waste for the purposes of the Directive. The ECJ concluded that leftover stone was not the main product sought by the quarry operator and was production residue. It was not certain on the facts of the case that the granite would be re-used, only that it was capable of re-use in the long term. Therefore the court concluded that the stone constituted waste. The court rejected the idea of a conclusive test for waste but reiterated that the term 'discard' had to be determined broadly in light of the general aims of the WFD.

(ii) Distinguishing between a 'by-product' and 'waste'

Production processes produce a range of substances. Some will be sought (ie they will be the products of the process) whereas as others will not (ie they will be residues of the production process). The latter may or may not be regarded as waste. Article 5(1) of the WFD lays down certain conditions which must be met if a substance is to be regarded as a by-product of a production process rather than waste for the purposes of Article 3(1). These include that:

- further use of the substance or object is certain;[13]
- the substance or object can be used directly without any further processing other than normal industrial practice;
- the substance or object is produced as an integral part of a production process; and
- further use is lawful, ie the substance or object fulfils all relevant product, environmental, and health protection requirements for the specific use and will not lead to overall adverse environmental or human health impacts.

Article 5(2) of the WFD enables additional criteria to be adopted for specific substances or objects to be regarded as non-waste by-products under a procedure known as 'comitology with scrutiny'. The initiative for proposing any such measures lies with the European Commission.

The twists in the European case law on the definition of waste have led to some uncertainty which can affect whether parties engaged in property transactions ought to regard themselves as subject to waste regulation.[14] The English courts have generally adopted a commonsense approach which is consistent with the WFD.[15] This approach was reflected in *Environment Agency v Thorn International UK Limited* which addressed the question of whether certain goods should properly be regarded as waste whilst they are being stored, pending possible repair and reuse.[16]

In *Thorn,* the Divisional Court considered the case of distributors of electrical equipment under 'new-for-old' schemes, whereby the old equipment was bought and refurbished for resale by a repair company. It held that the items bought by the repair company were not waste within the meaning of the WFD and EPA 1990 while awaiting such repairs. Simply because their owners no longer wanted the products, it was incorrect to regard the products as having been 'discarded'. When the goods were exchanged for replacement products, they could still be used for their original purpose. There was no rule that whenever a consumer let used goods go, those unwanted goods became and remained waste until the repair was complete.[17] Only those products which were found to be beyond repair would be discarded and considered as waste. The court distinguished between materials such as the woodchips destined for fuel (see *ARCO*), which were surplus to requirements and no longer required for their original purpose, and the electrical products in *Thorn*. The woodchips, although capable of economic reuse, were waste in the hands of the original manufacturer. By contrast, the electrical goods exchanged for replacement products were retained for their original purpose and did not undergo any material change in form. Therefore the court held that the goods held by Thorn were not waste.

(iii) When does waste cease to be waste?

Article 6 of the WFD outlines the conditions which must be fulfilled in order for a substance to reach end-of-waste status. Certain specified waste will cease to be waste once it has undergone a recovery operation, which could include a recycling operation[18] or an operation which prepares discarded substances for re-use, whether for their original or other purpose, provided that it satisfies criteria developed in accordance with the following conditions:

- the substance or object is commonly used for specific purposes;
- a market exists for such a substance or object;
- the substance or object fulfils the technical requirements for the specific purposes and meets existing legislation applicable to products;
- the use of the substance or object will not have an adverse impact on environmental and human health.

Article 6(1) and (2) enables the Commission to develop end-of-waste criteria for specific waste streams. For example, criteria have been developed for ferrous and aluminium scrap metal and glass.[19] Where no end-of-waste criteria have been set at an EU-level, member states may decide on a case-by-case basis whether certain waste has ceased to be waste, taking into account the applicable case law.

Once a substance becomes waste, a recovery process usually needs to be carried out in order for it to cease to be waste. An assessment of the discard test needs to be applied to any substance or object which results from a recovery operation. The European Court has considered the issue only generally with reference to the concept of a 'complete recovery operation'. Whether a recovery operation is complete and has transformed waste into a distinct product will be relevant to assessing the discard test, but is not determinative of whether the substance in question has ceased to be waste.[20] The lack of a clear distinction between waste and end-of-waste status has left national authorities with a wide discretion in how to apply the test to the cases which come before them.[21]

The question of whether a substance has ceased to be waste should not be determined by considering whether those subjecting it to a process of reclamation intend to discard it or not. If that were the test then the material in question would cease to be waste at the moment those subjecting it to such a process had the mere intention to reuse it. In *OSS Group Ltd v Environment Agency*, the Court of Appeal found that it was possible to recover a non-waste fuel from waste lubricating oil without waiting for the new fuel to be burned.[22] The Court of Appeal recognised that whilst a subjective intention to discard might be a useful guide to the status of material in the hands of the original producer, the material did not cease to be waste merely because it had passed into the possession of someone who intended to put it to a new use. The Court regarded it as relevant that the holder had converted the waste material into a distinct, marketable product that could be used in exactly the same way as an ordinary fuel, and with no worse environmental effects.[23]

A recovery operation will not result in 'end of waste' status where that operation does not alter the nature of substance, the substance retains its environmentally threatening nature or the process is merely a pre-treatment process.[24] Operations which merely dry, chip or grind waste to be used, say, as fuel are unlikely to rid a substance of its waste status before its final use. The Environment Agency has developed a number of national end-of-waste protocols which give examples of complete recovery operations.[25]

Summary of relevant factors to definition of waste

Drawing together the European court's jurisprudence and relevant guidance, the following factors indicate that a substance/object is likely to be waste. The substance/object:

- is commonly regarded as waste;
- has a low economic value
- is a production residue;
- is a residue for which no use other than disposal can be envisaged;
- is being transferred to a disposal or recovery operation;

- is a residue whose composition is not suitable for the use made of it or where special precautions must be taken when using it, owing to the environmentally hazardous nature of its composition.

In *R v Jagger*,[26] the Court of Appeal reviewed the definition of 'controlled waste' in the context of offences committed under s 33 of the EPA 1990.[27] Directive waste and controlled waste are effectively synonymous because any substance that is not Directive waste cannot be controlled waste.[28] In *Jagger*, the contractor acknowledged that he had been responsible for the collection of material from a building site and its deposit at another site on which demolition works were being carried out. However, he questioned the categorisation of the material in question as waste in circumstances where, he argued, the potential re-use of the material might take it outside of the definition of waste. The Court reiterated a number of key considerations relevant to determining whether the material deposited is waste. The material is more likely to be waste if it:[29]

- creates unacceptable risks to the environment or human health;
- is not suitable for re-use without further treatment;
- it is not certain that the material will be re-used as claimed;
- is present in excessive quantities.

1 A substance or object involuntarily discarded may also be waste. In Case C-1/03 *Van de Walle*, the hydrocarbons which were accidentally spilled and which caused soil and groundwater contamination were help by the ECJ to be waste even though no one knew at the time of the spill that it was happening.
2 Joined Cases C-206/88 and C-207/88 *Vessoso and Zanetti* [1990] 2 LMELR 133.
3 Joined Cases C-418/97 and C-419/97 *Arco*, para 41; Case C-194/05, para 52; and Case C-195/05.
4 Joined Cases C-418/97 and C-419/97 *Arco*, para 47.
5 Case C-359/88 *Zanetti*, para 9. For example, scrap metal is not recycled until it meets its end-of-waste criteria (Article 6). Someone who purchases scrap metal with the intention of reprocessing it into steel is still taken to have the intention to discard the material even though they may regard it as a valuable raw material.
6 Case C-129/96 *Wallonie*, para 29.
7 Case C-304/94 [1998] Env LR 59.
8 Case C-129/96 *Inter-Environment Wallonie ASBL v Region Wallonie* [1998] Env LR 625.
9 [2004] Env LR 6.
10 Case C-418/97 *Arco Chemie Nederland Ltd v Minister van Volkshuivesting and EPON* [2003] Env LR 40.
11 *Attorney General's Reference (No 5 of 2000)* [2000] Env LR 5.
12 *Palin Granit Oy v Lounais-Suomen Ymparistokeskus* [2002] Env LR 35.
13 See Case -114/01 *AvestaPolarit Chrome Oy*. In this case the European Court found the holder of leftover rock from a mining operation had discarded it with the consequence that it was classified as waste. However, the Court also found that the rock could have been classified as a non-waste by-product where the holder intended to use it lawfully for the necessary backfilling of the mine and provided guarantees that it would be definitely used for that purpose.
14 The definition is not so uncertain so as to breach Article 7. See *R (Rackham) v Swaffham Magistrates' Court and the Environment Agency* [2004] EWHC 17.
15 See eg *Environment Agency v Inglenorth* [2009] EWHC 670 (Admin). See Case -114/01 *AvestaPolarit Chrome Oy*.
16 [2009] Env. L.R. 10. See judgment of Moses LJ.
17 *Environment Agency v Thorn International UK Limited* [2009] Env. L.R. 10, Moses LJ at [22].
18 Recycling is defined in Article 3(17) of the WFD.
19 Council Regulation (EU) No 333/2011.
20 Joined Cases C-418/97 and C-419/97, *Arco Chemie Nederland Ltd*, paras 94–95. This was an example of a recovery operation which did not result in 'end-of-waste' status. In *Arco*, waste

in the form of wood chips containing toxic substances were ground into powder which could be burned in a power station. The European Court found the waste was being subjected to pre-processing rather than a complete recovery operation since these operations did not divest the wood of its toxic qualities or have the effect of transforming the wood into a product analogous to a raw material.

21 Defra, *Guidance on the legal definition of waste and its application* (August 2012), p 51.
22 *R (OSS Group Ltd) v Environment Agency and others* [2007] EWCA Civ 611.
23 *Scottish Power Generation Ltd v Scottish Environment Protection Agency (No 1)* [2005] Env LR 38 distinguished.
24 *Castle Cement v Environment Agency* (22 March 2001) (CO/2635/2000); *Scottish Power Generation Ltd v Scottish Environment Protection Agency* 2005 SLT 641.
25 See https://www.gov.uk/government/collections/quality-protocols-end-of-waste-frameworks-for-waste-derived-products.
26 [2015] Env. L.R. 25.
27 Controlled waste is defined as 'household, industrial or commercial or any such waste', s 75(4) EPA 1990, and applies to the environmental permitting system.
28 Controlled Waste (England and Wales) Regulations 2012, reg 3.
29 *R v Jagger* [2015] Env. L.R. 25 at [24].

Exclusions from the definition of waste

16.12 The WFD carves out various exclusions from the definition of waste which are set out in Article 2. Article 2 excludes from the scope of the Directive particular types of waste materials including radioactive waste, waste gaseous effluents emitted into the atmosphere as well as certain types of waste which are covered by other EU legislation.[1] Most relevant to those engaged in property transactions are the exclusions which apply to land (in situ) (Article 2(1)(b)) and uncontaminated soil or materials excavated in the course of construction activities (Article 2(1)(c)).

1. WFD, Article 2(1): The following shall be excluded from the scope of this Directive:
   a) gaseous effluents emitted into the atmosphere;
   b) land (in situ) including unexcavated contaminated soil and buildings permanently connected with land;
   c) uncontaminated soil and other naturally occurring material excavated in the course of construction activities where it is certain that the material will be used for the purposes of construction in its natural state on the site from which it was excavated;
   d) radioactive waste;
   e) decommissioned explosives;
   f) faecal matter, if not covered by paragraph 2(b), straw and other natural non-hazardous agricultural or forestry material used in farming, forestry or for the production of energy from such biomass through processes or methods which do not harm the environment or endanger human health.

2. The following shall be excluded from the scope of this Directive to the extent that they are covered by other Community legislation:
   a) waste waters;
   b) animal by-products including processed products covered by Regulation (EC) No 1774/2002, except those which are destined for incineration, landfilling or use in a biogas or composting plant;
   c) carcasses of animals that have died other than by being slaughtered, including animals killed to eradicate epizootic diseases, and that are disposed of in accordance with Regulation (EC) No 1774/2002;

d) waste resulting from prospecting, extraction, treatment and storage of mineral resources and the working of quarries covered by Directive 2006/21/EC of the European Parliament and of the Council of 15 March 2006 on the management of waste from extractive industries
3. Without prejudice to obligations under other relevant Community legislation, sediments relocated inside surface waters for the purpose of managing waters and waterways or of preventing floods or mitigating the effects of floods and droughts or land reclamation shall be excluded from the scope of this Directive if it is proved that the sediments are non-hazardous.

16.13 Article 2 of WFD lists the substances which are excluded from the scope of the Directive.[1] Of particular relevance to those involved in property transactions are the exclusion of land (in situ), including unexcavated contaminated soil and buildings permanently connected with the land (Article 2(1)(b)), and uncontaminated soil and other naturally occurring material excavated in the course of construction activities, where it is certain that the material will be used for purposes of construction in its natural state on the site from which it was excavated (Article 2(1)(c)).

Excavated soil is capable of being waste.[2] However, uncontaminated materials produced on site during construction works (including excavated soils) which are then re-used on site will not generally be regarded as discarded, provided:[3]

- They are suitable for that use and require no further treatment.
- Only the quantity necessary for the specified works is used.
- Their use is not a mere possibility but a certainty.

Whether the excavated soil becomes waste if it is moved off site or when it is in transit between sites is not entirely clear and will depend on the facts of the case. A decision of the Northern Ireland Court of Appeal found that where soil was excavated to prepare a site for the extension of a school and the soil was given to the owner of neighbouring property, the soil became controlled waste.[4] Although the judge acknowledged that soil and stones would not usually be regarded as waste material, the soil in this case was material which had to be disposed of, and therefore it came within the definition of controlled waste.

The approach taken in that decision is not always followed by the English courts.[5] It seems inconsistent that soils, which if used on site would not be waste, should automatically become waste as soon as they leave the site. The mere passing through the gates of the original site arguably does not constitute 'discarding' when the soils are intended for use on another site. The *Thorn* case, which found that goods remained non-waste whilst the receiver of goods stored them, pending the sorting of the goods into those which could be repaired and those which could not (and would therefore be discarded as waste) suggests that the soils are not inevitably waste simply because they are moved off-site.[6]

1 The Waste (England and Wales) Regulations 2011, reg 2.
2 *Ashcroft v Michael McErlain Ltd* QB Eng, 30 Jan 1985. In this old case, which relied on the dictionary definition of waste to construe COPA 1974, the excavated material was taken directly to a recipient for use at a paddock so was not regarded as waste.
3 Environment Agency Position Statement, *The Definition of Waste – Development of Greenfield and Brownfield Sites* (April 2006) (and any updates); See CLAIRE *Development Industry Code of Practice Version 2* (March 2011).

4 *Department of the Environment and Heritage Service v Felix O'Hare & Co Ltd and James Phillips* [2007] NICA 45.
5 See eg *Environment Agency v Inglenorth* [2009] EWHC 670 (Admin). However, the *O'Hare* decision was cited with approval in *R v W, C and C* [2010] EWCA Crim 927.
6 *Environment Agency v Thorn International UK Limited* [2009] Env. L.R. 10.

WASTE DISPOSAL AND PLANNING

16.14 The disposal of waste is regulated by land use law and planning policy. The Waste Framework Directive requires member states to produce a waste management plan covering its territory. National waste planning policy is contained in the Waste Management Plan for England (December 2013) and the National Planning Policy for Waste (Oct 2014).[1] These should be read in conjunction with the National Planning Policy Framework (NPPF), Planning Practice Guidance and, as relevant, the National Policy Statements for Waste Water and Hazardous Waste.

The Government's waste planning policies emphasise the importance of driving waste management up the waste hierarchy and the consideration of waste management alongside other spatial concerns such as housing and transport development. Waste planning authorities are required to prepare Local Plans which identify sufficient opportunities to meet the identified needs of their area for the management of waste streams, including the identification of specific sites for waste facilities. The NPPF identifies waste management as a 'strategic priority' and encourages cooperation between different local authorities.[2] This is especially important since waste management often involves transportation and disposal across administrative boundaries.

Development control

16.15 Responsibility for waste planning lies with waste planning authorities (normally county councils, metropolitan district councils, or unitary authorities in England and Wales).[3] Waste planning authorities must have regard to Article 13 of the WFD on the need to protect human health and the environment in carrying out their functions.[4]

The deposit of waste is regarded as development that requires planning permission.[5] Moreover, the use of land for waste management purposes may require planning permission if that use amounts to a material change of use. The deposit of waste materials on land will involve a material change in its use, if: (i) the superficial area of the deposit is extended, or (ii) the height of the deposit is extended and exceeds the level of the land adjoining the site.[6] Many activities, such as waste storage on land, will be incidental to the principle land use but whether a particular use requires consent will need to be determined on a case by case basis. Where land is subject to the requirement for an environmental permit, the permit shall not be granted unless there is prior planning consent for waste management activities.[7]

Planning conditions

16.16 Although policy on the use of planning conditions dictates that they should not duplicate controls under other statutory waste management regimes, in practice, there is often considerable overlap between planning and environmental permitting conditions. Any conditions attached to a planning permission should be imposed for a planning purpose and relate to the acceptability of the development in terms of land use rather than the regulation of the waste management processes per se. Such conditions may have important implications for property owners. Examples of waste matters which may fall within planning conditions include aftercare conditions requiring site restoration, post-development monitoring, the extent of tipping, transport access and the general type of waste which can be disposed of on the site. Operational controls will normally fall within the scope of the environmental permitting conditions. Examples include hours of operation, duration of operation, visual intrusion and noise levels. Whilst duplication and overlap between planning conditions and permitting conditions is undesirable it is not unlawful.

1 Department for Communities and Local Government, National Planning Policy for Waste, October 2014.
2 National Planning Policy Framework, para 156; Localism Act 2011, s 33A.
3 Designated by the Town and Country Planning (Prescription of County Matters) (England) Regulations 2003.
4 The Waste (England and Wales) Regulations 2011, reg 18.
5 Town and Country Planning Act 1990, s 55(1).
6 Town and Country Planning Act 1990, s 55(3)(b).
7 Environmental Permitting (England and Wales) Regulations 2010, Sch 9 para 2.

WASTE DUTY OF CARE

16.17 The statutory duty of care reflects the shift in UK waste law from an exclusive focus on waste disposal to the regulation of waste along the whole waste chain. The duty extends responsibility for the proper handling of waste to all persons in the waste chain from production through to disposal. Anyone who produces, imports, keeps, transports, stores, deals in,[1] treats or disposes of waste must take all reasonable steps to ensure that waste is managed appropriately. The duty of care imposed by s 34 of the Environmental Protection Act 1990 applies to anyone who is a holder of household, industrial and commercial waste, known as 'controlled waste' (this is effectively synonymous with Directive waste and does not include mining or agricultural waste).[2] The duty of care applies in addition to controls imposed through environmental permitting.

A person's duty of care extends beyond the point when they transfer the waste to another party.[3] When a person transfers waste to another waste holder they retain a responsibility to take all reasonable steps to ensure that the waste is managed correctly throughout its complete journey to disposal or recovery. In practice, this means checking the subsequent waste holder is authorised to take the waste and carrying out more detailed checks if a person suspects the waste is not being handled in accordance with the duty of care, for example, by requesting evidence that the waste has arrived at its intended destination.

There is a Code of Practice on the duty of care which provides practical guidance on discharging the duty. The Government recently published its revised Code in March 2016 bringing the existing code up to date.[4] Although a breach of the Code is not an offence, s 34(10) EPA 1990 provides that the Code should be taken into account in any legal proceedings in deciding whether the duty has been complied with.

Holders of controlled waste must take all reasonable steps to:

- prevent unauthorised or harmful deposit, treatment or disposal of waste (eg fly-tipping);
- prevent a breach by any other person to meet the requirement to have an environmental permit, or a breach of a permit condition;
- prevent the escape of waste from their control – this requires the proper storage and packaging of waste;[5]
- ensure that any person to whom you are transferring waste has the correct authorisation;
- provide an accurate description of the waste when it is transferred to another person;[6]
- take all reasonable steps to apply the waste hierarchy.[7]

The standard of reasonableness is objective and the duty of care is regarded as broken, regardless of whether harm is actually caused. Enforcement of the duty of care is undertaken by the Environment Agency in England and Natural Resources Wales in Wales. A breach of the duty of care can result in criminal sanction leading to an unlimited fine on a summary conviction or on a conviction in the Crown Court. The authority may give a person the opportunity of paying a fixed penalty (usually £300) as an alternative to prosecution.[8]

1 Waste brokers who arrange for the movement or disposal of waste without physically handling it are subject to controls under The Waste (England and Wales) Regulations 2011. Reg 25 creates an offence where a waste broker or dealer who deals in controlled waste without being registered with the Environment Agency. The EA is under a duty to maintain a register of all carriers, brokers and dealers of waste (reg 28).
2 The Controlled Waste (England and Wales) Regulations 2012, Sch 1.
3 See, for example, *Mountpace Ltd v Haringay LBC* [2012] EWHC 698 (Admin).
4 *Waste Duty of Care – Code of Practice (*March 2016) issued under s 34 of the Environmental Protection Act 1990 – https://www.google.co.uk/search?q=waste+duty+of+care+code+of+practice+2016&ie=utf-8&oe=utf-8&client=firefox-b&gfe_rd=cr&ei=YJtmV4H5H8vS8Ae1voHoCg.
5 An escape of waste is not the same as a deliberate deposit which is caught by s 33 EPA 1990. See *Gateway Professional Services (Management) Ltd v Kingston upon Hull City Council* [2004] Env LR.
6 Environmental Protection (Duty of Care) Regulations 1991, SI 1991/2839 requires that where controlled waste is transferred it must be accompanied by a transfer note, though this need not travel with the waste. The description can now be provided electronically (see www.edocoline) or on paper. A season ticket can be used for regular transfers of the same type of non-hazardous waste.
7 Waste (England and Wales) Regulations 2011, reg 12.
8 Section 34A of the Environmental Protection Act 1990.

Household duty of care

16.18 Householders must ensure that household waste is properly disposed of and are under a specific duty of care.[1] 'Household waste' is defined in s 75(5) of the EPA 1990 and includes waste from domestic properties, caravans and residential homes. A householder is required to take reasonable steps to check that the people removing waste from his premises are authorised to do so. A breach of the householder duty of care can also attract criminal penalties, leading to an unlimited fine on a summary conviction or on a conviction in the Crown Court.

1 Section 34(2A) of the Environmental Protection Act 1990.

Carriage of Waste

16.19 The requirement that all carriers of waste must be registered with the Environment Agency is inextricably linked to the duty of care. The Control of Pollution (Amendment) Act 1989 and the Waste (England and Wales) Regulations 2011 (the 2011 Regulations) require all carriers of waste to be registered with the Environment Agency. One of the principal aims of the regime is to reduce waste crime in the form of illegal fly-tipping.

The registration procedure for waste carriers is set out reg 29 of the 2011 Regulations. Registration may be refused if the EA considers the applicant is not a desirable carrier.[1] The EA has a wide range of enforcement powers concerning the carriage of waste including the power to inspect establishments and undertakings which collect or transfer waste, to make stop-checks on vehicles transporting waste, and to instantly seize vehicles used in unlawful waste operations.[2]

The carriage of waste regime provides for certain limited exemptions from the requirement to register.[3]

Waste carriers who transport waste without being registered are criminally liable.[4] The offence is punishable by an unlimited fine on summary conviction. Failure to produce a registration certificate on demand may also result in the grant of a fixed penalty notice[5] However, a person shall not be guilty of an offence in respect of the transport of controlled waste:

- within the same premises between different places in those premises;
- to its first point of arrival in Great Britain when imported; or
- when it is exported from Great Britain.[6]

Where the waste was transported in an emergency or the carrier had no knowledge or reasonable grounds to suspect he was carrying controlled waste, or the carrier was acting under employer's instructions, he will have a defence to the charge of unlawful carriage of waste.[7]

1 2011 Regulations, reg 29(5).
2 Environment Act 1995, ss 108–109; EPA 1990, s 71; Control of Pollution Act 1989, s 5.
3 CoP(A)A 1989, s 1(3); 2011 Regulations, SI 1991/1624, reg 26.

4 Control of Pollution (Amendment) Act 1989, s 1(1) and (5); Criminal Justice Act 1982, s 37.
5 Clean Neighbourhoods and Environment Act 2005, s 38.
6 Control of Pollution (Amendment) Act 1989, s 1(2).
7 Control of Pollution (Amendment) Act 1989, s 1(4). Clean Neighbourhoods and Environment
   Act 2005, Part 5, s 35.

THE ENVIRONMENTAL PERMITTING SYSTEM

16.20   Waste management licensing has been regulated under the environmental permitting system since 6 April 2008.[1] The Environmental Permitting Regulations are explained in Chapter 20.

The Government has prepared and is currently consulting on the draft Environmental Permitting (England and Wales) Regulations 2016 which it expects to come into force on 1 January 2017.

1 Environmental Permitting (England and Wales) Regulations 2010, SI 2010/675 (EP Regulations).

Who regulates waste?

16.21   In England and Wales, first tier local authorities, where they exist, are responsible for waste collection and county councils (or unitary authorities where there is no county council) are responsible for waste disposal. The Environment Agency (EA) in England (and Natural Resources Wales (NRW)) is responsible for applying and enforcing waste management law.

The draft EP Regulations are expected to strengthen the enforcement powers of the EA and NRW to tackle waste crime and poor performance in the waste industry.

Excluded and exempt waste operations

16.22   Certain waste operations are excluded from the permitting regime since they are covered by other regulatory regimes (reg 4). These exclusions include operations that:

- involve the disposal or recovery of waste that is not treated as industrial or commercial waste.[1]
- are disposals at sea under the Food and Environment Protection Act 1985.

Waste operations which pose a sufficiently low risk to the environment do not require an environmental permit (reg 4). Exempt waste operations must be consistent with the waste objectives in the WFD and must be registered with the regulator (Sch 2, para 3). In order to encourage more recycling, a wide variety of recycling activities are exempted, although such activities are in many cases subject to restrictions on quantity (for example, the collection of paper, cardboard and steel cans).

The four main waste exemption categories which are likely to be relevant to developers of land are listed in Schedule 3. They are:

- the direct uses of waste in operations such as construction, the manufacture of finished products, mixing plant ash into soil, spreading of certain wastes onto agricultural land as fertiliser;[2]
- the storage of waste pending its recovery;[3]
- waste treatment which results in change to the waste such as recovery of scrap metal, recovering of textiles, cleaning of certain wastes and treatment of waste food; and[4]
- the disposal of waste in operations that would lead to its destruction.[5]

1 Reg 3, Controlled Waste Regulations 2012.
2 EP Regulations 2010, Sch 3 ch 2, s 2, para U1–U16.
3 EP Regulations, Sch 3 ch 5, s 2, para S1–S3.
4 EP Regulations, Sch 3 ch 3, s 2, para T1–T33.
5 EP Regulations, Sch 3 ch 4, s 2, para D1–D8.

WASTE OFFENCES

16.23 There are offences which relate to waste operations at regulated facilities and general offences which apply to any activity concerning the handling of waste. Section 33 EPA 1990 (as amended)[1] makes it a criminal offence to:

- deposit controlled waste or knowingly cause or knowingly permit the deposit of controlled waste in or on land without, or otherwise than in accordance with, a permit;
- submit controlled waste, or knowingly cause or knowingly permit controlled waste to be submitted, to any listed operation[2] that is carried out in or on any land, or by means of any mobile plant, and is not carried out under and in accordance with an environmental permit;
- treat, keep or dispose of controlled waste in a manner likely to cause pollution of the environment or harm to human health.[3]

The Environmental Permitting (England and Wales) Regulations 2010 also contain stand-alone offences, such as for breaching permit conditions or enforcement notices, and corresponding penalties.[4]

Each limb of s 33 EPA 1990 creates a single offence that can be committed in a number of ways.[5] The prosecution can therefore frame an indictment in the alternative, for example, bringing a charge of disposing or treating and disposing of controlled waste in a manner likely to cause the pollution of the environment. This eases the evidential burden on the prosecution.

The offences fall into two categories: offences of strict liability and offences where the prosecutor must show that the offender 'knowingly' caused or permitted the deposit. The courts have taken a strict view of the term 'knowingly'.[6] The prosecution are only required to prove knowledge of the deposit of waste. It is not necessary to show that the defendant had knowledge of the breach of condition itself.

This means that operators of landfill sites are effectively under strict liability for any breaches of environmental permit conditions. Where a site operation is contracted out, a contractor can be convicted of an offence even though he is not the licence holder.[7] It should be noted that the offence under s 33(1)(c) applies whether or not a permit is in force. Any director, manager, company secretary or similar officer of a corporate body (ie part of the 'controlling mind' of the company) can be prosecuted personally if the offence has been committed with his or her knowledge or consent and is attributable to their neglect.[8]

1 See exemptions in 2010 Regulations, reg 68 and Sch 25.
2 Listed operation means anything falling within the categories of disposal and recovery operations listed in Annex I or II of WFD.
3 This offence applies regardless of the need for an environmental permit.
4 2010 Regulations, regs 38, 39.
5 *R v Leighton and Town and Country Refuse Collections Ltd* [1997] Env LR 411.
6 *Shanks & McEwan (Teesside) Ltd v Environment Agency* [1997]; *Ashcroft v Cambro Waste Products Ltd* [1981] 1 WLR 1349.
7 *Shanks McEwan (Midlands) Ltd v Wrexham Maelor Borough Council* [1996] Env LR (D) 26 *Times*, 10 April (1996).
8 Reg 41.

The meaning of 'deposit'

16.24   The meaning of 'deposit' in s 33 EPA 1990 has been interpreted broadly by the courts. Earlier restrictive definitions which found that waste was only 'deposited' when it reached its final resting place have been superseded by a wider definition which reflects a broader preoccupation with waste management rather than just disposal.[1] The courts have held that 'deposit' applies to temporary as well as permanent deposits[2] and that the term can cover continuing activities over a substantial period of time where an environmental permit allows for it.[3]

In *R (Thames Water Utilities Ltd) v Bromley Magistrates' Court (No 2)*,[4] the Administrative Court held that an unintended escape of untreated sewage on to surrounding land amounted to a 'deposit' under s 33, because the provisions of s 33(1)(a) revealed a legislative intention to impose strict liability in respect of the offence created by the first limb of the section.

1 *Leigh Land Reclamation Ltd v Walsall Metropolitan Borough Council* (1991) 155 JPL 547.
2 *R v Metropolitan Stipendiary Magistrate ex parte London Waste Regulation Authority* [1993] All ER 113.
3 *Thames Waste Management Ltd v Surrey County Council* [1997] Env LR 148. In *Milton Keynes DC v Fuller* [2011] Env LR 31 the court held that the moving of waste deposited by an unknown third party by a landowner to permit access onto his farm did not constitute 'depositing'. Aikens LJ observed at [40] that each case has to be decided according to its facts.
4 [2013] EWHC 472 (Admin); [2013] 1WLR 3641.

Defences

16.25   Section 33(7) of the EPA 1990 provides that a defendant will have a defence if he can prove that all reasonable steps were taken and all due diligence was exercised to avoid the commission of the offence. This defence may apply to any unpermitted activity.

The due diligence defence requires the defendant to show that he took all reasonable steps to avoid the offence, by for example setting up rigorous waste management systems in all the circumstances. In many respects this is similar to the requirements set down by the duty of care. For example, in *Environment Agency v Short* [1998] Env LR 300, the defendant left unused timber at the construction site relying on assurances given by the site owner that no waste management licence was required. The High Court held that the responsibility lay with the defendant to make inquires as to whether the exemption applied to the timber.[1]

There is also a specific defence to offences committed in an emergency in order to avoid danger to human health (but not danger to the environment) (reg 40). The burden of proof for establishing the defence lies with the defendant who must also show that he took all reasonable practicable steps in the circumstances to minimise pollution and notify the regulator after the event.[2]

1 See also *Durham County Council v Peter Connors Industrial Services Ltd* [1993] Env LR 197.
2 The courts take an objective view of what constitutes an 'emergency'. An emergency will only arise where a state of affairs arises unexpectedly, demanding urgent attention and it is impracticable to seek the waste regulator's approval: *Waste Incineration Services Ltd and Jacob v Dudley Metropolitan Borough Council* [1993] Env LR 29.

Penalties and remedies

16.26 A person who commits an offence under s 33 EPA 1990 is liable on conviction in the magistrates' court to an unlimited fine and/or imprisonment for a term of 12 months. On indictment in the Crown Court, the guilty party may receive an unlimited fine and/or up to five years imprisonment.[1] The sentencing court also has powers to order compensation in respect of the costs of removal of the waste and/or steps taken to eliminate or reduce the consequences of its deposit or disposal incurred by the Environment Agency, waste collection authority or occupier of the land on which the deposit has occurred.[2] There is also a power to confiscate any vehicles used in the commission of an offence.[3] A waste collection authority in England may issue a fixed penalty notice instead of prosecuting.[4] The amount of the fixed penalty is £200 unless the authority has specified an alternative amount not less than £150 and not more than £400.

The specific penalties and restorative remedies under the 2010 Regulations are set out at regs 38, 39, 44 and 57. The regulator also has power to apply for an injunction in the High Court in order to secure compliance with an enforcement notice, suspension notice, landfill closure notice or mining waste facility closure notice, whether or not it has taken other steps for that purpose.[5]

1 EPA 1990, s 33(8). Civil liability for the unlawful disposal of waste is provided for in s 73(6) of EPA 1990.

2 EPA 1990, s 33B. This applies also to offences under the EP Regulations. Section 59 of EPA 1990 gives the Environment Agency and waste collection authorities power to require the clean-up of land where controlled waste has been deposited in breach of s 33(1).
3 EPA 1990, s 33C.
4 EPA 1990, s 33ZA, added by the Unauthorised Deposit of Waste (Fixed Penalties) Regulations 2016, SI 2016/334
5 Environmental Permitting (England and Wales) Regulations 2010/675, reg 42.

HAZARDOUS WASTE

16.27 The amount of hazardous waste consigned in England is significant and rising. In 2010, 3.3 million tonnes were consigned, rising to 4 million tonnes in 2012. This waste arises from six main sectors of industry: chemicals, oils, construction and demolition, waste and water treatment and general industry. The Government's Hazardous Waste Strategy sets out the policy for reducing hazardous waste production and the management of such waste.[1]

Alongside the general waste management provisions additional controls apply to hazardous waste, which is often referred to as 'special waste'. The Hazardous Waste Directive (91/689/EEC) was replaced by the revised Waste Framework Directive (2008/98/EC). The WFD provides that additional record keeping, monitoring and control obligations from the 'cradle to the grave' are required when managing hazardous waste over non-hazardous waste, and that greater attention is required when different categories of hazardous wastes are mixed with each other or with non-hazardous wastes. In the UK, hazardous wastes are governed by the Hazardous Waste (England and Wales) Regulations 2005 (as amended).[2]

Regulation 6 of the Hazardous Waste Regulations 2005 defines hazardous waste as any waste:

- listed as a hazardous waste in the List of Wastes;[3]
- listed in regulations made under s 62A(1) of the Environmental Protection Act 1990 Act; or
- a specific batch of waste which is determined by the Secretary of State pursuant to reg 8 to be a hazardous waste.

The assessment and classification of hazardous wastes changed in July 2015. The Hazardous Waste Regulations have redefined certain wastes as 'hazardous' including paints, inks, batteries, detergents, oil filters, TVs, fridges and light bulbs. The Environment Agency's Technical Guidance WM3 provides a practical guide on how to determine whether the waste is hazardous.[4]

The Environment Agency must be notified of any premises where hazardous waste is produced or removed either by the producer or consignor of that waste.[5] Notification must be provided annually, unless premises are exempted, for example, because they are commercial or educational premises where no more than 200 kg of hazardous is being held or the waste has been fly-tipped.[6] Every movement of hazardous waste must be accompanied by a consignment note when collected by a registered waste carrier. Even if the waste is produced on premises which are exempt from the requirement to notify, a note is still required.[7] Producers, carriers and holders of hazardous waste must keep a record of these consignment notes in a register.[8] Anyone who deposits hazardous waste or recovers it is required to record the location of each deposit or recovery in site records.[9]

Failure to comply with the requirements of the Hazardous Waste Regulations 2005 is an offence.[10] A summary conviction may result in an unlimited fine, or on conviction on indictment (for certain offences only) an unlimited fine and/ or two years' imprisonment.[11] A range of civil sanctions are also available.[12] It is a defence to prove that due diligence was undertaken or that the failure to comply resulted from an emergency and all reasonable steps were taken to minimise the consequent environmental harm.[13]

1 See Defra, National Policy Statement on Hazardous Waste (2013) – https://www.gov.uk/government/uploads/system/uploads/attachment_data/file/205568/pb13927-hazardous-waste-policy-20130606.pdf.
2 Hazardous Waste (Miscellaneous Amendments) Regulations 2015/1360. These Regulations make amendments to enactments which concern hazardous waste or cross-refer to other enactments or European Union instruments concerning hazardous waste.
3 Wastes listed as hazardous in the List of Wastes are considered hazardous pursuant to the first indent of Article 1.4 of the Hazardous Waste Directive. See Hazardous Waste Regulations 2005, reg 4.
4 Environment Agency, Waste Classification – Guide on the classification and assessment of waste WM3 (May, 2015) https://www.gov.uk/government/uploads/system/uploads/attachment_data/file/427077/LIT_10121.pdf.
5 Hazardous Waste Regulations 2005, reg 21.
6 Hazardous Waste Regulations 2005, regs 22–23.
7 Hazardous Waste Regulations 2005, regs 35–38.
8 Hazardous Waste Regulations 2005, regs 49–51.
9 Hazardous Waste Regulations 2005, regs 47–48.
10 Hazardous Waste Regulations 2005, reg 65.
11 Hazardous Waste Regulations 2005, reg 69.
12 Hazardous Waste Regulations, regs 65A and 70.
13 Hazardous Waste Regulations, reg 66.

LANDFILL

16.28 The EU Landfill Directive 1991/31/EC (as amended) sets ambitious targets for the reduction of biodegradable municipal waste. A key objective of government policy is to reduce the amount of waste going into landfill and to encourage recycling. The Environmental Permitting Regulations 2010 and Landfill Allowance Scheme (Wales) give effect to the Landfill Directive 1991/31/EC (as amended) and impose restrictions on the type and amount of waste that can be disposed of in landfill in England and Wales.[1]

A landfill is defined as 'a waste disposal site for the deposit of waste onto or into land'.[2] The definition includes any permanent site that is used to store waste for more than a year prior to final disposal.[3] The main provisions in the Landfill Directive are as follows:

• all waste must be treated before being landfilled (Article 6(a));

- the following wastes may not be accepted in a landfill: liquid waste; flammable waste; explosive or oxidising waste; hospital and other clinical waste which is infectious; used tyres, with certain exceptions; any other type of waste which does not meet the acceptance criteria laid down in Annex II (Article 5(3));
- landfills must be classified into separate types – for hazardous, non-hazardous and inert waste (Article 6);
- detailed monitoring and technical requirements for all landfills (Annexes I and III);
- waste reduction targets for municipal biodegradable waste (Article 5(2)); and
- powers to close landfill sites and ability to enforce aftercare conditions (Article 13).

1 2010 Regulations, reg 35(2)(d), Sch 10.
2 2010 Regulations, Sch 10 para 1.
3 See *Blackland Park Exploration v Environment Agency* [2004] Env LR 33 which demonstrates the courts wide interpretation of the meaning of landfill.

LANDFILL TAX

16.29 The use of economic instruments in waste management is designed to reflect the true environmental cost of managing waste and to incentivise waste minimisation. The landfill tax introduced by the Finance Act 1996[1] provides that the majority of waste disposed of in landfill sites is taxable at the point of disposal. The Act categorises landfill waste and sets landfill tax levels according to whether the waste is taxable, 'inactive' or exempt from the tax altogether.

At the time of writing there were two different rates of landfill tax:

- less polluting wastes as listed in the Landfill Tax (Qualifying Material) Order 2011 – £2.60 per tonne;
- all other wastes – £82.60 per tonne.

1 Finance Act 1996, s. 40. See secondary regulations including The Landfill Tax Regulations 1996, The Landfill Tax (Qualifying Materials) Order 2011 and The Landfill Tax (Contaminated Land) Order 1996.

What is 'waste' for the purpose of landfill tax?

16.30 Section 64 of the Finance Act 1996 defines 'waste' for the purposes of the landfill tax. The definition is similar but not the same as the general definition under the EPA 1990 and the WFD. Therefore, it is possible that something which may be considered waste under the Directive might not be waste for the purposes of the landfill tax. This is because the legislative purpose of landfill tax, which emphasises the promotion of waste minimisation and recycling, is distinct from the WFD. The courts have held that materials deposited at a landfill site, which would come within the definition of Directive waste, but which are subsequently recycled and reused, are not waste for the purposes of landfill tax legislation.[1] The courts' reasoning is that to subject such materials to landfill tax would be contrary to its statutory purpose of promoting recycling.

The following types of waste are exempt from landfill tax, provided that all the required tests are met:

- dredgings – material removed from water;
- mining and quarrying waste;[2]
- pet cemeteries;
- filling of quarries;
- waste from visiting forces.

Tax credits

16.31 The Landfill Tax Credit Scheme allows operators to claim credit against landfill tax payments for any contribution made to an environmental project approved under the Landfill Tax Regulations 1996. These can include projects such as the remediation of contaminated land or the introduction of wildlife habitat. An operator is entitled to claim a credit on landfill tax of 90% of their contribution up to a maximum of 20% of their total landfill tax bill in a 12-month period. There has been criticism of the landfill tax credit scheme that it is unduly complex and open to abuse, being often used to secure public relations benefits for the contributing operator, rather than environmental improvements that are proportionate to the tax credit gained. The Landfill Allowance Trading Scheme which allowed for the allocation of tradable landfill allowances to each waste authority was ended in England in 2013 since it was thought to have a limited impact on landfill diversion.

1 *Parkwood Landfill v Customs & Excise Commissioners* [2003] Env LR 19. Applied by *Waste Recycling Group Ltd v Revenue and Customs Commissioners* [2008] Env LR 19.
2 Landfill Tax (Qualifying Material) Order 2011; Landfill Tax (Site Restoration and Quarries) Order 1999.

Chapter 17

Water

17.01 A prospective purchaser will need to obtain full information about the supply of water to the property and any rights to discharge waste water or other potentially polluting discharges from it. It will also be particularly necessary to know whether the property is susceptible to flooding[1] and what rights exist in relation to any rivers and streams flowing through or along the boundary of the land. A wide range of provisions relating to water may therefore be relevant to a property transaction, ranging from water supply and abstraction, through sewerage, to the general regulation of water quality and controls over pollution. These provisions represent some of the most complex and well-developed applying to any environmental medium, and have their most recent origins in the privatisation of the water industry carried out in 1989. The structure of the privatised water industry is still primarily contained in the Water Resources and Water Industry Acts 1991 (WRA 1991 and WIA 1991 respectively), as significantly amended by later legislation. On the regulatory side, the Environment Agency has inherited the National Rivers Authority's powers.[1] Ministers also retain important powers in addition to those exercised by the Agency, however. The Water Act 2014, although not fully in force at the time of writing, will further reform the market and introduce a greater degree of competition in respect of 'upstream' (ie non-retail) activities and retail to non-residential customers.

1 According to the Environment Agency, 2.3 million homes and 185,000 businesses are at risk of flooding in England and Wales representing property, land and assets to the value of over £200bn. The BBC Weather Centre notes that the rainfall in June and July 2007 was about 20% higher than ever seen before in records that go back to 1879. http://www.bbc.co.uk/climate/impact/flooding.shtml.
2 EA 1995, Part I. The NRA was abolished by s 2(3).

WATER SUPPLY

17.02 The usual pre-contract enquiries seek information about the supply of water to the property and whether it is metered. In general, each water undertaker is under a general duty to develop and maintain an efficient and economical system of water supply within its area and to ensure that all necessary arrangements have been made for providing water supplies to premises in the area and for making supplies available to those who demand them.[1] Water undertakers are also under specific duties to provide water mains and to make connections with water mains when required to do so. The first of these duties[2] requires the water undertaker to provide a water main[3] sufficient for domestic purposes[4] if required to do so by notice served by one or more of: (a) the owner or occupier of any premises in the locality; (b) the local authority; (c) where relevant, the new towns residuary body, urban development corporation or Mayoral development corporation for the area.[5]

1 WIA 1991, s 37(1).
2 Ibid, s 41(1).
3 A water main is any pipe vested in the water undertaker for the purpose of making a general supply of water available to customers or potential customers, as opposed to providing a supply to particular customers: WIA 1991, s 219(1).
4 'Domestic purposes' means drinking, washing, cooking, central heating and sanitary purposes, but not for the use of a bath having a capacity of more than 230 litres, for the purposes of a laundry business, nor for preparing food or drink for consumption off the premises: WIA 1991, s 218.
5 WIA 1991, s 41(2), as amended.

17.03 The premises to be supplied must consist of buildings or parts of buildings (existing or proposed).[1] Certain financial conditions must also be satisfied.[2] Under provisions due to be introduced by the Water Act 2014,[3] these will be calculated in accordance with charging rules to be made by Ofwat,[4] taking account of guidance issued by the Secretary of State. This regime will replace one in which the financial conditions were calculated with reference to the borrowing costs of the loan required to supply the main.[5] In practice the undertaker and the developer often entered into an agreement whereby the liability of the developer was discharged by a single agreed lump sum payment, so this change may have little practical effect other than to make the calculation of charges more transparent and flexible.

1 WIA 1991, s 41(1)(b).
2 Ibid, ss 41(1)(c) and 42 (as amended by the Water Act 2003).
3 Water Act 2014, ss 17–20, 38.
4 Ofwat or 'The Water Services Regulation Authority' is the economic regulator of the water and sewerage sectors in England and Wales. http://www.ofwat.gov.uk/
5 WIA 1991, s 43 before amendments introduced by the Water Act 2014.

17.04 The water undertaker has three months within which to comply with its duty to provide a water main. That period begins with the day after whichever is the later of: (a) the day on which the financial conditions referred to above are satisfied; or (b) the day on which the connection points between the service pipes to individual premises and the main are determined.[1] The three month period may be extended by agreement between the water undertaker and the person requiring the provision of the main. If there is a dispute as to whether the period should be extended, the matter is to be decided by reference to arbitration.[2] If the water undertaker is in breach of its duty to provide a water main, the breach is actionable by any person who requires provision of the main if he suffers loss or damage.[3] However, it is a defence for the undertaker to show that it took all reasonable steps and exercised all due diligence to avoid the breach.

1 WIA 1991, s 44(1). 'Service pipe' means so much of a pipe which is, or is to be, connected with a water main for supplying water from that main to any premises as: (a) is or is to be subject to water pressure from that main; or (b) would be so subject but for the closing of some valve, and includes part of any service pipe: WIA 1991, s 219(1). The places where the service pipes are to connect to the main are to be determined by agreement between the water undertaker and the person requiring the provision of the main. In default of agreement the places are to be

determined by reference to the Water Services Regulation Authority: WIA 1991, s 44(3)(b) and
(4) (as amended by the Water Act 2003).
2 Ibid, s 44(2) and (4).
3 Ibid, s 41(4).

17.05 The owner or occupier of any premises (existing or proposed) may serve
a connection notice on any water undertaker requiring it to connect a service
pipe from the premises to one of the undertaker's water mains in order to provide
a supply of water for domestic purposes.[1] The notice must be accompanied or
supplemented by all information which the undertaker reasonably requires.[2]
If the notice is served to comply with a local authority notice relating to an
unwholesome private supply of water to the premises and the connection must
be made across land owned or occupied by a third party who has unreasonably
refused consent, the notice must give details of those matters.[3] The connection
duty arises only if the water main in question is neither a trunk main,[4] nor is
intended solely for supplying water for non-domestic purposes and provided
that any conditions imposed by the undertaker in accordance with the WIA
have been satisfied.

1 WIA 1991, s 45(1), as amended by the Competition and Service (Utilities) Act 1992, s 43(1).
  Note also ss 45(1A) and 51D(1) (inserted by the Water Act 2003), which prohibit a water
  undertaker from allowing a service pipe to be connected to a water main unless it has vested in
  the undertaker.
2 WIA 1991, s 45(3)(a).
3 WIA 1991, s 45(3)(b).
4 A 'trunk main' means a water main which is or is to be used by a water undertaker for the
  purpose of: (a) conveying water from a source of supply to a filter or reservoir or from one filter
  or reservoir to another filter or reservoir; or (b) conveying water in bulk, whether in the course
  of taking a supply of water in bulk or otherwise, between different places outside the area of the
  undertaker from such a place to any part of that area or from one part of that area to another
  part of that area: WIA 1991, s 219(1).

17.06 Such conditions can only be imposed by serving a counter-notice
on the person who served the connection notice before the end of a 14-day
period beginning with the day after the service of the connection notice.[1] The
conditions may include the fulfilment of requirements as to the provision of
reasonable security,[2] the payment of outstanding water charges or reasonable
disconnection expenses resulting from any failure to pay charges, metering, the
provision of separate service pipes to each house or building on the premises
or to each part of a building which is separately occupied, the provision of a
system with a float-operated valve to maintain pressure, the compliance of
water fittings with the relevant regulations, and compliance with any notice
served in order to prevent damage, contamination or wastage.[2]

1 WIA 1991, s 47(3).
2 In accordance with the amendments to be introduced by the Water Act 2014, the amount of
  security that can be required will be determined in accordance with new Ofwat charging rules.
2 Ibid, s 47(1) and (2).

17.07 The duty on the water undertaker in respect of making connections
for domestic purposes includes the carrying out of certain additional works
in order to make the connection itself; the expenses of which are to be borne

by the person serving the notice (although this proviso is to be removed by the Water Act 2014).[1] These works may comprise three elements. First, the service pipe or any part of it must be laid in a street if necessary to connect it to the water main.[2] Second, and under certain circumstances, the water undertaker must lay any part of the service pipe between the street boundary and a stopcock fitted on the premises by the undertaker. These circumstances are where the water main is in a street, the premises abut the part of the street where the main is situated, the service pipe will not enter the premises through an outer wall of a building abutting on the street, and a stopcock will be fitted to the service pipe on the premises.[3] Third, the water undertaker must lay a service pipe in land owned or occupied by a third party if the connection notice is served in order to comply with a local authority notice relating to an unwholesome private supply of water to the premises.[4] However, the local authority must certify that the third party has unreasonably refused consent to the laying of the service pipe on the land or has sought to make consent subject to unreasonable conditions.[5] Under those circumstances, the water undertaker has power to lay the service pipe on the third party's land and to keep it there, in both cases without his consent.[6]

1 WIA 1991, s 46(1), and see amendments in the Water Act 2014, s 18(4).
2 Ibid, s 46(2).
3 Ibid, s 46(3).
4 Para **17.05**.
5 WIA 1991, s 46(4).
6 Ibid, s 159(1) and (2).

17.08 For the purpose of these ancillary duties, where a water main runs alongside a street and within 18 metres of its centre, any land between the water main and the boundary of the street which is not included in or occupied with the premises in question is treated as part of the street.[1] Finally, the undertaker must ensure that a stopcock belonging to it is fitted to the service pipe which is connected.[2]

1 WIA 1991, s 46(5).
2 Ibid, s 46(6).

17.09 A water undertaker is only in breach of its duty to lay or connect a service pipe where it fails to do so as soon as reasonably practicable after the relevant day, that is the latest of: (a) the day on which the connection notice is served on the undertaker; (b) the day on which a notice is served on the undertaker stating that the customer's pipe has been laid (where that is necessary); or (c) the day on which all conditions imposed by the water undertaker under the WIA have been complied with.[1] The reasonably practicable period is presumed to be 21 days, unless the contrary is shown, where the connection is to be made at the boundary of any premises abutting the part of the street where the main is situated.[2] The undertaker is also in breach of duty if it fails to make the connection before the end of the period of 14 days beginning with the relevant day where the duty is only to connect a service pipe, the whole of which has already been laid when the connection notice is served.[3] A water undertaker may delay its compliance with its connection duties until a reasonable time after any required information is provided which the undertaker has required to supplement the connection notice.[4]

1 WIA 1991, s 51(1)(a).
2 Ibid, s 51(2).
3 Ibid, s 51(1)(b).
4 WIA 1991, s 51(5).

17.10 Except where a water undertaker is required to lay a service pipe,[1] it is the responsibility of the customer to lay any service pipe required before the connection to the main can be made.[2] It follows that subject to those exceptions the permission of any third party landowner will be required to lay service pipes in his land. An example is a case where it is proposed to connect to the water main premises which do not abut on the street in which the water main is situated. In such cases, it will be desirable to obtain an easement rather than a licence to ensure that it binds third parties.[3] It is now established that contractual licences do not bind third parties[4] unless the licence is coupled with the grant of a proprietary interest or there is a proprietary estoppel.[5]

1 Paras **17.02–17.09**.
2 WIA 1991, s 51(3) and (4).
3 Such easements are overriding interests where title to the land is registered: Land Registration Act 1925, s 70(1)(a) and Land Registration Rules 1925, SI 1925/1093, r 258; *Celsteel Ltd v Alton House Holdings Ltd* [1985] 1 WLR 204.
4 *King v David Allen & Sons, Billposting Ltd* [1916] 2 AC 54; *Ashburn Anstalt v Arnold* [1989] Ch 1 (overruled on other grounds by *Prudential Assurance Co v London Residuary Body* [1992] 2 AC 386); *Camden London Borough Council v Shortlife Community Housing Ltd* (1992) 90 LGR 358.
5 *E R Ives Investment Ltd v High* [1967] 2 QB 379; *Crabb v Arun District Council* [1976] Ch 179.

17.11 The courts have accepted that the right to receive water through a pipe running through adjoining property can constitute an easement.[1] A theoretical difficulty arises in relation to this conclusion because of the general rule that a right cannot be an easement if it amounts to a right to exclusive possession or even joint use of the whole or part of the servient land.

On the other hand, there are cases of easements, apart from pipe easements, where the dominant owner is granted exclusive use of a part of the servient land.[2]

1 *Nuttall v Bracewell* (1866) LR 2 Exch 1 at 10; *Goodhart v Hyett* (1883) 25 Ch D 182 at 186; *Schwann v Cotton* [1916] 2 Ch 459 at 474.
2 *Wright v Macadam* [1949] 2 KB 744 (use of a coal shed).

17.12 It appears to be a question of degree whether the right granted amounts to an easement or not.[1] It is likely to be an easement provided that the servient owner's possession is not excluded to any substantial extent.[2] In the case of pipes passing beneath the land, there is unlikely to be any substantial exclusion. However, the precise circumstances of each case should be checked carefully. It is possible that if the landowner is effectively excluded from a sufficient portion of his land, a grant of a freehold (or leasehold) interest in that portion of the land has been made.[3] In the absence of an easement, a grant of land or a licence, laying a pipe in another person's land would constitute a trespass and the pipe when laid would belong to the owner of the land. If the right to receive a water supply across a neighbour's land involves any positive obligation on the servient owner, for example, to repair the pipes or to pay water supply charges, it is most unlikely to be accepted as an easement.[4]

1 *Gale on Easements* (19th edn), chapter 2.
2 It has also been observed that the fact that the exercise of a right involves the temporary exclusion of the servient owner is not incompatible with its status as an easement: *Megarry & Wade: The Law of Real Property* (8th edn, 2012), para 27–020.
3 *Metropolitan Rly Co v Fowler* [1893] AC 416; *Holywell Union v Halkyn Drainage Co* [1895] AC 117. In the case of land with registered title, a separate title would be required.
4 *Rance v Elvin* (1983) 49 p & CR 65; revsd (1985) 50 p & CR 9, CA but upheld on this point; cf (1985) CLJ 458 (A J Waite). The Court of Appeal held that there was a distinction between the right to a supply of water; and a right to an uninterrupted passage of water. A right of the passage of water through the service connection serving the property was not a right to be supplied with water by the servient owner at his expense, but to the uninterrupted passage of water and no more. It confers no right to insist upon the servient owner allowing water to enter his pipes. If, however, water does reach the pipes by any means whatever, that water must be permitted to pass through the pipes on the servient land so as to reach the dominant land. The court held that the servient owner is not bound to ensure that any water does reach the system, but if it does he cannot prevent its onward passage to the dominant tenement without being liable for action for interference with the easement.

17.13 A water undertaker supplying water to a house or any other building or part of a building which is separately occupied but does not have a separate service pipe may serve a notice on the consumer requiring the provision of such a pipe.[1] However, that power is restricted where water is supplied to two or more houses wholly or partly by the same service pipe, in which case further conditions apply.[2] When a notice is served requiring the provision of a separate service pipe, the same regime applies as if a connection notice has been served by the consumer.[3] The consumer is also required to lay within three months that part of the required pipe which the undertaker is not under a duty to lay.[4]

1 WIA 1991, s 64(1) and (3). The notice must set out the undertaker's power under s 64(4) to carry out the required works itself and recover its costs from the person required to carry them out.
2 Ibid, s 64(2).
3 Ibid, s 64(3)(b).
4 WIA 1991, s 64(3)(a).

17.14 Three additional points should be mentioned. First, planning permission will be required for the laying of any pipes which constitute engineering operations[1] unless deemed permission is granted under the Town and Country Planning (General Permitted Development) Order.[2] However, such works are excluded from the definition of development and hence from the requirement for planning permission when carried out by the water undertaker itself.[3]

1 Town and Country Planning Act 1990 (TCPA 1990), s 55(1).
2 Town and Country Planning (General Permitted Development) Order 1995, SI 1995/418, Sch 2 (as amended).
3 TCPA 1990, s 55(2)(c).

17.15 Secondly, a local authority must reject plans deposited under building regulations unless the proposal for providing the occupants with a supply of wholesome water sufficient for their domestic purposes appears to be satisfactory.[1] It is an offence for the owner to occupy the house or permit it to be occupied until the local authority has granted a certificate to the effect that it is satisfied that an adequate supply of wholesome water has been provided.[2] The maximum penalty on summary conviction is a fine not exceeding level 1 on the standard scale and a further fine for each day on which the offence continues after conviction.[3] A person who is aggrieved by a local authority's refusal to issue a certificate may apply to the magistrates' court for an order authorising the occupation of the house.[4]

1 Building Act 1984, s 25(1).
2 Ibid, s 25(4) and (6).
3 Ibid, s 25(6).
4 Building Act 1984, s 25(5).

17.16 Thirdly, unless it is impracticable to do so, six weeks' written notice of any proposal to supply water to any part of a fire authority's area must be given to the fire authority.[1] Failure to give such notice is an offence.[2]

1 Fire and Rescue Services Act 2004, s 43(1).
2 Ibid, sub-s (4).

Connection charges and infrastructure charges

17.17 The water undertaker is entitled to recover its reasonable expenses in carrying out its duties from the person serving the notice.[1] This will be amended by the Water Act 2014 to an entitlement to impose such charges as are in accordance with the charging rules to be set by Ofwat.[2] Water undertakers may also require the payment of infrastructure charges in respect of premises which are connected to the water supply for the first time.[2] The object is to impose the cost of improvements required as a result of the new demand on the developer rather than on all water consumers by way of water charges. Infrastructure charges can be levied only in respect of connections made on or after 1 April 1990,[3]and in accordance with a charges scheme which sets out the charges.[4]

1 WIA 1991, ss 45(2) and (6), 46(1) and (7).
2 Water Act 2014, s 18.
2 Ibid, s 146(2).
3 Water Act 1989 (Commencement No 1) Order 1989, SI 1989/1146, art 4.
4 This requirement is imposed by the water undertaker's Instrument of Appointment: Condition C.

17.18 The water undertaker is under a duty to supply premises connected to the water main with a supply of water sufficient for domestic purposes and to maintain the connection between the undertaker's main and the service pipe.[1] This duty only applies to household premises, which are premises in which, or in any part of which, a person has his home.[2] It also only applies where the total quantity of water estimated to be supplied to them annually is not less than 50 megalitres.[3] A demand has to be made by the occupier or by the owner (where different), in the latter case if he agrees to pay all the undertaker's charges in respect of the supply.[4] The duty applies only if there has been no disconnection under the undertaker's disconnection powers except to carry out necessary works or by reason only of a change of owner or occupier.[5] Breach of the duty is actionable by any person to whom the duty is owed who suffers loss or damage. However, it is a defence for the undertaker to show that it took all reasonable steps and exercised all due diligence to avoid the breach.[6]

1 WIA 1991, s 52(1), (3) and (4).
2 Ibid, ss 52(4A) and 17C(1) (inserted by the Water Act 2003).
3 Ibid, ss 52(4A)(c) and 17C(2).
4 Ibid, s 52(5).
5 Ibid, s 52(2) and (6).
6 Ibid, s 54.

17.19 If requested to do so by the owner or occupier of any premises, the water undertaker is under a duty to provide a supply of water: (a) to premises not consisting of the whole or any part of a building; or (b) for purposes other than domestic purposes. The supply must be made in accordance with such terms and conditions as may be determined by agreement or in default of agreement by the Water Services Regulation Authority according to what it considers to be reasonable.[1] This duty does not require the provision of a new supply of water to any premises if that would require the water undertaker to incur unreasonable expenditure in carrying out works to meet its existing and future obligations[2] or otherwise put at risk the undertaker's ability to meet any of those obligations.[3]

1 WIA 1991, ss 55(1), (2), and 56(1).
2 Existing obligations are those to supply water for domestic or other purposes. Future obligations are only those to supply buildings or parts of buildings with water for domestic purposes.
3 WIA 1991, s 55(3).

17.20 If requested to do so by the owner or occupier of a factory or place of business, a water undertaker is under a duty to fix a fire-hydrant on a suitable main or other pipe belonging to the undertaker which is as near as conveniently possible to the factory or place of business.[1] The water undertaker's expenses are payable by the owner or occupier who made the original request for the hydrant,[2] and notice of the installation must be given to the relevant fire authority.[3]

1 WIA 1991, s 58(1).
2 Ibid, s 58(4).
3 Fire and Rescue Services Act 2004, s 43.

17.21 Water undertakers are empowered to disconnect service pipes in order to carry out necessary works, for non-payment of charges, and at the request of a customer.[1] 'Disconnection' for these purposes includes disconnection of water by an automatic water metering device, activated as a consequence of failure to pay supply charges.[2] Further controls have now also been applied in respect of certain types of premises to limit the ability of water undertakers either to restrict the use that may be made of water at those premises, or to disconnect a water supply.[3] The premises in question begin with dwellings occupied by a person as their only or principal home and extend to hospitals, premises used for the provision of medical services, residential care homes, and the premises of emergency services.

1 WIA 1991, ss 60, 61 and 62 respectively.
2 *R v Director General of Water Services, ex p Lancashire County Council* [1999] Env LR 114.
3 WIA 1991, s 63A and 61(1A), respectively, taken with Sch. 4A: Water Industry Act 1999, s 1(1).

17.22 Water undertakers are under a general duty to supply only water which is 'wholesome', when supplied to any premises for domestic or food production purposes.[1] The standards of wholesomeness are set out by the Water Supply (Water Quality) Regulations 2000, as amended.[2] These Regulations transposed the EC Drinking Water Directive into UK law in respect of public water supplies.[3] The Regulations apply to public supplies that are provided by statutory water undertakers (and other licensed public water suppliers), and do not apply to private water supplies or to private distribution systems. The Private Water Supplies Regulations 2009[4] which implement and extend the requirements of the EC Drinking Water Directive apply to private water supply. Additional treatment obligations are placed on water undertakers by the Surface Waters (Abstraction for Drinking Water) (Classification) Regulations 1996.[5] It is a criminal offence for a water undertaker to supply water which is unfit for human consumption.[6] Prosecutions are relatively rare, but considerable financial penalties can be imposed. The first prosecution for this offence resulted in Severn Trent Water being fined £45,000 with £67,000 costs;[7] the most recent prosecution to date in 2013 was also of Severn Trent Water, leading to a fine of £66,000 and costs of £26,000.

1 WIA 1991, s 68(1).
2 SI 2000/3184.
3 80/778/EEC; OJ 1980 No L 229/1 as amended by Directive 98/83/EEC.
4 SI 2009/3101.
5 SI 1996/3001, see (1997) 9 *Environmental Law & Management* 5.
6 WIA 1991, s 70.
7 *Drinking Water Inspectorate and Secretary of State v Severn Trent Water* (1995) 243 ENDS Report 45.

WATER ABSTRACTION AND ABSTRACTION LICENSING

17.23 At common law the water in a stream may be used for the ordinary purposes of the riparian premises, for example, domestic purposes and for watering cattle (even if the stream is thereby exhausted),[1] and for such 'extraordinary' (or further) use in connection with the riparian premises as is reasonable.[2] However, in the latter case the water must be returned to the stream substantially unaltered in quality and quantity.[3] Landowners may also acquire an easement by grant or prescription to abstract water for the benefit of their land. However, the easement must have a lawful origin, and so cannot be created by prescription if the abstraction is unlawful during any part of the prescriptive period relied on (generally 20 years without significant interruption).[4] It follows that no easement can arise if any necessary licence to abstract is not in force throughout that period.

1 *Miner v Gilmour* (1859) 12 Moo PCC 131 at 156; *Swindon Waterworks Co v Wilts and Berks Canal Navigation Co* (1875) LR 7 HL 697 at 704.

2 An example of such a reasonable use is manufacturing but not supplying locomotives on land outside the riparian tenement: *McCartney v Londonderry and Lough Swilly Ry Co* [1904] AC 301.
3 *Rugby Joint Water Board v Walters* [1967] Ch 397, in which spray irrigation was held not to be a lawful extraordinary user because most of the water percolated into the soil or evaporated into the air.
4 *Cargill v Gotts* [1981] 1 WLR 441, CA.

17.24 Subject to the common law right of upstream riparian owners to abstract water, every riparian owner is entitled to the water of his stream in its natural flow, without sensible diminution or increase. Any invasion of this right causing actual damage, or calculated to found a claim which may ripen into an adverse right, entitles the party injured to the intervention of the court.[1]

1 *John Young & Co v Bankier Distillery Co* [1893] AC 691, HL, per Lord Macnaghten.

17.25 The right to abstract water is now also regulated by statute, thus creating an interlocking framework of common law and statutory rules. The present statutory regime under Part II of the Water Resources Act 1991 was significantly reformed by the Water Act 2003. This legislation introduced the preparation of Abstraction Management Strategies to describe the water resources position in each water catchment area and a strategy for addressing pressures on water resources in those areas (water resources management schemes).

Abstraction licensing: the current system

17.26 Subject to certain exceptions and to any drought order, it is an offence to abstract water from any source of supply or to cause or permit any other person to do so except in accordance with a licence granted by the Agency.[1] The prohibition extends to constructing or extending certain infrastructure works for abstracting water from underground strata.[2] Non-compliance with the provisions of a licence is also an offence even if no unauthorised abstraction takes place.[3] The maximum penalty on conviction for an offence is an unlimited fine on conviction by the magistrates' court or the Crown Court.[4] The following exceptions apply to the restrictions on abstractions.

(a) Abstraction of less than 20 cubic metres in any period of 24 hours, unless the abstraction forms part of a continuous operation, or series of operations, by which more than 20 cubic metres is abstracted during the period.[5]
(b) Abstraction for purposes of land drainage.[6]
(c) Abstraction for emergency purposes. An abstraction of water is an emergency abstraction if, in the opinion of the abstractor, an emergency has arisen which makes the abstraction necessary to prevent immediate danger of interference with any mining, quarrying, engineering, building or other operations (whether underground or on the surface), or, in relation to such operations, to prevent an immediate risk to a human being of death,

personal injury or harm to health, of serious damage to works resulting from any such operations; or of serious damage to the environment.[7]

1 WRA 1991, s 24(1); EA 1995, s 2. 'Source of supply' means any river, stream or other watercourse, any lake or pond, reservoir or dock, any channel, creek, bay, estuary or arm of the sea and any water-bearing underground strata. However, 'discrete waters', ie lakes, ponds or reservoirs (or one of a group of such connected waters) which do not discharge to any other inland waters are excluded from the definition: WRA 1991, s 221(1). 'Abstraction' is also defined in s 221(1). See British Waterways Board v National Rivers Authority [1993] Env LR 239, CA. An appeal decision of the Secretary of State has held that drawing from a discharge of water from an overflow is not an abstraction, since it flows undisturbed. On the other hand, drawing water from a reservoir by turning a valve or tap would seem to be an abstraction (Decision Letter WS/3471/521/13, 10 April 1969).
2 WRA 1991, s 24(2) and, (3).
3 Ibid, s 24(4).
4 Ibid, sub-s (5).
5 WRA 1991, s 27A (inserted by the Water Act 2003).
6 WRA 1991, s 29.
7 WRA 1991, s 29(2A), inserted by the Water Act 2003.

Offences

17.27 The control of abstraction is underpinned by a complex array of criminal offences, namely:

(a) failing to obtain an abstraction licence when one is required;[1]
(b) failing to comply with the conditions or requirements imposed by such a licence;[2] and
(c) failing to comply with a notice served by the Agency requesting information in relation to abstraction.[3]

It is also an offence to knowingly or recklessly make a statement which is false or misleading in a material particular when furnishing information or making an application for consent or a licence, or to wilfully alter or interfere with any meter or device used to measure the water abstracted so as to prevent it from measuring correctly.[4] If a record or journal is required to be kept by a condition on a consent or licence it is an offence to make a false entry or to knowingly or recklessly make a statement in that record or journal which is false in a material particular.[5] Each of these information-based offences is punishable by an unlimited fine or, on conviction on indictment, an unlimited fine and/or up to two years' imprisonment.[6]

1 WRA 1991, s 24(4)(a).
2 Ibid, sub-s (4)(b).
3 Ibid, s 201 as amended by the Water Act 2003.
4 Ibid, s 206 inserted by the Environment Act 1995, ss 112, 120(3), Sch 9, para 5, Sch 24.
5 Ibid, s 206(4).
6 Ibid, s 206(5).

17.28 The Agency is responsible for enforcing the provisions of the Act,[1] and enforcement proceedings may not be instituted except by the Agency or by, or with the consent of, the Director of Public Prosecutions.[2] The culpability of a corporate body may extend to its officers.[3] The Agency enjoys a wide discretion in the exercise of its enforcement powers, including whether to prosecute or, for offences committed after 6 April 2010, to seek to impose civil sanctions under the provisions of the Regulatory Enforcement and Sanctions Act 2008.[4] Guidelines for the exercise of these enforcement powers are set out in its *Enforcement and Sanctions – Statement* and *Guidance* documents. The latter makes further reference to the DEFRA guidance document *Civil Sanctions for Environmental Offences*. The focus in these documents is on a proportionate and flexible response to offending behaviour, with full criminal prosecution reserved for the most persistent, blatant or harmful breaches of the legislation.

1 WRA 1991, s 216(2).
2 Ibid, s 216(2).
3 Ibid, s 217.
4 The regime of this act was applied to environmental offences by the Environmental Civil Sanctions (England) Order 2010, SI 2010/1157. Various civil sanctions are available for most offences related to water abstraction licensing. For further details, consult the schedule 5 to the Order or the most recent version of the Agency's *Offence Response Options* document.

17.29 A person who abstracts water in accordance with a licence has a defence against a criminal prosecution or civil action in respect of the abstraction. However, such a defence is not applicable in an action for negligence or breach of contract.[1] It follows that the quantity of water permitted to be abstracted at common law may be exceeded if authorised by a licence. Subject to that the statutory restrictions do not affect private rights.[2]

1 WRA 1991, s 48.
2 Ibid, s 70; *Cargill v Gotts* [1981] 1 WLR 441. However, as stated in para **17.23**, the absence of the requisite licence does prevent time running for a prescriptive easement to abstract.

Applying for an abstraction licence

17.30 In relation to abstractions from any inland waters, a person shall be entitled to make an application for a licence if, as respects the place (or, if more than one, as respects each of the places) at which the proposed abstractions are to be effected, he satisfies the Agency that he has, or at the time when the proposed licence is to take effect will have, a right of access to land contiguous to the inland waters at that place (or those places); and he will continue to have such a right for the period of at least one year beginning with the date on which the proposed licence is to take effect, or until it is to expire (if sooner).[1] Similar provisions apply in respect of underground strata.[2] The Agency may take evidence of a person's occupation of land to be evidence of his right of access to it. A person who is negotiating to acquire an interest in the land which would entitle him to access it may also apply for an abstraction licence, as can a person who is or can be authorised to acquire land compulsorily.[3]

1 WRA 1991, s 35(2) as amended by the Water Act 2003.
2 Ibid, s 35(3) as amended by the Water Act 2003.
3 Ibid, s 35(4).

Types of licence

17.31 The Water Act 2003 created three types of abstraction licence. A full licence is a licence to abstract water from one source of supply over a period of 28 days or more for any purpose. A transfer licence is a licence to abstract water from one source of supply over a period of 28 days or more for the purpose of transferring water to another source of supply or transferring water to the same source of supply, but at another point, in the course of dewatering activities in connection with mining, quarrying, engineering, building or other operations (whether underground or on the surface), in either case without intervening use. A temporary licence is a licence to abstract water from one source of supply over a period of less than 28 days.[1]

1 WRA 1991 s 24A (inserted by the Water Act 2003).

17.32 The application must be made in the prescribed manner, include prescribed particulars and reports and be verified by such evidence as is prescribed.[1] The application must be made to the Agency on the appropriate form issued by and obtainable from the Agency. It must include such information, including maps, and must be accompanied by such reports as the Agency reasonably requires in order to determine it.[2] Notice of that application must be published in at least one newspaper circulating in the locality of the proposed point of abstraction or impounding and on the Agency's website.[3]

1 WRA 1991, s 34.
2 Water Resources (Abstraction and Impounding) Regulations 2006, SI 2006/641, reg 3
3 WRA 1991, s 37 (as amended) and Water Resources (Abstraction and Impounding) Regulations, reg 6.

17.33 The Agency must not determine an application for a licence before the end of the period allowed for making representations.[1] Subject to that and to the detailed provisions concerning publication requirements in the Regulations, the Agency must determine the application within four months after the relevant date. The relevant date is 21 days after receipt of the application or after the applicant has complied with an information request by the Agency in relation to the application.[2]

1 WRA 1991, s 38(1).
2 Part 2 of the Regulations contains detailed provisions as to the steps to be taken by the Agency in dealing with the application. In particular, they must give written notice of the application to any National Park Planning Authority in whose area the proposed abstraction is to take place. See also WRA 1991, s 34(3).

17.34 In dealing with applications the Agency is subject to a number of restrictions:

(a) The Agency must have regard to any written representations received before the end of the period allowed for making them and to the reasonable requirements of the applicant.[1]
(b) The Agency must not grant a licence derogating from 'protected rights' except with the consent of the person entitled to those rights.[2]

(c) Where the application relates to abstraction from underground strata, the Agency must have regard to the requirements of existing lawful uses of water abstracted from those strata for any purposes.[3]

(d) The Agency must have regard to the need to maintain the minimum acceptable flow of the waters in question.[4]

1 WRA 1991, s 38(3).
2 Ibid, s 39(1). Protected rights for the purposes of this Chapter of the Act are defined in s 39A. The Agency may be subject to an action for damages for breach of statutory duty if the grant of a licence infringes another person's protected rights: Water Resources Act 1991, s 60.
3 Ibid, s 39(2).
4 Ibid, s 40. The minimum acceptable flow is determined under s 21. If no minimum acceptable flow has been determined, the Agency must have regard to the considerations by which it would be determined: s 40(2).

17.35 Subject to these points, the Agency may grant a licence containing such provisions as it considers appropriate, or it may refuse the application if it considers it necessary or expedient to do so.[1] Licences which are issued must contain the following information:

(a) the person to whom the licence is granted;[2]

(b) the quantity of water which may be abstracted from the source of supply during specified periods;

(c) requirements as to determining the quantity of water abstracted and how it is to be measured or assessed;[3]

(d) the means authorised for abstraction;[4]

(e)   the purposes for which water abstracted in pursuance of the licence is to be used;[5] and

(f) whether the licence is to remain in force until revoked or is to expire at a specified time.[6]

1 WRA 1991, s 38(2).
2 Ibid, s 47(1).
3 Ibid, s 46(2).
4 WRA 1991, s 46(3).
5 Ibid, s 46(4).
6 Ibid, s 46(5).

17.36 The Secretary of State for the Environment may call in the application and decide it himself.[1] The applicant may appeal to the Secretary of State if he is dissatisfied with the Agency's decision, or if the Agency fails to give notice of its decision or of a call-in by the Secretary of State within the prescribed period[2] or any extended period agreed in writing between the parties.[3] Notice of appeal must be given within 28 days of the date of receipt of the Agency decision or of the expiry of the decision period[4]. Both in the case of called-in applications and appeals,[5] the Secretary of State may before making a determination hold a local inquiry or give the applicant and the Agency the opportunity of appearing before, and being heard by, an appointed person.[6]

1 WRA 1991, s 41.
2 The period is four months: Water Resources Regulations, reg 10.
3 WRA 1991, s 43.
4 The four-month period specified in the Water Resources Regulations, fn 2 above.

5 Water Resources Regulations, reg 12. This regulation sets out the appeal procedure.
6 WRA 1991, s 42 (called-in applications), and s 44 (appeals).

17.37 There are provisions for the revocation or variation of licences at the behest of the licence holder,[1] the Agency or the Secretary of State,[2] or the owner of fishing rights.[3] As in the case of other environmental licences, the Agency may be liable to pay compensation to the holder of a revoked or modified licence. In particular, compensation is normally payable in respect of expenditure incurred after the grant of a licence which has been rendered abortive, and other loss or damage directly attributable to the revocation or variation.[4] In addition, the Agency may serve notice imposing a temporary restriction on the abstraction of water for the purposes of spray irrigation in cases of exceptional shortage of rain or other emergency.[5] The Agency may revoke a licence by notice on the licence holder if charges payable are not paid within 28 days after the service of the notice demanding them.[6]

1 WRA 1991, s 51.
2 Ibid, ss 52–54.
3 Ibid, ss 55–56.
4 WRA 1991, s 61. In some cases, the Secretary of State may provide an indemnity: s 63(2), as amended by EA 1995, s 120, Sch 22, para 128.
5 WRA 1991, s 57.
6 Environmental Licences (Suspension and Revocation) Regulations 1996, SI 1996/508.

17.38 Decisions of the Secretary of State on appeals from the Agency on called-in applications and on proposals for the revocation or variation or licences, may be challenged in the High Court on a point of law within six weeks beginning with the date of the decision.[1]

1 WRA 1991, s 69.

Impounding works

17.39 It is an offence to begin (or cause or permit any other person to begin) to construct or alter any impounding works[1] at any point in inland waters which are not discrete waters[2] unless (a) a licence to abstract or impede the flow of waters at that point by the works is in force, (b) the impounding works will not obstruct or impede the flow of the waters except as authorised and (c) any other requirements of the licence are complied with.[3] Non-compliance with the provisions of a licence is also an offence even if no unauthorised impounding works are carried out.[4] The maximum penalty is an unlimited fine on conviction by a magistrates' court or by the Crown Court.[5]

1 'Impounding works' means any dam, weir or other works by which water may be impounded; or any works for diverting the flow of water in connection with the construction or alteration of any dam, weir or other works: WRA 1991, s 25(8).
2 'Inland waters' means the whole or part of any river, stream or other watercourse, any loch or pond, or any reservoir or dock and any channel, creek, bay, estuary or arm of the sea. 'Discrete waters' means lakes, ponds or reservoirs which do not discharge to any other inland waters or any group of two or more lakes, ponds or reservoirs and any watercourses connecting them where none of them discharges to any inland waters outside the group: WRA 1991, s 221(1).

3 WRA 1991, s 25(1) (as amended by the Water Act 2003).
4 Ibid, s 25(2)(b).
5 Ibid, s 25(3).

17.40 Charges may be made by the Agency on an application for, or grant of, an abstraction or impounding licence. In addition, single and/or periodic charges may be made while the licence is in force.[1] Charges may only be made under a scheme made by the Agency and approved by the Secretary of State. Each year the Agency adopts its *Abstraction Charging Scheme*, which contains details of how various charges are to be calculated.[2]

1 EA 1995, ss 41 and 42.
2 These schemes are adopted pursuant to EA 1995, ss 41–42.

Transfer of licences

17.41 With the exception of temporary licences, licenses can be transferred. This will be of crucial importance to those buying property which requires an abstraction licence in order to operate. Transfer of a licence is not automatic with transfer of the property; the Agency must be notified by the holder of the licence and the transferee. However, subject to the correct information being provided with the transfer notice, the Agency has a duty to transfer the licence.[1] This notice has to include such information as the Agency reasonably requires and (in the case of the transfer of a full licence or of a transfer licence) a declaration by the proposed transferee that he has, or at the time when the proposed transfer is to take effect will have, a right of access in relation to each point of abstraction; and he will continue to have such a right for the period of at least one year beginning with the date on which the proposed transfer is to take effect, or until the licence is to expire (if sooner), and may specify the date on which the holder and the transferee wish the transfer to take effect. Section 59B and 59C contain provisions regarding the vesting of licences on the death or bankruptcy of the licence holder and the apportionment of licences.

1 WRA 1991, s 59A(5) (as amended by the Water Act 2003).

Registers

17.42 The Agency must keep registers of prescribed information relating to the grant, revocation and variation of abstraction and impounding licences (including information as to how the applications have been dealt with), and persons becoming holders of abstraction licences by virtue of the rules on transfer and vesting of licences.[1] The registers must be available for inspection by the public at all reasonable hours at the Agency's regional offices. They are also now made available online via an interactive map.

The register must contain an index map to enable entries on the register to be traced. Entries must be made on the register within 14 days from the date of receipt of an application or of the decision.[2]

1 WRA 1991, s 189(1).
2 Water Resources Regulations, reg 17(1)–(5).

WATER DISCHARGE ACTIVITIES

17.43 Water pollution controls complement abstraction controls, although pollution controls are more clearly a creature of statute than their abstraction counterparts. As with abstraction, it is important for owners or occupiers of land to be aware of the general shape of the statutory regime, and the breadth of the obligations it creates. This statutory regime has now been integrated with various other permitting regimes into the Environmental Permitting (England and Wales) Regulations 2010,[1] which repealed the relevant parts of the WRA 1991.[2] In addition, it will be important for intending purchasers to have full details of any water discharge activities carried on from the property and of any relevant consent from the Agency. Vendors should also carefully consider what interests they retain when involved in site development, as retention of part of a site (for example) may mean retention of liabilities which may not be obvious.[3]

1 SI 2010/675, "the EP Regulations".
2 With the notable exception of s 104 of the WRA 1991 which contains the definitions of the water bodies to which these regulations apply. These include in essence all inland waters, ie, rivers and watercourses (other than public sewers or sewers or drains which drain into a public sewer) and lakes and ponds which discharge directly or indirectly into them, underground waters, coastal waters and territorial waters extending seaward for three miles from the baselines from which the breadth of the territorial sea is measured.
3 See *Taylor Woodrow Property Management v National Rivers Authority* [1995] Env LR 52, DC, considered at para **17.65**.

Principal offences

17.44 The EP Regulations create what is essentially a simple framework for environmental regulation, although the legislation is complex and obscurely drafted. The central requirement, as far as discharges to water are concerned, is not to cause or knowingly permit a water discharge activity other than under and in accordance with a permit.[1] 'Water discharge activity' is defined in expansive terms in Schedule 21. The core of the definition relates to the discharge or entry into waters of poisonous, noxious or polluting matter,[2] waste matter or trade or sewage effluent. However, it also includes matters such as cutting vegetation so that it falls into inland freshwaters and not taking reasonable steps to remove it. Certain water discharge activities are exempt from control under the EP Regulations providing that they are registered as exempt.[3] For all others, however, a permit is required and it is an offence to cause or knowingly permit such an activity to be carried on without a permit.[4] It is also an offence to breach the terms of any permit.[5]

1 Reg 12(1)(b).
2 Regs 12 and 38, Sch 21, para 3. 'Poisonous, noxious or polluting' are not defined in the EP Regulations, and must therefore be defined on a case by case basis. There has been little judicial consideration of the terms, but see (in relation to the same expression as used in the WRA 1991)

Express Limited v The Environment Agency [2004] EWHC 1710 Admin, [2005] 1 WLR 223, [2005] Env LR 7, *National Rivers Authority v Biffa Waste Services* [1996] Env LR 227 and W Howarth, '"Poisonous, Noxious or Polluting": Contrasting Approaches to Environmental Regulation' [1993] 56 MLR 171.
3 These activities are limited and relate to certain vegetation management activities and small discharges of sewage effluent.
4 Reg 38(1).
5 Reg 38(2).

17.45 The EP Regulations also create a number of other offences which may be relevant to the purchaser of land from which a water discharge activity has been carried out. The requirement for a permit discussed above also applies to the operation of any 'regulated facility'.[1] Somewhat confusingly, regulated facility is defined as including a water discharge activity. However, it also covers various other potentially polluting activities which require a permit, any one of which may be carried on jointly with a water discharge activity.[2] In practice, therefore, the regulated facility requirement will apply to operations which combine a number of different potentially polluting activities. The corresponding offence is slightly different. It is an offence to operate a regulated facility without a permit. It is also an offence to knowingly cause or knowingly permit the operation of a regulated facility without a permit.[3] It is also an offence under the EP Regulations to fail to comply with various notices served under the Regulations,[4] including those requiring information of an operator, and it is an offence intentionally to make false entries in any record required by an environmental permit condition.[5]

1 Reg 12(1)(a).
2 Reg 8.
3 Reg 38(1).
4 Reg 38(3), (4)(a).
5 Reg 38(4), (5).

17.46 The penalties available have been significantly increased compared to those available under the WRA 1991. This is no doubt partly because the EP Regulations cover a far wider range of potentially polluting activities, with a correspondingly larger range of potential harm. The maximum penalty for the principal offences of operating without a permit, contravening the conditions of a permit or breaching the terms of an enforcement notice is on summary conviction 12 months imprisonment and/or an unlimited fine. On conviction on indictment the maximum penalty is a hefty five years imprisonment and/or an unlimited fine.[1] The maximum penalties for offences related to the provision of information and record keeping are lower.[2] Once again, it should be noted that the Agency's flexible and proportionate approach to enforcement means that not every offence will be prosecuted,[3] but for those that are sentencing guidelines in force from 1 July 2014 onwards suggest fines of up to £3,000,000 for the largest and most serious offenders.[4] Custodial sentences for directors are also not uncommon in the most serious cases.

1 Reg 39(1).
2 Reg 39(3)–(4).
3 See discussion at para **17.28** above.
4 *Environmental Offences: Definitive Guideline* produced by the Sentencing Council.

'Causing or knowingly permitting'

17.47 Although any environmental permit will be an important factor in site acquisition (not least because of the implications for valuation), case law on the meaning of the phrase 'cause or knowingly permit' indicates that there are important liabilities which may arise under water pollution controls which might affect owners indirectly, and which may also be a relevant factor in drawing up leases for tenants whose activities might give rise to polluting discharges. A broad appreciation of the case law is therefore essential.

It should also be noted that the phrase to 'cause or knowingly permit' is not unique to water pollution control but in fact appears in a number of different regulatory contexts. Similar wording arises in connection with waste offences,[1] liability for the remediation of contaminated land under Part IIA of EPA 1990,[2] and now also liability under a 'works notice' in connection with anti (water) pollution works and operations.[3] Much of the case law has arisen in the context of water regulation, but it should also be considered mutatis mutandis in these other contexts.

1 It is an offence to 'knowingly cause or knowingly permit' the deposit of controlled waste otherwise than in accordance with the terms of an environmental permit: EPA 1990, s 33(1).
2 A person shall be an 'appropriate person' for the purposes of service of a remediation notice in relation to things which are to be done by way of remediation which are to any extent referable to substances which he 'caused or knowingly permitted' to be present in, on or under contaminated land: EPA 1990, s 78F(3).
3 WRA 1991, s 161A(1); inserted by EA 1995, Sch 22, para 162. This provision complements the amended s 161, which still enables the Agency itself to conduct certain clean-up operations where s 161A does not apply: WRA 1991, s 161(1A). See para **17.86** et seq.

17.48 This phrase creates two separate offences[1] which can be charged as alternatives on the same indictment without being bad for duplicity.[2] Further, it is well established that, at least in the case of 'causing', the offence is one for which liability is strict.[3] In practice, however, it would appear that polluters are unlikely to be prosecuted unless they in fact demonstrate some form of mens rea, albeit not mens rea in any strict legal sense, as described in successive regulators' enforcement policy documents.[4]

1 *McLeod v Buchanan* [1940] 2 All ER 179.
2 *R v Leighton and Town and Country Refuse Collections Ltd* [1997] Env LR 411, CA, a case which considered a charge (amongst others) of causing or knowingly permitting the deposit of controlled waste, contrary to Control of Pollution Act 1974, s 3(1)(a).
3 *Alphacell v Woodward* [1972] 2 All ER 475, HL.
4 Jewell 'Agricultural Water Pollution Issues and NRA Enforcement Policy' [1991] *Land Management and Environmental Law Report* 110; and see discussion of the Agency's enforcement current enforcement policy at para **17.28** above.

17.49 The addition of 'knowingly' to 'permitting' clearly adds a form of mental element to the second limb. The scope of this has been clarified in a recent Court of Appeal decision on the materially identical provisions in the Environmental Permitting (England and Wales) Regulations 2007. The Court held that the words 'knowingly' and 'permit' relate to the knowledge of the facts and not as to the existence and scope of the permission or conditions on a licence.[1] Therefore it will only be necessary for the prosecution to show that the defendant was aware of a water discharge activity, not that it was in breach of a permit. This clearly has serious implications for developers and landlords, who can much more easily be fixed with criminal liability as a result.

1 *Walker & Son (Hauliers) Ltd v Environment Agency* [2014] EWCA Crim 100 at [29].

17.50 The most established authority on the meaning of 'cause' in this context is the decision of the House of Lords in *Alphacell v Woodward*.[1] The defendants in that case constructed and operated two settling tanks near a river in connection with their paper manufacturing operations. Although frequent checks were made, pumps that were intended to prevent over-filling of the tanks became blocked by vegetation, and polluted water escaped into an adjacent river. In upholding the defendants' conviction of causing polluting matter to enter the river contrary to the (then applicable) Rivers (Prevention of Pollution) Act 1951, the House took a broad and pragmatic view of the meaning of 'cause':

> '... "causing" here must be given a common sense meaning ... The whole complex operation which might lead to this result was an operation deliberately conducted by the appellants and I fail to see how a defect in one stage of it, even if we assume that this happened without their negligence, can enable them to say that they did not cause the pollution.'[2]

1 [1972] 2 All ER 475.
2 Per Lord Wilberforce at 479b–c.

17.51 This general 'common sense' approach was reiterated by the remainder of the House. Their Lordships identified the 'deliberate and intentional' or 'positive' acts of the defendants in operating their works[1] and posed the question: if those acts did not cause the pollution, what did? As Lord Salmon put it:

> 'I consider ... that what or who has caused a certain event to occur is essentially a practical question of fact which can best be answered by ordinary common sense rather than abstract metaphysical theory. It seems to me that, giving the word "cause" its ordinary and natural meaning, anyone may cause something to happen, intentionally or negligently or inadvertently without negligence and without intention'.[2]

1 Per Viscount Dilhorne at 483e, and Lords Pearson and Cross at 488d and 489b respectively.
2 At 490a.

17.52 Further confirmation of this approach has been provided by the more recent, and robust, decision of the House of Lords in *Empress Car Co (Abertillery) Ltd v National Rivers Authority*.[1] The appellant company in that case had maintained an oil tank in a protective bund, but that protection was overridden by a connection to a smaller tank outside the bund. All that controlled escapes of oil from that second tank was an unlocked tap. The entire contents of both tanks escaped into a nearby river when an unknown person opened the tap, and the company was prosecuted under s 85 and convicted.

That conviction was ultimately upheld by the House of Lords. The principal speech, of Lord Hoffmann, confirmed the general thrust of *Alphacell*, but also provides some important elaboration. His Lordship firmly concluded that the question to be asked in prosecutions under engaging these provisions is not 'what caused the pollution?', but rather 'did the defendant cause the pollution?': 'The fact that for different purposes or even for the same purpose one could also say that someone or something else caused the pollution is not inconsistent with the defendant having caused it.'[2]

1 [1998] 1 All ER 481.
2 Ibid, at 487j.

17.53 *Empress Car Co*[1] further emphasised the requirement to show a positive act by the Defendant where the charge is 'causing'.[2] This is not because of anything inherent in the notion of 'causing', but is a consequence of the structure of the provisions, which leave cases of omissions to the 'knowingly permit' limb.[3] Lord Hoffmann therefore adopted the phrasing of the House in *Alphacell*.[4]

1 [1998] 1 All ER 481.
2 Ibid, per Lord Hoffmann, at 485.
3 See para **17.48**.
4 See para **17.51**.

17.54 The requirement to show a positive act by the defendant is not, however, to be interpreted too restrictively. Two examples of this are supplied by cases decided after *Alphacell* but rejected in *Empress Car Co*. In *Price v Cromack*[1] the Divisional court quashed the conviction of a landowner who had entered into an agreement by which industrial effluent ran onto his land for storage, that effluent having subsequently escaped. In *Wychavon District Council v National Rivers Authority*[2] the local authority failed to keep clear a sewer which it was obliged to maintain. Despite being notified that sewage was escaping into the River Avon, the Council took no action was subsequently convicted for causing sewerage effluent to enter the river on two successive days. The Council's appeal was allowed on the basis that there was no positive or deliberate act on its part.[3] The approach of the Divisional Court in both of these cases was roundly rejected by the House of Lords in *Empress Car Co*.[4] There is no requirement that the defendant's positive act should have been in some sense the immediate cause of the escape: '... the Act contains no such requirement. It only requires a finding that something which the defendant did caused the pollution.'[5] The requirement for a positive act is thus relatively easy to satisfy: 'The only question was whether something which the defendant had done, whether immediately or antecedently, had caused the pollution'.[6]

1 [1975] 2 All ER 113.
2 [1993] 1 WLR 125.
3 Eg, Tasker Watkins LJ at 137B–C.
4 *Empress Car Co (Abertillery) Ltd v National Rivers Authority* [1998] 1 All ER 481, per Lord Hoffmann at 485h.
5 Ibid, at 485j.
6 Ibid, at 486c.

17.55 Two cases helpfully illustrate the implications of this approach. The first, decided before *Empress Car Co* but endorsed in principle in that case,[1] was *CPC (UK) Ltd v National Rivers Authority*.[2] In that case, 165 gallons of cleaning fluid escaped from fractured piping into a river via a storm drain. The cause of the fracture was a defect in the piping when it was installed: an installation undertaken by specialist contractors *before* the defendants acquired any interest in the factory; and a defect which went undetected in the surveys undertaken on the acquisition in accordance with the custom and practice of the industry. Despite these circumstances, the defendants' conviction was upheld on the straightforward basis that since they were operating the factory when the escape occurred, the jury was entitled to find 'as a question of fact and common sense' that they caused the escape. Thus the question of causation is a question of fact, albeit delimited by law in respect of such matters as whether there is sufficient evidence to support a finding of causation, whether a cause is too remote, or whether knowledge or fault are relevant to the causation issue.[3]

1 [1998] 1 All ER 481, discussion at 491.
2 [1995] Journal of Environmental Law 69, [1995] Env LR 131, CA.
3 Generally see *Royal Greek Government v Minister of Transport (The Ann Stathatos)* (1949) 83 Ll L Rep 228, per Devlin J at 236–237.

17.56 In the second case, *Environment Agency v Brock plc*,[1] the company operating a landfill site extracted leachate from time-to-time via an extraction 'chimney'. A seal in the hose used for that extraction inexplicably failed after two months despite having an expected life of 12 months, and leachate entered controlled waters in consequence. While the acquitting magistrates did not have the benefit of the *Empress Car Co* decision when hearing the case, the Divisional Court concluded that even without it Brock plc should have been convicted. Had the company not been running the site and extracting the leachate, then the escape would not have occurred. The similarity between these facts and those of the *Empress Car Co* case makes this an unsurprising conclusion.

1 [1998] JPL 968, DC.

'Knowingly cause or knowingly permit'

17.57 One departure from the drafting of the WRA 1991 in the EP Regulations is that now, in addition to the familiar wording 'cause or knowingly permit', there is also an offence of knowingly causing or knowingly permitting the operation of a relevant facility otherwise than in accordance with a permit.[1] The addition of the word 'knowingly' would appear to add an element of mens rea to the 'causing' part of this offence. It seems likely that this will be construed in similar way to the mens rea requirement in respect of the expression 'knowingly permit', ie as requiring knowledge of the operations and their consequences leading to the offence but not requiring knowledge that there is no permit or that the operations are in breach of the terms of the permit.[2]

1 EP Regulations, reg 38(1)(b).
2 See discussion of *Walker & Son (Hauliers) Ltd v Environment Agency* [2014] EWCA Crim 100 at para **17.49** above.

Multiple defendants and separate acts

17.58 It clearly follows from the line of reasoning adopted in *Alphacell* and *Empress Car Co* that it is open to a court to find that more than one person was the cause of a discharge, either in the case of a joint enterprise or by their separate acts. This point was expressly not decided in *Alphacell v Woodward*,[1] but has been confirmed by the Court of Appeal in *A-G's Reference (No 1 of 1994)*.[2] In that case a company (the first respondent) was disposing of toxic waste in an area where sewage treatment was provided by a sewerage undertaker (the second respondent) whose statutory duties were performed on a day-to-day basis by the local borough council (the third respondent). The second respondents operated certain pumps which prevented untreated effluent from entering controlled waters. Failure by the second respondents to install appropriate pumps, and by the third respondents to adequately maintain them, resulted in the discharge into controlled waters of polluting effluent deposited by the first respondents in breach of consent conditions. The respondents were tried on separate counts which charged each with causing polluting matter to enter controlled waters, and were acquitted. As well as holding that the judge had erred in directing the acquittal of the second respondents (thus finding that a sewerage undertaker *could* be found to have caused pollution resulting from the operation of a sewage treatment works in an unmaintained state)[3] the Court of Appeal saw no difficulty in the concept of 'causing' by more than one defendant and by separate acts.[4] Lord Hoffmann's obiter remarks in the House of Lords in *Empress Car Co* lend further weight to this view.[5]

1 [1972] 2 All ER 475, per Lord Pearson at 488e.
2 [1995] 2 All ER 1007, [1995] 1 WLR 599.
3 Consistent with *CPC (UK) Ltd v National Rivers Authority* [1995] Env LR 131; see para **17.52**.
4 Per Lord Taylor CJ at 614a.
5 [1998] 1 All ER 481, at 487j, quoted in para **17.52**.

Acts of third parties

17.59 Although not directly considered in *Alphacell v Woodward*, that case did recognise the possibility that the acts of a third party or natural forces might affect determinations of whether a defendant caused a given escape. The starting point is a clear reluctance to complicate the 'common sense' meaning of 'cause' 'by the introduction of refinements such as causa causans, effective cause or novus actus'.[1] However, Lord Pearson did point out in that case that '[t]here was no intervening act of a trespasser and no Act of God. There was not even any unusual weather or freak of nature'.[2] Establishing the existence of such a situation is clearly not a 'defence' as such,[3] but it must equally clearly be part of the inquiry into whether the defendant caused the escape. This is doubly so since *A-G's Reference (No 1 of 1994)*[4] as it would be possible for both a site operator and, for example, a trespasser to be found to be 'causers': the test in law remains the same, its resolution is for the tribunal of fact.

1 [1972] 2 All ER 475, per Lord Wilberforce at 479b.
2 Ibid, at 488d. Similar phraseology is adopted by Lords Cross and Salmon at 489f and 490c.

3 Compare this with the statutory defences set out in the EP Regulations, reg 40, see paras **17.67–17.68**.
4 [1995] 2 All ER 1007; see para **17.58**.

17.60 The clearest consideration of the significance of intervening causes to the 'causing' test is also to be found in *Empress Car Co (Abertillery) Ltd v National Rivers Authority,* however.[1] On the basis of the structure of the liability introduced by the Act, imposed in the interests of protecting controlled waters from pollution, Lords Hoffmann and Clyde (giving the only speeches) both took a firm approach.[2] In particular, reliance on foreseeability as the determinant of whether the act of a third party or of God may defeat a defendant's liability was expressly rejected: '… forseeability is not the criterion for deciding whether a person caused something or not. People often cause things which they could not have foreseen'.[3] Instead, the House suggested that the true distinction is between acts and events which, although not necessarily foreseeable in the particular case, are in the generality a normal and familiar fact of life, and acts or events which are abnormal and extraordinary.[4] Neither leaky pipes nor acts of vandalism are anything out of the ordinary, in the way that (for example) an act of terrorism would be.[5] Whether this distinction will in fact enable the lower courts to apply the provisions more predictably remains to be seen, but annunciation of the 'new' test[6] did enable the House to set aside some of the least satisfactory decisions that had interpreted intervening causes broadly.[7] A useful summary of the effect of the *Empress Car Co* test is set out in Lord Hoffmann's speech.[8] An example of it in operation can be seen in *Express Ltd v Environment Agency,*[9] where a tyre blow-out on a (properly maintained) tanker caused part of the spray suppression system to become detached, in turn hitting the under-run protection barrier which itself became detached, shearing the delivery pipe. The driver of the lorry pulled over and a considerable quantity of milk escaped into nearby controlled waters. Despite evidence to the effect that each event in the sequence was unique and unusual, the Divisional Court upheld the magistrates' finding that the events, although 'unusual', were not 'extraordinary'.

1 [1998] 1 All ER 481.
2 Ibid, at 488b–492e and 494c–e respectively.
3 Per Lord Hoffmann, at 491e.
4 At 491e–f and 494d.
5 Lord Hoffmann's illustration, at 491h.
6 Lord Hoffmann was at pains to justify it by reference to *Alphacell*: 491j–492d.
7 Eg, *Impress (Worcester) Ltd v Rees* [1971] 2 All ER 357, DC (see 490d); *National Rivers Authority v Wright Engineering Co Ltd* [1994] 4 All ER 281, DC (see 492e).
8 [1998] 1 All ER 481, at 492f–493a.
9 [2003] EWHC 448 Admin, [2004] 1 WLR 579, [2003] Env LR 29, not to be confused with the case of the same name referred to at para **17.44** above.

Landlords' and lessors' liabilities

17.61 The broad interpretation of 'cause', with its emphasis on active operations or chains of operations, presents particular dangers for landlords and lessors. In some cases, despite having an arms-length relationship with the day-to-day operation of a site with polluting potential (that is, the act which might be the immediate cause of an unlawful escape), a landlord or lessor (perhaps a property developer) may have contributed to the underlying operations resulting in a discharge sufficiently to make them liable as a cause of it. In *Alphacell v Woodward* it was the construction of the effluent storage tanks, which subsequently operated imperfectly, which was sufficient to ground liability on those constructing the tanks. But in that case the defendants continued to operate the facilities on a day-to-day basis as well. Conversely, in *CPC (UK) Ltd v National Rivers Authority*[1] although the defendants were not responsible for the latent defect that resulted in the discharge, and indeed had taken all reasonable steps to locate such defects, as they did operate the factory they too were held liable. The question then remains: is the absence of that day-to-day involvement sufficient to escape liability?

1 [1995] Journal of Environmental Law 69 approved in *Empress Car Co (Abertillery) Ltd v National Rivers Authority* [1998] 1 All ER 481, 491; see para **17.56**.

17.62 The answer to this question appears to be 'no'. The court in *National Rivers Authority v Welsh Development Agency*[1] found otherwise on the facts before it. The Agency had built an industrial estate and let factory units on it. Under the terms of their leases, tenants undertook not to discharge polluting effluent through the estate's drainage system and thereby into controlled waters. Notwithstanding the lease, such pollution did occur and the Agency, as landlord, was prosecuted. The Agency's acquittal was upheld on appeal on the basis, first, that there was nothing in the design or construction of the drainage system which could be said to have caused the discharge and, secondly, that there was nothing else in the circumstances to show that the discharge was due to a 'positive and deliberate act' by the Agency. The latter reason has been rejected,[2] and the former might well be also. It is true that in *Alphacell* and *A-G's Reference (No 1 of 1994)*[3] there were *defects* in the operations which at least contributed to the discharges in those cases. There was no defect here. But to make that a precondition to liability would be to obviate the strict liability character of this offence, a possibility which was expressly rejected by Lord Wilberforce in *Alphacell*.[4] This case is therefore not consistent with current applications of the *Alphacell* test;[5] a point which is reinforced by the parallel drawn by Potts J between the respondents here and the local authority in the *Wychavon District Council v National Rivers Authority*,[6] a decision which has now been disapproved.

1 [1993] Env LR 407, DC.
2 See the discussion and conclusions at paras **17.55–17.57**.
3 Considered at para **17.58**.
4 [1972] 2 All ER 475, at 479d–e.
5 This conclusion is shared by another commentator: see Bell, McGillivray and Pedersen, *Environmental Law* (8ᵗʰ edn, 2013), p 650. See generally Burnett-Hall *Environmental Law* (3rd edn) 11-08-11-19.
6 [1993] 1 WLR 125; see para **17.54**.

17.63 More simply, as with the defendants in the *Welsh Development Agency* case, the second respondents in *A-G's Reference (No 1 of 1994)* played no active part in the day-to-day operations of the sewage treatment works, yet in the judgment of the Court of Appeal this should not have been sufficient in itself to prevent their actions from being considered by the jury to be a cause of the discharge. This is entirely consistent with the reasoning of the House of Lords in *Empress Car Co v National Rivers Authority*.[1]

1 [1998] 1 All ER 481; paras **17.52–17.56**.

17.64 The effect of the covenant in the lease in the *Welsh Development Agency* case is also significant. The Divisional Court *did not* endorse the stipendiary magistrate's view that the covenant effectively transferred the landlord's responsibilities to the tenants and that the landlord's obligations towards the stream were thus shifted to the tenants under the obligations created in those leases. Potts J was clear that 'obligations created by the lease do not, in my judgment, determine the crucial issue of fact …'. In terms of the 'causing' limb of the offence (and similar offences), the provisions of the lease are therefore more likely to affect enforcement behaviour than to have any other determinative legal consequences. This may be even more so in respect of the 'knowingly permitting' limb, where covenants in leases may be powerful evidence in some circumstances, if not in respect of the landlord/lessor's knowledge, then at least in respect of the issue of 'permission'. As a matter of good practice leases should therefore contain appropriate provisions relating to prohibited discharges, and landlords might also consider what systems are in place to ensure the observance of those covenants.

17.65 Finally, landlords should carefully consider what interests they *retain* when involved in site development. In *Taylor Woodrow Property Management v National Rivers Authority*,[1] for example, the defendant company retained control of an outfall which was the point of discharge into controlled waters of liquids drained from an industrial estate; it neither owned nor occupied the estate itself, as the site had been transferred to an associated company which undertook the development. Whilst the consented discharge was subject to a prohibition on the discharge of oil, such a discharge was in fact made by an occupant of the site. The defendants were not responsible for the discharge but were held to be guilty of a breach of consent conditions. The consent placed them under a positive obligation to avoid discharges of oil, even those which they did not themselves cause.

1 [1995] Journal of Environmental Law 55, [1995] Env LR 52, DC.

17.66 Where the purchaser of a site also takes on responsibilities under an existing environmental permit, they should also review any conditions to which that consent has been made subject. An important reason for this is that if the purchaser is later prosecuted for breach of these conditions it may not be possible for them to argue by way of 'defence' that the condition was not properly imposed. This sort of collateral challenge to consent conditions was rejected by the Court of Appeal as an abuse of process in *R v Ettrick Trout Co Ltd and Baxter*,[1] where it was held that the most appropriate means to challenge conditions in such cases was by way of judicial review. Although this must now be read in light of other collateral challenge cases,[2] this conclusion seems unlikely to be affected. This should therefore form part of a purchaser's review on taking on a discharge consent.

1 [1994] Env LR 165.
2 Eg, *Boddington v British Transport Police* [1998] 2 All ER 203.

Defences

17.67 A person shall not be guilty of any of the principal offences if the acts alleged to constitute the contravention were done in an emergency in order to avoid danger to human health. This is subject to the twin provisos that the person must have taken all reasonably practicable steps to minimise pollution and that particulars of the acts were furnished to the Agency as soon as reasonably practicable after they were done.[1]

1 EP Regulations, reg 40(1). This regulation also provides certain other more specific defences, eg in respect of water escaping from abandoned mines.

17.68 Discharges to sewers and from public sewers also fall within specific defences provided by the EP Regulations.[1] The Regulations make specific provision for which undertaker will be held to have 'caused' a discharge of sewage.[2] Similarly, there is a specific defence for sewerage undertakers in respect of contraventions attributable to discharges made into its sewers which it was not bound to receive and could nto reasonably be expect to have prevented.[3] On the other hand, if a person makes a discharge into a sewer which the sewerage operator *was* bound to receive, that person will not be guilty of an offence.[4]

1 Sch 21, para 6.
2 Sch 21, para 6(2)–(4)
3 Sch 21, para 6(5).
4 Sch 21, para 6(6) and reg 38(1).

Consents

17.69 If there is no existing permit and it is proposed to undertake a water discharge activity, an application for a permit should be made to the Agency. The basic elements of the consent process are set out in Part 2 and Schedule 5 of the EP Regulations. The Agency must consult on applications, subject to various exemptions.[1] The applicant must provide the Agency with such information as may be prescribed and such information as the Agency may reasonably require. The Agency may serve notice requiring further information to be supplied in respect of a duly-made application, and may deem the application withdrawn if the information is not supplied.[2]

1 Sch 5, paras 5 and 6.
2 Sch 5, paras 3 and 4.

17.70 The Agency is under a duty to determine (ie either grant or refuse) a duly made application.[1] It is also under a duty to periodically review permits and to carry out appropriate periodic inspections of regulated facilities.[2] A purchaser cannot assume that just because a permit has been granted it will be allowed to remain in place, or will necessarily be renewed on the same terms.

1 EP Regulations, Sch 5, para 12.
2 Ibid, reg 34 and see para **17.74** below.

Conditions on discharge consents

17.71 The Agency has a wide discretion as to the conditions which it may impose on permits,[1] and different conditions may relate to different periods. The previous legislation provided for the following conditions in particular, and it would seem that such conditions may still be imposed under the EP Regulations:

(a) places at which the discharges to which the consent relates may be made and as to the design and construction of any outlets for the discharges;

(b) nature, origin, composition, temperature, volume, and rate of the discharges and as to the periods during which the discharges may be made;

(c) steps to be taken, in relation to the discharges or by way of subjecting any substance likely to affect the description of matter discharged to treatment or any other process, for minimising the polluting effects of the discharges on any controlled waters;

(d) provision of facilities for taking samples of the matter discharged and in particular the provision, maintenance and use of manholes, inspection chambers, observation wells and boreholes in connection with the discharges;

(e) provision, maintenance and testing of meters for measuring or recording the volume and rate of the discharges and apparatus for determining the nature, composition and temperature of the discharges;

(f) keeping of records of the nature, origin, composition, temperature, volume and rate of the discharges and, in particular, of records of readings of meters and other recording apparatus provided in accordance with any condition attached to the consent; and

(g) making of returns and the giving of other information to the Agency about the nature, origin, composition, temperature, volume and rate of the discharges.[2]

The EP Regulations also include provision for permit conditions to require an operator to carry out works or do other things on land which is not within its ownership or control.[3] Where such conditions are imposed, the landowner of such land must grant the operator such rights as are necessary to comply with the condition; and there are provisions for the grant of compensation in such circumstances.[4] It is therefore worth purchasers of land adjoining existing or proposed regulated facilities checking whether any such conditions may be or have been imposed in respect of the land they seek to acquire.

1 The provision in EP Regulations, Sch 5, para 12(2) simply says that the Agency may grant a permit 'subject to such conditions as it sees fit'.
2 This list originally contained in WRA 1991, Sch 10, para 3(4).

3 EP Regulations, reg 15.
4 In Sch 5, Part 2.

17.72 The Agency is under a duty to exercise its powers to ensure, so far as is practicable, that any statutory water quality objectives laid down by the Secretary of State are achieved at all times.[1] The Agency is also influenced by the large number of EC directives relating to the aquatic environment in fixing the conditions on consents.

1 Water Resources Act 1991, s 84.

Transmission of applications to the Secretary of State

17.73 The Secretary of State has a broad power to give directions to the Agency as to the exercise of its functions under the EP Regulations. This includes the power to direct that specific applications or a class of applications be transmitted to him for consideration.[1] Such a direction is unlikely to be made except in cases of national importance. The Secretary of State may cause a hearing to be held, and if such a hearing is duly requested by the applicant or the Agency, must do so.[2]

1 EP Regulations, regs 61–62.
2 Reg 62(3).

Review of consents

17.74 The Agency must review permits from time to time and may by notice revoke or make modifications to a permit.[1] The revocation and variation of permits is subject to a right of appeal to the Secretary of State.[2]

1 EP Regulations, regs 34, 20, 22.
2 Reg 31.

Appeals and variation

17.75 Appeals against a decision of the Agency may be made to the Secretary of State. Schedule 6 of the EP Regulations sets out the detailed provisions on appeals. There is a general time limit of 6 months for the making of an appeal, although shorter time limits apply in certain cases, most notably in respect of enforcement notices and permit revocations.[1] These time limits may be extended in appropriate cases. The Secretary of State may cause a hearing to be held, and must do so if this is requested by the appellant or Agency.[2] Most appeals are in fact decided by an inspector from the Planning Inspectorate,[3] with only particularly important or controversial decisions being 'recovered' for the decision by the Secretary of State himself.[4]

1 Sch 6, para 3(1).
2 Sch 6, para 5(1).

3 Pursuant to Environment Act 1995, s 114.
4 Planning Inspectorate document *The Appeal Procedure Guidance*, March 2013. Appendix 2 sets out guidance on which cases will be 'recovered'.

Transfer of property

17.76 The EP Regulations continue the stance taken in the previous legislation of making permits personal to the operator who applies for them. It remains in existence unless revoked, surrendered or replaced with a consolidated permit.[1] It cannot be surrendered without either notifying or making an application to the Agency.[2] Further, on the death of a holder of a consent, the consent shall be regarded as property forming part of the deceased's personal estate, whether or not it would be so regarded otherwise, and shall accordingly vest in his personal representatives.[3] Such a permit remains in force for a limited period only unless action is taken to transfer it permanently.

1 EP Regulations, reg 19.
2 Ibid, regs 35–36.
3 Ibid, reg 67A.

17.77 In order to transfer a permit it is necessary for the current operator and the transferee to make a joint application to the Agency (unless the operator is an individual who cannot be found, in which case an application by the transferee alone is acceptable). Where the permit applies simply to a stand-alone water discharge activity, it is only necessary to notify the Agency, rather than making a full application.[1] These procedures will clearly need to be followed in any case where there is a change in the ownership or occupation of property where the new owner or occupier intends to continue the permitted water discharge activity. If this is not the case (for example, where the holder is transferring his interest in the property from which a discharge is made and the successor to that interest has no intention of continuing the discharge) it will be important for both vendor and purchaser to consider if the conditions on the consent place them under any continuing obligations.

1 EP Regulations, reg 21.

Charges

17.78 Charges may be made by the Agency under a scheme approved by the Secretary of State (inter alia) when applications for consent are made and during the continuation of a consent.[1] The Agency prepares a charging scheme, which is available online, for environmental permitting each year. In addition to dealing with charges for applications, the scheme also sets out how the annual or 'subsistence' charge is calculated for each permit. The amounts in the scheme are increased annually on 1 April, and the current policy states that the scheme of charges applicable to water discharge activities will soon be subject to significant change in that it will be migrated to the 'Unified Charging

Framework' which applies to other types of permit. The amounts collected are intended to cover the 'costs of regulation', not the other activites of the Agency.

1 EA 1995, s 41.

Public registers and commercial confidentiality

17.79 The Agency must maintain registers containing prescribed particulars including most applications, notices, appeals and information obtained by the Agency pursuant to its administration of the permit regime. The Agency has a duty to ensure that the contents of its registers are available for inspection by the public free of charge at all reasonable times. It must enable members of the public to obtain copies of entries on the registers on payment of reasonable charges.[1] There are certain exemptions from the requirement to include information in the registers. In particular, the EP Regulations provide for the exclusion of information in the interests of national security, and where information is 'confidential', ie commercial confidential.[2] The Secretary of State has a very wide power to give the Agency directions specifying the information or descriptions of information to be excluded 'in the interests of national security' or to be referred to the Secretary of State for his determination.[3]

1 EP Regulations, reg 46 and Sch 24. The information may also be subject to disclosure under the Environmental Information Regulations 2004; see Ch 4.
2 Regs 47, 48.
3 Reg 47(3).

17.80 The commercial confidentiality provisions are more complex. No information relating to the affairs of an individual or business which is commercially confidential shall be included in the register without the consent of that individual or business.[1] For this exemption to apply, the Agency, or the Secretary of State on appeal, must first determine that the information is 'confidential', that is, that including it in the register would prejudice to an unreasonable degree the commercial interests of the relevant individual or person.[2] This might be on the application of the person furnishing information on an application for a permit or its variation, or otherwise complying with a permit condition or requirement of the Agency, or where the Agency has otherwise obtained information which it considers may be confidential.[3] There is an appeals procedure where the Agency does not consider information to be confidential or where it fails to make a determination in time. In making a determination as to confidentiality, both the Agency and the Secretary of State apply a presumption in favour of inclusion on the register[4] and the Secretary of State also has a discretion to override a determination of confidentiality and direct that information is nevertheless to be included on the register.[5] Where information has been once found to be confidential, it will be presumed to continue to be confidential for four years or such shorter period as is specified in the confidentiality decision; the person to whom the information relates is however entitled to ask for it to continue to be treated as confidential.[6]

1 EP Regulations, reg 48(1).
2 Reg 51.

3 Reg 48(1).
4 Reg 51(2)(b).
5 Reg 56.
6 Reg 55.

Release of other confidential information

17.81 The release of information which is not required to be placed on the register will be inhibited by s 204 of the WRA 1991 which prohibits the disclosure of information with respect to any business which has been obtained by virtue of the provisions of the WRA 1991 and relates to the affairs of any individual or to any particular business, unless the consent of that individual or person carrying on the business has been obtained.[1] The prohibition lasts during the lifetime of the individual concerned or so long as the business continues to be carried on. The prohibition does not apply to the disclosure of information which is made for the purpose of carrying on certain governmental business or for the purposes of criminal or certain civil proceedings or in pursuance of a European Community obligation. Of particular note is that the prohibition does not apply to the disclosure of information made for the purpose of facilitating the carrying out by the Agency of its functions under the WRA 1991, EPA 1990, the Environment Act 1995, the Water Act 2003 or regulations under the Pollution Prevention and Control Act 1999.[2] It is an offence to contravene the prohibition on disclosing information. The penalties on summary conviction are an unlimited fine [3] and on conviction on indictment a term of imprisonment for a maximum of two years, or an unlimited fine or both.[4]

1 See also WIA 1991, s 206.
2 WRA 1991, s 204(2)(a), as amended by EA 1995, Sch 22, para 173, and by the Pollution Prevention and Control Act 1999, s 6, Sch 2, para 8 and Sch 3, and also by the Water Act 2003, s 101(1).
3 LASPO Act 2012, s 85.
4 The provisions of EC Directive 2003/4/EEC on the freedom of access to information on the environment and the Environmental Information Regulations 2004, SI 2004/3391, which implement the directive in the UK provide an exception to the disclosure obligations in the case of commercially confidential information protected by law but that is subject to demonstrating that disclosure would adversely affect the interests of the person who provided the material and whether it is in the public interest to maintain the exception. See further Ch 4 and in particular, paras **4.23–4.24** and **4.28**.

PROTECTION OF CONTROLLED WATERS

Precautions against pollution

17.82 The Secretary of State for the Environment has a general power to make regulations prohibiting a person from having custody or control of any poisonous, noxious or polluting matter unless prescribed steps have been taken to prevent or control the entry of that matter into any controlled waters.[1] These powers have been used in making various specific sets of regulations.[2]

1 WRA 1991, s 92.
2 Control of Pollution (Oil Storage) (England) Regulations 2001, SI 2001/2954, Water Resources (Control of Pollution) (Silage, Slurry and Agricultural Fuel Oil) (England) Regulations 2010, SI 2010/639, Nitrate Pollution Prevention (Amendment) and Water Resources (Control of Pollution) (Silage, Slurry and Agricultural Fuel Oil) (England) (Amendment) Regulations 2013, SI 2013/1001.

Anti-pollution works and operations

17.83 The Agency itself (and previously the NRA) has also long had powers to carry out prescribed works and operations where it appears that any poisonous, noxious or polluting matter or any solid waste matter is likely to enter, or to be or to have been present in, any controlled waters.[1] These are more specific than the regulation-making powers in s 92, in that they permit direct Agency intervention in individual cases, although nothing may be done under this section to impede or prevent the making of a consented discharge.[2] The works and operations which the Agency is entitled to carry out are confined to:

(a) in a case where the matter appears likely to enter controlled waters, works and operations for the purpose of preventing it from doing so; or
(b) in a case where the matter appears to be or to have been present in any controlled waters, works and operations for the purpose–
   (i) of removing or disposing of the matter;
   (ii) of remedying or mitigating any pollution caused by its presence in the waters; or
   (iii) so far as it is reasonably practicable to do so, of restoring the waters, including any flora and fauna dependent on the aquatic environment of the waters, to their state immediately before the matter became present in the waters.[3]

1 WRA 1991, s 161.
2 WRA 1991, s 161ZC(1).
3 Ibid, s 161(2)–(3) .

17.84 This power may only be used where it is necessary to do so 'forthwith' or where no person can be found upon whom to serve a 'works notice'.[1] In either case the Agency also has power to carry out investigations for the purpose of establishing the source of the matter and the identity of the person who has caused or knowingly permitted it to be present in controlled waters or at the place from which it was likely to enter them.[2] Where any works, operations or investigations are carried out by the Agency under s 161, the expenses reasonably incurred in doing so are recoverable from the person who caused or knowingly permitted[3] the matter in question to be present: in any controlled waters; or at the place from which it was likely, in the Agency's opinion, to enter any controlled waters.[4] This would include any person who has taken an interest in land, and has permitted matter to be present on it which in the Agency's opinion is likely to enter controlled waters. Liability in such cases may therefore precede water pollution itself. Unlike statutory nuisance powers there is no mechanism under this section by which those liable to bear the costs of the Agency's works and operations might themselves be compelled to carry them out. However, if a landowner were to take steps voluntarily to remove (or even lessen) the risk of an escape, then the Agency's ability to use its own powers may not arise. If the Agency does use its powers then this does not derogate from its ability to institute any other proceedings.[5]

1 WRA 1991, s 161(5). On works notices, see paras **17.86–17.93**.
2 WRA 1991, s 161(4).
3 For the meaning of this, see paras **17.47–17.66**.
4 WRA 1991, s 161ZC(2). For an illustration of recovery of such costs see *Bruton and the National Rivers Authority v Clarke* (1995) 7 *Environmental Law & Management* 93 in which the costs of post-incident pollution surveys, scientific and technical costs associated with investigations and restocking and rearing of fish were all recovered under similar provisions then contained in s 161.
5 Ibid, sub-s (6).

17.85 These powers to carry out anti-pollution works have also been widened in implementation of the Water Framework Directive.[1] Since December 2009, parallel provisions have existed allowing the doing of works designed to address 'harm' to controlled waters; the definition of harm for these purposes being tied back to the Water Framework Directive and the environmental quality objectives set under it.[2]

1 Directive 2000/60/EC.
2 WRA 1991, s 161ZA.

Works notices

17.86 Partly in consequence of problems associated with the underuse of s 161, new powers were introduced by additions to the WRA 1991 in respect of 'works notices' to enable the Agency to compel the prevention or remediation of water pollution.[1] These provisions came into force on 29 April 1999.[2] The effect of the works notice provisions is to add a power of compulsion to existing preventative and remediation powers: they enable the Agency to *require* works and operations to be carried out. In this sense, they complement other controls intended for the remediation of contaminated land.[3]

1 EA 1995, s 120, Sch 22, para 162, inserting ss 161A–161D into the WRA 1991. A consultation paper on implementation of these new powers was first issued in 1997: Anti-Pollution Works Regulations, DETR consultation Paper, August 1997.
2 Environment Act 1995 (Commencement No 15) Order 1999, SI 1999/1301.
3 See generally Ch 15.

17.87 The interaction between the contaminated land regime and the use by the Agency of works notices is potentially complex. The overlap has been reduced, however, by the alteration of the definition of contaminated land so that only cases of 'significant' actual or threatened pollution of controlled waters will engage the contaminated land regime.[1] This has the effect of disapplying that regime where the water pollution element is in reality minor. The presumption appears to be that, where the contaminated land regime applies, it should be used in preference to the WRA 1991 powers. The brief justification given for this is that Part 2A creates duties, whilst use of works notices is dependent on a power. Given the exceptions to the Part 2A duty, this justification is, at best, unconvincing. However, it is anticipated that works notices 'may be useful' in cases that otherwise would be cases of land contamination, where there is historic pollution of groundwater but Part 2A does not apply, for example, where pollutants are wholly in groundwater or the source of the pollution cannot be identified. The incidence of such cases remains to be seen, in light of experience with Part 2A itself.

1 The Water Act 2003, s 86, amending Environmental Protection Act 1990.

17.88 The Agency's 'entitlement'[1] to serve a works notice arises in exactly the same circumstances as those giving rise to its power to carry out works and operations under s 161 and s 161ZA,[2] namely, where it appears to the Agency that any poisonous, noxious or polluting matter or any solid waste matter is likely to enter, or to be or to have been present in, any controlled waters, or where it appears that harm to controlled waters is occurring or likely to occur.[3] Potential recipients of the notice are the same classes of persons who would be liable to meet the Agency's costs under s 161 or s 161ZA: 'causers' or 'knowing permitters'.[4] The works or operations which may be required by a works notice are, again, exactly those which the Agency would itself otherwise be entitled to carry out under the earlier section.[5]

1 The word used in WRA 1991, s 161A(1).
2 See para **17.83**.
3 WRA 1991, s 161A.
4 Set out in para **17.84**.
5 WRA 1991, s 161A(2)(a) and (b), set out in detail in para **17.83**(a) and (b), and s 161ZA(4).

17.89 A works notice must specify the periods within which the works or operations are required to be done,[1] and shall not normally be served before the intended recipient has been consulted as to its terms.[2] Additional detail is provided in regulations issued by the Secretary of State.[3] These dictate that the works or operations required to be carried out should be specified, along with the Agency's reasons both for serving the notice on that person and for specifying the works or operations in question.[4] In the case of an actual case of pollution, the nature and extent of the pollution must be described; in cases of threatened pollution, the description must be of the nature of the risk and the place from which the matter in question is likely to enter specified controlled waters.

1 Ibid, s 161AA(1).
2 Ibid, sub-s(2). Failure to consult shall not in itself invalidate a notice: s 161AA(4).
3 Under WRA 1991, s 161C: Anti-Pollution Works Regulations 1999, SI 1999/1006.
4 Ibid, reg 2.

17.90 The process of appeals in respect of the issue and enforcement of works notices has now also been determined.[1] There is no provision for the suspension of the effect of a works notice pending an appeal – a position which can be contrasted with that applying to appeals against, for example, statutory nuisance abatement notices, with which the new notices otherwise have many similarities. Strangely, the Regulations do not expressly state the period within which an appeal must be made: this must instead be specified in the notice itself.[2] However, representations on receipt of a notice of appeal must be received by the Secretary of State from parties to the appeal within fourteen days of receiving that notice. Appellants may choose the method of appeal, either by written representations or by a hearing[3] – again, a familiar pattern from other licensing contexts.

1 SI 1999/1006, regs 3–6.
2 SI 1999/1006, reg 2(e). The Consultation Paper proposed a period of 21 days beginning with the date of receipt: *Anti-Pollution Works Regulations*, DETR Consultation Paper, August 1997, para 3(1).
3 SI 1999/1006, regs 4–5.

17.91 Liabilities incurred through service of works notices may extend to other classes of person than those set out in s 161A. The Act expressly provides that a works notice may require a person to carry out works or operations in relation to any land or waters notwithstanding that the recipient is not entitled to carry out those works or operations,[1] for example, where the land or waters in question are not owned by the recipient of the notice. Any person whose consent is required before a works notice can be carried out must normally be consulted before service of the notice, but is nonetheless required to grant, or join in granting, any necessary rights.[2] In such a case, the recipient of the notice is required to pay compensation to the grantor of rights to carry out works on application by the grantor, and in the sum to be prescribed.[3] Enforcement of the duty to grant consent would, if necessary, be through a civil action brought by the recipient of the works notice, not the Agency.

1 WRA 1991, s 161B(1).
2 Ibid, sub-ss (2) and (3). Failure to consult will not in itself invalidate a notice subsequently served: s 161B(4).
3 WRA 1991, s 161B(5).

17.92 Applications for compensation under s 161B of the 1991 Act are to be made in accordance with regulations.[1] Applications are to be made within twelve months of granting rights, or twelve months of the determination or withdrawal of the appeal, or six months of the first exercise of the rights, whichever is the later.[2] The basis for the level of compensation payable is depreciation of the value of an interest in land, together with compensation for any loss of damage, including interest.[3] This is subject to express provisions in respect of valuation where an interest in land is mortgaged (the compensation shall be assessed as if the interest were not mortgaged), and whether or not mortgagees shall be entitled to receive any compensation.[4] The amount of any depreciation in the value of a relevant interest in land will be assessed in accordance with the relevant rules under s 5 of the Land Compensation Act 1961, with disputes over compensation to be determined by the Upper Tribunal (Lands Chamber).[5]

1 Anti-Pollution Works Regulations 1999, SI 1999/1006, reg 7, Sch.
2 Ibid, Sch, para 2.
3 Ibid, Sch, para 4.

4 Ibid, Sch, para 5(2).
5 Ibid, Sch, para 6.

17.93 Failure to comply with a works notice is an offence, punishable on summary conviction by three months' imprisonment or an unlimited fine or both, and on indictment by two years' imprisonment and/or a fine.[1] The Agency, in addition, has default powers to give effect to a notice, the cost of which may be recovered from the original recipient of the notice.[2] There is no power to secure any such charge on premises, although the Agency may seek enforcement of a notice in the High Court where it considers that criminal proceedings would afford an ineffectual remedy.[3]

1 WRA 1991, s 161D(1)–(2).
2 Ibid, s 161D(3).
3 Ibid, s 161D(4).

Water protection zones

17.94 As well as specific powers of direct intervention vested in the Agency, the Secretary of State is also given sweeping powers to designate an area as a water protection zone and restrict the carrying on in that area of specified activities in order to prevent or control the entry of any poisonous, noxious or polluting matter into controlled waters, and/or to regulate activities to reduce the causing of 'harm' in accordance with the Water Framework Directive.[1] However, despite its wide terms this power remains very little used. The only zone designated so far relates to the River Dee catchment area.[2] It effectively tightens control over the use of controlled substances within that zone through the introduction of a localised consent regime backed by criminal sanctions. It was made before the amendment of these provisions in 2009 to allow the use of water protection zones in pursuit of the objectives set out in and under the Water Framework Directive; these amendments have accordingly never been engaged and the proposal by DEFRA to use them to assist in controlling pollution from diffuse (ie agricultural) sources appears to have withered on the vine.

1 WRA 1991, s 93 and Sch 11.
2 Water Protection Zone (River Dee Catchment) Designation Order 1999, SI 1999/915.

Nitrate vulnerable zones

17.95 Previous editions of this work discussed the regime of 'nitrate sensitive areas' established under WRA 1991 and related regulations. This domestic regime has now been swept away, with the framework for dealing with nitrate pollution being firmly set by the Nitrates from Agricultural Sources Directive[1]. This directive is implemented in England by the Nitrate Pollution Prevention Regulations 2008,[2] which establish a network of nitrate vulnerable zones. These are areas draining into and contributing to the pollution of nitrate polluted waters.

17.96 Around 70% of England is covered by nitrate vulnerable zones, which equates to a much higher proportion of farmland once urban and other areas are excluded. The extent of the designation is apparent on interactive online maps maintained by the Agency. There are provisions for review of this designation, however, and even for expansion. In the event that the Secretary of State proposes to extend the designation to a new area, the landowner has a limited right of appeal against the designation.[1]

1 Nitrate Pollution Prevention Regulations 2008, reg 11B.

17.97 The effect where land is included in a nitrate vulnerable zone is to impose a heavy regulatory burden on the farmer. Parts 3 to 8 of the Regulations impose a large number of requirements. There are restrictions on the amount of organic manure which can be spread on a holding as a whole and particular hectares (and a mechanism for seeking derogation from these requirements where the land being farmed is grassland). In addition, there are detailed restrictions on how, when and where nitrogen fertiliser may be spread, and in terms of the plans that must be made and records that must be kept. All of these requirements imposed by the Regulations are backed by criminal sanctions in the form of fines.[1] Non-compliance can also have and effect on subsidy payments.

1 Nitrate Pollution Prevention Regulations 2008, reg 48.

17.98 Some insight into the perceived demands imposed within zones can be gained from the fact that designation of the zones was challenged in the High Court in 1997, questions from which were referred to the European Court of Justice.[1] The challenger was a farmer, concerned that the UK government's approach to implementation of the Directive would place a disproportionate burden on farmers as opposed to other contributors to the nitrates problem. However, that challenge failed.[2] The European Court of Justice adopted a broad interpretation of the purposes of the Directive, and confirmed member states' equally broad implementing discretion.

1 (1997) 268 ENDS Report 47.
2 *R v Secretary of State for the Environment, ex p Standley* (C-293/97) [1999] QB 1279, [1999] Env LR 801.

Groundwater protection

17.99 The protection of underground waters near the surface of land ('groundwaters')[1] was formerly effected largely by indirect or non-statutory means. For example, it may have been a consequence of good practice in regulating the discharge of polluting substances, or of regulating activities carried on on land (such as waste management and disposal). Also, the Agency (and the NRA before it) adopted a broad non-statutory approach to the protection of groundwaters. Non-statutory 'groundwater protection zones' were identified to inform the public as to which areas of the country are most sensitive to polluting activities that may affect groundwater, and also to give an indication of the Agency's likely approach to the exercise of its other powers, or its broad consultation responsibilities. The original purposes of the zones were set out in NRA documents.[2] These have been complemented by Agency policy statements,[3] and electronic resources.[4]

1 For a technical definition for certain statutory purposes see para **17.100**.
2 *Guide to Groundwater Protection Zones in England and Wales*, NRA, 1995; *Guide to Groundwater Vulnerability Mapping in England and Wales*, NRA, 1995.
3 *Groundwater Protection: Policy and Practice*, Environment Agency, 2006 (precursor first published in 1992).
4 Including access to groundwater vulnerability maps.

17.100 These disparate controls were re-focused, however, with the addition of direct legislative measures to protect groundwater. The Groundwater Regulations 1998[1] finally completed the implementation in England, Wales and Scotland of the first Groundwater Directive.[2] These provisions have themselves been superseded by the enactment of a new Groundwater Directive[3] (the first substantive daughter directive of the Water Framework Directive) and the introduction in England of environmental permitting as a comprehensive regime covering various different forms of potentially polluting activity. The purpose of the Directive is to prevent the pollution of 'groundwater' by two classes of substances, 'hazardous' and 'non-hazardous'.[4] Member States are required to take all measures necessary to prevent the introduction into groundwater of hazardous substances, and to limit the introduction into groundwater of non-hazardous substances such that they do not cause significant deterioration in the condition of the groundwater. This distinction is reflected in the EP Regulations by the distinction between hazardous substances, defined as substances which are toxic, persistent and liable to bio-accumulate, and other pollutants.[5]

1 SI 1998/2746.
2 Council Directive 80/68/EEC.
3 Council Directive 2006/118/EC.
4 Ibid, arts 1, 6. There is no definitive list of hazardous substances, and Member States are required to compile their own list. This is done in England by JAGDAG, the Joint Agency Groundwater Directive Advisory Group; in practice all substances formerly known as List 1 substances under the old Groundwater Directive are now be regarded as 'hazardous' substances.
5 See reg 2 and Sch 22, paras 4–5.

17.101 The mechanism of regulation is now similar to that imposed on water discharge activities and discussed in detail above;[1] a permit is required for groundwater activities as it is for water discharge activities. The discussion here is limited to those aspects of the scheme which are specific to groundwater activities. One key difference is that the definition of a groundwater activity is significantly wider than that of a water discharge activity. It includes not only the direct discharge of a pollutant to groundwater but also a discharge that 'might' lead to a direct or indirect input of a pollutant to groundwater.[2] No actual input of pollutants into groundwater is therefore required before an offence is committed; the mere possibility of such an input is enough. The Agency is able, however, to issue *ad hoc* 'determinations' that certain discharges will not be groundwater activities because they are too small, unexpected or difficult to prevent.

1 See paras **17.43–17.93**.
2 EP Regulations, Sch 22, para 3.

17.102 The distinction between hazardous and non-hazardous substances is reflected in the fact that the Agency must use its permitting and other powers to achieve the aims in respect of those substances set out in the directive. That is, it must prevent the input of any hazardous substance and limit the input of non-hazardous pollutants so that they do not cause pollution.[1] The rigour of these objectives is once again moderated by a list of exceptions, whereby pollution can be permitted as long as it does not compromise the objectives of the Water Framework Directive.[2]

1 EP Regulations, Sch 22, para 6.
2 Ibid, para 8.

DISCHARGE OF TRADE EFFLUENT INTO PUBLIC SEWERS

17.103 The rules in the WIA 1991 governing the discharge of trade effluent into sewers are quite separate from those dealing with discharges into controlled waters. There are two regimes governing the discharge of trade effluent into sewers: the first deals with ordinary trade effluent; the second, which is a modified version of the first, deals with 'special category effluent' which contains highly polluting substances. There is a right to make a connection to the public sewers for the purpose of making any lawful discharge of trade effluent.[1]

1 WIA 1991, s 118(3) and (4), applying WIA 1991, s 106 on which see paras **17.138–17.139**.

17.104 It should be noted that under its powers under the WIA 1991, the Government made the Water Industry (Schemes for Adoption of Private Sewers) Regulations 2011,[1] which came into effect on 1 July 2011. These provide for schemes to transfer ownership of private sewers, lateral drains and associated pumping stations into ownership of the regulated sewerage companies in England and Wales. The schemes for England and Wales were made on 1 July 2011. The effect was that on 1 October 2011:

(a) any private sewer (excluding pumping stations and highway drains or sewers) which, immediately before 1 July 2011, communicated with a public sewer; and

(b) any private lateral drain (excluding pumping stations) which, immediately before 1 July 2011, communicated with a public sewer, vested with the relevant sewerage company for the area.

1 SI 2011/1566.

17.105 On 1 October 2016, any pumping station which forms part of such a sewer or lateral drain which has not been transferred before that date will also vest with the relevant sewerage company for the area.

17.106 There are exceptions for the transfer in respect of Crown land (which includes land belonging to a government department). Furthermore, DEFRA's provisional non-statutory guidance on 'Private Sewers Transfer'[1] provides that some large sites with a number of individual properties under common ownership and which have common drainage arrangements by virtue, for example, of the site's freehold management should be regarded as having their own internally managed drainage system which would not be regarded as private sewers for transfer since the site itself comprises a single curtilage. This may include an industrial, business, retail or science park.

1 https://www.gov.uk/government/uploads/system/uploads/attachment_data/file/69356/private-sewers-transfer-guidance110928.pdf, see paras 18–19.

17.107 The undertaker must serve notice of the proposal to transfer the sewers and lateral drains on their owners at least two months before the date of transfer.[1] They must also publish notice of their proposal at least two months before the date of transfer.[2] Any owner of a private sewer, private lateral drain or pumping station or any other person affected by the proposal to adopt a private sewer, private lateral drain or pumping station, or the failure to do so, may appeal to the Water Services Regulation Authority (Ofwat) within two months of service or publication of notice of the adoption, whichever is the later.[3] The grounds of appeal are set out in s 105B(3) of the Water Industry Act 2011.

1 WIA 1991, s 105A.
2 Reg 6.
3 WIA 1991, s 105B(2) and 105B(4).

Applications for ordinary trade effluent consent

17.108 The occupier of any trade premises[1] within the area of a sewerage undertaker may only discharge trade effluent[2] from the premises into a public sewer[3] when it is done with the sewerage undertaker's consent. An application for a consent to discharge trade effluent into a public sewer must be by notice from the owner or occupier of the premises to the sewerage undertaker stating: (a) the nature or composition of the trade effluent; (b) the maximum daily quantity of trade effluent which it is proposed to discharged; and (c) the highest rate at which it is proposed to discharge the trade effluent.[4]

1 'Trade Premises' means any premises used or intended to be used for carrying on a trade or industry, including premises used for agricultural or horticultural purposes or for the purposes of fish farming or for scientific research or experiment: WIA 1991, s 141(1) and (2). Under s 88 of the Water Act 2003, the Secretary of State now has a power to amend this definition, or the definition of 'trade effluent', by order.
2 'Trade effluent' means any liquid, either with or without particles of matter in suspension therein, which is wholly or in part produced in the course of any trade or industry carried on

at trade premises, but does not include domestic sewage: WIA 1991, s 141(1). In *Thames Water Authority v Blue and White Launderettes Ltd* [1980] 1 WLR 700, effluent discharged from washing machines in a launderette was held to be trade effluent even though it is indistinguishable from effluent from domestic washing machines. The definition of trade effluent therefore relates to the purpose of the activity rather than the nature of the discharge.
3 WIA 1991, s 118(1).
4 Ibid, s 119.

Sewerage undertaker's decision

17.109 The sewerage undertaker may refuse consent[1] or give it either unconditionally or subject to such conditions as it thinks fit with respect to:

(a) the sewer or sewers into which any trade effluent may be discharged;

(b) the nature or composition of the trade effluent which may be so discharged;

(c) the maximum quantity of any trade effluent which may be discharged on any one day either generally or into a particular sewer;

(d) the highest rate at which trade effluent may be discharged either generally or into a particular sewer;

(e) the period(s) of the day during which trade effluent may be discharged;

(f) the exclusion from the trade effluent of condensing water;

(g) the elimination or diminution of any specified constituent of the trade effluent before it enters the sewer, where that constituent would, either alone or in combination with any matter with which it is likely to come into contact while passing through any sewers:

    (i) injure or obstruct those sewers, or make specially difficult or expensive the treatment or disposal of the sewage, or

    (ii) (where the trade effluent is to be, or is, discharged into a sewer having an outfall in any harbour or tidal water or into a sewer which connects directly or indirectly with a sewer or sewage disposal works having such an outfall) cause or tend to cause injury or obstruction to the navigation on, or the use of the harbour or tidal water;

(h) the temperature of the trade effluent when it is discharged into the sewer, and its acidity or alkalinity at that time;

(i) the payment by the occupier of the trade premises to the undertaker of charges for the reception of the trade effluent into the sewer, and for the disposal thereof;

(j) the provision and maintenance of an inspection chamber or manhole which will enable a person to take samples of what is passing into the sewer from trade premises;

(k) the provision, testing and maintenance of meters to measure the volume and rate of discharge of any trade effluent being discharged from the trade premises into the sewer;

(l) the provision, testing and maintenance of apparatus for determining the nature and composition of any trade effluent being discharged from the premises into the sewer;

(m) the keeping of records of the volume, rate of discharge, nature and composition of any trade effluent being discharged and in particular of records of readings of meters and other recording apparatus provided in compliance with any other condition attached to the consent; and

(n) the making of returns and giving of other information to the sewerage undertaker concerning the volume, rate of discharge, nature and composition of any trade effluent discharged from the trade premises into the sewer.[2]

1 No express power to refuse consent is given. However, this must be implied since the sewerage undertakers has a power rather than a duty to grant consent. In any case an appeal lies against a refusal to grant consent under s 122.
2 WIA 1991, s 121(1) and (2).

17.110 In deciding whether or not to grant a trade effluent consent and the conditions which should be imposed, a sewerage undertaker will take into account the conditions attached by the Agency to the undertaker's own consent to discharge from the sewerage works into controlled waters.[1] This is to ensure that the trade effluent will not result in the undertaker breaching its own discharge consent.[2]

1 Considered in paras **17.69–17.72**.
2 On offences in relation to controlled waters generally see para **17.44**.

Appeals

17.111 There is a right of appeal to the Director General of Water Services (ie OFWAT) against a refusal or failure to give consent, or against a condition attached to a consent.[1]

1 WIA 1991, s 122.

Review of consents

17.112 After granting consent, the sewerage undertaker may give a direction varying conditions attached to it, or adding or annulling conditions.[1] It must give notice of that direction to the owner or occupier of the trade premises affected, and must state in the notice the date on which it is to take effect (being not less than two months after it is given).[2] Subject to one exception, no direction may be given within two years from the date of the consent itself or a previous direction without the written consent of the owner and occupier.[3] The exception to the rule against giving directions within the two year period arises when the sewerage undertaker considers it necessary to give a direction within that period in order to provide proper protection for persons likely to be affected by discharges which could lawfully be made apart from the direction.[4] Under those circumstances the sewerage undertaker must pay compensation to the owner or occupier of the premises unless it believes that the direction is required as a result of an unforeseeable change of circumstances occurring since the beginning of the two year period. In that case it must give notice of its reasons to the owner and occupier.[5]

1 WIA 1991, s 124(1) and (7).
2 Ibid, s 124(5)–(6).
3 Ibid, s 124(2)–(3).
4 WIA 1991, s 125(1).
5 Ibid, s 125(2)–(3).

17.113 The owner or occupier may appeal against the direction to the Director General within two months of the notice being given to him (or later with the written permission of the Director General).[1] Provided that the appeal is brought before the date on which the direction takes effect, it does not take effect until the appeal is withdrawn or finally disposed of. The appeal may seek payment of compensation.[2] However, insofar as the direction relates to charges payable by the owner or occupier it may take effect on any date after the direction is given.[3] In determining the appeal the Director General may annul the direction or substitute another direction for it, whether more or less favourable to the appellant.[4]

1 WIA 1991, s 126(1).
2 Ibid, s 126(5)–(6).
3 Ibid, s 126(2)–(3).
4 WIA 1991, s 126(4).

Offence

17.114 It is an offence to discharge trade effluent from trade premises into a sewer without consent or in breach of condition. The maximum penalty is an unlimited fine on conviction by the magistrates' court or the Crown Court.[1]

1 WRA 1991, ss 118(5) and 121(5).

Trade effluent agreement

17.115 As an alternative to the consent procedure, a sewerage undertaker may enter into an agreement with the owner or occupier or any trade premises for the reception and disposal of any trade effluent produced on those premises.[1] Such an agreement, whilst a contract between the discharger and the sewerage undertaker, must be made available for inspection by the public.[2]

1 WRA 1991, s 129.
2 Ibid, s 196(1).

TRADE EFFLUENT CONTAINING SPECIAL CATEGORY EFFLUENT

17.116 Further controls apply in the case of discharges into public sewers of trade effluent containing prescribed substances or from prescribed processes. The prescribed substances are substances (the so called 'red list' substances which are the most harmful when entering the aquatic environment) and any other substances which are required to be controlled under the Dangerous Substances Directive.[1] Trade effluent is 'special category effluent' and therefore governed by the additional controls if: (a) prescribed substances are present in the effluent or are present in the effluent in prescribed concentrations; or (b) the effluent derives from a prescribed process or from a process involving the use of prescribed substances or the use of such substances in quantities which exceed the prescribed amounts.[2] These rules are elaborated by regulations.[3] The additional requirements apply to trade effluent in which any of the prescribed substances is present in a concentration greater than the background concentration, and to trade effluent deriving from a prescribed process if either asbestos or chloroform is present in a concentration greater than the background concentration.[4] However, trade effluent is not special category effluent if it is produced in any process which is subject to integrated pollution control under Part I of the EPA 1990.[5] In such cases the Agency will exercise control under that system, although the effluent remains trade effluent and discharges into sewers will therefore still be subject to the sewerage undertaker's consent.

1 Directive 76/464/EEC. These rules also enable the government to comply with the EC directive on asbestos pollution and the 1988 'black list' Directive in the case of discharges to sewers: Directive 87/217/EEC; Directive 88/347/EEC, amending Directive 86/280/EEC.
2 WIA 1991, s 138.
3 Trade Effluents (Prescribed Processes and Substances) Regulations 1989, SI 1989/1156, reg 3, as amended by the Trade Effluents (Prescribed Processes and Substances) (Amendment) Regulations 1990, SI 1990/1629 and the Trade Effluents (Prescribed Processes and Substances) Regulations 1992, SI 1992/339. The Regulations remain in force by virtue of the Water Consolidation (Consequential Provisions) Act 1991.
4 Ibid, reg 4.
5 WIA 1991, s 138(2), to be replaced by integrated pollution prevention and control: Pollution Prevention and Control Act 1999, s 6(2).

Table 17.1: Prescribed substances[1]

Mercury and its compounds

Cadmium and its compounds

Gamma-Hexachlorocyclohexane

DDT

Pentachlorophenol (and its compounds)

Hexachlorobenzene

Hexachlorobutadiene

Aldrin

Dieldrin

Endrin

Carbon Tetrachloride

Polychlorinated Biphenyls

Dichlorvos

1, 2-Dichloroethane

Trichlorobenzene

Atrazine

Simazine

Tributyltin compounds

Triphenyltin compounds

Trifluralin

Fenitrothion

Azinphos-methyl

Malathion

Endosulfan

1 SI 1989/1156, Sch 1.

Table 17.2: Prescribed processes[1]

Any process for the production of chlorinated organic chemicals.

Any process for the manufacture of paper pulp.

Any process for the manufacture of asbestos cement.

Any process for the manufacture of asbestos paper or board.

Any industrial process involving the use in any 12 month period more than 100 kg of the product resulting from the crushing of asbestos ore.

1 SI 1989/1156, Sch 2.

Procedure in case of special category effluent

17.117 Where a trade effluent notice is served on the sewerage undertaker or an agreement under s 129 is planned, in either case in relation to discharges of special category effluent, the sewerage undertaker must refer to the Agency the question whether the proposed discharges should be prohibited and, if not, whether any conditions should be imposed. In the case of a trade effluent notice, the reference to the Agency must be made within two months following the day of service of the notice. However, no reference needs to be made if the sewerage undertaker refuses its consent within that period.[1] It is an offence for an undertaker to fail to make such a reference before giving a consent or entering into an agreement.[2]

1 WIA 1991, ss 120(1)–(3) and 130(1)–(3).
2 WIA 1991, ss 120(9) and 130(7).

Appeals relating to special category effluent consents

17.118 If, on appeal under s 122, it appears to the Director General that the case is one in which a reference must be made to the Agency, he cannot determine the appeal except by upholding a refusal, unless he has himself referred the question to the Agency and obtained a copy of the notice of the Agency's determination.[1]

1 WIA 1991, ss 127(1) and 123.

17.119 The Agency may review (independently of a reference to it) consents and agreements relating to special category effluent to see whether authorised operations should be prohibited, or if not whether conditions should be imposed.[1] Generally, the Agency may not carry out a review within two years of the date of service of the notice of determination of a previous reference or review, unless there has been a contravention of a provision of a consent or agreement.[2] This limitation does not apply if the review is carried out to give effect to a European Community obligation or international agreement, or for the protection of public health or flora and fauna dependent on the aquatic environment.[3] Before determining the questions which are the subject of the reference or review, the Agency must give an opportunity to the sewerage undertaker and the owner or occupier to make representations or objections. It must consider any such representations or objections which are not withdrawn.[4] On determining any question on a reference or review, the Agency must serve notice on the sewerage undertaker and the owner or occupier stating any operations which are to be prohibited or any conditions which are to be imposed, or that it has no objection to the operations being carried out and does not intend to require conditions to be imposed.[5] In addition it may vary or revoke the provisions of a previous notice, consent or agreement.[6]

1 WIA 1991, ss 127(1) and 131(1).
2 Ibid, ss 127(2) and 131(2).
3 Ibid, ss 127(3) and 131(3).
4 WIA 1991, s 132(2).
5 Ibid, s 132(3) and (4).
6 Ibid, s 132(5).

Proposed variations of conditions

17.120 Sewerage undertakers must refer proposals to vary conditions to the Agency if the proposed variation would result in a discharge of effluent containing a concentration of a prescribed substance in excess of the background concentration.[1]

1 Trade Effluents (Prescribed Processes and Substances) Regulations 1989, SI 1989/1156, reg 5.

Compensation

17.121 Compensation is payable to the owner or occupier in respect of any loss or damage resulting from a review by the Agency carried out for the protection of public health or flora and fauna dependent on the aquatic environment within the two year period, unless the review has resulted from a change of circumstances which could not reasonably have been foreseen at the beginning of the two year period, or from a consideration by the Agency of material information which was not reasonably available to it at that time. Compensation is not payable if the review takes place following a breach of a condition of a consent or agreement.[1]

1 WIA 1991, s 134.

Transfer of property

17.122 It would seem that trade effluent consents relate to the point of discharge and are not personal to the discharger. They would therefore run with the land. This view is supported by the fact that the details which must be submitted in support of an application relate to the nature, quality and quantity of the discharge itself rather than to the identity of the discharger,[1] and also that the offence of discharging trade effluent without (or not in compliance with) a trade effluent consent is committed by an occupier of the property concerned.[2] It would seem to follow that there is no need to transfer the consent in the event of a change in ownership or occupation of the property. Whilst there are provisions relating to the transfer of environmental permits,[3] in the absence of equivalent provisions in respect of trade effluent consents, the general approach would still apply. Although there is no requirement to notify a sewerage undertaker of a change in occupation, it may be worth doing in the interests of good relations with the undertaker. Trade effluent agreements, as basically contracts between a discharger and sewerage undertaker, would not be transferable in the same way, and so purchasers of property in relation to which an agreement exists would normally need to ensure either completion of a new agreement or that an application for a consent was made before taking responsibility for an existing discharge.

1 WIA 1991, s 119.
2 Ibid, s 118. See para **17.114**.
3 EP Regulations, reg.21,see para **17.77**.

Trade effluent charges

17.123 A sewerage undertaker may require payment of trade effluent charges which can be either standard charges under a scheme or charges under a trade effluent agreement.[1] Under a charges scheme, a sewerage undertaker may make a charge when a trade effluent notice is served on it, when it grants a consent and when a consented discharge is made.[2] The charge may be a single amount for the whole period of the consent or a periodic (eg annual) charge during that time, or a combination of the two approaches.[3] The provisions under which charging schemes may be made or charges actually levied have been modified to provide the Secretary of State with more intrusive powers to control sewerage undertakers' behaviour.[4] In particular, these new provisions prevent undertakers from reaching agreements with householders for payment of water and sewerage charges in a way different to that set out in charging schemes.[5]

1 WIA 1991, s 143(1) and (5).
2 Ibid, s 143(1)(b).
3 Ibid, s 143(3).
4 WIA 1999, ss 3(1)–(2) and 4; commenced by SI 1999/3440 (C. 97) by 1 April 2000 at the latest.
5 The only limitations so far set relate to certain categories of 'vulnerable' occupiers: Water Industry (Charges) (Vulnerable Groups) Regulations 1999, SI 1999/3441 (as amended).

17.124 The person liable to pay trade effluent charges is the person to whom the trade effluent consent was granted or any person making a discharge pursuant to it as appropriate. Old trade effluent consents may contain conditions imposing trade effluent charges which may remain valid unless they have been varied subsequently.[1] The existence of a charging scheme does not prevent a sewerage undertaker from including terms as to payments in a trade effluent agreement.[2] Charges may be made on a metered or un-metered basis. There is a complex framework within which increases in charges may be provided for, in particular, increases may only be made up to a limit fixed in accordance with Condition B of the sewerage undertaker's Instrument of Appointment, following a periodic review undertaken by Ofwat. The Director General of Water Services is under a duty to ensure that the interests of every customer are protected in fixing charges and to ensure that no undue preference is shown and that there is no undue discrimination in the fixing of charges.[3] That duty is subject to the overriding duty on the Director General to secure that the functions of sewerage undertakers are properly carried out.[4]

1 Water Consolidation (Consequential Provisions) Act 1991, Sch 2, para 1.
2 WIA 1991, s 143(5)(b).
3 Ibid, s 2(3). A duty in the same terms is imposed on sewerage undertakers themselves through Condition E, para 2 of their Instrument of Appointment.
4 WIA 1991, s 2(2A).

Public registers

17.125 It is the duty of every sewerage undertaker to secure that copies of:

(a) every consent given,
(b) every direction by the sewerage undertaker varying consent,
(c) every trade effluent agreement, and
(d) every notice of determination of reference or review by the Secretary of State

are kept available at all reasonable times for inspection by the public free of charge at the office of the undertaker.[1] Sewerage undertakers must also supply copies on request to any person on payment of a reasonable sum. These requirements are more limited in scope than those applying to discharge consents,[2] largely because the undertaker will itself still be subject to the publicity and recording requirements applying to its own consent under the Water Resources Act 1991.

1 WIA 1991, s 196.
2 See para **17.79**.

Disclosure of other confidential information

17.126 It is a criminal offence for any person to disclose information relating to a business which has been obtained by virtue of the WIA 1991 and which relates to the affairs of any individual or to any particular business, during the lifetime of that individual or the continuance of that business, without the consent of the individual or person carrying on the business.[1] The prohibition does not apply if the disclosure is made for the purpose of carrying out functions under water legislation (including those of the Agency) or certain other law enforcement purposes or to fulfil an obligation under EU law.[2] It is also an offence for a person to disclose information furnished to him under the trade effluent provisions of the WIA 1991 unless he has the consent of the person who furnished it or the disclosure is made in connection with the execution of the Act or for the purpose of court proceedings or a report of such proceedings.[3] The latter prohibition does not appear to extend to information obtained by sewerage undertakers from tests carried out by their own officials. That information has not been 'furnished to' them and so is not covered by the prohibition. However, it may be caught by the earlier provision.[4]

1 WIA 1991, s 206(1) and (7).
2 Ibid, s 206(3); EA 1995, Sch 22, para 121; Pollution Prevention and Control Act 1999, s 6.
3 WIA 1991, s 206(2) and (7). This provision would not override any duties of disclosure imposed by the EC Directive on Freedom of Access to Environmental Information Transposed by the Environmental Information Regulation s 2004). See Ch 4.
4 Ie under the WIA 1991, s 206(1).

EC DIRECTIVE ON URBAN WASTE WATER TREATMENT

Principal provisions

17.127 In addition to the general legal frameworks controlling trade effluent discharges and the provision of a sewerage system, the Urban Waste Water Treatment (England and Wales) Regulations 1994[1] provide for the introduction of collection and treatment systems for urban waste water. The Regulations implement the EC Directive on Urban Waste Water Treatment,[2] Article 11 of which requires that discharges of industrial waste water[3] to sewerage or treatment plants must be subject to prior regulation or specific authorisation by the competent authority or appropriate body. This has been transposed into a duty[4] on sewerage undertakers, the Director General of Water Services and the Secretary of State to exercise their functions under Chapter III of Part IV of the WIA 1991[5] to secure that the requirements set out in Sch 4 are met. Further, trade effluent consents and agreements must be issued or reviewed in order to give effect to the requirements of these Regulations.[6] Accordingly, industrial waste water entering collecting systems and urban waste water treatment plants shall be subject to such pre-treatment as is required in order to:

(a) protect the health of staff working collecting systems and treatment plants;
(b) ensure that collecting systems, waste water treatment plants and associated equipment are not damaged;
(c) ensure that the operation of the waste water treatment plant and the treatment of sludge are not impeded;

(d) ensure that discharges from the treatment plants do not adversely affect the environment, or prevent receiving waters from complying with other Community Directives; and to

(e) ensure that sludge can be disposed of safely in an environmentally acceptable manner.

1 SI 1994/2841. For the equivalent Scottish controls see the Urban Waste Water Treatment (Scotland) Regulations 1994, SI 1994/2842.
2 91/271/EEC. On the interrelation of the UWWT Directive and Waste Framework Directive, see C-252/05 R *(Thames Water Utilities Ltd) v Bromley Magistrates' Court, Environment Agency (interested party)* [2007] 1 WLR 1945.
3 That is, any waste water discharged from industrial or trade premises other than domestic waste water and run-off rain water: SI 1994/2841, reg 2(1).
4 Ibid, reg 7.
5 WIA 1991, ss 118–140.
6 SI 1994/2841, reg 7. These correspond to Annex IC of the Directive.

17.128 More specifically, the Regulations provided a detailed rolling programme to ensure the design, construction and maintenance of collecting systems in accordance with the 'best technical knowledge not entailing excessive costs',[1] and also provision of treatment plants which provide secondary treatment (biological treatment with a secondary settlement or other process, which meets specified requirements in terms of reducing effluents' polluting characteristics).[2] Appropriate treatment plants were to be in operation at the latest by 31 December 2000 for all agglomerations[3] of more than 15,000 population equivalent ('pe')[4] and by 31 December 2005 for all discharges from agglomerations of between 10,000 and 15,000 pe, and for discharges to freshwater and estuaries from agglomerations of between 2,000 and 10,000 pe.[5] Failure to meet these requirements would place a sewerage undertaker in breach of its general duty to provide a sewerage system.[6]

1 SI 1994/2841, reg 4, Sch 2.
2 Ibid, reg 6, Sch 3, Table 1.
3 'Agglomeration' means an area where the population and/or economic activities are sufficiently concentrated for urban waste water to be collected and conducted to an urban waste water treatment plant or to a final discharge point: ibid, reg 2(1).
4 'Pe' is a measurement of organic biodegradable load.
5 On the definition of 'estuarial waters' by the UK government, and the ensuing controversy, see *R v Secretary of State for the Environment, ex p Kingston-upon-Hull City Council* [2000] Env LR 248, HC.
6 Under WIA 1991, s 94; SI 1994/2841, reg 4. See para **17.132**.

SENSITIVE AREAS AND HIGH NATURAL DISPERSION AREAS

17.129 More stringent treatment must generally have been applied by the end of 1998 to urban waste water entering collecting systems before discharge into 'sensitive areas' for all discharges from agglomerations of more than 10,000 pe.[1] Discharges to waters in sensitive areas must meet the same criteria as apply to other areas but to have done so by the earlier date of 31 December

1998. Sensitive areas are identified by the Secretary of State in accordance with specified criteria,[2] and include areas where further treatment is necessary to fulfil other Community Directives. Further sensitive areas were designated in 2002. Treatment of urban waste water discharged from agglomerations of between 10,000 and 150,000 pe to coastal waters in high natural dispersion areas and those from agglomerations of between 2,000 and 10,000 pe to estuaries in high natural dispersion areas may be less stringent than the norm prescribed in reg 5 provided that at least primary treatment is given,[3] and the Agency is satisfied that the discharges will not adversely affect the environment.[4] High natural dispersion areas are bodies of water identified by the Secretary of State into which the discharge of waste water would not adversely affect the environment as a result of hydrology, morphology or specific hydraulic conditions.[5] The power to define high natural dispersion areas was provided by way of derogation to the Directive, and the present government has stated its intention not to rely on that derogation.[6]

1 SI 1994/2841, reg 5(2).
2 Ibid, reg 3, Sch 1, Part I.
3 'Primary treatment' means treatment of urban waste water by a physical and/or chemical process involving the settlement of suspended solids, or other processes.
4 SI 1994/2841, reg 5(5)(b).
5 Ibid, reg 5, Sch 1, Part II.
6 *Raising the Quality*, DETR, September 1998, para 51.

Implications of the Directive

17.130 The result of the Directive is the substantial upgrading, and provision of new sewage works, a process which will increase charges payable in respect of trade effluent consents. The impact will obviously be greater where the sewage works discharge into waters in sensitive areas. Conditions of trade effluent consent will have to be varied, where necessary, to ensure compliance with the terms of the directive: the Regulations require that sewerage undertakers shall review consents or authorisations issued at 'regular intervals' with a view to modification, subject to the continuing oversight of the Agency.[1] Solicitors acting for purchasers will therefore need to check proposals to vary the charging scheme, proposals to vary conditions to trade effluent consents and whether the relevant sewage works discharges to sensitive waters, and the impact that is likely to have on the purchaser of the property.

1 SI 1994/2841, regs 7(4) and 11 respectively. On the interrelation of the UWWT Directive and Waste Framework Directive see C- 252/05 R *(Thames Water Utilities Ltd) v Bromley Magistrates' Court, Environment Agency (interested party)*, [2009] Env LR; *Times*, 28 August, 2008.

SEWERS

17.131 The law on sewers needs to be considered from two perspectives: first, from the viewpoint of the developer who needs to ensure that new sewers are constructed and, second, from that of the purchaser of an existing building who needs to ensure that the existing sewerage arrangements are adequate. These aspects will be dealt with in turn. It may help to clarify the terminology used at this stage. A 'drain' means a drain used for the drainage of one building or of any buildings or yards appurtenant to buildings within the same curtilage. 'Sewer' includes all sewers and drains (other than those defined in the previous sentence) which are used for the drainage of buildings and yards appurtenant to buildings.[1] In other words a drain serves a single building or more than one building within the same curtilage, whilst a sewer serves two or more buildings in separate curtilages. If private drains or sewers do, or in the future will, cross land belonging to a third party, it must be ascertained that the necessary private law rights do exist or can be acquired by agreement.[2]

1 WIA 1991, s 219(1).
2 The relevant law is discussed in paras **17.10** et seq.

SEWERS FOR NEW DEVELOPMENTS

Sewerage functions

17.132 Sewerage functions are, in general, carried out by private companies ('sewerage undertakers') which took over those functions from the public water authorities on privatisation in 1989. Local authorities are responsible for the control of drainage from buildings. Every sewerage undertaker is under a duty to provide, improve and extend an adequate system of public sewers and to cleanse and maintain them. It must also make provision for emptying the sewers and for disposing of the contents.[1] Sewerage undertakers are empowered to enter into agency arrangements with local authorities to carry out some or all of their sewerage functions.[2] Such arrangements do not affect any third party's remedy against an undertaker in respect of the carrying out (or failure to carry out) its functions.[3]

1 WIA 1991, s 94(1).
2 Ibid, s 97(1).
3 Ibid, s 97(2).

17.133 The provisions relating to the duty to provide public sewers are generally virtually identical *mutatis mutandis* to the duty on water undertakers to provide water mains.[1] In broad terms, they provide that certain specified persons or bodies (including the owner or occupier of any premises) may require the provision of (or 'requisition') a public sewer from a sewerage undertaker. The duty to comply with a sewer requisition only applies where the public sewer is to be used for domestic sewerage purposes.[2] It seems that there is some confusion amongst sewerage undertakers between their general duty to provide sewerage services[3] and this specific responsibility in respect of requisitioning. The government's view is that undertakers are under an absolute duty to provide new sewers to ensure effectual drainage, rather than one which is conditional on a requisition being made.[4]

1 WIA 1991, ss 98–101. For the provisions relating to the water mains duty see ss 41–44 and paras **17.02–17.06**. However, the sewerage undertaker's period for compliance is six months (s 101(1)) instead of three months (s 44(1)). Note also that the reasonable costs for the purpose of the relevant deficit, are those of the new sewer, pumping stations and a reasonable proportion of the cost of providing additional capacity in the earlier public sewers required in consequence of providing the new public sewer: s 100(4).
2 'Domestic sewerage purposes' in relation to premises means the removal from buildings and land occupied therewith of (a) the contents of lavatories, and/or (b) water which has been used for cooking or washing, and/or surface water: ibid, s 117(1).
3 WIA, s 94(1); para **17.132**.
4 *The Provision of New Drains and Sewers in England and Wales*, DETR, 1 March 2000, paras 4.3–4.4. See also 2010–2015 Government Policy: water and sewerage services, Appendix 4 drainage and sewers, DEFRA updated 8 May 2015.

17.134 Sewerage undertakers fall under a further duty to provide public sewers for domestic sewerage purposes in relation to premises completed before 20 June 1995 which are not currently connected to a public sewer, where the drainage of those premises is giving, or is likely to give, rise to adverse effects to the environment or amenity.[1] This duty was introduced to address some of the particular difficulties of sewerage in rural areas and whilst guidance has been issued on its application,[2] there is some suggestion that the duty is neither fully understood nor applied.[3]

1 WIA 1991, s 101A; inserted by EA 1995, Sch 22, para 103.
2 See eg *First Time Rural Sewage*, Ofwat Information Note 11.
3 *The Provision of New Drains and Sewers in England and Wales*, paras 4.8–4.10.

Adoption of sewers

17.135 A person constructing or proposing to construct a sewer may apply to the sewerage undertaker to enter into an agreement to adopt the sewer. The application must be accompanied by any information which the undertaker reasonably requires.[1] The undertaker may agree that if the sewer is constructed in accordance with the terms of the agreement, it will make a declaration vesting the sewer in itself on completion of the work, on a specified date or on the happening of a future event.[2] Agreements are generally in standard form and provide for the following matters: specified standards; inspection by the undertaker during the construction phase; re-opening of the works in appropriate cases; certificates of practical completion; maintenance periods; declaration and vesting of the sewer; a bond; connection to the public sewerage system; wayleaves and access; building over the sewer; and the payment of supervision fees and legal costs. Sewerage undertakers tend to be unwilling to negotiate the terms. An appeal lies to the Secretary of State if: (a) the application is refused; (b) the undertaker offers to enter into an agreement on terms which are unacceptable to the applicant; or (c) the undertaker fails to refuse or grant the application within two months from when it is made.[3] However, if the applicant fails to provide information required by the undertaker within the two month period, the period for responding is extended until a reasonable time after that information is provided.[4]

1 WIA 1991, s 104(2) and (3).

2 Ibid, s 104(1). The provisions relating to the adoption of sewers apply also to drains, except that, in the latter case, there must be a condition in any agreement that a declaration shall not be made until the drain becomes a sewer: s 104(6).
3 WIA 1991, s 105(2). For the time limits and procedure see s 105(3)–(7).
4 Ibid, s 104(4).

17.136 Any adoption agreement made by an undertaker is enforceable against it by the owner or occupier for the time being of any premises served by the sewer to which the agreement relates.[1] Accordingly, there is no need to assign the benefit of such an agreement. A sewerage undertaker may not make an agreement in relation to a sewer which is wholly or partly in the area of another undertaker, unless that other undertaker consents or the Secretary of State dispenses with the requirement for consent.[2]

1 WIA 1991, s 104(5).
2 Ibid, s 104(7).

17.137 In cases where the developer has failed to apply for an adoption agreement before the adoption of a sewer the following provision may be useful. A sewerage undertaker may adopt a sewer at its own volition or at the request of one or more owners of the sewer by means of a declaration that the sewer is to vest in it from a specified date.[1] The adoption may apply to part only of a sewer.[2] In deciding whether to make a declaration, the undertaker must have regard to all the circumstances and, in particular, to certain specified considerations.[3] The undertaker must give two months' notice to the owner(s) of its intention to adopt a sewer. If an appeal is lodged with the Secretary of State within that period, then no further action may be taken until the appeal has been determined.[4] A sewerage undertaker is not authorised to require any payment in relation to the adoption of a sewer or an agreement to adopt it.[5]

1 WIA 1991, s 102(1) and (2). These provisions apply also to sewage disposal works. The sewer or sewage disposal works must either be in the undertaker's area or serve the whole or part of the area. The power does not apply to sewers or works completed before 1 October 1937: s 102(7).
2 WIA 1991, s 102(3).
3 Ibid, s 102(5).
4 Ibid, s 102(4). See s 105 for the provisions on appeals. Additional requirements apply in the case of sewers which are wholly or partly in, or serve, another undertaker's area: s 103.
5 WIA 1991, s 146(3).

Drainage rights of owners and occupiers

17.138 The owner or occupier of any premises, or the owner of any private sewer which drains premises, shall be entitled to have his drains or sewer communicate with the public sewer of any sewerage undertaker and thereby to discharge foul water and surface water from those premises or that private sewer. [1] However, these drainage rights do not apply in the following cases except pursuant to a trade effluent consent:[2]

(a) discharging directly or indirectly into a public sewer any liquid from a factory (except domestic sewage or surface or storm water) or any liquid from a manufacturing process, or any other liquid or matter the discharge of which into public sewers is prohibited by legislation;

(b) discharging foul water into a surface water sewer, or vice versa (except, in the latter case, with the approval of the undertaker), if separate public sewers are provided for foul and surface water;

(c) having drains or a sewer made to communicate directly with a storm-water overflow sewer.[3]

1 WIA 1991, s 106(1) (as amended by the Water Act 2003).
2 See paras **17.103–17.114** on trade effluent consents.
3 WIA 1991, s 106(2).

17.139 Notice of the proposal to exercise drainage rights (a 's 106 notice') must be given to the sewerage undertaker.[1] The undertaker may serve a counter-notice within 21 days, refusing to permit the communication with the public sewer if it considers that it would be prejudicial to the sewerage system on account of the mode of construction or condition of the drain or sewer.[2] The undertaker may require the drain or sewer in question to be opened up for examination of its type of construction and condition.[3] In the case of communications with public sewers in Greater London which are used for the general reception of sewage from other public sewers and are not substantially used for the reception of sewage from private sewers and drains, the undertaker may refuse to permit the communication on any grounds it thinks fit. No application may be made to the Director General in respect of such refusal.[4]

1 WIA 1991, s 106(3).
2 Ibid, s 106(4).
3 Ibid, s 106(5), disputes as to these duties may be determined by the Water Services Regulation Authority on application to it: sub-s (6).
4 WIA 1991, s 106(8).

17.140 The sewerage undertaker may serve a counter-notice within 14 days of receipt of a s 106 notice (or of any relevant determination by the Authority stating that it intends to make the communication with the public sewer itself.[1] It is an offence for a person to make the communication after receipt of such a counter-notice.[2] The maximum penalty on conviction by a magistrates' court is level 4 on the standard scale. After giving the counter-notice, the undertaker is not obliged to make the communication until it has received payment of any sum required (not exceeding the undertaker's reasonable estimate of the cost of the work) or reasonable security. Any difference between the payment made and the reasonable cost of the work is repayable by, or payable to, the undertaker.[3] Disputes as to costs are referable to the Authority.[4]

1 WIA 1991, s 107(1).
2 Ibid, s 107(2).
3 WIA 1991, s 107(3) and (4).
4 Ibid, s 107(4A).

17.141 If the sewerage undertaker does not serve a counter-notice electing to make the communication itself, the person entitled to do so must, before commencing the work, give reasonable notice to the person directed by the undertaker to superintend the work and must give him all reasonable facilities for doing so.[1] An owner of occupier entitled to make the communication, or to examine, repair or renew a drain or private sewer has the same powers as a sewerage undertaker in respect of laying pipes in streets and carrying out other works for sewerage purposes.[2] However, if it is necessary to lay pipes in land belonging to third parties, the appropriate rights must be acquired by agreement.[3] It is an offence to cause a drain or sewer to communicate with a public sewer in contravention of these provisions or before the expiry of the period during which the undertaker any refuse permission to make a communication with a public sewer. The maximum penalty on conviction by the magistrates' court is a fine not exceeding level 4 on the standard scale. The undertaker also has the power to close any unlawful communication made and recover any expenses reasonably incurred from the offender.[4]

1 WIA 1991, s 108(1).
2 Ibid, s 108(2). The powers are contained in ss 158 and 161(1).
3 The relevant law is considered in relation to pipes for the supply of water. See paras **17.10–17.12**.
4 Ibid, s 109(2).

Construction of drain or sewer

17.142 If a person proposes to construct a drain or sewer which a sewerage undertaker considers is or is likely to be needed to form part of a general sewerage system, the undertaker may require it to be constructed differently from the original proposal.[1] A person aggrieved by such a requirement may appeal to the Authority within 28 days.[2] Subject to that, the undertaker has an action for damages if it suffers loss as a result of a failure to comply.[3] Any additional expenses reasonably incurred in complying with the undertaker's requirement or in repairing or maintenance which is attributable to the requirement until the drain or sewer becomes a public sewer, are repayable by the undertaker.[4] Infrastructure charges are also payable.[5]

1 WIA 1991, s 112(1).
2 Ibid, s 112(2).
3 Ibid, s 112(5).
4 WIA 1991, s 112(6).
5 See paras **17.17–17.22** in relation to infrastructure charges.

Building regulation consent: building over sewers

17.143 Paragraph H4 of Sch 1 to the Building Regulations[1] contains requirements on building over sewers. It applies only to work carried out over a drain, sewer or disposal main which is shown on any map of sewers, or on any site or in such a manner as may result in interference with the use of, or obstruction of the access of any person to, any drain, sewer or disposal main which is shown on any map of sewers.[2] It imposes the requirement that the erection or extension of a building or work involving the underpinning of a building shall be carried out in a way that is not detrimental to the building or building extension or to the continued maintenance of the drain, sewer or disposal main.

1 Building Regulations 2000 as amended.
2 The sewer maps must be kept by the undertaker under WIA 1991, s 199.

Building regulation consent: adequate provision for drainage

17.144 Paragraphs H1 and H3 of Sch 1 to the Building Regulations contains requirements in relation to the adequate provision for drainage. Where plans of a building or of an extension of a building are, in accordance with building regulations, deposited with a local authority, the local authority, or on appeal a magistrates' court, may require a proposed drain to connect with a sewer where the sewer is within 100 feet of the proposed or existing building, (b) it is at a level that makes the connection reasonably practicable, (c) it is a public sewer or one which the person constructing the drain is entitled to use, and (d) he is entitled to construct the drain through intervening land.[1] If the only impediment to requiring a connection is that the distance of the sewer is more than 100 feet, the local authority may still require the connection to be made if they undertake to pay so much of the expenses reasonably incurred as are attributable to the fact that the distance exceeds 100 feet.[2] Disputes with the local authority may be dealt with by a magistrates' court.[3]

1 Building Act 1984 s 21(4) as amended by the Building (Amendment Regulations) 2001 SI 2001/3335.
2 Ibid, s 21(5).
3 Building Act 1984, s 21(3); s 21(6) (the amount of a payment to be made under s 21(5)). In the latter case the matter can be referred to arbitration instead of decided by the magistrates' court.

Requirement for combined drainage

17.145 When the drains of two or more buildings are first laid, a local authority may require the buildings to be drained in combination into the existing sewer by means of a private sewer to be constructed by the building owners in accordance with the direction of the authority.[1] The authority may opt to do the work on behalf of the owners.[2] This power may only be exercised where the authority could require each of the buildings to be drained separately into an existing sewer,[3] but it appears that the buildings may be drained more economically or advantageously in combination.[4] Further, if drainage plans have already been passed, the authority may only exercise this power by agreement with the owners concerned.[5] The local authority must fix the proportions in which the expenses of constructing, maintaining and repairing the private sewer are to be borne by the owners concerned, or if the sewer is more than 100 feet from the site of any of the buildings, the proportions in which the expenses are to be borne by the owners concerned and the local authority. Notice of the decision must be given to each owner forthwith.[6] An appeal against the notice can be made to the magistrates' court within 21 days of service.[7] The grounds of appeal are listed in s 102. The time limit is strict.[8] If there is combined private drainage[9] enquiries need to be made of the vendor regarding obligations and disputes over maintenance.

1 Building Act 1984, s 22.
2 If the sewer is constructed by a local authority, it is not deemed to be a public sewer, even if the expenses are defrayed initially by the local authority: Building Act 1984, s 22(6).
3 Ie, under the Building Act 1984, s 21.
4 Building Act 1984, s 22(1).
5 Ibid, s 22(2).
6 Ibid, s 22(3). The expenses (in the proportions fixed) are recoverable by the local authority or the owners who incur them: s 22(5).
7 Building Act 1984, ss 22(4) and s 103(2).
8 Details of the grounds of appeal are set out in para **17.148**.
9 Prior to 2002, this was the subject of a Local Authority Enquiry.

Existing drains

Unsatisfactory drainage arrangements: local authority action

17.146 Section 59 of the Building Act 1984 imposes a duty on local authorities to take action in the case of unsatisfactory drainage arrangements relating to a building. The duty arises if it appears to the authority that any of the following circumstances exist:

(a) satisfactory provision has not been made, and ought to be made for drainage;
(b) a cesspool, private sewer, drain, soil pipe, rain-water pipe, spout, sink or other necessary appliance provided for the building is insufficient;
(c) a private sewer or drain communicating directly or indirectly with a public sewer is so defective as to admit sub-soil water;
(d) a cesspool or such other work or appliance as aforesaid provided for the building is in such a condition as to be prejudicial to health or a nuisance; or
(e) a cesspool, private sewer or drain formerly used for the drainage of the building, but no longer used for it, is prejudicial to health or a nuisance.

17.147 In any of those cases the authority must serve a notice on the owner of the building requiring him to take the appropriate remedial action.[1] The notice must indicate the nature of the works to be executed and state the time within which they are to be executed.[2] The same restriction applies in relation to the distance of the building from the public sewer as applies in the case of new buildings or extensions.[3]

1 Building Act 1984, s 59(1).
2 Ibid, s 99(1).
3 Ibid, s 59(3). See s 21(4), (5) and (6).

17.148 An appeal against the notice can be made to a magistrates' court within 21 days of service.[1] The notice itself must contain a statement indicating that there is a right of appeal and the time limit.[2] The grounds of appeal are that:

(a) the notice is not justified by the statute (it is *ultra vires*);
(b) there has been some informality, defect or error in, or in connection with, the notice;
(c) the requirements of the notice are unreasonable or unnecessary;
(d) insufficient time has been allowed for compliance;
(e) the notice might lawfully have been served on the occupier instead of the owner or vice versa, and such service would have been equitable;
(f) where the works are for the common benefit of the premises in question and other premises, that the owner or occupier of the other premises to be benefited ought to contribute towards the cost of any works required.[3]

1 Building Act 1984, s 103(2).
2 Ibid, s 103(3).
3 Ibid, s 102.

17.149 Subject to any appeal, if a person required by a notice to carry out works fails to do so within the time specified then the local authority is empowered to carry out the works and recover the reasonable expenses of doing so from that person. Also subject to an appeal, failure to carry out the required works is an offence punishable by a fine not exceeding level 4 on the standard scale on conviction by a magistrates' court, and by a further fine not exceeding £2 for each day on which the default continues after conviction.[1]

1 Building Act 1984, s 99(2).

Local authority powers to repair and unstop drains

17.150 Local authorities also have power, after serving the appropriate notice on the owner or occupier, to repair and/or unstop blockages in drains and to recover their reasonable expenses from the person or persons on whom the notice was served.[1] Where a notice is served on more than one person the costs may be apportioned. In the case of repairs the maximum recoverable cost is £250. These powers are not widely used since they involve the expenditure of funds by local authorities.

1 Public Health Act 1961, s 17, as substituted by the Local Government (Miscellaneous Provisions) Act 1982, s 27.

17.151 The following provisions apply in relation to soil and drainage pipes:

(a) a pipe for conveying rainwater from a roof must not be used to convey soil or drainage from a sanitary convenience;
(b) a soil pipe from a water closet must be properly ventilated; and
(c) a pipe for conveying surface water from premises must not be permitted to act as a ventilating shaft to a drain or sewer conveying foul water.[1]

1 Building Act 1984, s 60. Definitions of 'sanitary convenience' and 'water-closet' are contained in s 126.

17.152 In the event of a contravention of any of these provisions the local authority has power to serve a notice on the owner or occupier of the premises concerned requiring the necessary remedial work to be carried out. The provisions as to works in default, offences and appeals are the same as those relating to unsatisfactory drainage arrangements.[1]

1 Building Act 1984, ss 99, 102 and 103. See paras **17.146–17.149**.

Overflowing and leaking cesspools: local authority powers

17.153 If the contents of any cesspool soak from it or overflow, the local authority may serve a notice on the person by whose act, default or sufferance the soakage or overflow occurred or continued to execute the works or to take steps necessary to prevent it. However, this provision does not apply in the case of effluent from a properly constructed sewage tank, if the effluent by its character and means of conveyance and disposal is not prejudicial to health or a nuisance.[1] An appeal against a notice requiring the execution of works (as opposed to the taking of steps) may be made to the magistrates' court within 21 days.[2] Subject to that, if the person required to execute the works fails to do so within the time specified in the notice, the local authority may carry out the work and recover its reasonable expenses from the person in default.[3] The person in default in any event commits an offence for which the penalty is a fine not exceeding level 4 on the standard scale, together with a further fine not exceeding £2 for each day on which the default continues after conviction.[4] On the other hand, where the notice only requires a person to take steps other than the execution of works, there is no provision permitting an appeal or carrying out works in default. The person in default commits an offence for which the penalty is a fine not exceeding level 1 on the standard scale, together with a further daily fine of £2 if the default continues after conviction.[5]

1 Public Health Act 1936, s 50(1).
2 Ibid, ss 50(2), 290(3) and 300.
3 Ibid, s 290(6). Questions which could have been raised on an appeal cannot be raised in the proceedings for recovery of costs: s 290(7).
4 Public Health Act 1936, s 290(6).
5 Public Health Act 1936, s 50(3). The reasonableness of the local authority's requirements can be challenged in such proceedings.

Power of sewerage undertakers to alter drainage system of premises

17.154 Where premises have a drain or sewer which communicates with a public sewer or a cesspool, but that drainage system although sufficient to drain the premises properly is not adapted to the general sewerage of the area, or is otherwise objectionable in the opinion of the sewerage undertaker, the undertaker may at its own expense close the existing drain or sewer and fill up any cesspool and do any work necessary for that purpose.[1] This power may only be exercised if the undertaker first provides a drain or sewer in a position equally convenient to the owner of the premises which is equally effected for the drainage of the premises and communicates with a public sewer.[2] The sewerage undertaker must give prior notice of its proposal to carry out any such work to the owner of the premises, who may refer the matter to the Authority.[3] The sewerage undertaker has power to examine and test (if necessary by opening up the ground) any private drain or sewer which connects with a public sewer if the undertaker reasonably believes that it is injurious or likely to cause injury to health or a nuisance, or that it is so defective as to admit subsoil water.[4]

1 WIA 1991, s 113(1).
2 Ibid, s 97(1).
3 Ibid, s 113(3)–(5), as amended by the Competition and Service (Utilities) Act 1992, s 35(11).
4 Ibid, s 114.

Use of highway drains as sewers

17.155 A highway authority may agree with a sewerage authority that any drain or sewer vested in the former may be used by the latter for the purpose of draining surface water from premises or streets.[1] In practice sewers which are the subject of such an agreement are treated as public sewers. A Local Authority Enquiry formerly dealt with this point.

1 WIA 1991, s 115(1)(a).

Water supply and sewerage services

17.156 Water and sewerage undertakers have power to fix charges for the services they provide either in accordance with a charges scheme or agreements with the persons to be charged.[1] In practice the power to charge is regulated by the terms of the undertaker's instrument of appointment. Conditions B and C of the model instrument of appointment deal with increases in charges. The formula used to calculate the maximum permissible increase each year is RPI + K. K is an adjustment factor fixed periodically by the Authority to ensure that undertakers are able to finance the implementation of their functions properly whilst considering the need to obtain a reasonable return on capital. Reviews of the K factor are normally carried out at five yearly intervals, but they may be more frequent in the event of unexpected costs such as the need to comply with new EC legislation.

1 WIA 1991, s 142(1) and (2).

17.157 Undertakers have a wide discretion to charge differently in different circumstances,[1] but Condition E of the model instrument of appointment obliges undertakers to show no undue preference or discrimination in respect of any class of customers.[2] Undertakers will not be entitled to fix charges by reference to rateable values after 31 March 2000. For that reason meter charges or possibly standard rates are likely to be used. Details of current charges can be obtained from the appropriate undertaker. Subject to any agreement with the undertaker, charges are payable by the occupier of the premises to which the water or sewerage services are provided.[3] Where the charge relates to volume, the occupier may remain liable for a period after he ceased to be occupier unless he informs the undertaker of his intention to cease occupation at least two working days before that event. If the occupier informs the undertaker late, he remains liable to pay charges for 28 days after so informing the undertaker. If he does not inform the undertaker, the occupier remains liable until the next day on which the meter would normally be read or when a new occupier informs the undertaker that he has commenced occupation.[4]

1 WIA 1991, s 142(4).
2 See the corresponding obligation on the Secretary of State and Authority Services in WIA 1991, s 2(3). This discretion has itself been limited subsequently however: Water Industry Act 1999, s 5; para **17.123**.
3 WIA 1991, s 144(1) but see ibid for limitations applying in certain circumstances.
4 Ibid, s 144(2)–(4).

Sewage undertaker's liability for sewage flooding

17.158 The leading case on the issue of liability of sewage undertakers for the escape of sewage onto householder's property is *Marcic v Thames Water Utilities*.[1] Thames was responsible for the effective drainage of the area in which Marcic's house was situated. It frequently became flooded as a result of the failure of Thames to carry out repair work to its sewers in the vicinity of Marcic's property. The High Court held that although Marcic could not succeed by way of an action either for breach of statutory duty or nuisance, or under the rule in *Rylands v Fletcher*, his rights in terms of Art 8 and/or Art 1 of Protocol 1 to the European Convention of Human Rights had been infringed. Thames appealed against the latter finding. Marcic cross-appealed against the decision that his common law rights had not been infringed. The Court of Appeal held that whereas Marcic had no right of action for breach of statutory duty, the facts of which Marcic complained constituted a nuisance at common law. Thames appealed to the House of Lords. In allowing the appeal, the House of Lords held that the flooding of Marcic's premises did not constitute a nuisance at common law, because to so hold would run counter to the intention of Parliament which was enshrined in the Water Industry Act 1991. Furthermore, it was wrong to treat Thames as an ordinary owner of land in terms of nuisance law. Since sewerage undertakers such as Thames had no control over the volume of water which entered their sewerage systems, it was unlikely that Parliament had intended that every householder whose property was flooded could successfully sue Thames whenever flooding occurred. The House of Lords held that the only remedy, which was available to Marcic was under s 18 of the Water Industry Act 1991, which laid down detailed machinery in the event of an undertaker failing to effectually drain its area. Section 18(8) of the 1991 Act did not preclude a civil action in respect of an act or omission otherwise than by virtue of its being a contravention of a statutory requirement enforceable under s 18. Marcic claimed that the requisite adverse state of affairs of which he complained amounted to a nuisance and, therefore, did not fall within the ambit of circumstances falling under the exception to s 18. The House rejected this argument. It held that the nuisance was exactly a state of affairs, which was covered by the Act. It therefore fell to be dealt with solely by the machinery provided by the Act. According to Lord Hoffmann, the learning on the law of nuisance which was contained in *Sedleigh-Denfield v O Callaghan*,[2] *Goldman v Hargrave*[3] and *Leakey v The National Trust*[4] which the Court of Appeal had held was applicable to escapes from public sewers, was in fact relevant solely in relation to disputes between neighbouring proprietors of land. Lord Hoffmann took the view that such learning was inappropriate when dealing with the capital expenditure of a statutory undertaking, which provided public utilities on a large scale. Furthermore, the issue of the requisite priorities, which should be adopted by Thames Water *vis-à-vis* the provision of new sewers, should not fall to be determined by a judge. That would undermine the intention of the 1991 Act.

The House of Lords held that that claim under the Convention also failed. The claim did not take sufficient account of the statutory scheme under which Thames was operating the sewers which had given rise to the flooding. In determining the issue of liability, a fair balance had to be struck between the interests of the individual and those of the community as a whole. In the instant case the interests of the minority of customers of Thames whose properties were prone to sewer flooding had to be balanced against those of all the customers of Thames whose properties were drained by Thames's sewers and who would be required to meet the cost of building more sewers. The House of Lords held that the scheme[5] under the Water Utilities Act 1991 had struck a reasonable balance between the respective interests. In matters of general policy, on which opinions within a democratic society may reasonably differ widely, the role of the domestic policy maker should be given special weight. A fair balance had to be struck between the interests of the individual and the community as a whole. The scheme, which was set out in the 1991 Act, did so. A complaint against Thames could be pursued with the Director. The scheme was held to be Convention-compliant.

1 [2003] UKHL 66; [2004] 2 AC 42.
2 [1940] AC 880.
3 [1967] 1 AC 645.
4 [1980] 1 All ER 17.
5 Sewage undertakers operate a Customer Guarantee Scheme that provides very modest capped compensation to householders whose property has been flooded by sewage.

Water undertaker's liability for clean water flooding

17.159 Where an escape of clean water from a pipe causes loss or damage, the undertaker may be liable for the loss subject to the exceptions set out at s 209 of the Water Industry Act 1991 and s 208 of the Water Resources Act 1991. Where an escape is due wholly to the fault of the person who sustained the loss, or of any agent or contractor of that person, the undertaker will not be liable.[1] Accordingly, 'loss or damage' is restricted to loss or damage to property.[2] Where the escape of water has caused some physical damage, then prima facie it is only the cost of reinstatement of that physical damage which is recoverable.[3]

The fact that the act which caused damage is done under statutory authority is not a defence. Undertakers will be liable for any acts which are performed negligently.[4] Even if the undertaker is not negligent, it may remain liable for nuisance caused by the exercise of its powers. Where the nuisance is attributable to the undertaker's performance of a duty, as distinct from a power conferred by the statute, the undertaker is only liable if the duty is negligently performed.[5] The common law of nuisance does not impose obligations on a statutory sewerage undertaker inconsistent with the statutory scheme of the Water Industry Act 1991.

1 Section 209(1) of the Water Industry Act 1991 does not have the effect of extending liability beyond liability in negligence.
2 *Anglian Water Services Ltd v Crawshaw Robbins & Co Ltd* [2001] BLR 173.
3 *Skandia Property (UK) v Thames Water Utilities Ltd* [1999] All ER (D) 881.
4 Undertakers are guilty of negligence if they fail to take reasonable precautions in laying or maintaining their pipes, or in detecting or remedying any leaks that may occur. See *Manchester Corporation v Markland* [1936] AC 360 HL.
5 Thus where the damage is attributable to the undertaker's obligation to maintain pressure in its pipes (WIA 1991, ss 65–66) or to the performance of its duty to supply water under WIA 1991, s 55, the undertaker is not liable unless negligent.

Chapter 18

Built environment

INTRODUCTION

18.01 This is not a book on planning law. Neither will planning law necessarily play a central role in all property transactions.[1] Equally, whilst it is possible to characterise planning as 'environmental law', it would be more accurate to describe planning as having an important contribution to make to environmental protection, but having other purposes going far beyond that.

Planning is underpinned by the 'golden thread' of 'sustainable development'. Sustainable development is, broadly, meeting the needs of the present without compromising the ability of future generations to meet their own needs. Current government guidance however explains that sustainable development has economic and social aspects, in addition to the well-understood environmental one.[2]

1 Although the planning position in respect of land being transferred will be of interest, eg, whether any necessary permission exists, or whether any planning limitations apply: see Ch 5.
2 *National Planning Policy Framework*, March 2012. See in particular the Foreword and paragraphs 6–16, 'Achieving sustainable development'. Downloadable at https://www.gov.uk/government/uploads/system/uploads/attachment_data/file/6077/2116950.pdf

18.02 The full implications of planning controls for property transactions are best considered by reference to planning law texts.[1] What this Chapter seeks to do is to provide an overview of those aspects of planning law that are likely to be of concern or interest to developers. It alerts potential purchasers of land to the relevant development plans to which they must look in order to assess future development opportunities or threats. This chapter also seeks to provide a brief overview of how the system is structured, and how and when planning powers may be used to place environment-based or related controls upon development activity, principally through the use of conditions and/or planning obligations.

The specific contribution of planning to certain environmental issues affecting property transactions is considered in other chapters. For example, in respect of waste management,[2] contaminated land[3] and nature conservation.[4] Those accounts include illustrations of the controls which might be imposed in such cases.

1 Eg, accessible introductions such as Moore and Purdue *A Practical Approach to Planning Law* (13th edn, 2014, Bloomsbury Professional).
2 Ch 16.
3 Ch 15.
4 Ch 19.

PLANNING AUTHORITIES

18.03 Since 1 April 1996 the principal environmental regulators have been, in England, the Environment Agency (EA) and, in Scotland, the Scottish Environment Protection Agency (SEPA).[1] The EA also fulfilled the role of principal environmental regulator in Wales until 1 April 2013, when Natural Resources Wales (NRW) took over its functions.[2] The Environment Act 1995 made elaborate provision for the transfer of existing pollution control functions to the EA, including those of the National Rivers Authority (NRA) and previous waste regulation and disposal authorities, along with certain functions of the Secretary of State.[3] What have not been transferred to the EA and NRW are the functions of local authorities in respect of certain other pollution (or related) controls,[4] and planning controls.

The Planning and Compulsory Purchase Act 2004 brought about significant changes to the way in which planning control operates, with yet further changes being introduced by the Planning Act 2008, Localism Act 2011 and the Housing and Planning Act 2016.

Today, there still remains a two-tier system of planning authorities in most shire areas – counties being strategic authorities, and districts tactical authorities – with unitary authorities fulfilling both roles elsewhere (London boroughs, metropolitan districts and county boroughs in Wales).[5] Special arrangements still apply in some areas, in particular, the National Parks and the Norfolk and Suffolk Broads.[6]

Prior to the 2004 Act, county planning authorities were required to prepare and maintain a structure plan for their area. Structure plans were, for a time, replaced by 'Regional Spatial Strategies' with a wider coverage, prepared by Regional Planning Boards. RSSs were abolished by the 2011 Act, following a failed attempt by the Government to do this without primary legislation.[7] As a result, and with the exception of the London Plan, there is now no statutory regional planning policy. This change was intended to give effect to the concept of local planning ('localism').

At the district planning level, district authorities and unitary authorities which were formerly obliged to prepare a local plan or unitary development plan respectively now have a duty to prepare a local development scheme together with local development documents prepared in accordance with that scheme. These documents are considered later in this Chapter.

The 2011 Act introduced a further level of plan-making, known as neighbourhood planning. Neighbourhood planning covers both neighbourhood development orders and neighbourhood development plans. The former effectively grant planning permission for certain forms of development within a neighbourhood area; the latter are documents which sets out policies in relation to the development and use of land in the whole or any part of a particular neighbourhood area.[8] Neighbourhood areas are a statutory concept, being areas designated as such by a local planning authority following a request from a 'relevant body' such as a parish council.[9] As in previous years, the concept of the statutory 'development plan' remains central to planning control in England and Wales. Section 38 of the 2004 Act provides that, for any area in England (other than Greater London), the development plan shall be the Regional Spatial Strategy for the region in which the area is situated (as noted, none are now in force), and the development plan documents, taken as a whole, which have been adopted in relation to that area, and the neighbourhood development plans which have been made in relation to that area. Where regard is to be had to the development plan in any determination made under the Planning Acts (e.g. in deciding whether development should be granted planning permission or whether enforcement action should be taken), the determination *must* be made in accordance with the development plan unless material considerations indicate otherwise (s 38(6)). Much planning litigation concerns the proper scope of this section; in particular what is meant by the phrase 'material considerations'.

1 EA 1995, Pt I.
2 Pursuant to the Natural Resources Body for Wales (Establishment) Order 2013 and the Natural Resources Body for Wales (Functions) Order 2013 as amended by the Environment (Wales) Act 2016.
3 EA 1995, s 2(1)(a).
4 Eg, statutory nuisance: see Ch14 respectively.
5 TCPA 1990, s 1; Local Government (Wales) Act 1994.
6 EA 1995, s 63; TCPA 1990, ss 4A and 5.
7 LA 2011, s 109; *R (Cala Homes (South) Ltd) v Secretary of State for Communities and Local Government* [2010] EWHC 2866 (Admin), approved [2011] EWCA Civ 639.
8 PCPA 2004, ss 38A.
9 TCPA 1990, s 61G.

18.04 Although the trend in recent years has been to seek to concentrate planning policy and decision making at a more 'local' level, there have nonetheless been some planning powers formerly exercised at local level and which remain at, or have been recovered to, regional or national level.

In London and Wales, the Mayor and the National Assembly respectively exercise certain planning functions and responsibilities.[1] The Greater London Authority Act 1999 requires, for example, that the Mayor should prepare and keep under review a 'spatial development strategy' (known as the 'London Plan', referred to above).

The Planning Act 2008 excluded from the ordinary town and country planning regime applications for development falling within the description of nationally significant infrastructure projects (NSIPs). Developments comprising large-scale energy, transport, water and waste projects are amongst those covered by the 2008 Act regime. NSIPs are required to obtain 'development consent', rather than planning permission; development consent is obtained from the Secretary of State rather than the district and/or county planning authorities.[2]

The Housing and Planning Act received the royal assent on 12 May 2016. The 2016 Act contains a range of new powers and provisions.

In short under the Act starter homes are introduced as an affordable housing category on new build developments. Starter homes will be available to

461

first time buyers at a 20% discount off market value, subject to value caps. Provisions are introduced requiring councils to consider the sale of vacant council housing. The Act includes an extension of Right to Buy to housing associations. It introduces a 'rogues gallery' of landlords and letting agents with powers to ban repeat offenders. Agents will be able to keep clients' money in accounts separate to business accounts. Local Authorities are to grant planning permission on serviced plots, sufficient to meet the demand for self-build housing in their area.

'Planning permission in principle' (PPIP) may be granted automatically. Under the 2016 Act Councils are to compile and maintain registers of brownfields land, which may also be 'qualifying documents' for PPIP purposes. There are also enhanced powers for community liaison groups in local plan preparation and examination. The Secretary of State has power to intervene in neighbourhood planning. Starter homes are to be delivered on all 'reasonably sized' sites. Planning permission will be granted for homes in some circumstances under the NSIPs regime.

However, in keeping with the current trend, much of the details as to how these new provisions will actually apply has been left to statutory instruments yet to be drafted or enacted.

1 Town and Country Planning (London Spatial Development Strategy) Regulations 2000, SI 2000/1491, Town and Country Planning (Mayor of London) Order 2008, SI 2008/580; National Assembly for Wales (Transfer of Functions) Order 1999, SI 1999/672.
2 See generally, PA 2008 Part 3. Useful information can also be found on the National Infrastructure Planning website: http://infrastructure.planningportal.gov.uk.

18.05 The divisions of responsibility described have important practical implications. Law and policy – particularly policy – lay down guidance as to the practical division of responsibilities between local planning authorities and the statutory pollution regulators such as the EA.[1] Different bodies will have different priorities. Planning powers give the potential for local authorities to control local environmental impacts of development, particularly where there is ambiguity as to the borderline in some cases between specific pollution control powers, exercisable and enforceable by the environmental regulators, and general planning powers.

In some circumstances it may be quite proper for the local planning authorities to use their planning powers, even where this will to some degree duplicate measures possible under other regimes.[2] Developers who consider that such powers may have been used inappropriately may have to make a judgement as to whether compliance with such conditions would be cheaper or quicker than to challenge them, taking into account the costs of any consequent delay.

1 Para **18.07**.
2 See *W E Black Ltd v Secretary of State for the Environment and Harrow London Borough Council* [1997] JPL 37.

GENERAL POLICY POSITION

18.06 Until March 2012, national policy as to the general relationship between planning and pollution controls was set out in PPS 23, *Planning and Pollution Control.*[1] Paragraph 2 of the guidance summarised its contents as follows:

- Any consideration of the quality of land, air or water and potential impacts arising from development, possibly leading to impacts on health, is capable of being a material planning consideration, insofar as it arises or may arise from or may affect any land use.
- The planning system plays a key role in determining the location of development which may give rise to pollution, either directly or indirectly, and in ensuring that other uses and developments are not, as far as possible, affected by major existing or potential sources of pollution.
- The controls under the planning and pollution control regimes should complement rather than duplicate each other.
- The presence of contamination in land can present risks to human health and the environment, which adversely affect or restrict the beneficial use of the land but development presents an opportunity to deal with those risks successfully.
- Contamination is not restricted to land with previous industrial uses, it can occur on greenfield as well as previously developed land and it can arise from natural sources as well as human activities.
- Where pollution issues are likely to arise, intending developers should hold informal pre-application discussions with the LPA, the relevant pollution control authority and/or the environmental health departments of local authorities (LAs), and other authorities and stakeholder with a legitimate interest.
- Where it will save time and money, consideration should be given to submitting applications for planning permission and pollution control permits in parallel and co-ordinating their consideration by the relevant authorities.

PPS 23 was revoked on 27 March 2012, and replaced by the NPPF. The aim of the NPPF is to streamline national planning policy, and there is therefore considerably less detail about the relationship between planning and pollution controls in that document than in the document it replaced. The key text is now contained in para 122, which sits within Chapter 11, *Conserving and enhancing the natural environment.* Para 122 states that local planning authorities

> '... should focus on whether the development itself is an acceptable use of the land, and the impact of the use, rather than the control of processes or emissions themselves where these are subject to approval under pollution control regimes. Local planning authorities should assume that these regimes will operate effectively. Equally, where a planning decision has been made on a particular development, the planning issues should not be revisited through the permitting regimes operated by pollution control authorities.'

More detailed guidance on the interaction between the planning regime and matters such as air quality, hazardous substances, land affected by contamination, and waste, can however now be found in the Government's online National Planning Practice Guidance.[2]

Notwithstanding that PPS 23 has formally been cancelled, it is considered that the summary given in its para 2, as set out above, remains an accurate reflection of how the planning and other regimes relate to one another.

1 2005.
2 See http://planningguidance.planningportal.gov.uk.

DEVELOPMENT PLANS

18.07 Some reference has already been made in this Chapter to the central importance of the development plan in planning. The role of the development plan is to indicate the relative weight given by a LPA to different (often competing) planning considerations. As noted above,[1] all planning determinations must be made in accordance with the development plan unless material considerations indicate otherwise.[2] This inherent preference in favour of development consistent with the plan is now further reinforced by the policy contained in the NPPF, para 14 of which states that development proposals that accord with the development plan should be approved 'without delay'. It should however be noted that para 14 also provides that, where the development plan is absent, silent, or relevant policies are out-of-date, then permission ought to be granted, save in cases where either any adverse impacts of doing so would 'significantly and demonstrably outweigh the benefits, when assessed against the policies in the [NPPF] taken as a whole; or where specific policies in the [NPPF] indicate development should be restricted'.

Whether or not any given proposal is actually in accordance with the development plan is a question which ordinarily requires a value judgement to be made, and is thus a mixed question of fact and law.[3] It has been recognised by the courts that development plans may pull in different directions; thus it may be possible for development to conflict with the plan in certain respects, and yet still be 'in accordance' overall.[4]

1 Para **18.04**.
2 Section 38(6) of the Planning and Compulsory Purchase Act 2004, previously TCPA 1990, ss 54A and 70(2).
3 *City of Edinburgh Council v Secretary of State for Scotland* [1997] 1 WLR 1447, 1449 per Lord Clyde. This case was, in fact, dealing with s 18A of the Town and Country Planning (Scotland) Act 1972, which materially accords with the English provisions.
4 *R v Leomister District Council, ex p Pothecary* [1998] JPL 335, CA, overturning the decision of the High Court reported at [1997] JPL 835.

18.08 The development plan in any given area will comprise any pre-existing adopted development plan documents which continue in force (for example, unitary development plans prepared pursuant to 1991 legislation, or core strategies prepared pursuant to 2004 legislation), any Local Plan prepared and adopted pursuant to statute,[1] and any neighbourhood development plans which have been made in relation to that area.[2] As above, in London the development plan will also include the regional policies contained in the London Plan, but for the remainder of the country no regional spatial policies continue in force.[3] Local Plans should however be made having regard to regional considerations, by virtue of the existence of a duty upon LPAs and others to cooperate with one another in the preparation of their planning policy.[4]

The range of policies to be included in the development plan is very wide, in terms both of their substance and origin.

1 PCPA 2004; the Town and Country Planning (Local Planning) (England) Regulations 2012.
2 PCPA 2004, s 36(3).
3 Regional Spatial Strategies having been abolished by the Localism Act 2011.
4 PCPA 2004, s 33A.

18.09 Development plan documents form part of a wider class of documents known as 'local development documents', which also include 'supplementary planning documents'. Only the former form part of the statutory development plan, but the latter may be an important material consideration. Of the development plan documents, the most important for developers, where one has been produced,[1] is the Local Plan referred to above. The Local Plan should contain statements of: (i) the development and use of land which the local planning authority wish to encourage during any specified period; (ii) the allocation of sites for a particular type of development or use; and (iii) development management and site allocation policies, which are intended to guide the determination of applications for planning permission.[2]

Documents which were formerly required to form part of the development plan, namely those which set out any environmental, social, design and economic objectives which are relevant to the attainment of the development and use of land mentioned in the Local Plan, are now badged as supplementary planning documents (SPDs) instead. There is no longer any provision for documents known as 'area action plans'.

It can readily be seen that, even at the local level, local planning authorities are bound to be concerned about the impact of development on the wider community in social and environmental terms.

The NPPF offers considerable further guidance on the content of local plans. A full treatment of all relevant policies is beyond the scope of this work, but key points include: (i) plans should be prepared with the objective of contributing to the achievement of sustainable development; (ii) local planning authorities should seek opportunities to achieve each of the economic, social and environmental dimensions of sustainable development and net gains across all three; (iii) Local Plans should address the spatial implications of economic, social and environmental change; (iv) Local Plans should set out the opportunities for development and clear policies on what will or will not be permitted and where. Only policies that provide a clear indication of how a decision maker should react to a development proposal should be included in the plan.; and (v) Local Plans should set out the strategic priorities for the area.[3]

Local planning authorities must maintain an adopted policies map which expresses in geographical terms the adopted development plan policies. The text prevails in the case of any conflict between the text of the policies and the map.[4]

1 Many local planning authorities are behind schedule for the preparation of their up-to-date Local Plans, with the result that the development plan may only comprise development plan documents prepared under earlier legislation.
2 Section 17(7)(za) of the 2004 Act provides that regulations may prescribe which descriptions of documents are, or if prepared are, to be prepared as local development documents. The power to prescribe was exercised in the Town and Country Planning (Local Planning) (England) Regulations 2012 (the 2012 Regulations). Regs 4 and 5 contain the relevant provisions.
3 See generally NPPF paras 150–157.
4 2012 Regulations, reg 9.

18.10 The NPPF makes clear that local plans can prevent harmful development and mitigate the impact of potentially polluting developments. Its policies require that plans should contribute to conserving and enhancing the natural environment, minimising and reducing pollution. They should also prevent new and existing development from contributing to or being put at unacceptable risk from, or being adversely affected by unacceptable levels of soil, air, water or noise pollution or land instability. Allocations of land should be of land with the least environmental or amenity value, where consistent with the other policies in the NPPF.[1]

It is however to be noted that, where a site is affected by contamination or land stability issues, national policy is that responsibility for securing a safe development rests with the developer and/or landowner.[2]

1 See, for example, NPPF, paras 17, 109 and 110.
2 Ibid, para 120.

18.11 In preparing local development documents, other factors which LPAs must have regard include:

- policies developed by a local transport authority in accordance with s 108 of the Transport Act 2000;
- the objectives of preventing major accidents and limiting the consequences of such accidents by pursuing those objectives through the controls described in Article 12 of Council Directive 96/82/EC;[1]
- the need:
  (i) in the long term, to maintain appropriate distances between establishments and residential areas, buildings and areas of public use, major transport routes as far as possible, recreational areas and areas of particular natural sensitivity or interest, and
  (ii) in the case of existing establishments, for additional technical measures in accordance with Article 5 of Council Directive 96/82/EC; and
- the national waste management plan (which has the same meaning as in the Waste (England and Wales) Regulations 2011).[2]

1 On the control of major accident hazards involving dangerous substances.
2 2012 Regulations, reg 10.

18.12 In addition to the above considerations, certain other environment-related factors will arise in plans as a matter of course, including statutory and non-statutory designations to restrict development. Designation of a conservation area, for example, has particular legal consequences.[1] Non-statutory designations may include Green Belts, in which 'inappropriate' development will generally only be permitted in exceptional cases,[2] or a LPAs own local conservation designations.[3] Archaeological interests will also feature, and in fact are playing a far larger part in planning conditions (for example) than in years past.[4]

1 Generally see the Planning (Listed Buildings and Conservation Areas) Act 1990, ss 69–72 and see *R (Forge Field) v Sevenoaks District Council* [2014] EWHC 1895 (Admin).
2 NPPF, Ch 9.
3 NPPF, para 113.
4 NPPF, Ch 12.

DEVELOPMENT CONTROL

18.13 The exercise of development control powers therefore takes place within the broad framework which has just been described.

There remains an emphasis in planning guidance on close and early liaison between planning authorities and pollution regulators.[1] It is expressly provided in the NPPF, for example, that, wherever possible, parallel processing of other consents should be encouraged to help speed up the process and resolve any issues as early as possible. It is further stated that the participation of other consenting bodies in pre-application discussions should enable early consideration of all the fundamental issues relating to whether a particular development will be acceptable in principle, even where other consents relating to how a development is built or operated are needed at a later stage.[2]

1 As under the previous planning policy contained in PPS 23, paras 14 and 22.
2 NPPF, para 191.

18.14 Where such consultation does take place, LPAs are not permitted simply to substitute the consultee regulators' judgements for their own judgment. Not only would this be contrary to general principles of administrative law, but it is clearly the case that the views of pollution control authorities on the suitability of planning controls are not definitive.[1] In practice, of course, planning authorities do rely heavily on the judgement of environmental regulators, with whom considerable expertise lies – not only in deciding whether or not planning permission should be granted, but also in determining technical questions such as details of the conditions to which any permission might be subject. These might include steps to be taken to avoid pollution, such as protective works around oil or chemical storage facilities, or controls over dust or noise emissions, which continue for the duration of the construction process and/or the development itself.

1 See, for example, *R (Davies) v Stafford Borough Council* [2012] EWHC 971 (Admin).

18.15 Since the coming into force of s 93 of the Local Government Act 2003, developers can be charged for the cost to the LPA of pre-application consultation, reversing the position which existed previously.[1]

1 *R v Richmond-upon-Thames London Borough Council, ex p McCarthy & Stone (Developments) Ltd* [1992] JPL 467, HL.

Planning conditions

18.16 Local planning authorities may make planning permission subject to 'such conditions as they think fit' to regulate the development or use of any land under the control of the applicant, whether or not it is included in the application, where it appears expedient for the purposes of or in connection with the development permitted.[1] Although broadly stated, this power is not unlimited. The limitations are well known and, simply stated, are that conditions must:

(a) be necessary;
(b) be relevant to planning;
(c) fairly and reasonably relate to the development permitted;[2, 3]
(d) not be unreasonable in the *Wednesbury* sense;[4] and
(e) be precise and enforceable in all other respects.[5]

1 TCPA 1990, ss 70 and 72.
2 *Newbury District Council v Secretary of State for the Environment* [1981] AC 578. Amongst other things conditions often require sustainable drainage systems. Construction work which has drainage implications also requires prior approval of a drainage system by the approving body, which is the county council or unitary authority: Flood and Water Management Act 2010, Sch 3, para 7.
3 *Pyx Granite Co Ltd v Minister of Housing and Local Government* [1958] 1 QB 554, reversed on other grounds by the House of Lords: [1960] AC 260.
4 *Associated Provincial Picture Houses v Wednesbury Corpn* [1948] 1 KB 223.
5 On conditions generally see NPPF, paras 203 and 206.

18.17 Despite the breadth of this power, and as noted above,[1] it is not the function of planning to impose detailed limitations on site operations which are properly the function of pollution controls. *Gateshead Metropolitan Borough Council v Secretary of State for the Environment*[2] provides an example of what can be a difficult relationship.[3] That case concerned an application for permission to construct and operate an incinerator for the disposal of clinical waste. Applying a plan policy that such development should be permitted only if it would have 'acceptable consequences in terms of environmental impact', the LPA refused permission. On appeal, permission was granted – a decision upheld by both the High Court[4] and the Court of Appeal.

1 Para **18.07**.
2 [1994] 1 PLR 85; [1995] JPL 432, CA.
3 See Purdue, 'The relationship between development control and specialist pollution controls: which is the tail and which the dog?' [1999] JPL 585.
4 Reported at [1993] 3 PLR 100; (1994) 6 Journal of Environmental Law 93.

18.18 The Court of Appeal concluded (amongst other things not directly relevant here) that the LPA's concern that grant of planning permission would make the issue of the necessary environmental licence a *fait accompli*, was misguided. It was therefore not appropriate to refuse permission on the basis of matters which were clearly within the competence and jurisdiction of the pollution regulator. The decision at first instance elaborates on this. In particular, whilst it is clear that pollution is a relevant planning consideration, so too is the existence of 'a stringent regime' for preventing or mitigating the impact of pollution.[1] It was therefore not proper for the LPA to substitute its judgement for that of the pollution regulator.[2]

1 Per Jeremy Sullivan QC sitting as a deputy judge (as he then was); (1994) 6 Journal of Environmental Law 93, at 99.
2 See also *Derwentside District Council v Wheeler* [1994] PAD 403.

18.19 The local planning authority in the *Gateshead* case had refused permission on the basis of considerations held by the Court of Appeal to be properly within the responsibility of the Environment Agency. Their political motivation, it seems, had been to impose tighter local controls than they anticipated the Agency itself might apply. The converse situation was considered in *R v Bolton Metropolitan Council, ex p Kirkman*.[1] A local resident challenged by way of judicial review the decision of a local planning authority to grant planning permission for the installation of new flue gas cleaning equipment and a waste energy recovery system to an existing incinerator. One of the grounds on which the challenge was based was the contention that the planning authority had failed to address certain questions about what the applicant argued were potentially hazardous air emissions. Upholding the dismissal of the application, the Court of Appeal confirmed *Gateshead* to the extent that air emissions were found to be capable of being a material planning consideration, but so too was the existence of specialist pollution controls. The practical significance of the decision is enhanced, however, by the courts' further observations as to the extent of a local planning authority's discretion in applying pollution controls in the context of those other pollution-specific powers. In particular, the court concluded that 'while the dual system of controls permit the [local planning authority] to exercise greater control and conduct a greater degree of investigation than this LPA saw fit to do, it does not render it legally obligatory'. This approach was confirmed in *R v Leicestershire County Council, ex p Blackfordby*.[2]

A further, recent application of the decision in *Gateshead* is *R (An Taisce (National Trust For Ireland)) v Secretary of State for Energy and Climate Change*,[3] concerning the new Hinkley Point C nuclear power station. Patterson J held that it was acceptable for the Secretary of State, when considering whether or not to grant development consent for the project, 'not only to be cognisant of [the] existence' of the Office for Nuclear Regulation, but to 'leave matters [relating to the safety of the proposed power station] over for determination' by that body. The Secretary of State was entitled to conclude, solely because of the existence of a stringent future regulatory regime, that he had sufficient information to conclude that there would be no likely significant effect on the environment requiring the carrying out of a transboundary consultation with the Republic of Ireland.

1 [1998] JPL 787; [1998] Env LR 719, CA.
2 [2002] Env LR 2. See further *Hopkins Developments Ltd v Secretary of State* [2006] EWHC 2823 [2007] Env LR 14.
3 [2013] EWHC 4161 (Admin).

18.20 The above guiding statements do not cast much helpful light on the legal dividing line between planning and pollution controls. Instead, the practical consequence would seem to focus attention firmly on the need for liaison between planning authorities and pollution regulators. Best practice may be to focus on the purposes of the respective systems: the specificity of the objectives of pollution controls relative to the breadth of the land use orientation of planning also suggests priority to pollution controls, where they exist.[1] Yet this in itself confirms the view expressed in another case that environmental legislation is a 'different raft' from planning, with different considerations to be taken into account and having different consequences.[2] It therefore remains the case that planning permission can be refused if there is a likelihood of unacceptable harm being caused.[3] Where harm which is not unacceptable would (probably) arise, then the limits of acceptability will be determined by a combination of planning conditions and pollution controls (where they exist), with policy effectively dictating that specialist regulators can trump local planning authorities. The possibility of conflict may be lessened where – as the NPPF suggests[4] – planning and other licence applications are considered 'in parallel'. This will clearly not always be possible, but it does soundly place the onus on applicants to consult specialist regulators, and at an early stage. From the point of view of a third party, securing early access to information may thereby become crucial, although perhaps problematic.

1 Compare, eg, PPS 23, para 8 with EPA 1990, ss 3 and 7(2).
2 Per Turner LJ in *R v Kennet District Council, ex p Somerfield Property Company Ltd* [1999] JPL 361.
3 Per Glidewell LJ in *Gateshead*, considered by Purdue [1999] JPL 585, at 587.
4 NPPF, para 191.

18.21 In considering the proper extent of, and relationship between, planning and pollution controls, regard should be had to the purposes or objectives of the different regimes.[1] Related to this is that, often, the nature of the decisions being made may also differ: pollution controls are scientifically and technically driven, and whilst the significance of value judgements in the interpretation of apparently objective scientific 'facts' should not be understated,[2] planning is more obviously about making policy and value choices.[3] It is no surprise, therefore, that planning decisions may quite properly take account of a far wider range of non-scientific, even unscientific, factors, than generally feature in pollution licensing systems. Most obvious in this regard are public perceptions of environmental risk: perceptions that can be distinguished from scientifically demonstrable environmental risks. Such perceptions of risks may have the effect of blighting areas of land and therefore it is widely accepted that they may be material planning considerations.[4]

1 Para **18.12**.
2 Although it often is: *Setting Environmental Standards,* Twenty-first Report of the Royal Commission on Environmental Pollution, Cm 4053, 1998.
3 Exemplified in the decision in *R (May) v Rother DC* [2014] EWHC 456 (Admin) and affirmed by the Court of Appeal [2015] EWCA 610.
4 A view accepted by the parties, and apparently tacitly by the Court of Appeal, in *Newport County Borough Council v Secretary of State for Wales* [1998] JPL 377. See also *R v Broadland District Council, ex p Dore* [1998] PLCR 119 and *West Midlands Probation Committee v Secretary of State for the Environment* [1998] JPL 388, CA.

18.22 The *Newport* case concerned honestly-held, albeit not objectively justifiable, concern as to risks to public health and safety from a proposed chemical waste treatment plant. Although the court in *Newport* merely acquiesced in the parties' agreement as to the materiality of the honestly-held perception of risk, it appears clear from *Trevett v Secretary of State for Transport*[1] that it was correctly decided on that basis. The general rule would therefore still seem to apply: that the weight to be given to such concern is for the decision-maker, subject to review on the usual grounds. It is likely, however, that scientifically-informed views, including those of expert technical bodies, will continue to be given greater weight than those based on no technical knowledge or expertise at all. For example, it was held, in the wake of the *Newport* decision, that '… the inspector erred in [*Newport*] in treating the fears of the public as being of no relevance at all to the planning decision, as a matter of law. That does not mean that it would necessarily be reasonable for an authority to refuse a permission on the basis of unsubstantiated fears or, if they do so, that they are immune from the risk of an award of costs against them'.[2] The Court of Appeal confirmed the substantive decision in that case on the basis that, although objectively unjustifiable fears can be a legitimate factor for a local planning authority to take into account, and the weight to be given to them is a matter for the authority, it had not been shown that the authority had in fact failed to take those fears into account.[3]

1 [2002] EWHC 2996 Purdue, commenting on *Newport*, [1998] JPL 377, at 387, and referring, inter alia, to *Envircor Waste Holdings Ltd v Secretary of State for the Environment* [1996] JPL 489 and *Gateshead Metropolitan Borough Council v Secretary of State for the Environment* [1995] JPL 432, per Glidewell LJ.
2 Per Carnwath J (as he then was) in *R v Tandridge District Council and One-2-One Personal Communications Ltd, ex p Al Fayed* [1999] JPL 825, at 830.
3 [2000] JPL 604.

18.23 Nuisances, including statutory nuisances, will be of particular concern to local authorities. Although in principle the control of nuisance operates under a distinct statutory regime,[1] it should be noted that (i) the grant of planning permission of any type may change the character of the locality and therefore raise or lower the standard for statutory nuisance in that area;[2] (ii) nuisance regulation is stronger at a planning level however planning permission does not remove private law rights in common law nuisance which can be used for the protection of amenity;[3] and (iii) since a defence of best practicable means is available in the case of statutory nuisance, a local authority may not be able to abate its effects, which are therefore properly considered a matter for planning.[4] Notwithstanding that, in theory, the two regimes should be seen as complementary rather than duplicatory, in practice conditions are frequently imposed requiring applicants to take steps as agreed with the LPA to keep environmental nuisance within such limits as are compatible with the continued enjoyment of adjacent landowners. In some cases it may be that such conditions are imposed to ensure a higher standard of amenity than would be secured by the statutory nuisance regime,[5] but there are almost certainly other cases in which such conditions are imposed notwithstanding that they would appear to be unnecessary.[6]

1 EPA 1990, Part III, see ch 3.
2 Under common law nuisance the fact that the activity which was said to give rise to the nuisance had the benefit of a planning permission would normally be of no assistance to the defendant. *Coventry v Lawrence* [2014] UKSC 13, per Lord Neuberger at [90].

3 *Coventry v Lawrence* [2014] UKSC 13, per Lord Neuberger at [94].
4 These points were formerly made in Annex 1 to PPS 23, para 1.8. The points of principle hold good notwithstanding the cancellation of that advice.
5 An approach which was endorsed in Annex 1 to PPS 23, see 1.47–1.48.
6 Para **18.18**.

Planning obligations

18.24 Obligations are an important supplement to conditions in checking environmental harm. Any person interested in land in the area of an LPA may, by agreement or otherwise, enter into a planning obligation restricting the development or use of land, requiring specified operations or activities to be carried out, requiring the land to be used in any specified way, or requiring a sum or sums to be paid to the LPA.[1] The obligations created under s 106 of the TCPA 1990 run with the land to which they relate.[2] Obligations shall be a local land charge,[3] although general powers to discharge or modify restrictive covenants do not apply to planning obligations.[4]

1 TCPA 1990, s 106; PCA 1991, s 12.
2 TCPA 1990, s 106(3).
3 TCPA 1990, s 106(11).
4 Under the Law of Property Act 1925, s 84: TCPA 1990, s 106A(10). On obligations generally see NPPF, paras 203–205.

18.25 Policy and the courts have long required that planning obligations be:
(a) relevant to planning;
(b) necessary to make the proposed development acceptable in planning terms;
(c) directly related to the proposed development;
(d) fairly and reasonably related in scale and kind to the proposed development;[1] and
(e) reasonable in all other respects.[2]

However, since the coming into force of regulation 122 of the Community Infrastructure Levy Regulations 2010 ('CIL Regulations'), satisfaction of the tests listed at (b)–(d) above have had the force of statute, at least if the obligations are to be relied upon as a reason for granting planning permission. Consequently, to ensure compliance with these tests, LPAs requesting obligations have in recent years been expected to provide detailed justification for each measure sought. Developers may themselves wish to request such justification before committing to any particular course of action or payment.[3]

An Inspector, or a court, will be vigilant to ensure that a planning obligation is not simply being used as a mechanism which allows planning permission to be 'bought'. The tests at (c) and (d) above are a particularly important check in this regard.

It is also noteworthy that a planning obligation can provide for the transfer of an interest in land. If a planning obligation so provides, it will therefore be subject to the provisions of the Law of Property (Miscellaneous Provisions) Act 1989.[4] For example, if a purported transfer is to be effective, both parties to that transfer must be parties to the obligation (as required by s 2 of the 1989 Act).

1 *Tesco Stores Ltd v Secretary of State for the Environment* [1995] 2 All ER 636, HL.
2 *R v Plymouth City Council, ex p Plymouth and South Devon Co-operative Society* [1993] JPL 1099, CA.
3 See the online National Planning Practice Guidance, paragraph: 004, Reference ID: 23b-004-20150326.
4 *Jelson Ltd v Derby City Council* [2000] JPL 203 (Chancery Division).

18.26 It can be seen, therefore, that a number of the tests as to the validity of planning conditions[1] apply to obligations, although for the different purpose of determining an obligation's materiality to a planning determination. Reg 123 of the CIL Regulations has the effect of restricting the use of pooled contributions. If there are agreements in place for more than five s 106 contributions after April 2010 for a project or type of infrastructure, from April 2015 or the date CIL is adopted if earlier, a Local Planning Authority will not be able to collect any contributions for that purpose.

1 Para **18.16**.

18.27 Obligations may clearly involve binding obligations of a sort not possible to effect through conditions: not least in that they may provide for the payment of money to an LPA.[1] Others might include obligations to:

(a) offset (through substitution, replacement or regeneration) the loss of or impact on a resource present on a site or nearby, for example, loss of habitats; or
(b) protect or reduce harm to protected sites or species, acknowledged to be of importance. This might include developers creating nature reserves, planting trees, establishing wildlife ponds or providing other nature conservation benefits.

1 TCPA 1990, s 106(1)(d).

Environmental impact assessment

18.28 Part of the property developer's broader concern will be the possibility that, in addition to normal planning procedures, he will be required to undertake an environmental impact assessment (EIA). Originally introduced as a response to European initiatives by regulations in the UK in 1988,[1] the environmental impact assessment process was then substantially modified in 1999[2] with further modifications in 2011. The Town and Country Planning (Environmental Impact Assessment) Regulations 2011 (hereafter, the EIA Regulations) currently apply.

1 Town and Country Planning (Assessment of Environmental Effects) Regulations 1988, SI 1988/1199, as amended and supplemented, implementing Council Directive 85/337/EEC on the assessment of the effect of certain public and private projects on the environment (hereafter, the EIA Directive).
2 By the Town and Country Planning (Environmental Impact Assessment) (England and Wales) Regulations 1999, SI 1999/293. These took on board changes made by European Directive 97/11/EEC.

18.29 The EIA process is intended to provide a full and systematic account of a development's likely effects on the environment – including those subject to pollution controls – and the measures intended to avoid, reduce or remedy significant adverse effects. This involves the compilation of expert quantitative and qualitative analyses of a project's environmental effects, and the presentation of the results in a way which enables them to be properly assessed by planning decision-makers.[1] The results of the scientific and technical assessment, presented in the form of an 'environmental statement' are material to the determination of planning decisions, and are to be compiled in accordance with the procedure set out in the EIA Regulations.[2] This involves public consultation and publicity in addition to that applying under normal planning procedures.[3] EIA is therefore properly considered to be a process rather than just the scientific and technical assessment required for the preparation of the environmental statement itself.

1 DETR Circular 2/99, *Environmental Impact Assessment*, 12 March 1999.
2 EIA Regulations, Part IV.
3 Ibid, Part 5 and regs 37, 39 and 40.

The continuing significance of the EIA Directive

18.30 EIA is not required in the case of all applications for planning permission, but only in specified classes of cases.[1] The source of this obligation is the EIA Directive, which requires EIA in respect of 'development consents' of specified types.[2] The European origins were initially the source of some difficulty in the UK, where the requirement to undertake an EIA was superimposed on an already complex planning system. In the earliest cases on the application of the 1988 Regulations, for example, the courts demonstrated a marked reluctance to overturn planning decisions that were formally subject to an obligation to conduct an EIA where there has been approximate substantive, but not formal, compliance with the Directive[3]. However, in a much more robust decision, the House of Lords then concluded that failure to consider whether a major development required EIA was not overcome by proof of 'substantial compliance' with the Directive.[4]

1 Para **18.36**.
2 Directive 85/337/EEC, now consolidated with amendments by Directive 2011/92/EU, art 1.2.
3 Eg, *Twyford Parish Council v Secretary of State for the Environment and the Secretary of State for Transport* (1992) 4 Journal of Environmental Law 273, HC.
4 *Berkeley v Secretary of State for the Environment and Fulham Football Club* [2001] 2 AC 603; [2000] 3 WLR 420.

18.31 The House of Lords took an equally strong view towards the direct effect of the Directive, despite the absence of a categorical statement of the European Court of Justice (now known as the CJEU) to the effect that the Directive is indeed directly effective.[1] In *R v North Yorkshire County Council, ex p Brown*[2] the House concluded that the Directive did require an EIA to be conducted in respect of the registration of, and determination of (potentially) revised conditions on, an old mining consent under unusual statutory provisions intended to modernise minerals consents.[3] Despite the fact that those registration powers had been introduced after the 1988 implementing regulations, their Lordships interpreted the 'wide scope and broad purpose' of the Directive as imposing an obligation to conduct an EIA where that was necessary to ensure that planning decisions affecting the environment were made in the basis of full information.[4] Although Lord Hoffmann did not himself expressly describe this obligation as being directly effective, it was subsequently described as such in *R v Durham County Council and Sherburn Stone Co Ltd, ex p Huddleston*[5] where the Court of Appeal held that a failure to require an EIA may in principle be challenged by another individual by way of judicial review, despite the fact that this in effect gives the directive obligation horizontal direct effect. The approach of the Court of Appeal in *Huddleston* was endorsed both as to horizontal direct effect and the implication of direct effect for individual rights by the ECJ in *R (Delena Wells) v Secretary of State for Transport, Local Government and the Regions*.[6]

1 The Advocate General was more direct in this point than the court itself in *Aannamaersbedrijf PK Kraaijveld & others v Gedeputeerde Staten van Zuid-Holland* (Case C-72/95) [1997] Env LR 265.
2 [1999] 1 All ER 969.
3 Under the Planning and Compensation Act 1991, s 22, Sch 2.
4 Per Lord Hoffmann, giving the only speech, at 974j.
5 [2000] 1 WLR 1484.
6 [2004] 1 CMLR 31.

18.32 While the statutory provisions in issue in *Brown* were unusual,[1] it is submitted that the principles set out in that case may have broader application.[2] For example, if there is a delay between determination of a planning permission and consideration of any other necessary environmental licence, then it may be arguable that the latter process becomes a 'new and free-standing examination of the issues' such as to make it susceptible to EIA, rather than merely detailed regulation after environmental concerns have been considered in granting the principal consent. Local planning authorities should certainly be very careful to ensure that they have full information of the potential impacts of applications for outline planning permission, where there will certainly be a time lag between any outline application and approval of reserved matters.[3] There is now, however, authority to the effect that approval of reserved matters will not amount to a 'development consent' within the meaning of the Directive, and so an 'updated' EIA *may* not be necessary; the EIA can still accompany the application for outline permission, *provided that* the level of information provided at the outline stage is sufficient for the environmental effects of the development properly to be assessed at the reserved matters stage[4] It appears also that, at least in the context of the pollution control regimes, the requirements of EIA may be satisfied by providing the necessary information (through the necessary process), albeit under the guise of a permit application, rather than in an 'environmental statement' labelled as such.[5]

Those involved in purchasing property should be particularly astute to assess whether the requisite planning permission has been obtained. The courts have made clear that the grant of retrospective consent for unauthorised EIA development carried out without prior compliance with the requirement of the EIA Directive is only permissible exceptionally.[6] The consequence may therefore be that the development has to be removed before a lawful application for planning permission can be made.

1 Although not unique, as Lord Hoffmann suggested they may be (at 974c): see, for example, Environment Act 1995, Schs 13 and 14.

2 See also Purdue, commenting on *Brown* at [1999] JPL 616.

3 *R v Rochdale Metropolitan Borough Council, ex p Tew* [2000] EnvLR 1.

4 The specific question of the need for EIA at the reserved matters stage in planning, was referred to the ECJ by the House of Lords in *R v Bromley LBC ex p Barker* ([2002] Env LR 631 (CA)), which reached the ECJ at the same time as two sets of infraction proceedings (*Commission v UK*, Case C-508/03) which raised the same issues. The ECJ judgments are reported at [2006] 1 QB 764. The House of Lords' judgment which then followed the reference is reported at [2006] 3 WLR 1209. See in particular the speech of Lord Hope at paras [22]–[29].

5 *R (Blewett) v Derbyshire County Council* [2004] Env LR 29 at para 41, per Sullivan J. In *R (Edwards & Pallikaropoulos) v Environment Agency* [2008] UKHL 22 at para 61, Lord Hoffmann considered there to have been 'substantial compliance' with the EIA Directive in that the information provided under Sch 4 to the Pollution Prevention and Control (England and Wales) Regulations 2000 SI 2000/1973 (which included a non-technical summary) sufficed for EIA purposes. He distinguished the situation from that in *Berkeley v Secretary of State for the Environment* [2001] 2 AC 603 in which the alleged 'environmental statement' had to be pieced together from a number of documents emanating from different sources. Lord Carnwath revisited the exercise of the court's discretion in *R (Champion) v North Norfolk DC* [2015] 1 WLR 3710 (there the specific context was compliance with the EIA and Habitats Directives and their transposing regulations) where he also considered the decision of the CJEU in *Gemeinde Altrip v Land Rheinland-Pfalz (Vertreter des Bundesinteresses beim Bundesverwaltungsgericht intervening)* Case C-72/12 [2014] PTSR 311 which he found consistent with the Supreme Court's own dicta in *Walton v Scottish Ministers*. He held at [58] that those authorities left it: open to the court to take the view, by relying 'on the evidence provided by the developer or the competent authorities and, more generally, on the case file documents submitted to that court' that the contested decision 'would not have been different without the procedural defect invoked by that applicant'.

6 *R (Ardagh Glass Ltd) v Cheshire West and Chester Council* [2010] EWCA Civ 172.

The EIA Regulations

18.33 The essential substance of the EIA process is as follows. Applications for planning permission for the largest and/or potentially most significant developments must be accompanied by an environmental statement (Sch 1 development),[1] while certain other categories of project will only be subject to the EIA process if the particular proposal is likely to have significant effects by virtue of factors such as its nature, size or location (Sch 2 development).[2] The discretion as to whether to require an assessment in such cases falls to the relevant planning authority.[3] If this discretion is to be delegated to officers, then that delegation must be done formally.[4]

1 EIA Regulations, reg 2(1), Sch 1.

2 Ibid, Sch 2; *R v Swale Borough Council and Medway Port Authority, ex p Royal Society for the Protection of Birds* [1991] JPL 39.

3 *R v Poole Borough Council, ex p Beebee* [1991] JPL 643.

4 *R v St Edmundsbury Borough Council, ex p Walton* [1999] JPL 805, HC.

18.34 The EIA Regulations set out a procedure by which the need for an EIA is determined. First, the terminology of 'screening' and 'scoping' (which previously was frequently used by environmental consultants) is formally embedded in EIA. There is a 'screening' procedure for determining whether development is indeed EIA development.[1] All proposals for Schedule 2 development must be subject to a 'screening opinion' of the local planning authority or a 'screening direction' of the Secretary of State. In order properly to 'screen' the proposal, the authority must ensure that it has sufficient information available to it to form a judgment as to the development's likely effects; however the authority need not require the degree of information which would later form part of the EIA itself.[2] Where something purporting to be an environmental statement is submitted, then that conclusively renders the project EIA development for the purposes of considering the planning permission. Both opinions (issued by a local planning authority) and directions (given by the Secretary of State) are required to include a written statement giving 'clearly and precisely the full reasons' for the conclusion.[3] The Court of Appeal held in *R v Secretary of State for the Environment, Transport and the Regions, ex p Marson*,[4] however, that no duty to give reasons arose if the Secretary of State refused to give a direction.

'Scoping' is a further procedure which requires the relevant planning authority, on a request from a person minded to make an application for planning permission for EIA development, to state in writing its opinion as to the information to be provided in the environmental statement.[5] The Secretary of State is given a complementary power to make a 'scoping direction'. Consultation with both the applicant and statutory consultees is required, and an opinion must be adopted within five weeks of the request, unless a longer period is agreed in writing with the person making the request.[6] Importantly, the opinion (or direction) does not preclude the local planning authority or Secretary of State from subsequently requiring further information to be provided with any statement submitted.[7]

1 EIA Regulations, Part 2.
2 *R (Jones) v Mansfield District Council* [2003] EWHC (Admin) (HC); [2004] Env LR 21 (CA). See further the helpful summary of Elias J. in *R (Hereford Waste Watchers) v Hereford CC* [2005] Env LR 29 at para 34.
3 Reg 4(7).
4 [1998] 3 PLR 90; [1998] JPL 869.
5 EIA Regulations, Part IV.
6 EIA Regulations, reg 13(4).
7 Ibid, reg 13(6).

18.35 The formalisation of consultation is also an important feature of the scoping procedure, which is designed to assist applicants in the preparation of any environmental statement. Applicants who intend to submit an environmental statement may give notice of that fact in writing to that authority or the Secretary of State. The relevant planning authority or Secretary of State is thereafter obliged to notify the consultation bodies in writing of the name and address of the person who intends to submit an environmental statement and of the duty imposed on them to make information available to that person which is considered relevant to the preparation of the environmental statement. Whilst such bodies were formerly given a power to charge for doing so, the current EIA Regulations do not make any such provision. Particular consultees may, of course, continue to have a power to charge under general empowering provisions contained within their guiding legislation.[1]

1 For example, Natural England has power to charge for certain services pursuant to Natural Environment and Rural Communities Act 2006, s 11.

18.36 One further aspect of the EIA Regulations of which developers should be aware is the criteria to be applied in deciding whether an EIA is required. In deciding whether a project is Sch 2 development, and then whether an EIA is required, complex conditions apply. First, development will only be Sch 2 development if it falls within the familiar categories set out in the Schedule and it is either in a 'sensitive area',[1] or the development meets or exceeds certain thresholds or criteria set out in the Schedule itself.[2] Having applied this definition, it should be clear whether or not development is, in fact, Sch 2 development. But before that development is required to be subject to EIA it must also be established that it is likely[3] to have significant environmental effects.[4] Schedule 3 provides guidance on making this decision, which must be taken into account by the relevant planning authority,[5] while Schedule 4 sets out the information to be required in the statement itself. Schedule 3 includes (where relevant) the:

(a) characteristics of the development, for example, its size, any 'cumulation' with other development, the use of natural resources, and any consequential pollution and nuisances;

(b) location of the development, that is, its environmental sensitivity having regard to factors including the existing use of land, the relative abundance, quality and regenerative capacity of natural resources in the area, and the absorption capacity of the natural environment; and

(c) characteristics of the potential impact, in relation to the other criteria, including the extent, magnitude and complexity, probability, and duration, frequency and reversibility of the impact.

Even in the short space which this book dedicates to EIA, a sense of its complexity can readily be appreciated.

1 Essentially, defined statutory and extra-statutory designations: regulation 2(1).
2 This obligation arises not from a clear statement, but – confusingly – from the definition of Schedule 2 development in regulation 2(1).
3 'Likely' not meaning 'unlikely', see *R (An Taisce (National Trust For Ireland)) v Secretary of State for Energy and Climate Change* [2013] EWHC 4161 (Admin).
4 Para **18.38**.
5 EIA Regulations, reg 4(5).

Strategic environmental assessment

18.37 Just as EC Directive 85/337/EEC led to the introduction of the EIA Regs (above), EC Directive 2001/42, *The Assessment of the Effects of Certain Plans and Programmes on the Environment* (hereafter, the SEA Directive), was implemented in England by the Environmental Assessment of Plans and Programmes Regulations 2004 (SI 2004/1633) (hereafter, the SEA Regulations).The requirement for strategic environmental assessment applies, inter alia, to plans or programmes prepared for agriculture, forestry, fisheries, energy, industry, transport, waste management, water management, telecommunications, tourism, town and country planning or land use, which set the framework for future development consents of certain projects listed in Annex I or II to EC Directive 85/337/EC (see above), and to any plan or programmes which has been determined to require an assessment pursuant to Articles 6 or 7 of Directive 92/43/EC on the conservation of natural habitats and of wild flora and fauna.[1] The requirements for SEA are likely to be of less direct interest to developers promoting particular proposals than EIA, but may be of interest where challenges to other development are being considered.

1 Reg 5(1)–(3) of the SEA Regulations and Article 3.2 of the SEA Directive.

18.38 The SEA Regulations require the responsible authority to determine whether or not a plan, programme or modification is likely to have significant environmental effects.[1] In so doing, the authority must take into account certain criteria specified in Schedule 1 to the Regulations, and the views of 'consultation bodies'. An example of a criterion is the characteristics of the plan or programme, having regard to the relevance of the plan or programme for the integration of environmental considerations in particular with a view to promoting sustainable development. Another is the characteristics of the effects and of the area likely to be affected, having regard to the probability, duration, frequency and reversibility of the effects or the transboundary nature of the effects. Under reg 10, the Secretary of State has power to require a responsible authority to provide him with relevant documents, and to direct that any particular plan or programme has significant environmental effects.

1 Reg 9.

18.39 Part 3 of the SEA Regulations deals with the meaning of 'environmental assessment'. It explains that, where such an assessment is required, the responsible authority must prepare an environmental report. The report must identify, describe and evaluate the likely significant effects on the environment of implementing the plan or programme, and reasonable alternatives taking into account the objectives and the geographical scope of the plan or programmes.[1] Schedule 2 to the Regulations contains the information required to be included in the report. This includes a non-technical summary of the information provided under the previous paragraphs (one of which requires an assessment of the likely significant effects on the environment of the plan or programme).

Reg 13 also provides that every draft plan or programme for which an environmental report is prepared (together with its accompanying environmental report) shall be made available for consultation. The consultation bodies are defined in reg 4 as Historic England (previously English Heritage), Natural England (previously English Nature) and the Environment Agency. The functions of the now-defunct Countryside Agency now lie with Natural England. By virtue of reg 8, a plan or programme for which an assessment is necessary may not be adopted or submitted for adoption until completion of that process.

1 Reg 12(2).

18.40 Since the last edition of this work, there has been some litigation in England on the effect of SEA. One key issue to have emerged has been whether or not certain planning policy documents or planning instruments (such as development briefs, masterplans, etc.) require SEA, where the adoption of such documents provided for, but not made compulsory by, national legislation. Lindblom J (as he then was), following the approach of the CJEU in *Inter-Environnement Bruxelles ASBL v Region de Bruxelles-Capitale*,[1] held that a Supplementary Planning Document prepared in respect of the redevelopment of Earls Court did require SEA, on the particular facts of that case, notwithstanding that the preparation of such documents is not mandatory.[2]

The decision in *Inter-Environment Bruxelles* was however the subject of subsequent criticism by the Supreme Court, with Lord Neuberger PSC stating in *R (Buckinghamshire CC) v Secretary of State for Transport* that he considered the legislation to be have been given a meaning which the European legislature clearly did not intend, and that, had the opportunity arisen in that case, he would have referred the matter back to Europe for reconsideration.[3] It remains to be seen whether the present wide scope of the requirement for SEA will be addressed in further litigation, but given the Supreme Court's strong indications, the matter seems ripe for challenge.

Reference is also made to the consideration of the Directive, as purportedly transposed by the Northern Ireland Regulations, in the Northern Ireland High Court in *Seaport Investment Limited*.[4] In that case, Weatherup J held that, as in the case of EIA, a court will not examine the fine detail of the contents of an environmental report but will ensure, nevertheless, that there has been 'substantial compliance' with the information required by Sch 2.[5] Also of interest is the judge's holding that the draft plan, and the environmental report, had to be developed at the same time, or at a time sufficiently close to each other that the content of the latter could properly inform the content of the former.[6] It also remains to be seen whether these principles will be applied in England in the same way.

1 Case C-567/10. The CJEU held that plans and programmes whose adoption is regulated by national legislative or regulatory provisions, which determine the competent authorities for adopting them and the procedure for preparing them, must be regarded as 'required' within the meaning, and for the application, of the SEA Directive notwithstanding that their adoption is not compulsory.
2 [2013] EWHC 2834. It is however submitted that the finding was a fact sensitive one. Lindblom J relied on the fact that in several places in their core strategies the planning authorities had announced their intention to prepare a supplementary planning document. All of [the relevant] passages in the core strategies made clear what the local planning authorities were going to do to provide detailed guidance supplementing the policies and provisions of the development plan, and thus finish the framework of policy and guidance within which proposals for development in the Opportunity Area would be considered. Lindblom J considered that it followed that the framework of policy and guidance did require the SPD if that framework was to be complete, and that that was enough to amount to a requirement in an administrative provision within the ambit of Article 2(a) of the SEA directive.
3 [2014] 1 WLR 324 at [187]–[189]. The UK Supreme Court gave judgment in *R (HS2 Action Alliance Ltd) v Secretary of State for Transport* [2014] UKSC 3 held that 'High Speed Rail: Investing in Britain's Future – Decisions and Next Steps' (Cm 8247, 10 January 2012) was not a 'plan or programme' covered by the SEA directive. The Supreme Court refused to refer the matter to the CJEU but the matter has been taken before the Aarhus compliance committee by campaigners. As of May 2016 a decision was awaited.

4 [2007] NIQB 62, [2008] Env LR 23. The Department appealed the High Court's findings to the Court of Appeal, which referred the following questions to the European Court of Justice:

'1. On the proper construction of Directive 2001/42/EC ("the Directive") where a state authority which prepares a plan falling within Article 3 is itself the authority charged with overall environmental responsibility in the member state, is it open to the member state to refuse to designate under Article 6.3 any authority to be consulted for the purposes of Articles 5 and 6?

2. On the proper construction of the Directive, where the authority preparing a plan falling within Article 3 is itself the authority charged with overall environmental responsibility in the member slate, is the member state required to ensure that there is a consultation body which will be designated that is separate from that authority?

3. On the proper construction of the Directive, may the requirement in Article 6(2) to the effect that the authorities referred to in Article 6 (3) and the public referred to in 6 (4) be given an early and effective opportunity to express their opinion "within appropriate timeframes", be transposed by rules which provide that the authority responsible for preparing the plan shall authorise the time limit in each case within which opinions shall be expressed, or must the rules transposing the Directive themselves lay down a time limit, or different time limits for different circumstances, within which such opinion's shall be expressed?'

The reference was heard by the CJEU in 2011 (reported at [2012] Env LR 21). In respect of the first and second questions the CJEU concluded that, in circumstances such as those in the main proceedings, art.6(3) of the SEA Directive does not require that another authority to be consulted as provided for in that provision be created or designated, provided that, within the authority usually responsible for undertaking consultation on environmental matters and designated as such, a functional separation is organised so that an administrative entity internal to it has real autonomy, meaning, in particular, that it is provided with administrative and human resources of its own and is thus in a position to fulfil the tasks entrusted to authorities to be consulted as provided for in art.6(3) and, in particular, to give an objective opinion on the plan or programme envisaged by the authority to which it is attached, thus disagreeing with the view taken by the trial judge.

In respect of the third question, the CJEU held that art.6(2) of Directive 2001/42 must be interpreted as not requiring that the national legislation transposing the directive lay down precisely the periods within which the authorities designated and the public affected or likely to be affected for the purposes of art.6(3) and (4) should be able to express their opinions on a particular draft plan or programme and on the environmental report upon it. Consequently, art.6(2) does not preclude such periods from being laid down on a case-by-case basis by the authority which prepares the plan or programme. However, in that situation, art.6(2) requires that, for the purposes of consultation of those authorities and the public on a given draft plan or programme, the period actually laid down be sufficient to allow them an effective opportunity to express their opinions in good time on that draft plan or programme and on the environmental report upon it.

On the original decision, see also Gregory Jones 'Strategic Environmental Assessment: the *Seaport* Case' (2008) 20 ELM 282.

5 [2008] Env LR 23], para 26.

6 Ibid paras 47–49.

Chapter 19

Nature conservation

INTRODUCTION

19.01 Nature conservation law is unlike most other forms of environmental regulation. It seeks to protect interests which may be further removed from public health or amenity interests than other areas of environmental law (such as pollution control or the remediation of contaminated land). Further, rather than being concerned with defining what *is* permitted in terms of environmentally harmful behaviour (as in the case of, for example, pollution authorisations and planning consents, where a general statutory prohibition on pollution or development is coupled with a licensing system), conservation law and conservation authorities are frequently concerned with defining what is *not* permitted by reference to individual areas of land or particular conservation interests. This has a number of consequences.

First, conservation law lacks the statutory cohesion of other areas of environmental law. It is drawn from a variety of statutory sources, dealing with a variety of interests: from protection of individual species, through site designation, to general controls on development affecting conservation interests. This makes the area rather confusing, a situation exacerbated by EC and international measures superimposed on the existing UK statutory framework.[1]

1 See eg Habitats Directive 92/43/EEC; Conservation of Habitats and Species Regulations 2010, SI 2010/490. On the latter, see paras **19.42–19.57**.

19.02 Secondly, the different regulatory philosophy that has arisen in the context of conservation law as opposed to other areas of environmental law may seem very abstract but it has important practical implications. The potential conflict between any absolute protection of conservation interests and property interests is well-recognised, and makes this area prone to a type of legal response that promotes negotiation and agreement between public bodies and private individuals or companies, and which places less emphasis on the sort of criminal sanctions more common in pollution control. The implications of conservation for property values are recognised too, and the law may make provision for the payment of money under the terms of management agreements or in the form of grant aid. The identity of the parties to that negotiation is therefore crucial, along with the approach they adopt. The policy of statutory regulators in general and conservation agencies in particular[1] therefore has a central role in determining the effect of conservation law in practice.

19.03 Thirdly, the likelihood of conservation law affecting those with an interest in land is initially more a question of where a person's land is than what that person seeks to do with it (although, of course, this is not invariably the case). This is clear from the different forms of site designation which may be made: National Parks, Areas of Outstanding Natural Beauty, Sites of Special Scientific Interest, Special Areas of Conservation, Special Protection Areas, Ramsar Sites or simply the known habitat or migratory routes of species with legal protection. In these cases, only once the relevant conservation interest has been identified will statutory controls come into play. This is unlike pollution controls where legal prohibitions will apply universally, without any initial designation or identification of environmental interests, and so the practical effects of conservation law will be very different to the effects of pollution control law. Nonetheless the law does not generally provide compensation for the loss of value of land designated for nature conservation or landscape protection.[1]

1 For a recent case where Natural England's application of an undisclosed policy on licences to kill common buzzards was held by the High Court to be unlawful because it was arbitrary see *R (McMorn) v Natural England* [2015] EWHC 3297 (Admin).

19.04 Fourthly, the implications of conservation law for property are as great for subsequent purchasers as for present owners.[1] Conservation interests are tied to the land in question, and will affect the asset value of sites. Designations made and agreements entered into may confine purchasers' freedom of action, as well as providing for additional civil and criminal liabilities when conservation interests are interfered with. For example, designation of a site of special scientific interest carries with it certain presumptions as to notification of subsequent purchasers.[2] Similar implications flow from reliance on restrictive covenants. Equally, potential purchasers of residential property should be wary of known conservation interests affecting land.[3]

1 See *MWH Associates Ltd v Wrexham CBC* [2012] EWCA Civ 1884; [2013] Env LR 27.
2 *Southern Water Authority v Nature Conservancy Council* [1992] 3   All ER 481, see paras **19.34–19.38**.
3 See paras **19.17ff**.

19.05 Finally, the negotiations which take place under the broad umbrella of conservation law have a political complexion unlike those in pollution control. Absence of absolute legal protection may operate to limit the usefulness of site designation (from a regulator's point of view), whilst some gaps in the incomplete statutory framework may be filled by planning powers, which then makes the political character of conservation explicit by giving local authorities an important role. In fact, and as will become clear, local authorities have a central role in the implementation of conservation policy.

STATUTORY REGULATORS

19.06 Primary statutory responsibility for conservation falls to Natural England (previously known as the Nature Conservancy Council for England[1], and then English Nature[2]), Scottish Natural Heritage, and Natural Resources Wales (which has taken over the responsibilities of the Countryside Council for Wales) ('the conservation bodies'). In Northern Ireland, the relevant body is the Council for Nature Conservation and the Countryside. All three of the conservation bodies in Britain were originally set up (as 'the conservancy councils') by Part VII of EPA 1990 and the Natural Heritage (Scotland) Act 1991 (NHSA 1991) and replaced the previous unitary Nature Conservancy Council (NCC) – a reorganisation which ran counter to integrationist trends in other areas of environmental law, and which gave rise to considerable controversy during the course of the Bill through Parliament. The functions of the conservancy councils were set out in broad terms in EPA 1990, s 132. These included: specific functions previously exercised by the NCC under, for example, the National Parks and Access to the Countryside Act 1949 (NPACA 1949), the Countryside Act 1968 (CA 1968) and the Wildlife and Countryside Act 1981 (WCA 1981),[3] relating in particular to designation of sites of special scientific interest and licensing of activities in respect of protected species; the establishment, maintenance and management of nature reserves; provision of advice for the Secretary of State or any other Minister on the development and implementation of policies for or affecting nature conservation in their area; the provision of advice and the dissemination of knowledge about nature conservation; and commissioning and providing support for research.[4] For the conservancy councils' purposes, 'nature conservation' meant the conservation of flora, fauna or geological or physiographical features.[5] Although, broadly speaking, these functions subsist today, they now need to be considered in the light of subsequent legislation which has brought about a reorganisation of the way in which conservation bodies operate.

1 As originally set up by the EPA 1990, Part VII.
2 As it became under the Countryside Rights of Way Act 2000, s 73(1).
3 See EPA 1990, Sch 9.
4 See also EPA 1990, Sch 6: constitutions of the conservancy councils.
5 EPA 1990, s 131(6), as originally enacted.

19.07 The way in which these bodies are now organised is attributable in large part to amendments to the EPA 1990 made by the Natural Environment and Rural Communities Act 2006. Under s 2 of NERCA 2006, Natural England's general purpose is today to ensure that the natural environment is conserved, enhanced and managed for the benefit of present and future generations, thereby contributing to sustainable development.[1] To that end, its purpose includes: (a) promoting nature conservation and protecting biodiversity; (b) conserving and enhancing the landscape; (c) securing the provision and improvement of facilities for the study, understanding and enjoyment of the natural environment; (d) promoting access to the countryside and open spaces and encouraging open-air recreation; and (e) contributing in other ways to social and economic well-being through management of the natural environment.[2]

The functions, powers and duties of the Countryside Council for Wales were transferred to Natural Resources Wales as of 1 April 2013, along with certain devolved functions of the Environment Agency Wales and other functions carried out directly by the Welsh Government.[3] Under s 132 of the EPA 1990, National Resources Wales has many of the functions initially bestowed when the EPA was first enacted (see above). Its role however is to be redefined and extended by the Environment (Wales) Bill that was agreed by the Assembly on 2 February 2016 and is due to become law in Spring 2016. The functions, powers and duties of Scottish Natural Heritage remain essentially those in the NHSA 1991.[4]

As was the case under the previous regime, NERCA 2006 aims to ensure that the national conservation bodies with responsibility for improving nature conservation do not do so in isolation from one another, concerned only with the position in their own country. All of the bodies have the function of providing advice to the appropriate authorities on the development and implementation of policies for or affecting any nature conservation matter which: (i) arises throughout the United Kingdom and raises issues common to England, Wales, Scotland and Northern Ireland; (ii) arises in one or more (but not all) of those places and affects the interests of the United Kingdom as a whole; or (iii) arises outside the United Kingdom.[5] To a similar end, all bodies are concerned with establishing common standards throughout the United Kingdom for the monitoring of nature conservation and for research into nature conservation and the analysis of the resulting information.[6]

Since cross-border co-ordination remains complex, however, none of the above functions may be discharged by the conservation bodies unless through the Joint Nature Conservation Committee, originally set up by the EPA 1990, and which has been preserved by NERCA.[7] The Constitution of the Committee is dealt with in Sch 4 to NERCA. Its members include the chairman or deputy chairman of each of the conservation bodies and one other member of those bodies appointed by the body in question.[8] Under s 35(1) of NERCA, the Committee may give advice or information to any of the UK conservation bodies on any matter which is connected with the functions of that UK conservation body, and, in the opinion of the joint committee, arises throughout or in part only of the United Kingdom, or arises outside the United Kingdom. This transnational dimension to conservation problems in the UK stands comparison with the approach of international co-operation that features in much European environmental law.

The Marine Management Organisation (MMO) was established under the Marine and Coastal Access Act 2009 (MCAA 2009). The MMO inherited the functions of the Marine and Fisheries Agency and acquired several important new roles, principally an extended marine licensing role, marine planning and, together with Natural England and the Joint Nature Conservation Committee, the creation of a network of marine protected areas (including marine conservation zones and European marine sites). The MMO's jurisdiction covers the UK marine area, which is the territorial sea, exclusive economic zone and continental shelf, including the waters of every estuary, river or channel, so far as the tide flows at mean high water.[9] It does not include the Scottish inshore region, which is regulated by Marine Scotland, a body that was established at the same time.

1 NERCA 2006, s 2(1).
2 Ibid, s 2(2).
3 A similar merger between Natural England and the Environment Agency in England is periodically discussed.
4. See s 2(1).
5 NERCA 2006, s 34(2)(a).
6 Ibid, s 34(2)(c).
7 EPA 1990, s 132(1), NERCA, s 31(a).
8 Ibid, Sch 4(1)(c).
9 MCAA 2009, s 42.

19.08 The borderline between nature conservation and matters of countryside or landscape protection has been somewhat simplified in England by the merging of the Countryside Agency, created in 1999,[1] with English Nature (and the Rural Development Service) to form Natural England.[2] This has brought England in line with both Scotland and Wales, where countryside matters fell to the relevant conservation bodies.[3] Natural England's functions concern the provision, development and improvement of facilities for enjoying the countryside and to the conservation and enhancement of its natural beauty and amenity. These functions relate more to matters of general amenity and recreation than to conservation proper, and in addition to the potential overlap with the conservancy councils' specific powers, these functions may also impact on the exercise of general planning powers by local authorities.[4]

1 NPACA 1949, s 1; Development Commission (Transfer of Functions and Miscellaneous Provisions) Order 1999, SI 1999/416.
2 Natural Environment and Rural Communities Act 2006, s 1(4).
3 EPA 1990, s 130; NHSA 1991, s 1.
4 The exercise of planning powers in respect of conservation is considered in paras **19.62–19.66**.

19.09 There is a broader category of bodies whose functions have implications for conservation, although their powers are not so much concerned with promoting conservation interests as having the potential to damage them. Typically, such bodies fall under statutory duties to consider conservation interests in the exercise of their functions. The Environment Agency, for example, is required to 'have regard to' the desirability of conserving and enhancing the conservation and enhancement of natural beauty and the conservation of flora, fauna and geological or physiographical features of special interest in exercising its pollution control functions, and to exercise its other functions 'so as to further' those interests.[1] The purposes of National Parks have also been broadened to include conserving and enhancing natural beauty, wildlife and cultural heritage,[2] a provision which has particular implications for the exercise of planning powers by National Parks Authorities. By s 40(1) of NERCA 2006 *all* public authorities must in exercising their functions have regard to the purpose of conserving biodiversity. Planning policy, such as the National Planning Policy Framework and the internet-based National Planning Policy Guidance,[3] also sets out nature conservation criteria and considerations to which local planning authorities should have regard in making decisions on the development of land.[4]

1 EA 1995, s 7(1).
2 NPACA 1949, s 5.

3 http://planningguidance.communities.gov.uk/
4 See paras **19.62–19.66**.

19.10 The exercise of statutory regulators' powers in respect of conservation has traditionally been the subject of less attention than their pollution control counterparts. This has important consequences. Regulators have scientific and legal discretions to exercise, which comprise some of the most significant conservation powers in the UK. The absence of express criteria in the legislation as to how those powers are to be exercised places the emphasis on internal procedures. Regulators' working practices have not been free from criticism by the courts.[1] It is notable, for instance, that the detail of site designation notices is subject to no statutory template, and so falls to be negotiated on a case-by-case basis.

In *R (McMorn) v Natural England* the English statutory regulator's approach to determining applications for licensing to kill common buzzards under WCA 1981 came under sustained criticism by the High Court. Ouseley J 'was struck by NE's emphasis on DEFRA policy and its lack of emphasis on the law'.[2] Natural England had acted arbitrarily, inconsistently with its policy on other species, and disproportionately. The case highlights the problems that can arise for landowners in not knowing the policy approach that will be applied. The applicant gamekeeper's business had suffered as he had failed over many years to obtain licences. The judge found it 'quite disturbing that, as the problems faced by the Claimant grew, so did the demands of NE for evidence proving what it had hitherto appeared to accept'.[3]

1 See eg *R v Nature Conservancy Council, ex p Bolton Metropolitan Borough Council* [1996] JPL 203.
2 [2015] EWHC 3297 (Admin) at para 134.
3 Ibid, para 210.

19.11 While the UK conservation bodies differ in some respects, they are all bodies of appointed expert members, constitutionally independent from local and national government and established to provide advice on habitats and species protection, with certain specific responsibilities. They are therefore absolutely key to the conservation of nature, especially where they have enforcement functions. In *R (Morge) v Hampshire CC* Lord Brown considered that:

> 'After all, even if development permission is given, the criminal sanction against any offending (and unlicensed) activity remains available and it seems to me wrong in principle, when Natural England have the primary responsibility for ensuring compliance with the Directive, also to place a substantial burden on the planning authority in effect to police the fulfilment of Natural England's own duty.'[1]

Given in that case that Natural England was satisfied that the proposed development would comply with the legislative duty, the Supreme Court held that the local planning authority was 'entitled to presume that that is so'.[2]

However, enforcement in this area is not straightforward. In the past there have at the very least been difficulties in co-ordinating practices between different areas of the country.[3] In part this is down to limited resources; in part it is down to fragmentation. Natural England's role is often only advisory and, contrary to dicta from the courts, it does not have a monopoly on enforcement action, but shares it with the police. Finally, the wider responsibilities of the nature conservation bodies have the potential to confuse priorities. Natural Resources Wales for example has both flood defence and nature conservation responsibilities that may conflict. Natural England is charged with promoting recreation as well as biodiversity.

Variations in enforcement practice have important implications for the likelihood and manner of prosecution under conservation law, an important consideration given that it is often landowners and occupiers who will be most susceptible to such action.[4] There are certainly reported examples of prosecutions *not* having been initiated against owners on the basis of 'sufficient personal reasons' and so in theory the converse might also apply.

1 [2011] UKSC 2; [2011] 1 WLR 268 at para 29
2 Ibid, para 30, see also para 45 per Lady Hale; Lord Kerr dissenting.
3 Eg, Withrington and Jones 'The Enforcement of Conservation Legislation: Protecting Sites of Special Scientific Interest', in Howarth and Rodgers (eds) *Agriculture, Conservation and Land Use* (1992).
4 See para **19.26**.

19.12 Following consultation, Natural England published an overarching enforcement policy in March 2009. This makes clear that the organisation's main aim is to prevent harm to the natural environment, to which end it states that Natural England 'will use all its regulatory levers, including providing advice, guidance and land management incentive schemes, to encourage compliance with the law and ensure that the natural environment is conserved, enhanced, protected and restored.' The overall aims of deterrence, eliminating financial gain from non-compliance and changing behaviour are reiterated as are the enforcement principles: action that is consistent, proportionate, transparent, targeted and accountable.

A non-exhaustive list of public interest factors given for deciding whether or not to prosecute are as follows:

(a) impact on the natural environment;
(b) foreseeability of the offence and the circumstances leading up to it;
(c) grounds for believing that the offence is likely to be continued or repeated, for example, by a history of recurring conduct;
(d) the offence, although not serious in itself, is widespread in the area where it was committed;
(e) a prosecution would have a significant positive impact on maintaining community confidence;
(f) the deterrent effect of the prosecution and
(g) the intent and attitude of the offender.

The policy clearly provides significant scope for landowners and other interested parties to negotiate following alleged environmental infringements.

The picture is further complicated by a limited, but increasing, range of offences where Natural England, Natural Resources Wales and the Marine Management Organisation have access to the alternative of civil sanctions under the Regulatory Enforcement and Sanctions Act 2008 (RESA 2008).[1]

Natural England has had these powers since 3 January 2012 in respect of a variety of offences concerning protected species, SSSIs, habitat protection and environmental damage. Civil sanctions are potentially very significant, enabling the regulator among other things to impose fixed penalties as well as variable fines of up to £250,000. The powers are circumscribed by statutory guidance on their use and application.[2]

In practice civil sanctions are rarely issued. They apply to only a limited range of offences. The most used to date has not been a sanction set by the regulator, but enforcement undertakings whereby the regulated party can design its own civil sanction for acceptance by the regulator, usually a payment of money to a good cause (but it could include commitments to restore land or change practices), and thereby avoid all other regulatory liability.[3] Breach of the undertaking is a criminal offence.[4] Where available, enforcement undertakings present a novel and significant opportunity for landowners to negotiate with the relevant conservation body to limit the negative consequences of breaches of nature conservation law.

1 See eg Environmental Civil Sanctions (England) Order 2010 and the Environmental Civil Sanctions (Miscellaneous Amendments) Regulations 2010.
2 RESA 2008, ss 63–65.
3 RESA 2008, s 50; Environmental Civil Sanctions (England) Order 2010, Sch 4.
4 Environmental Civil Sanctions (England) Order, Sch 4, para 7(3).

PROTECTION OF INDIVIDUAL ANIMALS AND PLANTS AT NATIONAL LEVEL

19.13 Individual birds, animals and plants are subject to differing levels of legal protection: some extensive and general; some more focused and species-specific. These are likely to be of less direct impact in property transactions than some other aspects of conservation,[1] although provisions in respect of, for example, nesting sites (and their animal equivalents) may be important. The most general level of protection is provided by Part I of the Wildlife and Countryside Act 1981 (WCA 1981), as amended by the Countryside Rights of Way Act 2000, which is concerned with wildlife. EU law imposes separate controls that are considered below.[2]

1 Habitat protection, for example (paras **19.17** et seq.), or the impact of planning controls (paras **19.62–19.66**).
2 See paras **19.42–19.57**.

19.14 Birds are generally subject to a high level of protection.[1] For example, it is an offence intentionally to: kill, injure or take any wild bird;[2] to take, damage or destroy nests of wild birds while in use or being built; or to take or destroy wild bird eggs.[3] Certain offences also apply to persons having possession or control of wild birds (or parts thereof) and their eggs,[4] to employing prohibited methods of killing or taking, and to selling wild birds.[5] Certain defences and exceptions apply, particularly in respect of game birds,[6] where what would otherwise be an offence is committed by an 'authorised person'.[7]

In addition, no offence is committed by reason of any of those prohibited acts, if the act is the incidental result of a lawful operation and could not reasonably be avoided.[8] Accordingly, there is no offence if a bird's nest is destroyed in the course of development for which planning permission has been obtained, provided that all reasonable steps have been taken to avoid the destruction. For this purpose it is arguably unnecessary to delay the project by six months in order to avoid the nesting season if that would render the project economically unviable. There is also a defence if the act is authorised by a licence granted by 'the appropriate authority'.[9] A person convicted of an offence under this part of WCA 1981 is liable on summary conviction to imprisonment for a term not exceeding six months or an unlimited fine.[10]

1 WCA 1981, ss 1–8.
2 Ibid, s 21(1) defines 'wild bird' to be any bird of a kind normally resident in or as a visitor to Great Britain in a wild state (subject to certain exceptions).
3 WCA 1981, s 1(1).
4 Ibid, s 1(2).
5 Ibid, ss 5 and 6 respectively.
6 Listed in WCA 1981, Sch 2, Part I. On defences and exceptions see ss 1(3), 2, 4 and 5(4) and 5(4A).
7 Meaning: the owner or occupier, or a person authorised by them, of the land on which the action authorised is taken; and a person authorised by a local authority or other defined body. See WCA 1981, s 27(1).
8 WCA 1981, s 4(2)(c).
9 Ibid, s 16(1); for the English inshore region 'the appropriate authority' is the MMO: MCAA 2009, s 10, see para **19.07** above. Although this licensing power may be curtailed in certain areas protected under European law: *Royal Society for the Protection of Birds v Secretary of State for Scotland* (2000) GWD 26–961; *Times* 12 September.
10 WCA 1981, s 21; Legal Aid, Sentencing and Punishment of Offenders Act 2012, s 85.

19.15 The presumption that birds are protected does not apply to animals, where similar protection only applies where species are expressly named in Schedules to WCA 1981.[1] The prohibition of certain methods of killing or taking wild animals applies to all wild animals, however, not just to those listed,[2] with further limitations applying to particular species.[3] Wild plants, on the other hand, are subject to very wide offences, although enforcement of these is notoriously difficult. It is an offence for anyone intentionally to pick, uproot or destroy any scheduled wild plant,[4] or for anyone other than an authorised person (a group that includes a landowner)[5] to intentionally uproot any wild plant not included in the Schedule.[6] However, it is a defence to show that that act was an incidental result of a lawful operation and could not reasonably have been avoided.[7]

1 WCA 1981, s 9 and Sch 5, which includes bats. See also s 10(5), limiting defences in respect of both.

2 Ibid, s 11(1). 'Wild animal' means any animal other than a bird which is or was (before it was killed or taken) living wild: s 27(1).
3 Ibid, s 11(2) and Sch 6.
4 Ibid, Sch 8.
5 Ibid, s 27(1).
6 Ibid, s 13(1).
7 Ibid, s 13(3).

19.16 Part I of the 1981 Act also contains provisions in respect of 'areas of special protection' for birds (formerly known as bird sanctuaries)[1] and release into the wild of animal species which are not normally resident in Great Britain.[2] It is an offence for any person intentionally to kill, injure or take any scheduled wild animal[3] or to damage, destroy or obstruct access to, any structure or place which it uses for shelter or protection, or to disturb it while occupying such a structure or place.[4] A number of defences apply[5] including showing that what was done was the incidental result of a lawful operation and could not reasonably have been avoided;[6] and action authorised by a licence granted by the appropriate authority.[7] Certain aspects of species protection are however dealt with by specific regimes. For instance, badgers, seals and deer are subject to special controls,[8] fish may benefit from measures intended to prevent over-exploitation and to protect private fishing rights,[9] and a different regime applies to imports and exports of endangered species.[10]

The most controversial culls of animals in recent years were the pilot badger culls in Somerset and Gloucestershire promoted with the intention of preventing the spread of bovine tuberculosis. Two rounds of judicial challenges to the pilot cull, attacking the policy behind the culls and the compliance of the Secretary of State with that policy were dismissed by the High Court and the Court of Appeal.[11] However, in another case concerning the culling of Gulls in the Ribble estuary,[12] the Secretary of State's decision was quashed by the Court of Appeal. Whilst decisions concerning the issue of licences, and decisions to cull animals at a national level, may be difficult to quash, it is also the case that the Secretary of State can misdirect himself as to the proper approach to the complex statutory requirements in this area.

1 WCA 1981, ss 3 and 4.
2 Ibid, s 14 and Sch 9; the Wildlife and Countryside Act 1981 (Variation of Schedule 9) Order 1997, SI 1997/226.
3 Ibid, s 9 Sch 5.
4 Ibid, s 9(1) and (4).
5 Ibid, ss 9(3), (10).
6 Ibid, s 10(3)(c). See also para **19.14**.
7 Ibid, s 16(3).
8 The Protection of Badgers Act 1992, the Conservation of Seals Act 1970 and the Deer Act 1991, respectively.
9 See generally *Reid Nature Conservation Law* (3rd edn, 2009), pp 125–144.
10 Eg EC Regulations 338/97 and 939/97 on the protection of species of wild flora and fauna by regulating trade: Control of Trade in Endangered Species (Enforcement) Regulations 1997, SI 1997/1372, noted at (1997) 9 Environmental Law and Management 151.
11 *R (Badger Trust) v SSEFRA* [2012] EWCA Civ 1286 and [2014] EWCA Civ 1405.
12 *RSPB v SSEFRA* [2015] Env. L.R. 24.

SITE DESIGNATION AND HABITAT PROTECTION AT NATIONAL LEVEL

Private law measures

19.17 Even before statutory nature conservation powers were introduced, some landowners took responsibility on themselves for conservation. Through the use of devices such as restrictive covenants some environmentally-aware landowners privately initiated and enforced local systems for the protection of amenity, both in relation to individual sites and to wider areas or estates. However, under the normal principles of property law covenants which bind successors in title are the exception rather than the rule in such cases,[1] and so they are of limited use for contemporary environmental or conservation purposes.

1 Eg, *Tulk v Moxhay* (1848) 2 Ph 774. See Bell [1983] Conveyancer 327.

19.18 To be effective, the burden of restrictive covenants must have been intended to run with the land,[1] it must be a negative burden,[2] the covenant must have been made for the benefit of land retained by the covenantee,[3] and the covenant must normally have been registered.[4] Further, it is normally only the covenantee who can enforce a restrictive covenant. There are now certain statutory modifications to these general rules which allow the enforcement of restrictive covenants for conservation purposes. These generally only apply in respect of covenants entered into by statutory or public authorities, for example, the National Trust,[5] local authorities[6] or conservation authorities.[7]

1 This is presumed to be the case in relation to covenants made after 1925 unless the contrary intention appears: Law of Property Act 1925, s 79.
2 *Haywood v Brunwick Permanent Building Society* (1881) 8 QBD 403. Confirmed by the House of Lords in *Rhone v Stevens* [1994] 2 AC 310.
3 *Re Gadd's Land Transfer* [1965] 2 All ER 800.
4 See Land Charges Act 1972 s 2: Class D(ii) *Restrictive Covenants*; Land Registration Act 2002, Schs 1 and 3.
5 National Trust Act 1937, s 8 excepts the Trust from the requirement that a covenant be made for the benefit of land that the Trust retains, and so the Trust can enforce restrictive covenants against persons deriving title under the other party to the same extent as if the Trust were possessed of or entitled to or interested in adjacent land for the benefit of which the covenant was made. See also *Gee v National Trust for Places of Historic Interest or Natural Beauty* [1966] 1 WLR 170, CA; *Re Whittings Application* (1998) 58 p & CR 321.
6 Eg TCPA 1990, s 106, planning obligations; Housing Act 1985, s 609.
7 Eg NPACA 1949, s 16, provision for restrictive covenants to bind successors in title; WCA 1981, s 39(3), management agreements; Ancient Monuments Act 1979, s 17(5).

19.19 Other than in these cases, if the land benefited by the covenant changes hands, then the new owner may in some situations enforce the covenant against the covenantor and his successors in title. The rules concerning transfer of the benefit of a restrictive covenant are complex, and there are different legal and equitable rules.[1] As in most cases the remedy sought will be an injunction – an equitable remedy – it will normally be the equitable rules which are of most relevance. In essence these are, first, that the covenant must 'touch and concern' the land of the original covenantee,[2] and, secondly, that nothing is done in the transfer to stop the benefit passing (for example, the use of express words).[3] The latter would seem to have replaced the earlier requirement that the benefit of the covenant must be annexed to the land, or expressly assigned – rules which now apply only to covenants made before 1926.[4]

On 23 June 2014 the Law Commission published recommendations for the introduction of a new statutory regime for conservation covenants in England and Wales.[5] Conservation covenants are voluntary bilateral agreements between landowner and a responsible body (such as charity or public body) which can contain both positive or negative obligations to use land for conservation purposes, such as to maintain woodland or to refrain from using pesticides. Such covenants are common in other jurisdictions; what is proposed is a draft bill that would put them on a statutory footing in the UK. They would be registered and long-lasting, only capable of amendment by application to the Lands Chamber of the Upper Tribunal. Breach of the covenant would be enforceable in the courts and damages would be payable. The proposal presents a powerful mechanism for philanthropic landowners and conservation organisations to secure biodiversity benefits privately. It is yet to be taken up in the legislative agenda.

1 See generally *Megarry & Wade: The Law of Real Property*, (8th edn, 2012), 32–059–32–082.
2 *Smith and Snipes Hall Farm Ltd v River Douglas Catchment Board* [1949] 2 KB 500.
3 *Roake v Chadha* [1983] 3   All ER 503.
4 These conditions were rejected in *Federated Homes Ltd v Mill Lodge Properties Ltd* [1980] 1 All ER 371, CA, and now seem to be accepted without comment: *Megarry & Wade* above, at 32–064–32–065.
5 Law Commission report No 349.

19.20 Leases taken by persons concerned to protect conservation interests may also be a significant private law mechanism in this regard. A reasonably long lease would normally be necessary, with lessees also being granted full management rights. Repairing obligations will also need close consideration, as the lessee may be best equipped to maintain a site for particular conservation purposes.

Public law measures

19.21 More extensive controls, established expressly for the purposes of conservation, operate under public law. A range of provisions are relevant, many of which are concerned with the designation of sites with recognised conservation value (see Table 1). Here too the law is somewhat uncoordinated, however. For example, different designations may be made for different purposes, not only under different procedures, but carrying with them different implications for persons with property interests. Similarly, a single site may be the subject of more than one designation, with a consequent accumulation of protection, or overlapping controls in respect of different parts of the same site. The broadest forms of classification are those which are 'structural': relatively large areas within which general constraints apply (often through the planning system) but which have broader purposes than conservation. The best example might be National Parks, strictly a landscape and recreational designation, where a special institutional framework applies within a specific legal and policy context. Areas of Outstanding Natural Beauty are another example of controls applying to large areas, the effect of which is generally through the planning system.

Table 19.1: Principal terrestrial conservation designations

Importance	Site designations and explanation	Common acronym or abbreviation
Sites of International Importance	(a) Ramsar Sites listed under the Convention on Wetlands of International Importance.	Ramsar, usually also SSSI
	(b) Special Areas of Conservation under the EC Directive on the Conservation of Natural habitats and of Wild Flora and Fauna.	SAC, usually also SSSI
	(c) Special Protection Areas under the EU Directive on the Conservation of Wild Birds.	SPA, usually also SSSI
	(d) Sites in respect of which a Nature Conservation Order has been made under the WCA 1981, s 29.	NCO
Sites of National Importance	National Nature Reserves under NPACA 1949, s 19 or WCA 1981, s 35.	NNR
	Sites of Special Scientific Interest under WCA 1981, s 28.	SSSI
Sites of Regional/ Local Importance	Local Nature Reserves under NPACA 1949, s 21.	LNR
Non-statutory Nature Reserves	Non-statutory.	N/A
Sites of Importance for Nature Conservation (etc)	Non-statutory, generally adopted for planning purposes and having a wide range of names and differing status.	SINCs (etc)
Local Green Space	Non-statutory, referred to in the National Planning Policy Framework at paragraph 76.	N/A

19.22 More specific controls with more specific implications often relate to (generally smaller) areas of land designated under statutes specifically for the purposes of conservation. These include Sites of Special Scientific Interest (SSSIs), sites to which Nature Conservation Orders apply, Local and National Nature Reserves, Environmentally Sensitive Areas (ESAs), Special Areas of Conservation (SACs) under the EC Habitats Directive, and Special Protection Areas (SPAs) under the now consolidated EU Wild Birds Directive. Although generally different provisions relate to different designations, some of them (including

SACs and SPAs) fall under the umbrella designation of 'European Sites' to which the Conservation of Habitats and Species Regulations 2010 apply.[1]

In *Western Power Distribution Investments Ltd v Cardiff CC*[2] the High Court considered the lawfulness of the designation of land as a local nature reserve under s 21 of NPACA 1949. The case related to land at two reservoirs that was held on statutory trust for use as public walks and pleasure grounds under the Public Health Act 1875. The local authority considered that the land could be managed for both conservation and recreational purposes, but it would be important to ensure that managing it for a recreational purpose did not compromise its management for a conservation purpose under s 15(1)(b) of the 1949 Act. Ouseley J rejected the argument that there would always be inevitable conflict between the statutory regimes so that designation of land held on public trust under the 1875 Act was incapable of designation as a local nature reserve. However he held that there was on the facts of the case an inevitable conflict between the designations under the two Acts that could not lawfully be resolved so the nature conservation designation had to be quashed. The existing status of land may therefore be very important if biodiversity protection conflicts with some other purpose and may have application in National Parks and Areas of Outstanding Natural Beauty, which are not primarily designated for nature conservation.

1 SI 2010/490, considered in paras **19.41–19.53**.
2 [2011] EWHC 300 (Admin).

SITES OF SPECIAL SCIENTIFIC INTEREST

19.23 SSSIs are the most familiar form of statutory site designation. Although having the original purpose of safeguarding important areas of specifically scientific interest, SSSIs are now used for wider environmental ends: a role enhanced by European Community and International measures, such as the EC Habitats Directive[1] and the Ramsar Convention on Wetlands of International Importance (1971) which are dependent for their implementation in the UK at least in part on SSSIs. The relative effectiveness of the SSSI system was subject to criticism in the 1990s, culminating in the reform brought about by the Countryside and Rights of Way Act 2000.

Traditionally there has been an overlap between the 'conservation objectives' used for the protection of sites that are protected under national and international law, although since 2012 Natural England has sought to distinguish the conservation goals for European sites and SSSIs in England and Wales.[2] SSSI designation originally could extend as far as the jurisdictional limit of local authorities, generally mean low water (with slight variations between England, Northern Ireland, Scotland and Wales). The Marine and Coastal Access Act 2009 (MCAA 2009) amended WCA 1981 to define the circumstances when SSSIs may extend below the mean water mark in England and Wales.[3] As such, SSSIs will be one of six designations contributing to an ecologically coherent network of marine protected areas.

In Scotland, the Nature Conservation (Scotland) Act 2004, which came into force on 29 November 2004, replaced s 28 of WCA 1981 and created a code for the protection of SSSIs north of the border. This Chapter focuses on the provisions in England and Wales.

1 92/43/EEC, see paras **19.42–19.57.**
2. The distinction is not simple and led to litigation in *RSPB v SSEFRA* [2014] EWHC 1645 (Admin); [2014] Env LR 29 and [2015] EWCA Civ 227; [2015] Env LR 24.
3 MCAA 2009, Sch 13; WCA 1981 ss 28, 28B and 28C.

19.24 Where a conservation body is of the opinion that any land is of special interest by reason of its flora, fauna, or geological or physiographical features, that fact must be notified to specified persons, namely the local planning authority (LPA), the Secretary of State and every owner and occupier of any of the land.[1] The notification must specify the features by reason of which the site is of special interest and any operations which would be likely to damage it ('potentially damaging operations').[2]

1 WCA 1981, s 28(1).
2 Ibid, s 28(4). On the meaning of 'operations', see *Sweet v Secretary of State and Nature Conservancy Council* [1989] JEL 245. On the meaning of 'likely to damage', see *North Uist Fisheries Ltd v Secretary of State for Scotland* 1992 SLT 333.

19.25 It is the act of notification which gives rise to legal protection of a site, although it is important to note that such notification is subject to confirmation within nine months.[1] During the process of confirmation any person notified can make representations in respect of the notification, which the body is bound to consider (see s 28(3)). Section 28 creates a *duty* to notify once a conservation body has applied its own guidelines to a site, and has formed an opinion as to its special interest. However, there remains a discretion to be exercised or a judgment to be made in confirming that notification, the exercise of which could in practice amount to the effective withdrawal of notification.[2]

Landowners and occupiers should therefore carefully scrutinise a conservation body's reasoning in its notification document, as substantive or procedural errors could compromise the confirmation of a new site on their land. Confirmation of sites has been successfully challenged by way of judicial review, which is one indication of the perceived (potential) impact of notification on property interests.[3]

An important challenge in this area was the case of *R (Boggis) v Natural England*.[4] The claimant, Mr Boggis, sought judicial review of Natural England's decision to notify and confirm its decision to declare a section of coastline an SSSI. Natural England had considered the site to be of special scientific interest because, as the cliff faces naturally eroded, fossils of scientific interest were exposed. The claimant, whose property was located close to the cliff edge, had constructed artificial sea defences to prevent the erosion from taking its course. The effect of the designation was that the claimant's consent would be required to maintain the defences.

There were two main strands to the claimant's arguments. The first related to the act of designation and confirmation itself. The claimant argued that

Natural England had acted unlawfully in designating the land as an SSSI, as it had misconstrued what constituted a 'geographical feature' for the purposes of s 28. He argued that the act of exposure of a cliff face through erosion by the sea did not constitute a 'geological feature', and that s 28 only allowed designation in a case where there was current and not future scientific interest in an area. He argued, further, that the effect of the designation was not conservation at all, but destruction. In the High Court,[5] Blair J had rejected this argument, noting that the wording used in s 28 in relation to the size of an SSSI was deliberately vague. An exposed cliff face, the judge held, was plainly capable of being a geological feature for the purposes of s 28, and Natural England had not misconstrued s 28 by interpreting a geological feature in terms of the feature as maintained by erosion. Further, the fact that the fossils were currently unexposed did not mean that the land was not of current interest; conservation was a dynamic concept which might involve allowing natural processes to take their course, as in the case of erosion by the sea. The Court of Appeal (Sullivan LJ) upheld the decision, confirming that conservation does not necessarily mean preservation of the *status quo*; in the present case the geological exposure itself was capable of being a geological feature meriting protection under the SSSI designation.

The claimant's second argument was that Natural England had wrongly failed to carry out an appropriate assessment of the SSSI designation as it was a 'plan or project' likely to have significant effects on a nearby European conservation site under Council Directive 92/43.[6] The argument succeeded before the High Court, but was rejected in the Court of Appeal where Sullivan LJ held without qualification that the designation is neither a plan or a project and does not, in itself, amount to an intervention in the natural surroundings.

While conservation bodies have a generally wide discretion to formulate criteria for notification, *Boggis* demonstrates that there is scope for litigation, especially where wider public law duties are engaged. A decision *not* to select a site that otherwise meets the criteria for notification is more likely to be open to challenge.[7]

1 WCA 1981, s 28(5).
2 *R v Nature Conservancy Council, ex p Bolton Metropolitan Borough Council* [1996] JPL 203; *R v Nature Conservancy Council, ex p London Brick Property Ltd* [1996] JPL 227; cf *R (Fisher) v English Nature* [2004] Env LR 7 (HC); [2005] Env LR 10 (CA).
3 See, eg *R v Nature Conservancy Council, ex p Bolton Metropolitan Borough Council* [1996] JPL 203, where the decision to confirm the notification of a site was quashed on the basis that the Conservancy Council had failed to observe principles of natural justice in its negotiations with the landowner. For the implications of designation, and / or confirmation of designation of a site as an SSSI on Human Rights, see *R (Aggregate Industries Ltd) v English Nature* [2003] Env LR 3 (compatibility of the process with the 'due process' protections afforded by Article 6 of the European Convention in Human Rights); *Fisher v English Nature* [2005] Env LR 10 and *R (Trailer and Marina (Leven) Ltd) v Secretary of State for the Environment, Food and Rural Affairs* [2004] EWCA Civ 1580 (whether s 28 violates the right to property under Article 1 of the First Protocol to the Convention).
4 [2009] EWCA Civ 1061; [2010] PTSR 725.
5 [2008] EWHC 2954 (Admin); [2009] 3 All ER 879.
6 See para **19.42** below et seq.
7 See *R (Fisher) v English Nature* [2004] Env LR 7 (HC) per Lightman J at para 18.

Implications for owners and occupiers of SSSI notification

19.26 Almost since its inception, the fragmented system for the protection of conservation interests created by the 1981 Act had been subject to severe criticism. The main criticisms of the system in general, and of s 28 and SSSIs in particular, concerned the perceived lack of a coercive edge: designation of an SSSI did not oblige the owner or occupier to take steps to conserve the habitat that was its subject, nor refrain from doing damage to it, but required only that the owner or occupier notify the Conservancy Council (as it was then called) of the intention to carry out any 'potentially damaging operations', giving the Council an opportunity to attempt to negotiate a habitat-friendly management agreement with the individuals concerned. The second area of criticism concerned the reliance on, and the operation of, management agreements, which many felt allowed landowners too easy an 'escape route' from conservation obligations.

19.27 Against this background, significant reform was introduced through the Countryside and Rights of Way Act 2000 (CROWA). As well as those relating to SSSIs, CROWA contained controversial provisions in respect of access to the open countryside and to registered common land, and certain other proposals concerning public rights of way and road traffic. The relevant provisions came into force on 30 January 2001.[1]

1 CROWA, s 103(2).

19.28 Following these amendments, the protection for SSSIs may be summarised as followed. First, and fundamentally, they enable the conservation bodies to impose permanent restrictions on land in SSSIs in place of the previous temporary restrictions, together with powers to secure positive management of SSSIs. CROWA also added further detail than was originally provided for in WCA 1981 in respect of the notification and denotification of sites, and provided for increased penalties applicable for damage to an SSSI by owners, occupiers and by other persons. In summary, the amendments (i) affirmed the duty on the conservation bodies to notify land that is of special interest, (ii) set out the procedures and timetable that is to be followed, including a formal opportunity on those notified to make representations concerning – but not to appeal against – notification,[1] (iii) required the relevant conservation body to set out in the notification of a site the body's views about the appropriate management of the land and (iv) provided detailed powers by which the bodies may vary a notification after it has been made. Bodies also now have express power to denotify a site.[2] Also, CROWA introduced a formal mechanism for the notification of Ramsar sites.[3]

1 Such a right does apply in respect of Scotland: Natural Heritage (Scotland) Act 1991, s 12.
2 WCA 1981, s 28D.
3 Convention on Wetlands of International Importance especially as Waterfowl Habitat, signed at Ramsar on 2 February 1971; WCA 1981, s 37A.

19.29 The 'coercive edge' of the present system derives from the duty on owners or occupiers of land within an SSSI not to carry out, or cause or permit to be carried out, on that land any operation specified in the notification, unless (i) they give Natural England notice of the proposal to carry out the prohibited operation(s) *and* (ii) they do so within the terms of a management agreement,[1] a 'management scheme'[2] or 'management notice',[3] or with the written consent of the conservation body.[4] A relatively extensive obligation rests on the body to justify its decision in respect of any consent granted or refused,[5] and this may facilitate reliance on the right of appeal to the Secretary of State against refusal or conditional consent.[6] Modification or withdrawal of consent may, in some circumstances, give rise to liability on the body to pay the owner or occupier compensation.[7] A person who, without reasonable excuse, contravenes s 28E(1) of the Act is guilty of a criminal offence and liable to an unlimited fine on conviction by a magistrates' court or the Crown Court.[8] A convicting court can also require a person convicted of an offence under the amended 1981 Act to carry out, within such period as it specifies, such operations for the purpose of restoring the land to its former condition as is specified (a 'restoration order').[9] The technical complexities of making any intelligible order should perhaps not be underestimated. It is a 'reasonable excuse' for a person to carry out an operation (or to fail to comply with a requirement to send a notice about it), if the operation in question was authorised by a planning permission, or the operation in question was an emergency operation particulars of which were notified to Natural England as soon as practicable after the commencement of the operation.[10]

Offences may also be committed by so-called 'section 28G authorities', essentially all public bodies including statutory undertakers, who carry out operations likely to damage an SSSI without complying without first notifying the conservation body and complying with the notification and assent requirements in s 28H.[11] A further offence applies to any person who intentionally or recklessly destroys or damages the flora, fauna or other features of an SSSI either with or without knowledge that the relevant feature is within an SSSI.[12] The defence of 'reasonable excuse' applies to all the offences within s 28P.

In *Natural England v Day*[13] a fine of £450,000 (and a costs order in excess of that amount) was upheld on appeal against for an offence under s 28E(1). The landowner had constructed a wide track through an acre of woodland designated as a SSSI on his estate in Cumbria. The very high fine was justified because of the landowner's wealth, the fact that he had damaged nature conservation in pursuit of commercial gain and the gravity of his conduct. At para 43 Lord Thomas LCJ concluded:

'It was the judge's duty to impose a fine that would not only punish the appellant for what he had done for commercial gain but which would also deter others and protect the public. As the judge rightly identified, the protection of the environment and particularly protection of SSSIs are of great importance. SSSIs represent the common heritage of mankind; they are not subject to the commercial interests of a person who holds the land for the time being. It is also important to take account of the obvious fact that Natural England has significant difficulties in monitoring SSSIs; deterrence is of considerable importance. The fine therefore had to be of such a size that it would achieve each of these objectives.'

The case demonstrates a tend in the courts to take environmental offences more seriously[14] and the Court of Appeal noted that a fine 'in seven figures' would not be inappropriate were it necessary.[15]

In England and Wales the conservation bodies now have the option of imposing civil sanctions instead of prosecution, including enforcement undertakings put forward by the regulated party, as discussed above.[16]

1 For example under s 16 of NPACA 1949.
2 Under s 28J of WCA 1981.
3 Under s 28K of WCA 1981.
4 WCA 1981, s 28E.
5 Ibid, sub-s (7) and (8).
6 WCA 1981, s 28F.
7 Ibid, s 28M.
8 Ibid, s 28P.
9 Ibid, s 31(1).
10 Ibid, s 28P(4).
11 Ibid, s 28P(2) and (3).
12 Ibid, s 28P(6) and (6A) respectively.
13 [2014] EWCA Crim 2683; [2015] Env LR 15.
14 The Court of Appeal referred to its earlier decision in *R v Sellafield* [2014] EWCA Crim 49; [2014] Env LR 19.
15 Ibid, para 46.
16 See para **19.12**.

19.30 The idea behind the system of management schemes and new management notices is that conservation bodies can better secure the positive management of SSSIs.[1] Management schemes can be prepared by the body for conserving or restoring the characteristics of the site by reason of which it was designated, and where it appears to the body that an owner or occupier is not giving effect to the scheme, then a management notice may be used as a means of enforcement.[2] Such a notice can require the owner or occupier to carry out work or do other things on the land in question, although it is a precondition to its service that the body cannot secure an agreement with that person by which those things would be carried out. The owner or occupier affected has an opportunity to challenge the fact of its service or its content by an appeal, which might include a public inquiry.[3]

1 WCA 1981, ss 28J–28L.
2 Ibid, s 28K.
3 Ibid, s 28L(4).

19.31 Although no exhaustive list of potential grounds of appeal is provided by the Act, it is clear that an appeal may be on the ground that some other owner or occupier of the land should take all or any of the measures specified in the management notice, or pay part of their cost.[1] It will therefore be apparent that, in determining appeals under this section, the Secretary of State is involved in just the sort of apportionment exercise that has so strenuously been avoided elsewhere in environmental law.[2] Some assistance is contained in the Act as to how the Secretary of State must exercise this appeal power. This – conversely – does reveal the influence of those other licensing provisions. In particular, in considering appeals under this provision, the Secretary of

State must take into account, as between the appellant and any other owner or occupier: their relative interests in the land, considering both the nature of the interests and the rights or obligations arising under or by virtue of them; their relative responsibility for the state of the land which gives rise to the requirements of the management notice; and the relative degree of benefit to be derived from carrying out the requirements of the management notice.[3] In practice, other parts of the contaminated land regime can provide fruitful ground for informing the arguments that might be raised in these appeals.

1 WCA 1981, s 28L(2).
2 Most obviously, in connection with the remediation of contaminated land; paras **15.95–15.98**.
3 Ibid, s 28L(7).

19.32 As well as the enhanced powers of enforcement surveyed above, the amended WCA 1981 also gives conservation bodies enhanced powers of entry to land and of compulsory purchase in connection with it.[1] There is also provision for enforcement powers of broader application than merely in respect of SSSIs, extending to wildlife crime under the Act generally,[2] and including extensive powers to take samples for enforcement purposes.[3] The circumstances in which a conservation body may seek to compulsorily purchase land are that the body is satisfied that it is unable to conclude, on terms appearing to it to be reasonable, an agreement with the owner or occupier as to the management of the land; or has entered into such an agreement, but the body is satisfied that it has been breached in such a way that the land is not being managed satis-factorily.[4] Disputes about whether or not a management agreement has been breached will be referred to arbitration.[5] Once compulsorily purchased, the relevant conservation body can choose to manage the land itself, or dispose of it, or any interest in it, on terms designed to secure that the land is managed satisfactorily.[6]

1 WCA 1981, s.51(1) and s.28N respectively.
2 Ibid, s 19ZA.
3 Ibid, s 19ZB.
4 Ibid, s 28N(2).
5 Ibid, sub-s(3).
6 Ibid, sub-s(4).

19.33 It should be noted that the amended WCA 1981 places duties on statutory undertakers and certain public bodies in respect of SSSIs, and imposes restrictions on them when carrying out or authorising activities which affect an SSSI (whether within the site or not). For example, Ministers, the National Assembly of Wales, local authorities, statutory undertakers, and other public bodies are under a duty to take reasonable steps, consistent with the proper exercise of their functions, to further the conservation and enhancement of the flora, fauna or geological or physiographical features by reason of which the site is of special interest.[1] Certain statutory undertakers have specific consultation and decision-making duties.[2]

1 WCA 1981, s 28G.
2 Ibid, ss 28H and 28I.

19.34 A key feature of s 28 remains the use of 'owner' or 'occupier' to trigger criminal liability. 'Owner' is defined broadly, and in fairly standard terms, as a person, other than a mortgagee not in possession, who, whether in his own right or as a trustee or agent for any other person, is entitled to receive the rack rent of the land or, where the land is not let at a rack rent, would be so entitled if it were so let.[1] 'Occupier' is more problematic as it is not defined in the Act. There is, however, House of Lords authority on the meaning of this word; authority which may also be significant for the purposes of other statutory regimes.[2] It should be noted, however, that the definition of 'owner' will often depend on the particular statutory context, and so the simple transposition of definitions is not advisable.[3]

1 WCA 1981, s 52(4) applying the definition in NPACA 1949, s 114(1).
2 Eg, new controls over contaminated land: see generally Ch 15.
3 Compare, eg, *Walton v Sedgefield Borough Council* [1999] JPL 541, considering 'owner' for the purposes of TCPA 1990, s 179 with *Camden London Borough Council v Gunby* [2000] 1 WLR 465, considering whether managing agents can be 'owners' for the purpose of statutory nuisance proceedings.

19.35 The limitation on occupiers' liability was confirmed by the case of *Southern Water Authority v Nature Conservancy Council* concerned an SSSI on the Isle of Wight designated in 1982.[1] Notification was sent to the Southern Water Authority (SWA) and two farmers, each of whom owned part of the site. Across the two farmers' land ran a ditch, which was part of the SSSI but which did not encroach upon SWA's land. In 1987 the farmers asked SWA to dredge the ditch to alleviate flooding, despite dredging being amongst the notified potentially damaging operations. Neither the Nature Conservancy Council's consent nor planning permission was granted for any dredging operations. In February 1989 SWA entered the farmers' land and dredged the ditch, taking almost four weeks to do so. In January 1990 SWA were charged, being the occupier of land within the SSSI and without reasonable excuse, with carrying or causing or permitting to be carried out potentially damaging operations contrary to s 28. The farmers were not prosecuted.

1 [1992] 3 All ER 481; see Jewell 'Conservation and Crime' (1992) 142 NLJ 1370.

19.36 While accepting that SWA's entry upon the land to carry out the operations did not amount to 'ownership', the justices found that the continuous work for four weeks, physically preventing others from enjoying the full use of the land and being akin to SWA treating it as their own, did amount to 'occupation' and so SWA was convicted. However, the High Court quashed the conviction, and that decision was upheld by the House of Lords, addressing two questions of statutory interpretation. First, as SWA was not the owner of the land upon which they carried out the operations, could it instead be an 'occupier'? Second, could SWA, coincidentally being the owner of other land within the same SSSI, commit an offence under s 28 on part of the SSSI not in its ownership? On the first point, Lord Mustill, giving the only speech, held that the word 'occupier' should be interpreted in its context and according to its purpose; it has no fixed meaning. His Lordship stated that amongst the 'kinds of occupier [who] must have

503

been intended to fall within the prohibition' are three obvious categories: occupiers at the time of designation who are recipients of the notification, occupiers after designation who can be 'presumed' to have been notified, and subsequent purchasers who are alerted by the SSSI's registration as a local land charge.[1] The proposition that there might be a fourth category of occupier whose occupation is created only by carrying out operations on the land was rejected.

1 Under provision then contained in the WCA 1981, s 28(11).

19.37 The notion of an 'operational occupier' was rejected due to the absence of 'such a comprehensive and stable relationship with the land as to be … someone to whom the Act can sensibly be made to apply'. From the acceptable kinds of occupier described, whether a person *is* someone to whom the Act can 'sensibly be made to apply' hinges upon whether they have been notified on designation, or can be presumed to have been notified of designation. Thus the definition of 'occupier' under s 28 comprises both some sort of physical 'occupation' and actual or presumed notification. Also, Lord Mustill stated that it can be presumed that persons coming into 'occupation' after designation have received notification and that there would be no hardship caused by the imposition of strict liability, as the new 'occupier' would have knowledge of that liability through its registration as a local land charge. In the context of land transactions this may be significant, as this conclusion may depend upon the nature of the subsequent occupation, in particular, whether there was reason to consult the land charges register. The acquisition of certain forms of interest in land would not always demand recourse to the register, and so the question of what amounts to occupation sufficient to give rise to the presumption of notification remains.

19.38 On the second question of interpretation, the House was equally unconvinced: '[t]he accidental feature that the person who comes on to one part of the land to perform potentially damaging operations at the request or with the consent of the owner is himself the owner of a different part cannot make him the owner of 'that land" for the purposes of sub-section (5)'. The House of Lords therefore took a restrictive interpretation of the meaning of 'occupier' under the 1981 Act, albeit before the CROWA reforms. The implications for owners are limited, but *Southern Water Authority* perhaps makes it more likely that owners will be targeted as defendants where offences have been committed by third parties on their land.[1]

It should be noted that the House of Lords considered 'occupation' purely by reference to its 1981 statutory context. Under the amendments made by CROWA, a statutory undertaker such as SWA could be liable for committing a separate offence under s 28P(2) of the WCA 1981.[2]

1 Para **19.34**.
2 As a 'section 28G authority', see para **19.29**.

MANAGEMENT AGREEMENTS

19.39 The conservation bodies have express powers to enter into management agreements in respect of both SSSIs[1] and nature reserves.[2] By s 7 of NERCA 2006, Natural England now enjoys wider powers to make agreements with persons with an interest in land about the management or use of the land, if doing so appears to it to further its general purposes,[3] and whether or not the land is the subject of an SSSI or nature reserve designation. In addition to these particular powers vested in the conservancy councils, strategic planning authorities (generally unitary authorities and county councils) may enter into management agreements for the purpose of conserving or enhancing the natural beauty or amenity of any land which is both in the countryside and within their area, or promoting its enjoyment by the public.[4] Each power is broadly the same.

1 Countryside Act 1968, s 15; NERCA 2006 s 7.
2 NPACA 1949, s 16. Nature reserves themselves are considered in paras **19.58–19.59**.
3 See above para **19.07**.
4 WCA 1981, s 39.

19.40 Under the 1968 Act, where the relevant conservation body considers it expedient to do so, it may enter into an agreement with the owners, lessees and occupiers of designated land, or of any other land, which imposes restrictions on the exercise of rights over land by the persons who can be bound by it.[1] This includes making agreements in respect of land adjacent to sites themselves.[2]

The conservation bodies and local authorities are able to enforce restrictions in agreements against successors in title to the land to which they relate, despite the fact that they may not have been made for the benefit of land retained by the authority.[3] This avoids some of the problems associated with restrictive covenants noted above.[4] Any management agreement may:

(a) provide for the carrying out of works or other things;
(b) provide for the costs of those works to be defrayed by the land's owners or other persons or the relevant conservancy council; and
(c) contain other provisions as to the making of payments.[5]

1 CA 1968, s 15(2).
2 Amendments made by EPA 1990, Sch 9, para 4(1); CROWA 2000 s 75(3).
3 CA 1968, s 15(4); NPACA 1949, s 16(3); WCA 1981, s 39(3).
4 Paras **19.17–19.20**.
5 CA 1968, s 15(3); NPACA 1949, s 16(3). The wording in the WCA 1981, s 39(2) is rather different.

19.41 The level of any payments made under the terms of a management agreement will normally be set in accordance with ministerial guidance.[1] Where an offer is made to enter into a management agreement providing for the making of payments to the owner or occupier of land within an SSSI or land to which a nature conservation order relates who has given notice of their intention to carry out potentially damaging operations, that owner or occupier may seek arbitration as to the level of payment offered.[2] The manner of assessing compensation equates with normal cases of contractual or tortious liability, that is pecuniary loss directly and naturally flowing from the designation, with a corresponding obligation on the claimant to act reasonably to mitigate that loss.[3] However, an owner or occupier is still under no obligation to enter into a management agreement even after arbitration. Arbitration is also available to those seeking grant aid to carry out works on agricultural land, where an application for a farm capital grant[4] has been refused in consequence of an objection by the relevant authority or conservation body.

1 WCA 1981, s 50(2). *See Guidelines on Management Agreement Payments and Other Related Matters* (DETR, 2001).
2 Ibid, s 50(3).
3 *Thomas v Countryside Council for Wales* [1994] 4 All ER 853, HC.
4 Agriculture Act 1970, s 29.

CONSERVATION OF HABITATS AND SPECIES REGULATIONS 2010

19.42 The domestic regulations which were first made to implement Directive 92/43/EEC[1] on the conservation of natural habitats and of wild flora and fauna ('the Habitats Directive') were the Conservation (Natural Habitats &c) Regulations 1994. Those Regulations also served to implement part of Directive 79/409/EEC.[2] The 1994 Regulations needed to be read in conjunction with pre-existing conservation legislation as well as with the terms of the Directives. In some cases the words of the Directive were directly transposed into the domestic Regulations; in others there were important differences between the Regulations and the existing legal position.[3]

The 1994 Regulations have since been entirely replaced, in England and Wales, by the Conservation of Natural Habitats and Species Regulations 2010.[4] Those regulations are similar in approach and structure to the 1994 Regulations. In Scotland the Habitats Directive is transposed through a combination of the 2010 Regulations, in relation to reserved matters, and the original 1994 Regulations.

New provisions in the 2010 Regulations implement aspects of the Marine and Coastal Access Act 2009, including the transfer of certain licensing functions from Natural England to the Marine Management Organisation; and the appointment of Marine Enforcement Officers to use powers under the 2009 Marine Act to enforce certain offences under the Habitats Regulations.

1 OJ L206/7, 21.05.92.
2 OJ L103, 25.4.79 (On the Conservation of Wild Birds).
3 Eg, the Regulations (reg 41) prohibit the 'deliberate' killing of protected animals, whereas the 1981 Act criminalises 'intentional' killing.
4 Conservation of Natural Habitats and Species Regulations 2010, SI 2010/490, as subsequently and variously amended.

European legal background

19.43 The 1994, and 2010, Regulations have emerged from a complex European framework, and one which continues to evolve. Whilst the Habitats Directive built on the much earlier Birds Directive, a series of cases from the Court of Justice of the European Union ('CJEU') has also elaborated on their implications. Of particular significance are the *Leybucht Dykes*,[1] *Santoña Marshes*[2] and *Lappel Bank*[3] decisions, complemented by important Scottish authority on the implementation of the Directives.[4]

1 *Commission v Germany* (Case C-57/89) [1991] ECR I-883; (1992) 1 Journal of Environmental Law 139.
2 *Commission v Spain* (Case C-355/90) [1993] ECR 4221.
3 *R v Secretary of State for the Environment, ex p Royal Society for the Protection of Birds* (Case C-44/95) [1997] QB 206.
4 *WWF (UK) v Secretary of State for Scotland*, 1998 GWD 37–1936; [1999] 1 CMLR 1021. See below para **19.46** et seq.

19.44 The Birds Directive requires Member States to classify 'special protection areas' (SPAs) for the purpose of ensuring the survival and conservation of certain species.[1] This extends to protection for migratory species, with particular regard to wetlands of international importance.[2] The Habitats Directive builds on (and amends) the Birds Directive. Its principal object is the creation of a coherent ecological network of 'special areas of conservation' (SACs – the network is referred to as 'Natura 2000') to maintain or restore natural habitats and species of wild flora and fauna of Community interest. It also gives legal force at Community level to a further international convention, the Bern Convention.[3] The site designation approach favoured by both of these measures has enabled their implementation through the adaptation of existing UK mechanisms, essentially a broadening of the SSSI network. The approach of the CJEU to interpreting the Directives is obviously important to their implementation in the UK.

1 Article 4. Note that, under the Directive, Member States are placed under a general obligation to take measures to maintain a sufficient diversity of habitats for all European Bird Species (Arts 1, 2 nd 3).
2 Particularly those protected under the *Convention on Wetlands of International Importance especially as Waterfowl Habitat*, 1971 (the Ramsar Convention).
3 *Convention on the Conservation of European Wildlife and Habitats*, 1979.

19.45 The CJEU has taken a strict approach to the interpretation of the Directives, in respect both of the initial designation of sites and their subsequent protection, once designated. This has been elaborated in a Scottish context, although the Scottish courts have a rather more chequered history in this regard. Taking designation first, it is clear that the obligation imposed by the Birds Directive (and by the Habitats Directive) to designate SPAs is a strict one: it cannot be achieved by adopting other special conservation measures.[1] When choosing sites to be designated, the CJEU has emphasised the primary role of the ornithological criteria set out in the Directive.[2] The consequence is that the discretion that member states have when choosing to designate a site is very limited: designation of SPAs and SACs is an objective exercise, to which economic criteria (among others) are irrelevant.[3] Once designated, proposals that may deleteriously affect sites might then be considered to be permissible on grounds of imperative overriding reasons, but the CJEU seems clear that this should not affect the initial designation decision itself.

1 *European Commission v Netherlands* (Case C-3/96) [1999] Env LR 147; cf *Bown v Secretary of State for Transport* [2004] Env LR 26.
2 *Santoña Marshes, Commission v Spain* (Case C-355/90) [1993] ECR 4221.
3 *R v Secretary of State for the Environment, ex p Royal Society for the Protection of Birds* (Case C-44/95) [1997] QB 206. The CJEU has rejected a number of factors for not designating SPAs, including the effect of the Common Agriculture Policy (Case C-96/98 *Commission v France* [2000] 2 CMLR 681); waiting for public consultation and the fact that the land is state-owned (Case C-166/97 *Commission v France* [1999] Env LR 781). As to the strictness of the criteria to be applied by Member States in designating SACs, see Case C-371/98 *R v Secretary of State for the Environment, Transport and the Regions, ex p First Corporate Shipping Ltd* [2001] ECR I9235.

19.46 What has proved more complex in a UK context has been the closely-connected problem of determining the boundaries of SPAs and SACs as part of the designation process. In particular, the Outer House of the Court of Session in Scotland has considered the applicability of the strict approach adopted by the CJEU in setting the boundaries of sites when designating them.[1] The case concerned a challenge to the decision to designate an area of the Cairngorms as both an SPA and SAC.[2] In issue was the exclusion from the site when designated of the summit of Cairn Gorm itself and another area intended for development for recreational use, when these areas had been included in the original designation proposals and when their exclusion was clearly based on economic and recreational grounds.[3] At first glance, *Lappel Bank* and *Santoña Marshes* would seem to be determinative: those cases emphasise that designation must be based on ornithological (and ecological) criteria alone. However, after a close analysis of these cases the court concluded that they were not concerned with the issue of site boundaries, but with whether a clearly defined and agreed area should in fact be designated.[4] This left the court more scope to conclude on the relevance of economic factors at the earlier stage of site designation: the definition of its boundaries.[5] As to this, Lord Nimmo-Smith concluded that designation of sites and determination of their boundaries were linked processes, requiring the exercise of discretion throughout. Consequently, there was no absolute obligation on member states to include all contiguous or linked qualifying habitats or species populations within a site.

1 *WWF (UK) v Secretary of State for Scotland*, 1998 GWD 37–1936; [1999] 1 CMLR 1021.
2 Lord Nimmo-Smith accepted that the decisions of the CJEU on the Birds Directive applied *mutatis mutandis* to the Habitats Directive.
3 It should be noted that Lord Nimmo-Smith also rejected the substantive application on grounds of delay, so his later conclusions may, strictly speaking, be obiter.
4 Eg, it was agreed what 'the Santoña Marshes' actually were.
5 Also see *Commission v Netherlands* [1999] Env LR 147, 178 at paras 59 et seq.

19.47 On most readings, the *WWF* decision looks like a dilution of the *Lappel Bank* and *Santoña Marshes* cases. However, it does not undermine them entirely: the discretion of member states to refuse to designate a site, even though its boundaries may be modified, remains very narrow. Equally, the conclusion has received some support from the opinion of Advocate General Leger in a subsequent case.[1] The decision of the court reiterated the conclusion reached in *Lappel Bank*, but did not directly address the point at issue in *WWF (UK)*, or the decision in that case. The issue of European law therefore remains: was Lord Nimmo-Smith actually correct in distinguishing the European cases as he did? As to the *outer* geographical extent of SPAs and SACs, the High Court has held that the Directive applies as far as the continental shelf.[2]

1 *R v Secretary of State for the Environment, Transport and the Regions, ex p First Corporate Shipping Ltd* (Case C-371/98).
2 *R v Secretary of State for Trade and Industry, ex p Greenpeace* (No 2) [2000] Env LR 221. See further the Offshore Petroleum Activities (Conservation of Habitats) Regulations 2001 (SI 2001/1754).

19.48 When it comes to potentially harmful effects on an SAC or SPA after designation the CJEU has taken a similarly strict initial line, although this too has been moderated – in this case, by the member states. In the *Leybucht Dykes* case,[1] the court concluded that the power of member states to reduce the extent of an SPA once it has been designated only arose in exceptional circumstances. The grounds on which this might be done did not include economic or recreational requirements. However, the effect of this decision has subsequently been side-stepped by amendment of the Directive itself to allow 'imperative reasons of public interest, including those of a social or economic nature' to prevail in some cases.[2]

1 Case C-57/89 [1991] ECR I-833.
2 Habitats Directive, arts 6(4) and 7. See generally on the amendments to Article 6 of the Directive: *Royal Society for the Protection of Birds v Secretary of State for Scotland* [2001] Env LR 19 (on the obligation under Article 6(2) to 'take appropriate steps to avoid the deterioration of the sites and significant disturbance of the species for which the areas have been designated'); Case C-127/02 *Landelijke Vereniging tot Behoud van de Waddenzee, Nederlandse Vereniging tot Bescherming van Vogels v Staatssecretaris van Landbouw, Natuurbeheer en Visserij* (CJEU, 7 September 2004), (on the meaning of 'plan or project' in Article 6(3)); *R (Medway Council) v Secretary of State for Transport* [2002] EWHC 2516 (on the justification for carrying out actitivities harmful to an SPA where there may be no other alternative).

Designation of European Sites

19.49 The Regulations provide for a number of things, including the designation of European Sites; site (and thus habitat) protection stemming from that designation; the making of special nature conservation orders (SNCOs); the grounds upon which consent for interference in designated sites might be given, both by the conservation bodies and by planning authorities; and plant and animal protection. The Regulations rest on a philosophy which, notwithstanding the otherwise apparent similarity to sites of special scientific interest under the 1981 Act, is clearly genuinely orientated towards conservation interests. This is clear from the duty imposed on the Secretary of State, the conservation bodies, and the competent authority (for the purposes of a Marine Area) to exercise their functions under a specified list of enactments so as to secure compliance with the Habitats Directive. Other competent authorities, such as Local Planning Authorities, must have regard to the provisions of the Directive in the exercise of their functions.[1]

1 The Conservation of Habitats and Species Regulations 2010, (hereafter 'the 2010 Regulations'), reg 9.

19.50 The principal designation under the Regulations is that of 'European Site'. This category comprises:[1]

(a) SACs, designated by the Secretary of State from a list of sites of community importance nominated by the Secretary of State by 5 June 1995 and thereafter approved by the European Commission.

(b) Sites of community importance, designated by the Commission on Member States' nomination. Such sites are 'automatically' designated once they are included in the Secretary of State's list of nominations for designation (SACs), thus avoiding the need to await the Commission's approval and thus speeding up their protection.

(c) Sites the status of which is unclear, but which appear to meet the Directive criteria as priority sites but which have been omitted from the Secretary of State's nomination list, pending the Commission's final decision.

(d) SPAs under the Birds Directive.

(e) Candidate SACs.

1 2010 Regulations, reg 13.

19.51 There are complex notification and registration requirements attached to designation as a European Site, including notice to the conservation bodies, which in turn must notify landowners, occupiers and local authorities, and then compile their own register of sites. Such sites are registrable as local land charges.[1]

1 2010 Regulations, regs 13–15.

Implications of designation

19.52 The implications of site designation for a European Site are similar to those arising under other conservation law, with it being envisaged that the principal mechanism of ensuring control will be the management agreement. Until the 2010 Regulations were amended in 2012 it was an offence to carry out potentially damaging operations on a European Site unless done within the terms of a management agreement, with the relevant council's consent, or after allowing a period of four months to elapse.[1] One difference between the legislation and that relating to SSSIs is that the list of potentially damaging operations can be amended at any time. The Regulations also provide far more detail than the provisions of the 1981 Act in relation to the basis on which the nature conservation bodies can grant consent. Where the proposed operations are not directly concerned with or necessary to the management of the site and are likely to have significant effects on the site, the relevant body must make an 'appropriate assessment' of the implications for the site of the proposed operations in view of its nature conservation objectives, and may only give consent 'after having ascertained that the plan or project will not adversely affect the integrity of the site'.[2]

1 2010 Regulations, reg 20; subsequently repealed, subject to transitional arrangements, by the Conservation of Habitats and Species (Amendment) Regulations 2012/1927, reg 12
2 2010 Regulations, reg 21.

19.53 The CJEU has confirmed that, when considering whether proposed operations are likely to have an 'adverse effect' on a site within the Regulations, the proper approach for the decision-maker is as follows:

> 'a risk exists if it cannot be excluded on the basis of objective information that the plan or project will have significant effects on the site....'[1]

Where no consent has been given, but there is a risk that an operation will be carried out anyway the Secretary of State may consider exercising his powers under reg 25 to issue an SNCO.

1 Case C-127/02 Landelijke Vereniging tot Behoud van de Waddenzee, Nederlandse vereniging tot Bescherming van Gogels v Staatssecretaris van Landbouw, Naturbeheer en Visserij (Waddenzee), at paras 43–44.

19.54 SNCOs provide the second level of protection under the Regulations. The consent of the relevant nature conservation body is a necessary precondition to carrying out potentially damaging activities. That consent can only be given on the same basis as applies to European Sites generally.[1]

1 Paras **19.56–19.57**.

19.55 As with other sites protected under the WCA 1981, the grant of planning permission constitutes a 'reasonable excuse' for what would otherwise be the offence of carrying out prohibited operations on a designated site. Unless it is part of the management of a site, development which is likely to have a significant effect on a European site (whether the development is on the site or not) can only be given planning permission after an assessment of the implications of the proposal for the site.[1] If there is a negative assessment, the development can be approved only if there are no alternative solutions and the project must be carried out for 'imperative reasons of overriding public importance'. If the site contains a priority habitat or species, only a limited number of such reasons are relevant to the making of such a determination, namely, reasons relating to human health, public safety or beneficial consequences of primary importance to the environment, or other reasons recognised by the European Commission as imperative reasons.[2] In other circumstances, the factors which a competent authority may take into account are not expressly limited, and may include reasons of a social or economic nature.[3] Development materially affecting a European Site is therefore only likely to be permitted in fairly unusual circumstances.

1 2010 Regulations, reg 61.
2 Ibid, reg 62(2).
3 Ibid, reg 62(1).

19.56 The Regulations go further, however, in requiring a review of existing planning consents. Where a consent was granted, before the coming into force of the Regulations for development which might now have a significant effect on a European Site, that decision must be reviewed in like manner as if it were newly proposed. Planning authorities are then required to 'affirm, modify or revoke' such decisions.[1] Such modifications are effected through established planning powers and will, therefore, normally give rise to the possibility of compensation of the developer. This review does not apply to development which has been completed, nor to that granted or deemed to be granted under the Town and Country Planning (General Permitted Development) Order 1995 or the Town and Country Planning (General Permitted Development) (England) Order 2015·

1   2010 Regulations, reg 63.

19.57 In respect of permitted development rights, the 1994 Regulations introduced a major change (carried through into the 2010 Regulations): if permitted development which is 'not connected with or necessary to the management of the site' is likely to have a significant effect on a European Site, the permission granted by the 1995 or 2015 General Permitted Development Order is subject to a condition that it shall not be begun until the relevant planning authority's written consent has been given.[1] This applies equally where such development has started but has not been completed: it must not continue without written permission. In deciding whether to give permission, the authority may only give permission if satisfied that the development will not adversely affect the integrity of the site. If approval is not given, then planning permission proper must be sought, at which point considerations which might override the conservation value of the site may be relevant. The Regulations also consider the implications of the designation of European Sites for various other legislation, including electricity works, pipelines, works conducted under the Transport and General Works Act, development consent orders under the the Planning Act 2008, and various powers relating to marine sites.[2]

1   2010 Regulations, regs 73–76.
2   2010 Regulations, regs 81–101.

OTHER CONSERVATION DESIGNATIONS

Nature reserves

19.58 A further form of 'designation' is the nature reserve: an area of land managed for the preservation of flora, fauna or geological and physiographical features of special interest, and for enabling research into them.[1] By June 2015 there were 224 National Nature Reserves in England (compared to 222 in 2006), covering over 94,000 hectares. Unlike SSSIs, however, the premise on which nature reserves are based is agreement. The 1949 Act enables management agreements[2] to be entered into by the conservation bodies for the establishment of nature reserves,[3] and subsequently for byelaws to be made 'for the protection of the reserve'.[4] Byelaws may not interfere with the exercise by any person of a right vested in them as an owner, lessee or occupier of land in a reserve.[5] The method by which reserves are created is a simple declaration that land is to be a reserve.[6] Land may be compulsorily acquired for the establishment of a reserve,[7] but this power is used infrequently.

1 NPACA 1949, s 15.
2 Paras **19.39–19.41**.
3 NERCA 2006, s 7 (for England); NPACA 1949, s 16 (for Scotland and Wales).
4 Ibid, s 20. A non-exhaustive list of matters for which byelaws may provide is set out in s 20(2).
5 Ibid, s 20(2).
6 NPACA 1949, ss 19 and 21; WCA 1981, s 35(2).
7 Ibid, s 17.

19.59 There is a further distinction between national and local reserves, which affects who manages a site and for what purposes they may do so. Where land has been declared to be a nature reserve and is managed for that purpose by either a conservation body or an approved body (such as a Wildlife Trust),[1] and the land is of national importance then it may be declared to be a national nature reserve (NNR).[2] Alternatively, a county council, district or county borough council may provide, or secure the provision of, nature reserves in the interests of the locality (LNRs).[3] These may not include areas managed as reserves by the conservation bodies. While there are far more LNRs than NNRs, they tend to be smaller: the 1,280 LNRs in existence at the end of July 2006 occupy a far smaller area than the 200 or more national reserves.

1 WCA 1981, s 35(5).
2 Ibid, s 35(1).
3 NPACA 1949, s 21.

Environmentally sensitive areas and countryside stewardship

19.60 Agriculture law is not the particular focus of this book. However, two particular conservation schemes should be mentioned: environmentally sensitive areas (ESAs) and the countryside stewardship schemes (CSSs). First, the Secretary of State has power to designate 'environmentally sensitive areas' where it appears that it is particularly desirable to:

(a) conserve and enhance the natural beauty of the area;
(b) conserve the flora and fauna and geological and physiographical features of the area; or
(c) to protect buildings and other objects of historic interest,

and that the maintenance or adoption of particular agricultural methods is likely to facilitate those purposes.[1] The Act further enables the Minister to enter into management agreements with any person having an interest in agricultural land by which that person agrees to manage the land as specified by the Order in consideration for payments made by the Minister.[2] A large number of these orders have now been made, and so their ability to affect agricultural landowners is marked.[3]

1 Agriculture Act 1986, s 18(1).
2 Ibid, s 18(3)–(8).
3 See generally the Environmentally Sensitive Areas (England) Designation Orders (Amendment) Regulations 1996, SI 1996/3104, as amended.

19.61 The same observation can be made for activities relating to 'countryside stewardship'. Under new regulations,[1] the Secretary of State has provided for the payment of grants to any person who enters into a 'stewardship agreement' requiring the carrying out of activities conducive to specified purposes on land in which that person has an interest.[2] Those purposes are:

(a) the conservation or enhancement of the natural beauty or amenity of the countryside, including its flora and fauna and geological or physiographical features, or of any features of archaeological interest there; or

(b) the promotion of the enjoyment of the countryside by the public.[3]

Detailed provisions in respect of agreements and grants are set out in the Regulations, although it should be noted that an obligation is placed on an agreement-holder to notify the Minister in the event of a change in occupation of the land to which it applies.[4] That notification must normally be given within three months after the change in occupation concerned, and the minister may then decide to enter into an agreement with the new occupier of the land for the remainder of the term of the original agreement.

More recently, the Environmental Stewardship Scheme has been introduced in England, which aims to secure widespread environmental benefits across agricultural land. There are three tiers to the scheme. First there is 'Entry Level Stewardship', a 'whole farm scheme' open to all farmers and land managers. 'Organic Entry Level Stewardship' is a similar scheme, but only open to those farmers or land managers who farm all or part of their land organically. Finally, 'High Level Stewardship' applies in high priority situations and areas, and concentrates on the more complex types of management where land managers need advice and support and where agreements need to be tailored to local circumstances. Financial support for commitments in respect of land management on each of these schemes is available to varying degrees. Existing ESAs and CSSs are able to be transferred to the ESS.

1 The Countryside Stewardship Regulations 1998, SI 1998/1327.
2 SI 1996/695, reg 4. These schemes replace those previously made with the Countryside Commission under CA 1968, s 4, as amended by WCA 1981, s 40.
3 SI 1998/1327, reg 3(1).
4 Ibid, reg 9.

NATURE CONSERVATION AND PLANNING LAW

19.62 The fragmented nature of conservation law and site designations serves to emphasise the important 'background' role of planning powers. This is particularly so in respect of the principal designation of SSSI, where effective control in many cases is ceded to planning authorities, who can provide a 'reasonable excuse' to a site-related offence in many cases through the grant of planning permission.[1] The ability to do so is more qualified in the cases of European sites: the same 'defence' applies, but the basis on which planning consent may itself be granted has been modified.[2] The detail of planning law cannot be considered here, but it will be important to note the implications of specific planning policy in respect of conservation. That policy will guide the exercise by local planning authorities of their powers; it also provides a residual framework where nature conservation law itself does not apply (for example, local non-statutory site or area designations).

1 WCA 1981, s 28P(4).
2 Paras **19.55–19.57**.

General policy framework

19.63 National planning policy is set out in the National Planning Policy Framework (April 2014) (NPPF). More detailed development control policies will be found in the Statutory Development Plan which is adopted by a local planning authority for its area. According to the NPPF, the purpose of the planning system is to contribute to the achievement of 'sustainable development', a concept which has three dimensions. One of those is 'the environmental role', which means:

> 'contributing to protecting and enhancing our natural, built and historic environment; and, as part of this, helping to improve biodiversity, use natural resources prudently, minimise waste and pollution, and mitigate and adapt to climate change including moving to a low carbon economy'.[1]

1 NPPF para 7.

19.64 Conservation interests generally are likely to be a material planning consideration in development control decisions, as will be the fact of a particular site designation.

19.65 Local planning authorities should adopt criteria-based policies against which proposals for any development on or affecting protected wildlife or geodiversity sites will be judged. Distinctions should be made between the hierarchy of international, national and locally designated sites so that protection is commensurate with their status and gives appropriate weight to their importance and the contribution that they make to wider ecological networks.[1]

1 NPPF para 113; see also para 114.

Development control

19.66 According to the NPPF, planning decision makers should:

> '[approve] development proposals that accord with the development plan without delay; and

- • where the development plan is absent, silent or relevant policies are out of date, [grant] permission unless:
  - – any adverse impacts of doing so would significantly and demonstrably outweigh the benefits, when assessed against the policies in this Framework taken as a whole; or
  - – specific policies in this Framework indicate development should be restricted.'[1]

1 NPPF para 14.

Chapter 20

Environmental permitting and atmospheric pollution

INTRODUCTION

20.01 As a non-exhaustive explanation of environmental law in property transactions, this book cannot set out the detail of the Environmental Permitting regime established by the Environmental Permitting (England and Wales) Regulations 2010 ('the EP Regulations').[1] This area of the law is complex and has evolved significantly in the recent past. In England and Wales the EP Regulations replaced the Pollution Prevention and Control (England and Wales) Regulations 2000 (the 'PPC Regulations') from 6 April 2008. The EP Regulations bring together the PPC and Waste Management Licensing Regulations into one new regulatory system. Apart from combining the two sets of Regulations to which other licensing regimes have been added, there have been no major changes to the PPC aspects. A permit issued under the PPC Regulations is regarded as having been issued under the EP Regulations. Both sets of regulations were introduced under the Pollution Prevention and Control Act 1999 and build on the system which existed under Part I of the EPA 1990. The PPC Regulations replaced the pollution control regimes called Integrated Pollution Control (IPC) and Local Air Pollution Control which had been set up under Part I of the Environmental Protection Act 1990 (EPA 1990).[2]

1 Originally SI 2007/3538 but replaced by SI 2010/675.
2 It should be noted that s 6(2) of the Pollution Prevention and Control Act 1999 has not yet been commenced, as a result of which Part I of the 1990 Act is only prospectively repealed.

20.02 Part I of the EPA 1990 did make an important shift towards a more structured and centralised approach to the control of pollution from the largest and most polluting industrial processes. It is therefore an important part of the backdrop to the exercise of other pollution-related powers by both the Environment Agency and by local authorities. This shift in pollution controls was achieved through the creation of two separate, but conceptually and practically interconnected, systems of control. The first was the IPC system itself, under which emissions into *all* environmental media from the most polluting industrial processes are supervised by the Environment Agency.[1] That system was intended to 'prevent or minimise pollution of the environment due to the release of substances into any environmental media'[2] and was itself extended – and deepened – by the integrated pollution prevention and control (IPPC) system which was in turn replaced by the environmental permitting regime.[3] The second is local air pollution control (APC), under which local authorities supervise less complex or polluting processes and their emissions to air, but not their emissions to other environmental media. Here too, these powers were modified, so that local authorities exercise 'integrated' controls over some processes regulated by the environmental permitting regime.

1 EPA 1990, s 4.
2 Pollution Prevention and Control Act 1999; see paras **20.06.**
3 Paras **20.06–20.15.**

20.03 Whilst the IPC system had some distinctive characteristics in itself,[1] its contribution to atmospheric pollution control is also important. Historically, such controls have been complex and disjointed. Statutory controls over smoke have existed for some parts of the country (notably London) since the thirteenth century, and have always complemented regulation through the law of nuisance.[2] Newer statutory powers therefore add to an existing legal framework, which also includes controls over smoke and smoke-producing activity.[3] It has been sought to bring a more structured approach to the exercise of these historically fragmented powers by the further superimposition of a strategic air quality planning process.[4] As discussed below, this has more of a co-ordinating role than certain apparently similar policy statements, and in any event is quite limited in scope.[5]

1 In particular, the application of the 'best practicable environmental option' requirement.
2 Which may still apply: see Chs 13 and 14.
3 Eg, Clean Air Act 1993; paras **20.15–20.17.**
4 Eg, the publication of a new *Air Quality Strategy for England, Scotland, Wales and Northern Ireland*, Cm 4548, January 2000.
5 Paras 20.04–20.05.

THE STRATEGIC CONTEXT

20.04 There is a trend in UK environmental law generally towards greater definition of strategic objectives, partly in response to European initiatives.[1] This trend is confirmed in the context of integrated controls and atmospheric pollution. In particular, under the Environment Act 1995, the Secretary of State may for the first time prepare a national strategy with respect to the assessment or management of the quality of air.[2] Originally published in 1997,[3] that strategy was reviewed in 1998 and a revised version published in early 2000 with an Addendum in 2003. The latest strategy was published in July 2007.[4] The strategy is intended to set out objectives for the management of ambient air quality in the long term, focusing on the 10 air pollutants considered to have the greatest impact on human health: oxides of nitrogen, benzene, ozone, 1,3-butadiene, polycyclic aromatic hydrocarbons, carbon monoxide, lead, amonia, certain particulates and sulphur dioxide. As such, the strategy is also the principal vehicle for giving effect to obligations imposed by the Ambient Air Quality Directive.[5]

1 Eg, Ambient Air Quality Directive (2008/50/EC) and the Industrial Emissions Directive (2010/75/EU).
2 EA 1995, ss 80–81.Under EPA 1990, s 3.

3 *The Unitied Kingdom National Air Quality Strategy*, Cm 3587, 1997.
4 *The Air Quality Strategy for England, Scotland, Wales and Northern Ireland.*
5 2008/50/EC.

20.05 The strategy relies for its implementation on the whole raft of controls considered here. One of the most important sets of controls is that operated by local authorities. Not only does the strategy provide a framework within which individual air pollution authorisations are determined,[1] but in conjunction with the statutory air quality standards made in support[2] it may also trigger the exercise by local authorities of their powers to secure the achievement of strategic objectives through 'air quality management areas' and associated 'action plans'.[3] For example, where any of the objectives prescribed in the relevant air quality regulations are not likely to be achieved within any part of a local authority's area within periods that are also prescribed,[4] the authority concerned is required to designate that part of its area as an air quality management area.[5] An action plan must then be prepared setting out how the authority intends to exercise the whole range of its powers in pursuit of the objectives.[6] The time allowed for compliance, coupled with the fragmentation of the powers themselves, makes the significance of these provisions in particular cases hard to assess. As the planning framework may also prompt the exercise of other powers – traffic control or reduction most obviously – concern in practice may focus on the particular implementation framework rather than these 'umbrella' provisions.

1 Eg, the Agency must 'have regard' to the strategy in exercising its functions: EA 1995, s 81(1).
2 Air Quality (England) Regulations 2000, SI 2000/928, 6 April 2000; for Wales, SI 2000/1940, 1 August 2000; and for Scotland, SI 2000/97, 6 April 2000.
3 EA 1995, ss 82–4.
4 Eg, SI 2000/928, reg 3.
5 EA 1995, s 83(1).
6 See *Local Air Quality Management*, Technical Guidance LAQM. TG(09), DEFRA February 2009.

THE DIRECTIVES ON INTEGRATED POLLUTION PREVENTION AND CONTROL AND INDUSTRIAL EMISSIONS

20.06 The implementation in the UK of the Council Directive 91/61/EC on integrated pollution prevention and control was preceded by a complex and lengthy consultation process, including the publication of three consultation papers before the PPCA 1999 received the Royal Assent,[1] and one afterwards.[2] Although the Directive borrowed heavily from the UK's own IPC system, it was not identical to it, and its implementation therefore brought some important changes to industrial pollution control. The UK therefore had some advantage relative to other member states in implementing the obligations under the Directive,[3] but there were also some important difficulties arising in connection with the superimposition of IPPC on the UK's IPC system. These were summarised in the course of Parliamentary consideration of the (then) PPC Bill:[4]

(a) the range of environmental impacts addressed by IPPC was wider than IPC;

(b) the Directive extended the number of installations subject to integrated controls to apply to some 6,000 installations rather than the 2,000 subject to IPC. These included: about 1,000 landfill sites previously regulated under EPA 1990, Part 2; installations subject to a combination of local air pollution controls, trade effluent or waste discharge consenting under WIA 1991 or WRA 1991; and installations whose emissions as a whole were not currently controlled by a permitting regime, but whose discharges to water were subject to the consent of the Agency or a sewerage undertaker and other specific controls applied, such as those within a nitrate vulnerable zone;[5]

(c) in some cases the IPC system was wider than IPPC; and

(d) it had always been the government's intention to take the opportunity of implementing IPPC to make some improvements to the IPC regime in light of experience since 1990, including in respect of public consultation and transparency.

1 DETR, July 1997, January 1998 and January 1999; considered at (1997) 9 Environmental Law & Management 215; (1998) 10 Environmental Law & Management 28 (1999) 11 Environmental Law & Management 87, respectively.
2 DETR, August 1999, considered at (1999) 58 EnvLBull 1. The final outcome of the consultation process was reported at (2000) 66 Environmental Law Bulletin 1.
3 Tromans, Annotations to the Pollution Prevention and Control Act 1999, *Current Law Statutes*, 1999, Vol 1, p 24–2.
4 Lord Whitty, *Official Report*, HL, Vol 595, col 780.
5 Eg, intensive poultry and pig farms.

20.07 Rather than extending or supplementing IPC controls by use of delegated powers under the European Communities Act 1972, the approach adopted was to introduce new primary legislation, supported by regulations, in the hope of introducing a more cohesive and intelligible new system. The purpose of the PPCA 1999 is therefore to 'enable a single, coherent pollution control system to be set up by regulations which will apply to all the installations to which the Directive applies and to those installations previously regulated under Part I of the 1990 Act but to which the Directive did not apply.' The practical problem, however, was the limited time available to complete this process. The solution was to introduce a 'skeletal' bill, with almost all matters of detail to be left to implementing regulations. The consequence was considerable Parliamentary controversy. For example, the first draft of the Bill extended to just four substantive sections and three short schedules. This prompted referral of the Bill to the House of Lords Select Committee on Delegated Powers and Deregulation, which produced a 'damning indictment' of the Bill and the extent to which it proposed to delegate powers to the Secretary of State.[1] The Committee's fundamental concern was '. . . whether it can ever be right to legislate on a topic of such importance, which provides for widespread controls and affects the activities carried on both on a commercial and private basis, leaving everything of substance to be determined either by or under the regulations.'

1 *Official Report*, HL, 15 February 1999, col 466.

20.08 As a consequence of this stormy Parliamentary passage,[1] the Bill which received the Royal Assent on 27 July 1999 was markedly changed, although it still delegates considerable powers to the Secretary of State and its brevity continues to belie its importance. The main features of the Act are as follows:

(a) Section 1 sets out a threefold general purpose for powers exercised under the Act, being to: implement Council Directive 96/61/EC concerning integrated pollution prevention and control; regulate, otherwise than in pursuance of that Directive, activities which are capable of causing any environmental pollution; and otherwise to prevent or control emissions capable of causing such pollution. This is not a narrow purpose, and certainly enables the Secretary of State to go some way beyond the Directive in extending integrated controls to industrial processes not previously subject to IPC, or to pollution control at all.

(b) Schedule 1 to the Act sets out the further detailed purposes for which the regulation-making power provided by the Act may be used.[2] This is a very elaborate list, which does not restrict the Secretary of State's powers in any meaningful sense. This is apparent from the Regulations which have subsequently been adopted.[3]

(c) The IPPC Directive applied to large combustion plants on offshore oil and gas installations, and so the Act was used to implement the requirements of the Oslo and Paris Convention of 1992 (the Ospar Convention) on the use and discharge of chemicals from offshore platforms.[4]

(d) Responsibility for implementation of IPPC and the Industrial Emissions Directive in Scotland falls to the Scottish Parliament,[5] while the Regulations made under the Act are expressed to apply to England and Wales.[6]

1 Considered in greater depth by Tromans, Annotations to the Pollution Prevention and Control Act 1999, *Current Law Statutes*, 1999, Vol 1, pp 24–3 to 24–4.
2 PPCA 1999, s 2.
3 Environmental Permitting Regulations, SI 2010/675.
4 PPCA 1999, s 3.
5 Scotland Act 1998, s 53; PPCA 1999, s 5(3), Pollution Prevention and Control (Scotland) Regulations 2012 (SI 2012/360).
6 SI 2010/675, reg 1(1)(c).

20.09 The original IPPC Directive was replaced by an updated directive in 2008[1] which was in turn replaced by the Industrial Emissions Directive[2] (IED) which required transposition over an extended period between 2013 and 2016. The IED repealed and replaced within its scope seven earlier directives including the IPPC Directive,[3] the Large Combustion Plant Directive,[1] the Waste Incineration Directive[4] the Solvent Emissions Directive[5] and three directives on titanium dioxide.[6] The new directive generally builds on and improves the controls under the former IPPC directive. It contains common provisions on permitting followed by provisions applicable to particular industries. Detailed emission limit values for individual processes are set in Annexes to the IED.

The general provisions of the IED include:

(a) an obligation on the operator of an installation to hold a permit;[7]
(b) a power for member states to include requirements for certain categories of plant in general binding rules;[8]
(c) a requirement for operators to inform the competent authority immediately in the event of any incident or accident significantly affecting the environment and to take measures to limit the environmental consequences and prevent further occurrences, and to take appropriate complementary measures considered necessary by the competent authority.[9]

The provisions in Chapter II of the IED apply to the installations listed in Annex I which comprises an extended version of the installations listed in the former IPPC Directive. Again, the provisions of the IED expand on the equivalent provisions in the latter directive. The general principles of the IED governing the basic obligations of the operator are that:[10]

(a) the operator must take all appropriate preventive measures against pollution;
(b) the best available techniques[11] must be applied;
(c) no significant pollution must be caused;
(d) the waste hierarchy must be applied to the generation and management of waste in accordance with the Waste Framework Directive;[12]
(e) energy must be used efficiently;
(f) necessary measures must be taken to prevent accidents and limit their consequences;
(g) on final cessation of activities steps are taken to avoid any risk of pollution and return the site to a satisfactory state.[13]

'Pollution' is defined as the introduction of harmful substances, vibrations, heat or noise into air, water or land, which expands on the earlier IPC model in the UK.[14]

One of the most significant innovations of the IED relates to site closure. Whereas the IPPC Directive simply required that competent authorities must ensure that the necessary measures are taken upon definitive cessation of activities to avoid any pollution risk and return the site of operation to a satisfactory state,[15] the IED is much more specific.

Before starting to operate an installation (or before a permit is updated for the first time after 7 January 2013), the operator must submit to the competent authority a baseline report which demonstrates the state of soil and ground contamination for the purpose of a quantified comparison with its state on definitive cessation of activities.[16] On definitive cessation of activities, the operator must assess the state of soil and groundwater contamination caused by the operation of the installation. Where significant soil or groundwater pollution has been caused compared to the condition of the site demonstrated by the baseline report, the operator must take the necessary measures to return the site to that 'baseline' state, taking account of the technical feasibility of those measures.[17] Where soil and groundwater contamination at the site poses a significant risk to human health or the environment as a result of the operator's activities carried out prior to the baseline report produced for the first update of the permit after 7 January 2013, (or in the absence of any requirement for a baseline report) the operator must take the necessary remedial action so that the site, taking into account its current or approved future uses, ceases to pose such a risk.[18]

1 2008/1/EC.
2 2010/75/EU.
3 2001/80/EC.
4 2000/76/EC.
5 1999/13/EC.
6 1978/176/EEC, 1982/883/ECC and 1992/112/EEC.
7 Article 4. The obligation to hold a permit also applies to combustion plants, waste incineration plans and co-incineration plants. 'Installation' is defined as 'a stationary technical unit within which one or more [listed] activities ... are carried out, and any other directly associated activities on the same site which have a technical connection with the activities listed.... and which could have an effect on emissions and pollution': Article 3(3). See *Burnett-Hall on Environmental Law*, 3rd edn (2012) 23-018-23-028. 'Operator' is defined as 'any natural or legal person who operates or controls ... the installation ... or, where this is provided for in national law, to whom decisive economic power over the technical functioning of the installation ... has been delegated': Article 3(15).
8 Article 6.
9 Article 7.
10 Article 11.
11 Article 3(10) BAT builds on the concept of Best available techniques not entailing excessive cost (BATNEEC) in Part I of the Environmental Protection Act 1990 (now repealed). Provision is made in the IED for BAT reference documents and BAT conclusions to describe what BAT is in practice: Article 13.
12 2008/98/EC.
13 Articles 11(h) and 22.
14 Article 3(2).
15 Article 3.1(f) of 2008/1/EC.
16 Article 22.2.
17 Article 22.3.
18 Article 22.3 and 22.4. In deciding the necessary measures, account must be taken of the condition of the site established by the description in the permit application (in accordance with Article 12.1(d), which was a requirement under Article 6.1(d) of the earlier IPPC Directive 2008/I/EC).

The Environmental Permitting Regulations 2010

20.10 The structure and details of IPPC controls that were contained in the PPC Regulations have now been replaced by the EP Regulations.[1] They have been made under s 2 of the Act: a provision which sets out an exclusive list of the matters for or in connection with which the regulations may be made; and one which is subject to the general purpose of the Act itself.[2] Neither of these lists is narrow.[3] The EP Regulations do not make substantive changes to the PPC Regulations. While the EP Regulations as the PPC Regulations did before reflect in large part the structure of controls under Part I of EPA 1990, there are significant differences, the first of which is the activities to which the EP Regulations apply.

1 Originally SI 2007/3538, now SI 2010/675 which are due to be replaced by new EP Regulations in 2016.
2 PPCA 1999, s 1.
3 For the latter, see para 20.08.

20.11 The general effect of the EP Regulations is to produce a single regulatory framework for activities governed by the IED, local air pollution control and mobile plant, as well as waste and mining waste operations, radioactive substances, water discharge, groundwater and solvent emission activities and small waste incineration plants.

The common regulatory framework is contained in the main part of the EP Regulations, supplemented by Schedules 5 and 6 which contain detailed provisions on environmental permits and appeals respectively. Most of the other Schedules impose duties on the regulators to exercise their functions so as to comply with specified EU Directives which fall under the umbrella of the EP Regulations:

Directive	Schedule to the EP Regulations
Industrial Emissions Directive (2010/75/EU)	Schedules 7A, 13A, 14, 15A, 17A
Energy Efficiency Directive (2012/27/EU)	Schedule 8A
Waste Framework Directive (2008/98/EC)	Schedule 9
Landfill Directive (1991/31/EC)	Schedule 10
End-of-Life Vehicles Directive (2000/53/EC)	Schedule 11
Waste Electrical and Electronic Equipment Directive (2012/19/EU)	Schedule 12
Asbestos Directive (87/217/EEC)	Schedule 16
Petrol Vapour Recovery Directives (94/63/EC and 2009/126/EC) Directive)	Schedule 18
Batteries and Accumulators (2006/66/EC)	Schedule 19
Water Framework Directive (2000/60/EC) and Groundwater Daughter Directive (2006/118/EC)	Schedules 21 and 22

Schedule 8 contains the provisions governing the regulators' duties to exercise their powers in respect of local authority air pollution controls which are not covered by EU law.

Which Regulator?

20.12 Schedule 1, Part 2 of the EP Regulations divides installations[1] into three categories according to which authority will be the regulator: Part A(1), Part A(2) and Part B. The regulatory functions for all regulated facilities[2] governed by the EP Regulations are allocated as follows:[3]

'(1) Functions in relation to a Part A(1) installation1 or Part A(1) or Part A(2) mobile plant are exercisable by the Environment Agency.
(2) Functions in relation to a Part A(2) installation, a Part B installation, a Part B mobile plant, a small waste incineration plant or a solvent emissions activity are exercisable by the local authority in whose area the installation is or will be operated.

(3)   If the operator of Part B mobile plant has his principal place of business in England and Wales, functions in relation to that plant are exercisable by the local authority in whose area the place of business is.

(4)   If the operator of Part B mobile plant does not have his principal place of business in England and Wales, functions in relation to that plant are exercisable by—

(a)   the local authority which granted the environmental permit authorising the operation of the plant; or

(b)   if no permit has been granted, the local authority in whose area the plant is first operated, or is intended to be first operated.

(5)   Functions in relation to a waste operation (unless it is a Part B activity) a mining waste operation, a water discharge activity or groundwater activity, are exercisable by the Agency even if carried on at a Part B installation or Part B mobile plant.'

1 'Installation' means (except where used in the definition of 'excluded plant' in s 5.1 of Part 2 of Sch 1): (a) a stationary technical unit where one or more activities are carried on; and (b) any other location on the same site where any other directly associated activities are carried on. The definition reflects that in the IED – See para **20.09**, n 7. 'Activities' are those listed in Schedule 1, Part 2 which cover operations governed by the IED as well as local authority air pollution control. EP Regulations, reg 2(1).
2 Defined in EP Regulations, reg 8 – see para **20.18**.
3 EP Regulations, reg 32.

20.13 The basic criminal backbone to the PPC Regulations is that no person may operate a regulated facility[1] except under and to the extent authorised by an environmental permit.[2] An environmental permit is granted by the the appropriate regulator.[3] Schedule 5 makes detailed provision in respect of the granting and content of permits.

Whilst the general principles to be taken into account in determining the conditions to which permits are to be subject were set out in unusual detail in the PPC Regulations, the EP Regulations do not replicate that detail and leave the conditions wholly in the regulator's discretion. However, reg 64 provides that the Secretary of State may issue guidance to a regulator with respect to the exercise of its functions under the Regulations. The regulator must have regard to any such guidance.

1 EP Regulations, reg 8 – see para **20.18**.
2 EP Regulations. reg 12.
3 Ibid, reg 13(1).

20.14 A substantial amount of guidance has been issued by the Secretary of State: the Environmental Permitting Core Guidance (which describes the general permitting and compliance requirements); and guidance on the European Directives implemented through the regime including the Industrial Emissions Directive (2010/75/EU), Waste Framework Directive (2008/98/EC), End-of Life Vehicles Directive (2000/53/EC), Waste Electrical and Electronic Equipment Directive (2002/96/EC), Landfill Directive (1999/31/EC), and Petrol Vapour Recovery Directives (94/63/EC and 2009/126/EC). DEFRA has also issued section guidance notes for Part A installations and process guidance notes for Part B installations.

20.15 As is the case in other environmental licensing contexts, permits are subject to periodic review.[1] Correspondingly, conditions may be varied, and permits may be transferred or revoked.[2]

1 EP Regulations, reg 34.
2 Ibid, regs 20, 21 and 22.

20.16 Further provisions of the EP Regulations include: enforcement and offences (Part 4) public registers (Part 5); powers and functions of the regulator and the appropriate authority (Part 6); and transitional and consequential provisions.

20.17 The Government has prepared and is currently consulting on draft Environmental Permitting (England and Wales) Regulations 2016 which it expects to come into force on 1 January 2017. The purpose of the 2016 Regulations will be to consolidate the numerous amendments made to the 2010 Regulations and also to take account of amendments made by other legislation. Whilst the draft regulations do not contain any major policy changes, they are expected to strengthen the enforcement powers of the Environment Agency and Natural Resources Wales to tackle waste crime and poor performance in the waste industry. A review of the EP Regulations will be undertaken in England in 2019 as part of a broader statutory review.

When is a permit required?

20.18 Under the EP Regulations only 'regulated facilities' require a permit. The definition of a 'regulated facility'[1] includes:

(a) Installations – ie those activities controlled under the IED together with others regulated under the Local Authority Air Pollution regime.
(b) Waste operations – ie any disposal or recovery of waste not carried out at an installation. (See *R (on the application of Tarmac Aggregates Ltd) v The Secretary of State for Environment, Food and Rural Affairs & Anor* for the approach to waste recovery.)
(c) Mobile plant.
(d) Radioactive substances activities.
(e) Water discharge and groundwater activities.
(f) Small waste incineration plants.
(g) Solvent emissions activities.
(h) Flood risk activities.

The Environmental Permitting (England and Wales) (Amendment) (No 2) Regulations 2016 bring flood risk activities[2] within the framework of regulated facilities under the EP Regulations from 6 April 2016. These are governed by a new Schedule 23ZA. A long list of exemptions in a new Part 4 of Schedule 3 relieve low risk activities from the permitting requirement. There is also a long-standing proposal to regulate water abstraction under the EP Regulations but so far this has not materialised.

However, the following are not regulated facilities:[3]

(a) Exempt facilities.[4]
(b) Excluded waste operations.[5]
(c) The disposal or recovery of household waste from a domestic property within the curtilage of that property by a person other than an establishment or undertaking.

A single environmental permit can cover multiple regulated facilities listed in Schedule 1. This means that on a site where different activities take place, there is no need for multiple permits.[6] However, a single permit cannot cover similar activities carried out by different operators.

1 EP Regulations, reg 8.
2 SI 2016/475. The definition of flood risk activities covers erecting structures in, over or under a main river (currently regulated under s 109 of the Water Resources Act 1991, which will be repealed) as well as many other activities currently regulated under byelaws.
3 EP Regulations, reg 8(2).
4 EP Regulations, reg 5, Sch 3.
5 EP Regulations, reg 2.
6 This has raised questions in some cases as to extent to which physically discrete installations actually form part of the same site. See *United Utilities v Environment Agency* [2006] EWCA 633. In that case the company operated several sludge treatment facilities which were linked to a facility for final treatment some 700m away. The Court discussed the coherence of the 'regulated facility' in terms of the coherence of the 'site'. Proximity was relevant but not determinative. On the facts of the case, 700m was considered too far away to form a single site.

Applications for an environmental permit

20.19 Only the operator of a regulated facility can apply for an environmental permit (reg 13). An operator is defined by reference to the degree of 'control' exercised over the facility (reg 7). No person may operate a regulated facility except under and to the extent authorised by an environmental permit. Operators are advised to undertake pre-application discussions with the regulators to establish whether there is a need for a permit and to discuss the procedure for granting it.[1]

The requirements for applications are set out in Schedule 5 to the 2010 Regulations. The application must be made by the operator or his agent in the correct form and enclose the prescribed information and the relevant fee. The periods for determining applications are two months for an application to transfer a permit; three months to surrender or vary a permit and four months for a fresh application for the grant of a permit (other than a mobile plant and most standard facilities) or to vary a permit where public participation is required.[2] These determination periods are not fixed and may lengthen where further information is required or the information being dealt with is of a sensitive nature.[3] The regulator must notify the applicant of its decision and the reasons for it.[4] The determination must be published on the regulator's website. In the interests of clarity, the regulator should issue a new permit consolidating any changes as a result of the application. The Secretary of State has the power to 'call in' applications which give rise to issues of substantial regional or national significance (reg 62). In those circumstances, the regulator will send any consultation representations to the Secretary of State who will issue the final decision.

1 See DEFRA, *Environmental Permitting Guidance - Core Guidance* (March 2013) https://www.gov.uk/government/uploads/system/uploads/attachment_data/file/211852/pb13897-ep-core-guidance-130220.pdf.
2 2010 Regulations, Sch 5, Pt 1, para 15.
3 2010 Regulations, Sch 5, Pt 1, para 4.
4 2010 Regulations, Sch 5, Pt 1, para 17.

Determining applications

20.20 The regulator must determine whether a permit application accords with the relevant requirements of the EU Directives and thereby provides the necessary level of environmental protection. The regulator must either grant the permit, usually subject to conditions, or refuse it (reg 13). The determination involves the exercise of expert judgment and is therefore difficult to challenge.[1] A regulator must refuse a permit application if it considers the applicant will not be the operator of the facility or it doubts the competence of the operator and his ability to comply with any permitting conditions.[2] Reasons for doubting an operator's competence may include doubts as to management competence, technical competence, financial competence or a poor record of compliance with previous regulatory requirements.[3]

1 See eg *Levy v Environment Agency* [2003] Env LR 11.
2 2010 Regulations, Sch 5, Pt 1, para 13. The second requirement does not apply in the case of applications for a stand-alone water or groundwater activity: Sch.5, para 13(3), EP Regulations.
3 See Environmental Permitting Guidance, Gore Guidance, DEFRA 2013, section 9.

Permit conditions

20.21 The regulator can impose any conditions it sees fit when granting a permit.[1] It has a duty to do so in order secure the objectives that apply to the particular category of facility. All permit conditions should be necessary and enforceable. The conditions may stipulate objectives or outcomes, set standards for mitigating a specific risk or directly address a legislative requirement.[2] The conditions may pertain to steps which are required to be carried out before, during or after the operation of the facility. There are deemed conditions (unless expressly included) in every permit governed by the IED, requiring the operator:

(a) to report to the regulator incidents and accidents which significantly affect the environment and to take necessary measures to limit the environmental consequences and prevent further possible incidents and accidents;

(b) to report to the regulator the breach of any permit condition and to ensure that compliance is restored within the shortest possible time; and

(c) in the event of a breach of a permit condition which poses an immediate danger to human health or threatens an immediate significant adverse effect on the environment to suspend the operation of the facility (or relevant part of it) immediately until compliance with the condition has been restored.[3]

The regulator is under a statutory duty to ensure compliance with specified provisions in the relevant Directives. Regulators can impose permit conditions requiring operators to do things which they are not entitled to do without obtaining the consent of another person.[4] For example, the conditions may be used where it is necessary to monitor the effects of an activity on another person's land. The person who owns, occupies or with the ability to grant rights of access to the relevant land must be notified by the regulator.[5] The person whose consent is required must grant consent. However, they will be entitled to compensation from the operator.[6]

1 EP Regulations, Sch 5, Pt 1, para 12(2).
2 Environmental Permitting, Core Guidance DEFRA 2013, sections 7.8–7.11.
3 EP Regulations, Sch 5, para 20.
4 EP Regulations, reg 15(1).
5 EP Regulations, Sch 5, Part 1, para 9.
6 EP Regulations, Sch 5, Part 2.

Transfer applications

20.22 The EP Regulations allow for the transfer of permits from one operator to another.[1] A permit can be transferred completely or partially, so that the original operator retains control of some of the facility and another operator takes over the operation of the transferred part. A joint application must usually be made by the transferor and the transferee. However, where the operator (or one or more of two or more joint operators) cannot be found, a transfer may still take place on the application of the transferee alone or of the transferee and the joint operators who can be found as appropriate. In the case of a stand-alone water discharge activity, stand-alone groundwater activity or stand-alone flood risk activity, the transfer may be effected by the regulator on a notification by the operator and proposed transferee, with equivalent provisions where the operator (or one or more of two or more joint operators) cannot be found.

The regulator must refuse the application if it considers that the proposed transferee would not be the operator or would not operate the facility in accordance with the permit.[2] There is a two month time limit for determining a transfer application. If no determination has been made in that window and no extension of time has been agreed by the parties the application is deemed to have been refused.[3]

1 EP Regulations, reg 21. See ch 12.
2 EP Regulations, Sch 5, para 13.
3 EP Regulations, Sch 5, para 15.

Surrender of a permit

20.23 A permit imposes continuing obligations on an operator even after those activities have ceased until the operator formally surrenders the permit. There are two methods for surrender of a permit. Operators of certain regulated facilities (Part B installations, mobile plants, solvent emission activities, and stand-alone water discharge activities, groundwater activities and flood risk activities – in the latter case, except where a permit condition is to operate after the activity is complete) may simply notify the regulator. In all other cases the operator must apply to the regulator to surrender.[1] It is possible to surrender *part* of the permit for a regulated facility. This is the only method for reducing the extent of the site of the regulated facility covered by the permit.

The regulator must accept an application to surrender if it is satisfied that the necessary measures have been taken to:[2]

(i)   avoid any pollution risk from the operation of the regulated facility;
(ii) return the site of the regulated facility to a satisfactory state, having regard to the state of the site before the facility was put into operation; and
(iii) to avoid any specified risk in the case of permits authorising a flood risk activity.

The requirement to avoid any pollution risk must be interpreted in a proportionate way. In practice, the operator should address the risks of any pollution that could occur, unless the risk is so small that action is not justified. The regulator will hold the operator responsible for any contamination to the land unless it is not reasonable to do so or the operator is able to prove that the contamination occurred before the permit was issued. The operator is responsible for any change between the condition of the site as described in the original information supplied with the permit application and the application to surrender. The operator must return the site in a 'satisfactory state' i.e. to its original condition (although clearly this will not always be possible for example where the land has been used for landfill). This may be significantly stricter than the 'suitable for use' test under the contaminated land regime in Part 2A of the EPA 1990.[3]

1 EP Regulations, regs. 24 and 25.
2 EP Regulations, Sch.5, para 14.
3 See Regulatory Guidance Note, RGN9: Surrender, Environment Agency, May 2013.

Variation

20.24 The regulator may vary an environmental permit on the application of the operator or on its own initiative.[1] A variation application may include an increase to the area over which the regulated facility operates. Where this occurs, issues such as the protection of the land and, where relevant, land use planning must be addressed. A variation cannot reduce the area covered by a permit except in the case of a Part B installation (not relating to a waste operation) and a stand-alone water discharge or ground water activity.[2] Where a substantial change is proposed there must be public participation or the regulator may request public consultation on its own initiative.[3] The regulator must not, without the agreement of the operator, vary on its own initiative any permit condition relating to a stand-alone water discharge activity within four years of the grant of the permit or earlier variation of a condition. There is an exception in the case of a standard facility where the variation is necessary, to comply with EU obligations or a direction by the Secretary of State or Welsh Ministers, or where the variation is the consequence of the partial transfer of the permit.[4] There are also restrictions on the regulator's power to vary a permit for a stand-alone flood risk activity unless the operator agrees.[5]

1 EP Regulations, reg 20(1).
2 EP Regulations, reg 20(2) and (3).
3 EP Regulations, Sch 5 Part 1, para 5.
4 EP Regulations, reg 20(4) and (5).
5 EP Regulations, reg 20(7).

Standard permits

20.25 A key innovation under the EP Regulations is the power of the Environment Agency to draw up standard rules.[1] The standard rules must achieve the same level of environmental protection as site-specific conditions. Standard rules, applicable to different classes of facilities, are being developed in consultation between the EA and the relevant industries. There is a duty on regulators to ensure the standard rules are kept under review.[2] Where revisions are proposed, fresh consultation may be required. It is the operator's decision whether to apply to the EA to be allowed to operate under the standard rules. These standard rules cannot be appealed since applying for such a permit is voluntary.[3] No additional site-specific risk assessment will be necessary for a standard facility once the standard conditions have been attached to the permit. If the rules are modified, the operators subject to the standard rules will be notified[4] and given three months to decide whether they wish to continue to operate under the revised rules. The standard rules may also be revoked altogether but the rules will remain in force until the regulator has varied the conditions of the permit.[5]

1 2010 Regulations, reg 26. See Defra, *Environmental Permitting Core Guidance*, Ch 8.
2 2010 Regulations, reg 26(4).
3 2010 Regulations, reg 27(3).
4 2010 Regulations, reg 28.
5 2010 Regulations, regs. 29, 30.

Public consultation and participation

20.26 The EP Regulations require public consultation on environmental permit applications but do not prescribe the methods of consultation. This allows flexible approaches to public participation to be developed by the regulators. The regulator has a duty to consider representations made during the determination process. [1]The meaning of 'public consultee' is given in Schedule 5, Part 1, paragraph 1 to the EP Regulations and includes anyone who the regulator considers will be (or is likely to be) affected by the application and anyone who will have an interest in the application.

Representations may be received from members of the public, persons with rights to the land in question or other EU Member States. The EA is required to prepare a statement of its policies on public participation in accordance with Cabinet Office guidelines.[2] It is envisaged that this will enable a flexible and proportionate approach to public participation although it might also lead to inconsistent levels of public input.[3] Subject to exceptions, public consultation is required for every application for the grant of an environmental permit[4] and for every variation of an environmental permit which entails a substantial change or if the regulator decides that public consultation should apply.[5] Where an operator wishes to operate under the standard rules, consultation will have already taken place at the development stage of those rules.

1 2010 Regulations, Sch 5, Part 1, para. 11. Defra, *Environmental Permitting Core Guidance*, Ch 10.
2 2010 Regulations, reg 59.
3 Defra, *Environmental Permitting Core Guidance*, Ch 10.
4 EP Regulations, Sch 5, paras 5(1) and 6. It does not apply to applications relating to mobile plants, standard permits, certain small Part B installations, a mining waste operation not involving a mining waste facility to which Article 7 of the Mining Waste Directive applies or radioactive substances activities.
5 EP Regulations, Sch 5, paras 5(2), (3) and (4) and 6.

Public information

20.27 Information relevant to environmental permitting is available through public registers and under the Environmental Information Regulations 2004.[1] Regulators must maintain registers containing information on all the regulated facilities for which they are responsible.[2] The registers must be available for public inspection free of charge at all reasonable times.[3] Registers may take any form, either hardcopy or electronic, and must contain copies of permits, applications, enforcement notices and monitoring information.[4] The regulator is not required to publish information relating to criminal proceedings while they are in progress.[5] No information should be included in a register if it would be contrary to the interests of national security.[6] Information may also be withheld where the regulator considers that it may be commercially confidential.[7] Where information is excluded from the register on grounds of confidentiality, a statement must be placed on the register indicating the existence of that information.[8] An operator can request that confidential information be excluded at the time the information is submitted. It will not be enough to assert commercial prejudice: the operator must substantiate that confidentiality is required by law to protect a legitimate economic interest. However, information relating to emissions must be included on the register.[9]

1 SI 2004/3391, reg 4.
2 2010 Regulations, reg 46. See Defra, *Environmental Permitting Core Guidance*, Ch 14.
3 EP Regulations, reg 46(9).
4 EP Regulations, Sch 24 para 1.
5 EP Regulations, reg 46(2).
6 EP Regulations, reg 46(2).

7 EP Regulations, regs. 48, 51. See DEFRA, *Environmental Permitting Core Guidance* paras 14.17–14.33.
8 EP Regulations, reg 46(8).
9 EP Regulations, reg 51.

Enforcement powers

20.28 The regulators have a suite of enforcement powers to ensure the effectiveness of the environmental permitting system.[1] The regulators are under a duty to undertake appropriate, periodic inspections of regulated facilities.[2] The inspection process can include reviewing information, site-inspections and in-depth audits.[3]

Regulators are encouraged to adopt a risk-based approach to compliance targeting those facilities that pose the greatest risk to the environment or human health and those which have poorer standards of operation. Part of the aim is to reduce the regulatory burden on operators with high operating standards. Operators may also have significant responsibility for self-monitoring under the terms of their environmental permits. Permit conditions may require the provision of monitoring data and evidence that the conditions are being met.

The regulator may serve an enforcement notice where it believes an operator has contravened, is contravening or is likely to contravene any permit conditions.[4] Enforcement notices will specify the steps required to remedy the problem and the timescale in which they must be taken.

Where there is a risk of serious pollution or specified risks in relation to flood risk activities, a suspension notice may be served whether or not the operator has breached a permit condition.[5] The same applies where the manner of operating the facility is in breach of a permit condition and the contravention involves a risk of pollution (not necessarily serious).[6] It is an offence not to comply with any such notice.[7]

The regulator has a broad power to revoke an environmental permit which is likely to be exercised where it has exhausted other means of enforcement. On revocation, the permit will cease to authorise operations although any post-operation obligations, such as site restoration, may remain in force.

Where an operator has committed a criminal offence under the EP Regulations, regulators should consider whether to bring a prosecution.[8] A person convicted of an offence under the EP Regulations may be ordered by the convicting court to remedy the matter if it appears to be within the person's power to remedy it.[9]

The Environment Agency has power (since 6 April 2015) to accept enforcement undertakings from suspected offenders instead of prosecuting.[10]

The regulator now has power to apply for an injunction in the High Court to secure compliance with an enforcement notice, suspension notice, landfill closure notice or mining waste facility closure notice (whether or not it has taken other steps for that purpose).[11]

1 Defra, *Environmental Permitting Core Guidance* Ch 11.
2 EP Regulations, reg 34(2). There is also a duty to carry out periodic inspections of exempt waste operations (Sch 2, para 15).
3 The regulator should have regard to the recommendation of the European Parliament and Council (2001/331/EC) on the minimum criteria for environmental inspection.
4 EP Regulations, reg 36.
5 EP Regulations, reg 37(2).
6 EP Regulations, reg 22.
7 EP Regulations, reg 38(3).
8 EP Regulations, reg 38.
9 EP Regulations, reg 44.
10 EP Regulations, reg 44A and Sch 23ZA.
11 EP Regulations, reg 42. Prior to 30 October 2015, the power to seek an injunction only applied if the regulator considered that prosecution for failure to comply with any of those notices would afford an ineffectual remedy.

Remediation

20.29 If a regulated facility gives rise to a risk of serious pollution or a specified risk in relation of a flood risk activity (whether or not exempt), a regulator may arrange for the risk to be removed.[1] If an operator[2] commits an offence that causes pollution, the regulator may arrange for steps to be taken to remedy pollution. In either case, the regulator may recover its costs from the operator,[3] unless it is shown that there was no risk of serious pollution or that the regulator's cost were incurred unnecessarily.[4]

Site protection must be addressed throughout the life of a permit. Even where an operator is under an obligation to restore a site at closure, that does not justify the operator contaminating the site during the operation of the facility. It will not usually be desirable to wait until the regulated facility ceases to operate before removing any contamination or remedying any harm at the site. Where an incident such as a spillage occurs, the regulator should be notified and the operator should take all practical steps to address any contamination at the time of the incident and a record of the steps taken to return the site to a satisfactory state should be made available to the regulator.[5]

1 EP Regulations, regs 57 and 57A.
2 In this section 'operator' refers to the operator of an installation, an establishment or undertaking carrying on an exempt waste operation or a person carrying on a water discharge or groundwater activity: EP Regulations, reg 57(6).
3 EP Regulations, reg 57(4).
4 EP Regulations, reg 57(5).
5 See the operator's duty to report and remedy incidents and accidents under EP Regulations, Sch 5, para 20.

Appeals

20.30 A person may appeal when the regulator has refused their application for a permit or to vary, transfer or surrender that permit.[1] It is also possible to appeal against an enforcement notice, suspension notice, revocation notice, prohibition notice, landfill closure notice, mining waste facility closure notice, flood risk activity emergency works notice, flood risk activity notice of intent or flood risk activity remediation notice and a determination to publish certain confidential information on the public register.[2] An appeal is made to the Secretary of State although it will normally be administered by the Planning Inspectorate which has drawn up its own procedural guidance on appeals for environmental permitting.[3] Time limits for appeals vary according to the basis of the appeal.[4] An appeal must be made:

(a) before a revocation notice takes effect;
(b) not later than 15 working days after the date of notice of deemed withdrawal of a permit application for failure to provide additional information requested by notice by the regulator;
(c) within two months from the date of a suspension, enforcement landfill closure or mining waste facility closure notice or a regulator initiated variation;
(d) not later than 21 days after the date of a prohibition notice regulator initiated;
(e) within 15 working days after receiving notice that certain information must be included on the public register;[5] or
(f) in all other cases, within six months of the decision.

While an appeal is being considered, the conditions or suspension must be complied with. However, a revocation notice has no effect until the appeal has been determined.[6] The appeal may be conducted by written representations or an oral hearing or inquiry. The appellant and regulator will normally be expected to bear their own costs of the appeal but where there is a hearing or inquiry an application for costs can be made. Appeal decisions may also be challenged by judicial review on a point of law.

1 EP Regulations, reg 31. DEFRA, *Environmental Permitting Core Guidance* Ch 13.
2 EP Regulations, reg 53.
3 Available at www.planninginspectorate.gov.uk.
4 EP Regulations, Sch 6, para 3.
5 EP Regulations, reg 53(1).
6 EP Regulations, reg 31(9).

CONTROLS UNDER THE CLEAN AIR ACT 1993

20.31 Where a process is not subject to the EP Regulations,[1] emissions of smoke or particulate matter may nevertheless be subject to regulation by a local authority under the provisions of the Clean Air Act 1993 (CAA 1993), or under the statutory nuisance provisions of EPA 1990.[2] The 1993 Act (which consolidated the Clean Air Acts of 1956 and 1968) prohibits:

(a) the emission of 'dark smoke' from the chimney of any building, or from a chimney which serves the furnace of any fixed boiler or industrial plant;[3]
(b) the emission of dark smoke from industrial or trade premises;[4]

(c)   the installation of smoke-emitting, non-domestic furnaces without the relevant local authority's approval;[5]

(d)   the emission of grit and dust from non-domestic furnaces at a rate exceeding limits prescribed by the Secretary of State, when the 'best practicable means' have not been used to minimise those emissions;[6] and

(e)   the burning in non-domestic furnaces of of solid, liquid or gaseous matter in excess of specified limits without the installation of equipment for the arrestment of grit and dust approved by the local authority.[7]

1   Clean Air Act 1993, s 41A.
2   See Ch 14.
3   CAA 1993, s 1(1)–(2).
4   Ibid, s 2.
5   Ibid, s 4.
6   CAA 1993, s 5. On 'best practicable means' generally, see Edwards v National Coal Board [1949] 1 All ER 743, CA.
7   Ibid, s 6.

20.32   In most of these cases it will be the occupier who is liable to prosecution for failure to comply with the CAA 1993.[1] However, liability will also fall on a person causing or permitting the emission of dark smoke from industrial or trade premises whether an occupier or not,[2] and on the installer of unauthorised furnaces or the person on whose instructions such a furnace was installed.[3] The meaning of 'cause or (knowingly) permit' is considered extensively above.[4] Liability may therefore fall on landlords as well as on tenants for certain smoke-related offences, for example, where the emission of smoke from trade or industrial premises has been permitted by a lease without a corresponding term requiring consent to be gained from a local authority.

1   CAA 1993, ss 1, 2, 5 and 6.
2   Ibid, s 2(1).
3   Ibid, s 4(4).
4   In respect of water and waste-related offences, see paras **17.55–17.75** and **16.43–16.48**.

20.33   Chimney heights are also subject to regulation under the 1993 Act, where they are used for certain purposes.[1] Local authorities may also declare the whole or any part of their area to be a smoke control area, one consequence of which is a general prohibition on the emission of smoke in that area.[2] The Secretary of State or, in Wales, the National Assembly may by order exempt specified classes of fireplaces from that prohibition if satisfied that they can be used for burning fuel other than authorised fuels without producing any smoke or substantial quantity of smoke.[3] It is also a defence to a prosecution under section 20 to show that the alleged emission was caused solely by the use of an authorised fuel.[4]

1   CAA 1993, s 14.
2   Ibid, ss 18 and 20.
3   Ibid, s 21. See the Smoke Control Areas (Exempted Fireplaces) (England) (No 2) Order 2015, SI 2015/307.
4   The Smoke Control Areas (Authorised Fuels) (England) Regulations 2014, SI 2014/2366.

PART III
PRECEDENTS

A   DEFINITIONS

A.1.1   Authorities

Any authority with jurisdiction in respect of any Hazardous Substance in on over or under the Property including without any limitation the local planning authority the Environmental Health Department of the [local authority] the Environment Agency or any successor bodies of any such authority.

A.1.2   Environment (wide definition)

All or any of the following media: land (including without limitation any building structure or receptacle in on over or under it) water (including without limitation surface coastal and ground waters) and air (including without limitation the atmosphere within any natural or man-made structure or receptacle above or below ground) [and any living organisms or eco-systems supported by those media].

A.1.3   Environment (narrow definition)

All or any of the following media: land (excluding any building structure or receptacle) water (excluding the high seas and coastal waters) and air (excluding the atmosphere within any natural or man-made structure or receptacle).

A.2   Environmental Consultant

An appropriately experienced qualified and competent environmental consultant experienced in undertaking environmental investigations and assessments of a similar size scope nature and complexity to the work required in clause [ ] of this Deed appointed by [ ] to carry out that work.

A.3   Environmental Engineer

An appropriately experienced qualified and competent environmental engineer experienced in supervising remediation works of a similar size scope nature and complexity to the Remediation Works appointed by [ ] to carry out the Remediation Works.

A.4   Environmental Information

[*Reports provided to the Buyer*]

A.5.1   Environmental Law (wide definition)

European Community legislation (including without limitation any regulation or directive) the common law legislation (including without limitation subordinate legislation statutory guidance and any order or notice made pursuant to such legislation) any byelaw or judgment or order of any court or administrative tribunal in each case relating to the protection of the Environment matters affecting human health [and safety] the health of other living organisms and/or the disposal spillage release emission or migration of any Hazardous Substance and any code of practice procedure or standard compliance with which is required in order to discharge any duty [or to conform with any practice recommended by any governmental or regulatory body] in relation to any matter referred to in this definition [in any such case whether or not the same has been enacted or is in force at the date of this Agreement].

A.5.2   Environmental Law (narrow definition)

United Kingdom legislation relating to the disposal spillage release emission or migration of any Hazardous Substance [which has been enacted and is in force at the date of this Agreement].

A.6   Hazardous Substance (wide definition)

Any substance (whether in solid liquid or gaseous form) which alone or in combination with one or more others is any one or more of the following: waste capable of polluting the Environment capable of causing harm to human health any living organism or ecosystem or property or likely to cause an actionable nuisance.[1]

1 For a narrow definition of 'Hazardous Substance' see para **9.12**.

A.7   Named Authorities

The Environmental Health Department of the [local authority] and the Environment Agency or any successor bodies.

A.8   Permit

Any consent approval authorisation permission permit licence registration or notification required under any Environmental Law.

A.9   Remediation Contractor

An appropriately experienced and competent contractor experienced in carrying out remediation works of a similar size scope nature and complexity to the Remediation Works appointed by [ ] to carry out the Remediation Works.

A.10   Remediation Method Statement

A statement of the proposed method and extent of remediation works in relation to the Property produced in accordance with clauses [ ] and [ ] of this Deed.

A.11   Remediation Works

The remediation works described in the Remediation Method Statement.

B PROVISIONS DESIGNED TO CHANNEL LIABILITIES TO THE BUYER UNDER THE GENERAL LAW

B.1   [The Seller/Buyer] agrees with [the Buyer/Seller] that [the Seller/Buyer] will pay and satisfy any and all liabilities (whether current or arising in the future whether falling on the Seller or the Buyer and this shall include without limitation complying with any requirement imposed by any competent authority) in relation to any Hazardous Substance in on or under the Property [at any time] [at the date of Completion][1] (and it shall be for [the Seller/Buyer] to prove that any Hazardous Substance was not in on or under the Property at that date)[2] and the [Seller/Buyer] also agrees that in the event of an investigation of Hazardous Substances at the Property by any Authority it will join with the [Buyer/Seller] in notifying that Authority of and confirming to it the contents of the agreement in this clause [B.1] and the continuing effect and application of the said agreement and in requesting the Authority to give effect to the said agreement including without limitation for the purposes of paragraph 7.29 of the Contaminated Land Statutory Guidance under the Environmental Protection Act 1990, Part 2A (April 2012) (or the equivalent under any statutory guidance which replaces or amends it).

B.2   The [Seller/Buyer] agrees with [the Buyer/Seller] to make no claim of any nature (including without limitation a claim for a contribution or indemnity) against [the Buyer/Seller] in relation to any Hazardous Substance in on or under the Property [at any time] [at the date of Completion][1] nor to take any step which is likely to lead to the imposition of any liability relating to any such matter on [the Buyer/Seller].

B.3   The Buyer acknowledges that:

B.3.1 It has been given permission by the Seller and has had full opportunity to inspect, survey, and investigate the condition of the Property;

B.3.2 It is a large commercial organisation;

B.3.3 It has been provided with the Environmental Information prior to the date of this Deed;

B.3.4 The Environmental Information is sufficient to make the Buyer aware of the presence and extent of any Hazardous Substances referred to in the Environmental Information;

B.3.5 With respect to the contents of any report, plan and other written material or information (including without limitation the Environmental Information) either disclosed to it and/or orally communicated to it by

the Seller both as to the condition of the Property and as to the nature
and effect of any remedial work which has been carried out:
(i) it relies on it at its own risk; and
(ii) no warranty is given, or representation as to its accuracy is made
by the Seller;

B.3.6   the Purchase Price takes into account the condition of the Property.

1 Delete inapplicable alternative.
2 The wording in round brackets should only be used if the Buyer is assuming liability for
hazardous substances present on the Property at the completion date.

C   WARRANTIES

C.1   There is and has been in relation to the Property no actual pending
or threatened civil criminal or administrative action communication
notice claim demand enforcement action prosecution prohibition or
order relating to:
(i)   the presence in or discharge emission or migration to or from the
Property of any Hazardous Substance
(ii)   any failure to comply with any Environmental Law or Permit
(iii) any withdrawal revocation variation absence of refusal of or
failure to renew any Permit.

C.2   The Seller is unaware of any circumstance which may lead to any
event referred to in clause [C1].

D   WIDE INDEMNITY

The [Seller/Buyer] shall indemnify the [Buyer/Seller] in respect of all and
any actions losses damages liabilities judgments charges claims [costs
(including without limitation legal and consultancy fees) and expenses
(including without limitation the cost of any work reasonably required
to avoid or mitigate any such actions losses damages liabilities charges
claims costs or expenses]¹ [together with any costs and expenses
directly relating to any thereof (including without limitation legal
and consultancy fees and the cost of any work reasonably required to
avoid or mitigate any such actions, losses, damages, liabilities, charges
or claims costs and expenses)]¹ which may be paid incurred suffered
or sustained by the [Buyer/Seller] arising (directly or indirectly) out of
or in connection with any Hazardous Substance present in on or under
the Property [at any time] [at the date of Completion].¹

*(Note that the indemnitor will normally wish to qualify the
indemnity by provisions such as E2 and E3.)*

1 Delete inapplicable alternative.

E LIMITED INDEMNITY BY THE SELLER AND COUNTER INDEMNITY BY THE BUYER

E.1 Subject to the provisions of Clauses [E.2] and [E.3] the Seller undertakes to indemnify the Buyer in respect of any factually and legally sustainable claims under Environmental Law against the Buyer by third parties arising out of the migration of any Hazardous Substance present on the Property at Completion from the Property on or after Completion.

E.2 It shall be a precondition of the Buyer's right to claim under this indemnity that:

E.2.1 The Buyer shall use all reasonable endeavours to avoid (and if impossible to avoid to minimise the size or extent of) any liabilities which are the subject of this indemnity;

E.2.2 Any liability the subject of this indemnity shall not have been aggravated or increased or caused in any way by the Buyer or by any third party subsequent to Completion or at the direction of the Buyer prior to Completion or by any matters subsequent to Completion and outside the Seller's control;

E.2.3 Written notification of the liquidated liability is received by the Seller no later than the [...] anniversary of the date of this Agreement;

E.2.4 The Buyer shall to enable the Seller to assess its liabilities (if any) and to determine appropriate courses of action under this indemnity and to take such action as it considers appropriate in the circumstances to minimise its liabilities under the terms of this indemnity:

E.2.4.1 Keep the Seller at all times fully informed of any circumstances that give rise or may give rise to or otherwise relate to any liabilities which are the subject of this indemnity whether existing or potential;

E.2.4.2 Supply to the Seller such information (including copies of relevant documents) as the Seller reasonably requires;

E.2.4.3 Permit the Seller and its representatives access to the Property for the purpose of undertaking tests on and taking samples from the Property and carrying out such preventive or remedial work as it reasonably thinks fit (subject to the Seller making good after the completion of such work and taking reasonable steps to minimise disturbance to the Buyer); and

E.2.4.4 Give such co-operation as is reasonably requested by the Seller (including but without limitation meeting with and reviewing matters with the Seller);

E.2.5 The Buyer shall consult fully with the Seller and comply with the Seller's reasonable requirements as to whether and how any matters which may be the subject of this indemnity shall be defended satisfied remedied settled compromised or in any way dealt with, provided that without limitation the Buyer shall at the Seller's request permit the Seller to have conduct of any such matter;

E.2.6   The Buyer shall not acknowledge the validity or quantum of any claim or settle or compromise any claim or proceedings without the prior approval (not to be unreasonably withheld or delayed) of the Seller;

E.3   The Seller's liability under this indemnity shall be limited as follows:

E.3.1   This indemnity does not apply in any case where the Property is used for a purpose other than that of [   ];

E.3.2   This indemnity does not extend to loss of profits or any other form of economic loss;[1]

E.3.3   The Seller's liability shall be limited to an aggregate of [£];

E.3.4   The Seller shall not be liable in respect of any claim the value of which is less than [£];

E.3.5   The Seller's liability shall be limited to that part of any claim which exceeds the sum specified in clause [E.3.4];

E.3.6   The Seller's liability in respect of any individual claim shall be limited to the minimum amount required to undertake remediation works to prevent any further material migration of the relevant Hazardous Substance from the part of the Property in respect of which the claim shall have arisen to any land outside the boundaries of the Property.

E.4   Subject to the preceding provisions of this Clause [E] the Buyer undertakes to indemnify the Seller in respect of all and any liabilities and expenses which may be incurred by the Seller arising out of or in connection with the presence of any Hazardous Substance in on or under the Property or the migration of any Hazardous Substance from the Property on or after Completion.

E.5   The provisions of Clause [E.2] shall mutatis mutandis apply to any claim by the Seller against the Buyer under the terms of Clause [E.4].

1 An alternative limitation based on the rule in *Hadley v Baxendale* is as follows:
   'The Seller's liability under this indemnity shall be limited to such liabilities in relation to any Hazardous Substance present in on or under the Property at Completion as may:
   (i) fairly and reasonably be considered arising according to the usual course of things; or
   (ii) reasonably be supposed to have been in the contemplation of both parties at the date of granting this indemnity.'
   The Seller's liability under the indemnity for loss of profits or other economic loss will not generally be excluded by this wording. See Chapter 9, para **9.10**.

F LEASE PROVISIONS – TENANT'S COVENANTS

The Tenant covenants with the Landlord during the Term as follows:

F.1 [To ensure that the Property below ground 'level' is at all times kept free from Hazardous Substances;]

[To ensure that no Hazardous Substances in on or under the Property cause or may cause harm to people, property or the Environment whether or not within the Property;]

[To maintain the Property in no worse state and condition than that at the commencement of the Lease as evidenced by the Environmental Report;]1

1 Delete inapplicable alternatives.

F.2 Not to commit or allow to be committed any act or make or allow to be made any omission which would or may cause any Hazardous Substance to escape leak or be spilled or deposited on the Property or discharged from the Property or migrate to or from it and to notify the Landlord immediately of any such occurrence;

F.3 Not to store in on or under the Property any petrol or other specially inflammable explosive or combustible substance nor any other Hazardous Substance (excluding any Hazardous Substance in general use for domestic purposes) except any such approved in writing by the Landlord which is used in connection with the Tenant's business on the Property;

F.4 Not to discharge or cause or permit to be discharged into any pipe drain or sewer serving the Property any Hazardous Substance or without limitation any deleterious matter (including without limitation oil or grease) but to keep thoroughly cleaned the Property and the pipes drains and sewers serving the Property whenever necessary;

F.5 Not to use the Property

F.5.1 Except for the business of [   ] or for such other purpose as the Landlord shall in its discretion approve and in any case only to the extent that it does not cause a nuisance;

F.5.2 In any manner which would cause or may lead to a breach of the provisions of clause [F.2];

F.6 Not to erect nor install in or on the Property any engine furnace plant or machinery which would or may:

F.6.1 Cause noise fumes or vibration which can be heard smelled or felt outside the Property; or

F.6.2   May lead to a breach of the provisions of clause [F.2].

F.7   Not to carry out or cause or permit to be carried out in on or under the Property any excavations tunnelling engineering or building or exploratory works or without limitation other operations involving the disturbance or penetration of the surface or subsoil of the Property;

F.8   To obtain maintain and comply with all the Permits necessary to carry out [the Permitted Use] and on the termination of the Lease (for whatever reason) to take all steps available to the Tenant to ensure that all such Permits are (at the direction of the Landlord) duly transferred to the Landlord or to any other person or surrendered.

F.9   To comply with good industrial practice in relation to any activity carried on at the Property which may affect the Environment and/or the health or comfort of human beings and/or other organisms.

F.10   Prior to commencing [the Permitted Use] to obtain a report from a suitably qualified environmental consultant and to comply with its recommendations in relation to any activity carried on at the Property.

F.11   To notify the Landlord forthwith of any complaint from any person or any notice or proceedings against the Tenant relating to any matter affecting the Property concerning the Environment or the health or comfort of human beings or other organisms and to provide the Landlord with copies of any correspondence notices proceedings or other documents relating thereto.

F.12   At the termination of the Lease for whatever reason to obtain a report from a suitably qualified environmental consultant as to the steps required to put the Property including without limitation the subsoil into such condition as is:

F.12.1   Suitable for [the Permitted Use];

F.12.2   Necessary to ensure that no Hazardous Substance will cause harm to human health or the Environment or migrate from the Property;

and to comply with the recommendations of that report and to obtain a further report from such environmental consultant stating that the requirements of this clause [F.12] have been complied with.

F.13   To ensure that any plant and equipment on the Property are capable of functioning so as to comply with all applicable Environmental Law.

F.14   To permit the Landlord and its employees or agents at all reasonable times after giving to the Tenant forty eight hours written notice (except in an emergency) to enter:

F.14.1   To inspect and view the Property and examine its condition;

F.14.2   To undertake investigations (including without limitation the taking of samples) in on and/or under the Property to ascertain the condition of the Property and (without limitation) the nature extent and mobility of Hazardous Substances in on and/or under the Property;

F.14.3   To undertake any works which the Landlord deems necessary (and for which the Tenant is not responsible under clause [F.15]) to avoid or minimise the risk of any Hazardous Substance in on or under the Property polluting the Environment causing harm to human health or to any other living organism or damaging property provided that the Landlord shall make good after the completion of such work and take reasonable steps to minimise disturbance to the Tenant provided further that the Tenant shall not be entitled to any compensation in respect of the exercise by the Landlord of the rights in this clause [F.14].[1]

1 The landlord's right to undertake remedial work may lead to the conclusion that the landlord is a 'knowing permitter' under the contaminated land legislation. See paras 10.05 and 15.75–15.77.

F.15   (Where by reason of breach by the Tenant of its obligations under this clause [F] works are required to remedy such breach and such works relate in any way to any Hazardous Substance) to carry out and complete at the expense of the Tenant to the satisfaction of the Landlord and in accordance in all respects with the Landlord's specifications and under the Landlord's supervision all remediation and works as shall be required by the Landlord by notice to the Tenant and within such reasonable period as is specified in the notice provided that the Landlord may itself or by its employees or agents enter and remain upon the Property (with plant equipment and materials) as necessary to execute such remediation and works if:

F.15.1   The Landlord in its notice to the Tenant incorporates a notification of its election to carry out the same; or

F.15.2   The Tenant fails to comply with a notice under this clause [F.15].

F.16   To pay the Landlord on demand all expenses and costs directly or indirectly incurred by the Landlord under clause [F.15] (such expenses and costs and any interest on them calculated from the date the expenditure is incurred to be recoverable as if they were rent in arrear).

F.17   To keep the Landlord indemnified in respect of all and any actions losses damages liabilities charges claims costs and expenses which may be paid incurred suffered or sustained by the Landlord arising (directly or indirectly) by reason of breach by the Tenant of its obligations under this clause [F].

1 Delete inapplicable alternatives.

G   LEASE PROVISIONS – LANDLORD'S COVENANTS

G.1   The Landlord shall treat or remove any Hazardous Substances present in on or under the Property at the commencement of the Lease in accordance with the recommendations of the Environmental Report.

G.2   The Landlord reserves all such rights as are necessary to enable the Landlord to the exclusion of the Tenant to investigate, monitor, take samples of, remediate, remove or otherwise manage any Hazardous Substances present in on or under the Property at the commencement of the Lease, provided that the Landlord covenants in exercising any such rights to minimise disruption to the Tenant and following any intrusive work promptly to reinstate the Property to the reasonable satisfaction of the Tenant. [1]

1 This type of provision should not be used if the tenant may need to disturb the ground.

G.3   The Landlord agrees with the Tenant to pay and satisfy any and all liabilities in relation to any Hazardous Substance present in on or under the Property at the commencement of this Lease whether current or future and whether falling on the Landlord or the Tenant without limitation under Part 2A of the Environmental Protection Act 1990 and/or any legislation which amends or replaces it.

G.4   The Landlord shall indemnify the Tenant in respect of all and any actions losses damages liabilities judgments charges claims costs (including without limitation legal and consultancy fees) and expenses (including without limitation the cost of any work reasonably required to avoid or mitigate any such actions losses damages liabilities judgments charges claims costs or expenses) which may be paid incurred suffered or sustained by the Tenant arising (directly or indirectly) out of or in connection with the presence of any Hazardous Substance in on or under the Property at the commencement of the Lease.

G.5   It is hereby agreed and declared that no covenant by the Tenant in this Lease shall extend to any Hazardous Substance present in on or under the Property at the commencement of this Lease.

H   LOAN AGREEMENT CLAUSES

Warranties

H.1   The Borrower has obtained all Permits requisite for the operation of its business and has at all times complied in all material respects with the terms of those Permits and all other applicable Environmental

Laws including without limitation all lawful requirements of any environmental regulatory authority relating to the Property and its business.

H.2   [So far as the Borrower is aware] there are no Hazardous Substances in on or under the Property which are likely to give rise to liabilities on the Borrower or any owner or occupier of the Property.

H.3   No notification has been received by the Borrower suggesting that the Borrower or any other owner or occupier of the Property is in breach of any Environmental Law in relation to the Property or that a claim may be made against the Borrower in relation to any such matter.

H.4   The Borrower is unaware of any circumstances which may give rise to a claim in relation to the Property against the Borrower or any owner or occupier of the Property under any Environmental Law.

Covenants

H.5   The Borrower shall comply with all Environmental Laws relating to the Property and the Borrower's business.

H.6   The Borrower shall obtain and maintain in force all Permits relating to the Property and the Borrower's business and fully comply in all material respects with the terms and conditions of all such Permits.

H.7   The Borrower shall promptly upon receipt of the same notify the Lender of any claim notice or other communication served on it in respect of any alleged breach of any Environmental Law which might reasonably be expected if substantiated to have a material adverse effect on the ability of the Borrower to perform its obligations under this Agreement.

H.8   The Borrower shall provide to the Lender on request all information relating to the Borrower's compliance with Environmental Law including without limitation compliance with the conditions of any Permit.

H.9   The Borrower shall obtain and maintain in full force and effect environmental insurance on terms acceptable to the Lender (provided that such insurance is obtainable in the European Union on reasonable terms and at commercially reasonably rates) in relation to the condition of the Property and liabilities resulting from the operation of the Borrower's business.

H.10   The Borrower shall comply with environmental best practice in operating its business.

H.10.1 The Borrower shall not keep Hazardous Substances at the Property unless they are required for carrying on the Borrower's business and they are kept in compliance with all applicable Environmental Laws.

Indemnity

H.11 The Borrower shall indemnify the Lender in respect of all and any actions losses damages liabilities charges claims costs (including without limitation legal and consultancy fees) and expenses (including without limitation the cost of any work reasonably required to avoid or mitigate any such actions losses damages liabilities charges claims costs or expenses) arising directly or indirectly as a consequence of:

H.11.1 The presence of any Hazardous Substance in on or under the Property

H.11.2 A breach of any Environmental Law by the Borrower or any of its officers employees or agents.

Conditions Precedent

Environmental Report

H.12 The Lender receiving a report addressed to the Lender prepared by an environmental consultant [acceptable to] [approved by] the Lender stating that:

H.12.1 There are no conditions associated with the Property which may adversely affect the Environment or the health or comfort of human beings or other organisms or without limitation give rise to liabilities under Environmental Law;

H.12.2 The operations on the Property comply with Environmental Law in all material respects;

H.12.3 The Property is not contaminated land as defined in Part IIA of the Environmental Protection Act 1990.

Environmental Insurance

H.13 The Lender receiving evidence of environmental insurance which is acceptable to the Lender having been issued in respect of the Property [and the operation of the Borrower's business] (provided that such insurance is available in the European Union upon reasonable terms and at commercially reasonable rates).

Early Repayment Clauses

Event of default

H.14   The Borrower is in breach of any Environmental Law or any warranty covenant representation obligation or undertaking given in respect of the Property or the Borrower's business relating to the Environment or the health or comfort of human beings or other organisms.

H.15   Any Environmental Permit required for the operation of the Borrower's business on the Property is revoked suspended withdrawn or cancelled.

H.16   Any Environmental Law is modified amended or changed such that there is a material risk of liability attaching to the Lender in connection with the Property or the operation of the Borrower's business.

I   A LETTER OF APPOINTMENT OF ENVIRONMENTAL CONSULTANT

(Note that this letter is designed to commission a survey dealing with all environmental issues. If a survey limited to contamination is required, numbered paragraphs I 9–13 should be deleted)

[Name and Address of Environmental Consultant]

Dear Sirs

[Desktop Study]/[Phase I Survey] of *[name of property]*

We set out below our proposed terms of engagement.

I.1   We require a [Desktop Study]/[Phase I Survey] of *[name of property]*. The purpose is to enable us to understand any environmental issues relating to the property which may require expenditure by or involve liabilities on the owner or otherwise affect the value.

I.2   You will prepare a report dealing with all relevant environmental issues including but not limited to the potential for land contamination at the property and its surrounds, and its significance in relation to the environmental setting and current use of the property as well as regulatory issues. Such a report will include the following:

I.3   A review of historical land uses and operations at the property and on neighbouring land to assess the potential for soil, groundwater or surface water contamination.

I.4   A review of available geological, hydrogeological and hydrological data associated with the property. This will include a review of data relating to the underlying geology; depth, characteristics and use of local aquifers; possible contaminant migration routes into these aquifers; licensed abstractions from underlying aquifers; and surface waters in the vicinity of the property. It will allow the significance of contamination to be put into context in terms of the potential for third party or regulatory authority actions.

I.5   A description of environmental conditions at the property based on a physical inspection, together with interviews with property management and personnel regarding on-property environmental issues, if they are available.

I.6   Such an inspection would include a review of at least the following features:
- surface water and foul drainage systems;
- paving of loading, unloading, storage and handling areas;
- above and below ground hazardous materials storage and containment facilities;
- evidence of asbestos-containing and other deleterious materials;
- the nature of adjacent land uses;
- the environmental setting of the property; and
- areas of stained ground and other evidence of ground contamination.

I.7   Review of Regulatory Authority databases (particularly the Local Authority Environmental Health and Planning Departments, and the Environment Agency) to determine whether they have any records of environmental issues pertaining to the property (i.e. pollution and contamination incidents and/or remediation; proximity of licensed landfill properties; groundwater and surface water designations and abstractions; authorised facilities).

I.8   Recommendations in respect of the need for and form of any intrusive property investigations (soil and groundwater sampling).

I.9   A review of the processes carried on at the property and the emissions (including noise), discharges and spillages therefrom into all environmental media.

I.10   A review of all waste streams from the property.

I.11   A review of relevant licensing issues.

I.12   A review of all matters likely to give rise to any environmental liability or significant expense on the part of any Buyer of the property.

I.13   A review of all environmental matters likely to affect the occupation or use of the property.

I.14 The review will be based on publicly available information, previous reports (if available), property inspection, discussions with management and contact with the relevant regulatory authorities. You give no warranty or representation that all relevant matters will be discovered in the course of your work, although you will endeavour to provide a comprehensive appraisal of any significant environmental issues associated with the property. Specific assumptions and limitations which you identify as being relevant in the course of your work are to be set out in the report. No sampling or testing will be included in the audit.

I.15 You agree that you have performed and will perform the work detailed above ('the Services') fully and faithfully in accordance with the terms of this letter. You have exercised and will continue to exercise in carrying out the Services, all such professional skill, care and diligence as may reasonably be expected of a properly qualified and competent environmental consultant experienced in the provision of such services in respect of work of a similar scope, nature and complexity to the Services. You have kept and will continue to keep us fully and properly informed on all aspects of the progress and performance of the Services and will provide us with all such other information in connection therewith as we may reasonably require.

I.16 You agree to maintain with reputable insurers carrying on business in the European Union, from the date hereof and for a period of at least [6][12]¹ years from delivery to us of your final report (or from the date of termination of your engagement by us for any reason), professional indemnity insurance to cover each and every professional liability which you may incur in relation to the Services, with a limit of indemnity of not less than [£5 million] in relation to any one claim and in total during each twelve month period, provided that such insurance continues to be available in the European Union market on reasonable terms and at commercially reasonable premium rates. You will inform us immediately if the insurance ceases to be available on such terms. Such insurance shall be subject to such conditions as may be usual from time to time in the European Union market. You will provide us with documentary evidence that the insurance is being properly maintained if we so require.

1 The 12 year alternative applies if the appointment is in the form of a deed.

I.17 You will provide a draft report in relation to the property covering the above within [   ] days of this letter. The cost of such work for the property will be [   ] (exclusive of VAT and general reasonable expenses, incurred directly in connection with the Services which will be charged at cost (and, in the case of VAT payable subject to production of a valid VAT invoice)).

I.18   Any additional work beyond the scope of the audit, as set out above (e.g. follow up work, meetings, ongoing liaison, presentations, etc.) will be charged at £[   ] per hour. No changes will be made to the scope of your work without prior authorisation by [   ].

I.19   Your invoice may be issued after submission of your audit report and will be payable within twenty-eight days of issue.

I.20   Whilst the copyright in the report remains vested in you, you grant us an irrevocable royalty-free non-exclusive licence to use and to reproduce any part of the report for any purpose whatsoever in connection with the property.

I.21   You will not at any time for any reason disclose to any person nor otherwise make use of any confidential information which has or may come into your possession in the course of this engagement relating to us, the property or any activities carried out thereon unless such information comes properly into the public domain through no fault of yours or unless you are required by law to disclose such information.

I.22   You will at our request in relation to the property execute up to [   ] collateral warranties (in the form attached to this letter) in favour of any Buyer or other person with an interest in the property including mortgagees and tenants who may be nominated by us.

I.23   We may transfer the benefit of this agreement to any other person at any time, provided that we notify you that we have done so.

I.24   The application and interpretation of this letter shall be governed by English Law and any disputes or differences arising under it shall be referred to the English courts.

Yours faithfully

[*Signature of client*]

We acknowledge receipt of the letter of appointment above and confirm our acceptance thereof.

Signed: .

Name: .

Position: .

Company: .

Date: .

J   DEED OF COLLATERAL WARRANTY

(This is designed for use in connection with the appointment of an environmental consultant – see Precedents I and K. It will need to be adapted when used with Precedent I).

DATE:

PARTIES:

(1)   CONSULTANT [   ] [Company Number [   ]] of/whose registered office is at

(2)   BUYER   [   ]   [Company   Number   [   ]]   of/whose registered office is at

(3)   CLIENT   [   ]   [Company   Number   [   ]]   of/whose registered office is at

RECITALS:

J(A)   *Interpretation*

J(A1)   In this Deed the following words and expressions shall, where the context so admits, be deemed to have the following meanings:

'the Appointment' means the agreement dated the [   ] between the Client (1) and the Consultant (2) (and includes any further agreement varying or supplementing such agreement) under which the Consultant has agreed to perform the Services.

'the Client' means the persons named as the third party above and includes any person to whom the benefit of the Appointment has been validly assigned in accordance with its terms.

'the Consultant' means the person named as the first party above.

'Practical Completion' has the meaning given to it in the Appointment.

'the Project' has the meaning given to it in the Appointment.

'the Proprietary Material' has the meaning given to it in the Appointment.

'the Buyer' means the person named as the second party above and includes any person to whom the benefit of this Deed and/or any rights arising under it shall have been validly assigned in accordance with clause [J4].

'the Services' has the meaning given to it in the Appointment.

'the Site' has the meaning given to it in the Appointment.

J(A2)   The clause headings in this Deed are for the convenience of the parties only and do not affect its interpretation.

J(A3)   Words importing the singular meaning shall include where the context so admits the plural meaning and vice versa.

J(A4)   Words denoting the masculine gender shall include the feminine and neuter genders and words denoting natural persons shall include corporations and firms and all such words shall be construed interchangeably in that manner.

J(A5)   Where the context so admits, references in this Deed to a clause or a Schedule are to a clause or Schedule of this Deed.

J(A6)   References in this Deed to any statute or statutory instrument shall include and refer to any statutory amendment or re-enactment thereof from time to time and for the time being in force.

J(A7)   Words and expressions in this Deed imposing an obligation on a party to do any act or thing shall include an obligation to procure that such act or thing is done, and words and expressions placing a party under any restriction include an obligation not to permit any infringement of such restriction.

J(B)   *Circumstances and Agreement*

J(B1)   By the Appointment the Client has engaged the Consultant to perform the Services.

J(B2)   The Buyer wishes to buy the Site subject to receiving an environmental report from the Consultant following Practical Completion such as would induce a reasonable buyer to acquire the Site on the terms proposed by the Client.

J(B3)   As a condition of and in consideration of the Buyer's agreement as aforesaid the Consultant has agreed to enter into this Deed for the benefit of the Buyer.

OPERATIVE PROVISIONS:

J.1   Consultant's Warranties

J.1.1   The Consultant warrants and undertakes to the Buyer that he has observed and performed and will continue to observe and perform each and all the obligations on his part to be observed and performed under the Appointment in accordance with the terms of the Appointment provided always that the Consultant shall owe no greater obligations to the Buyer under this Deed than he would have owed had the Buyer been named as a joint client with the Client under the Appointment.

J.1.2   Without prejudice to the generality of clause [J1.1] the Consultant warrants and undertakes to the Buyer that in the performance of the Services he has exercised and will continue to exercise all such professional skill care and diligence as may reasonably be expected of a properly qualified and competent consultant of the relevant discipline experienced in the provision of such services in respect of works of a similar size scope nature and complexity to the Project.

J.1.3   The Consultant extends to the Buyer the benefit of all warranties and undertakings on the part of the Consultant contained in the Appointment.

J.1.4   The Consultant acknowledges that the Buyer shall be deemed to have relied and shall continue to rely upon the warranties and undertakings given by the Consultant under this clause [J1].

J.1.5   The Consultant acknowledges to the Buyer that, at the date of this Deed the Appointment remains in full force and effect and the Client has paid all sums properly due to the Consultant under the Appointment.

J.2   **Use of Proprietary Material**

J.2.1   The copyright in the Proprietary Material shall remain vested in the Consultant but the Consultant grants to the Buyer an irrevocable royalty-free non-exclusive licence to use and to reproduce any or all of the Proprietary Material for any purpose whatsoever connected with the Project and/or the Site including but without limitation the execution completion maintenance letting occupation management sale advertisement extension alteration reinstatement and repair thereof. Such licence shall carry the right to grant sub-licences and shall be transferable to third parties and shall subsist notwithstanding the termination (for any reason) of the Consultant's engagement under the Appointment provided always that the Consultant shall not be liable for the consequences of any use of the Proprietary Material for any purpose other than that for which it was prepared.

J.2.2   The Consultant shall provide a complete set of copies of the Proprietary Material to the Buyer without charge on Practical Completion and thereafter shall provide further copies of any or all of the Proprietary Material to the Buyer upon request and upon payment by the Buyer of the Consultant's reasonable copying charges.

J.3   **Insurance**

J.3.1   The Consultant undertakes to the Buyer to maintain with reputable insurers carrying on business in the European Union from the date hereof and for a period expiring no earlier than twelve (12) years after the date of Practical Completion and notwithstanding the termination for any reason of the Consultant's engagement under the Appointment professional indemnity insurance to cover each and every professional liability which he may incur under this Deed with a limit of indemnity of not less than [five million pounds (£5 million)] in relation to any one claim and in total during each twelve month period in respect of claims arising from pollution or contamination and in relation to each and every claim in respect of all other circumstances provided always that such insurance continues to be available in the European Union market upon reasonable terms and at commercially reasonable premium rates.

J.3.2   Such insurance shall be subject to such conditions as may be usual from time to time in the European Union market and in particular (but without limitation) such insurance shall not include any condition which may adversely affect the right of the Buyer to proceed directly against the insurers pursuant to and in the circumstances contemplated by the Third Parties (Rights Against Insurers) Act 1930.

J.3.3   As and when he is reasonably required to do so by the Buyer the Consultant shall produce for inspection by the Buyer documentary evidence that such insurance is being properly maintained.

J.3.4   The Consultant shall forthwith notify the Buyer if such insurance ceases to be available upon reasonable terms and at commercially reasonable premium rates or if for any other reason the Consultant is unable to continue to maintain such insurance.

J.4   **Assignment**

The Buyer may at any time assign charge or transfer the benefit of this Deed and/or any rights arising under it to any mortgagee of the Buyer and/or to any Buyer of the Site or any part or parts thereof from the Buyer upon notice to the Consultant without the consent of the Consultant being required provided there shall only be two such assignments or transfers to Buyers.

J.5   **Other Remedies**

Nothing in this Deed shall in any way prejudice or affect any other rights or remedies (whether under any contract at law in equity or otherwise) which the Buyer would have against the Consultant in the absence of this Deed.

J.6   **Limitation**

No action or proceedings for any breach of this Deed shall be commenced against the Consultant after the expiry of twelve (12) years following Practical Completion.

J.7   **Third Parties**

Unless that right of enforcement is expressly granted, it is not intended that a third party should have the right to enforce a provision of this deed pursuant to the Contracts (Rights of Third Parties) Act 1999.

J.8   **Notices**

Any notice or other communication required under this Deed shall be given in writing and shall be deemed to have been properly given if compliance is made with Section 196 of the Law of Property Act 1925 (as amended by the Recorded Delivery Service Act 1962).

J.9   **Governing Law and Disputes**
The application and interpretation of this Deed shall in all respects be governed by English law and any dispute or difference arising under this Deed shall be subject to the jurisdiction of the English Courts.

DELIVERED as a deed on the date of this document.

Executed as a deed by [CONSULTANT] acting

by (or, where the common seal of [CONSULTANT]

is affixed) in the presence of:

_ Director

_ Director/Secretary

K   DEED OF APPOINTMENT OF ENVIRONMENTAL CONSULTANT TO UNDERTAKE SITE INVESTIGATION – PHASE II (INTRUSIVE WORKS)

DATED:

PARTIES:

(1)   [CLIENT]

(2)   [CONSULTANT]

OPERATIVE PROVISIONS:

K.1   Interpretation

K.1.1   In this Deed the following words and expressions shall, where the context so admits, be deemed to have the following meanings:-

'the Buyer' means [   ] and any other buyer of the Client's interest in the Site or any part of it.

'the Client' means the persons named as the first party above and includes (except for the purpose of clause [K.6]) any person to whom the benefit of this Deed and/or any rights arising under it shall have been validly assigned under clause [K.10.2].

'the Consultant' means the person named as the second party above, and includes, in the case of a partnership any person who may become a partner of the Consultant after the date of this Deed.

'the Fee' means the lump sum stated in paragraph E of Schedule 1 or any adjusted sum agreed pursuant to clause [K.7.2] payable to the Consultant for the proper performance of the Services.

'Practical Completion' means practical completion of the Services and any other services performed by the Consultant in accordance with clause [K.7.3].

'the Project' means the investigative works to be carried out at the Sites as briefly described in paragraph B of Schedule 1.

'the Proprietary Material' means all drawings details plans specifications schedules reports calculations software (whether or not computer generated) and other work (and any designs, ideas, concepts and inventions contained in them whether patentable or not) which may be prepared conceived or developed by or on behalf of the Consultant in the course of or as a result of performing the Services.

'the Services' means the services that have prior to the date hereof been performed and will after the date hereof be performed by the Consultant in connection with the Project as set out in Schedule 2 and includes (except for the purpose of clause [K.6.1]) any additional services instructed by the Client under clause [K.7.3].

'the Site' means the sites defined and described in paragraph A of Schedule 1.

K.1.2 The clause headings in this Deed are for the convenience of the parties only and do not affect its interpretation.

K.1.3 Words importing the singular meaning shall include where the context so admits the plural meaning and vice versa.

K.1.4 Words denoting the masculine gender shall include the feminine and neuter genders and words denoting natural persons shall include corporations and firms and all such words shall be construed interchangeably in that manner.

K.1.5 Where the context so admits, references in this Deed to a clause or Schedule are to a clause or Schedule of this Deed.

K.1.6 References in this Deed to any statute or statutory instrument shall include and refer to any statutory amendment or re-enactment thereof from time to time and for the time being in force.

K.1.7 Words and expressions in this Deed imposing an obligation on a party to do any act or thing shall include an obligation to procure that such act or thing is done and words and expressions placing a party under any restriction include an obligation not to permit any infringement of such restriction.

K.1.8 All covenants agreements and obligations of the Consultant to the Client are made or given to the Client joint and severally.

K.2   Circumstances and Agreement

K.2.1   The Client intends to sell the Site and the Buyer wishes to buy the Site subject to receiving an environmental report from the Consultant following Practical Completion such as would induce a reasonable Buyer to acquire the Site on the terms proposed by the Client.

K.2.2   The Client has resolved to appoint the Consultant to act as his environmental consultant for the Project and to perform the Services on the terms and conditions set out in this Deed.

K.3   Consultant's General Obligations

K.3.1   The Client appoints the Consultant and the Consultant agrees to perform the Services on the terms of this Deed. Where, in the performance of the Services the Consultant seeks or is obliged to seek the Client's approval or agreement to any matter the Client's approval or agreement shall not in any way derogate from the Consultant's obligations under this Deed nor diminish his liability for any breach of such obligations.

K.3.2   The Consultant warrants to the Client that he has exercised and will continue to exercise in the performance of the Services all such professional skill care and diligence as may reasonably be expected of a properly qualified and competent environmental consultant experienced in the provision of such services in respect of works of a similar size scope nature and complexity to the Project.

K.3.3   The Consultant warrants to the Client that he has complied and will continue to comply with all relevant statutory requirements regulations and permissions applicable to the Project.

K.3.4   The Consultant shall keep the Client fully informed on all aspects of the progress and performance of the Services and shall provide the Client with all such other information in connection with the Project as the Client reasonably requires.

K.3.5   The Consultant acknowledges that nothing contained in this Deed shall prejudice or affect his liability in tort to the Client or any other person.

K.3.6   The Consultant shall within 14 days of the request of the Client to do so execute a deed of warranty in favour of the Buyer in the form set out in Schedule 3 or in such similar or varied terms if the parties agree and shall deliver it duly executed to the Client. If the Consultant fails to deliver any deed of warranty validly requested under this clause within 14 days of such request the Consultant shall be obliged to repay to such Client any payment made by the Client to the Consultant under this Deed such repayment being made without prejudice to any rights and remedies of the Client which will remain in full force and effect.

K.3.7 The Consultant indemnifies the Client against each and every liability which the Client may incur to any person to the extent that liability arises by reason of any negligence omission or default on the part of the Consultant in the performance of his obligations under and in connection with this Deed provided that the Consultant shall not have any liability under this Clause in respect of claims made more than twelve years after the date of this Deed.

K.4 **The Client's Obligations**

K.4.1 The Client shall if requested by the Consultant supply to the Consultant within a reasonable time (having regard to the time and nature of any such request) any necessary and relevant data and information in the possession of the Client.

K.5 **Consultant's Personnel**

K.5.1 The Consultant has appointed the person named in Schedule 1 who has directed and controlled and will continue to direct and control the performance by the Consultant of the Services. Such person or any replacement approved by the Client pursuant to clause [K.5.3] or clause [K.5.4] shall have full authority to act on behalf of the Consultant for all purposes in connection with this Deed.

K.5.2 The Consultant shall, subject to clauses [K.5.3] and [K.5.4], use the key person named in Schedule 1 in connection with the performance of the Services and such person's services shall subject to clauses [K.5.3] and [K.5.4] be available for so long as may be necessary to ensure the proper performance of the Services.

K.5.3 The Consultant shall not remove from the performance of the Services any person referred to in clause [K.5.1] or clause [K.5.2] nor any person approved by the Client pursuant to clause [K.5.3] or clause [K.5.4] without the prior approval of the Client which approval shall not be unreasonably withheld or delayed. If such approval is given the Consultant shall be responsible for replacing such person with a person who shall previously have been approved by the Client. Save in emergency there shall be an appropriate handover period between the person being removed and his replacement.

K.5.4 The Client shall have the right after consultation with the Consultant to request the removal of any person engaged in the performance of the Services if in the Client's opinion his performance or conduct is or has been unsatisfactory and the Consultant shall promptly remove such person and replace him with a person who shall previously have been approved by the Client.

K.6   **Remuneration**

K.6.1   The Client shall pay to the Consultant the Fee as full remuneration
(subject to clause [K.7.3]) for the proper performance of the Services
in accordance with this Deed. Invoices shall comply with Regulations
13 and 14 of the Value Added Tax Regulations 1995 (SI 1995/2518)
and shall be supported by documents vouchers and receipts necessary
for computing and verifying them.

K.6.2   The Fee shall be paid by instalments as provided in Schedule 1 subject
to Clauses [K.6.3] and [K.6.4], provided that the Client shall be entitled
to reschedule the instalments if in his reasonable opinion the amount
of the Fee which would otherwise be payable does not substantially
correspond as a proportion of the whole of the Fee to the Services
properly performed by the Consultant at that time.

K.6.3   The Consultant shall on the dates set out in Schedule 1 submit to
the Client a tax invoice showing the instalment of the Fee which the
Consultant considers due and any other sums which the Consultant
considers due to it under this Deed together with Value Added Tax less
any sums previously paid by the Client. Payment shall be due to the
Consultant on the date the Client receives each invoice.

K.6.4   Within 5 days after the date on which any payment becomes due to the
Consultant the Client shall give notice to the Consultant specifying the
amount of the payment which he proposes to make in relation to the
Consultant's invoice and the basis on which that amount is calculated.
If no notice is given the Client shall be treated as having notified the
Consultant that he proposes to make payment of the amount stated in
the Consultant's invoice.

K.6.5   Where the Client intends to pay less than the sum stated in any
Consultant invoice under clause [K.6.3] the Client shall give written
notice to the Consultant (a **'pay less notice'**) not later than three days
before the final date for payment (the **'prescribed period'**). The pay less
notice shall specify the sum that the Client considers to be due on the
date on which the pay less notice is served and the basis upon which
that sum is calculated.

K.6.6   The Client shall pay the Consultant all sums due under this Deed on or
before the final date for payment which shall be the expiry of 30 days
from receipt of the Consultant's invoice under Clause [K.6.3].

K.6.7   If any amount due under this Deed is not paid in full by the final date
of payment under Clause [K.6.6] and no effective notice has been given
under Clause [K.6.5] the Consultant shall be entitled (without limiting
any other right or remedy of the Consultant) to suspend performance
of its obligations under this Deed by giving not less than 7 days' notice
to the Client to that effect. The right to suspend performance shall
cease when the Client makes payment in full of the amount due and
any period during which the performance is validly suspended under

this clause shall be disregarded in computing the time taken by the Consultant to complete any of the Services affected by the suspension.

K.7 Additions to and Deductions from the Fee

K.7.1 Subject to clause [K.7.3] as appears below the Fee shall be inclusive payment for the Services and all other matters relating to this Deed and for all costs disbursements, expenses and overheads of every kind incurred by the Consultant in connection with the Project.

K.7.2 If at any time the nature and scope of the Project is materially altered in accordance with the Client's requirements the Client and the Consultant shall agree a fair and reasonable adjustment to the Fee to reflect any substantial increase or decrease in the work required of the Consultant resulting from such alteration.

K.7.3 In addition to the Services the Consultant shall perform such other services in relation to the Project as the Client may from time to time instruct. The Client shall pay to the Consultant in respect of such services an additional fee to be agreed between the parties based on the hourly rates set out in paragraph G of Schedule 1 unless the Client in his sole discretion shall elect that such additional fee shall be calculated solely on the basis of such hourly rates provided that it shall be a condition precedent to the Consultant's right to payment under this clause [K.7.3] that he shall have notified the Client prior to commencing the performance of such services that he intends to seek additional payment therefore and shall have obtained the Client's agreement thereto.

K.8 Insurance

K.8.1 Without prejudice to his other obligations under this Deed or otherwise at law the Consultant shall maintain with reputable insurers carrying on business in the European Union from the date hereof and for a period expiring no earlier than twelve (12) years after Practical Completion and notwithstanding the termination for any reason of the Consultant's engagement under this Deed professional indemnity insurance to cover each and every professional liability which he may incur under this Deed with a limit of indemnity of not less than [five million pounds (£5 million)] in relation to any one claim and in total during each twelve month period in respect of claims arising from pollution or contamination and in relation to each and every claim in respect of all other circumstances provided always that such insurance continues to be available in the European Union market upon reasonable terms and at commercially reasonable premium rates.

K.8.2 Such insurance shall be subject to such conditions as may be usual from time to time in the European Union market and in particular (but without limitation) such insurance shall not include any condition which may adversely affect the right of the Client to proceed directly against the insurers pursuant to and in the circumstances contemplated by the Third Parties (Rights Against Insurers) Act 1930.

K.8.3   As and when he is reasonably required to do so by the Client the Consultant shall produce for inspection by the Client documentary evidence that the insurance required by clause [K.8.1] is being properly maintained.

K.8.4   The Consultant shall forthwith notify the Client if the insurance required by clause [K.8.1] ceases to be available upon reasonable terms and at commercially reasonable premium rates or if for any other reason the Consultant is unable to continue to maintain such insurance.

K.9   **Copyright and Confidentiality**

K.9.1   The copyright in the Proprietary Material shall remain vested in the Consultant but the Consultant grants to the Client an irrevocable royalty-free non-exclusive licence to use and to reproduce any or all of the Proprietary Material for any purpose whatsoever connected with the Project and/or the Site. Such licence shall carry the right to grant sub-licences and shall be transferable to third parties and shall subsist notwithstanding the termination (for any reason) of the Consultant's engagement under this Deed provided always that the Consultant shall not be liable for the consequences of any use of the Proprietary Material for any purpose other than that for which the same was prepared.

K.9.2   The Consultant or the Client shall if so requested by the other at any time execute such documents and perform such acts as may be required fully and effectively to assure to the other the rights referred to in clause [K.9.1].

K.9.3   The Consultant shall not without the prior approval of the Client take or authorise the taking of any photographs of the Project for use in any publicity or advertising nor publish alone or in conjunction with any other person any articles photographs or other illustrations relating to the Project or any part thereof nor shall he impart to any publication journal or newspaper or any radio or television programme any information regarding the Project.

K.9.4   The Consultant shall not either during the period of his engagement under this Deed (except as necessary for the proper performance of the Services) or at any time after its expiry or termination for any reason disclose to any person nor otherwise make use of any confidential information of which he has or may in the course of his engagement become possessed relating to the Client the Project or otherwise nor shall he disclose to any person whatever (except his insurance or other professional advisers) anything contained in this Deed without the prior authority of the Client. The above restriction shall continue to apply without limitation in point of time unless and until such information comes properly into the public domain through no fault of the Consultant.

K.10 Assignment and Sub-Letting and Third Parties

K.10.1 The Consultant shall not assign his interest in this Deed or any part thereof nor any right arising hereunder to any person without the prior consent of the Client.

K.10.2 The Client may at any time assign upon notice to the Consultant without charge or transfer the benefit of this Deed and/or any rights arising under it to any person without the consent of the Consultant being required.

K.10.3 Unless the right of enforcement is expressly granted it is not intended that a third party should have the right to enforce a provision of this deed pursuant to the Contracts (Rights of Third Parties) Act 1999.

K.10.4 The parties may rescind or vary this deed without the consent of a third party to whom an express right to enforce any of its terms has been provided.

K.11 Time for Performance

The Consultant shall subject to the provisions of this Deed proceed with the Services regularly and diligently and shall perform the same as may be necessary having regard to the reasonable instructions of the Client. If at any time the Consultant is prevented or delayed in the performance of the whole or any part of the Services for any reason (whether by reason of force majeure or otherwise) the Consultant shall forthwith so notify the Client giving the specific reason for such delay or prevention and shall use his best endeavours as soon as practicable to resume and expedite the performance of the Services so as to complete the same with all reasonable speed.

K.12 Alterations to Terms

K.12.1 All additions amendments and variations to this Deed shall be binding only if in writing and signed by the duly authorised representatives both of the Client and of the Consultant.

K.12.2 This Deed supersedes any previous agreement or arrangements between the parties in respect of the Services (whether oral or written) and represents the entire understanding between the parties in relation to the Services.

K.12.3 Notwithstanding the date of this Deed it shall have effect as if it had been executed upon the actual commencement of the Services by the Consultant.

K.13 Notices

Any notice or other communication required under this Deed shall be given in writing and shall be deemed to have been properly given if compliance is made with Section 196 of the Law of Property Act 1925 (as amended by the Recorded Delivery Service Act 1962). The addresses and numbers for service of the Client and of the Consultant shall be those stated in Schedule 1 or such other address or number for service as the party to be served may previously have notified to the other party.

K.14   Disputes

K.14.1 Any dispute or difference arising under or in connection with this deed may in the first instance be referred to an adjudicator appointed on the request of either party by [   ]¹ for a decision in accordance with the provision of Part II of the Housing Grants Construction and Regeneration Act 1996.

1 The person who will appoint an adjudicator at the request of either party

K.14.2 The adjudication shall be undertaken in accordance with the rules and provisions of the Scheme for Construction Contracts (England and Wales) Regulations 1998 (SI 649) ('the Scheme').

K.14.3 The Scheme shall be amended by adding the following wording to paragraph 7(2)B:
'provided that the referral notice together with accompanying documents shall not exceed 20 single sided pages and any further documentation will be disregarded by the adjudicator.'

K.14.4 The adjudicator shall have the discretion to award either party the costs of any adjudication.

K.14.5 If the adjudicator fails to give a decision in accordance with paragraph 20 of the scheme [   ] shall appoint another person to act as adjudicator in his place.

K.14.6 The adjudicator's decision shall be final and binding unless and until the dispute or difference is finally determined by the Technology and Construction Court.

K.14.7 Subject to clauses [K.14.1] to [K.14.5], the parties agree that all differences or disputes of whatever nature arising under this Deed shall be tried by a Judge sitting as such in the Technology and Construction Court in London.

K.14.8 If and insofar as this Deed leaves any matter or thing to the decision or opinion of any person (including any account requirement or notice) the same shall not prevent the Court in determining the rights and liabilities of the parties from making any finding necessary to establish that such decision or opinion was correctly made or expressed on the facts found by the Court or to establish what or what other decision or opinion should have been made or expressed and giving effect thereto as if no decision or opinion had been made or expressed.

K.15   Governing Law
> The application and interpretation of this Deed shall in all respects be governed by English law.

> DELIVERED as a deed on the date of this document.

> EXECUTED under the Common Seal of

Director
Director/Secretary

> EXECUTED under the Common Seal of

Director
Director/Secretary

SCHEDULE 1

A.   *The Site*

B.   *The Project* comprises [*environmental ground investigation works at the Site*].

C.   *Person* referred to in clause [K.5.1] is [   ].

D.   *Key person* referred to in clause [K.5.2] is [   ].

E.   *The Fee* shall be the sum of £[   ]

F.   The Fee is [   ] payable as follows:

G.   Hourly rates referred to in clause [K.7.3] shall be as follows:

H.   The Client's address and number for service are as follows:

Address:

Tel:

Fax no:

The Consultant's address and number for service are as follows:-

Address:

Tel:

Fax:

SCHEDULE 2

The Services

> [*Insert detailed specification agreed with Environmental Consultant*]

SCHEDULE 3

Form of Deed of Warranty

(referred to in clause [K.3.6])

Annexed hereto

[Insert document J]

L   REMEDIATION WORKS

L.1   Investigation and Assessment

L.1.1   The Buyer shall procure that the Environmental Consultant using all the skill care and diligence as may reasonably be expected of a properly qualified and experienced environmental consultant experienced in undertaking work of a similar size scope nature and complexity as the work required in this clause [L.1] undertakes [within …days/weeks/ months from][1] [as soon as reasonably practicable after][1] the date of this Deed:

(i)   investigations (including without limitation intrusive investigations) in order to obtain such information as to the presence, nature and extent of Hazardous Substances in on or under the Property as is sufficient for the purposes of clauses [L.1(ii)-(iv)] of this Deed;

(ii)   an assessment of the need for and nature and extent of remediation works in order to ensure that on completion of the Remediation Works the Property will be in a condition which complies with clause [L.4.3] of this Deed;

(iii)   an assessment of the risks to the Environment and human health posed by Hazardous Substances in on or under the Property both before and after the Remediation Works are carried out;

(iv)   an assessment of the risk of liabilities which may fall on owners and occupiers of the Property both before and after the Remediation Works are carried out;

(v)   preparation of a report detailing the investigations and assessments undertaken in accordance with clauses [L.1(i)-(iv)] of this Deed and shall procure that a copy is provided forthwith to the Seller.

L.2   Remediation Method Statement

L.2.1   The Buyer shall prepare a draft of the Remediation Method Statement [within … months from the date of this Deed][1] [as soon as reasonably practicable following the preparation of the report required under clause [L.1(i)-(v)] of this Deed][1] and submit it forthwith to the Seller for information only.

1 Delete inapplicable alternative.

L.3 **Approval/Modification of Remediation Method Statement**

L.3.1 The Remediation Method Statement shall be submitted forthwith to the Named Authorities for approval and shall be modified in accordance with any reasonable requirements of either of the Named Authorities. In the absence of approval by the Named Authorities the Buyer shall consider and implement any modification which should be made to the Remediation Method Statement.

L.3.2 Any modification to the Remediation Method Statement effected in accordance with clause [L.3.1] of this Deed or otherwise shall be notified forthwith to the Seller.

L.4 **Remediation Works**
The Buyer shall:

L.4.1 procure that the Remediation Works are carried out and completed [no later than [ ] from the date of this Deed][1] [as soon as reasonably practicable][1] under the supervision of the Environmental Engineer using all the skill care and diligence as may reasonably be expected of a properly qualified and competent environmental engineer experienced in supervising remediation works of a similar size scope nature and complexity to the Remediation Works;

L.4.2 procure that the Remediation Works are carried out by the Remediation Contractor using all the skill care and diligence as may reasonably be expected of an appropriately experienced and competent remediation contractor experienced in undertaking works of a similar size scope nature and complexity to the Remediation Works;

L.4.3 procure that on completion of the Remediation Works the condition of the Property shall be fit for use as [industrial premises][2] and such as would be acceptable to any reasonable owner or occupier of the Property;

L.4.4 comply with and procure the compliance with all applicable legal requirements and all reasonable requirements (whether or not under compulsion of law) of any Authorities (including without limitation the Named Authorities) in connection with the implementation of the Remediation Works;

L.4.5 procure that the Remediation Works are completed to the reasonable satisfaction of the Named Authorities;

L.4.6 use all reasonable endeavours to obtain satisfactory evidence that the Remediation Works have been completed to the satisfaction of the Named Authorities.

1 Delete inapplicable alternative.
2 Amend as necessary.

L.5   **Step in Rights**

L.5.1   If the Remediation Works are not completed in accordance with clause [5] of this Deed by [ ], or if at any time prior to the completion of the Remediation Works the Seller reasonably considers that the Buyer is failing to fulfil its obligations under this Deed in a material manner and has not rectified any such breaches after written notice thereof and a reasonable opportunity to remedy them (being a period not less than 28 days from the date of such written notice), the Seller shall be entitled (but without any obligation to do so) at its own discretion and at the reasonable cost of the Buyer to assume all the obligations and entitlements of the employer under the appointments of the Environmental Consultant and the Environmental Engineer and the contract with the Remediation Contractor by giving notice in writing to that effect to the Seller and to the Environmental Consultant and the Environmental Engineer and the Remediation Contractor, and the Buyer shall grant to the Seller all such rights in respect of the Property as are necessary for that purpose.][1]

1 Delete if not required.

L.6   **Information and Miscellaneous**

L.6.1   Until completion of the Remediation Works the Buyer and/or its representatives will attend monthly meetings with the Seller and/or its representatives.

L.6.2   During the carrying out of the Remediation Works, the Buyer shall provide to the Seller:
(i)   copies of any scopes of work, specifications, assessments, audits or reports including without limitation any sampling, testing and/or monitoring data or other information prepared by the Environmental Consultant and/or the Environmental Engineer and/or the Remediation Contractor and/or any of their sub-contractors in respect of the Remediation Works;
(ii)   at any time on request in writing full written details of the Remediation Works carried out up to the date of such request;
(iii)   a reasonable opportunity to attend any Site visits or meetings with the relevant regulatory authorities and to inspect the carrying out of the Remediation Works.

L.6.3   The Buyer shall provide to the Seller copies of the appointment of the Environmental Consultant and the Environmental Engineer and of the contract with the Remediation Contractor promptly after each such appointment and contract is entered into.

L.6.4   Within four weeks from the date of practical completion of the Remediation Works the Buyer will provide to the Seller:

    (i)   a full record of all steps taken in carrying out the Remediation Works including without limitation a written description, diagrams, plans and photographs;

    (ii)   a report detailing the steps taken to comply with the Buyer's obligations under clause [L.5] of this Deed, together with documentary evidence of those steps, and copies of all approvals and permissions issued by and correspondence with the Authorities relating to the Remediation Works and/or the Property.

L.7   Warranties

L.7.1 The Buyer shall:

    (i)   provide within two weeks from the date of practical completion of the report prepared in accordance with clause [L.1.1] of this Deed a warranty from the Environmental Consultant in favour of the Seller in respect of that report and the work carried out in connection with that report substantially in the form set out in Schedule [1] of this Deed, subject only to such amendments as maybe reasonably required by the Environmental Consultant to the extent that such amendments do not materially diminish the position of the Seller under that warranty;

    (ii)   provide within two weeks from the date of practical completion of the Remediation Works a warranty from each of the Environmental Engineer and the Remediation Contractor in favour of the Seller in respect of the Remediation Works substantially in the forms set out in Schedules [2] and [3] of this Deed respectively subject only to such amendments as may be reasonably required by the person or body corporate giving the warranty to the extent that such amendments do not materially diminish the position of the Buyer under that warranty (always provided that there shall be included a warranty that the condition of the Property is such as is required by clause [L.4.3] of this Deed and that the requirements of clauses [L.4.4] and [L.4.5] of this Deed have been complied with).

SCHEDULES 1, 2 and 3

[Insert appropriate forms of deed of warranty.]

Index

[*all references are to paragraph number*]

Aarhus Convention
implementation, 1.40, 4.01

Abatement expenses
charge on premises, as, 14.61–14.62
generally, 14.58–14.60

Abatement notices
appeals
'best practicable means', 14.38–
14.39
effect, 14.40
generally, 14.36
grounds, 14.38
orders consequent on, 14.47–14.49
procedural and evidential issues,
14.42–14.46
relevant date, 14.39–14.41
defences
'best practicable means', 14.54–
14.56
reasonable excuse, 14.50–14.53
duty to serve, 14.12–14.18
expenses incurred in undertaking
work
charge on premises, as, 14.61–
14.62
generally, 14.58–14.60
format, 14.26–14.29
introduction, 14.25
recipient
generally, 14.30–14.33
owner, 14.34–14.35
restrictions on service, 14.36–14.37

Abstraction of water
common law rights, 17.23–17.24
enquiries about
generally, 7.11
preliminary, 3.21
impounding works, 17.39–17.40
licensing
applications, 17.30–17.38
background, 17.22–17.26

Abstraction of water – *contd*
licensing – *contd*
impounding works, 17.39–17.40
registers, 17.42
transfer, 17.41
types of, 17.31
offences, 17.27–17.29
preliminary enquiries, and, 3.21
statutory rights
current system, 17.26
defence, 17.30
offences, 17.28–17.29
regulation, 17.25
transfer of permits, and, 12.08

Adequacy of information
lender liability, for, 10.57–10.61

Adoption of sewers
generally, 17.135–17.137

Affected parties
considerations, 1.12–1.13
generally, 1.05
landlords, 1.08
lenders, 1.10
purchasers, 1.07
tenants, 1.09
vendors, 1.06

**Agricultural land agreements,
management of**
contents, 19.40
local land charges, and, 5.28
payments, 19.41
purpose, 19.39

Air pollution control (APC)
clean air, 20.32–20.34
introduction, 20.01–20.03
strategic context, 20.04–20.05

Amenity notices
appeal, 15.25–15.26
criteria, 15.24
enforcement, 15.27

Amenity notices – *contd*
generally, 15.23
non-compliance, 15.25

Animals, protection of
areas of special protection, 19.16
generally, 19.13
scope, 19.15

Anti-pollution works
controlled waters, protection of
17.83–17.85

Appeals
abatement notices
'best practicable means', 14.38–
14.39
effect, 14.40
generally, 14.36
grounds, 14.38
orders consequent on, 14.47–
14.49
procedural and evidential issues,
14.42–14.46
relevant date, 14.39–14.41
abstraction licences, as to, 17.36
amenity notices, as to, 15.25–15.26
discharges into controlled waters, as
to, 17.75
discharges of trade effluent into sewers,
as to, 17.111
environmental permits, applications
for, 16.32
remediation notices, against
generally, 15.71
grounds, 15.72–15.73

Apportionment
remediation liability, of, 15.93–
15.96

Areas of archaeological importance
local land charges, 5.31

**Areas of outstanding natural beauty
(AONB)**
local authority enquiries, 6.22

Areas of special protection
protection of animals and birds, and,
19.16

Asbestos
preliminary enquiries, 3.14

Assessment of risk
see Risk assessment

Assignment, prohibition against
environmental study, and, 8.16
liability under leases, and, 10.15–10.17

Atmospheric pollutions
clean air, 20.32–20.34
introduction, 20.01–20.03
strategic context, 20.04–20.05

Birds, protection of
areas of special protection, 19.16
EC law, 19.44
generally, 19.13
scope, 19.14

Brine extraction
searches, 7.31

Building preservation notices
local land charges, 5.24

Building regulations
sewers, building over
drainage provision, 17.144
generally, 17.143
water supply connections, and, 17.15

Built environment
conditions, 18.16–18.23
development control
conditions, 18.16–18.23
generally, 18.13–18.15
obligations, 18.24–18.27
development plans, 18.07–18.12
environmental impact assessment
introduction, 18.28–18.29
regulations, 18.33–18.36
significance, 18.30–18.32
strategic, 18.37–18.40
introduction, 18.01–18.02
obligations, 18.23–18.27
planning authorities, 18.03–18.05
planning conditions, 18.16–18.23
planning obligations, 18.24–18.27
policy, 18.06

'Buyer beware' rule
alterations
duty of disclosure, and, 2.18–2.20
effect, 2.40–2.42
encumbrances affecting land, 2.39
physical condition of land, 2.37–
2.38
conditions of sale
duty of disclosure, and, 2.18–2.20
effect, 2.40–2.42

'Buyer beware' rule – *contd*
  conditions of sale – *contd*
    encumbrances affecting land,
      2.39
    physical condition of land, 2.37–
      2.38
  defective building
    liability for, 2.28–2.31
  duty of disclosure
    contractual terms, 2.18–2.21
    generally, 2.20
    local land charges, 2.21
    planning matters, 2.22–2.24
    relevant matters, 2.25
    remedies, 2.20
  encumbrances affecting land, 2.39
  exceptions
    defective building, liability for,
      2.28–2.31
    duty of disclosure, 2.20–2.26
    fraudulent concealment, 2.17
    misdescription, 2.07–2.10
    misrepresentation, 2.11–2.16
    negligent workmanship, 2.27
  fraudulent concealment, 2.17
  introduction, 2.07
  leaving waste, 2.32–2.33
  limits, 2.34–2.36
  misdescription, 2.07–2.10
  misrepresentation
    civil actions, 2.11–2.15
    criminal actions, 2.16–2.16
  negligent workmanship, 2.27
  physical condition of land, 2.37–
    2.38
  purpose, 2.01–2.05
  seller's position, 2.44–2.46
  waste on the premises, 2.32–2.33

Canal and River Trust
  enquiries, 7.32

Carbon tetrachloride
  preliminary enquiries, 3.15

Category 4 screening levels
  remediation, and, 15.44

Causation
  civil liability, 13.58

Caveat emptor rule
  see 'Buyer beware' rule

Certificates of title
  risk assessment, and, 9.32

Cesspools
  local land charges, and, 5.11
  overflowing and leaking powers,
    17.153

Charging notices
  remediation, and, 15.101

Chlorofluorocarbons (CFCs)
  preliminary enquiries, 3.15

Civil liability
  causation, 13.58
  contributions, 13.60–13.61
  contributory negligence, 13.59
  damages, 13.53–13.56
  generally, 13.01–13.03
  independent contractors, for torts of,
    13.57
  injunction, 13.51–13.52
  limitation period, 13.50
  negligence, 13.48–13.49
  nuisance
    defences, 13.37–13.46
    introduction, 13.04
    private, 13.05–13.33
    public, 13.34–13.36
    remedies, 13.50–13.56
  private nuisance
    defences, 13.37–13.46
    defendant, 13.13–13.18
    entitlement to sue, 13.11–13.12
    generally, 13.05–13.10
    landlords and tenants, 13.20–
      13.23
    natural nuisances, 13.19
    non-natural use, 13.24–13.33
    remedies, 13.50–13.56
  public nuisance
    defences, 13.37–13.46
    generally, 13.34–13.36
    remedies, 13.50–13.56
  remedies
    damages, 13.53–13.56
    injunction, 13.51–13.52
    limitation period, 13.50
    Rylands v Fletcher, 13.24–13.33
    trespass, 13.47

Clay extraction
  searches, 7.31

Clean air
  integrated pollution control, and,
    20.32–20.34

Closets
local land charges, 5.12

Coal extraction
searches, 7.31

Coast protection
local land charges, 5.15

Coastal erosion
local land charges, 5.32

Collateral warranties
environmental study, and, 8.16
precedent, J.1–J.9

Condition of property
conditions of sale, 2.37–2.38
preliminary enquiries, 3.06

Conditions of sale
duty of disclosure, 2.18–2.20
effect, 2.40–2.42
encumbrances affecting land, 2.39
physical condition of land, 2.37–
2.38

Conditions precedent
loan agreement clause, H.12–H.13

Confidentiality
environmental study, and, 8.16

Connections to water supply
ancillary duties, 17.07–17.08
breach of duty, 17.09
building regulations, 17.15
charges, 17.17–17.22
customer's obligations, 17.10
easements, 17.10–17.13
fire authority, notice to, 17.16
general duty, 17.05–17.06
planning permission, 17.14

Consents
discharges into controlled waters
appeals, 17.75
application, 17.69–17.70
charges, 17.78
conditions, 17.71–17.72
confidentiality, 17.80–17.81
registers, 17.79
review, 17.74
Transfer or property, 17.76–
17.77
transmission of applications to
Secretary of State, 17.73
variation, 17.75

Consents – *contd*
discharges of trade effluent into sewers,
for
appeals, 17.111
application, 17.108
conditions, 17.109–17.110
criteria, 17.110
review, 17.112–17.113
transfer, 17.122
environmental permits
appeals, 16.32
application for, 16.23
competence assessment and
enforcement, 16.31
conditions, 16.27
consultation, participation in,
16.30
determining applications, 16.26
exempt operations, 16.22
offences, 16.36
regime, 16.19
registers, 16.33
regulations, structure of, 16.20
requirement of, 16.21
standard, 16.30
surrender, 16.28
transfer applications, 16.25
variation, 16.24

Conservation areas
local authority enquiries, 6.13–6.14
local land charges, 5.24

Construction site noise
regulation of, 14.73–14.76

Contaminant linkage
remediation, and, 15.45–15.47

Contaminated land
amenity notices
appeal, 15.25–15.26
criteria, 15.24
enforcement, 15.27
generally, 15.23
non-compliance, 15.25
development control, 15.15
enquiries about
duty of disclosure, 2.25
generally, 7.15
local land charges, 5.20
Environmental Liability Directive,
15.105–15.110
Green Card warning, 1.13
introduction, 15.01–15.02

Contaminated land – *contd*
lender liability, and
  causing pollution, 10.46
  knowingly permitting pollution,
    10.47
  occupier, 10.50
  owner, 10.49
local authority enquiries
  consultation with adjoining or
    adjacent landowners, 6.18
  notice of identification, 6.15–6.16
  register entries, 6.17
meaning, 15.40–15.42
planning issues
  development control, 15.15
  introduction, 15.10
  planning conditions, 15.16–15.20
  planning obligations, 15.21–15.22
  strategic planning, 15.11–15.14
planning conditions, 15.16–15.20
planning obligations, 15.21–15.22
policy, 15.03–15.06
principles
  polluter pays, 15.08
  property values, 15.09
  suitability for use, 15.07
registers, 15.102–15.103
remediation *see* **Remediation**
reports, 15.104
risk, 15.42
statutory nuisance, and, 15.32–15.33
strategic planning, 15.11–15.14
waste management, and, 15.28–
  15.31

Contamination
long form enquiries, 7.15

Contributions
civil liability, 13.60–13.61

Contributory negligence
civil liability, for, 13.59

Controlled waters
discharges to
  consents, 17.69–17.81
  defences, 17.67–17.68
  generally, 17.43
  landlords and lessors' liability,
    17.61–17.66
  multiple defendants, 17.58
  offences, 17.44–17.57
  separate acts, 17.58
  third party acts, 17.59–17.60

Controlled waters – *contd*
protection of
  anti-pollution works and operations,
    17.83–17.85
  groundwater protection, 17.99–
    17.102
  nitrate sensitive areas, 17.95–17.98
  nitrate vulnerable zones, 17.98–
    17.98
  pollution precautions, 17.82
  protection zones, 17.94
  works notices, 17.86–17.93

Cooling towers
preliminary enquiries, 3.16

Cost recovery
remediation, and, 15.99–15.103

Counter-indemnities
risk assessment, and, 9.19

Countryside
areas of outstanding natural beauty,
  6.22
national parks, 6.23–6.25

Countryside Agency
nature conservation, and, 19.08

Countryside Council for Wales
generally, 19.06

Countryside stewardship
nature conservation, and, 19.60–19.62

Covenants
loan agreement clauses, H.5–H.10.1

CRC Energy Efficiency Scheme
leases, and, 10.31

Culverts
local land charges, 5.13

Damages
civil liability, in case of, 13.53–13.56

Deed of collateral warranty
environmental study, and, 8.16
precedent, J.1–J.9

Defective buildings
'buyer beware' rule, and, 2.28–2.31

Definitions
authorities, A1.1.1
environment, A.1.3–A.1.3
environmental consultant, A.2
environmental engineer, A..3

Definitions – *contd*
environmental information, A.4
environmental law, A.4.1–A.4.2
hazardous substance, A.5.1–A.5.2
named authorities, A.7
permit, A.8
remediation contractor, A.9
remediation method statement, A.10
remediation works, A.1158

Delay
transfer of permits, and, 12.13

Derogate from grant, obligation not to
liability under leases, and, 10.34

Development control
contaminated land, and, 15.15
planning issues, and
conditions, 18.16–18.23
generally, 18.13–18.15
obligations, 18.24–18.27
nature conservation, and, 19.66

Development plans
generally, 18.07–18.12
waste policies in, 16,18

Discharges and deposits
trade effluents into sewers
agreements, by, 17.115
charges, 17.123–17.124
compensation, 17.121
consents, 17.103–17.113
introduction, 17.103–17.107
offences, 17.114
registers, 17.125–17.126
sewerage undertaker enquiries, and,
7.23
special category effluent, 17.116–
17.120
transfer of consent, 17.122
transfer of permits, 12.04
waste
preliminary enquiries, 3.20
public registers, 7.02
water
consents, 17.69–17.81
defences, 17.67–17.68
generally, 17.43
landlords and lessors' liability,
17.61–17.66
multiple defendants, 17.58
offences, 17.44–17.57
separate acts, 17.58
third party acts, 17.59–17.60

Discharges into water
consents
appeals, 17.75
application, 17.69–17.70
charges, 17.78
conditions, 17.71–17.72
confidentiality, 17.80–17.81
registers, 17.79
review, 17.74
Transfer or property, 17.76–17.77
transmission of applications to
Secretary of State, 17.73
variation, 17.75
defences, 17.67–17.68
generally, 17.43
landlords and lessors' liability,
17.61–17.66
multiple defendants, 17.58
offences
causing or knowingly permitting,
17.47–17.56
generally, 17.44–17.55
knowingly cause, 17.57
knowingly permit, 17.57
penalties, 17.46
separate acts, 17.58
third party acts, 17.59–17.60
transfer of permits, and, 12.04

Discharges of trade effluent into
sewers
agreements, by, 17.115
charges, 17.123–17.124
compensation, 17.121
consents
appeals, 17.111
application, 17.108
conditions, 17.109–17.110
criteria, 17.110
review, 17.112–17.113
transfer, 17.122
introduction, 17.103–17.107
offences, 17.114
registers
confidential information, 17.126
generally, 17.125
introduction, 7.02
sewerage undertaker enquiries, and,
7.23
special category effluent
appeals, 17.118
generally, 17.116
procedure, 17.117

Discharges of trade effluent into
  sewers – *contd*
  special category effluent – *contd*
    prescribed substances and processes,
      17.116
    review, 17.119
    variation of conditions, 17.120
  transfer of consent, 12.07, 17.122

Disclosure duty
  contractual terms, 2.18–2.20
  generally, 2.20
  local land charges, 2.21
  planning matters, 2.22–2.24
  relevant matters, 2.25
  remedies, 2.20

Ditches
  local land charges, 5.13

Drainage
  and see Sewers
  local authority enquiries
    adoption agreement, 6.44–6.46
    foul, 6.40–6.43
    general matters, 6.07–6.08
    surface water, 6.40–6.43
  local land charges, 5.11, 5.34
  preliminary enquiries, 3.05

Dust
  statutory nuisance, 14.04

Early repayment
  loan agreement clause, H.14–H.16

Easements
  indemnities, and, 9.31
  water supply connections, and,
    17.10–17.13

Encumbrances affecting land
  'buyer beware' rule, and, 2.39

Energy Performance Certificates
  leases, and, 10.32
  preliminary enquiries, and, 3.10

Enforcement notice
  duty of disclosure, and, 2.25

English Nature
  creation, 19.06
  enforcement, 19.11–19.12
  powers, 19.10

Environment
  definitions, A.1.2–A.1.3

Environment Agency (EA)
  aim, 1.30
  creation, 1.42
  functions
    generally, 1.43,
    regulated matters, 7.04
    transfer, 18.03
  long form enquiries
    contamination, 7.15
    fisheries, 7.19
    flood defence, 7.13
    industrial activities, installations and
      mobile plant, 7.18
    invasive species, 7.16
    land drainage, 7.13
    navigation, 7.20
    providers, 7.06–7.09
    radioactive substances, 7.17
    typical information in, 7.10–7.20
    waste management, 7.14
    water abstraction, 7.11
    water pollution, 7.12
  nature conservancy, and, 19.09
  offices, 7.21
  other authorities, enquiries of 7.04
  pollution inventory, 7.03
  property search reports, 7.05

Environmental consultant
  deed of appointment, K.10–K.15
  deed of collateral warranty, J.1–J.9
  definition, A.2
  letter of appointment, I.1–I.24

Environmental engineer
  definition, A.3

Environmental impact assessment
  introduction, 18.28–18.29
  regulations, 18.33–18.36
  significance, 18.30–18.32
  strategic, 18.37–18.40

Environmental information
  Aarhus Convention, 4.01
  charging, 4.34
  Code of Practice, 4.03
  commercial confidentiality, 4.23
  confidential proceedings, 4.22
  course of justice, 4.19
  criminal offences, 4.35
  defence and security, 4.18
  definition, 4.09–4.10, A.4
  DEFRA Guidance, 4.04
  Directive, 4.01

Environmental information – *contd*
  disclosure adversely effecting course of
    justice, 4.19
  disclosure adversely affecting
    intellectual property rights, 4.20
  emissions, 4.21
  enforcement, 4.36
  environment to which relating, 4.25
  excepted information
    categories, 4.10
    commercial confidentiality, 4.23
    confidential proceedings, 4.22
    course of justice, 4.19
    criteria, 4.11
    defence, 4.18
    emissions, 4.21
    environment to which relating, 4.25
    incomplete documentation, 4.16
    industrial confidentiality, 4.23
    intellectual property rights, 4.20
    internal communications, 4.17
    international relations, 4.18
    interpretation, 4.10
    historical records, 5.09
    manifest unreasonableness, 4.14
    national security, 4.18
    not held by authority, 4.13
    personal data, 4.26
    public security, 4.18
    general request formulated in
      manner, 4.15
    separating out, 4.12
    voluntary supply by third party, 4.24
  form and content, 4.33
  Freedom of Information Act 2000
    generally, 4.01
    relationship with EIR 2004, 4.02
  general request formulated in manner,
    4.15
  historical records, 4.10
  ICO guidance, 4.05
  incomplete documentation, 4.16
  industrial confidentiality, 4.23
  intellectual property rights, 4.20
  internal communications, 4.17
  international relations, 4.18
  introduction, 4.01–4.02
  legislative basis, 4.01
  manifest unreasonableness, 4.14
  meaning, 4.09–4.10
  national security, 4.18
  neither confirming of denying, 4.32
  not held by authority, 4.13

Environmental information – *contd*
  organisation and dissemination, duty
    of, 4.39
  personal data, 4.26
  public authorities
    charging, and, 4.35
    generally, 4.07
    holding requirement, 4.08
    judicial or legislative capacity, in,
      4.06
    meaning, 4.06
    requests, and, 4.02
  public interest test, 4.27
  public security, 4.18
  quality of information, 4.28
  refusal notice, 4.31
  Regulations (EIR) 2004
    application, 4.06
    Code of Practice, 4.03
    DEFRA Guidance, 4.04
    generally, 4.01
    ICO guidance, 4.05
    public authorities, 4.07–4.09
    relationship with FOIA 2000, 4.02
  remedies
    application to Information
      Commissioner, 4.38
    Information Tribunal's powers, 4.38
    internal reviews, 4.37
  request formulated in general manner,
    4.15
  request to public authority
    generally, 4.02
    procedure, 4.29
  separating out, 4.12
  statutory basis, 4.01
  time limits, 4.30
  voluntary supply by third party, 4.24

Environmental insurance
  conditions, 9.41
  disclosure, 9.43–9.44
  extent of cover, 9.37–9.40
  generally, 9.33–9.36
  limits, 9.41
  placing policy, 9.42
  types of, 9.37–9.40
  vendor's or purchaser's advisors and
    contractors, policies for, 9.45

Environmental law
  breach, 1.14
  conveyancing context, 1.01
  definitions, A.5.1–A.5.2

Environmental law – *contd*
development, 1.17
environmental principles, and, 1.31
European Community
  extent of, 1.18
  impact of, 1.21, 1.25
  implementation and enforcement,
    1.26
  sustainable development, meaning
    and implications, 1.24
  Treaty-based, 1.22
  Treaty of Amsterdam, 1.22–1.23
  UK law, influence on, 1.25
framework, 1.15–1.20
impact, 1.19
influence of policy trends, 1.32
international, 1.18
issues, 1.04
lawyers, and, 1.20
legislative authority
  EC law, 1.18,, 1.21–1.26
  generally, 1.15–1.20
  regulators, 1.41–1.43
  UK law, 1.27–1.35
legislative provisions, 1.16
meaning, 1.02
offences, 1.14
penalty powers, 1.34
policy trends, 1.32
sanctioning regimes, 1.34
significance, 1.03–1.04
voluntarism, and, 1.33

Environmental liabilities
dealings with, 9.03–9.04
effect, 9.02

Environmental Liability Directive
land, damage to, 15.107
liability, 15.106
pollution or contamination not
  remediated after coming into
  effect, 15.105
primary remediation, 15.109
water, damage to, 15.108

Environmental permits
appeals, 16.32
applications, 16.23
competence assessment and
  enforcement, 16.31
conditions, 16.27
consultation, 16.30
determining applications, 16.26

Environmental permits – *contd*
exempt operations, 16.22
offences, 16.36
participation in consultation, 16.30
regime, 16.19
registers, 16.33
regulations, 16.20
requirement of, 16.21
standard, 16.30
structure of regulations, 16.20
surrender, 16.28
transfer
  applications, 16.25
  generally, 12.04
variation, 16.24

Environmental permitting
amending regulations, 20.17
appeals, 20.31
applications for permit
  determination, 20.20
  generally, 20.19
  public consultation and
    participation, 20.26
category of installations, 20.12
conditions of permit, 20.21
consultation and participation, 20.26
criminal liability, 20.13
enforcement powers, 20.28
general effect, 20.11
guidance, 20.14
introduction, 20.10–20.11
other provisions, 20.16
periodic review, 20.15
permit conditions, 20.21
public consultation and participation,
  20.26
public information, 20.27
regulated facility, 20.18
Regulations, 20.10
regulatory functions, 20.12–20.17
remediation, 20.29
requirement for permit, 20.18
review, 20.15
standard permits, 20.25
surrender of permit, 20.23
transfer applications, 20.22
variation of permit, 20.24

Environmental surveys
buyers' considerations, 8.17
commissioner, 8.09–8.10
consultant
  appointment, 8.15–8.16

Environmental surveys – *contd*
consultant – *contd*
selection, 8.12–8.14
desk top assessment, 8.04–8.05
disadvantages, 8.11
existing reports, and, 8.17
importance, 8.01
phase I study, 8.06
phase II study, 8.07–8.08
types
desk top, 8.04–8.05
generally, 8.02–8.03
phase studies, 8.06–8.08

Environmentally sensitive area (ESA)
generally, 19.22
purpose, 19.60–19.62

Estate agents
misrepresentation, 2.16

EU law
environment, and, 1.21–1.26

European sites
designation, 19.51
effect, 19.52–19.57
generally, 19.49
types, 19.50

Evaporative condensers
preliminary enquiries, 3.16

Explosives
preliminary enquiries, 3.24

Financial charges
cesspools, 5.11
closets, 5.12
coast protection, 5.15
contaminated land, 5.20
culverts, 5.13
ditches, 5.13
drains, 5.11
general, 5.06
pests, 5.16
petrol tanks, 5.18
remedial work expenses, 5.21
search of, 5.03
sewers, 5.11
smoke control areas, 5.17
specific, 5.11–5.21
statutory nuisances, 5.19
verminous premises, 5.16
watercourses, 5.13
wholesome water supply, 5.14

Fire authorities, notice to
water supply connections, of, 17.16

Fisheries
long form enquiries, 7.19

Flood defence
local authority enquiries, 6.38
long form enquiries, 7.13

Flood risk
local land charges, 5.32
transfer of permits, 12.04

Flooding
Environment Agency enquiries, 7.13
preliminary enquiries, 3.05

Flora and fauna
background, 19.43–19.48
designation of European sites
effect, 19.52–19.57
generally, 19.49–19.51
types, 19.50
generally, 19.42

Foul sewers
local authority enquiries, 6.40–6.43

Fraudulent concealment
'buyer beware' rule, and, 2.17

Fraudulent misrepresentations
'buyer beware' rule, and, 2.15

Fumes
statutory nuisance, 14.04

Gases
statutory nuisance, 14.04

Greenhouse gas permits
transfer, 12.10

Groundwater
discharge of water, and, 17.99–
17.102
transfer of permits, and, 12.04

Habitat protection
private law, 19.17–19.20
public law, 19.21–19.22

Halons
preliminary enquiries, 3.15

Hardship
remediation, and, 15.99–15.103

Hazardous substances
definitions, A.6

Hazardous substances – *contd*
enquiries
local authority enquiries, 6.31–6.32
local land charges, 5.24
public registers, 7.02
risk assessment, 9.12
transfer of permits, 12.06
waste, 16.40

Hazardous waste notifications
transfer, 12.12

Hedgerow notices
local authority enquiries, 6.35–6.37

**Her Majesty's Inspectorate of Pollution
(HMIP)**
creation, 1.42
functions, 18.03

Highway drains
use as sewers 17.157

Human Rights Act 1998
generally, 1.36–1.39

Hydro-chlorofluorocarbons (HCFCs)
preliminary enquiries, 3.15

Indemnities
caps on liability, 9.18
certificates of title, 9.32
claims regime, 9.21
counter-indemnities, 9.19
covenants, 9.31
definitions
environment, 9.11
environmental law, 9.13
hazardous substances, 9.12
easements, 9.31
Eastern Counties Leather case
background, 9.22
claim issue, 9.24
Clause 4.1 issue, 9.26
Implied term issue, 9.27
Lessons from, 9.28–9.31
notification issue, 9.25
pollution indemnity agreement, 9.23
extent of cover, 9.09–9.10
introduction, 9.06–9.08
limitations, 9.16
precedents
limited, E.1–E.5
loan agreement clauses,
H.11–H.11.2
wide, D.1

Indemnities – *contd*
proof, 9.20
standard conditions, 9.29
standard of remedial work, 9.15
subject to planning, contract being,
9.30
time limits, 9.17
trigger event, 9.14

Independent contractors
civil liability for torts of 13.57

**Industrial activities, installations and
mobile plant**
long form enquiries, 7.18

Information
and see **Environmental information,
Local authority enquiries**
Canal and River Trust, 7.32
caveat emptor rule, and
alterations, 2.37–2.42
exceptions, 2.07–2.31
generally, 2.06
limits, 2.34–2.36
commercial property search reports
contamination, 7.15
fisheries, 7.19
flood defence, 7.13
industrial activities, installations and
mobile plant, 7.18
invasive species, 7.16
land drainage, 7.12
navigation, 7.20
providers, 7.06–7.09
radioactive substances, 7.17
typical information in, 7.10–7.20
waste management, 7.14
water abstraction, 7.11
water pollution, 7.12
Environment Agency
function of 7.04
long form enquiries, 7.10–7.20
offices, 7.21
pollution inventory, 7.03
property search reports, 7.05
extent, 2.03–2.04
introduction, 2.01–2.04
mineral extraction, 7.31
Natural England, 7.26–7.30
Natural Resources Wales, 7.26–7.30
preliminary enquiries
air conditioning, 3.10
asbestos, 3.14

Information – *contd*
  preliminary enquiries – *contd*
    building regulation, 3.08
    condition of property, 3.06–3.07
    discharges and deposits, 3.20
    disputes, 3.13
    energy performance certificates, 3.10
    environmental matters, 3.11
    explosives, 3.24
    generally, 3.01–3.05
    grants, 3.09
    hazardous substances, 3.11
    highway agreements, 3.09
    infrastructure, 3.09
    legionella, 3.16
    noise, 3.19
    notices, 3.12
    ozone-depleting substances, 3.15
    physical condition of property, 3.06
    planning regulation, 3.08
    polychlorinated biphenyls, 3.22
    radioactive substances, 3.23
    radon gas, 3.18
    sick building syndrome, 3.17
    standard forms, 3.05
    statutory agreements and infrastructure, 3.09
    statutory requirements, 3.10
    storage tanks, 3.07
    utilities and services, 3.07
    water abstraction, 3.21
  public registers, 7.02
  seller's position, 2.44–2.46
  sewerage undertakers
    charges and sewers, 7.24
    generally, 7.22
    model enquiries, 7.23–7.24
    office addresses, 7.25
    trade effluent, 7.24
  sources
    commercial property search providers, 7.06–7.09
    Environment Agency, 7.03–7.05
    generally, 2.05
    introduction, 7.01
    local authority enquiries, 6.01–6.51
    local land charges, 5.01–5.33
    preliminary enquiries, 3.01–3.24
    public registers, 7.02
    sewerage undertakers, 7.22–7.25
    water companies, 7.22–7.25

Information – *contd*
  water companies
    charges and sewers, 7.24
    generally, 7.22
    model enquiries, 7.23–7.24
    office addresses, 7.25
    trade effluent, 7.24

Injunctions
  civil liability remedy, 13.51–13.52
  statutory nuisance, 14.20–14.24

Inland waterways
  enquiries, 7.32

Inspection of premises by landlord
  leases, and, 10.22

Inspection of sites
  remediation, and, 15.53–15.59

Insurance
  environmental
    conditions, 9.41
    disclosure, 9.43–9.44
    extent of cover, 9.37–9.40
    generally, 9.33–9.36
    limits, 9.41
    placing policy, 9.42
    types of, 9.37–9.40
    vendor's or purchaser's advisors and contractors policy, 9.45

Integrated pollution control (IPC)
  clean air, 20.32–20.34
  introduction, 20.01–20.03
  public registers, 7.02
  strategic context, 20.04–20.04

Integrated pollution prevention and control (IPPC)
  generally, 20.06–20.09
  public registers, 7.02

Intellectual property rights
  environmental study, and, 8.16

Intimation notices
  liability under leases, and, 10.27

Invasive species
  long form enquiries, 7.16

Joint Nature Conservation Committee (JNCC)
  generally, 19.07

Land, agreements for management of
  contents, 19.40

Land, agreements for management of – *contd*
local land charges, and, 5.28
payments, 19.41
purpose, 19.39

Land drainage
local authority enquiries, 6.38
long form enquiries, 7.13

Landfill tax
exemptions
contaminated land, 16.46
site restoration and quarries, 16.47
introduction of, 16.44
landfill allowance and trading scheme, 16.49
rate, 16.44
tax credits, 16.48
'waste', 16.45

Landlords
considerations, 1.08

Lease liabilities
assignment prohibition, 10.15–10.17
clean and tidy, 10.14
covenant for quiet enjoyment, 10.33
covenant not to operate noisy, noxious or offensive trade or business, 10.21
covenant to allow inspection of premises by landlord, 10.22
CRC Energy Efficiency Scheme, 10.31
energy performance certificates, 10.32
inspection of premises by landlord, 10.22
intimation notices, 10.27
introduction, 10.01
keeping clean and tidy, 10.14
keeping in repair, 10.11–10.13
landlord and tenant, between
assignment, 10.15–10.17
clean and tidy, 10.14
inspection of premises, 10.22
introduction, 10.07
noisy, noxious or offensive trade or business, 10.21
nuisance, 10.19–10.20
payment of outgoings, 10.08–10.09
permitted use, 10.18
repair, 10.11–10.13
statutory works, 10.10

Lease liabilities – *contd*
landlord and tenant, between – *contd*
underletting, 10.15–10.17
use, 10.18
works, 10.10
new
introduction, 10.35
landlord's position, 10.36
tenant's position, 10.37–10.40
noisy, noxious or offensive trade or business, 10.21
non-derogation, 10.34
nuisance
introduction, 10.02
prohibition, 10.19–10.20
statutory, 10.06
obligation not to derogate from grant, 10.34
payment of outgoings, 10.08–10.09
permitted use, 10.18
pollution of controlled waters, and 10.03–10.05
precedents
landlord's covenants, G.1–G.3
tenants' covenants, F.1–F.17
prohibition against assignment, 10.15–10.17
prohibition against underletting, 10.15–10.17
quiet enjoyment, 10.33
repairs, 10.11–10.13
statutory appeal provisions, 10.23–10.26
statutory nuisance, and, 10.06
statutory works, 10.10
third party, to
introduction, 10.02
pollution of controlled waters, and 10.03–10.05
statutory nuisance, 10.06
underletting prohibition, 10.15–10.17
undertaking statutory works, 10.10
use, 10.18
waste
generally, 10.30
permissive, 10.29
voluntary, 10.28
works, 10.10

Legionella
preliminary enquiries, 3.16

Lender liability
adequacy of information, 10.57–10.61

Lender liability – *contd*
  channelling to purchaser, B.1–B.3
  considerations
    adequate information, 10.57–10.61
    direct liability, 10.45–10.55
    enforcement, 10.63
    generally, 1.10
    introduction, 10.41
    model clauses, 10.62
    non-payment by borrower, 10.42–
      10.43
    priority of rights, 10.56
    securitisation, 10.64
    value of security, 10.44
  contaminated land
    causing pollution, 10.46
    Green Card warning, 1.13
    knowingly permitting pollution,
      10.47
    occupier, 10.50
    owner, 10.49
  direct liability on lenders
    causing pollution, 10.46
    introduction, 10.45
    knowingly permitting pollution,
      10.47
    occupier, 10.52–10.54
    owner, 10.49–10.51
    receivers' acts, for, 10.55
    responsible person, 10.48
  generally, 1.10
  impact on value of security, 10.44
  introduction, 10.41
  model clauses, 10.62
  mortgagee in possession
    occupier, 10.54
    owner, 10.50
  non-payment by borrower, 10.42–
    10.43
  priority of rights, 10.56
  purchaser channelling, B.1–B.3
  receivers' and administrators' acts, for,
    10.55
  sites of special scientific interest
    occupier, 10.53
    owner, 10.51
  statutory nuisance
    occupier, 10.50
    owner, 10.49
    responsible person, 10.48
  waste removal notices, occupier, 10.50
  water pollution
    causing pollution, 10.46

Lender liability – *contd*
  water pollution– *contd*
    knowingly permitting pollution,
      10.47
    occupier, 10.50

Liability
  and see under individual headings
  civil
    causation, 13.58–13.61
    generally, 13.01–13.03
    independent contractors, 13.57
    negligence, 13.48–13.49
    nuisance, 13.04–13.46
    remedies, 13.50–13.56
    trespass, 13.47
  contaminated land
    generally, 15.01–15.06
    Green Card warning, 1.13
    planning powers, 15.10–15.104
    principles, 15.07–15.09
  lease, under
    landlord and tenant, between,
      10.07–10.20
    new leases, 10.35–10.40
    quiet enjoyment, 10.33–10.34
    statutory appeal provisions, 10.23–
      10.27
    third party, liabilities to, 10.02–
      10.06
    waste, for, 10.28–10.30
  lender
    adequate information, 10.57–10.61
    direct liability, 10.45–10.55
    enforcement, 10.63
    generally, 1.10
    introduction, 10.41
    model clauses, 10.62
    non-payment by borrower, 10.42–
      10.43
    priority of rights, 10.56
    securitisation, 10.64
    value of security, 10.44
  statutory nuisance
    abatement *see* **Abatement notice**
    considerations for assessing, 14.11
    construction site noise, 14.73–14.76
    definition, 14.04–14.11
    generally, 14.01–14.03
    nuisance, definition, 14.08–14.11
    prejudicial to health, definition,
      14.06–14.07
    summary proceedings, 14.63–14.67

Licences
abstraction of water
applications, 17.30–17.38
background, 17.22–17.26
impounding works, 17.39–17.40
registers, 17.42
transfer, 17.41
types, 17.31
discharges into water
appeals, 17.75
application, 17.69–17.70
charges, 17.78
conditions, 17.71–17.72
confidentiality, 17.80–17.81
registers, 17.79
review, 17.74
transfer or property, 17.76–17.77
transmission of applications to
Secretary of State, 17.73
variation, 17.75
discharges of trade effluent into sewers
appeals, 17.111
application, 17.108
conditions, 17.109–17.110
criteria, 17.110
review, 17.112–17.113
transfer, 17.122
transfer
discharges into controlled waters,
17.76–17.77
discharges of trade effluent into
sewers, 17.122
generally, 12.04

Limestone extraction
searches, 7.31

Limestone pavement order
duty of disclosure, and, 2.25

Limitation period
civil liability, for, 13.50

Listed building enforcement notices
local land charges, 5.24

Litter control areas
public registers, 7.02

Loan agreement clauses
conditions precedent, H.12–H.13
covenants, H.5–H.10.1
early repayment clauses, H.14–
H.16
indemnities, H.11–H.11.2
warranties, H.1–H.4

**Local authority air pollution control
(LAAPC)**
clean air, 20.32–20.34
introduction, 20.01–20.03
strategic context, 20.04–20.05

Local authority enquiries
abatement zones, 6.27
adoption agreements, 6.44–6.46
areas of outstanding natural beauty,
6.22
conservation areas, 6.13–6.14
contaminated land
consultation with adjoining or
adjacent landowners, 6.18
notice of identification, 6.15–6.16
register of entries, 6.17
countryside
areas of outstanding natural beauty,
6.22
national parks, 6.23–6.26
drainage
adoption agreements, 6.44–6.46
foul, 6.40–6.43
general matters, 6.07–6.08
standard for, 6.39
surface water, 6.40–6.43
foul drainage, 6.40–6.43
generally, 6.01
hazardous substance consents,
6.31–6.32
hedgerow notices, 6.35–6.37
national parks, 6.23–6.26
noise
abatement zones, 6.27
register entries, 6.28–6.30
outstanding notices, 6.09–6.10
pollution notices, 6.33–6.34
radon gas precautions, 6.19–6.21
rights of way, 6.02–6.06
sewers
boundaries, within, 6.47–6.48
general matters, 6.07–6.08
nearby, 6.49–6.51
surface water drainage, 6.40–6.43
tree preservation orders, 6.11–6.12

Local Better Regulation Office
establishment, 1.35
function, 1.35

Local land charges
areas of archaeological importance,
5.31

Local land charges – *contd*
building preservation notices, 5.24
cesspools, 5.11
closets, 5.12
coast protection, 5.15
coastal erosion risk, 5.32
conservation area designations, 5.24
contaminated land, 5.20
culverts, 5.13
ditches, 5.13
drainage schemes, 5.34
drains, 5.11
duty of disclosure, and, 2.25
enforcement
  generally, 5.04
  specific financial charges, 5.22
flood risk, 5.32
hazardous substances contravention
  notices, 5.24
listed building enforcement notices,
  5.24
management of agricultural land
  agreements, 5.28
miscellaneous charges
  areas of archaeological importance,
    5.31
  coastal erosion risk, 5.32
  flood risk, 5.32
  management of agricultural land
    agreements, 5.28
  nature conservation orders, 5.28
  scheduled monument consent, 5.31
  sewers, 5.30
  smoke control areas, 5.29
nature conservation orders, 5.28
permitted development restriction
  directions, 5.24
pests, 5.16
petrol tanks, 5.18
planning charges
  building preservation notices, 5.24
  conservation area designations, 5.24
  generally, 5.23
  hazardous substances contravention
    notices, 5.24
  listed building enforcement notices,
    5.24
  permitted development restriction
    directions, 5.24
  planning obligations, 5.24
  tree preservation orders, 5.24
  waste land notices, 5.24
planning obligations, 5.24

Local land charges – *contd*
register *see* **Local land charges register**
remedial work expenses, 5.21
scheduled monument consent, 5.31
search of, 5.03
sewers, 5.11, 5.30
smoke control areas, 5.17, 5.29
specific financial charges
  cesspools, 5.11
  closets, 5.12
  coast protection, 5.15
  contaminated land, 5.20
  culverts, 5.13
  ditches, 5.13
  drains, 5.11
  pests, 5.16
  petrol tanks, 5.18
  remedial work expenses, 5.21
  search of, 5.03
  sewers, 5.11
  smoke control areas, 5.17
  statutory nuisances, 5.19
  verminous premises, 5.16
  watercourses, 5.13
  wholesome water supply, 5.14
statutory nuisances, 5.19
tree preservation orders, 5.24
types
  drainage scheme, 5.34
  financial, 5.06–5.22
  generally, 5.05
  listed buildings, 5.33
  miscellaneous, 5.26–5.32
  planning, 5.23–5.25
verminous premises, 5.16
waste land notices, 5.24
watercourses, 5.13
wholesome water supply, 5.14

Local land charges register
drainage scheme charges, 5.34
financial charges
  general, 5.06
  specific, 5.07–5.22
form
  drainage scheme charges, 5.34
  general financial charges, 5.06
  generally, 5.05
  listed buildings charges, 5.33
  miscellaneous charges, 5.26–5.32
planning charges
  general, 5.23–5.25
  specific financial charges, 5.07–5.22

Local land charges register – *contd*
general financial charges, 5.06
generally, 5.01–5.04
listed buildings charges, 5.33
miscellaneous charges, 5.26–5.32
planning charges, 5.23–5.25
specific financial charges
enforcement, 5.22
generally, 5.07–5.09
types, 5.10–5.21

Local nature reserves (LNR)
nature conservation, 19.21

Local Planning Authorities (LPA)
built environment, and, 18.03–
18.05

Macrory Review
recommendations, statutory
implementation, 1.35
sanctioning and penalty regimes,
examination of, 1.34

Mains water supply
charges, 17.17–17.22
generally, 17.02–17.04

**Management of agricultural land
agreements**
contents, 19.40
local land charge enquiries, 5.28
payments, 19.41
purpose, 19.39

Marine licences
transfer, 12.11

Methyl bromide
preliminary enquiries, 3.15

Mineral extraction
searches, 7.31

Miscellaneous charges
areas of archaeological importance,
5.31
coastal erosion, 5.32
flood risk, 5.32
management of agricultural land
agreements, 5.28
nature conservation orders, 5.28
scheduled monument consent, 5.31
sewers, 5.30
smoke control areas, 5.29

Misdescription
'buyer beware' rule, and, 2.07–2.10

Misrepresentation
civil actions
fraudulent misrepresentations,
2.15
generally, 2.11–2.14
criminal actions, 2.16

Money laundering
definition, 1.14
offences, 1.14
reporting obligations, 1.14

Mortgagees
considerations, 1.10

National nature reserves (NNR)
nature conservation, 19.21

National parks
local authority enquiries, 6.23–6.26

National Rivers Authority (NRA)
creation, 1.42
functions, 18.03

Natural England
generally, 7.26–7.30
regulator, as, 1.43

Natural habitats
background, 19.43–19.48
European sites
designation, 19.51
effect, 19.52–19.57
generally, 19.49
types, 19.50
generally, 19.42

Natural Resources Wales
creation, 19.06
generally, 7.26–7.30
introduction, 7.04
regulator, as, 1.43

**Nature Conservancy Council for England
(English Nature)**
creation, 19.06
enforcement, 19.11–19.13
powers, 19.10

Nature conservation
animals
areas of special protection, 19.16
generally, 19.13
scope, 19.15
birds
areas of special protection, 19.16
EC law, 19.44

Nature conservation – *contd*
  birds – *contd*
    generally, 19.13
    scope, 19.14
  countryside stewardship, 19.60–19.62
  development control, 19.66
  environmentally sensitive areas (ESA)
    generally, 19.22
    purpose, 19.60–19.62
  flora and fauna
    background, 19.43–19.48
    designation of European sites,
      19.49–19.57
    generally, 19.42
  habitats
    private law, 19.17–19.20
    public law, 19.21–19.22
  introduction, 19.01–19.05
  management agreements for land
    contents, 19.40
    payments, 19.41
    purpose, 19.39
  natural habitats
    background, 19.43–19.48
    European sites, 19.49–19.57
    generally, 19.42
  nature reserves
    generally, 19.58
    types, 19.59
  plants
    generally, 19.13
    scope, 19.15
  planning law, and
    development control, 19.66
    generally, 19.62
    policy, 19.63–19.65
  regulators
    conservation, 19.06
    co-ordination, 19.07
    enforcement, 19.11–19.12
    landscape and countryside, 19.08
    other authorities, 19.09
    powers, 19.10
  site designation
    private law, 19.17–19.20
    public law, 19.21–19.22
  sites of special scientific interest (SSSI)
    effect, 19.26–19.38
    generally, 19.23–19.24
    notification, 19.25
  special areas of conservation (SAC)
    designation, 19.51
    effect, 19.52–19.56

Nature conservation – *contd*
  special areas of conservation (SAC)–
    contd
    generally, 19.49
    types, 19.50
  special nature conservation order
    (SNCO)
    generally, 19.49
    scope, 19.53
  special protection areas (SPA)
    designation, 19.51
    effect, 19.52–19.56
    generally, 19.49
    types, 19.50
  stewardship, 19.60–19.62

Nature conservation areas
  local land charges, and, 5.28

Nature reserves
  generally, 19.58
  types, 19.21, 19.59

Navigation
  long form enquiries, 7.20

Negligence
  civil liability for 13.48–13.49

Negligent workmanship
  'buyer beware' rule, and, 2.27

Neighbour disputes
  preliminary enquiries, 3.05

Nitrate sensitive areas
  controlled waters, 17.95–17.98

Nitrate vulnerable zones
  controlled waters, 17.98–17.98

Noise
  construction site, 14.73–14.76
  local authority enquiries
    abatement zone, 6.27
    public registers, 7.02
    register entries, 6.28–6.30
  preliminary enquiries, 3.19
  statutory nuisance, 14.04

**Noisy, noxious or offensive trade or
  business**
  leases, and, 10.21

Notices
  preliminary enquiries, 3.12

Nuisance
  civil liability
    defences, 13.37–13.46

Nuisance – *contd*
  civil liability – *contd*
    introduction, 13.04
    private, 13.05–13.33
    public, 13.34–13.36
    remedies, 13.50–13.56
  defences
    easements, 13.35–13.36
    generally, 13.37
    statutory authority, 13.37–13.46
  liability under leases, and
    introduction, 10.02
    prohibition against, 10.19–10.20
  private nuisance
    defences, 13.37–13.46
    defendant, 13.13–13.18
    entitlement to sue, 13.11–13.12
    generally, 13.05–13.10
    landlords and tenants, 13.20–13.23
    natural nuisances, 13.19
    non-natural use, 13.24–13.33
    remedies, 13.50–13.56
  public nuisance
    defences, 13.37–13.46
    generally, 13.34–13.36
    planning permission or permits, 13.43–13.46
    prescriptive easements, 13.38–13.40
    remedies, 13.50–13.56
    statutory authority, 13.41–13.42
  remedies
    damages, 13.53–13.56
    injunction, 13.51–13.52
    limitation period, 13.50
    Rylands v Fletcher, 13.24–13.33
  statutory *see* **Statutory nuisance**

1.1.1-Trichloroethane
  preliminary enquiries, 3.15

Orphan linkage
  remediation, and, 15.83

Outgoings, payment of
  liability under leases, and, 10.08–10.09

Ozone-depleting substances
  preliminary enquiries, 3.15

Parties
  considerations
    environmental, 1.12
    generally, 1.05
    landlords, 1.08
    lenders, 1.10

Parties – *contd*
  considerations– *contd*
    purchasers, 1.07
    tenants, 1.09
    values and liabilities, [1.11
    vendors, 1.06
  protection
    contractual terms, 2.37–2.42
    defective building, liability for, 2.28–2.31
    duty of disclosure, 2.20–2.26
    fraudulent concealment, 2.17
    generally, 2.01–2.06
    misdescription, 2.07–2.10
    misrepresentation, 2.11–2.16
    workmanship, negligent, 2.27

Permit
  definition, A.8

Permitted development restriction directions
  local land charges, 5.24

Pests
  local land charges, 5.16

Petrol storage certificates and licences
  transfer, 12.05

Petrol tanks
  local land charges, 5.18

Physical condition of land
  'buyer beware' rule, and, 2.37–2.38

Planning
  'buyer beware' rule, and, 2.22–2.24
  conditions, 18.16–18.23
  construction noise, 14.73–14.76
  development control
    conditions, 18.16–18.23
    generally, 18.13–18.15
    obligations, 18.24–18.27
  development plans, 18.07–18.12
  environmental impact assessment
    introduction, 18.28–18.29
    regulations, 18.33–18.36
    significance, 18.30–18.32
    strategic, 18.37–18.40
  introduction, 18.01–18.02
  local land charges, and
    and see **Planning charges**
    generally, 5.23
    types, 5.24
  nature conservation, and
    development control, 19.66

Planning – *contd*
nature conservation, and – *contd*
generally, 19.62
policy, 19.63–19.65
obligations, 18.24–18.27
planning authorities, 18.03–18.05
policy, 18.06

Planning charges
building preservation notices, 5.24
conservation area designations, 5.24
generally, 5.23
hazardous substances contravention
notices, 5.24
listed building enforcement notices,
5.24
permitted development restriction
directions, 5.24
planning obligations, 5.24
tree preservation orders, 5.24
waste land notices, 5.24

Planning conditions
contaminated land, in case of, 15.16–
15.20
generally, 18.16–18.23

Planning obligations
contaminated land, and, 15.21–15.22
generally, 18.24–18.27
local land charges, and, 5.24

Planning permission
water supply connections, for, 17.14

Plants, protection of
generally, 19.13
scope, 19.15

Pollutant linkage
remediation, and, 15.45–15.47

Pollution notices
local authority enquiries, 6.33–6.34

Pollution of controlled waters
liability under leases, and, 10.03–
10.05

Pollution, prevention and control
generally, 20.06–20.09
public registers, 7.02

Polychlorinated biphenyls (PCBs)
preliminary enquiries, 3.22

Polychlorinated terphenyls (PCTs)
preliminary enquiries, 3.22

Preliminary enquiries
air conditioning, 3.10
asbestos, 3.14
building regulation, 3.08
condition of property, 3.06–3.07
discharges and deposits, 3.20
disputes, 3.13
energy performance certificates, 3.10
environmental matters, 3.11
explosives, 3.24
generally, 3.01–3.05
grants, 3.09
hazardous substances, 3.11
highway agreements, 3.09
infrastructure, 3.09
legionella, 3.16
noise, 3.19
notices, 3.12
ozone-depleting substances, 3.15
physical condition of property, 3.06
planning regulation, 3.08
polychlorinated biphenyls, 3.22
radioactive substances, 3.23
radon gas, 3.18
sick building syndrome, 3.17
standard forms, 3.05
statutory agreements and
infrastructure, 3.09
statutory requirements, 3.10
storage tanks, 3.07
utilities and services, 3.07
water abstraction, 3.21

Private nuisance
damages, 13.53–13.56
defences
generally, 13.37
planning permission or permits,
13.43–13.46
prescriptive easements, 13.38–13.40
statutory authority, 13.37–13.46
defendant, 13.13–13.18
easements, 13.38–13.40
entitlement to sue, 13.11–13.12
generally, 13.05–13.10
injunctions, 13.51–13.52
landlords and tenants, 13.20–13.23
limitation period, 13.50
natural nuisances, 13.19
non-natural use, 13.24–13.33
planning permission or permits,
13.43–13.46
prescriptive easements, 13.38–13.40

Private nuisance – *contd*
  remedies
    damages, 13.53–13.56
    injunctions, 13.51–13.52
    limitation period, 13.50
  Rylands v Fletcher, 13.24–13.33
  statutory authority, 13.41–13.42

Prohibition notice
  duty of disclosure, and, 2.25

Property development business
  misrepresentation, 2.16

Public nuisance
  defences
    generally, 13.37
    planning permission or permits,
      13.43–13.46
    prescriptive easements, 13.38–
      13.40
    statutory authority, 13.37–13.46
  generally, 13.34–13.36
  planning permission or permits,
    13.43–13.46
  prescriptive easements, 13.38–13.40
  remedies
    damages, 13.53–13.56
    injunction, 13.51–13.52
    limitation period, 13.50
  statutory authority, 13.37–13.46

Public registers
  abstraction of water, 17.42
  contaminated land, 15.102–15.103
  discharges into water, 17.79
  discharges of trade effluent into sewers
    confidential information, 17.126
    generally, 17.125
  environmental permits, 16.33
  generally, 7.02
  impounding of water, 17.42
  remediation, and, 15.102–15.103
  water abstraction activities, 17.42

Purchasers
  considerations, 1.07

Quiet enjoyment, covenant for
  liability under leases, and, 10.33

Radioactive substances
  enquiries, and
    generally, 7.17
    preliminary, 3.23
  transfer of permits, 12.04

Radon gas
  local authority enquiries, 6.19–
    6.21
  preliminary enquiries, 3.18

**Ramsar Convention on Wetlands of
  International Importance (1971)**
  enquiries, and
    duty of disclosure, 2.25
    generally, 7.26
  generally, 19.21

Receivers
  lender liability, and, 10.55

Reclaimed land
  preliminary enquiries, 3.05

Registers
  abstraction of water, 17.42
  contaminated land, 15.102–15.103
  discharges into water, 17.79
  discharges of trade effluent into
    sewers
    confidential information, 17.126
    generally, 17.125
  environmental permits, 16.33
  generally, 7.02
  impounding of water, 17.42
  remediation, and, 15.102–15.103
  water abstraction activities, 17.42

Remedial work agreements
  adjudication under HGCRA 1996,
    11.24
  assessing problem, 11.06
  beneficiary's viewpoint, 11.02
  carrying out works, 11.09
  collateral warranties, 11.12
  completion certificate, 11.10
  construction operations, and, 11.14
  contract, 11.04
  information, 11.11
  investigation of site condition, 11.06
  meetings, 11.11
  parties to, 11.05
  precedent, L.1–L.7
  records, 11.11
  remediation method statement, 11.07
  remediation standard, 11.08
  remediator's viewpoint, 11.03
  site condition, 11.06
  step-in rights, 11.13

Remedial work expenses
  local land charges, 5.21

Remediation
agreement for works
  adjudication under HGCRA 1996, 11.24
  assessing problem, 11.06
  beneficiary's viewpoint, 11.02
  carrying out works, 11.09
  collateral warranties, 11.12
  completion certificate, 11.10
  construction operations, and, 11.14
  contract, 11.04
  information, 11.11
  investigation of site condition, 11.06
  meetings, 11.11
  parties to, 11.05
  precedent, L.1–L.7
  records, 11.11
  remediation method statement, 11.07
  remediation standard, 11.08
  remediator's viewpoint, 11.03
  site condition, 11.06
  step-in rights, 11.13
appeals
  generally, 15.71
  grounds, 15.72–15.73
apportionment, 15.93–15.96
appropriate persons, 15.75–15.79
assessment criteria, 15.43
charging notices, 15.101
contaminant linkages, 15.45–15.47
'contaminated land'
  Category 4 screening levels, 15.44
  generic assessment criteria, 15.43
  introduction, 15.40–15.45
  risk, 15.42
  significant harm, 15.48–15.50
  significant pollutant linkages, 15.45–15.47
  soil guideline values, 15.43
  special sites, 15.51–15.52
'contractor', A.9
cost recovery, 15.99–15.103
definitions
  contaminant linkages, 15.45–15.47
  contaminated land, 15.40–15.52
  orphan linkages, 15.84
  special sites, 15.51
designation of sites, 15.53
escaped substances
  non-statutory exclusions, 15.90
  statutory exclusions, 15.84

Remediation – *contd*
exclusions
  non-statutory, 15.84–15.92
  statutory, 15.80–15.83
extent of contaminated land, 15.59
features, 15.37
generally, 15.34–15.37
generic assessment criteria, 15.43
guidance, 15.38–15.39
hardship, 15.99–15.103
inspection of sites, 15.53–15.59
liability
  apportionment, 15.93–15.96
  appropriate persons, 15.75–15.79
  exclusions, 15.80–15.92
  generally, 15.74
  regimes, 15.110
method statement, 11.07, A.10
non-statutory exclusions
  changes to substances, 15.89
  escaped substances, 15.90
  excluded activities, 15.86
  introduction, 15.84–15.85
  pathways, 15.91
  payments made for remediation, 15.87
  receptors, 15.91
  sold with information, 15.88
orphan linkage, 15.83
pollutant linkage, 15.45–15.47
primary, 15.109
principal features
  charging notices, 15.101
  cost recovery, 15.99–15.103
  definition of contaminated land, 15.40–15.52
  duty of inspection, 15.53–15.59
  duty to require remediation, 15.60–15.63
  hardship, 15.99–15.103
  introduction, 15.36–15.39
  liability, 15.74–15.96
  registers, 15.102–15.103
  risk summaries, 15.58
registers, 15.102–15.103
remediation notices
  appeals, 15.71–15.73
  contents, 15.62–15.63
  duty of disclosure, and, 2.25
  generally, 15.60–15.63
  requirements, 15.68–15.70
  restrictions on service, 15.64–15.67
risk, 15.42

Remediation – *contd*
risk summaries, 15.58
screening levels, 15.44
significant harm, 15.47
significant contaminant linkages,
15.45–15.47
soil guideline values, 15.43
special sites, 15.51–15.52
standard, 11.08
statutory exclusions
escaped pollution, 15.84
no appropriate person remaining,
15.83
owners or occupiers, 15.80
professional capacity, persons in,
15.81
statutory guidance, 15.38–15.39
undertaking for, 11.01
works
definition, A.11
precedent, L.1–L.7

Repairs
liability under leases, and, 10.11–10.13
sewers, to, 17.150–17.152

Reports
remediation, and, 15.104

Reservoirs
local authority enquiries, 7.02

Rights of way
local authority enquiries, 6.02–6.06

Risk assessment
certificates of title, 9.32
claims regime, 9.21
counter-indemnities, 9.19
environmental liabilities, and
dealings with, 9.03–9.04
effect, 9.02
indemnities
caps on liability, 9.18
definitions, 9.11–9.13
Eastern Counties Leather case,
9.22–9.31
extent of cover, 9.09–9.10
introduction, 9.06–9.08
limitations, 9.16
proof, 9.20
standard of remedial work, 9.15
time limits, 9.17
trigger event, 9.14
introduction, 9.01
warranties, 9.05

Risk summaries
remediation, and, 15.58

River work consents
transfer, 12.09

Rylands v Fletcher
civil liability, and, 13.24–13.33

Scheduled monument consent
local land charges, 5.31

**Scottish Environment Protection Agency
(SEPA)**
creation, 1.42
transfer of functions, 18.03

Scottish Natural Heritage
generally, 19.06

Screening levels
remediation, and, 15.44

Securitisation
lender liability, and, 10.64

Sewerage undertaker
generally, 7.22
model enquiries
charges, 7.24
sewers, 7.24
trade effluent, 7.23
office addresses, 7.25

Sewers
adoption, 17.135–17.137
building regulations
drainage provision, 17.144
generally, 17.143
construction, 17.142
discharges of trade effluent
agreements, by, 17.115
charges, 17.123–17.124
compensation, 17.121
consents, 17.103–17.113
introduction, 17.103–17.107
offences, 17.114
registers, 17.125–17.126
sewerage undertaker enquiries, and,
7.23
special category effluent, 17.116–
17.120
transfer of consent, 17.122
existing development, under
alteration of system of premises,
17.154
charges, 17.156–17.158

Sewers – *contd*
existing development, under – *contd*
generally, 17.146–17.149
highway drains, use of, 17.155
overflowing and leaking cesspools, 17.153
repair and unstopping, 17.150–17.152
highway sewers, use of, 17.155
introduction, 17.131
liability of undertaker for flooding, 17.158
local authority enquiries
boundaries, within, 6.47–6.48
general matters, 6.07–6.08
nearby, 6.49–6.51
local land charges, 5.11, 5.30
new developments, for
adoption, 17.135–17.137
building regulations, 17.143–17.144
combined drainage, 17.145
construction, 17.142
generally, 17.132–17.134
owners and occupiers, rights of, 17.138–17.143
overflowing and leaking cesspools, 17.153
repair and unstopping, 17.150–17.152
undertaker's liability for sewage flooding, 17.158
water supply, and, 17.156–17.158

Sick building syndrome
preliminary enquiries, 3.17

Single European Act 1986
generally, 1.22

Site of special scientific interest (SSSI)
effect, 19.26–19.38
enquiries, and
duty of disclosure, 2.25
generally, 7.28
generally, 19.23–19.24
lender liability, and
occupier, 10.53
owner, 10.51
notification
effect, 19.26–19.38
generally, 19.25–19.26

Smells
statutory nuisance, 14.04

Smoke
statutory nuisance, 14.04

Smoke control areas
local land charges, 5.17, 5.29

Special areas of conservation (SAC)
designation, 19.51
effect, 19.52–19.57
generally, 19.21, 19.49
types, 19.50

Special category effluent
compensation, 17.121
consent
appeals, 17.118
review, 17.119
variation of conditions, 17.120
generally, 17.116
procedure, 17.117
prescribed substances and processes, 17.116
transfer of property, 12.04, 17.122

Special nature conservation order (SNCO)
duty of disclosure, and, 2.25
generally, 19.49
scope, 19.53

Special protection areas (SPA)
designation, 19.51
effect, 19.52–19.57
generally, 19.21, 19.49
types, 19.50

Special sites
remediation, for, 15.51–15.52

Specific financial charges
cesspools, 5.11
closets, 5.12
coast protection, 5.15
contaminated land, 5.20
culverts, 5.13
ditches, 5.13
drains, 5.11
pests, 5.16
petrol tanks, 5.18
remedial work expenses, 5.21
search of, 5.03
sewers, 5.11
smoke control areas, 5.17
statutory nuisances, 5.19
verminous premises, 5.16
watercourses, 5.13
wholesome water supply, 5.14

Statutory appeals
liability under leases, and, 10.23–10.26

Statutory nuisances
abatement expenses
charge on premises, as, 14.61–14.62
generally, 14.58–14.60
abatement notice
appeals, 14.38–14.49
defences, 14.50–14.56
duty to serve, 14.12–14.18
expenses incurred in undertaking work, 14.58–14.62
format, 14.26–14.29
introduction, 14.25
owner, identifying, 14.34–14.35
recipient, 14.30–14.33
restrictions on service, 14.36–14.37
background, 14.02–14.03
construction site noise, 14.73–14.76
contaminated land, 15.32–15.33
definition
generally, 14.04–14.05
nuisance, 14.08–14.11
prejudicial to health, 14.06–14.07
dust, 14.04
establishment of, 14.05
fumes, 14.04
gases, 14.04
injunction, power to seek, 14.20–14.24
introduction, 14.01–14.03
liability under leases, and, 10.06
legislation, 14.01
lender liability, and
occupier, 10.50
owner, 10.49
responsible person, 10.48
local land charges, and, 5.19
noise
construction site, 14.73–14.76
generally, 14.04
offences
commission of nuisance, 14.57
summary proceedings, 14.50–14.56, 14.63–14.67
smells, 14.04
smoke, 14.04
steam, 14.04
summary proceedings by person aggrieved
costs, recovery of, 14.70–14.72
procedure, 14.63–14.67
service of notice, 14.68–14.69
third parties, liability to, 10.06

Steam
statutory nuisance, 14.05

Stewardship
nature conservation, and, 19.60–19.62

Storage tanks
preliminary enquiries, 3.07

Street litter control notices
public registers, 7.02

Super SSSI (nature conservation order)
enquiries, and
duty of disclosure, 2.25
generally, 7.28
generally, 19.21

Surface water drains
local authority enquiries, 6.40–6.43

Surveys
buyers' considerations, 8.17
commissioner, 8.09–8.10
consultant
appointment, 8.15–8.16
selection, 8.12–8.14
desk top assessment, 8.04–8.05
disadvantages, 8.11
existing reports, and, 8.17
importance, 8.01
phase I study, 8.06
phase II study, 8.07–8.08
types
desk top, 8.04–8.05
generally, 8.02–8.03
phase studies, 8.06–8.08

Sustainable development
general concept, 1.28
key objectives, 1.29
meaning and implications, 1.24
revision of strategy, 1.28

Tenants
considerations, 1.09

Tenants' covenants
assignment prohibition, 10.15–10.17
clean and tidy, 10.14
covenant for quiet enjoyment, 10.33
intimation notices, 10.27
introduction, 10.01
keeping clean and tidy, 10.14
keeping in repair, 10.11–10.13

Tenants' covenants – *contd*
new
introduction, 10.35
landlord's position, 10.36
tenant's position, 10.37–10.40
nuisance
introduction, 10.02
prohibition against, 10.19–10.20
payment of outgoings, 10.08–10.09
permitted use, 10.18
precedents, F.1–F.17
prohibition against assignment,
10.15–10.17
prohibition against underletting,
10.15–10.17
quiet enjoyment, 10.33
repairs, 10.11–10.13
statutory appeal provisions, 10.23–
10.26
statutory nuisance, 10.06
statutory works, 10.10
underletting prohibition, 10.15–10.17
undertaking statutory works, 10.10
use, 10.18
waste, and
generally, 10.30
permissive, 10.29
voluntary, 10.28
works, 10.10

Third parties
contractual rights, 8.16

**'This Common Inheritance' (White Paper
Cm 1200, 1990)**
generally, 1.27

Tin extraction
searches, 7.31

Trade effluent discharge
agreements, by, 17.115
charges, 17.123–17.124
compensation, 17.121
consents
appeals, 17.111
application, 17.108
conditions, 17.109–17.110
criteria, 17.110
review, 17.112–17.113
transfer, 17.122
introduction, 17.103–17.107
offences, 17.114
public registers
confidential information, 17.126

Trade effluent discharge – *contd*
public registers – *contd*
generally, 17.125
introduction, 7.02
sewerage undertaker enquiries, and,
7.23
special category effluent
appeals, 17.118
generally, 17.116
procedure, 17.117
prescribed substances and processes,
17.116
review, 17.119
variation of conditions, 17.120
transfer of consent, 12.07, 17.122

Transfer of permits
consent to river works, 12.09
delay, and, 12.13
environmental permits, 12.04
flood risk activities, 12.04
generally, 12.01–12.04
greenhouse gas permits, 12.10
groundwater discharges, 12.04
hazardous substances consent, 12.06
hazardous waste notifications, 12.12
marine licences, 12.11
petrol storage certificates and licences,
12.05
radioactive substance activities, 12.04
summary table, 12.14
trade effluent consent, 12.07
waste, 12.04
water abstraction licences, 12.08
water discharge activities, 12.04
watercourse works, 12.09

Treaty of Amsterdam
generally, 1.22–1.23

Tree preservation orders
local authority enquiries, 6.11–6.12
local land charges, 5.24

Trespass to land
civil liability, and, 13.47

1.1.1-Trichloroethane
preliminary enquiries, 3.15

UK environmental law
generally, 1.27–1.35
Human Rights Act 1998, 1.36–1.39

Underletting, prohibition against
liability under leases, and, 10.15–10.17

Urban waste water
Directive
  implications, 17.130
  principal provisions, 17.127–17.128
high natural dispersion areas, 17.129
sensitive areas, 17.129

Use, permitted
liability under leases, and, 10.18

Vendors
considerations, 1.06

Verminous premises
local land charges, 5.16

Warranties
assessment of risk, and, 9.05
precedents
  generally, C.1–C.2
  loan agreement clauses, H.1–H.4

Waste
carriage of, 16.41–16.42
definition
  'discard', 16.12–16.15
  evolution, 16.10
  general, 16.11
Directive
  introduction, 16.04
  legal status of objectives, 16.08–
    16.09
'discard', 16.12–16.15
duty of care, statutory, 16.39
economic management instruments
  landfill tax, 16.44–16.49
  use, 16.43
environmental permits
  appeals, 16.32
  application for, 16.23
  competence assessment and
    enforcement, 16.31
  conditions, 16.27
  consultation, participation in, 16.30
  determining applications, 16.26
  exempt operations, 16.22
  offences, 16.36
  regime, 16.19
  registers, 16.33
  regulations, structure of, 16.20
  requirement of, 16.21
  standard, 16.30
  surrender, 16.28
  transfer applications, 16.25
  variation, 16.24

Waste – *contd*
hazardous, 16.40
historical development, 16.03
introduction, 16.01–16.05
landfill tax
  exemptions, 16.46–16.47
  introduction of, 16.44
  landfill allowance and trading
    scheme, 16.49
  rate, 16.44
  tax credits, 16.48
  'waste', 16.45
law and policy, 16.01
legislative background, 16.01–16.04
lists of, 16.11
offences
  defences, 16.38
  deposit, meaning, 16.35–16.36
  Environmental Permitting
    Regulations, under, 16.37
  generally, 16.34
planning controls
  conditions, 16.18
  development plans, 16.17
  introduction, 16.16
policy
  convergence, 16.06
  domestic, 16.07
problem, scale of, 16.02
producer responsibility, 16.50
tax credits, 16.48
tort, as
  generally, 10.30
  permissive, 10.29
  voluntary, 10.28
transfer of permits, and, 12.04
urban waste water Directive
  implications, 17.130
  high natural dispersion areas, 17.129
  principal provisions, 17.127–
    17.128
  sensitive areas, 17.129

Waste management
contaminated land, 15.28–15.31
economic management instruments
  landfill tax, 16.44–16.49
  use, 16.43
enquiries, 7.14
transfer of permits, 12.04

Waste removal notice
duty of disclosure, and, 2.25
lender liability, and, 10.50

Water
abstraction
common law rights, 17.23–17.24
impounding works, 17.39–17.40
licensing, 17.22–17.26, 17.30–17.42
offences, 17.27–17.29
statutory rights, 17.25–17.30
anti-pollution works, 17.83–17.85
connections
charges, 17.17–17.22
procedure, 17.05–17.15
discharge of water
anti-pollution works and operations, 17.83–17.85
groundwater protection, 17.99–17.102
nitrate sensitive areas, 17.95–17.98
nitrate vulnerable zones, 17.98–17.98
pollution precautions, 17.82
protection zones, 17.94
works notices, 17.86–17.93
discharge of trade effluent into sewers
agreements, by, 17.115
charges, 17.123–17.124
compensation, 17.121
consents, 17.103–17.113
introduction, 17.103–17.107
offences, 17.114
registers, 17.125–17.126
sewerage undertaker enquiries, and, 7.23
special category effluent, 17.116–17.120
transfer of consent, 17.122
environmental damage to, 15.108
generally, 17.01
groundwater protection, 17.99–17.102
impounding works, licences for
applications, 17.40
charges, 17.40
liability of undertaker for flooding, 17.159
mains supply
charges, 17.17–17.22
procedure, 17.02–17.04
nitrate sensitive areas, 17.95–17.98
nitrate vulnerable zones, 17.98–17.98
protection zones, 17.94
sewers
and see **Sewers**
existing development, for, 17.146–17.158

Water – *contd*
sewers – *contd*
generally, 17.131
new developments, for, 17.132–17.145
supply
charges, 17.17–17.22
connections to mains, 17.05–17.16
generally, 17.02
mains, 17.02–17.04
trade effluent discharge
agreements, by, 17.115
charges, 17.123–17.124
compensation, 17.121
consents, 17.103–17.113
introduction, 17.103–17.107
offences, 17.114
registers, 17.125–17.126
sewerage undertaker enquiries, and, 7.23
special category effluent, 17.116–17.120
transfer of consent, 17.122
undertaker's liability for flooding, 17.159
urban waste water Directive
implications, 17.130
high natural dispersion areas, 17.129
principal provisions, 17.127–17.128
sensitive areas, 17.129
water discharge activities
consents, 17.69–17.81
defences, 17.67–17.68
generally, 17.43
landlords and lessors' liability, 17.61–17.66
multiple defendants, 17.58
offences, 17.46–17.57
separate acts, 17.58
third party acts, 17.59–17.60
wholesome, 17.22
works notices, 17.86–17.93

Water abstraction
common law rights, 17.23–17.24
enquiries about
generally, 7.11
preliminary, 3.21
impounding works, 17.39–17.40
licensing
applications, 17.30–17.38
background, 17.22–17.26
impounding works, 17.39–17.40

Water abstraction – *contd*
  licensing – *contd*
    registers, 17.42
    transfer, 17.41
    types of, 17.31
  offences, 17.27–17.29
  preliminary enquiries, and, 3.21
  statutory rights
    current system, 17.26
    defence, 17.30
    offences, 17.28–17.29
    regulation, 17.25
  transfer of permits, and, 12.08

Water companies
  generally, 7.22
  model enquiries
    charges and sewers, 7.24
    trade effluent, 7.24
  office addresses, 7.25

Water connections
  charges, 17.17–17.22
  procedure, 17.05–17.16

Water discharge activities
  consents
    appeals, 17.75
    application, 17.69–17.70
    charges, 17.78
    conditions, 17.71–17.72
    confidentiality, 17.80–17.81
    registers, 17.79
    review, 17.74
    Transfer or property, 17.76–17.77
    transmission of applications to
      Secretary of State, 17.73
    variation, 17.75
  defences, 17.67–17.68
  generally, 17.43
  landlords and lessors' liability,
    17.61–17.66
  multiple defendants, 17.58
  offences
    causing or knowingly permitting,
      17.47–17.56
    generally, 17.44–17.55
    knowingly cause, 17.57
    knowingly permit, 17.57
    penalties, 17.46
  separate acts, 17.58
  third party acts, 17.59–17.60
  transfer of permits, and, 12.04

Water pollution
  Environment Agency enquiries, 7.12
  lender liability, and
    causing pollution, 10.46
    knowingly permitting pollution,
      10.47
  occupier, 10.50

Water protection zones
  controlled waters, 17.94

Water service companies
  generally, 7.22
  model enquiries
    charges and sewers, 7.24
    trade effluent, 7.24
  office addresses, 7.25

Water supply
  charges, 17.17–17.22
  connections
    ancillary duties, 17.07–17.08
    breach of duty, 17.09
    building regulations, 17.15
    charges, 17.17–17.22
    customer's obligations, 17.10
    easements, 17.10–17.13
    fire authority, notice to, 17.16
    general duty, 17.05–17.06
    planning permission, 17.14
  generally, 17.02
  mains, 17.02–17.04
  metering, and, 3.05
  sewers, and, 17.156–17.158

Watercourses
  local land charges, 5.13
  transfer of consent to works, 12.09

Waterways
  enquiries, 7.32

Wholesome water supply
  local land charges, 5.14

Workmanship
  'buyer beware' rule, and, 2.27

Works notices
  duty of disclosure, and, 2.25
  generally, 17.86–17.93

Works, undertaking statutory
  liability under leases, and, 10.10